COMMON LIFE in the EARLY CHURCH

COMMON
LIFE *in*
the EARLY
CHURCH

ESSAYS HONORING GRAYDON F. SNYDER

Edited by Julian V. Hills
with Richard B. Gardner, Robert Jewett, Robert Neff,
Peter Richardson, David M. Scholer, and Virginia Wiles

TRINITY PRESS INTERNATIONAL
Harrisburg, Pennsylvania

Trinity Press International, P.O. Box 1321, Harrisburg, PA 17105
Trinity Press International is a division of the Morehouse Group

Library of Congress Cataloging-in-Publication Data

Common life in the early church : essays honoring Graydon F. Snyder /
  edited by Julian V. Hills ; with Richard B. Gardner, ... [et al.].
      p.   cm.
    Includes bibliographical references and index.
    ISBN 1-56338-254-7 (alk. paper)
    1. Christian communities – History of doctrines – Early church, ca.
  36-600. 2. Community – Religious aspects – Anabaptists. I. Snyder,
  Graydon F. II. Hills, Julian Victor. III. Gardner, Richard B.,
  1940- .
  BV4405.C64 1998
  270.1 – dc21   98-39934

Printed in the United States of America

98   99   00   01   02   10   9   8   7   6   5   4   3   2   1

Contents

Preface

I could never have imagined, twenty-one years ago, that the privilege would fall to me to edit this Festschrift for Graydon F. Snyder. I met him then as team-teacher (with Robin Scroggs) of a course on the sociology of the New Testament — a class that would open the eyes of this young, traditionally educated master's student to an extraordinary range of new possibilities for interpreting the scriptures. I admit that when I cross-registered for the course, "Snyder" was but a name to me. But I was quickly captured by his exceptional learning, by his quick wit, and above all by his humility before questions of exploration and analysis that in the modern era he was among the first to ask. His was the kind of vision I wanted to share; his were the kind of theories that I wanted to know about. Those, of course, were the days before *Ante Pacem* — Snyder's magnum opus, as one of our contributors has dubbed it. But *Ante Pacem* was already more than a glint in Snyder's eye, since much of the research for it had been completed by then; and it was clear that we were being let in on a rather big secret — an open secret, as the publication of that great monograph would make it.

Doubtless each of the other twenty-six contributors to this volume has his or her story to tell about how and when and why Graydon Snyder became much more than one name among many in a list of former teachers or scholarly influences. Some of them briefly tell their story, or at least allude to it. But I am also confident that the essays gathered here go far beyond mere reminiscence or the re-presentation of some academic status quo, and that they do so in two complementary ways.

First, while these essays attest to the breadth of Snyder's interests, both in his published writings and in the implications that others have found in them, the scholars whose work is here offered to Snyder and the wider world have clearly done their best to demonstrate that some new awareness — an original hypothesis, some unconventional perspective — can yield questions, and even data, with which all of us must now reckon. Only rarely will biblical exegetes, historians of religion, theologians, and historians of art have the opportunity to see their work collected in one volume, not as random samples of what has preoccupied these disciplines but as a coherent attempt to show that some shifting of the boundaries has taken place, or needs to. Many positions hitherto reckoned unassailable must now be put to the test, rephrased, reformulated, in light of fresh advances across these many fields.

Second, these essays are united not only in their inspiration but also in their deliberate focus on the "common" life. Now, "common," the key word in this volume's title, will mean many things to many people: shared, communal, equal, everyday, and the like. But it also includes what is regular, down-to-earth, even vulgar — what the proverbial "man or woman in the street" thought or had to say or simply had to endure about the way things were, back then. It evokes, that is to say, how he or she actually experienced the theological propositions and social realities that have all too often been consigned to the realm of the history of ideas. And so again and again our contributors have reflected not only on the high culture of learned literacy and fine art but also on the common lot of the majority — not only the leaders but the led, those who themselves had no voice, those whose names we shall never know. These now nameless men and women, of course, constituted the vast numerical majority in the movements that these essays consider. Those untold thousands are now given a place, a forum, a hearing — from members of the earliest Jesus movement, through the writings of Paul and the later New Testament authors, to those, five or six centuries later, who were unknowingly patronized by an official judgment that Christian art — icons, images, visual narration — could be acceptable only as a second best for those who could neither read nor interpret the great tradition of the leaders, whose major voices are names immortalized in hagiography.

All of us who join in honoring Graydon Snyder owe some special debts of gratitude that need to be recorded here. To Richard B. Gardner, Peter Richardson, David M. Scholer, and Virginia Wiles, for their prompt and careful fulfillment of their role as coeditors as the essays began to appear; many of our authors have privately told me of the thanks due to these critical but supportive readers. To Robert Jewett, who first conceived of this endeavor, identified those of us who might see it through, and took account of both the intellectual and the practical dimensions of the project. To Robert Neff, recently retired as president of Juniata College, and Joanne M. Park, his assistant, who with great devotion coordinated the initial round of solicitations of commitments from those who are listed in the following pages as "Partners in Publication." To Estella B. Horning, Graydon's sister-in-law, who graciously assumed Neff's role after his retirement; her readiness to take up this onerous administrative task has been a great gift.

Our debts continue. To Jeanine Wine, longtime friend of Graydon and Lois Snyder, whose artwork graces this volume in a delicate but forceful interpretation of Snyder's reconstruction of the actual visual images that most deeply impressed early Christians' hearts and minds in the *ante-pacem* period. To my colleague at Marquette University, the Reverend Thomas A. Caldwell, S.J., for translating the essay by Andreas Lindemann. To the Reverend Donald L. Hays, of Waverly, Ohio, who diligently pored over the holdings of Bethany Theological Seminary library, Richmond, Indiana, to secure the final references that would make as complete as possible the comprehensive bibliography of Snyder's work that precedes the index to this volume. To those within the Anabaptist faith community whose financial and moral support has made all the difference at decisive moments as we went ahead with this substantial undertaking.

The entire editorial team and I are likewise indebted to Harold Rast and Laura Barrett, of Trinity Press International, for their willingness to go along with our daring scheme to compile, edit, and submit a volume such as this for publication within a year of its acceptance by the Press. Such courage as this was nothing less than an act of faith, and we are most grateful for it.

In sum, it is as much by the strength of all these fine colleagues as by my own that I have done what I can, on behalf of those named below as Partners in Publication and of countless others, to honor our mutual friend and beloved honoree, Graydon F. Snyder.

JULIAN V. HILLS

July 20, 1998

Partners in Publication

Persons making financial contributions toward the publication
of this honorary volume

Philip G. Abruzino
Glen Ellyn, Illinois

Anna Achleitner
Washington, District of Columbia

Homer L. Ash
Keene, New Hampshire

Craig K. and Carol J. Bailey
Springfield, Illinois

Justin and LaVonne Beeson
The Lyle Lichtenberger Family
Morgantown, West Virginia

R. Russell Bixler
Pittsburgh, Pennsylvania

Ron and Mary Boose
Hopewell, Pennsylvania

Robert L. Brawley
McCormick Theological Seminary

Glendon and Wanda Button
Conrad, Iowa

Clyde and Karen Carter
Daleville, Virginia

David and Jane Cox
Kokomo, Indiana

Merle and Jean Crouse
Saint Cloud, Florida

Roger and Finney Cruz
Chicago, Illinois

Nils A. Dahl
Oslo, Norway

Barry and Arlene Deardorff
Glenview, Illinois

Allen and Joan Deeter
North Manchester, Indiana

Robert E. and Nancy R. Faus
Richmond, Indiana

Chalmer E. Faw
McPherson, Kansas

Earle and Jean Fike
Bridgewater, Virginia

Robert C. Ford
Chicago, Illinois

Richard B. Gardner
Bethany Theological Seminary

Thomas W. Geiman
Port Republic, Virginia

Jay and June Gibble
Elgin, Illinois

John and Jacki Gingrich
Claremont, California

LeRoy and Kathi Griffin
Grand Rapids, Michigan

Warren and Ruth Groff
Bartlett, Illinois

Terry L. Grove
Winter Park, Florida

Allen and Lois Hansell
Mountville, Pennsylvania

Per K. Hanson
Northbrook, Illinois

A. Blair and Patricia Helman
Manchester College

Francis and Jean Hendricks
Eudora, Kansas

Paul and Ruth Hersch
La Verne, California

Luise Höhn
Frankfurt am Main

Donald J. Hoover
Alexandria, Virginia

Marlin and Mary Neil Hoover
Flossmore, Illinois

Warren Hoover
Fort Washington, Maryland

Lynne L. Hoppes
Sacramento, California

John and Estella Horning
Lombard, Illinois

Jonathan Hunter
Le Mesa, California

Robert and Janet Jewett
Evanston, Illinois

Earl and Harriet Kaylor
Huntingdon, Pennsylvania

J. Calvin Keeling
Bakersfield, California

Thomas D. Kinzie
Portland, Oregon

Robert Knechel
McPherson College

Edgar Krentz
Lutheran School of Theology
   at Chicago

Richard R. Kurrasch
Royal Oak, Michigan

Richard L. Landrum
Fort Wayne, Indiania

Thomas Liby
South Bend, Indiana

Mark Lichtenberger
Saint Joseph, Michigan

David Lindberg
Lutheran School of Theology
   at Chicago

Richard A. Livingston
Glenview, Illinois

Koloman Karl Ludwig
Hammond, Indiana

Joseph M. Mason
Greenville, Ohio

W. Robert McFadden
Bridgewater College

Wilbur and Joyce McFadden
North Manchester, Indiana

Edgar V. McKnight
Furman University

Donald and Phyllis Miller
Richmond, Indiana

Olden D. Mitchell
North Manchester, Indiana

Paul and Connie Williams Moodie
Onarga, Illinois

Carol Munro Mosley
St. Pauls United Church of Christ
Chicago, Illinois

Harold S. Moyer
Roanoke, Virginia

Robert Neff
Juniata College

Theresa Clingenpeel Parakh
Bellingham, Washington

Marian Patterson
Milledgeville, Illinois

J. Bentley Peters and Linda G. Wallon
Elgin, Illinois

William Puffenberger
Elizabethtown, Pennsylvania

Frank and Jennie Ramirez
Elkhart, Indiana

John and Martha Reumann
Philadelphia, Pennsylvania

David Rhoads
Lutheran School of Theology
    at Chicago

Peter Richardson
University of Toronto

Donald L. Robinson
Wyomissing, Pennsylvania

Paul and Mary Robinson
Sebring, Florida

Eugene and Delora Roop
Bethany Theological Seminary

Steven J. Rosenberg
Chicago, Illinois

Robert L. Rotgers
Wauwatosa, Wisconsin

Jane E. Salinger
North Manchester, Indiana

Alvin Schmucker
Milford, Indiana

David M. Scholer
Fuller Theological Seminary

Kenneth M. Shaffer, Jr.
Brethren Historical Library and
    Archives

John and Beverly Shepard
Long Beach, California

Barry Shutt
Harrisburg, Pennsylvania

Joseph N. Simmons
South Holland, Illinois

Lois Mow Snavely
Loris, South Carolina

Anna Snyder
Syracuse, New York

Darrell and Ruth E. Snyder
North Manchester,
    Indiana

Jonathan E. Snyder
Tokyo, Japan

Stephen Snyder
St. Louis, Missouri

William Richard Stegner
Garrett-Evangelical Theological
    Seminary

Michael and Renate Stratton
Liestal, Switzerland

Ellen and Ray Swihart
Sebring, Florida

Walter Thurman, Jr.
Chicago, Illinois

Murray Wagner
Bethany Theological Seminary

Robert and Shirley Wagoner
Huntingdon, Pennsylvania

Guy and Linda Wampler
Lancaster, Pennsylvania

Bev Weaver and Duane Grady
Indianapolis, Indiana

Mary Elizabeth Wieand
Lombard, Illinois

Jacob C. and Jean Wine
East Petersburg, Pennsylvania

David Zersen
Concordia University at Austin

Table of Congratulations

John E. Alsup

Mary K. Anderson

Robert Atkins

Robert J. Banks

William A. Beardslee

Pier Franco Beatrice

Hans Dieter Betz

Bible College of Victoria

C. Clifton Black

Marcus Borg

William S. Campbell

D. A. Carson

Nelda Rhoades Clarke

Adela Yarbro Collins

Raymond F. Collins

Rudiger and Mireio Corsten

Charles H. Cosgrove

John M. Court

John Dominic Crossan

Goeffrey Curtiss

Peter H. Davids

R. Conrad and Lucinda M. E.
  Douglas

James D. G. Dunn

David Eastis

École Biblique, Jerusalem

Richard A. Edwards

David Eller

Keith Elliott

Eldon Jay Epp

Norman R. Ericson

Craig A. Evans

Gordon D. Fee

Herbert A. Fisher

Dan Fraikin

Wesley Fuerst

W. Ward Gasque

Lawrence T. Geraty

Neil Gerdes

Robert H. Gundry

Adolf Hansen

Don Haymes

Richard B. Hays

Charles W. Hedrick

David and Anne Hendricks

James D. Hester

Lyndon C. Hills

Paul Hoffmann

Kenneth O. Holderread

Stewart and Karen Hoover

Friedrich W. Horn

Bruce E. Huffman

Wesley W. Isenberg

Robert M. Johnston

Ann and Cliff Joseph

Calvin Katter

Hans-Josef Klauck

Hans Kvalbein

James LaGrande

Wally Landes

Calvin Lee Lawyer

Werner E. Lemke

Wilhelm Linss

Troy W. Martin

Doreen McFarlane

B. H. McLean

Robert P. Meye

David R. Miller

Blaine Miner

Margaret M. Mitchell

Walter F. Nickeson

Lloyd Prince Nyce

Eric Osborn

Larry and Debra Palguta

Joanne M. Park

Linda Parrish

Clayton N. Pheasant

Plough Publishing House

Barbara E. Reid

C. Truman Reinoehl

David and Shirley Rogers

Eva Salmons

Dieter Sänger

Roberta Schaafsma

John J. Schmitt

Benedikt Schwank

Donald Senior

Stephen S. Smalley

Carolyn Snyder and
  Chuck Sain

Graham Stanton

Jay H. Steele

Willard M. Swartley

William R. Telford

Pauline and Lolita Thornton

Thomas H. Tobin

Etienne Trocmé

Joseph B. Tyson

Bastiaan Van Elderen

John J. Vincent

Benedict T. Viviano

Delia and Tim Waits

William O. Walker, Jr.

Brenda Jones Watkins

Thomas and Ethel Wilson

Wilhelm Wuellner

Contributors
and Editors

Thomas M. Bolin
Assistant Professor of Hebrew Bible
St. Mary's University
San Antonio, Texas

Peder Borgen
Professor Emeritus
President of the Royal Norwegian Society of Sciences and Letters
President of Studiorum Novi Testamenti Societas
University of Trondheim
Trondheim, Norway

Barbara E. Bowe
Associate Professor of Biblical Studies
Catholic Theological Union
Chicago, Illinois

David R. Cartlidge
Beeson Professor Emeritus
Maryville College
Maryville, Tennessee

Richard B. Gardner
Academic Dean and Professor of New Testament
Bethany Theological Seminary
Richmond, Indiana

Lloyd Gaston
Professor of New Testament Emeritus
Vancouver School of Theology
Vancouver, British Columbia
Canada

Robert C. Helmer
Assistant Professor of Religious Studies
Lourdes College
Sylvania, Ohio

Julian V. Hills
Associate Professor of Theology
Marquette University
Milwaukee, Wisconsin

Robin M. Jensen
Associate Professor of the History of Christianity
Andover Newton Theological School
Newton Centre, Massachusetts

Robert Jewett
Harry R. Kendall Senior Professor of New Testament Interpretation
Garrett Evangelical Theological Seminary
Evanston, Illinois

John Kampen
Vice President and Dean of Academic Affairs
Bluffton College
Bluffton, Ohio

William Klassen
Visiting Research Professor
Director of the Library Project
École Biblique, Jerusalem

Edgar Krentz
Christ Seminary–Seminex Professor of New Testament, Emeritus
Lutheran School of Theology at Chicago
Chicago, Illinois

James LaGrand
Pastor
Beacon Light Christian Reformed Church
Gary, Indiana

Andreas Lindemann
Professor of New Testament Studies
Kirchliche Hochschule Bielefeld
Bielefeld, Germany

Donald E. Miller
Emeritus Professor of Ministry Studies
Bethany Theological Seminary
Richmond, Indiana

Robert W. Neff
President
Juniata College
Huntington, Pennsylvania

J. C. O'Neill
Professor Emeritus of New Testament Language, Literature and Theology
New College
University of Edinburgh
Edinburgh, Scotland

Carolyn Osiek
Professor of New Testament
Catholic Theological Union
Chicago, Illinois

John Reumann
Ministerium of Pennsylvania Professor, Emeritus
Lutheran Theological Seminary at Philadelphia
Philadelphia, Pennsylvania

Peter Richardson
Professor of Religion
University of Toronto
Toronto, Ontario
Canada

Calvin J. Roetzel
Arnold Lowe Professor of Religious Studies
Macalester College
St. Paul, Minnesota

Daryl D. Schmidt
Professor of Religion
Texas Christian University
Fort Worth, Texas

David M. Scholer
Professor of New Testament
Fuller Theological Seminary
Pasadena, California

Robin Scroggs
Edward Robinson Professor of Biblical Theology, Emeritus
Union Theological Seminary in New York
New York, New York

Kenneth M. Shaffer, Jr.
Librarian/Archivist
Brethren Historical Library and Archives
Elgin, Illinois

Klyne Snodgrass
Paul W. Brandel Professor of New Testament Studies
North Park Theological Seminary
Chicago, Illinois

William Richard Stegner
Senior Professor of New Testament Interpretation
Garrett Evangelical Theological Seminary
Evanston, Illinois

Robert E. Wagoner
Professor of Philosophy
Juniata College
Huntingdon, Pennsylvania

Virginia Wiles
Assistant Professor of Religion
Muhlenburg College
Allentown, Pennsylvania

Stephen G. Wilson
Professor of Religion
Carleton University
Ottawa, Ontario
Canada

Jeanine Wine
Artist
5440 S. Dorchester Avenue
Chicago, Illinois 60615

Introduction to the Artwork

BY JEANINE WINE

Adapted from Graydon F. Snyder, *Ante Pacem*

Illustrations for this book are adaptations of images commonly found in art-work before the fourth century CE. Theoretically, early Christian communities utilized these common forms to host the theological symbol systems of their newfound faith.

Part 1: The Legacy of Graydon F. Snyder

Reading the Law. A popular portrayal on pre-Christian sarcophagi is that of a seated man reading to a standing boy. When viewed outside the Christian community it could be interpreted as a father reading to his son or as an adult teaching a youth. More than likely, within the Christian context the man depicts Jesus reading the revelation and the child symbolizes someone new to the faith community. At a later date, the seated figure becomes Saint Peter reading the Law.

Part 2: Common Life in Judaism and Christianity

Fractio Panis. The breaking of the bread reflects the *agape* meal of the early church. The scene, which occurs in early Christian art nearly as often as the Jonah cycle, shows seven men and women at a curved table. They are eating two fish and drinking wine. In front of the table are five loaves of bread.

Part 3: Common Life in the Gospels and Acts

Feeding the Five Thousand. This story, rather than the Passover, forms the model for the Lord's Supper. Depictions of the event are frequent, especially on sarcophagi. Early Christian artists commonly showed Jesus blessing fish and baskets of bread. At a later date artists sometimes had two disciples giving the loaves and fishes to Jesus.

Part 4: Common Life in the Letters and Other Writings

The Orante. The *orante* is a female figure with arms lifted upward. She is an ancient symbol found in various types of plastic art, particularly on coins of the Roman Empire. On coins she bears the epithet *pietas*. She appears frequently in early Christian art, especially where deliverance is involved (e.g., Noah and the Ark, Daniel in the Lion's Den). Alone as a symbol, she is most commonly seen on sarcophagi. She stands for the Christian who has been delivered from threats such as persecution, famine, floods, and death. This symbol disappears after the Peace of the Church.

Part 5: Common Life in Art, Architecture, and Music

The Good Shepherd. The Good Shepherd is a significant symbol in the early church, possibly derived from ancient Near Eastern plastic art that depicts the shepherd as one who offers a gift to a god. In the early church this imagery reflects the hospitality offered by the faith community. Eventually, the Good Shepherd symbolizes Jesus himself, who cares for the lambs. This particular Good Shepherd utilizes the iconography of Orpheus, with pipe and sheep that rest nearby.

Part 6: Graydon F. Snyder: Curriculum Vitae and Comprehensive Bibliography

The Jonah Cycle. In *Ante Pacem*, Graydon F. Snyder shows that the primary artistic representation of early Christianity is the Jonah Cycle.

Jonah Cast Out of the Boat. While the biblical story has Jonah cast out of the boat because his disobedience was threatening the boat's destruction, the early Christian Jonah is always shown as an *orans*. Rather than one running from God, Jonah is a believer who enters the chaos of the Roman culture.

Jonah Spewed Out of the Sea Animal. In the biblical story a sea monster swallows Jonah after he is cast out of the boat, the monster perhaps representing maximum distance from God. In early Christian art it may refer to the distance of Roman culture from God. Jonah is swallowed by the culture but emerges, as an *orans*, in a victorious manner.

Jonah at Rest. In the biblical narrative the pouting Jonah rests under a bush. In early Christian art Jonah reclines victoriously after his encounter with the monster. The iconography of Jonah at Rest probably comes from that of Endymion, who can be found in a prone position on several non-Christian sarcophagi, resting after acting as a consort for the moon goddess, Selene.

Abbreviations

AB	Anchor Bible
ABD	D. N. Freedman, ed., *Anchor Bible Dictionary*
ABRL	Anchor Bible Reference Library
ACW	Ancient Christian Writers
ALGHJ	Arbeiten zur Literatur und Geschichte des hellenistischen Judentums
ANF	Ante-Nicene Fathers
ANRW	*Aufstieg und Niedergang der römischen Welt*
ASB	American Standard Bible
ASOR	American Schools of Oriental Research
ASTI	*Annual of the Swedish Theological Institute*
AV	Authorized Version (also KJV)
BA	*Biblical Archaeologist*
BAGD	W. Bauer, W. F. Arndt, F. W. Gingrich, and F. W. Danker, *Greek-English Lexicon of the New Testament*
BAR	*Biblical Archaeologist Reader*
BARev	*Biblical Archaeology Review*
BDF	F. Blass, A. Debrunner, and R. W. Funk, *A Greek Grammar of the New Testament*
BETL	Bibliotheca ephemeridum theologicarum lovaniensium
BHT	Beiträge zur historischen Theologie
Bib	*Biblica*
BibLeb	*Bibel und Leben*
BibRev	*Bible Review*
BJRL	*Bulletin of the John Rylands University Library of Manchester*
BJS	Brown Judaic Studies
BLead	*Brethren Leader*
BLT	*Brethren Life and Thought*
BR	*Biblical Research*

BTB	*Biblical Theology Bulletin*
BWANT	Beiträge zur Wissenschaft vom Alten und Neuen Testament
BZ	*Biblische Zeitschrift*
BZAW	Beihefte zur ZAW
BZNW	Beihefte zur ZNW
CBQ	*Catholic Biblical Quarterly*
CBQMS	Catholic Biblical Quarterly – Monograph Series
CHR	*Catholic Historical Review*
ChrCent	*Christian Century*
ChrMin	*Christian Ministry*
ConBNT	Coniectanea biblica, New Testament
CR	*Critical Review of Books in Religion*
CRINT	Compendia rerum iudaicarum ad novum testamentum
CTSReg	*Chicago Theological Seminary Register*
Diss SR	Dissertations – Studies in Religion
DJD	Discoveries in the Judaean Desert
DSD	*Dead Sea Discoveries*
DSS	Dead Sea Scrolls
Ebib	*Études bibliques*
EDNT	*Exegetical Dictionary of the New Testament*
EKKNT	Evangelisch-katholischer Kommentar zum Neuen Testament
EPRO	Études préliminaires aux religions orientales dans l'empire Romain
EstBib	*Estudios bíblicos*
ET	English Translation
ETL	*Ephemerides theologicae lovanienses*
ETS	Erfurter theologische Studien
EvT	*Evangelisches Theologie*
EWNT	H. Balz and G. Schneider, eds., *Exegetisches Wörterbuch zum Neuen Testament*
ExpTim	*Expository Times*
FAT	Forschungen zum Alten Testament
FC	Fathers of the Church
FFNT	Foundations and Facets: New Testament

FRLANT	Forschungen zur Religion und Literatur des Alten und Neuen Testaments
GMess	*Gospel Messenger* (Church of the Brethren)
GTA	Göttinger theologische Arbeiten
HBT	*Horizons in Biblical Theology*
HDR	Harvard Dissertations in Religion
HKNT	Handkommentar zum Neuen Testament
HNT	Handbuch zum Neuen Testament
HNTC	Harper's New Testament Commentaries
HR	*History of Religions*
HSS	Harvard Semitic Studies
HTKNT	Herders theologischer Kommentar zum Neuen Testament
HTR	*Harvard Theological Review*
HTS	Harvard Theological Studies
HUCM	Monographs of the Hebrew Union College
HUT	Hermeneutische Untersuchungen zur Theologie
IBS	*Irish Biblical Studies*
ICC	International Critical Commentary
IDB	G. A. Buttrick, ed., *Interpreter's Dictionary of the Bible*
Int	*Interpretation*
JAAR	*Journal of the American Academy of Religion*
JAC	Jahrbuch für Antike und Christentum
JB	Jerusalem Bible
JBL	*Journal of Biblical Literature*
JBR	*Journal of Bible and Religion*
JETS	*Journal of the Evangelical Theological Society*
JJS	*Journal of Jewish Studies*
JJSSup	Journal of Jewish Studies – Supplement Series
JR	*Journal of Religion*
JRS	*Journal of Roman Studies*
JSNTSup	Journal for the Study of the New Testament – Supplement Series
JSOTSup	Journal for the Study of the Old Testament – Supplement Series
JSSSup	Journal of Semitic Studies – Supplement Series

JTC	*Journal for Theology and the Church*
JTS	*Journal of Theological Studies*
KEK	Kritisch-exegetischer Kommentar über das Neuen Testament
KJV	King James Version (also AV)
KNT	Kommentar zum Neuen Testament
KVR	Kleine Vandenhoeck Reihe
LCL	Loeb Classical Library
LD	Lectio divina
LPGL	G. W. H. Lampe, *Patristic Greek Lexicon*
LSJ	Liddel-Scott-Jones, *Greek-English Lexicon*
LUÅ	Lunds universitets årsskrift
MeyerK	H. A. W. Meyer, Kritisch-exegetischer Kommentar über das Neue Testament
MTZ	*Münchener theologische Zeitschrift*
NAB	New American Bible
NCB	New Century Bible
NEB	New English Bible
NICNT	New International Commentary on the New Testament
NIV	New International Version
NovT	*Novum Testamentum*
NovTSup	Novum Testamentum, Supplements
NPNF	Nicene and Post-Nicene Fathers
NRSV	New Revised Standard Version
NRT	*La nouvelle revue théologique*
NTAbh	Neutestamentliche Abhandlungen
NTOA	Novum Testamentum et Orbis Antiquus
NTS	*New Testament Studies*
OTL	Old Testament Library
OTP	J. H. Charlesworth, ed., *The Old Testament Pseudepigrapha*
PCB	M. Black and H. H. Rowley, eds., *Peake's Commentary on the Bible*
PG	J. Migne, *Patrologia graeca*
PL	J. Migne, *Patrologia latina*
PSTJ	*Perkins (School of Theology) Journal*

RAC	*Reallexikon für Antike und Christentum*
RB	*Revue biblique*
REB	Revised English Bible
RechBib	Recherches bibliques
RelSRev	*Religious Studies Review*
RevQ	*Revue de Qumran*
RHPR	*Revue d'histoire et de philosophie religieuses*
RSV	Revised Standard Version
SANT	Studien zum Alten und Neuen Testament
SBL	Society of Biblical Literature
SBLDS	SBL Dissertation Series
SBLMS	SBL Monograph Series
SBLRBS	SBL Resources for Biblical Study
SBLSBS	SBL Sources for Biblical Study
SBLSCS	SBL Septuagint and Cognate Studies
SBLSP	SBL Seminar Papers
SBLSS	SBL Semeia Studies
SBS	Stuttgarter Bibelstudien
SBT	Studies in Biblical Theology
SC	Sources chrétiennes
SecCent	*Second Century*
SJLA	Studies in Judaism in Late Antiquity
SJT	*Scottish Journal of Theology*
SMB	Série monographique de "Benedictina"
SNTSMS	Society for New Testament Studies Monograph Series
SPB	Studia postbiblica
SR	*Studies in Religion/Sciences religieuses*
STDJ	Studies on the Texts of the Desert of Judah
StPatr	*Studia Patristica*
Str-B	H. Strack and P. Billerbeck, *Kommentar zum Neuen Testament*
TCGNT	B. M. Metzger, *A Textual Commentary on the Greek New Testament*
TDNT	G. Kittel and G. Friedrich, eds., *Theological Dictionary of the New Testament*

TDOT	G. J. Botterweck and H. Ringgren, eds., *Theological Dictionary of the Old Testament*
TEV	Today's English Version
THKNT	Theologischer Handkommentar zum Neuen Testament
TLZ	*Theologische Literaturzeitung*
TRE	*Theologische Realenzyklopädie*
TSK	*Theologische Studien und Kritiken*
TToday	*Theology Today*
TU	Texte und Untersuchungen
TZ	*Theologische Zeitschrift*
UBSGNT	United Bible Societies, *Greek New Testament*
UUÅ	Uppsala universitetsårsskrift
VC	*Vigiliae christianae*
WBC	Word Biblical Commentary
WUNT	Wissenschaftliche Untersuchungen zum Neuen Testament
ZAW	*Zeitschrift für die alttestamentliche Wissenschaft*
ZKG	*Zeitschrift für Kirchengeschichte*
ZNW	*Zeitschrift für die neutestamentliche Wissenschaft*
ZTK	*Zeitschrift für Theologie und Kirche*

PART ONE

THE LEGACY OF GRAYDON F. SNYDER

1

GRAYDON F. SNYDER AS ETHICIST AND EDUCATOR IN THE ANABAPTIST TRADITION

Donald E. Miller

The purpose of this article is to pay tribute to the contribution of Graydon F. Snyder as ethicist and educator in the Anabaptist tradition. Others are more qualified to speak about biblical scholarship, but since I have been engaged in a lifetime of study as an ethicist and educator, I highlight those aspects of Snyder's contribution. My comments also come from a friendship of more than fifty years as well as twenty-five years of teaching together as colleagues.

Graydon Snyder has lived a life informed by the Anabaptist tradition both as practitioner and interpreter. He grew up in a Church of the Brethren family in Huntington, West Virginia, and came to Brethren-related Manchester College in Indiana in 1947 with the intention of going into medicine. Teachers like Gladdys Muir and T. Wayne (Tim) Rieman influenced him to change his vocational direction and attend Bethany Theological Seminary, a school affiliated with the Church of the Brethren. Before doing so he married Lois Horning, whose parents had been missionaries to China.

In seminary he chose to specialize in NT studies and after graduating proceeded to Princeton Theological Seminary, where he received a doctorate under Otto Piper. He did postgraduate work in Oslo, Norway, along with Nils Dahl, following which he taught at Bethany Theological Seminary for twenty-seven years. He began his Bethany career teaching OT, but soon changed to the field of study in which he would become best known; he later became academic dean of the seminary. In 1986 Snyder moved to Chicago Theological Seminary as dean and professor of New Testament.

During these years the range of his scholarly contributions is evident in his bibliography and his professional affiliations. What is not evident are the many occasions when he preached, taught classes in local congregations, served on numerous committees, and kept a wealth of contacts with former students. In particular he served on the board of Bethany Hospital, which is situated on Chicago's West Side. He and his wife, Lois, have been pillars in the intercultural, interracial Chicago First Church of the Brethren near Bethany Hospital. He and Lois have also been active in establishing and supporting the Association of Brethren Caregivers.

Such a very brief synopsis of events in Snyder's life underlines the fact that he has spent his life within the circle of Anabaptism both as a faith participant and as a creative interpreter. This is not to suggest that his contributions are narrowly defined by tradition. Quite the contrary is true. The focus of his concern is the whole of the Christian tradition, but he clearly works from a stance nourished by Anabaptism. He is eager to address any question put by a student, and he is bold in proposing innovative, creative answers; but in doing so his Anabaptist stance becomes evident.

The characteristics and normative practices of Anabaptism are discussed throughout Snyder's writings. A most useful summary is given in his *Health and Medicine*.[1] Here he suggests six characteristics of Anabaptist groups:

1. *Separation of church and state.* The life and practices of the church are neither authorized nor required by the power of the state. Anabaptists see the Emperor Constantine's official authorization of Christianity as the fall of the church.

2. *Adult baptism.* For Anabaptism, "freedom of choice,... multiplicity of faith responses, and... an informed decision to join a family of faith... are crucial aspects of the Christian faith" (pp. 8–9).

3. *No force in religion.* "Anabaptists do agree that Christians would not use violence or force to compel another into an unwanted agreement. For that reason Anabaptists are inevitably pacifistic" (p. 9).

4. *Mutual assistance.* "(A)ll Anabaptists are driven toward communal life, but that often takes the form of mutual assistance rather than common ownership of property" (p. 9). Anabaptists help one another in times of disaster, emergency, or other need.

5. *No oaths and no creeds.* Anabaptists are not willing to give undivided loyalty to anyone or any group except to Christ.

6. *A communitarian emphasis.* "A primary virtue for Anabaptists is *Gelassenheit*, or submission to the Will of God and the direction of the community" (p. 10).

When it come to the practices of the Anabaptists, Snyder mentions first

---

1. Snyder, *Health and Medicine in the Anabaptist Tradition* (Health/Medicine and the Faith Traditions; Valley Forge, Pa.: Trinity Press International, 1995).

of all restitutionism (p. 11). Anabaptists want to restore the church of the NT and of the early church prior to the time that the Roman Empire established Christianity. This is not to be understood as a narrowly monolithic view because it allows for the variety that was already present in the NT and the early church.

Anabaptist practice is characterized by discipleship, which is a willingness to leave the ways of the world and to follow the way of Jesus, wherever that may lead. Part of discipleship is peacemaking. Disciples are to live at peace with one another and with all persons so far as possible. They are to be reconciled to one another as Christ has reconciled us to God. Believers are to be reconciled before taking communion together.

Another practice is that of baptism, which is a sign of the new community God is bringing about. Anabaptists are committed to simplicity of living, which means a simple devotion to Christ's call unencumbered by materialism and a willingness to move about according to the call of Christ as that may be interpreted by the community.

Anabaptists believe in discipline. The community of believers expects individual believers to hear the call of God as that is interpreted by the community. When reconciliation fails, the separation may be openly acknowledged with admonishment or avoidance. Finally, Anabaptists live in anticipation of the new community God is bringing about: "Early Christians shifted their allegiance from a specific nation to the world" (p. 17). With the Edict of Milan in 313 and its aftermath, establishing Christianity as the official religion of the Roman Empire, came the fall of the church: "The faith once again became identified with a land, with a people, and with specific immovable centers" (p. 18).

With these characterizations Snyder indicates what he means by Anabaptism, and therefore what is meant by saying that he stands within the Anabaptist tradition in his work as biblical scholar, teacher, and ethicist. The centrality of the NT in the Anabaptist vision is seen in the focus of Snyder's scholarship on the NT. His concern is to see the inculturation of the Jesus tradition into the Greco-Roman social matrix. This relates directly to the Anabaptist concern about the legitimizing of Christianity as a state religion under Constantine. Primary elements of the Jesus tradition are peace, reconciliation, and healing, which are also central to the Anabaptist orientation. The purpose of this article is to show how the main themes in the development of Snyder's career and scholarship stand within that tradition.

Interpretation

As has already been suggested, Snyder is not a passive interpreter of the Anabaptist tradition, particularly that of the Church of the Brethren. His is a

dramatic, creative, historical approach, open to innovation and reinterpretation. I am giving special attention to Snyder as ethicist and educator, both of
which rest fundamentally upon interpretation. Ethics has to do with understanding a situation deeply enough to perceive the alternatives available for
response. Both understanding and perception of alternatives require interpretation. Indeed, some ethicists suggest that the most important element of
ethics is interpretation.[2]

In a more obvious way the work of an educator requires interpretation.
An educator is constantly interpreting a body of knowledge or tradition to
those who are learning. Whereas this can intend to be simply an unchanging
reproduction, it is commonly accepted that education requires interpretation. Snyder as educator understood his calling as that of interpreting and
reinterpreting the materials that were being addressed. His interpretation
often involved dramatic new historical evidence as well as striking analogies
to common, everyday contemporary experience. His work as both ethicist and educator can be better understood in relation to the principles of
interpretation he follows.

For Snyder the principal focus of interpretation has been the scriptures,
particularly the NT. John Howard Yoder has suggested that Snyder's approach to scripture accepts the liberal position of a gap between the text
and the context (an article proposed to Snyder, but never written), but that
he doesn't move in the liberal direction of thereby dismissing the text. Rather
he asks the reason for the dissonance as a way of understanding how the text
can be taken seriously in another context. Therefore he takes the conservative position that all scripture is useful for the instruction of contemporary
believers.

An example of how this process of interpretation is carried out can be
found in Snyder's unpublished doctoral dissertation.[3] There he has a discussion of the eucharist, the substance of which is also found in many of his
later writings, for example the commentary on 1 Corinthians. When Jesus
broke the bread and said, "This act of breaking the bread shares in the breaking of my body for all of you," the emphasis is upon the action of breaking
bread. Snyder then goes on to propose that the traditional centering of the
celebration upon the bread cannot be correct:

> First, we are dealing here [in 1 Corinthians 11] with an action, not a
> substance. As both v. 24 and v. 25 make it clear, we are to do what the
> Lord says. Second, the word "this" does not refer to the bread.... In
> Greek the word "bread" is masculine, but the word "this" is neuter.

2. See, e.g., Paul L. Lehman, *Ethics in a Christian Context* (New York: Harper & Row, 1963).
3. "The Continuity of Early Christianity: A Study of Ignatius in Relation to Paul" (Th.D.
diss., Princeton Theological Seminary, 1961).

There might be other explanations, but most likely the Greek means either "That is to say" or "This action is." Finally, in Judeo-Christian practice, normally the celebration involves a dramatic reinvolvement in the redemptive or paradigmatic event.[4]

Snyder concludes that in the eucharist the community participates in the death and resurrection of Jesus by itself being willing to die to the past and be open to the possibility of the new community coming in the future.

The principle of interpretation becomes evident in the illustration. The meaning of the text is not on the surface so that every reader can quickly agree as to its meaning. Nor is the meaning to be found by an inspired true meaning that is self-evident to all genuine believers. Rather, one must look at the text in its historical, social, and cultural setting. This includes an understanding of the meaning and use of words at the time, as well as an understanding of the common social and cultural practices at the time. Such considerations give a present-day reader the most likely meaning of the text for a reader at the time it was written. Thereby the gap between the text and the context is taken seriously and better understood. The textual phrase "This is my body" is usually understood to refer to the bread. Snyder gives textual, grammatical, and historical arguments that a different meaning was more likely for the readers at that time. This different meaning has a dramatic impact upon how the text is to be understood today.

The rendering of a text's meaning in its context is never absolute. It is always a matter of selecting the most probable meaning on the basis of the historical data available. In the illustration above Snyder speaks of the "normal" usage in the Greek language, of the "most likely" meaning, and of the "normal" Judeo-Christian religious practice. Clearly the interpretation depends upon making judgments based upon historical data. The interpretation of historical data is a matter of discerning what is more or less probable. So the rendering of the phrase "This is my body" is based upon probable historical data, which means that new historical studies could change the probabilities. For this reason any text is always open to reinterpretation based upon new evidence.

This openness of interpretation may be illustrated by a book that Snyder wrote together with Kenneth M. Shaffer Jr., entitled *Texts in Transit*.[5] They chose texts according to three criteria: "those sections of the New Testament most frequently used in worship, hymns, and study; those topics most important to the Brethren; and those texts most frequently used to support the

---

4. Snyder, *First Corinthians: A Faith Community Commentary* (Macon, Ga.: Mercer University Press, 1992) 158.

5. Snyder and Shaffer, *Texts in Transit* (Elgin, Ill.: Brethren Press, 1976).

most important teachings of the church."[6] For the Church of the Brethren
the majority of texts chosen were from the Gospel of Matthew. The selection indicates that interpretation is influenced by what is of most interest
to present-day believers. Nevertheless Snyder holds that all biblical texts are
important and can serve to edify readers in our day.

In *Texts in Transit* the authors raise the question of how a text can mean
one thing at one time and another thing at another time. There are in their
view three ways in which the meaning of a text can change. First, "we can
discover information today which can change the longstanding meaning of a
text" (p. 7). There have been many significant discoveries of ancient manuscripts during the past century. Information from those documents can alter
the understanding of a biblical text:

> For example, in John 4:9 we normally translate a word there as "Jews
> *have no dealings with* Samaritans." We could assume that means no so-
> cial or economic dealings. But investigations of ancient texts would
> indicate that it means Jews did not use vessels in common with non-
> Jews, a point which is quite pertinent between Jesus and the Samaritan
> woman at the well. (p. 8)

A second way in which the meaning of a text can be altered is through
a change of circumstances. Adult baptism in the early eighteenth century,
when the Brethren arose, was universally rebaptism (anabaptism) because
all persons were baptized at birth by the church and under compulsion by
the state. Adult baptism was therefore a challenge to the authority of both
the church and the state. The circumstances today are quite different for
Brethren in the U.S. Freedom of belief is guaranteed by the Constitution, and
most churches accept the possible doctrinal validity of adult baptism. Often
adult baptism is not rebaptism because the person was not baptized as a child.
Brethren also accept by reaffirmation of faith without rebaptism those who
were previously baptized even when the previous baptism was in infancy. Part
of the changed circumstance is that in the U.S. infant baptism is no longer
done by requirement of the state. The meaning of baptism in the U.S. today is
that of moving from the family of orientation into the family of faith, from the
biological community into the new community of Christ. The circumstances
have changed, and so the meaning of the text has also changed.

Similarly, passages about bearing arms change their meaning when there
is no military draft. Such passages are currently interpreted in relation to
working for peace and reconciliation. Snyder comments that it "is part of the
genius of the Church of the Brethren that it can keep its heritage texts, and
therefore its identity, but yet see how these texts apply to modern life in a

---

6. Snyder, "*Texts in Transit* Reconsidered: Great Passages of the Bible for Brethren," *Guide*
96/4 (September–November 1981) 2–9.

way they did not necessarily apply either in the New Testament or at the birth of the Church of the Brethren" (p. 8).

A third way that the meaning of a text can change is when social pressures

> force the change of the meaning of a text, or at least create the cli-
> mate in which the meaning of a text will be altered.... Texts which we
> thought had one meaning have, under pressures of racial freedom, a
> desire for stronger family life, the equality of the sexes, or the nature of
> sexuality, come to mean something other than what we had supposed.
> It seems to me inappropriate for a biblical text to be twisted to mean
> something that it does not. It also seems to me inappropriate for a bib-
> lical text to be used for a form of advocacy which was not intended by
> the original text. (p. 8)

The meaning of a passage may change according to new discoveries about the original context, or according the changing circumstances of the contempo-rary interpreter. So the interpreter must be aware of the historical context, the contemporary context, and the analogy by which the two can be brought together. Traditions of interpretation develop, but they may be altered by new historical facts or by new contemporary concerns. Clearly Snyder's principles of interpretation are tied neither to a single inspired meaning for each passage nor to the standard rendering of any particular tradition. His method of in-terpretation is that of "an arrow in flight," i.e., a text in transit. This view fits well with an Anabaptist stance that is ever open to new truth about the NT and the early Christian church in order that contemporary life may be edified.

Teaching

Grady was popular as a teacher of the OT. He brought a wealth of historical information to the text as well as boldness of interpretation. Some students refused to have their traditional biblical understanding shaken, but most be-came radically engaged with the text. Early in his teaching career Grady wrote a survey of the Bible for senior high youth, entitled *In His Hand*.[7] In it he could make use of his classroom teaching of OT. It was one of the earliest of many writings for laypeople in the church wherein he served as educator.

We can see Grady's teaching method, and equally his method of inter-pretation, by reviewing a lesson of his. One of the best-known OT stories is that of David and Goliath. After commenting that in the encounter with Goliath, "David was hardly a little boy," Snyder goes on to say, "It is true that David was not accustomed to military armor, but all we know of the rest of David's life spoke of his great military prowess. He must have been a powerful warrior" (part 2, p. 146). But what of the weapons?

---

7. Snyder, *In His Hand* (Elgin, Ill.: Brethren Press, 1964).

David was as well armed as the giant Goliath was. To be sure, he did not have the customary dueling weapons which Goliath expected, but the sling was a real weapon. The sling was used by armies not only in the Near East (2 Kings 3:25) but later in the Roman army as well. The stone was a special smooth ball, usually of flint, carried in a shoulder bag (1 Samuel 17:40). In several excavations in the Near East, ammunition depots have been discovered filled with these slingstones. With some practice the slinger could become a crack shot. Judges 20:16 states that the Benjaminite army had 700 left-handed slingers who were so accurate they could hit a hair with a stone. (ibid.)

After briefly rehearsing David's career, Snyder comments that the "story of David's rise to power is loaded with shrewd maneuvers and political savvy, but David was not an evil man or an evil king." Instead,

the point is that political maneuvers can also be used by God. God's will is expressed through social forces. David could act as a politician and as a man of faith simultaneously. Somehow we expect the man of God to be a sensitive saint. We expect this so much that we fail to see what is plainly in the biblical record: the great man of God, David, was a man who knew and worked with the great political forces of his time.... (p. 151)

In Snyder's rendition of the biblical story of David we see his method of interpretation being brought to bear in the teaching of high school youth in the church. When asked why he had given so much space to the OT account, Snyder responded with three closely connected affirmations. "First, God's self-revelation is bound to his people." Here we see a fundamental theme of Snyder's teaching. It is through a people that God is revealed. Revelation is not a matter of doctrines passed from one generation to another without regard to the life of the people. Genuine doctrine is born of the experience of a people. "Second, just as the Old Testament shows how impossible it is for mankind to live under the law, so also the Old Testament is a crucial aspect of our personal lives." By this he means that every person in her or his own individual life cannot avoid the struggle with what it means to live under the law. Coming to terms with this struggle is a basic developmental task of all persons.[8] His third stated reason for studying the OT was that it is

---

8. One of Snyder's popular topics in the classroom was the question whether the fall of humankind is actually good. Since all persons fall short of the divine expectation, which is experienced as expectations between one another, and since the forgiveness for such fallenness leads to maturity, are not Adam and Eve in their fallen state more mature than in their innocence? Otherwise stated, would an adult individual who retained all the innocence of childhood be more mature than someone who had fallen and been forgiven? Or, theologically stated, is not the person in Christ more mature than the innocent in the Garden of Eden?

a part of our world in its own right. We cannot understand our own culture without understanding the OT as one of the most basic elements evident in literature, music, drama, and history.[9]

Leading Themes

I wish to take several themes from Snyder's teaching and writing in order to illustrate further the method and content of his interpretation, as well as to refer to his ethical teachings. In particular, I shall consider the themes of community and the individual, freedom and bondage, promise and fulfillment, the local and translocal, Jesus and the church. Perhaps these are sufficient to give us a glimpse into his contribution as educator and ethicist.

Regarding community and the individual, Snyder holds that the individual is formed and sustained in the community. The individual has no identity outside a community or a group of communities. Individuals can influence their communities and the community can shape individuals, but the two are not independent of one another. The reality of a community is in the obligations and narratives that give identity to the community. Individuals participate in the community identity by a process of socialization. Separation from the community is "death," and participation in the community with hope, joy, and freedom is "life."[10]

In explaining the meaning of the Greek word *soma*, normally translated "body," Snyder notes that while there are several instances when it refers to a physical body, normally it refers "to that which defines who we are. Hence it refers to the primary human community." While a westerner usually thinks of himself or herself as a body that contains a soul, the Bible speaks of a corporate body, i.e., a community wherein individuality is expressed as personhood. Only in this sense can one understand the Pauline reference to Christians as members of the body of Christ (1 Cor 6:12–20; 12:12–26) or to the body of Christians as the temple of the Holy Spirit (1 Cor 6:19).[11]

The body of obligations that constitute the identity of the people is called the covenant. In the Bible the people agree with God to fulfill certain obli-

---

9. Snyder, "Why I Wrote What I Wrote in the New Youth Curriculum," *BLead*, September 1964, 22. In another place Snyder argues that one can avoid the problem of Marcion, who rejected the OT "god of wrath and judgment" in favor of a NT "God of love," by seeing the NT as fulfilling the OT: "The unity of the Bible lies in its eschatological expectation, that is, the understanding of the fulfillment. That fulfillment will be a time of justice and peace, when the faults of creation will be resolved" ("Peace from a Biblical Perspective" [unpublished MS from a symposium at McCormick Theological Seminary, Chicago, 1987] 2). Hence while affirming the OT, Snyder clearly is Anabaptist in seeing the NT as normative.

10. Snyder seldom refers to Émile Durkheim, but their views often closely correspond; see, e.g., Durkheim, *The Elementary Forms of the Religious Life* (New York: Macmillan, 1915; repr. New York: Free, 1965).

11. Snyder, *First Corinthians*, 227.

gations, and God agrees to give life to the people (Genesis 15, 17). The
covenant, intentional in origin, tends to wane and become traditional as
it passes from one generation to the next. Eventually it becomes "habitual
and pro forma." Jesus called for a renewal of the original sense of covenant; similarly, "Paul says the covenant cannot be passed on through law,
but only through promise (Gal. 3:15–18)." The apostle Paul recognized that
even though the covenant is permanent, it must be constantly renewed.[12]

Snyder then goes on to say that Christianity fell into the same problem
that faced Judaism, the fall of the covenant into habit. This happened as
Christianity became the dominant religion of the Roman Empire in the fourth
century. The empire stressed faith as assent to doctrine, and enforced it by
law and imperial force; it would take "the Left Wing of the Reformation to
return Christianity to a covenant sense of faith shared by adults."[13] Here
again we see the interpretive stance within the Anabaptist tradition.

Another of Snyder's leading themes is that of freedom and bondage. In an
article entitled "Obedience or Disobedience?" concerning Rom 13:1–7 and
obedience to the state, he does not find a radical opposition between obedience to the state in Romans 13 and the teaching of Romans 12, which
reads like the Sermon on the Mount.[14] Whereas modern persons tend to see
a contradiction between freedom and obedience to the institutions that have
authority over them, Paul does not. Modern readers think of freedom as getting out from underneath oppressive authority. But "the New Testament does
not see it that way at all. For Paul especially, freedom is to be restored to authority so that one is no longer forced to react to it. Man's necessity to react
to authority is what is called 'demonic power'" (p. 9).

When one is unable to do what one knows one ought to do because one
is reacting to authority, then one is in bondage to sin. Here Grady uses an
illustration from contemporary life that so many of his classes have heard:

If a wife comes and reminds us this is the day to play with the children,
we are in a problem. We may recognize that, indeed, this is the day to
play with the children, and in fact we may have been thinking about
it, but now that she has mentioned it we find it nearly impossible to do
so. In Paul's terms that is sin. Sin is when you cannot do what is good
and right because of reaction to authority. (ibid.)

There is a worse condition, namely, doing something you do not want to do
in order to avoid doing what you are asked to do even though you know the
request is right. In the illustration above, watching a TV program one does

not like to watch in order to avoid playing with the children would be worse: "Paul would call that 'death.'" When our reaction to God drives us to do what is destructive or wrong, then we are in bondage to evil, the satanic, the demonic. "The good news, then, is not that we are free from authority, but that we are free from our hangup — our reaction to authority" (ibid.).

Freedom in Christ means that we are free to obey the state. When the state asks of us something against God's will, then we are free to follow God's will. This is not "disobedience" to the state. Rather it is obedience to the real authority of the state. Asked by a Roman soldier to carry luggage one mile, the one asked can carry it farther because he is doing it voluntarily. In the same way, "called to go to Vietnam he does go, but as a volunteer reconciler, not as a paid killer. Called to quell a riot in the city he responds by working for the free movement of all citizens and the abolition of ghettos. If the state cannot accept his obedience as obedience, then that is a condemnation of the state, not of the Christian" (p. 10).

Another theme in Snyder's teaching is promise and fulfillment, which can be seen in four subthemes. The Bible promises Israel *shalom* (peace) if and when they keep the Ten Commandments. Christianity sees the fulfillment of this promise in the universalization of the covenant. Not killing one another within the tribe is universalized to the whole of humanity. Christians live in the expectation of the coming of such a time. Another subtheme is the move from landedness to mobility. Israel is mobile in the desert, but becomes attached to a land upon settling in Palestine. Christianity sees itself as released from the land to go forth in mission to the whole world. Still another subtheme is the shift from theocracy to parabolic community. Israel becomes an established kingdom under God, but this kingdom becomes the promise of a parabolic community that will witness to the nations about the true role of political and social institutions. A final subtheme is the move from act to intention. The law of Israel centers upon acts rather than intentions. The Sermon on the Mount can be read as focusing on intentions rather than acts. The one who is angry with the neighbor has already committed murder. The one who lusts has already committed adultery.

This movement from promise to fulfillment is basic to biblical faith. Israel and Christianity are always oriented to the endtime, the "day of the Lord," the time when the promises of God will be fulfilled. Prophets spoke of the endtime being at hand to motivate people in their righteousness. In times of discouragement they spoke of the delay of the day of the Lord. Early Christians saw in Jesus the beginning of the endtime: in Christ the believer already participates in the endtime even though the fulfillment of the promise is not yet complete.

Still another of Snyder's themes is that of the local and the translocal. The local refers to the close-knit relationships of a congregation, the translocal to the more complex and cosmopolitan relationships in a large community.[15] The church's vitality and power comes from the local congregations, but its response to political and economic forces is led by the translocal church. The local church tends to be acculturated, related to land, to kinship, law and tradition. The translocal church is more likely to be urban, pluralistic, nontraditional, and responsive to larger cultural trends. In the early Christian period the conflict between the translocal church in, say, Rome and the local churches in the outlying areas was decisive for the future of Christianity. In the contemporary church there is a considerable rift between many local congregations and the translocal denominational structures.

One more important theme for Snyder is that of Jesus and the church. Very little is known about the man Jesus except what has been preserved in the NT gospels. The early church "called forth the synoptic Gospels for direction in its daily life, its worship, its preaching, its relationship to nonbelievers, and its own structure." It is impossible to separate these accounts of Jesus from the man himself. There is so little that can be established with historical certainty about the man behind the gospels that the effort to do so is useless. The gospel accounts are part and parcel of the life of the early church. The effort to find the historical Jesus "necessitates a Jesus not related to his community. To the contrary, the resurrected Lord formed and was formed by the early church."[16]

In the very early church two traditions about Jesus arose. One was the story of Jesus, evident in the Gospel of Mark. The other was the sayings of Jesus as found, for example, in the *Gospel of Thomas*. In Matthew and Luke the two are combined. Those who saved only the sayings became more and more spiritualistic and detached from history. They became the gnostics. The gospel accounts of Jesus were brought together by the church, and they had the power to shape the church. Further, they took on the characteristics of the cultures into which they were brought, and they were able to transform the culture from within. This power of inculturation and transformation gave Christianity its vitality. Christianity could have disappeared in the cultures it encountered, or it could have remained aloof like the gnostics. In either case Christianity would have had no historical power.

While working with scholarly materials, Snyder continued to teach not only in the seminary but in the wider church. I have already mentioned *Texts in Transit*, which was written for the instruction of laypersons in the Church of the Brethren. It offered interpretations of passages on opposition to oaths and to retaliation, simple living, settling differences, service to strangers, mis-

---

15. This is similar to Ferdinand Toennies's distinction between "community" and "society" (*Gemeinschaft* and *Gesellschaft*). Snyder is informed especially by Robert Redfield's studies of peasant societies.

16. Snyder, *First Corinthians*, 249, 250.

sion, discipleship, the prayer veil, the secular world, healing, the love feast, communion, and the state. I have also mentioned the youth curriculum, *In His Hand*. Snyder also coauthored a set of volumes for youth entitled *Using Biblical Simulations*.[17] These were extended creative dramas in which the participants would improvise a given biblical scene.

For example, one simulation took as its subject the occasion when Jesus is brought before the Sanhedrin in John 18. Participants divide themselves into four groups: the Sadducees, the Pharisees, the Herodians, and the Apocalypticists. The respective group leaders are to take the roles of Caiaphas, Nicodemus, Antipater, and Saul. Each group is given a set of biblical passages to study in order to understand the attitude of that particular group. The Sadduccee group is given Mark 12:18–27; Acts 4:1–4; 5:17–28; and several other passages. Each of the four groups appoints a chairperson and a chronicler, examines the biblical texts, and decides the group's identity and their strategy for persuading others of their point of view. All the groups then come together as the Sanhedrin. They elect a chair and then discuss the following questions: Who is Jesus and what is his purpose? What should be done with Jesus? Who will carry out the decision about Jesus? The situation develops naturally according to the interactions as they occur, rather than according to a given script. When the simulation is completed, all participants reconvene to share with one another their plans, strategies, and feelings about what happened.

The uniqueness of this form of Bible study is that it combines careful consideration of the text with a situation that has spontaneity and drama. It is designed to awaken the participants' sense of the historical present when decisions are actually being made, and when the outcome is not yet a part of a given tradition. The groupings also give participants a sense of the social realities of the time and of the larger political forces bearing upon them. The simulations are a fine illustration of Snyder's effort to have participants historically informed, politically aware, and open to changing understandings within the text.

Archaeological Evidence

Snyder's scholarship on and teaching of the NT took a decided turn when he began to study the archaeological evidence. He began to look at the nonliterary evidence for the lives of the early Christians. The interpretation of early Christianity for nearly two thousand years has depended upon the writings of important literary figures. But the literary accounts can be far different from

---

17. Donald E. Miller, Graydon F. Snyder, and Robert W. Neff, *Using Biblical Simulations* (2 vols.; Valley Forge, Pa.: Judson, 1973–75).

the actual lives of ordinary Christians. Again we note the Anabaptist stance of interest in everyday life and interaction rather than simply the transmission of creed and doctrine.

Snyder suggests that there are at least three possible sources of error when history is reconstructed with reference only to the sacred literature of the early church:

> First, it is often assumed that the literature represents rather accurately the historical situation when actually it may have a tendentious purpose. Second, it is assumed the literature speaks with a single voice when actually other voices have been ignored, repressed, or assimilated. Third, it is assumed the literature represents a reflective or literary level of popular religion, whereas actually literature and practice often stand in tension with each other.[18]

Snyder's method is to examine archaeological remains to discover to what extent the early gospel tradition transformed the local culture or was transformed by the local culture. One must also attempt to discern whether the evidence indicates genuine transformation or merely nonnormative presence.[19] Noting that little archaeological data appears before AD 180, he begins at that date and concludes at AD 313, when Christianity began to become the official religion of the state. Prior to 180 nothing can be shown to be distinctively Christian: "Whatever estimate one makes of the profuse Christian literature of that time, it took over a century for the new community of faith to develop a distinctive mode of self-expression."[20]

Space precludes review of all the early Christian symbols that Snyder discusses, but we can look at several documented in *Ante Pacem*. The *orante* was a female character with uplifted praying hands. It appeared on Roman coins and in sepulchral art, and was therefore quite familiar to Christians. It apparently had the cultural meaning of filial piety: "In the Christian culture that emerged about A.D. 180, no symbol occurs more frequently and integrally than this female figure with lifted arms. Not only does she exist as a separate symbol, but she is also the main figure in almost every biblical scene, both fresco and sculpture" (p. 19). Snyder concludes that for Christians the *orante* was probably a symbol of security and communal tranquility, the "community"

---

18. Snyder, *Ante Pacem: Archaeological Evidence of Church Life before Constantine* (Macon, Ga.: Mercer University Press, 1985) 8.

19. Ibid., 10.

20. Ibid., 2. Cf. Rodney Stark, *The Rise of Christianity: A Sociologist Reconsiders History* (Princeton, N.J.: Princeton University Press, 1996) 9: "The lack of anything surviving prior to 180 must be assessed on the basis of the tiny number of Christians who could have left such traces. Surely it is not surprising that the 7,535 Christians at the end of the first century left no trace. By 180, when I project that the total Christian population first passed the 100,000 mark, there would finally have been enough Christians so that it is probable that traces of their influence would survive."

now being the church. So in biblical scenes of threat like those of Noah, Jonah, and Daniel, the *orante* signifies God's peace, as also in funerary art (p. 20).

Another widely used symbol was that of the fish. Snyder judges that there were two uses of the fish symbol. The earlier arose with other sea symbols — the ship and the anchor, for example — to represent living in an alien environment. Later, as Christianity became more acceptable, the fish became a symbol of baptism. Very early the fish could stand for the communion meal because of the story of the feeding of the five thousand. The acronym ICHTHYS for the Greek phrase "Jesus Christ, Son of God, Savior" spells out the word "fish" in Greek. Only well after Constantine did the fish come specifically to signify the sacramental Christ.[21]

Snyder proposes that the early church avoided two pitfalls that would have precluded it from becoming a universal religion. First, it did not reject accommodation to the cultural matrix, as the gnostics were to do. One can see this accommodation taking place in the pastoral epistles, but it continued strongly thereafter: "Without this adaptation or conventionalization, early Christianity might have shifted into a nonviable spiritualization." Second, the early church also avoided overintellectualism: "The presence of the original genius of Christianity and the ability of Christianity to attract intellectual leaders surely set the stage for the universal acceptance of the Church, but it was the rapid accommodation to and alteration of the social matrix that enabled Christianity to become a universally practiced religion" (p. 164).

Snyder observes that the late second and third centuries saw a conflict develop between the urban group and the extra-urban group. The former "placed more emphasis upon the growing tradition of the Christian faith and at the same time held a more flexible attitude toward personal and social ethics." The latter was more concerned to maintain the adaptations that had been achieved with the local cultures. An "incredible battle" arose between the "city church leaders," represented by Callistus, and the "cemetery leaders," represented by Hippolytus. Indeed, "perhaps there was no more crucial event in this period of church history than when Callistus was elected bishop of Rome over his 'cemetery' opponent." So it was that urban translocal Christianity gained the ascendancy. When the emperor Constantine came to power, he supported the popular local Christianity that had accommodated to the social matrix. The fourth- and fifth-century church leaders in Rome were able to meld the local traditions of fellowship in the social matrix with the urban memory orientation to create Christian orthodoxy (pp. 164–65).

These changes can be observed in the development of christology. The early images of Jesus were as wonder-worker and deliverer. Only in the fifth

---

21. Ibid., 25. ΙΧΘΥΣ stands of course for the Greek, "Jesus Christ, Son of God, Savior" (note the first letter of each word): Ἰησοῦς Χριστὸς Θεοῦ Υἱὸς Σωτήρ.

century does the suffering Christ on a cross appear. Early Christianity "offered a single figure, Jesus, who could bring peace and opportunity to those in desperate circumstances. The effective agent of that deliverance was none other than the early Christian faith community." The changes can be observed in ecclesiology as well. The church began to have a dramatic impact upon the social hierarchy of the time. In particular, local congregations tended toward the equality of men and women, master and slave: "One can see this fact in two distinct ways: the rapidity with which Roman family names were dropped and the total lack of reference to slaves." And with regard to worship, the fifth-century transformation combined the memory tradition and the house church tradition, but when buildings were built, seldom were they on the sites of older house churches (p. 166).

Attitudes toward the state were not so confrontational as is often assumed by later generations. More likely Christians had little concern for state activities. Property rights in the catacombs were publicly registered, as were house churches. Legal transactions could not be hidden, so clearly most Christians were not in hiding from the state.

In summary, early Christianity adapted in many ways to the social matrix of the time, but in doing so it had a significant influence upon that matrix: "It created a new Christian community that knew it had been differentiated from that Hellenistic society, expressed itself in terms of small-group caring and hospitality, offered deliverance from the personal and social entrapments of life, and infused people with a vision of cross-cultural universality." Constantine gave this Christianity a public role, and the church leaders of the late fourth and fifth centuries altered it to create what came to be Christian orthodoxy (p. 169).

Inculturation and Ethics

A significant development came in Snyder's career when he spent a sabbatical in Zimbabwe lecturing and studying African Christianity. This led him to raise the question of what would have happened if the Jesus tradition had been inculturated elsewhere than in the Greco-Roman context.[22]

At the obvious risk of oversimplification, the earliest Jesus tradition can be summarized in this way: "(1) healings of persons regardless of their status as clean or unclean; (2) universal commensality regardless of class distinctions; (3) a constant tension with the social matrix (as seen in Jesus' crucifixion

---

22. Snyder credits the African scholar Itumeleng Mosala with raising this question for him. See his "Before the Canon: The Pre-Cultural Jesus Tradition," in Isabel Mukonyora, James L. Cox, and Frans J. Verstraelen, eds., "Rewriting" the Bible — The Real Issues: Perspectives from within Biblical and Religious Studies in Zimbabwe (Gweru/Harare, Zimbabwe: Mambo, 1993) 81; also idem, Health and Medicine, 111.

by the social matrix) and in his constant use of apocalyptic reversal (in the Beatitudes, for example); and (4) subversion of political limitations (as seen in Jesus' sending of the disciples to create inclusivity and in his apocalyptic vision of a universal community)."[23]

This Jesus tradition is precultural, which is to say that it is prior to the Greco-Roman inculturation. This has led Snyder to study how the Jesus tradition was embodied in other cultures, such as Africa or Ireland. And it is here that we discover the intersection of inculturation and ethics because Snyder understands the early church and local churches in general to be focused on relationships and engagement with the culture at least as much as on doctrine — on orthopraxis as much as on orthodoxy. This concern for fellowship, for transforming the social matrix, and for relationships is ethical in nature.

In an article on ethics Snyder identifies several contemporary ethical dilemmas. With regard to whether Christian ethics is public or private, he suggests that the dichotomy is false. Every personal decision affects the corporate life, and every public issue becomes personal for those who are affected by it. There is a difference between local and translocal ethics, as has been noted above, but it would be better to drop the private/public dichotomy. Likewise, to the question of whether the gospel is separate from social action Snyder suggests that the gospel can never be simply accepted without challenging the social context. Too often it is assumed that the American context is thoroughly Christian. The gospel always pulls toward what ought to be.[24]

Whether the gospel is apocalyptic or pragmatic is fundamental. A pragmatic ethic takes responsibility for the whole society, "but more and more Christians are becoming aware that the church is not responsible for a universal ethic." Rather the gospel involves a vision of the human good that will inevitably challenge some existing institutions. In that sense it is apocalyptic. The question of principle and context may seem to be critical, but is only an apparent dilemma. Christianity can relate to a variety of cultures. Nevertheless there are certain basic ethical "directions" in the gospel. These include an "affirmation of the meaning of life as it is (incarnation), an openness to the future (resurrection), and love of neighbor as the expression of self-love (covenant)."[25]

We have already seen that freedom consists of accepting God's authority, thereby living in peace rather than in bondage to sin. Peace is a fundamental theme in Snyder's ethics. He staunchly defends the position that the Bible teaches pacifism: "I believe that every Christian is a pacifist. It would seem

---

23. Snyder, "Before the Canon, 83.
24. Snyder, "Christian Ethics," *ChrMin*, July 1970, 33–34.
25. Ibid., 34–35.

to me that what we have seen in the entire Bible is so convincing, that one could hardly come to any other conclusion." He proceeds to describe the things that make for peace. They include the power of the universal vision, the teleological suspension of reified cultural values, the ministry of reconciliation, and the destruction of dividing walls. It is tribal and familial loyalties, faith bound to a certain land or location, the authorizing of the church by the state, and the view that intentions do not matter that lead to violence.[26]

Early in his career Snyder accepted a position on the Board of Bethany Hospital on the West Side of Chicago. This has led him to have an intense and continuing interest in medical ethics. Recent discussions of medical ethics tend to emphasize the categories of autonomy, beneficence, nonmaleficence, and justice. Autonomy points to the right of a person to decide what treatment she or he will receive. Beneficence refers to the fact that on balance the treatment should benefit the patient. Nonmaleficence is the principle that at the very least no harm should be done. And justice refers to the fact that the benefits of treatment should be as widely and equally distributed as possible. In this conversation, Snyder repeatedly points out that the Bible does not assume solitary individuals but rather embodied people — persons within social groups. Medical decisions should therefore include significant other persons, such as family members, the church community, as well as an ethics advisory group.

Regarding "doing no harm," the Bible teaches that humanity should protect and cultivate the creation, but should also work for the coming of the new creation. With regard to calculating the benefits of a remedy, Snyder suggests that the love ethic is much more than that of "a minimally decent Samaritan." Christian love takes the radical stance of caring for another without counting the cost to the giver: "The Jesus of the Gospels called on us to sell all we have and give to the poor, to turn the other cheek when attacked, to love the neighbor as ourselves."[27]

With regard to justice, strictly speaking the Bible does not teach that each person is to be considered equally. It refers to peace (shalom) rather than justice, if the latter means equality. "Each individual is received in the faith community as a legitimate and full member," which means that every person is to be fully included in the community on the basis of talent and circumstances. Therefore those who are poor, ill, or otherwise marginalized will receive special treatment. The result is an embodied shalom rather than an abstract equality.[28]

26. Snyder, "Peace from a Biblical Perspective," 7–8.
27. Snyder, Tough Choices (Elgin, Ill.: Brethren Press, 1988) 40.
28. Ibid., 42.

This discussion makes clear that Snyder believes that ethical issues must be considered from the point of view of both what will serve the common good (utilitarianism) and generally accepted moral norms (deontology), for both have a basis in the Judeo-Christian tradition. However, they must always be set within the biblical narrative. He therefore opts for a "virtue ethic," or what he would prefer to call a "narrative ethic." He believes that the biblical narrative, and within it the Jesus story, can relate to different cultures and different situations in different ways. It is the calling of the body of believers to search together for the fitting faithful action. This leads to a life of peacemaking, reconciliation, hospitality, service to the disinherited, sometimes suffering within a community of believers, often tension with the current culture, but always a life infused with hope for a time of greater wholeness.

The Legacy to Chicago

Snyder's talent as educator should be evident throughout what has been said above. He is first and foremost an interpreter and an educator as well as a scholar. His teaching has taken place in the seminary classroom, the Sunday school, adult study groups, at the lecture podium, through sermons, written curricular materials, and constant informal discussions with students and friends. Snyder spent many years as a seminary dean. His vision of seminary education is consonant with his vision of the church. Basic to the formation of a pastor is a thorough study of scripture. Such study, as we have seen, should make the student aware of the historical setting of the text, the probable meaning of the text at the time of the writer, and the meaning of the text for contemporary listeners.[29] As a seminary dean he worked for a viable cluster of seminaries in the Chicago area. That cluster would use the strengths of each school to produce a many-faceted curriculum in which students had a wide range of cross-registration options.

In Snyder's view, seminary education is more than an exercise in intellectual disciplines. The relationships of students to one another are a part of the setting for learning. Snyder pioneered the use of colloquium groups of students and faculty looking at ministerial issues as a part of their relationship to one another. He believes that seminaries should teach for both local and translocal ministries. Therefore students should be able to minister in various congregational settings, but they should also understand the wider church issues and the international outlook of the church.[30] As women and minorities

---

29. Snyder, "Present Trends in Theological Education," *BLT* 23/3 (Summer 1978) 165.
30. Ibid., 166–67.

assume leadership in the church and come to seminary for training, the seminary should seek to find the way in which they can best relate to the whole, and hence achieve more than merely abstract equality.

To comprehend Snyder's contribution as educator, one most know something of his teaching style. He is not only articulate in presenting the concepts I have been discussing, he also loves to be engaged in debate. He likes the use of story and has been adept at keeping in mind and retelling the stories of many of his students and friends. He believes deeply that such storytelling is basic to community formation. He is also intensely competitive, whether in the classroom or on the handball court. Seldom does one best him in intellectual exchange (or in handball volleys!).

His classroom style might be called one of dramatic dissonance. He will present a position or a stance that may seem on the surface to be disconnected. Then he will debate the issue with students until they must concede. Some students are uncomfortable at not being able to make their case, yet not wanting to change. His goal is to cajole students into creative thinking. Those who engage with him are very often highly stimulated and challenged. Many students are lifelong friends and carry on the method of interpretation he taught them.

A story Snyder tells about himself, though not about a classroom event, may serve to illustrate his teaching method:

I was standing near a bench at the Illinois Central Railway station on 57th Street in Hyde Park on Chicago's South Side. An older man was sitting on the part of the bench with four slats. So I sat on the part of the bench with three slats as we waited for the train.

The man said, "Do you suppose there are any good public benches in Chicago?"

"No, I don't suppose so."

"Do you think there are any good benches in the United States?"

I thought of New York, and San Francisco. "No, I don't think so."

"Do you think there are any good benches in the world?"

"Well, yes. There are good benches in Turkey in front of the Hagia Sophia."

"Have you ever been there?"

"Yes."

"What were you doing?"

"I was looking at archaeological sites and giving lectures."

"Do you travel much?"

"Quite a bit."

"Why do you travel?"

"I am an educator in professional organizations, and I travel once overseas and once in the U.S. each year."

"What do you do?"

"I am a professor."

"At the university?"

"Well, more or less."

"How can you be a professor at the university more or less?"

"I teach at Chicago Theological Seminary, where the students are covered by the university's health plan, have privileges in the gymnasium, and other university benefits."

"Oh, I see. That is more or less."

At this time the train stopped and we stood up to get in the train.

He said, "We can continue our conversation on the train."

I said, "If you like."

As we sat down, he said to me, "What are the four most important archaeological discoveries with regard to Christianity?"

"I would say the Dead Sea Scrolls, the gnostic writings in Egypt, the excavation beneath St. Peter's basilica in Rome, and a number of others."

He quickly said, "Some people think the Dead Sea Scrolls were not written by the Qumran community. They are a later forgery."

"Goldman has suggested that, but it is not the accepted opinion."

"What do you think of the view that the apostle Paul was a spy of the Roman government sent to disrupt the Hebrew community?"

"It's baloney. There is not one shred of evidence to support it."

I had discovered that my protagonist was a retired journalist, and I could have said that his proposal about Paul sounded like something a journalist would make up, but I didn't. By this time I noticed that a number of people in our car were gathered around listening to the conversation.

Suddenly he said, "There's no use for us to talk any more. You are committed to an orthodox version of Christianity, and you have a closed mind."

I said, "Have you heard the story about the two men working on a telephone pole?"

"No."

"Well, this is how it was:

The telephone pole was right above a community college. The one had always wanted to take college courses, something he told the other man.

The other man said, "Why don't you see if you can enroll. Perhaps they will take you."

So the first man slid down the pole and walked into the community col-lege. There the dean greeted him. He told the dean he would like to take courses.

The dean said, "Indeed you are qualified, and we can admit you. But there is only one class open this term. All the others are filled."

"What is the open class?"

"Deductive reasoning."

"What is that?"

"Let me explain it this way. I recently asked someone, 'Do you have a weed whacker?'

" 'Yes, I do,' was the reply.

" 'Then you must have a lawn.'

" 'Well, yes I do.'

" 'Then you must have a lawnmower.'

" 'Yes, I do.'

" 'Then you must have a sizable lawn.'

" 'Yes, it is.'

" 'And you must have a rather large house.'

" 'Yes, I do.'

" 'And then you must have a sizable family.'

" 'I have two girls and two boys.'

" 'And then you must be heterosexual.'

" 'I am as straight as they come.'

"Now that is deductive reasoning," said the dean.

The man was very, very impressed with this, so he took the application forms and quickly climbed back up the pole.

The other man said to him, "Well, what did you find out?"

He retorted, "Do you have a weed whacker?"

"No," was the answer.

"Then you must be gay," he said.

The retired journalist said to me, "What does that have to do with anything?"

"You took one statement of mine about the apostle Paul and decided I am orthodox and closed-minded. My statement gave no hint whether I am orthodox or closed-minded. You should have known better than to make a statement like that."

The train stopped and I got off.

Graydon Snyder is a bold, resourceful, imaginative, scholarly ethicist, educa-tor, and interpreter of the Anabaptist tradition. He has made a significant contribution to his field of study. He supports his tradition in a creative, non-defensive manner; in fact he seldom mentions it. Rather he uses disciplined historical research, logic, and interpretation to persuade others, whatever their tradition. He focuses upon the NT and the pre-Constantinian church as a way of presenting a world-historical vision of the future. He has lived a life dedicated to service, ministry, and teaching at all levels of the life of the church. It is a privilege to pay this tribute to him.

2

ANALOGIES FOR OUR COMMON LIFE

Reflections on Graydon F. Snyder
as Teaching Theologian

Virginia Wiles

Any student of Graydon Snyder's knows much about his personal life. Its many and varied particulars that have entwined themselves through his lectures, discussions, and arguments in the classroom have more to do with the NT than with him personally. Any student who has understood the process of the class knows that what students affectionately call "Grady's stories" are not, in the end, about Snyder at all. Or rather, they are about him only to the extent that they are about the students themselves, about the original hearers of the NT texts, indeed, about humanity with all its great diversity. These stories are "analogies for our common life."

As someone who has sat in many of Snyder's classes and spent uncounted hours discussing the NT and its theologies with him, nothing is clearer to me than that analogy is the key mode of his thinking. I have rarely ever had a conversation with him that did not draw its life and structure from some analogy. And yet when I turn to read his published works, there is relatively little direct evidence of the use of analogy. Why is this? Why does Snyder the teacher and friend so consistently draw on analogies in his teaching and in personal conversations, while Snyder the scholar usually leaves them out of his published writings?

Two answers to this question are ready at hand. Perhaps his analogies are used only for teaching purposes and thus are not needed when he is writing for his peers. Surely this is true for many scholar-teachers: they use many illustrations in the classroom in order to explain the difficult concepts that their peers can grasp without the "crutch" of an illustration. Or one might seek the answer to this question by suggesting that since he has taught in a seminary, his illustrations are efforts to help his students apply the theologies of the NT to present-day church life. Here again, NT scholarship does not need the analogies, for such scholarship has traditionally sought a historical truth that is not dependent upon the present-day churches' needs or experiences. To include such analogies in his scholarly writing would be to confuse the historical task of discerning "what it meant" with the theological and pastoral tasks of "what it means."[1] In either case, whether the analogy is used for purpose of explanation or of application, the analogy could appear to be "tacked on" to the principal scholarly purpose of investigating the socio-historical contexts and meanings of the NT texts and the life of the early church.

Had I not spent so many hours in personal conversation with Graydon Snyder, I might stop my inquiry at this point, for these two answers seem quite plausible from a distance. Perhaps the need to explain or apply the NT texts can account for some of the stories that Snyder tells. But these needs cannot account for his persistent use of analogy in private conversation. My intuition and experience tell me that Snyder does not merely "use" analogy. Rather, *his entire mode of thinking* is analogical. This leaves me, however, with a quandary: How can I make assertions about Snyder's "analogical" mode of thinking based merely on my own individual experience or intuition? Would this not violate the standards of scholarship, standards that we surely want to uphold in this collection of scholarly articles written in his honor?

Fortunately there are hints in Snyder's writings that can point the way. It will be helpful, first, to offer a few of "Grady's stories" as examples of what I am calling "analogies." Then, secondly, there is at least one place in his scholarly writing where we can catch a glimpse of how Snyder assumes analogy as a form of theological expression. Finally, from these few written examples I will attempt to describe how analogy functions in Snyder's intellectual work.

"Grady's Stories"

As a young scholar-teacher, Snyder wrote a series of youth lessons entitled *In His Hand* for his denomination.[2] It is in these lessons that we can catch a

---

1. See Krister Stendahl, "Biblical Theology, Contemporary," *IDB* 1.418–32. See my brief critique of this distinction in "On Transforming New Testament Theology: (Re)Claiming Subjectivity," in Virginia Wiles, Alexandra Brown, and Graydon F. Snyder, eds., *Putting Body and Soul Together: Essays in Honor of Robin Scroggs* (Valley Forge, Pa.: Trinity Press International, 1997) 319–20.

2. *In His Hand* (Elgin, Ill.: Brethren Press, 1964).

glimpse of the kinds of analogies used in his classroom. These few examples may shed light on how and why Snyder appears to use analogies.

1. A Comparison. Snyder tackles the task of explaining the relationship between faith and works in the epistle of James by narrating what he calls a "comparison":

> A young man and a young woman may fall in love with each other without saying anything to each other. By expressions of "faith" such as signals and smiles, they may communicate to one another the trust and loyalty that have developed between them. We call this love.... Eventually the boy and girl who have whispered their love to each other will make public that confession and will promise to each other and to their friends and family that they will take on certain obligations to each other and to society....
>
> At the same time those persons who indicate that they love one another and then never carry out that expression of love in a marriage ceremony are regarded as warped personalities who would not make desirable mates. To put it another way, if love does not lead to confession of love, and to a concrete expression of love, it is not likely love at all. But concrete expressions of love and confessions of love which do not have love behind them are hypocrisy and are worthless.
>
> So it is with faith. Concrete expressions of faith, such as creedal statements and ethical actions, are of no value unless there is a true, faithful communion with God that brought about these concrete expressions. But at the same time a faith which does not give concrete expressions is not likely a faith at all.[3]

Snyder uses this analogy to "explain" the theological concepts of *fides, fiducia,* and *credentia* as they apply to the theology of James. As is frequently the case, the analogy draws in fundamental ways upon human experience of relationships.

2. A "Multiple Choice" Analogy. Early in the series of lessons, Snyder establishes what might be called a "multiple choice" analogy. He uses this analogy in his discussion of Genesis 2–3:

> Suppose I have a small son named Jimmy. Suppose I own a vase which I treasure very much. I would like to enjoy the beauty of the vase along with my friends and Jimmy, too. In order to do this I might handle Jimmy and the vase in several ways:
>
> 1. I could place the vase on a stand in my front room. In order to protect the vase I could tie Jimmy hand and foot, place him near the vase, and say, "Jimmy, have a good time."

---

3. Ibid., 469–71.

2. I could refuse to risk the vase and put it in one room and then take Jimmy to another room which is completely lacking in breakable items. I could lock Jimmy in the second room and say, "You are completely free here, Jimmy. Have a good time."

3. I could place both Jimmy and the vase in the room without any mention of the value of the vase or any command not to break it. Jimmy might never touch the vase, and even if he did, he would not be aware of the fact that he did something displeasing to his father.

4. I could place both the vase and Jimmy in the room and explain very carefully to him the value of the vase. I could then say, "Jimmy, you are free to have a good time, but if you break the vase, you will be punished."[4]

In this use of analogy, Snyder has set up a "thought experiment," whereby he expects his reader to think through various possibilities. He follows his multiple-choice scenarios with an explanation of why only the fourth choice "will suit." The brevity of his explanation, however, makes it clear that he has anticipated that his reader was imagining these possibilities one by one. We can begin to see that such analogies have been forged in the classroom. Although it takes a reader but a few minutes at most to read through his analogy and its explanation, one can imagine that the process of "thinking through" this analogy might well take a full class period of an hour or more. Indeed, there might be extensive discussion and disagreement among the students as to which of these four scenarios would be preferable. Such analogies, then, take on the characteristic of being "means of thought" rather than simple explanations of a foregone conclusion.

Such "thought experiments" can be extended to relate to other texts. For example, Snyder returns to this analogy in a later lesson where he wants to explain "the law written on the heart" in Jeremiah:

> To illustrate this, let us return to the case of Jimmy and the vase (page 30). You will remember that his father gave a law: "Do not break the vase." This was a good law, but suppose that in his freedom the boy, Jimmy, did break it. For this he would be punished by his father. It is the very nature of freedom that after this punishment the boy would feel ambivalent toward his father. He wishes to please him and obey him, but at the same time he wishes to show him that he is still free. The power of his father to judge him and punish him becomes a reason for Jimmy to rebel even more against his father — it "tempts" him to disobey his father. The situation now becomes serious. Since his father is both a loving father and a judge, his presence with Jimmy serves

---

4. Ibid., 30–31.

both to attract his son to him and to repel him. His father is caught: any new law that he might make, *no matter how good and reasonable,* will only serve to drive his son away from him. This son is also caught: if he obeys the law of his father, he gives up his own sense of freedom and finally destroys his own self-esteem.[5]

Having encouraged his reader to think through various scenarios regarding law and free will in relation to Jimmy, the vase, and Jimmy's father, Snyder can now count on his reader following him through yet one more logical argument regarding law and freedom.[6] The force of this argument depends more upon what might be called "experiential logic" than on analytic or conceptual logic.[7] Again, this experience is not purely "individual" experience but rather "relational" experience.

3. Theology by Analogy. Occasionally Snyder speaks directly of analogy, as in this instance when he is explaining Paul's notion of "slavery to righteousness":

Perhaps an analogy would help. A young man may resent the fact that his parents try to force him to comb his hair and wear a tie. Combing one's hair and wearing a tie may be good things, but the young man, in his struggle against his parents and against social custom, will find in this particular law a threat to his own individuality. So combing his hair and wearing a tie becomes a major point of debate between himself and his parents. But one day he meets a girl that he likes. The next day he combs his hair and wears a tie! Combing his hair and wearing a tie is now no longer a law; it is something he wants to do in order to find favor in the eyes of his new friend. So, following his "conversion," he does live according to the law; but he does not know it — for the law is really what he wants to do![8]

What is most interesting at this point in Snyder's discussion is that the current experience of faith is employed to explain Paul's analogy. He writes:

The analogy used here in chapter 6 [of Romans] by Paul is that of slavery.... Paul says that the new [human] situation is indeed a slavery, a slavery to God or a slavery to righteousness. But this new slavery is really freedom, because now we are free to live according to life itself

---

5. Ibid., 224–25; emphasis original.
6. See also Snyder's discussion of Romans 1, where he again returns to the analogy of Jimmy, referring both to Genesis and Jeremiah (ibid., 340–41).
7. By "experiential logic" I mean something akin to what David Tracy refers to as the criterion of "meaningfulness" (see Tracy, *Blessed Rage for Order: The New Pluralism in Theology* [New York: Seabury, 1975] 71).
8. Ibid., 410. In Snyder's explanation of this analogy he again refers to the "nature of freedom in our Genesis discussion" — that is, to Jimmy, the vase, and Jimmy's father.

without struggling against the law or trying in some way to establish ourselves as free individuals. . . . He says that while it may appear to each of us in our alienation from God that true freedom is escape from the law, actually this attempt to escape from the law is nothing else but sin. We are enslaved to the law because we are forced to run from it. The attempt to escape law results in death because it forces us to live in that way which is contrary to life itself. When we give up trying to find freedom for ourselves and die to ourselves with Christ in baptism, then we are raised to a new life. In this new life we no longer know the law or think about it. Instead, we live a life of righteousness, joyfully accepting God's will for us and working for his goal. . . .[9]

It is possible to reconstruct Snyder's argument from back to front. He begins with (a) a statement of "what Paul wants to say"; then he articulates (b) the analogy (=slavery) that Paul himself used in order to make clear his meaning; and finally he sets forth (c) his own analogy (=combing hair) in an effort to make clear the meaning of Paul's analogy and corresponding meaning.

Snyder's double use of the term "analogy" in this explication of Romans 6 hints that his earlier reference to his own analogies as "illustrations" or mere explanations is not quite adequate. The analogies themselves participate in the forming of the theology. This dynamic can be seen most clearly in Snyder's major exegetical work on Paul, *First Corinthians*.[10]

"Paul's Stories"

Thirty years after publishing his youth lessons on the Bible, Snyder published his commentary on 1 Corinthians. His understanding of analogy had grown significantly during this time. In one of the "Summary Essays" at the end of the commentary Snyder emphasizes the importance of analogy for reading Paul's letters:

[Paul] clearly uses many analogies. . . . When does Paul use an analogy? The inability to discern analogy in Paul has caused considerable trouble in Christian history. Some readers take literally what Paul meant as analogy. In that way they seriously alter the meaning of both the text and Paul's message. . . . Sometimes Paul signals to us that an analogy is coming. . . . But more often there is no signal. . . . Even when we have determined we are in an analogy, our problems are not all solved. . . . In

---

9. Ibid., 409–10.
10. Snyder, *First Corinthians: A Faith Community Commentary* (Macon, Ga.: Mercer University Press, 1992).

any case a good reading of Paul's letters requires close attention to the meaning (tenor) of analogies.[11]

This indicates the importance that Snyder attaches to analogy as a mode of thought and presentation. The role of analogy is seen most strikingly in Snyder's exegesis of 1 Corinthians 5–6. The subtitle of this section is "Two Case Studies at Corinth."[12] In the introduction to this section Snyder raises the question of the relation between 1 Corinthians 5–6 and the rest of Corinthians. Specifically, he asks whether these chapters are "really discussions of immorality."[13] He concludes that they were rather "case studies" exemplifying and elaborating the theology that Paul had set forth in chapters 1–4:

> Chapters 5 and 6 actually continue the discussion of chapters 1–4. Chapter 5 is addressed to the Christ house church. It is a specific demonstration (case study) that their living in the endtime has already backfired. Chapter 6 is addressed more to the other three groups. It shows them (by means of a second case study) that their secular practicality has kept them from living in the endtime.[14] In chapters 1–4 Paul has responded to the problem of divisions at Corinth. In 5:1–13 he gave a case study on the problems of an endtime reached too quickly; an immorality done in the name of the Lord. In 6:1–11 he addressed, by means of another case study, those who were still living in the old age: a failure to trust within the community. Now, before starting the answer to their questions (7:1), he draws this "letter" to a close with a unifying summary. Both elements of the Corinthian church are addressed in one image — that of the body.[15]

It is in the final section of these chapters that the analogical method becomes fully explicit. Snyder denies that this passage can "be taken simply as a warning against sexual immorality." Rather it should be understood "as a teaching about the corporate life of the new age."[16] In 6:12–14 Paul uses analogies of eating and sexuality in order to instruct the Christ church that "the corporate body is not made for immorality (an alienating or competing allegiance)."[17] He does not assume that immorality as such was the problem

---

11. See the essay entitled "Analogy" (ibid., 221–22).

12. I wonder why Snyder did not call these analogies in the subtitle. He does refer to them as analogies later in the text; see ibid., 81, 83, 222. In any case, the terminology of "case studies" does point to an important element in Snyder's use of analogies. Case studies are not mere application of a concept to a specific situation. They invite the participant to "think through" the concept so that it might be applied to a variety of situations. That is, they are primarily a learning technique, not a prescribed application.

13. Ibid., 56.

14. Ibid.

15. Ibid., 77.

16. Ibid., 80.

17. Ibid., 81.

of the Christ church. Rather, their problem consisted of what he calls "the ideology of freedom."[18] Whether that "ideology of freedom" led to immorality or excessive "morality," it was the ideology that was the point of Paul's instruction, not any specific result of that ideology. Paul uses the analogy/case study to get at the root of the problem. The "fruit" of an ideology of freedom may well be immorality, and surely Paul would oppose immorality. But the deeper problem is the "root," which is the ideology itself.

After addressing the Christ church, Paul then turns the same analogy towards the others at Corinth in 6:15–18. Here the problem is not an ideology of freedom but "the extent to which the early Corinthian Christians have actually shifted from the unrighteous age to the community of the endtime."[19] Snyder's comments on analogy become more explicit in this section:

> Some readers have confused the literal analogy (the vehicle) with the actual situation addressed (the tenor). *Paul was not addressing a case of immorality at Corinth.* Granted the analogy bears truth and there were likely some cases of immorality in the Corinthian church; *nevertheless the topic is the return of some Corinthian Christians to the old age of unrighteousness.* Depending on the old age for body-network functions (legal judgments in this case, 6:1–8) creates or preserves a self-identity outside the faith community. To be sure, association with the old age is required (5:10), but one's self-identity (*psyche*) comes from the community of the endtime. It comes from joining to that community where Christ is Lord (v. 17).[20]

The emphasized sections of this quotation highlight Snyder's insistence that Paul is here employing analogy in order to teach a theological truth. The "ethical instruction" in these chapters is really theological instruction. Paul writes about immorality because he wants to instruct the Christ church regarding the inadequacy of their "ideology of freedom." He writes about lawsuits because he wants to instruct the other Corinthian churches regarding their wrongheaded dependence upon the old age. In terms of analogy, the ethical issues addressed are the vehicle for conveyance of the tenor or "focal meaning,"[21] namely, laying a theological foundation that will overcome the divisions at Corinth (1 Cor 1:10). These divisions, according to Snyder, have

---

18. Ibid.

19. Ibid., 82.

20. Ibid., 83 (emphasis added). Snyder's phrase "the actual situation addressed" could be confusing here. The tenor, in this instance, is the return of the Corinthians to the "old age"; this, rather than immorality, is the "actual situation addressed." Thus, the tenor might more accurately be described as a theological "idea" (as it is lived out in an actual situation — which for Snyder would be true of any genuinely theological idea).

21. See the summary essay on "Analogy" (ibid., 220–22) for Snyder's use of the terms "vehicle" and "tenor."

"arisen between those who are above the law and those who feel caught in
the web of this age."[22] In Snyder's reading, then, 1 Cor 6:20 concludes not
only 6:12–20 but the whole of 1 Corinthians 1–6: "The message is simple.
In the life of the body Christians do not act for themselves or for their own
self-interest. Christians give honor and obedience to God — in that way the
body will not be divided against itself."[23]

In reading this section (on 1 Corinthians 5–6) of Snyder's commentary,
one might easily get lost. This is perhaps to be expected as we read an analogical thinker who is dissecting another analogical thinker. Snyder thinks that
Paul is writing on two levels at once — on the level of vehicle, Paul speaks
about immorality; on the level of tenor, Paul is addressing the Corinthian
need for a unity consistent with the "already but not yet" reality of the endtime. Snyder thus needs to exegete the dual levels of the text. He constantly
shifts back and forth between making assertions about the logic of the vehicle and the logic of the tenor. Further, he needs to explain whether and how
the vehicle adequately conveys the tenor.

Snyder is not unaware of the complexity of this task. In his essay on analogy at the conclusion of the commentary he outlines the difficulties in using
(and interpreting) analogies.[24] He identifies three specific challenges in regard
to analogies. First, the vehicle must be "true to life." But because the vehicle is true to life, there is often the danger that the interpreter will assume
that the vehicle itself is the message and will thus misread the text. Second,
the vehicle must relate adequately to the tenor. Otherwise the vehicle will
miscommunicate the tenor. Of course, no vehicle is ever perfectly adequate
to convey the nuances and tensions of the tenor, but the vehicle must be
adequate to what one wishes to communicate. Third, the tenor needs to be
evident in the way the vehicle is used; otherwise the interpreter may read
the vehicle as carrying an entirely different meaning than what the author
intends.

If there are so many difficulties in using analogies, why would we bother
using them? Are they merely crutches for less sophisticated minds? Do they
simply assist one until she or he is able to state the "meaning" in precise conceptual language? Would the "meaning" be the same without the analogy?
Or is the analogy somehow essential not only to the conveying of the meaning but even to the meaning itself? No doubt the answers to these questions
depend upon the nature of the analogies used and the kinds of meanings
one is wishing to convey. I want to propose, however, that in Graydon Sny-

22. Ibid., 21.
23. Ibid., 85.
24. Ibid., 221–22.

der's teaching and in his theological reflection, analogies are essential to the message he wants to communicate.

The Analogical Life

In a series of lectures that Snyder gave in 1970, there is a revealing comment. After describing the power that spouses and children have to create and to influence one another, he asserts:

> Our covenant with God is not dissimilar to these human phenomena. As a side comment I might say I believe the human necessities are God given, that is, *ontologically the same as the divine necessities.* But since we normally separate the two, I will conform at this point to the usual means of communication.[25]

Snyder goes on to speak of the power of God, concluding as follows:

> God's power is the drive of the covenant. *On the human level* it is the ultimate hope to know and be known by someone else. *On the divine level* it is the hope that life has ultimate significance and the drive to achieve that hope.[26]

Here, I would claim, is clear evidence of Snyder's analogical method. To use the language he employed for analogy in his commentary, we could say that the "human level" corresponds to the "vehicle" and that the "divine level" corresponds to the "tenor." Indeed, this is precisely my experience of Snyder's teaching and thinking. He is "theological" through and through. By this I mean to say that I do not believe that he ever speaks about "purely" human phenomena. Every comment, description, narration of human action, motivation, or imagining is (at least potentially) a theological assertion. Human life is, in short, the "vehicle" for the divine.[27]

In Snyder's language, human life is always penultimate at best.[28] Yet it is none other than human life that conveys the divine, or ultimate; in Snyder's view, the only way we know the divine.[29] In the terms of analogy, the only

---

25. Snyder, "Power and Violence: A Biblical Study," *Colloquium* 1 (Bethany Theological Seminary Monograph Series; Oak Brook, Ill.: Bethany Theological Seminary, 1971) 33 (emphasis added).

26. Ibid., 34 (emphasis added).

27. For Snyder "human life" always means "relational existence." See his "Power and Violence," 32.

28. See, for example, his use of this language in "Power and Violence," 38–40, and in *First Corinthians,* 113.

29. Such a relation between the divine and human is true to an Anabaptist hermeneutic. See, e.g., Nadine Pence Frantz, "Theological Hermeneutics: Christian Feminist Hermeneutics and the Believers Church Tradition" (Ph.D. diss., University of Chicago, 1992).

way we can know the tenor (=meaning) is to hear and understand the vehicle. The human and the divine are inextricably bound through analogy. One
might even say that human existence is dependent upon its participation in
this analogy. Although a particular vehicle may not be necessary to the (universal) tenor, some vehicle is needed in order to convey the tenor. At least
in terms of the human world (the only world we know) analogy is essential
to meaning. Analogy is what binds together the human and the divine.

This sounds very much like a Johannine approach to truth and reality.
Certainly it is a radically incarnational view of God (or Christ). In the Gospel of John, Jesus' revelation of God's reality is an analogy writ large. An
analogy proper must consist of both vehicle and tenor.[30] If there is only "vehicle," then there is no analogy, only an interesting or entertaining story —
only a "sign" misunderstood. If there is only "tenor," then there is no analogy, only an abstract concept. Jesus' revelation of God (analogy) occurs in
human words and actions (vehicle) that inherently point toward (or allude
to) the divine reality (tenor). The power of John's gospel lies precisely in the
analogy, in the inextricable relationship between the vehicle and the tenor.
To "believe" in the Gospel of John is to grasp the analogy — both the vehicle (as vehicle and thus penultimate) and the tenor (as ultimate). In this
I think Snyder would agree with the Johannine method, for he, like John,
assumes that theology or God-language is necessarily analogical.[31] The goal
for the Johannine community is not that the hearers grasp the tenor without any further need of an analogical vehicle. Rather, the community is to
become a vehicle for the tenor of the ultimate reality. The community is to
live analogically.

Here, then, lies the key to Snyder's use of analogies both as theologian and
as teacher. Theology, for Snyder, is irreducibly analogical. Just as theology
cannot be reduced to tenor, since that would reduce theology to creedal or

---

30. It is crucial to remember that the analogy does not equal the vehicle, which would result
in a radical reductionism. (Reduction of the vehicle to "mere" story divorced from the tenor is to
assign ultimacy to what is inescapably penultimate. It is to live a "false reality." The meaning of
the penultimate lies in the tenor, not the vehicle, in the divine, not the human.) Rather, the term
"analogy" refers to the complex of relations between the vehicle and the tenor. In the language
of David Tracy, these relations consist of "similarities-in-difference, continuities-in-discontinuity
and ordered relationships-in-disorder" (The Analogical Imagination [New York: Crossroad, 1981]
420–21). As an aside it might be important to point out that simple "word-pictures" or simple
(i.e., nontensive) life-situations do not qualify as true analogies. They may illustrate a conceptual
truth, but some tensive relations within the vehicle are necessary in order for the story to count
as an analogy. It is these tensions that give the analogy the sense of malleability and "play."
Although Snyder's own assertions that reality is found neither in the subject nor the object but
rather in the "betweenness" of relationships were made in reference to other philosophical issues,
they are apropos here as well. See, e.g., "Power and Violence," 52–53.

31. See a similar assessment of the gospels by Tracy in Analogical Imagination, 410: "A
first-order tensive religious language like the metaphorical language in the parables of Jesus
may receive a distinct, but never separate, reflective sublation into the second-order reflective
language of theological analogy — as they do in the Johannine tradition."

doctrinal assertions, neither can "Grady's stories" be reduced to mere "illustrations" of an essentially conceptual "theology." "Tenor" without "vehicle" is gnostic. Some story, if not one of "Grady's stories," is necessary in order to think theologically. The goal of "Grady's stories" in the classroom is to teach the students to interpret all of human life (not just some specifically "religious" experiences or symbols or texts) theologically.[32]

If the danger in Gnosticism is "forgetting the vehicle" and striving for a nonanalogical tenor, there is a counterdanger in a reductionistic historicism, in confusing the vehicle for the tenor. Modern biblical scholarship has at times reduced the text to its historical, sociological, or literary reality. But if, as in Snyder's understanding, the text is a vehicle that intends to communicate a tenor beyond itself, a refusal to acknowledge this referent results in a severe misreading of the text.[33] This is the danger of historicist scholarship gone to seed. In the words of David Tracy:

> Insofar as we dare not ask the fundamental questions that these strange texts articulate, . . . all is opinion, all thinking is doxic thinking, all philosophy is the history of those opinions, all art is history of changing tastes, all religion the history of curious psyches and shifting social patterns, all history at best gossip. All indeed is ultimately a tale told by an idiot, signifying nothing.[34]

Thus a reduction of analogy either to its tenor on the one hand or to its vehicle on the other destroys the possibility of genuine theology. "Grady's stories" are not incidental — either as explanation or application. To be sure, none of these particular stories is essential; other stories could be substituted. Yet why has Snyder the scholar and theologian not published more of "Grady's" stories?

I would wish for time and space to make a proposal for how scholar-teachers like Graydon Snyder might include such analogical thinking more explicitly in published scholarship. I believe that we NT scholars should be sophisticated enough to interpret analogies as analogies and not as illustrations or applications or, worse yet, as personal, confessional statements. More

---

32. This is not to imply that there is a single, "correct" NT theology that Snyder teaches his students. Rather, he teaches them to think theologically with John, with Paul, with James, with Matthew, etc. The final class of his "New Testament Theologies" course consists of a challenge to the students to take a single story and tell and retell the story according to these various NT theologies. Many stories emerge as various theologies are explored.

33. See Tracy's distinction between the "sense" of a text and the "referent" of a text in *Blessed Rage for Order*, 51; also 76–78. The "referents" of the text do not pertain to the meaning "behind" the text (e.g., the author's real intention or the social-cultural situation of the text). Rather, to shift metaphors, "referent" basically manifests the meaning "in front of" the text, i.e., that way of perceiving reality, that mode of being-in-the-world which the text opens up for the intelligent reader.

34. Tracy, *Analogical Imagination*, 106–7.

work needs to be done by NT scholars on the character and function of analogy, drawing from theologians such as David Tracy.[35] Unlike propositional or
conceptual language (which yearns for univocity and finality), analogy makes
sport of language, lying as it does halfway between univocity and equivocity.[36]
Analogy proper depends upon the "relationship" between vehicle and tenor
(and the relationships within the vehicle and tenor) — upon understanding
that truth lies in the "misty betweens" rather than in a single identifiable element. Analogies yield more readily to, indeed, they invite, conversation as
the primary mode of truth speaking. To the extent that scholarship is com-
bative rather than conversational, analogies will always be suspect, for no
one ever won an argument by analogy. But for those who advance intellectual endeavor through critical collaboration and conversation, analogy may
open as-yet-unseen paths for our corporate thinking.

Finally, one important thing we can learn even from Snyder's "nonanalogical" writings is the importance of community and relationship, both
topically (i.e., as a topic of study) and functionally (i.e., as a mode of study).
Some of Snyder's most recognized contributions are those that elaborate this
relational "betweenness": between the Great Tradition and the Local Tradition,[37] between the vehicle and the tenor, between the "Jesus tradition" and
the canon.[38] This relatedness, for Snyder, gives evidence of the power of God:

> I believe we know the power of God through covenant necessity.... I
> believe the Judeo-Christian understanding of [humanity] portrays us
> as relational beings rather than individuals. Each of us was created by
> others and in turn we create others.... In fact human life is not possible
> apart from relational creation. That is the real power of God.[39]

Here are the decisive "analogies for our common life." They are among us
as we, by telling our shared or conflicting stories, become together — in
our teaching, in our conversations, and in our scholarship — the vehicles
of divine covenant.

---

35. I would especially point to the work of Tracy in developing criteria for the critical use
of analogy and for his articulation of a "mutually critical correlation" between human situation
and the tradition. One fear of many NT scholars is that the use of analogy appears to be wholly
"unmethodological." Tracy certainly challenges such a view; see his *Analogical Imagination*, 438
n. 2, for a substantial bibliography on analogy.

36. See William C. Placher's discussion of Aquinas's understanding of the nature of analogical
predication in *The Domestication of Transcendence: How Modern Thinking about God Went Wrong*
(Louisville, Ky.: Westminster/John Knox, 1996) 28–31.

37. See Snyder, *Ante Pacem: Archaeological Evidence of Church Life before Constantine* (Macon,
Ga.: Mercer University Press, 1985) 9–11.

38. See Snyder's recent essay, "Before the Canon: The Pre-Cultural Jesus Tradition," in Isabel
Mukonyora, James L. Cox, and Frans J. Verstraelen, eds., *"Rewriting" the Bible — The Real Issues*
(Gweru/Harare, Zimbabwe: Mambo, 1993) 81–89.

39. Snyder, "Power and Violence," 32.

3

"BY THEIR FRUITS
YOU WILL RECOGNIZE THEM"

*Trenches into the Theological and Exegetical Directions
of Graydon F. Snyder*

ROBIN SCROGGS

To write an appraisal of the intellectual output of Graydon Snyder requires more skills in more areas than I possess. Just who is Snyder the thinker? Is he principally an exegete? A theologian? An archaeologist? An ethicist? A sociologist? A health expert? A church leader? The answer to these questions has to be "all of the above."

Trained as a NT scholar, one would of course expect him to be an exegete. Indeed, nothing he writes is without some exegetical component, because he is always thinking about the biblical grounding of his topic, whether it is health care or Christian education. And yet specific exegetical writings — those whose primary purpose is to explain a text — are limited to a few articles and the major commentary on 1 Corinthians.[1] Even these works clearly have larger goals than the explication of a text. Snyder refuses to compartmentalize. Each piece implies a whole world of meaning, and it seems that this "whole world" is consciously present in his thinking, even if only implied

---

1. Snyder, *First Corinthians: A Faith Community Commentary* (Macon, Ga.: Mercer University Press, 1992). Other exegetical papers show a great variety of interests; I cite here a few examples. On 1 Corinthians 7: Snyder, "Jesus Power: A Confrontation with Women's Lib at Corinth," *BLT* 16/3 (Summer 1971) 161–67; idem and Lauree Hersch Meyer, "Sexuality: Its Social Reality and Theological Understanding in 1 Corinthians 7," SBLSP 19 (1980) 359–70. On 1 Thessalonians: Snyder, "Apocalyptic and Didactic Elements in 1 Thessalonians," SBLSP 1 (1972) 233–44; idem, "A Summary of Faith in an Epistolary Context: 1 Thess. 1:9, 10," SBLSP 2 (1972) 355–65. On apocalyptic materials: Snyder, "The Literalization of the Apocalyptic Form in the New Testament Church," *BR* 14 (1969) 5–18; idem, "Sayings on the Delay of the End," *BR* 20 (1975) 19–35.

in the particular document under discussion. Snyder is, of course, an exegete, but he seems to be uninterested in exegesis in and of itself.

How could he help but be a theologian? For him, coming out of a specific religious tradition, teaching at his denominational seminary for most of his career, asking theological questions seems the natural thing to do. And, indeed, those theological questions are either explicit in his writings or seething just below the surface. But again, Snyder does not seem interested in being an armchair theologian any more than an armchair exegete.

To the outside world, Snyder is probably known more as an archaeologist than any other of the above suggested categories.[2] From his early article on the bones of St. Peter[3] to what is perhaps his magnum opus, Ante Pacem,[4] Snyder has maintained not only an interest in the subject but even a leading role in the rethinking of how to evaluate artifacts and what that reevaluation means for the reconstruction of the understanding of the history of the pre-Constantinian church. This is surely his outstanding intellectual achievement, a mind-boggling reinterpretation that seems far too little observed by scholars and churchpeople alike.

Yet if I were forced to accept a pigeonhole for our honoree, perhaps "ethicist" is the one that I would choose. Snyder seems always centrally concerned with how people in community are to live their lives. His concern for health care certainly fits within this category, although his expertise in the area transcends that of simply a "concerned citizen." Does he not then care about how exegetical and theological groundings affect the ethical positions he argues for? Yes, in most instances. His most recent writings about a "cultureless Jesus," however, may raise questions in this regard and perhaps give away what is the essence for him: ethical performance. To these issues we shall return.

Undergirding everything is Snyder's location as a churchperson. Why bother with exegesis or theology or ethics? Because the church matters, and when he thinks of church I take it that he thinks of the church as community, as a corporate, integrated body and not just as a collection of individuals. The church as community is more than the sum of its parts. One has only to look at the many items in his bibliography that were written to serve this body

---

2. See, e.g., his numerous articles on archaeological and patristic topics in several comprehensive dictionaries: Watson E. Mills, ed., *Mercer Dictionary of the Bible* (Macon, Ga.: Mercer University Press, 1990); Everett Ferguson, ed., *Encyclopedia of Early Christianity* (1st ed., 1990; 2d ed.; New York: Garland, 1997); David Noel Freedman, ed., *The Anchor Bible Dictionary* (New York: Doubleday, 1992); Richard P. McBrien, ed., *The HarperCollins Encyclopedia of Catholicism* (New York: HarperCollins, 1995).

3. Snyder, "Survey and 'New' Thesis on the Bones of St. Peter," BA 32 (1969) 2–24.

4. Snyder, *Ante Pacem: Archaeological Evidence of Church Life before Constantine* (Macon, Ga.: Mercer University Press, 1985).

to grasp Snyder's commitment.[5] Exegesis and theology are subordinate to the community: that is, theology emerges from the community; theology does not determine the community. To a skeptical rationalist like myself, the aura with which he clothes the church community approaches mystical proportions.

If I read our author correctly, however, it is a sociological/anthropological model around which his thinking whirls and which seems to pervade his analyses, whether exegetical, theological, ethical, or archaeological. This may even suggest that the model is so important to him because it becomes a creative model for the church itself. Surprisingly, I cannot find one writing in which this model is explained in detail. Snyder briefly describes it in *Ante Pacem,* and in a few other places.[6] But the observant reader can see allusions to this model scattered through all his later writings. Once one knows how this model works for him, it is easy to see how it has become the organizing principle for his assessment of the data. I suspect, however, that to him the import lies deeper. It may actually give him a perspective from which to understand how the church throughout history "works." The model might even be used to locate a scholar (Snyder) in relation to the community of faith (the Brethren). The importance of this principle for Snyder necessitates a description in some detail.

The Great and the Local Tradition

This model goes back to the different approaches of Max Weber and Émile Durkheim. Weber saw the creative force in religious groups to be the leader, the "charismatic prophet" who provided the ideas and inspiration for the determinative ideas. Durkheim, on the other hand, saw the group itself as the catalyst: for him, the ideas emerged from the long-term impulses of the communities. The theological superstructure was just that — an expression (Sigmund Freud might say a "projection") of the interests and values of the group.[7] But Snyder has relied primarily on three anthropologists who, in his interpretation, have brought Weber and Durkheim into a both/and rather

---

5. See, e.g., Snyder, Donald E. Miller, and Robert W. Neff, *Using Biblical Simulations* (2 vols.; Valley Forge, Pa.: Judson, 1973–75); Snyder, *Tough Choices: Health Care Decisions and the Faith Community* (Elgin, Ill.: Brethren Press, 1988); idem, *Health and Medicine in the Anabaptist Tradition: Care in Community* (Valley Forge, Pa.: Trinity Press International, 1995); and already in idem, *In His Hand* (Elgin, Ill.: Brethren Press, 1964–65).

6. Snyder, *Ante Pacem,* 9–11; idem, *Health and Medicine,* 111; idem, "Before the Canon: The Pre-Cultural Jesus Tradition," in Isabel Mukonyora, James L. Cox and Frans Verstraelen, eds., *"Rewriting" the Bible — The Real Issues: Perspectives from within Biblical and Religious Studies in Zimbabwe* (Gweru/Harare, Zimbabwe: Mambo, 1993) 82.

7. Snyder appeals to Weber (*The Sociology of Religion* [Boston: Beacon, 1963]) and to Durkheim (*The Elementary Forms of the Religious Life* [London: Allen and Unwin; New York: Macmillan, 1915]).

than an either/or relationship.[8] In Snyder's synthesis, any specific religious phenomenon is the result of an encounter, sometimes conflictive, between these two forces: the leadership from above and the community from within. The leadership Snyder calls the "great tradition"; this side emphasizes religious tradition, "revelation," and scripture. The community he identifies as the "local tradition," which takes its cue from the surrounding culture, the "social matrix": these people honor ritual, a strict morality, and "family values."

As early as 1978 I was able to characterize Snyder's views as follows:

> Any specific religious phenomenon, Snyder argues, will be a result of the tension between the two traditions in a given time and space. At times the translocal tradition may dominate, at other times the local. Usually there will be some compromise, such that a phenomenon will rarely be a pure example of either tradition. Since writings are usually suspect as being primarily creations of the trans-local tradition, Snyder begins only in the post–New Testament period, when archaeological artifacts are available. In conversation, however, Snyder and I have concluded that it may be possible to use this typology as a grid to understand movement within trajectories in the New Testament itself. For example, it is possible that Paul himself represents a decisive victory of the trans-local tradition over the local, while the Pastorals reflect increasing assimilation by the local tradition of the Pauline thought world.[9]

Snyder himself summarizes the interplay of the two traditions in *Ante Pacem:*

> I would suggest the following processes are always at work as a revealed body of truth affects a social situation:
>
> 1. Some elements of the great tradition are being accepted in the social matrix.
>
> 2. Some elements of the great tradition are being accepted in the social matrix in a non-normative manner.

---

8. Robert H. Thouless, *Conventionalization and Assimilation in Religious Movements as Problems in Social Psychology* (Oxford: Oxford University Press, 1940); Robert Redfield, *Peasant Society and Culture: An Anthropological Approach to Civilization* (Chicago: University of Chicago Press, 1956); Melford E. Spiro, *Buddhism and Society: A Great Tradition and Its Burmese Vicissitudes* (London: Allen and Unwin, 1971).

9. Scroggs, "The Sociological Interpretation of the New Testament," in idem, *The Text and the Times: New Testament Essays for Today* (Minneapolis: Fortress, 1993) 58. I was able to make such a report at the time because of unpublished work and conversation with Snyder, although my report antedated *Ante Pacem* by seven years. Grady once told me that this was a unique moment in scholarship, in which a book had been reviewed before it was published! The dating is important, however, because it shows for how long these ideas had been fueling Snyder's thought.

3. Some elements of the social matrix are being adapted by the great tradition.

4. Some elements of the social matrix are being accepted by the great tradition in a non-normative manner.[10]

What emerges from all of this is a fascinating and seductive model for the study of religious phenomena. As I have discovered for myself, once it is in mind, it is hard not to approach the data from this perspective. There is a certain "common-senseness" to the theory that is almost overpoweringly strong. How could an expression not be influenced by the prophets and the texts of the tradition — how could that same expression not be molded by the community and bent to serve its own sense of needs? What Snyder has done is to give us a model that is always useful in any situation. It is, in short, a brilliant contribution to our search for a social location that does not minimize the theological dimension.

Is there, for Snyder, a normative force to this model? I suspect that there may be. What would be excluded from "valid" expressions are only these extremes: (1) the scholar who sits aloof from any community involvement and (2) the community that refuses to live in any way under the influence of the great tradition. One can imagine (or even claim to know) such extremes. Certainly the extreme (at either end) is fearful of those at the other end. The community is suspicious of the scholar who sits in his or her ivory tower; likewise, the scholar is fearful of the community whose main aim is to provide respectability (and even fun) for its members, or which is so moralistic as to have no flexibility (sophistication?) in ethical matters. Barring these extremes, Snyder's model calls for a sensitivity that might lead to acceptance of virtually any religious expression. After all, no community exists without some influence of the great tradition, and no scholar exists without some awareness of the inevitable liturgies and familial concerns of the community. We all have some vision; we all must die. In a remarkable way, Snyder's model is nonjudgmental.

It may also be suggested, at least, that this model helps Snyder to find himself within the Anabaptist communities of which he is a part. If that is the case, then he can be an example of how we all — especially those of us who are academic types — struggle to find a comprehensible location within our own communities. The Anabaptist communities can be seen as very much informed by the local tradition. Granted, they are certainly sectarian and thus set over against the larger local traditions of the surrounding secular and religious realities. But within they seem to have developed their own well-established local traditions. Their own sense of rituals is strong; they lay

---

10. Snyder, Ante Pacem, 10.

great stress on rectitude within the community; and they eschew the most obvious signs of the great tradition: the acceptance of formal creeds. Snyder, on the other hand, is inevitably a person of the great tradition. His model, meanwhile, shows how the two entities live together, indeed, belong together. His model explains (away?) tension and makes acceptable seemingly conflicting urges. Whether my analysis is on target or not, it shows how useful the model is for grasping the dynamics of the individual within the community.

The Thesis

Apart from the specific ideational contribution a doctoral thesis makes, perhaps the most important thing one learns from reading in retrospect is how the young scholar is already sowing seeds of later maturation. Snyder's thesis was entitled "The Continuity of Early Christianity: A Study of Ignatius in Relation to Paul."[11] The title itself suggests what could be seen as the period of church history our Anabaptist scholar is interested in. "Early Christianity" for the thesis means from the beginnings until the early second century. Later it will become clear that Snyder is concerned with the entire period *ante pacem* — an era ending with Constantine. According to Anabaptist interpretation, Snyder says, Constantine marks the beginning of the decline of (the purity of?) the church: "The church began to fall on October 28 of the year 312, when the Roman emperor Constantine received his vision and was instructed to conquer in the name of Christ. The subsequent Edict of Milan in 313 sealed the fate of the church."[12] The fall seems to be attachment to a land, a people, and specific immovable centers. As a wandering people, "early Christians [the true church?] shifted their allegiance from a specific nation to the world."[13]

For the thesis itself, however, the key problem is that of continuity or discontinuity within this earliest period. The sense that somewhere the vision of the earliest church was lost or compromised has haunted scholars and theologians for centuries. For religionsgeschichtliche scholars such as Wilhelm Bousset, the break occurred between Jesus (who remained the only "pure" example of Christianity) and Paul and his contemporaries, who become those responsible for the hellenization of an original, Jewish (but more than Jewish) religion. Albert Schweitzer attempted to show that the break happened

---

11. Snyder, "The Continuity of Early Christianity" (Th.D. diss., Princeton Theological Seminary, 1961). The director was Otto A. Piper, the German theologian called to Princeton as professor of NT literature and exegesis. Piper, to judge from his bibliography (see William Klassen and Graydon F. Snyder, eds., *Current Issues in New Testament Interpretation: Essays in Honor of Otto A. Piper* [New York: Harper, 1962] 247–60), seems to have remained primarily a theologian. It is of interest to note that in the bibliography of Snyder's thesis there is not a single item of Piper's.

12. Snyder, *Health and Medicine*, 18.

13. Ibid., 17.

after Paul, since Paul was himself thoroughly enmeshed in apocalyptic, Jewish mysticism.

Snyder tackles the problem by raising the question whether and to what extent and in what way Ignatius might be in some continuity with Paul. On the surface, there would seem to be little relationship. In general, in the second century, Paul is quoted but the church seems to move toward a position closer to the Gospel of John.[14] The hands are the hands of Paul, but the voice is the voice of John. So how does it go with Ignatius?[15]

Obviously Ignatius and Paul show little continuity in relation to specific doctrines. For Snyder, this is not crucial since what is important is how each man viewed himself in relationship to God and the mission of the church. And in this respect Ignatius was in conscious dependence on the apostle: "In his dependence on Paul for his eschatological self-awareness, Ignatius shows conclusively that he has not deviated from New Testament Christianity."[16] This self-awareness, however, is not to be seen as an individualistic perception; rather it cannot be separated from the church as the vehicle of God's activity in history. Thus Snyder establishes continuity, but not one that has much to do with doctrine. Instead it lies with the reality of community and prophet. The signs of continuity — hence the marks of authenticity? — lie in faithful response of individual and community to the plan of God for God's world. If the unspoken agenda in the thesis is to deny a "fall" in the pre-Constantinian church, Snyder has contributed to that agenda.

Certainly it would be unfair to apply Snyder's later model of great/local traditions to his analysis at an earlier phase of his career — unfair but fun! In his thesis, does the great or local win? Probably "win" is a term inapplicable to the complex interwovenness of historical ambiguity; but, in my judgment, Snyder does seem a bit suspicious of the great tradition. Yes, the prophets stand over the community, but they do not live independently of the community. What unites, perhaps even subordinates, the prophets to the community is the obedience the prophets owe to God and God's plan, a plan whose goal is the community. Prophets must not be allowed to become mystagogues — Wilhelm Bousset's term for Paul.

Archaeological Evidence for the Local Tradition

Snyder very soon turned to archaeology to pursue his search for the local tradition. In a startling 1969 article he debunked the pope's recent (1968)

---

14. Snyder, "Continuity of Early Christianity," 132.
15. Despite the title, the exegetical part of the thesis focuses on Ignatius; indeed, the thesis really belongs in the category of early church history.
16. Snyder, "Continuity of Early Christianity," 255.

claim that the bones of Peter had been "convincingly identified."[17] I cannot
repeat the details of his debate with the consensus thesis about the bones
and the role that a church called St. Sebastian's had with regard to the relics.
I do think it fair to label the consensus theory — with the pope's interest
in assuring the historical presence of Peter and Paul in Rome in accordance
with ancient legends and church politics — an attempt to impose the great
tradition over what Snyder thinks were local tradition phenomena.

Indeed, Snyder's interest in archaeology stems, it would seem, from the
possibility that artifacts may give us the precious few extant records of the
local tradition. Texts, to the contrary, are almost always reflections of the
great tradition.[18] Snyder suggests that a correct reading of the artifacts we
possess will show that the early church lived out of a reality significantly different from what the theological texts of the patristic writers would have us
believe. His revisionist portrait is remarkable: "The early Christians continued the feasts of the dead, the old Roman Parentalis." That is, an important
dimension of life "baptized into Christ" was the custom of eating with the
dead — with deceased family members, for example, but also with important
local heroes, such as saints and martyrs: "The special role of the martyr probably compares to the hero cult of pagan Rome;...feasts for the dead were
likely early in the church but regular feast days for the martyrs began late
in the 2nd century....Many of the earliest buildings for Christian worshipers
were covered cemeteries, connected with Christian burial areas, specifically
the catacombs." Snyder then argues that the edifice of St. Sebastian's was
just such a covered cemetery.[19]

Whatever the outcome of this particular theory, the image of early Christians sitting at the graves of their ancestor, eating with them, jolts the mind
of someone whose image of what went on in the church has been formed
by the NT and patristic writings. These ceremonies, Snyder argues, were not
only popular; they could become riotous, drunken feasts. What we know as
normative Christianity was a post-Constantinian forcing of the mass onto the
ceremony of eating with the dead, so that the mass gradually assumes the
dominant role. The great tradition hedges in the local.[20]

In Ante Pacem, Snyder's marvelous summary of early Christian archaeology, the author furthers his interpretation by exploring the implication of
artifacts for understanding popular theology of the period. Anything like
a "theology of the cross" was nonexistent in mainstream Christianity. The

17. Snyder, "Survey," 2; this article was considered of sufficient import to be reprinted in
Edward F. Campbell and David Noel Freedman, eds., The Biblical Archaeologist Reader, vol. 3
(Garden City, N.Y.: Anchor, 1961–70).
18. I.e., the "ecclesiastical tradition" (Ante Pacem, 9).
19. Snyder, "Survey," 17–22.
20. Ibid., 22.

first cross-symbols are at the earliest mid-fourth century, while "the first clear crucifixions are known to us from the fifth century." There is no evidence before Constantine of christological symbols which signify "suffering, death, or self-immolation. All stress victory, peace, and security in the face of adversity.... There is no place in the third century for a crucified Christ, or a symbol of divine death." The *ante-pacem* Jesus brings peace and rescues believers from difficult circumstances. The community was itself non-hierarchical: "The pre-Constantinian Church was remarkably democratic"; "Social class structures were all but destroyed"; "People found in the new faith community a place of deliverance and peace." The movement toward hierarchical structure seems to have been an attempt by the leadership to secure the dominance of the great tradition, or at least to control the local.[21]

In the conclusion of *Ante Pacem* Snyder draws together his assessment of the movement and conflict of the different dynamics through the fourth century. He is too wise and clever to make either the great or the local tradition savior or Satan. Snyder assumes, I think, that any social manifestation of one extreme or the other would not survive. The church has survived because it continues to be a blend, although at different times one or the other dynamic dominates. Snyder's judgments are important and justify my listing them in some detail.

What enabled Christianity to become a "universal religion"? The way Snyder answers that question is interesting. The underlying answer is that Christianity accepted and embraced the "social matrix"; that is, it accommodated itself to the surrounding culture through the local tradition. Had it not, it might have succumbed to a "nonviable spiritualization" (e.g., gnosticism) or to an "intellectualism" which would have isolated itself from the masses. *Without the local tradition there would have been no Christianity* as we know it today.[22] For example, Paul and the Gospel of John take stands typical of the great tradition. But the NT also contains the deutero-Pauline and deutero-Johannine writings, in which the great tradition is accommodated to the social matrix. "It is significant," Snyder writes, "that the formation of the canon includes those books that call for social adaptation."[23]

On the other hand, *without the great tradition Christianity could not have distinguished itself from its matrix*. Thus the very fact that Christian artifacts begin to "appear" around 180 CE indicates that the great tradition is beginning to alter the local tradition so that Christianity becomes differentiated from other social groups. This tension, between accommodation and differentiation, continued through the third century.

---

21. Snyder, *Ante Pacem*, 27, 29, 165–66.
22. Ibid., 163–65.
23. Ibid., 164.

The most interesting question, perhaps, is what Constantinian Christianity represented. Here Snyder's answer is initially surprising, in view of the Anabaptist bias that it is specifically Constantinian Christianity that represents the fall of the church. Snyder argues, however, that Constantine supported a Christianity "based upon popular Christianity derived from the social matrix." It is, rather, church theologians and politicians such as Damasus, Augustine, and Ambrose who successfully fought to control the local tradition, such that "the bishops were elevated and the cult of the dead was controlled." But though controlled, not eliminated. Indeed what was finally reached was a compromise, which Snyder politely dubs a "consensus." It is that fourth/fifth century consensus which he calls "orthodoxy."[24]

His analysis is breathtaking, combining sociological/anthropological dynamics, archaeology, and theology. It is the most successful application that I know of the principles of the sociology of knowledge to this swath of four centuries of church existence. Questions do arise for the *post-pacem* period. Given what was obviously the strength of the local tradition, especially as supported by Constantine, it is not easy to see how individual thinkers could so successfully oppose the Christianity of the local tradition that a compromise was even necessary. What made the views of Damasus, Augustine, and Ambrose so powerful, especially if the imperial version of Christianity was on the "other side"? And how is Constantine the cause of the fall of the church if he so strongly upheld the local tradition, without which Christianity could not have become a universal religion?

Snyder's views of these dynamics are complex, no doubt correctly so. The interweaving of the two traditions in the actual manifestations of the church, without a simplistic direction of one over the other, and Snyder's refusal to applaud one at the expense of the other keep his analysis from being a pat, theoretical forcing of the data. His refusal to opt for one over the other also, perhaps, shows Snyder's own ambiguity about these dynamics. How does Snyder the intellectual relate to Snyder the churchperson? And where does poor Constantine stand in all this? Is he savior or Satan? But then pigeonholes are not really appropriate in an analysis which stresses the stubborn ambiguity of history.

Exegesis

Snyder's only work of sustained exegesis is his commentary on 1 Corinthians.[25] I wish to focus on this production as an exemplar of how our honoree approaches a text. Reviewing or assessing commentaries is a precarious task,

---

24. Ibid., 165.
25. Snyder, *First Corinthians.*

and potentially boring at best. The commentator who produces an interpretation that is amazingly consistent and provocative is easy to review, but one suspects it as being more the commentator's view than that of the original author. A text such as 1 Corinthians is a very curvy road and not easily susceptible to manipulation by any commentator, although some come close. Snyder is sensitive to the curves, but that means that any assessment of his commentary is not easy reading.

This commentary, however, is interesting because Snyder explicitly writes it from a perspective of the "Radical Reformation churches." This is the significance of the subtitle: A Faith Community Commentary. Once again our author's religious views as an Anabaptist emerge as a major dimension of his hermeneutic. Snyder makes it clear that he does not see his reading as a deconstructionist one. That is, he is not saying: "This is the way we Anabaptists read the text, regardless of what Paul intended." Rather, he argues that there are significant similarities between the Pauline communities then and communities today in the radical reformation. As a result his interpretation should be closer to, not further from, the original intent of the text:

> I have . . . come to the conviction that a community close to the original community can perceive things not apparent to a different type of social structure. I agree with those who say the early church was a close community with a fairly high sense of personal individuation. Coming from a similar modern community, though the historical circumstances are vastly different, makes it possible for us to empathize with the material in a manner not available to everyone.[26]

The possibilities in this hermeneutic are intriguing. How does it work out in this commentary?

According to Snyder the most significant thing about 1 Corinthians is that it "marks the literary beginning of Christianity." Paul's basic theological framework was the apocalyptic idea of two ages: the present (evil) age and the future (blissful) era of God's kingdom. At first Paul views the resurrected Jesus as the one who will bring in the new age (1 Thessalonians). Although resurrected in the past, his work is essentially future. By the time of 1 Corinthians, however, Paul has introduced a paradigm shift: "The endtime is not something toward which Christians live, but, because of our intense hope and expectation, is already partially present. . . . The shift was from a Jewish apocalyptic hope in the coming new age to a Christian faith in the *presence* of the resurrection community."[27] Snyder is here close to defining the essence of Christianity as a partially realized resurrection community. It is no accident that the words "resurrection" and "community" are linked.

---

26. Ibid., vii.
27. Ibid., 7–8 (emphasis added).

In general Snyder's presentation of the background of the letter presents no surprises. One suggestion is, however, important for his reading of the text. While for Snyder the letter has integrity, it was written in two "sittings." The first was caused by a letter from the Corinthians. As a response to this letter Paul wrote chapters 7–16. Before he could send this, however, he received additional news from Corinth — "an oral report from his friend Chloe." To deal with this disturbing news describing sharp divisions within the community, Paul adds to his planned, original letter, chapters 1–6.[28]

Snyder connects this conflict with failure of some of the Corinthian leaders to understand what Paul has tried to communicate about the "paradigm shift" mentioned above — the presence of and yet tension between the old and the new age in the life of the community: "A true leader lives in the old age with all of its problems, yet exhibits the life and faith of the new age." This is why, contrary to many scholars, Snyder ties closely together chapters 1–4, where Paul speaks about the conflict of the ages, and chapters 5–6, which seem on the surface to deal with miscellaneous problems at Corinth he has heard about. For Snyder these are not miscellaneous; they rather "illustrate the nature of the conflict between the two ages.... Chapters 5 and 6, then, illustrate the continuing, constant conflict between the ages, a conflict which does not allow any to think of themselves as already 'in' the new age. Quarrels, pride and position belong to the old age."[29] I mention this perspective in some detail because it changes how the text of chapters 5–6 is read. And since some of Snyder's most creative readings lie in these chapters, I will use them to illustrate his exegetical work.

One thing Snyder's perspective does is to remove "immorality" from center stage. Indeed, he argues, 1 Corinthians does not have to do with immorality in any significant way. For example, "Chapter 5:1–8 has more to do with the Christ house church living above the law than it does with a gross sexual sin. The discussion of prostitution in 6:12–20 refers more to betrayal of the faith community than it does to brothers visiting the temple brothel." In 5:1–8 the issue is really the arrogance of part of the community in sanctioning what is (for Paul) an obviously sinful situation. That is, Paul is focused on the community, not the individual. In Snyder's reading of v. 5, "flesh" means living according to "human aspirations," while "spirit" refers to the community, especially that of the Christ house church: "It is necessary for the Christ house church to recognize its own spiritual arrogance." By removing that individual from its community, it will demonstrate its awareness of what is involved in living as a true faith community and will, it is to be hoped, lead the individual to repentance.[30]

---

28. Ibid., 11–13.
29. Ibid., 12.
30. Ibid., 56, 61–62. The term "Christ house church" refers to a group in Corinth that was

Even more remarkable is Snyder's interpretation of 6:12–20. He tries to give a consistent metaphorical interpretation based on the OT analogy between sexual immorality and defection from faith. It is best, he suggests, to read "body" to refer to the faith community. And this means that the purpose of the passage, as the climax of chapters 1–6, is to warn the community at Corinth of the need to preserve its faithfulness, i.e., its stance between the ages, in the face of temptations to live either completely in the old or completely in the new: "Paul closes this 'letter' (chapters 1–6) with a metaphorical summary on the nature of the body of Christ."[31]

Regardless of whether one agrees or not with these exegetical moves, they demonstrate how Snyder is constantly thinking of the corporate reality of the faith community. The individual so much belongs to the community that Paul, so Snyder seems to think, is not really interested in the individual at all. It is the body as corporate that is central to Paul's concern. Nowhere is this clearer than in Snyder's exegesis of chapter 15. In startling words he writes: "Resurrection for Paul is communal. Death also then is a communal loss.... The New Testament teaching on resurrection, like its teaching about life, views the afterlife of the individual as a participation in the ongoing community. *It can hardly be otherwise.*" The individual has meaning — and reality? — only as he or she "participates" in the community. I am not entirely sure I grasp all that our honoree means, but I do know that many folk, church people and scholars, think it can, indeed, be otherwise. Snyder knows this very well. Thus the sentence that follows the one just quoted, while directed at Paul's original audience, may just as well refer to a contemporary one: "Paul is writing to an audience that does not understand these things"![32]

My purpose here is not to criticize Snyder's exegesis, a criticism which would certainly be judged by him to stem from an individualistic, secular, Western mentality, but to demonstrate how a person in the tradition of the radical reformation can read the text. More, to open our minds to the possibility that such a person can, in Snyder's words quoted above, "empathize with the material in a manner not available to everyone." Snyder has thus thrown down the gauntlet before us individualistic secular westerners. Shall we pick it up? I am sure we have much to learn.

A final question: How does this exegesis fit into the model of the great vs. the local tradition? Let me put the issue as provocatively as possible. Does Snyder's Paul belong to the great or to the local tradition? Given Snyder's model, no historical phenomenon (even that of a prophet or an apostle) can

---

heavily responsible for the conflict within the churches. This group thought that the new age was already present and thus that "everything is lawful" (1 Cor 6:12; 10:23).

31. Ibid., 80.

32. Ibid., 196 (emphasis original).

be simply one or the other. Any phenomenon is a combination, a compromise along the line of a continuum between the extreme points. So Paul the apostle is by definition both. But where is he on the continuum? By this time we should expect from Snyder some curious amalgam, and this is, I think, what we get. One would expect Paul to represent the great tradition. He certainly transcends the geographical local community. He certainly proclaims the gospel. I think Snyder implies that he transcends compulsive concern about morality ("Sin boldly," he might tell Timothy). He does not demonstrate an overemphasis upon ritual — at least that of baptism (evaluation of his interest in the eucharist is more complicated).

At the same time, Snyder's Paul does not present the truth as a monolithic revelation. Indeed, the apostle is not primarily concerned with proclaiming Truth but with forming communities "in which love, understanding, and forgiveness are operative." That is, the overcoming of divisions within the churches is not to be achieved primarily by having everyone think the same thing but by mutual acceptance of the persons in the community. Paul sees his task not as promoting Truth but as showing "how people may act together as a primary community without destroying their deep individual convictions."[33]

Thus a Paul emerges whose primary reality is community in which certain acts are practiced. Could one go so far as to say that what a community *believes* is not important, that it is what the community *does* that is essential? That may be going beyond what Snyder wants to say. He does show Paul as pointing to a certain understanding of the cross as decisive for understanding what God is about, but Snyder's comments about the significance of the cross are provocative and revealing. He seems to separate the "gospel" from the "cross"; nevertheless, "however the Gospel may be presented, it needs to be congruent with the cross." The context suggests that what Snyder means by "gospel" is intellectual theology, while the cross is "a symbol of self-giving and mutuality with full sharing in each other's social context."[34]

At first it may strike one as surprising that in just this section ("The Foolishness of the Cross: 1:18–25") Snyder raises the problem of mission and Third-World churches. The issue is becoming crucial for our author, as we shall see below. Here he speaks negatively of "a Jesus Christ clothed in the garb of Western culture."[35] What seems to be set up here is a distinction: true Christian reality lies in a community of self-giving and mutuality, while theology (inevitably bound to cultural expressions) represents the nonessential dimension of Christianity. Clearly this is Snyder's version of the old debate

33. Ibid., 22, 25.
34. Ibid., 33; see also p. 34 on the significance of the cross.
35. Ibid., 33.

between the eternal and the temporal in Christianity. The question for us is whether this is also Paul's version. I am not so sure.

But to return to my question: Where does Paul fit on the continuum? Does his view of the faith community belong to the great or the local tradition? In my judgment, Snyder's Paul comes out ultimately on the side of the local tradition. His Paul is not really interested in "revelation" or "the Book" as a source of divine truth that can be collected in sentences. Snyder's Paul is centrally concerned with the local community, rather than with some abstract collective unity, and with the community as it *acts*. Granted, Paul is not a moralist, but it seems to me that the view of the faith community that Snyder upholds as Pauline is essentially that of a moral community.[36] It may even be that the "Christ house church" exhibits more signs of the great tradition than does Paul.

A Jesus without Culture?

Graydon Snyder does not sit still. Who is to say where he will appear next? One catches a glimpse of perhaps a new direction in the section of the commentary mentioned above, where he grapples with the possibility of a Christianity unbound from Western culture. In two recent publications he specifically raises the question of a cultureless Jesus, how one would find such a Jesus, and what that would mean.[37]

He proceeds through several stages in relation to the basic question he poses: "What is that Christianity which stands in dialectical tension with any social matrix?" He locates this in the Jesus tradition which he (too?) optimistically thinks can be reasonably determined, so that "one can see original actions of Jesus."[38] It is not accidental that the sentence reads "actions" and not "teachings."[39] His summary of the Jesus tradition is worth quoting at some length:

> One could conclude that the Jesus tradition at its earliest level consisted of (1) healings of persons regardless of their status as clean or unclean; (2) universal commensality regardless of class distinctions; (3) a constant tension with the social matrix and in his constant use of apocalyptic reversal; (4) subversion of political limitations.[40]

---

36. One must remember that one person's morality is another's moralism.

37. Snyder, "Before the Canon"; idem, *Health and Medicine.*

38. Snyder, "Before the Canon," 82.

39. That is, Snyder here sides with E. P. Sanders (e.g., in *Jesus and Judaism* [Philadelphia: Fortress, 1985]) over against Rudolf Bultmann (e.g., in *Jesus and the Word* [New York: Scribner, 1934]).

40. Snyder, "Before the Canon," 83.

These traits mark the "pre-Christian cultural period," which as we have seen above ends for Snyder the archaeologist about 180 CE. At that point it becomes clear that "Christianity took on a particular cultural form based on a symbol system rooted in the Greco-Roman tradition."[41] Snyder insists, correctly of course, that Christianity could have gone through some other cultural system. That is, the form Christianity took due to Greco-Roman culture is *not essential* to Christianity.

The lesson to be learned is not hard to see. Other cultural forms of Christianity are potentially equally legitimate as the Greco-Roman. This is possible because "the pre-Christian cultural Jesus tradition stands in dialectical relationship to any new social matrix." For non-Western believers it is their "right to seek the marks of Christianity at the earlier stage and to isolate the Jesus tradition. They may use that tradition as a guide/critique of their own culture."[42]

I would have serious questions to put to Snyder, were we to dialogue about his proposal. First, is the earliest Jesus tradition purely an ethical tradition, as not only Snyder but also some Q scholars would have it?[43] (And would one have any need for such a Jesus?) Second, was there a cultural void in early Christianity before 180 CE? Surely the NT documents already reflect Greco-Roman culture. And just as surely the earliest Jesus tradition, however one describes it, is from its inception in a cultural form. Can there be a Jesus — any Jesus — not embedded in a social matrix? Does Snyder implicitly privilege a Jewish matrix?[44]

Such a dialogue is not in place here. What is in place is to honor Graydon Snyder for his prolific range, his constant probing and imaginative questing, and his stubborn wrestling to hold together issues of scholarship and faith. No, he does not sit still. Where he will provoke us next we await with anticipation. One thing is sure: that provocation will push us to new thinking, and that is the highest compliment I can pay to any scholar.

41. Ibid., 83, 85.

42. Ibid., 85, 86.

43. This seems to me the clear implication of Burton L. Mack, *The Lost Gospel: The Book of Q and Christian Origins* (San Francisco: Harper, 1993).

44. I and many scholars would assume the culture to be Jewish; others, such as Mack, think it already Greco-Roman.

PART TWO

COMMON LIFE
IN JUDAISM AND
CHRISTIANITY

4

"A STRANGER AND AN ALIEN AMONG YOU"
(Genesis 23:4)

The Old Testament in Early Jewish and Christian Self-Identity

THOMAS M. BOLIN

One of Graydon Snyder's enduring contributions to the study of early Christian art is his informed use of the concepts of the Great and Little Traditions formulated by sociologist Robert Redfield. Snyder's application of this analytical tool solidly grounds early Christian art in the cultural context of the lives of ordinary Christians in the Roman Empire. This in turn has required us to look at Christian art in a fresh light and advanced our understanding of it as extensively as the work of Adolf Deissmann a century ago did for the language of the NT by establishing its context in koine Greek. Snyder argues that the interpretive locus of Christian pictorial depictions of biblical scenes lies not in texts but rather in the nonliterary strata of early Christianity, the local or Little Tradition.[1] The following paragraphs will briefly summarize the work of Redfield and Snyder's use of it before bringing the latter's conclusions to bear on the cycle of stories dealing with Abraham in Genesis 12–25. This

---

1. Snyder, *Ante Pacem: Archaeological Evidence of Church Life before Constantine* (Macon, Ga.: Mercer University Press, 1985) 9–11; Snyder often refers to the Little Tradition as the social matrix. For another use of Redfield's categories, see John Dominic Crossan, *The Birth of Christianity: Discovering What Happened in the Years Immediately after the Execution of Jesus* (San Francisco: Harper, 1998). This same distinction, albeit with different terminology, is used in the analysis of OT texts in Philip R. Davies, "Scenes from the Early History of Judaism," in Diana Vikander Edelman, ed., *The Triumph of Elohim: From Yahwisms to Judaisms* (Contributions to Biblical Exegesis and Theology 13; Kampen: Kok/Pharos, 1995) 155, 178–79.

investigation will show that the same kind of worldview and self-definition that guided early Christian pictorial depiction of OT personages is also one of the motivations behind the Jewish authors' composition of this important section of the OT.

On the Great and Little Traditions

Redfield's elaboration of these terms occurs in his discussion of peasant society and culture.[2] Each tradition stems from a different locus in a society. The Great Tradition is that of the schools and temples, consciously cultivated and communicated, while the Little Tradition is that of the peasants, developed in the lives of the illiterates and accepted without question or scrutiny. This distinction between the two traditions is only a necessary first step to analysis of their interaction and mutual influence, and Redfield goes so far as to understand civilization as "a persisting and characteristic but always changing interaction between little and great traditions."[3] This influence is either the impact of the Little Tradition upon the Great, i.e., "universalization," or its reverse, i.e., "parochialization."[4]

In examining the early Christian pictorial scenes drawn from the OT, Snyder states that the artists' understanding of these scenes does not come from actual reading of the texts to which they refer, but rather is informed by the variant interpretations given to them by the Little Tradition.[5] Consequently, the selection and depiction of these figures are influenced by the world views of the illiterate nonelite. Noting that the majority of OT scenes are pictured in such a way so that the main figure is understood to be in a foreign or hostile environment and in need of divine succor, Snyder arrives at his main conclusion: this portrayal is informed by individual Christians' experience of the pre-Constantinian Greco-Roman milieu as inimical:

> It now appears that Old Testament Stories provided the artistic possibility of representing peace (the Orante [=one praying]) in moments of extreme threat (Noah and the Flood, Jonah in the Sea, Daniel and the Lions, Susannah and the Elders, the Three Young Men in the Fiery Furnace).[6]

---

2. Redfield, *Peasant Society and Culture: An Anthropological Approach to Civilization* (Chicago: University of Chicago Press, 1956).

3. Ibid., 50.

4. Ibid., 54–55. Snyder also utilizes these terms (*Ante Pacem*, 9–10). Both writers borrow the terms from McKim Marriott.

5. *Ante Pacem*, 45–55. The OT figures are Adam and Eve, Noah, Isaac, Moses, Jonah, Daniel, Susannah, and the Three Men in the Fiery Furnace.

6. Ibid., 55; cf. also Snyder's remarks in regards to the depiction of Jonah, but applicable to the other biblical scenes: "After the peace of Constantine the Jonah cycle waned sharply in popularity. When the environment was no longer hostile to the Christian, when the Chris-

It would be fitting to call this process parochialization, since we have liter-ary figures being absorbed and reinterpreted by the nonliterary environment. Likewise, the reverse process of universalization is also observable in early pa-tristic texts that contain references to biblical figures and stories which are clearly influenced by pictorial depictions of them. A discussion of Jonah by Augustine in *Ep.* 102 is an illustrative case. Augustine surmises that when Jonah was cast into the sea and swallowed by the fish, he must have been nude. There is nothing in the biblical text of Jonah to explain or support this observation; however, in artistic depictions of Jonah it is common for the prophet to be naked.[7] Here in the area of early Christian depictions of OT figures one can see the interplay between Great and Little Traditions as understood by Redfield and Snyder.

The component of Snyder's work that I wish to isolate and apply to the Abraham stories in Genesis concerns the early Christians' understanding of the world as hostile and the impact of this perspective on their visual por-trayal of biblical figures. Snyder's argument can be summarized as follows: (1) the overwhelming majority of pre-Constantinian Christian depictions of OT figures portray them in situations of danger or in hostile environments; (2) the status of Christianity as an illicit religion would doubtless cause Chris-tians to view their larger social world as potentially threatening;[8] and (3) the social reality of the latter impacts the artistic depiction of the former. It is my contention that an analogous argument can be made concerning the compo-sition of the Abraham stories in Genesis where, similar to the figures in early Christian art, Abraham is portrayed as an outsider, constantly moving in a land that is never truly his and interacting with members outside of his group in potentially hostile relationships that imply his status as foreigner. The cru-cial component in this argument is that which corresponds to item 2 in the outline of Snyder's conclusion, i.e., the independent knowledge of Christian self-perception as strangers in an alien climate because of their illicit status. Evidence of Jewish understanding of the world as a hostile environment and of both Jewish and non-Jewish perceptions of Jews as strangers in that cul-

---

tian community was no longer harassed qua Christian, then the pictorial symbol of the peaceful Orante amidst critical (biblical) situations no longer served a useful purpose. It lost its value in the social matrix" (49).

7. Further discussion on this in Thomas M. Bolin, *Freedom beyond Forgiveness: The Book of Jonah Re-Examined* (JSOTSup 236; Sheffield: Sheffield Academic Press, 1997) 26–28. For the influence of artistic representations of Jonah on remarks in the writings of Origen, see William S. Babcock, "Image and Culture: An Approach to the Christianization of the Roman Empire," *PSTJ* 41 (1988) 1–10.

8. I do not intend to say that Christianity was in a constant state of persecution during the three centuries prior to its legalization; literary and archaeological evidence would not bear this out. However, given the nature of the sporadic outbreaks of persecution of Christians, not just by the government but by other groups in the Greco-Roman urban culture, the potential for hostility could be and was viewed by early Christians as more or less constant.

ture would provide, as concomitant evidence does for early Christian art, a
historical context which would explain the portrayal of Abraham in Genesis.
Historical investigation reveals this world view and attitude present for the
first time in the hellenistic period (333–63 BCE), and I maintain that it is in
that period that the composition of the Abraham stories as they are found in
the OT must be placed. Elaboration of these observations will comprise the
remainder of this essay, and I begin with the investigation of the hellenistic
period.

Hellenism and Its Impact on the Ancient Near East

Most historians agree that the military victories of Alexander the Great
throughout Asia and the Mediterranean in the last half of the fourth century BCE inaugurated not only political but also cultural and religious changes
of great magnitude. Alexander and his successors engaged in a vigorous
program of building and colonization that resulted in the widespread dissem-
ination of Greek language and culture. The ensuing picture of antiquity is
frequently described by the term "hellenistic," a category that refers to anything having to do with ancient Greek culture from Alexander to the advent
of Roman hegemony. Modern understanding of the term traces its origins to
nineteenth-century German historiography and philosophy of history, particularly the work of J. G. Droysen, who distinguished Hellenism from classical
Greek culture by the former's contact with neighboring Mediterranean cultures, e.g., Egyptian, Mesopotamian, Anatolian. In its ancient Greek usage
"Hellenism" and its related terms (Ἑλληνικός, Ἑλληνιστής, Ἑλληνιστί)
refer to Greek language and/or customs.[9]

Comparison of the ancient and modern understandings of Hellenism reveals both an important convergence and contrast. The convergence lies in
that the two understandings each see Hellenism as a phenomenon with cultural ramifications. To speak of Hellenism according to its ancient sense of
the use of the Greek language is to acknowledge implicitly that a particular language is more than just one of a variety of forms of communication,
but is also the bearer and creator of a particular cultural identity. This is
amply evident in the debates that surround the ideological assumptions behind some groups' acceptance or rejection of language, and one need look no
further for examples than the dispute surrounding so-called "English only"
laws in the U.S. or the political motivations underlying the use of Gaelic in

---

9. For background, see Martin Hengel, *Judaism and Hellenism: Studies in Their Encounter in
Palestine during the Early Hellenistic Period* (2 vols.; Philadelphia: Fortress, 1974) 1. 1–5; Hans
Dieter Betz, "Hellenism," *ABD* 3.127–35; and Helmut Koester, *Introduction to the New Testament*,
vol. 1: *History, Culture, and Religion of the Hellenistic Age* (2d ed.; Berlin: De Gruyter, 1995)
41–71.

Ireland. The contrast in understandings is equally as meaningful. For historians after Droysen, Hellenism means the amalgamation of Greek and Oriental cultures, but in its ancient Greek usage "Hellenism" is a term that distinguishes Greek culture from others.[10] One was said to follow hellenistic custom when one adapted the Greek language and way of life (e.g., dress, food) as opposed to other languages and modes of living. The disjunctive understanding of Hellenism in antiquity plays an important role in its interaction with Judaism. A working definition that functions as a starting point for further discussion is that of John M. G. Barclay, which describes Hellenism as "the common urban culture in the eastern Mediterranean, founded on the Greek language . . . typically expressed in certain political and educational institutions and largely maintained by the social élite."[11]

Two key components for the ensuing discussion of Judaism in the hellenistic period come out of this investigation. First, Hellenism understood as Greek language and culture functions to distinguish it from the many other languages and cultures with which it interacts. Put another way, contact between members of Greek and non-Greek culture is characterized by each culture's experience of the opposing culture as foreign or alien. Second, as the combination of Greek language and a "common urban culture . . . largely maintained by the social élite," Hellenism is clearly to be understood as a Great Tradition of the ancient Mediterranean. Its location in cities and expression in political and educational systems serve to distance it from the rural locale of the illiterate peasantry.[12] These two elements come together in the Abraham stories which, as a literary product, are the expression of the Jewish Great Tradition generated in response to the experience of the hellenistic world as other.

In his influential study of the late Roman Empire, Peter Brown has recounted the displacement of long-held religious beliefs and the growth of ennui regarding personal identity that arose from the experience of the world as Roman *imperium*.[13] Jonathan Z. Smith has argued for the presence of these

---

10. So, e.g., Herodotus *Hist.* 4.78; Diodorus Siculus *Hist.* 17.110.5.

11. Barclay, *Jews in the Mediterranean Diaspora: From Alexander to Trajan (323 BCE–117 CE)* (Edinburgh: T. & T. Clark, 1996); cf. Hengel's characterization: "Hellenism, then, must be treated as a complex phenomenon which cannot be limited to purely political, socio-economic, cultural or religious aspects, but embraces them all" (*Judaism and Hellenism* 1. 3).

12. While Koester emphasizes the public and international aspects of hellenistic culture and learning, he notes that they are limited to certain population groups in cities (*History, Culture, and Religion*, 97–103).

13. Brown, *The Making of Late Antiquity* (Cambridge, Mass.: Harvard University Press, 1978). In this context Brown describes the Christian experience of the Roman world as other, and the consequent reaction of Christianity in the redefinition of personal relationships: "The Christians of the third century loved their neighbors, but this may have been because they belonged to a growing body of people who were a little more determined than in any previous period of ancient history to choose their neighbors" (78). John North aptly characterizes this transformation as a "development from religion as embedded in the city-state to religion as choice of differen-

same phenomena in the hellenistic era.[14] For Smith the hellenistic under-standing of the world as a unified whole, and a Greek one at that, results in a "radical revaluation of the world" and a shift in the understanding of the purpose of religion. Prior to this period, religion serves to create stabil-ity by envisioning an ordered universe and reaffirming humanity's place in it. The rise of Hellenism precipitates the realignment of relationships between cities and people, resulting in a view of the world as unstable, foreign, and hostile. Because of this the task of religion becomes that of providing the be-liever the means of escape from a threatening environment. Smith describes this shift as one that moves from a closed to an open universe: "Suffering from what might be termed 'cosmic paranoia' man sees danger and threat everywhere . . . a grim system of aggressors, an openly hostile army which seeks to chain him. . . . Hellenistic man discovered himself to be an exile from his true home, a home beyond the borders."[15]

Smith understands this sense of alienation and escape in cosmic terms, but I wish to argue that, given their perception by themselves and others as a distinct people, hellenistic Jews had a heightened awareness of the world as a hostile realm not only in a cosmological but also in a cultural dimension.[16] In a position similar to that of Smith, Thomas L. Thompson has character-ized the political and economic landscape of second-century BCE Palestine as an open world of religious syncretism to which Judaism responded in terms of what he calls exclusive monotheism, i.e., a theological outlook in which "the exclusivity of an alternative and traditional regional deity . . . represented for many the sole signification of the heavenly spirit."[17] Put another way, in the face of a homogenizing religious outlook which understands differing gods as the multiple manifestations of the one true god, some Jews respond with the claim that their particular god alone is the only true god; all other worship is false. This portrayal of the Jewish reaction to Hellenism opens

---

tiated groups offering different qualities of religious doctrine, different experiences, insights, or just different myths and stories to make sense of the absurdity of human experience" ("The De-velopment of Religious Pluralism," in Judith Lieu, John North, and Tessa Rajak, eds., *The Jews among Pagans and Christians in the Roman Empire* [London and New York: Routledge, 1992] 178).

14. Smith, "The Temple and the Magician," in idem, *Map Is Not Territory: Studies in the History of Religions* (SJLA 23; Leiden: Brill, 1978; repr. Chicago: University of Chicago Press, 1993) 172–189; originally published in Jacob Jervell and Wayne A. Meeks, eds., *God's Christ and His People: Essays in Honour of Nils Alstrup Dahl* (Oslo: Oslo University Press, 1976) 233–47 (references are to the reprint edition).

15. "The Influence of Symbols on Social Change: A Place on Which to Stand," in *Map Is Not Territory*, 138, 140; first published in *Worship* 44 (1970) 457–74 (references are to the reprint edition).

16. This combination of cosmological and cultural alienation is apparent in apocalyptic writ-ings, the most well-known literary product of hellenistic Judaism, where cultural injustice and evil earn cosmological recompense.

17. "The Intellectual Matrix of Early Biblical Narrative: Inclusive Monotheism in Persian Period Palestine," in Edelman, *Triumph of Elohim*, 123.

up the question of cultural identity, given exclusive monotheism's emphasis on a people's ancestral and/or national god. Thompson's claim merits further investigation, in particular by expansion beyond the chronological and geographic parameters of Seleucid-era Palestine.

The Impact of Hellenism on Judaism

Although Greek contact with Palestine is much older than Alexander the Great,[18] the commonly held view of the meeting between hellenistic culture and Judaism describes it as a reaction of the latter against the former, typified in the Maccabean revolt of 166–60 BCE. Read out of 1–2 Maccabees, Hellenism is seen as the vigorous attempt to introduce Greek culture, specifically religion, into Judaism, which valiantly resists any such measures. While it is true that the Maccabean revolt was fueled by Jewish resistance to enforced hellenization, it should not be held up as the archetypal model of hellenistic-Jewish contact. To do so runs the risk of appropriating the polemic of 1–2 Maccabees, which flattens its picture of both Hellenism and Judaism into the caricatures of the evil Seleucid king Antiochus IV and the brave Jewish warrior Judah Maccabee. The cultural pull of Hellenism on Judaism is older and often less overt than the legal measures enacted by Antiochus IV in Jerusalem. Jewish reactions, encompassing both approval and condemnation, were not limited to Jerusalem or Palestine.

Concerning the degree of hellenization among Palestinian Jews, scholarly debate ranges along a wide spectrum between the two boundary positions of Martin Hengel, who argues for sustained interaction between the two, and Louis H. Feldman, who maintains that Judaism resisted any attempts at hellenization because of its own internal cohesion and, ultimately, the admiration of political authorities.[19] Given the understanding of Judaism in the hellenistic period as an ethnic identity apart from the issue of where Jews lived, any discussion of Hellenism and Judaism should encompass both Palestinian and diaspora Judaism.[20] Indeed, the understanding of these two aspects of Judaism as distinct should be abandoned in favor of one that con-

---

18. See Morton Smith, *Palestinian Parties and Politics That Shaped the Old Testament* (New York: Columbia University Press; London: SCM, 1971) 43–61.

19. Hengel, *Judaism and Hellenism* 1. 310–14; Feldman, *Jew and Gentile in the Ancient World: Attitudes and Interactions from Alexander to Justinian* (Princeton, N.J.: Princeton University Press, 1993) 416–46. Hengel, while arguing for a prolonged and profound contact between Judaism and hellenistic culture, nevertheless makes the careful observation that "it is not possible to say that Palestinian Judaism ... maintained a straight course through the Hellenistic period untouched by the alien civilization and completely faithful to the Old Testament tradition. Still less can it be claimed that it was completely permeated by the Hellenistic spirit.... The truth lies between the extremes" (ibid., 1. 310).

20. See Davies's discussion of the emergence of "Juda-ism" as a conscious ethnic idea ("Scenes," 151–54).

trasts urban, elite Judaism with its rural peasant counterpart, in other words,
a view that envisages ancient Jewish culture as Great and Little Traditions
rather than as something with a dual existence in and out of Palestine. As
Snyder's utilization of Redfield's categories reinterpreted the early Christian
nonliterary data in terms apart from notions of perceived early Christian
"orthodoxy" extrapolated from written sources, so too an understanding of
hellenistic Judaism as Great and Little Traditions frees the discussion from
the privileging of Palestinian Judaism as normative over that of the diaspora.[21]
This alternative interpretative model allows one to see connections between
Jews on the basis of their social position rather than geographic location. For
example, members of the Jewish elite in Alexandria would have more in common with their cultured counterparts in Jerusalem than with poorer Jews in
the Egyptian countryside.[22]

A further help in making sense of the data is provided by the careful and
critical work of Barclay on diaspora Judaism in the hellenistic period.[23] Barclay gives a nuanced analysis of the extent of hellenization among diaspora
Jews by interpreting the evidence according to the criteria of assimilation,
i.e., the level of social integration, and acculturation, i.e., the impact of
"the linguistic, educational and ideological aspects of a given cultural matrix."[24] These two factors are not necessarily related concomitantly. Some
Jews could be fairly integrated into hellenistic society without appropriating
the nonmaterial aspects of its culture, while others could have knowledge
of hellenistic language and education without maintaining sustained contact
with non-Jews. As in the case with diaspora and Palestinian Judaism, the
distinction here is according to social location. Those Jews understood to
be acculturated are those who could avail themselves of hellenistic language
and education.[25]

While Barclay observed that one cannot generalize about Jewish identity

---

21. Barclay discusses the problems and assumptions that accompany scholarly use of categories such as orthodoxy, heterodoxy, and deviation in regards to ancient Judaism (*Jews in the
Mediterranean Diaspora*, 83–88).

22. By way of example is the partially disdainful evaluation of manual labor found in Sir
38:24–39:5, a literary product of the hellenistic Jewish elite. However, it should be noted that
this "Satire of the Trades" is a literary motif present in Egyptian scribal traditions centuries prior
to the writing of the OT.

23. *Jews in the Mediterranean Diaspora*; Barclay's work should be read in tandem with Edith M.
Smallwood, *The Jews under Roman Rule: From Pompey to Diocletian* (2d ed.; SJLA 20; Leiden:
Brill, 1981). Because I am limiting my discussion to pre-Roman Judaism, I will not deal with
Smallwood's work.

24. Barclay, *Jews in the Mediterranean Diaspora*, 92.

25. Although the assimilation and acculturation have many points of contact, a distinction
between the two is valid. By way of example Barclay asks us to consider the difference between a
Jewish slave in a non-Jewish household, immersed in hellenistic society while unlearned in Greek
language and thought, and a Jew learned in Greek culture who nevertheless limits his contact
with non-Jews (ibid., 92).

in the diaspora or speak of its typical characteristics, he nevertheless outlines certain recurring traits that emerge in the evidence, particularly when
Judaism comes in contact with outsiders. Barclay discerns a powerful sense
of ethnicity among many hellenistic Jews, maintained by observance of distinguishing practices such as circumcision and continuance of a common
ancestry through endogamy.[26] He designates four traits as "Practical Distinctions" which, because of their visibility, serve to distinguish Jews from others.
They deal with worship (e.g., rejection of foreign cult, Sabbath observance)
and socialization (e.g., dietary restrictions, circumcision); each carries significant social ramifications. For example, dietary restrictions would severely
limit the role well-to-do Jews could play in the developed interplay of hospitality and reciprocity surrounding meals in the ancient world.[27] Refusal to
participate in any non-Jewish cult would narrow the social and political are-
nas into which one could travel. These characteristics serve both to give
Jews a sense of distinction from their neighbors and to foster non-Jewish
perceptions of Jews as a unique people. This is abundantly clear from the
literary evidence, as is the animosity engendered among both groups by this
perceived difference.[28]

Among Jewish authors of the period, distinctive Jewish practices are dealt
with in a number of ways. Apart from those texts that are not openly inimical to outsiders (e.g., 1–4 Maccabees, Esther) two approaches are taken.
The first acknowledges Jewish distinction and claims its superiority over other
modes of living. This is apparent in the *Letter of Aristeas*, a second-century
BCE work which serves as a Jewish apologetic to hellenistic society by recounting a legendary story of the translation of the Pentateuch into Greek
for the great library of Alexandria. While preparing to send translators to
Egypt from Palestine, the high priest Eleazar answers questions put to him
from King Ptolemy II through a messenger (*Ep. Arist.* 128–70). Eleazar's responses are an extended defense of both Jewish dietary practice and aniconic
monotheism, not surprisingly two of Barclay's practical distinctions, i.e., identifying cultural markers visible to outsiders. Considering monotheism, Eleazar
remarks that "all the rest of mankind (*except ourselves*, as he said) believe
that there are many gods...they make images of stone and wood.... Those
who have invented these fabrications and myths are usually ranked to be the

26. Ibid., 402–13. Ethnicity is here understood as "a combination of kinship and custom,
reflecting both shared genealogy and common behavior" (402).

27. "It was hardly possible to cement friendships without accepting Gentile invitations, and
choosing separate or select food did not accord with common notions of sociability" (ibid., 435).

28. The first sentence of Barclay's book, commenting on Num 23:9, notes "the sense of distinction which lies at the heart of the Jewish tradition" (ibid., 1); here Barclay is following Philo's
reading of the same verse (*Mos.* 1.278). Similarly, North claims for both early Judaism and Christianity "the existence of separate values and principles, unacceptable to other members of the
society but required of members" ("Development," 184).

wisest of the Greeks" (*Ep. Arist.* 134–38).[29] Eleazar then contrasts all others
with the Jews: "God . . . surrounded us with unbroken palisades and iron walls
to prevent our mixing with any of the other peoples in any matter, being thus
kept pure in body and soul, preserved from false beliefs" (139).

In discussing dietary regulations, Eleazar gives an allegorical reading of
the biblical laws regarding the eating of cloven-hoofed animals, seeing in the
division of the hoof a symbol of the division or separation of the Jews from
all others.[30]

Another way Jewish authors deal with the distinctive elements of their
culture is to argue for the antiquity of those practices and to trace them to
great figures in Greek culture. This is different from the approach in *Aristeas*
in that it attempts to use the finest traits of hellenistic culture and heritage against its heirs by claiming them for Judaism, specifically in regards to
those distinguishing features of Jewish life. An example of this is in the fragments of Aristobulus, an Alexandrian Jew of the second century BCE versed
in Greek language and thought. In defense of Sabbath observance (again, one
of Barclay's practical distinctions), Aristobulus appeals to the presence of the
numeral seven in the cycles of nature and invokes Homer and Hesiod for further support: "Indeed all the cosmos of all living beings and growing things
revolves in series of sevens. Its being called 'sabbath' is translated as 'rest.'
And both Homer and Hesiod, having taken information from our books, say
clearly that the seventh day is holy" (frg. 5.13).[31] Aristobulus's rhetorical aims
are baldly apparent in his spurious claim that Homer and Hesiod draw ideas
from the OT. Moreover, two of the texts he cites that purport to be from
these Greek authors do not occur in their writings. This is further indication
of Aristobulus's ultimate aim of claiming classical Greek support for precisely
one of the practices that distinguished Judaism in the hellenistic age.[32]

What is important to note about these two texts is that to a great extent
they both view certain aspects of hellenistic culture favorably, e.g., the asceticism of certain philosophical ideas. However, despite this positive evaluation,
both the author of *Aristeas* and Aristobulus are at pains to stress the pre-

---

29. *OTP* 2. 21–22 (emphasis added). Barclay (*Jews in the Mediterranean Diaspora*, 138–50)
speaks of the "sense of religious incommensurability" in the text, reflected in the repeated
expression of gentile admiration for Judaism that lacks a Jewish response in kind (143–44).

30. *Ep. Arist.* 150–52 (*OTP* 2. 22–23). This leads immediately to a comparison between Jews
and "the majority of other men" (πλείονες τῶν λοιπῶν ἀνθρώπων), who engage in deviant and
lascivious behavior.

31. *OTP* 2. 842; see Barclay's analysis in *Jews in the Mediterranean Diaspora*, 150–58.

32. This strategy is also evident in Aristobulus's allegorical reading of biblical texts. Its irony
is eloquently expressed by Barclay: "[Aristobulus] draws out from the text what his Hellenistic
education demands must be there, but then asserts that his Hellenistic concepts are themselves
derived from Moses' genius. In other words, he claims to own what he has in fact been mastered
by" (ibid., 156).

eminence and fundamental importance of distinctive Jewish practice.[33] This is significant because it underscores the sense of difference that character-ized the relationship between Jews and outsiders in the hellenistic era. Even among those Jews who embraced some of the fundamental characteristics of hellenistic culture, such as language and philosophy, there were a number who still understood the encounter with that culture as something alien and potentially detrimental.[34]

One cannot deal with the portrayal of Judaism in this era by non-Jewish authors without also treating the issue of anti-Semitism. In the aftermath of the Holocaust there has been a considerable amount of scholarship on the origins of anti-Semitism in antiquity. The works of Jules Isaac and Marcel Simon have drawn attention to its presence in pagan society and raised the question of whether this presence exerted any influence on Christian anti-Semitism.[35] The answer to this question is crucial because it determines the degree of Christian culpability for both ancient and modern anti-Semitism. Feldman maintains that Greco-Roman anti-Semitism was minimal and that Jews were esteemed by outsiders. Similarly, while John G. Gager acknowl-edges anti-Semitism on the part of Greco-Roman society, he characterizes it as a series of responses to particular political situations (e.g., the Maccabean and First Revolts, conversions to Judaism) rather than as a predominant atti-tude.[36] In response to both of these authors, Peter Schäfer's recent work on the subject attempts to deal with the ambiguous and varying nature of opin-

---

33. So Barclay writes concerning the author of *Aristeas*: "Though he accommodates his Ju-daism to many aspects of the Hellenistic tradition, he never abandons the Jewish sense of difference; indeed he uses Hellenistic categories to define the terms of Jewish superiority. By presenting the Jews as purer than others, fenced off from their 'perversions,' he defends the preservation of Jewish distinction as a moral and theological necessity" (ibid., 147–48).

34. Cf. Barclay's remarks on accommodation, i.e., the various means to which Jews put their hellenistic education to use (ibid., 96–98).

35. See the survey in John G. Gager, *The Origins of Anti-Semitism: Attitudes toward Judaism in Pagan and Christian Antiquity* (New York: Oxford University Press, 1983) 13–23. The currency of this issue is confirmed by the Vatican document on the Holocaust released March 16, 1998 (Pontifical Commission for Religious Relations with the Jews, "We Remember: A Reflection on the 'Shoah,'" *Origins* 27 [1998] 670–75). The text's surprising claim that the Holocaust "was the work of a thoroughly neopagan regime" whose "anti-Semitism had its roots outside of Chris-tianity" (673) has stirred up a great deal of debate on the origins of Christian anti-Semitism. I wish to make clear that my remarks here are, due to the nature of my investigation, limited to the pre-Christian era and are in no way an attempt to mitigate the sad historical reality of Christian anti-Semitism.

36. Feldman's view (*Jew and Gentile*, 84–287) is critiqued by Peter Schäfer: "The emphasis upon both sympathy for the Jews and their achievements in the Greco-Roman world is also the declared purpose of . . . Louis Feldman, which being overly apologetic, however, grossly overshoots its mark" (*Judeophobia: Attitudes toward the Jews in the Ancient World* [Cambridge, Mass.: Harvard University Press, 1997] 6). Gager's approach (*Origins of Anti-Semitism*, 39–88) is characterized by Schäfer as "functionalist" and is contrasted with an "essentialist" understanding which sees anti-Semitism as stemming from opposition to fundamental characteristics of Judaism (*Judeophobia*, 2–5). A good example of the essentialist approach is J. N. Sevenster, *The Roots of Pagan Anti-Semitism in the Ancient World* (NovTSup 41; Leiden: Brill, 1975).

ions about Jews among Greco-Roman writers. While this is not the place to delve into anti-Semitism and its origins, several aspects of Schäfer's position are worth mentioning. The first is the caution against saying that Jewish distinctiveness is the cause of, rather than the rationale for, anti-Semitism, since the implication is to make Judaism the cause of its own mistreatment.[37] The second deals with the specific Jewish practices used to warrant anti-Semitism. Schäfer discusses several factors which, not surprisingly, correspond with Barclay's practical distinctions: monotheism, dietary practices, circumcision, and Sabbath observance. Third and most important, Schäfer traces the origin and development of the recurring slander of Jewish hatred of outsiders (μισοξενία), which occurs in several discussions of Judaism by outsiders spanning the hellenistic and Roman periods.[38] The earliest account of the charge is found in the fragments of the historian Hecataeus of Abdera, who flourished ca. 300 BCE and wrote a history of Egypt. In discussing the Exodus as part of Egyptian history, Hecataeus maintains that the Jews were expelled from Egypt and that, under the leadership of Moses, they took possession of Palestine and established a social order complete with a temple and cultus: "The sacrifices that he [Moses] established differ from those of other nations as does their way of living, for as a result of their own expulsion from Egypt he introduced a way of life which was unsocial and hostile to foreigners (ἀπάνθρωπόν τίνα καὶ μισόξενον βίον)."[39]

Again, in regards to this charge, Jewish distinctiveness is not the cause of the negative depiction, but rather particular Jewish practices are used as a justification for polemic on the part of outsiders. Schäfer maintains that this hostile response to Judaism presupposes an already existing Egyptian anti-Judaism coupled with the new phenomenon of hellenistic culture. The earliest evidence of this combination is, not coincidentally, in the treatment of the Jews by Hecataeus, the Greek author drawing upon native traditions for his historical survey of Egypt. Schäfer concludes:

> [Since] this conscious perversion of the "truth" [distinctive Jewish practices], the phobic mystification of the outgroup . . . is the peculiar result of the amalgamation of Egyptian and Greek prejudices, one might argue

---

37. "It is true that the allegation of the Jewish 'separateness' and 'strangeness' does have a *fundamentum in re*, but to argue that it is the *reason* for pagan anti-Semitism is to confuse cause with pretext, to hold the Jews themselves responsible for what others do to them" (Schäfer, *Judeophobia*, 209); cf. the similar position of Gager (*Origins of Anti-Semitism*, 31).

38. Schäfer, *Judeophobia*, 167–69, 177–79, 194, 208–11.

39. Fragment of Hecataeus preserved in Diodorus Siculus *Hist.* 40.3. Translation, partial transliterated Greek text, and discussion in Schäfer, *Judeophobia*, 15–16; *contra* Gager, *Origins of Anti-Semitism*, 39–41. Translation and discussion in Menahem Stern, ed., *Greek and Latin Authors on Jews and Judaism* (3 vols.; Jerusalem: Israel Academy, 1974–84) 1. 20–35; and Louis H. Feldman and Meyer Reinhold, eds., *Jewish Life and Thought among Greeks and Romans: Primary Readings* (Minneapolis: Fortress, 1996) 7–10. While intriguing, the contradictions between the accounts of the Exodus in Hecataeus and in the OT are beyond the scope of the discussion.

that only the idea of a world-wide Greco-Hellenistic civilization made it possible for the phenomenon we call anti-Semitism to emerge.[40]

What I hope to have accomplished in this brief treatment of a very complex topic is to establish several historical observations concerning Judaism in the hellenistic period. The first is that Hellenism as an influential cultural phenomenon should be understood as a Great Tradition encompassing members of the educated and elite classes. Second is that some Jews, confronting an alien culture in Hellenism, experienced this new social world as a foreign environment, a place where they were not at home. This experience was most apparent at those junctures where Jewish culture was visible as an alternative to the Greek manner of living, i.e., forms and object of worship, regulations on diet, and concrete designations of ethnicity such as circumcision and Sabbath observance. This is true even of those Jews who find much to esteem in hellenistic culture. Third and finally, these points of contact between Judaism and Hellenism generate a considerable amount of animosity in the literature of both groups. In the Great Traditions of both cultures one sees attempts to justify antipodal positions on the same datum: the uniqueness of certain aspects of Jewish life. Turning now to the premiere product of the ancient Jewish Great Tradition, the OT, the cultural context of hellenistic Judaism outlined here will furnish an interpretive matrix for the wanderings of the figure looked upon by Jews as the father of their people.

The Abraham Stories and Their Context

The search for the historical context of the patriarchal stories is nothing new to biblical scholarship. Although Julius Wellhausen claimed over a century ago that the stories did not allow for historical reconstruction beyond that dealing with the time of their composition, during this century archaeologists and exegetes developed elaborate historical tableaux founded upon perceived points of contact between elements in the biblical texts and archaeological data of various kinds from all over the Levant.[41] The resultant "Patriarchal Age" was dated roughly to the first half of the second millennium BCE — beyond this broad estimate scholars parted ways — and its proponents drew upon the burgeoning pool of written and material remains uncovered

---

40. Schäfer, *Judeophobia*, 206.

41. Wellhausen's oft-quoted remark is that "we attain no historical knowledge of the patriarchs, but only of the time when the stories about them arose in the Israelite people" (*Prolegomena to the History of Israel* [Edinburgh: Black, 1885; repr. Atlanta: Scholars Press, 1994] 318–19 [German original 1883]). Well-known examples of historical reconstructions of the patriarchal age are William F. Albright, *From the Stone Age to Christianity: Monotheism and the Historical Process* (2d ed.; Garden City, N.Y.: Doubleday/Anchor, 1957) 236–49; and John Bright, *A History of Israel* (Philadelphia: Westminster, 1959) 60–94.

in Mesopotamia, Anatolia, and Palestine for support. Additionally the stories themselves were subjected to a rigorous source-critical analysis, and their
various traditions and compositional strata were given dates and a detailed
developmental history both for their oral and written stages.[42]

While attempts to discover the historical background of the patriarchs
themselves have been subjected to extensive criticism and have, for the most
part, been discontinued, the search for the contextual framework of the stories about them continues apace.[43] John Van Seters has published extensively
in this regard, arguing that the traditions behind the stories stem from the
exilic and postexilic periods. Van Seters establishes his conclusions by comparison of Genesis 12–50 with biblical and extrabiblical texts from the sixth
to the fourth centuries BCE, including among the latter Greek historiographical traditions.[44] Another recent and important study is that of E. Theodore
Mullen, which merits special mention because it describes the Pentateuch as
a document whose purpose is to create and sustain Israelite ethnic identity in
the wake of the exile and restoration. For Mullen the Israelites were in need
of a national history to sustain their identity while in exile and to substanti-
ate their claims to the land against those of the indigenous inhabitants upon
their return to Palestine under Cyrus the Great.[45] Drawing upon studies of
ethnicity which delineate the elements necessary to define an ethnic group,
such as a common ancestor, territory, genealogy, and practices, Mullen shows
that these factors are central to the entire Pentateuch. In this regard Mullen
and I both think the purpose of the Abraham stories to be the creation of an
ethnic identity, i.e., the endorsement of a particular group and their way of

---

42. Examples include Gerhard von Rad, "The Form-Critical Problem of the Hexateuch," in
The Problem of the Hexateuch and Other Essays (Edinburgh: Oliver and Boyd, 1966) 1–78 (Ger-
man original 1938); and Martin Noth, *A History of Pentateuchal Traditions* (Englewood Cliffs, N.J.:
Prentice-Hall, 1972) (German original 1948).

43. Thompson offers sustained critique of the idea of a patriarchal age (*The Historicity of the
Patriarchal Narratives* [BZAW 133; Berlin: De Gruyter, 1974]).

44. Van Seters isolates features in the Abraham cycle which correspond to historical realia in
the neo-Babylonian and Persian periods (*Abraham in History and Tradition* [New Haven, Conn.:
Yale University Press, 1975]) and shows extensive points of contact between Genesis and the
Greek traditions of antiquarian and historiographical writing (*Prologue to History: The Yahwist
as Historian in Genesis* [Louisville, Ky.: Westminster/John Knox, 1992]). Although diverging from
Van Seters's analysis in several key respects, Joseph Blenkinsopp also understands the Pentateuch
as the product of the Jewish community in exile: "Learned priests and their associates were
engaged in constructing, in response to the experience of deprivation and exile, a conceptual
world of meaning in which historical reconstruction, the recovery of a usable past, played an
important role. We have good reason to find in Genesis 12–50 ... the fruits of these labors"
(*The Pentateuch: An Introduction to the First Five Books of the Bible* [New York: Doubleday, 1992]
120–21).

45. Mullen states that the Pentateuch was written "to define the concept of the people 'Israel'
on the basis of the changing cultural situations introduced by both the exile and the restoration
of the Judahite community with the beginning of the Persian period" (*Ethnic Myths and Pentateuchal Foundations: A New Approach to the Formation of the Pentateuch* [SBLSS; Atlanta: Scholars
Press, 1997] 64–65; cf. also 77–78).

life as distinct from others. However, Mullen understands this as a response to an inner-Jewish conflict concerning the rightful possessors of the land of Palestine, while I see it as the result of an external confrontation between Judaism and the larger hellenistic world.[46]

My treatment of the Abraham stories does not profess to be an exhaustive discussion of the texts with all of their attendant issues. I wish to focus on certain essential features and to show that they are best explained when interpreted against the background of Judaism in the hellenistic period. The biblical material examined here spans the middle third of Genesis. It begins in 12:1 and, with an interruption in Genesis 24 where Rebekah is betrothed to Isaac, ends in 25:7–10 with the death of Abraham. While the arrangement of the episodes exhibits signs of linear progression, these stories remain highly episodic, so that it is fitting to look at them as variations on a small number of repeated themes.

The first is the repeated description of Abraham as a foreigner/alien residing in Canaan. This is expressed by use of the verb גור (12:10 [Egypt]; 20:1 [Gerar]; 21:34 [land of the Philistines]) and its nominal form, גר (17:8; 23:4).[47] Abraham's continuous wandering across vast expanses of the known world further emphasizes his status as a foreigner. In just the first ten verses of the account he moves from Mesopotamia (Ur) to Egypt with stops in Syria (Haran) and Palestine (Shechem, Bethel, the Negev, 12:1–10). As already mentioned, one of the results of the spread of hellenistic culture was the shift from understanding the world as a stable environment with its center in a temple to a view of the world as an open, chaotic, and hostile realm where one did not belong.[48] The motif of Abraham's wandering presupposes such a world.

Tension is created by the combination of Abraham's wandering with God's repeated promise to Abraham that he and his descendants will possess the land of Canaan.[49] The rationale given by the text and many commentators for this seeming contradiction is that Abraham is taking the customary in-

---

46. So also Davies: "Behind its [the OT] production and development lie two distinct motives: one was to generate a cultural and social identity, the other to refine that identity and oppose it to the identities that other cultures and peoples were furnishing for themselves" ("Scenes," 170). Mullen is open to the possibility of a hellenistic dating for some of the Pentateuch; see his remarks on similarities to the writings of Berossus and Manetho: "that the Biblical historiography should be dated even later than the Persian period remains a real possibility" (*Ethnic Myths*, 84 n. 95; see also 328).

47. Van Seters stresses this recurring theme (*Abraham*, 16).

48. From this standpoint, wandering plays an important metaphorical role: "In a world experienced in this way, liminality becomes the supreme goal rather than a moment in a rite of passage" (Smith, "Birth Upside Down or Right Side Up?" *Map Is Not Territory*, 170; first published in *HR* 9 [1970] 281–303 [references are to the reprint edition]).

49. Discussion on the promises in Genesis is vast; see Van Seters, *Prologue to History*, 215–76. While acknowledging that their names are changed in Genesis 17, for the sake of simplicity I will use "Abraham" and "Sarah" throughout the discussion. Also, the toponyms used here are

spection tour by walking around and through the land he is to occupy. So in 13:17 God commands him to "walk through the length and breadth of the land, for I will give it to you."[50] Abraham's perambulation would be explained in this light if in fact he did take possession of the land. However he does not and remains an alien there. In this respect it is significant that even God refers to him with this label in 17:8. Indeed the only land that Abraham comes to own in the story is the cave where he and Sarah are buried, and rather than having it given to him by God, Abraham acquires it through the more mundane means of purchase.

I want to emphasize this point because it is too often neglected in commentaries: Abraham never possesses the land promised him by God. He dwells on it as a resident alien his entire life and at his death owns only his burial place.[51] The close attention to the details of proper land transaction in Genesis 23 only accentuates the fact that this, Abraham's only acquisition of land, has nothing to do with God's pledge to him. That promise involved the gift of a vast expanse of land in which to live. This story deals with the purchase of a small plot on which to die and be buried. The powerful statement about human life gleaned from this is that to be a human being in this world is to be an alien. The only true homeland, in the sense of a place of peace and safety, is the grave.[52]

This is one of the viewpoints Snyder perceives at work behind Christian burial art as a reaction to the hostile Roman world. Likewise its presence here in Genesis reflects a similar experience of the larger world on the part of its Jewish author and audience. Scholars differ concerning whether the audience is meant by the author to identify in the promise of land with Abraham or his offspring. For Blenkinsopp, Abraham symbolizes the returnees from exile who are to rebuild the Israelite culture. Abraham's purchase of a burial place, replete with commercial details, "would more naturally re-

---

those given in the story. No attempt is made to clarify or correct them in the light of historical geography.

50. Claus Westermann cites other ancient witnesses to this practice (*Genesis 12–36* (Minneapolis: Augsburg, 1985] 180). Leo Tolstoy utilizes this practice as a plot device to illustrate the destructive power of human greed ("How Much Land Does a Man Need?" in D. Tippens, S. Weathers, and J. Welch, eds., *Shadow and Light: Literature and the Life of Faith* [Abilene, Tex.: Abilene Christian University Press, 1997] 119–32).

51. Similarly, Tolstoy ends his story with the answer to the question that is its title: "Six feet from his head to his heels was all he needed" ("How Much Land Does a Man Need?" 132). Blenkinsopp speaks of the paradox of Genesis 12–50 in that its central theme involves the land of Canaan and yet at crucial points in the story, including both its beginning and its end, the main characters are not in it (*The Pentateuch*, 110).

52. See also Abraham's reference to himself as "a stranger and an alien" (גר־ותושב, 23:4) in his dealings with the Hittites even after, according to the narrative's chronology, having lived in Palestine for close to a century. I should mention that this is a main theme in the Garden Story (Gen 2:4–3:24) where, as a punishment, the man is alienated from the ground that gave him life and can only be reconciled to it in death (Gen 3:17–19).

fer to the reappropriation of land after the return from exile." Mullen notes
those promises which are directed to Abraham's offspring and maintains that
the postexilic community would have seen themselves as those descendants
and hence, the rightful heirs to the land.[53] The distinction is perhaps too
subtle, as both Blenkinsopp and Mullen acknowledge in their discussion. To
see oneself as the descendant of an ancestor can imply identification with
that ancestor and an understanding of events in his life as having an almost archetypal significance for his progeny. As lived Abraham, so live his
offspring.[54] The familiar text of Deut 26:5, "a wandering Aramean was my
ancestor," which occurs in a command to the Israelites to remember the
homelessness of Abraham, illustrates this awareness on the part of the biblical authors. This portrayal of Abraham as a wandering sojourner with no true
home deserves a second look in light of what it can reveal about those who
created the stories about him.

Closely related to the portrayal of Abraham as an alien is his interaction
with outsiders, all of whom are understood to be indigenous to the regions
where Abraham travels.[55] Many of these encounters involve antagonism and
hostility. In the dual story of Sarah's pretending to be Abraham's sister (Gen
12:10–20; 20:1–17), Abraham's deception is motivated by his perception of
outsiders as potentially hostile.[56] In both stories he suspects that his hosts will
kill him on account of his wife, and in Genesis 20 he charges the residents of
Gerar with having no reverence for God (20:11). In Genesis 12 he and Sarah
are expelled from Egypt for their deception. Abimelech, on the other hand,
allows Abraham to continue to reside on his lands. He and Abraham strike a
bargain not to deal falsely with each other (21:22–24). However, immediately
afterward a dispute arises between the two men concerning the ownership of
a well. Abraham lays claim to the well by making a gift to Abimelech, and at
the resolution of this dispute, we are told that he continued to reside there as
an alien (ויגר אברהם בארץ פלשתים ימים רבים, 21:34). The meaning here is
clear: Abraham assumes that outsiders will deal with him harshly, and even
when an agreement governing relations is formally concluded, such peaceful
coexistence is uneasy at best and does not change the status of the alien.[57]

---

53. Blenkinsopp (The Pentateuch, 102; cf. also 125); Mullen (Ethnic Myths, 137).
54. "As stories about the fathers they have validity for the story of all their posterity"
(Westermann, Genesis 12–36, 25).
55. These outsiders are the Egyptians and their king (12:10–20); Melchizedek, king and priest
of Salem (14:18–20); the king of Sodom (14:21–24); Abimelech, the king of Gerar, and his
servants (20:1–18; 21:22–34); and Ephron and the other Hittites (23:3–20).
56. Van Seters gives an overview and source-critical analysis (Abraham, 167–91).
57. One perhaps could also include Abraham's encounter with the king of Sodom (Genesis
14) and the Hittites (Genesis 23). However, the latter text bears a strong resemblance to neo-
Babylonian and Persian contracts (Van Seters, Abraham, 98–100), and both are similar in tone
to the common, unwritten rules of commercial interaction still practiced in the Levant.

Another main theme in the Abraham stories deals with the problem of an heir. The author uses the time-honored motif of the aged, childless couple to make two claims. First, God's promise of land and blessing to Abraham's descendants is only for those who are traced through Isaac.[58] Even though Ishmael is Abraham's seed, he is rejected by God because he is not the off-spring of both Abraham and Sarah. Though God will bless Ishmael, he will not be the inheritor of the promise (17:18–21). The ethnic implications are clear. Ishmael is not the bearer of God's blessing because he has a foreign (Egyptian) mother. This is apparent in the repeated reference to Hagar's eth-nicity (הגר המצרית, 16:3; 21:9). The connection of such a story with the maintenance of ethnic identity through endogamy is striking, and this is a particular concern for Judaism in the hellenistic period. The heir to God's promise cannot have a foreign mother.

Second, Abraham is, true to his name, the father of many nations. In addition to the Israelites and the Ishmaelites, born from Sarah and Hagar re-spectively, Gen 25:1–6 recounts a genealogy descended from Abraham and "another wife," Keturah. As Van Seters has pointed out, stories of the ances-tors of ethnic groups which trace the development of those groups through use of genealogies are a distinctive feature of Greek historiographical and antiquarian writing.[59] These two purposes underlying the stories of Abraham and his descendants are the same as those at work in *Aristeas* and the writings of Aristobulus discussed above. Just as *Aristeas* emphasizes the distinctiveness of the Jews from all others, so too does Genesis stress that God's promises are valid only for those children of Abraham descended through Isaac (and later, Jacob), i.e., the Israelites. And, as Aristobulus attempts to prove that the great figures of Greek culture are dependent upon Jewish thought, Gen-esis also gives Abraham special status by making him the ancestor of many peoples while maintaining his special relationship with the Israelites.

The most important indicator of the historical background to the Abra-ham stories involves the institution of circumcision in Genesis 17. As with all aetiological tales, Genesis 17 presupposes the custom by offering a rationale for it. As Claus Westermann notes, the Babylonians did not practice circum-cision during the time of the exile. However, this fact alone does not provide support for interpreting Genesis 17 as an exilic text meant to safeguard Jewish identity in Babylon because there is no other evidence that this practice was at issue there.[60] However, circumcision was one of the practices during the hellenistic period that distinguished the Jews as an ethnic group from others. In fact, circumcision is as controversial as it is in the hellenistic age because

---

58. So Blenkinsopp (*The Pentateuch*, 109); Mullen (*Ethnic Myths*, 140).
59. Van Seters, *Prologue to History*, 86–103.
60. *Pace* Westermann, *Genesis 12–36*, 256, 264–66.

Greek culture found such ritual mutilation curious at best and repugnant at worst.[61] More important, given the prominent social role played by the gymnasium in the spread of the hellenistic Great Tradition, for the first time a forum exists where one could distinguish between those who were circumcised and those who were not. As Robert G. Hall points out, in cities such as Alexandria the gymnasium was one of the primary means of perpetuating Greek culture and learning. It was also the avenue to citizenship, something we know that Alexandrian Jews aspired to in the first century CE.[62]

This is the proper background to understand the categorical nature of God's command to Abraham and the fundamental role circumcision plays in the covenant story of Genesis 17. It is the sine qua non of the covenant between Yahweh and Abraham, and the promise of the land is contingent upon its observance. After a lengthy exposition of the promises, Yahweh deals with Abraham's obligations. The transition to the command to circumcise in v. 8 is emphasized in the Hebrew by the addition of the pronoun to the inflected form of the verb (תשמר...ואתה), so that the sense is: "As for *you*, you shall keep my covenant" (NRSV). This mark of the covenant is to be perpetually observed and extends to all males connected with Abraham's household. The penalty for ignoring it is simple and severe: the uncircumcised male is "cut off from his people" (17:14). It is no coincidence that immediately after this command God makes clear to Abraham that the promises apply only to the child he will bear with Sarah. As we have seen above, this text carries with it a strong sense of Jewish ethnic identity, and it is here coupled with one of the distinguishing physical features of that identity.

And so in the Abraham stories there are themes and elements whose presence can best be explained by looking at the historical situation of Judaism in the hellenistic period. Abraham functions as a symbol of the individual Jew. The world he moves in is one in which he has no home, where he is a stranger in temporary residence. This reflects part of a larger response by many to the world that emerged after the conquest of Alexander and the struggles of his successors. The interaction between Abraham and outsiders is often characterized by mistrust and hostility. This perception of non-Jews as other, and conversely of Jews as a unique people, is a common theme in the literature of both groups in the hellenistic era. Some of the ways Jewish authors understand the engagement of Judaism and Hellenism are also present in the Abraham stories. Key texts in the Abraham material stress the necessity of circumcision and endogamy for Israelite identity. God's promises are made only to the offspring of Abraham and Sarah, and their validity is

---

61. See Davies, "Scenes," 175–76. For analysis of Greco-Roman attitudes toward circumcision, see Schäfer, *Judeophobia,* 93–105.

62. Hall, "Circumcision," *ABD* 1.1027–28.

contingent upon the practice of circumcision. Again, it is peculiarly in the hellenistic period that circumcision becomes a unique marker of the newly emerging idea of Jewish ethnicity.

This study of the Abraham stories is analogous to Snyder's analysis of early Christian art, which draws upon the social reality of cultural hostility towards early Christianity and shows how it is interpreted and expressed in the Christian Little Tradition. Similarly, the Jewish Great Tradition that created Genesis 12–25 experienced the world as foreign and often antagonistic. Such an outlook is best explained in the historical context of the hellenistic period which, it is hoped, sheds a little more light on the purpose and meaning of these stories.

5

THE CROSSING OF THE RED SEA AS INTERPRETED BY PHILO

Biblical Event – Liturgical Model – Cultural Application

PEDER BORGEN

It is a privilege and a pleasure for me to contribute an essay to the Festschrift in honor of my good friend and treasured colleague Graydon Snyder. I first met Graydon in the late 1950s, when he was a Fulbright Fellow at the University of Oslo. Both then and later I have learned much from his keen interest in the community life of early Christianity and of patristic times, as well as in the complex life of the world today. In his historical research Graydon has demonstrated how literary texts and ancient art mutually enrich each other. Together they give a better picture of the symbols, concepts, and religious activities that have had a decisive impact on the life of Christians. The following essay explores a related field of texts and images in the spirit of much of Snyder's most influential writing.[1]

The relationship between the law of Moses and the cosmos is a central theme in Philo's works.[2] One of the places where he deals with this theme

1. On a more personal level I should mention a very memorable experience when, in 1959, Graydon and his wife, Lois, asked me to join them on a trip to the Soviet Union in a Volkswagen. In Moscow, on May Day, we saw the parading communists greeting Nikita Khrushchev as he stood on the top of the Lenin Mausoleum. May I add that my wife, Inger, and I wish to thank Graydon and Lois for their generous hospitality and for the many pleasant get-togethers we have had at conferences and other times.

2. See Harry Austryn Wolfson, *Philo: Foundations of Religious Philosophy in Judaism, Christianity, and Islam* (2 vols.; Cambridge, Mass.: Harvard University Press, 1948) 2. 189–92; Valentin Nikiprowetzky, *Le Commentaire de l'Écriture chez Philon d'Alexandrie* (ALGHJ 11; Leiden: Brill, 1977) 115–55; David Winston, "Philo's Ethical Theory," *ANRW* 2.21.1 (1984) 386–88; Peder Borgen, *Philo of Alexandria: An Exegete for His Time* (NovTSup 86; Leiden: Brill, 1997) 140–57. I have in mind especially *Ques. Exod.* and *Abr.* 1–6.

Abbreviations for works of Philo quoted in this essay are as in Samuel Sandmel, *Philo of*

in a principal way is *Mos.* 2.45–52. He writes: "Thus whoever will carefully
examine the nature of the particular enactments (τὰ διατεταγμένα) will find
that they seek to attain to the harmony (ἁρμονία) of the universe (τὸ πᾶν)
and are in agreement with (συνᾴδω) the principles of eternal nature" (2.52).
The plural participle used as a noun, τὰ διατεταγμένα, means the "enactments" or "ordinances" of a code of law. The particular enactments referred
to are the specific laws and regulations in the Mosaic law. This conclusion is
in accordance with *Abr.* 3, where the patriarchs are understood to be the
more general archetypes as distinct from the particular (ἐπὶ μέρους) laws
which follow in the treatises *On the Decalogue* and *On the Special Laws.*[3]

In the context of *Mos.* 2.52 Philo narrates two events from biblical history,
the deluge and the cities destroyed by fire. On the higher level of interpretation they exemplify ethical virtues in contrast to vices: those who followed
injustice and vices were counted as enemies not of humankind but of the
whole of heaven and the universe. They were punished by the deluge — with
Noah and his family as exceptions — and by the fire which destroyed the
cities (2.53–65).

From this analysis a hermeneutical key can be formulated: the particular ordinances of the Jewish law coincide with universal cosmic principles.
Thus to Philo universal and general principles do not undercut or cancel the
specific ordinances or events of the Mosaic law. This hermeneutical insight
implies that Philo can in different ways interpret one and the same biblical text basically on two, sometimes on three, levels, e.g., on the concrete
and specific level, the level of the cosmic and general principles, and the
level of the divine realm of the beyond. Within Philo's two- or three-level
hermeneutical perspective there is therefore room for various emphases.

The treatises *Against Flaccus* and *On the Embassy to Gaius* belong to the
kind of writing in which concrete historical events are interpreted. In other

---

Alexandria: An Introduction (New York: Oxford University Press, 1979) xii–xii; English titles in
the LCL edition appear in parentheses): *Abr.=De Abrahamo* (*On Abraham*); *Agr.=De agricul-
tura* (*On Husbandry*); *Conf.=De confusione linguarum* (*On the Confusion of Tongues*); *Congr.=De
congressu quaerendae eruditionis gratia* (*On Mating with the Preliminary Studies*); *Decal.=De decal-
ogo* (*On the Decalogue*); *Det.=Quod deterius potiori insidiari soleat* (*The Worse Attacks the Better*);
Deus=Quod Deus sit immutabilis (*On the Unchangeableness of God*); *Ebr.=De ebrietate* (*On Drunkenness*); *Flacc.=In Flaccum* (*Against Flaccus*); *Fug.=De fuga et inventione* (*On Flight and Finding*);
Gig.=De gigantibus (*On the Giants*); *Jos.=De Josepho* (*On Joseph*); *L.A.=Legum allegoriae* (*Allegorical Interpretation*); *Leg.=De legatione ad Gaium* (*On the Embassy to Gaius*); *Mig.=De migratione
Abrahami* (*On the Migration of Abraham*); *Mos.=De vita Mosis* (*On the Life of Moses*); *Mut.=De
mutatione nominum* (*On the Change of Names*); *Post.=De posteritate Caini* (*On the Posterity and
Exile of Cain*); *Sac.=De sacrificiis Abelis et Caini* (*The Sacrifices of Abel and Cain*); *Sob.=De so-
brietate* (*On Sobriety*); *Som.=De somniis* (*On Dreams*); *Spec.=De specialibus legibus* (*On the Special
Laws*); *Virt.=De virtute* (*On the Virtues*); *Vita=De vita contemplativa* (*On the Contemplative Life*);
in addition, *Ques. Gen.* (or *Exod.=Questions and Answers on Genesis* (or *Exodus*).

3. A detailed examination of Philo's use of the term confirms this understanding; see *Mos.*
2.15, 138; *Decal.* 158, 174; *Spec.* 2.1, 250; *Deus* 87; *Conf.* 2; *Leg.* 210 (Borgen, *Philo of Alexandria*,
146–47).

writings the focus may be placed primarily upon the higher level of general cosmic principles and God's realm above the created world. The *Allegorical Interpretation* qualifies for this classification. Another possibility is to place both levels together in immediate sequence, as is the case especially in several entries in the *Questions and Answers on Genesis and Exodus* and parts of *On Abraham* and *On Joseph*. In Philo's rewriting of the laws of Moses in *On the Life of Moses, On the Decalogue, On the Special Laws, On the Virtues,* and *On Rewards and Punishments*, the main emphasis is on concrete biblical history, with various aspects of the higher level woven into the paraphrase. It should be added that typological interpretation is also used by Philo, as in *On the Contemplative Life* 85–87, where a concrete biblical event of old — the Crossing of the Sea (Exodus 14–15) — is told because it is a model for the liturgical reenactment in the main feast of the Therapeutae.[4]

Biblical Event

The aim of the present study is to illustrate aspects of Philo's two-level exegesis in his treatment of Exod 13:17–15:21. In his commentary on Exodus, Brevard S. Childs gives a survey of the history of interpretation of the biblical story of the Crossing of the Sea. Referring to Philo, he states that Philo is, of course, fully acquainted with the biblical tradition, but also that the more typical allegorical approach appears in other references to the Crossing.[5] Childs's brief reference demonstrates the need for a discussion of the relationship between Philo's recounting of the story and his allegorical exposition of it.

In Philo's writings there are three places that deal with Exod 13:17–15:21 as a specific event in biblical history: the one referred to by Childs (*Mos.* 1.163–80); another in 2.246–56; and a briefer version in *Vita* (83) 85–89. In all three, Philo's report of the Crossing of the Red Sea takes the form of a paraphrase of the biblical story.

Now, the two treatises *On the Life of Moses* are organized around the idea of the four offices of Moses: as king, lawgiver, high priest, and prophet. Book 1 is largely devoted to Moses as king; 2.12–65 presents Moses as law-giver; 2.66–186 presents him as high priest; and 2.187–292 as prophet.[6] The story of the Crossing of the Sea is part of Moses' activities as king and as prophet.

As for the context of the story of the Crossing in *Mos.* 1.163–80, an outline of the book should be given. In 1.1–148 Philo gives an account of Moses'

---

4. See Borgen, *Philo, John and Paul: New Perspectives on Judaism and Early Christianity* (BJS 131; Atlanta: Scholars Press, 1987) 17–59.

5. Childs, *Exodus: A Commentary* (OTL; London: SCM, 1974) 231.

6. In Judaism, the three offices (king, priest, prophet) could be united in one person; Josephus says that John Hyrcanus possessed all three (*Ant.* 13.299–300). The office of law-giver had to be added as an office uniquely connected with Moses, since the laws were given by him.

life from his birth to God's use of Moses as an agent in the punishments of the Egyptians and subsequently to the departure of the Hebrew people from Egypt. What follows (1.149–62) is an excursus that breaks off from the Pentateuchal narrative; it gives a characterization of Moses' kingship. He became, it suggests, god and king and the model for the Hebrew nation to follow in their exodus as they faced attacks from the king of Egypt and other enemies.[7]

In the transitional words of *Mos.* 1.163, Philo refers back to a main point in the preceding section and outlines the purpose of their wandering: "So, having received the authority, which they willingly gave him, with the sanction and assent of God, he proposed to lead them to settle in Phoenicia and Coelesyria and Palestine, then called the land of the Canaanites. . . . " It is to be noted that Philo places this event in the past, since he refers to the land of the Canaanites as a name of the past, different from the present name of Palestine.

The main parts of the biblical story of the Crossing (Exod 13:17–15:21) are included in Philo's paraphrase in *Mos.* 1.163–80: (1) the beginning of the journey from Egypt to the Red Sea (1.163–65; cf. Exod 13:17–18); (2) the cloud goes before them (1.163–66; cf. Exod 13:21–22); (3) the king of Egypt changes his mind and pursues the Hebrews and reaches them as they are encamped on the shores of the sea (1.167–69; cf. Exod 14:5–9); (4) the people are panic-stricken and address Moses in their despair, at which Moses encourages the people and prophesies (1.170–75; cf. Exod 14:10–18); (5) Moses smites the sea with his staff, the water is divided, and the guiding cloud turns back and forms the rearguard of the people (1.176–78a; cf. Exod 14:19–22); (6) the Hebrews are saved through the Sea, while the Egyptians are drowned (1.178b–79; cf. Exod 14:23–29); (7) the Hebrews find themselves unexpectedly victorious, form two choirs, and sing hymns of thanksgiving (1.180; cf. Exod 14:30–15:1a, 20–21a).[8] The Song of Thanksgiving at the Sea is mentioned briefly, and the references to Moses in Exod 15:1 and to his sister Miriam in 15:20 are coordinated into the picture of the two choirs being formed. The further content of the hymn (Exod 15:1–21) is not given. Then in *Mos.* 1.181 the Hebrews continue their journey into the desert.

Philo focuses on certain points in the biblical story. One of these is Moses' role as the authorized leader of the people. Thus in *Mos.* 1.164 he writes that "he [Moses] led them . . . ," while in Exod 13:18, 21 LXX God is the subject. Similarly, in 1.170 Philo reads "they [the Hebrews] . . . began to accuse their ruler," while Exod 14:10–11 LXX reads "the children of Israel cried to the Lord; and they said to Moses. . . . " Again, Exod 14:13 LXX reads "Moses said to the people," and Philo elaborates on this, picturing how Moses mediates between God and the people: "using his mind and speech simultaneously

---

7. See Borgen, *Philo of Alexandria*, 197–205.
8. Philo does not mention that in Exod 13:19 Moses takes the bones of Joseph with him.

for different purposes, with the former he silently interceded with God to save them from their desperate affliction, with the latter encouraged and comforted the loud-voiced malcontents" (*Mos.* 1.173).[9]

As in the biblical story, the king of Egypt and the Egyptians are the enemies. In his description of the Egyptians, Philo stresses their bitterness and wrath (1.172). So it is relevant to make the observation that Philo in his own time sees the Egyptians as the enemies of the Jewish people, in that they had an innate hostility to the Jews (*Flacc.* 29; cf. *Leg.* 162–71.205).[10]

As stated above, Philo also uses the story of the Crossing of the Sea to illustrate Moses' role as a prophet. The section on Moses as prophet is divided according to the way in which an oracle is received — as an answer to a question asked by Moses or as a direct inspiration. Of the latter type Philo gives four examples: Moses' prophecies (1) of the destruction of the Egyptians (*Mos.* 2.246–57); (2) of the manna and the Sabbath (258–69); (3) of the slaughter of the idolaters (270–74); and (4) of the destruction of Korah and his companions (275–87).[11]

An outline of the example in *Mos.* 2.246–57 is as follows: (1) time and place: when they set out as colonists from Egypt to Syria and reach the Red Sea (2.246–47a); (2) situation: their desperate situation at the Sea, as they are pursued by the king of Egypt (2.247b–50); (3) prophecy: as an extended speech Moses utters his inspired prophecy about the destruction of the Egyptians (2.251–52); (4) result: what Moses prophesied comes to pass; the enemy meets their doom by drowning in the Sea, while the Hebrew nation makes its passage as on a dry path (2.253–55); (5) reaction: the Song of Thanksgiving. Moses leads the choir of men, and appoints his sister to lead the women. They sing a song of harmony and joy, and all the myriads of people take part.

Biblical Event and Liturgical Use in a Pagan Context

While the story of the Crossing of the Sea in *Mos.* 1.163–80 is seen as an event on the journey of the Hebrew people under the leadership of the di-

---

9. Philo has an interesting interpretation of the cloud in the form of a pillar: "Perhaps indeed there was enclosed within the cloud one of the lieutenants (ὑπάρχοντες) of the Great King — an unseen angel, a forerunner..." (*Mos.* 1.166). In a similar manner it is said in *Pirqe R. El.* 42 that the angel Michael had the function of the pillar.

10. Borgen, *Philo of Alexandria*, 197–205.

11. So Philo divides prophecies into three groups: (1) prophecies spoken by God in his own person; (2) prophecies in which the revelation comes through question and answer; and (3) prophecies which, through inspiration, are spoken by Moses in his own person. Philo leaves the first kind out of the discussion in *Mos.* 2.181–287. A similar division is found in Cicero; see Émile Bréhier, *Les Idées philosophiques et religieuses de Philon d'Alexandrie* (1st ed., 1908; 3d ed; Paris: Vrin, 1950) 179–205; Walther Völker, *Fortschritt und Vollendung bei Philo von Alexandrien* (TU 49/1; Leipzig: Hinrichs, 1938) 292. In various ways the nature of Moses' prophetic utterances is discussed in rabbinic writings; see, e.g., *Lev. Rab.* 1.14; *b. Yebam.* 44b.

vinely authorized king, Moses, and in 2.246–57 as an example of Moses' role
as prophet, it is in *Vita* 85–89a referred to as an event of old which serves as
a model for liturgical reenactment when the Therapeutae during their sacred
vigil form a joint choir of men and women and sing in harmony.

The outline of the treatise *On the Contemplative Life* is as follows: the Therapeutae and their worship are contrasted with pagan polytheistic worship, of
which the Egyptian animal worship is the worst (*Vita* 1–9); the Therapeutae
concentrate on the vision of God and renounce all thoughts of private property (10–20); their Sabbath-centered life at their central place is a spot near
the Mareotic lake (21–39); as a contrast to their symposia Philo describes the
pagan feasts and among them the two symposia described by Xenophon and
Plato (40–63); Philo gives an account of the festal meeting and symposium
of the Therapeutae, of which the sacred vigil is a part (64–90).

The account of the Crossing of the Sea is found in *Vita* 85–89a.[12] After
the supper the Therapeutae hold the sacred vigil and form two choirs, one of
men and one of women. When each choir separately has done its own part
in the feast, they mix and become a single choir, a copy of the choir set up of
old beside the Red Sea due to the wonders there wrought (83–85). Then the
story of the actual crossing of the Red Sea is told as a paraphrase of parts of
Exodus 14 together with points about the singing in Exodus 15. In his paraphrase of the biblical story, Philo places the emphasis on the reaction by the
men and the women when they saw this wonderful sight: filled with ecstasy
they formed a single choir and sang hymns of thanksgiving. The focus is on
the performance of the choristers rather than on the content of the Song.

It is outside of the scope of the present essay to discuss details about the
ways in which the choir sings. Instead the question to be asked is this: What
can be learned about Philo's interpretation of the OT in this treatise? As
an event "of old" (πάλαι, *Vita* 85) in the biblical history of the past, it has
a "second level" of meaning, in this case in the form of its reenactment in
the present. Philo says that the ecstatic effect of the event in the present is
piety: "Lovely are the thoughts, lovely the words and worthy of reverence
the choristers, and the end and aim of thoughts, words and choristers alike is
piety (εὐσέβεια)." Thus, although the Therapeutae, according to Philo, took
great interest in the allegorical meaning of the sacred scriptures (*Vita* 28,
78), the Crossing is not in 85–89a developed into general abstract ethical or
cosmic principles. There is rather a typological and liturgical interpretation
of the biblical event.

---

12. Concerning the general understanding of the treatise and in particular the problem of
the dating of the feast and the banquet, see among others Valentin Nikiprowetzky, "Le 'De Vita
Contemplativa' révisité," in *Sagesse et Religion: Colloque de Strasbourg, Octobre 1976* (Paris: Presses
Universitaires de France, 1979) 105–25. In the present essay attention is focused on Philo's
understanding and interpretation and not on the historical questions related to the Therapeutae.

Ethical and religious ideas of a more general nature are present in the treatise, however, when the worship and life of the Therapeutae are described in contrast to pagan polytheistic worship and immoral life. Philo also touches on the ethical aspect in his characterization of the participants in the vigil: they experienced an ethically noble (καλή) drunkenness (*Vita* 89).

Philo develops the religious and ethical aspects from the etymological meaning of the name "Therapeutae":

> [It is] a name derived from θεραπεύω, either in the sense of "cure," because they profess an art of healing better than that current in the cities — the latter cures only the bodies, but theirs also treats souls oppressed with grievous and well-nigh incurable diseases, inflicted by pleasures and desires (ἡδοναὶ καὶ ἐπιθυμίαι) and griefs and fears, by acts of covetousness, folly and injustice and the countless host of the other passions and vices; or else in the sense of "worship," because nature and the sacred laws have schooled them to worship the Self-existent, who is better than the good, purer than the One and more primordial than the Monad. (*Vita* 2)

This contrast is further spelled out in *Vita* 3–9, and "as for the gods of the Egyptians it is hardly decent even to mention them" (8) since the Egyptians even worship irrational animals (8–9). Pagan immorality is in particular seen in the savage violence, drunkenness, and debauchery at pagan feasts, such as at Xenophon's and Plato's Symposia (40–63). The Therapeutae, in contrast, "soar above the sun of our senses" (11) and follow the truly sacred instructions of the prophet Moses (64b).

A Second Level Meaning: A Cultural Application

In *On the Contemplative Life* Philo presents the Crossing of the Sea as a specific event in the past biblical history which serves as a model for the liturgical reenactment by the Therapeutae. As a contrast, in other sections of the treatise he describes the pagan polytheism and immorality. In his *Allegorical Interpretation* Philo weaves such words for passions and idolatry, virtues and vision, directly together with words from the biblical stories. Such expositions of the Crossing are found in several places in Philo's writings, for example, *L.A.* 2.102–4; *Agr.* 79–83; *Ebr.* 111; *Sob.* 13; *Som.* 2.268–69. In the present study only the brief passage in *Ebr.* 111 will be analyzed.

The three treatises *On Husbandry*, *Concerning Noah's Work as a Planter*, and *On Drunkenness* are all exegetical elaborations of parts of Gen 9:20–21 LXX. The words elaborated upon in *On Husbandry* are the phrase "And Noah began to be a husbandman"; the treatise on *Noah's Work as a Planter* is largely founded on the phrase "and he planted a vineyard"; and *On Drunkenness* is primarily an elaboration of "And [Noah] drank of the wine and became drunken."

For an understanding of *Ebr.* 111 the context should be outlined. In *Ebr.* 4 Philo says that liquor is a symbol for (1) folly and foolish talking, (2) complete insensibility, (3) greediness, (4) cheerfulness and gladness, and (5) nakedness. Point 1, folly and foolish talking, occupies, with digressions, *Ebr.* 11–153. Within this context Deut 21:18–21, about the disobedient son, is quoted in *Ebr.* 14:

> For if anyone...has a disobedient and contentious son who does not listen to the voice of his father and mother, and they discipline him and he does not hearken to them, his father and mother shall take him and bring him forth to the assembly of the elders of his city and to the gate of his place, and shall say to the men of their city, "This our son is disobedient and contentious, he does not listen to our voice, he is a riotous liver (συμβολοκοπῶν) and a wine-bibber, and the men of the city shall stone him with stones and thou shalt remove the evil one from among yourselves."

The exegesis of this passage covers *Ebr.* 15–96. According to Philo, the accusations brought against the son are "disobedience, contentiousness, paying of contributions and drunkenness" (15). He interprets συμβολοκοπῶν to mean the "paying of fees" (συμβολῶν εἰσφορά), which means that the person joins a social association or club.[13] Religious activities always play a role at such gatherings. On the whole Philo sharply criticizes the practices of the club. He argues that the lifestyle in the club is characterized by gluttony and indulgence, so that by paying their contributions they are actually mulcting themselves in money, body, and soul (20–22). Philo implies that some Jews join such clubs, and thus he connects the participation in such associations with the story of the golden calf in Exod 32:1–19 (*Ebr.* 95–96). In doing this he has an Egyptian setting in mind, since he identifies the golden calf in Exodus 32 with the bull Apis. In this way the disobedient son makes a god of the body and unites idolatry and immorality.

The story of the golden calf concludes the expository elaborations on the theme of the disobedient son (*Ebr.* 14–96). At the same time parts of the same story are elaborated upon in a lengthy exposition in *Ebr.* 95–125. In *Ebr.* 96, Exod 32:17–19 is quoted:

---

13. See T. Seland, "Philo and the Clubs and Associations of Alexandria," in John S. Kloppenborg and Stephen G. Wilson, eds., *Voluntary Associations in the Graeco-Roman World* (London and New York: Routledge, 1996) 110–27; Peder Borgen, *Early Christianity and Hellenistic Judaism* (Edinburgh: T. & T. Clark, 1996) 28–30, 35; idem, *Philo, John and Paul*, 227–28; idem, *Bread from Heaven* (NovTSup 10; Leiden: Brill, 1965; repr. 1981) 124–25; Isaak Heinemann, *Philons griechische und jüdische Bildung* (1932; repr. Hildesheim: Olms, 1962) 431.

For we are told that

(a) when Joshua heard the voice of the people as they shouted, he said to Moses,

(b) "There is a voice of war in the camp." And he said,

(c) "It is not the voice of men raising the shout through might, nor of those who raise it for being overcome,

(d) but it is the voice of men who raise the shout over the wine that I hear."

(e) And when he drew nigh to the camp, he saw the calf and the dances.

In a systematic way this quotation is interpreted in *Ebr.* 96–125. The short exposition of (a) is given in 98a, followed by a longer exposition of (b) in 98b–104. Item (c) is interpreted in 105–21, (d) in 122–23, and finally (e) in 124, which is followed by a concluding prayer in 125. In the present study Philo's interpretation of point (c) is of primary interest, since elements from Exodus 14 and 15 are drawn into the exposition.

Philo begins the section by giving the example of Abraham, taken from Genesis 14 (*Ebr.* 105–110). Abraham's victory included the rebuke of polytheism and idolatry. The next example is the Crossing of the Sea and the Song at the Sea, in Exodus 14–15, which mean punishment of impiety and passions and salvation of the spirit that sees God (111). Positively, victory means the appropriation of wisdom, as exemplified in the song led by Moses at the well (Num 21:16–18; *Ebr.* 112–13).[14] In *Ebr.* 114–18, Num 31:49–50 is quoted, and the virtues of courage and harmony are praised and so also the acknowledgment that the whole cosmos is a gift of God. The particular gifts of virtues and activities which correspond to them are the theme of *Ebr.* 119–20, with Gen 27:20 as the biblical reference. Finally, in the *inclusio* in *Ebr.* 120 parts of the wording of point (c) are repeated. This sentence from Exod 32:17–19 has framed the expositions of various other scriptural quotations in *Ebr.* 105–21.

Philo introduces point (c) in this way: "For in the phrase 'it is not the sound of those who raise the song through might' the last words mean 'those who have been victorious in war.'" This interpretation serves as a heading for examples of songs of victory in such a war. As in the case of the worship of the (Egyptian) golden bull, so also here in the example of Abraham (*Ebr.* 105–10) the polemic is raised against idolatry and immorality: Abraham had routed the nine kings, meaning the four passions and the five sense-faculties, which were rising in unnatural rebellion.[15] Philo understands Gen 14:22–23 within a cosmic setting:

---

14. Cf. the similar interpretation in *Som.* 2.268–71.
15. For Abraham as a warrior, see *Abr.* 225, 231–35.

"I will stretch forth my hand to the most high God who made heaven and earth, if I will take from a rope to a shoe's latchet of all that is thine." He points in these last words, I think, to the whole of creation, heaven, earth, water, the air we breathe, to animals alike.

Abraham "has the vision of the Existent" as "the Cause, and [who] honors the things of which He is the cause only as second to Him" (*Ebr.* 107).

The contrast is "the man of no discernment, whose understanding, by which the Existent can be comprehended, is blinded." He sees only the material contents of this world as shown him by his senses, and these material things he believes to be the causes of all that comes into being. And therefore he starts fashioning gods and fills the inhabited world with idols of stone and wood and numberless other figures wrought in various materials, and decrees great prizes and magnificent honors, public and private, to painters and sculptors, whom the lawgiver had banished from the boundaries of his commonwealth (πολιτεία; *Ebr.* 109–10).[16] Philo brings his exposition of the victory won by Abraham to a close by an *inclusio*: "Such persons did Abraham rebuke and we shewed that it was with this thought that he raised his hymn of victory" (110b).

Philo's next example is the song of victory at the Red Sea, where the evil passions were destroyed (111). Here he weaves words from Exodus 14 and 15 together with words about misconceptions and passions. The passage should be quoted in full (words taken from LXX are emphasized):[17]

So too with the song of Moses:
When he had seen *the king of Egypt* (τὸν βασιλέα τῆς Αἰγύπτου),
the boastful mind,
with his *six hundred chariots* (ἑξακοσίοις ἅρμασι, cf. Exod 14:7 LXX),
that is, the *six* (ἕξ) movements of the organic body,
adjusted for the use of the *princes* (τριστάταις, cf. Exod 14:7; 15:4 LXX) who ride upon them,
who, though no created object can be stable, think it right to aver that all such are firmly established and unsusceptible of change,
suffering the penalty due to its impiety,
and the Practising One escaping the onset of enemies and in an unexpected way being saved with might,
then he hymns God, the righteous and true arbitrator, initiating the most fitting and suited songs to the occasion.
The horse and his rider He has thrown into the sea (ἵππον καὶ ἀναβάτην

---

16. It is worth noting that the terms ξόανα (images carved of wood, statues) and ἀγάλματα (statues in honor of a god) are used in *Vita* 7 in the description of idolaters in contrast to the community of the Therapeutae. See further *Decal.* 66; *Mos.* 2.205.

17. The translation in the LCL is modified.

ῥίψας εἰς θάλασσαν, cf. Exod 15:1 LXX), that is, having done away with the mind which rode upon the unreasoning impulses of passion, that four-footed beast which knows not the rein, He has shown himself the *helper* (βοηθός, Exod 15:2 LXX) and champion of the seeing soul, to bestow on it full *salvation* (σωτηρίαν, Exod 15:1 LXX).

The structure of the passage is simple. A temporal clause introduced by ἐπειδάν ("when") is followed by a main clause. In the temporal clause what Moses saw is reported, and in the main clause it is said that on that basis he hymns God.

As can be seen from the quotation, Philo makes expository supplements to the emphasized words from parts of Exodus 14 and 15. These added explanations call for comment. As for the definition of the king of Egypt as "the boastful mind" (ὑπέραυχος νοῦς), it should be noted that in *Agr.* 62 Philo states that the Egyptian spirit is boastful (ὑπέραυχος) by nature. Passages such as Exod 5:2 LXX give the basis for such a characterization: "And Pharaoh said, 'Who is he that I should hearken to his voice . . . ? I do not know the Lord, and I will not let Israel go.'" Philo paraphrases this verse in *Mos.* 1.88 as evidence of the arrogance (τῦφος, ὕβρις) of the Egyptian king. Of special interest for the understanding of *Ebr.* 111, which concerns the king of Egypt and the six hundred chariots, is the *Mekilta* on Exod 15:1, where it says that the Egyptians prided themselves before God as they took the six hundred chariots (Exod 14:7).

The six hundred chariots are interpreted to mean the six movements of the organic body (ταῖς τοῦ ὀργανικοῦ σώματος ἓξ κινήσεσιν). The basis for this exegesis is the number 6 in 600 and the idea of movement connected with "chariots." In *L.A.* 1.4 and *Conf.* 139 Philo lists the six movements of the body: forwards, backwards, upwards, downwards, to the right, and to the left.[18]

The princes (τριστάται) are seen as standing upon the chariots. The "standing" is understood to mean standing firm, being stable (cf. ἑστάναι). Philo sees this as an expression of the view that all things are stable and unsusceptible to change, and he makes clear that no created object can be stable. His understanding here is based on his view that the Egyptians represent the realm of the body and the world of the senses. Philo is influenced by the Aristotelian and Peripatetic view that God is wholly stable and immobile but is the source of movement for all other beings.[19]

The Crossing and its dual results are referred to in general terms. The two

---

18. See Karl Staehle, *Die Zahlenmystik bei Philon von Alexandreia* (Leipzig and Berlin: Teubner, 1931) 34; David T. Runia, *Philo of Alexandria and the Timaeus of Plato* (Philosophia antiqua 44; Leiden: Brill, 1986) 189. Cf. Aristotle *E.N.*. 3.1.16 (1110a).

19. Runia, *Philo of Alexandria*, 434. See further *Post.* 28–30; *Gig.* 48–49; *Deus* 27–28; *Mut.* 54.57; *Som.* 2.219–27; *Ques. Gen.* 1.32; *Ques. Exod.* 2.37.

fates are "judgment" and "penalty," in contrast to escape from the onset of
the enemies and to salvation.

Philo refers to Moses' hymn to God by quoting a phrase from Exod 15:1:
"The horse and his rider He has thrown into the sea." In his exposition he
interprets "the rider" to mean the mind and "the horse," the four-footed
[animal], to mean "rebellious passions."

Philo draws on Platonic ideas when he associates passions with horses.
In *Phaedr.* 246a–b and 253d–e, for example, the charioteer is interpreted as
reason and the two horses as high spirit and desire.[20] An even more direct use
of this Platonic tradition is seen in *Agr.* 72; *L.A.* 1.72–73; and *Virt.* 13. Philo
relies on Stoic ideas, however, when he tells that the horses are four-footed
beasts which, ethically interpreted, mean the four passions, i.e., "pleasure,
greed, pain and fear."[21]

So far Philo's interpretations of the Egyptian side of the Crossing have
been discussed. Then the Hebrew side needs to be treated. He says that God
"has shown himself the helper (βοηθός) and champion of the seeing soul
(τῆς ὁρατικῆς ψυχῆς)." "The seeing one" is an etymological interpretation
of the name Israel, based on the incident when Jacob, after his wrestling, was
given this name (Gen 32:24–28; see *Mig.* 199–201; *Mut.* 81–82. As in *Ebr.*
111, elsewhere Philo also uses "the seeing one" to characterize the (Hebrew)
nation over against Pharaoh (*Det.* 91–95) or the Egyptians (*L.A.* 2.34; *Sac.*
134; *Conf.* 91–92).

Philo usually sees Jacob as the "Practicer."[22] Jacob's wrestling provides
Philo with a metaphor to describe the Practicer who struggles against passions (*L.A.* 3.190–91). But he can also apply the term to the people. Thus
in *Ebr.* 24 he refers to the experience of the nation as they came out of
Egypt: Amalek attacked them and "cut off the rearguard of the practicer"
(τοῦ ἀσκητοῦ, Deut 25:18). It should be added that already in the biblical
use the names Jacob and Israel could mean both the person and the nation
(Num 23:7).

Corresponding to *Ebr.* 24 and *Conf.* 91–92, "the practicing mind" and "the
seeing soul" have "the king of Egypt" and his chariots and princes as enemies
in *Ebr.* 111.

---

20. Runia, *Philo of Alexandria*, 320 n. 23.

21. See Johannes von Arnim, ed., *Stoicorum Veterum Fragmenta* (4 vols.; Leipzig: Teubner,
1903–24) 3. 381–83.

22. According to J. W. Earp's "Indices," s.v. ἀσκητής (*Philo* [10 vols. and supp.; LCL; Cambridge, Mass.: Harvard University Press; London: Heinemann, 1962] 10. 336–37), there are
nearly a hundred occurrences of this and cognate words in Philo's writings. He often interprets
the patriarchs Abraham, Isaac, and Jacob as representing "teaching," "self-teaching," and "practice," respectively; see, e.g., *Mos.* 1.76; *Abr.* 52; *Jos.* 1; *Som.* 1.167–68; *Congr.* 34–36 (Borgen,
Bread from Heaven, 103).

Biblical Event – Liturgical Model – Cultural Application

How is the deeper interpretation in *Ebr*. 111 to be related to the versions in *Mos*. 1.163–80; 2.246–56 and *Vita* 85–89, where the Crossing of the Sea is presented as an event from past biblical history? When the phrase "the king of Egypt" in *Ebr*. 111 is spiritualized to mean "the boastful mind," does it still retain a specific and concrete reference?

Although in *Ebr*. 111 Philo interprets the Crossing by using ideas with Peripatetic, Platonic, and Stoic backgrounds, the context in the treatise *On Drunkenness* supports the understanding that he applies his exposition to the life of the Jews in their pagan cultural context. Hence, first, in the exposition of Deut 21:18–21 in *Ebr*. 15–96, the disobedient son is criticized for joining a social association with its lifestyle of gluttony and indulgence. Second, Philo implies that some Jews join such clubs, make a god of the body, and worship the vanity most honored by the Egyptians (Apis), whose biblical symbol is the golden bull (Exod 32:1–19). In this worship of the body, idolatry and immorality are united, and the pagan setting in Egypt is here evident. Third, in the immediately preceding context (*Ebr*. 109–10), Philo is quite concrete and specific about the making of idols of stone and wood, etc. He states that Moses, the lawgiver, has banished such painters and sculptors from his commonwealth (πολιτεία). Here, then, he refers to the Jewish community, where the One God is worshiped, in contrast to pagan society, where idols are worshiped. This understanding is supported by *Virt*. 219, where it is said that the proselytes "abandon customs which assign divine honors to stocks and stones and settle in a commonwealth (πολιτεία) full of true life and vitality."[23]

Against this background the view expressed in *Ebr*. 111 that created objects are stable and the picture given of uncontrolled passions are meant to refer to pagan views and ways of life. Thus although "the king of Egypt" is spiritualized to mean "the boastful mind," the phrase still retains its specific reference to the pagan impiety of the Egyptians.

The use of the Crossing of the Sea (Exodus 14–15) in *On the Contemplative Life* points in the same direction, since the Jewish community life of the Therapeutae is pictured in contrast to pagan idolatry — the sharpest criticism being leveled against Egyptian animal worship — and to pagan immorality. It should be added that in *On the Embassy to Gaius* and *Against Flaccus*, where Philo recounts the persecution suffered by the Alexandrian Jews under the emperor Caligula and the governor Flaccus respectively, he sees it basically as a dualistic conflict against the evil Egyptian force with its polytheistic worship of animals. It is a dualism between the people whose "vision has soared

---

23. See Borgen, *Philo of Alexandria*, 220–23.

above all created things" (*Leg.* 5) and the Egyptians, who put the world upside down by preferring earth above heaven (cf. *Fug.* 180). Gaius's claim to
be worshiped as a god belongs to this earthly form of pagan religion.[24]

In conclusion, it has been shown that for Philo the Crossing of the Sea is,
to be sure, an event of the past in biblical history. In the section on Moses
as king, in *On the Life of Moses*, book 1, he saw it as part of the journey of
the nation from Egypt under the leadership of Moses as king. Likewise, in the
section on Moses as prophet (*Mos.* 2.187–292), the story of the Crossing is
given as an example of his role as a prophet. The above analysis has shown,
however, that the story of the Crossing in all three cases has been consciously
placed in interpretative contexts. Thus these rewritings of the event in biblical history play an integral and important part in Philo's expository activity
and do more than simply demonstrate that he is acquainted with the biblical
tradition.

As for a second level of interpretation, a typological usage is pictured in
Vita 85–89. As an event of the past it serves as a model for liturgical reenactment in the feast of the Therapeutae who, according to Philo, lived a life that
contrasted with that of their pagan environment, the latter characterized by
polytheism and immorality.

While the rewriting of the Crossing and the description of pagan life are
kept apart in *On the Contemplative Life*, the two aspects are woven together
in *Ebr.* 111. Different facets of the second level of interpretation can be seen:
the cosmic aspect and the aspect beyond, where different views as to the relationship between God and creation are discussed — the question of stability
over against instability; the different level of ethical observance and the conflict between disorderly passions and the life of the Practicer; and the level of
the beyond, where God is seen as the arbitrator and helper of the seeing soul.

Although Philo in this way brings his interpretation of the Crossing up to a
second level of meaning — by using ideas with Peripatetic, Platonic, and Stoic
backgrounds — several observations in the treatise *On Drunkenness* show that
he applies this exposition to the life of the Jews in a pagan cultural context.
For Philo, this setting is identified as that of a distinctly Egyptian outlook and
way of life. It is therefore evident that Philo can deliberately interpret the
biblical story in different ways and on various levels: on its concrete level as
an event of the past; on another level as a typological event of the past now
used as liturgical reenactment in the present; and on a yet higher level as an
event which points to the conflict of principles and ethical struggle in a
pagan and literally Egyptian context.

---

24. Ibid., 184–87, 189–90.

6

NORMATIVE SELF-DEFINITIONS OF CHRISTIANITY IN THE NEW TESTAMENT

WILLIAM KLASSEN

It was fashionable at one time, when trying to describe or define Christianity, to speak about the "essence" of Christianity.[1] For a variety of reasons we no longer use that terminology without serious qualification or reservations. Instead we talk more readily about "normative self-definitions" of Christianity and Judaism.[2] That terminology also has limitations, for it is a curious mixture of psychological and legal terminology. Furthermore, the way in which it is generally used has a sociological connotation because it is applied to a group.

---

1. On the origin of the expression, see the exchange between Hermann Mulert ("Wann kam der Ausdruck 'das Wesen des Christentums' auf?" *ZKG* 45 n.F. 8 [1926] 117) and Heinrich Hoffmann ("Zum Aufkommen des begriffes 'Wesen des Christentums,'" ibid., 452–59).

2. Scholars familiar with the Canadian religious studies scene will know that the phrase "normative self-definition" as applied to religion received widespread attention in the 1970s, in large part through the government-funded McMaster Project. Ben F. Meyer records that "it was dedicated to discovering how and why, by the mid-third century of the common era, Judaism and Christianity alike had achieved a socially effective self-definition: comprehensive, flexible, normative, open to adjustment but firm enough to allow each to discern and reject self-negating revisions" (*The Early Christians: Their World Mission and Self-Discovery* [Wilmington, Del.: Glazier, 1986] 9). According to one participant, "the process of achieving normative self-definition in Judaism and Christianity [amounted to] the process whereby the two religions narrowed the options of what it meant to be Jewish or Christian, excluded other options, and took measures to assure that favoured positions would become normative" (Lawrence H. Schiffman, *Who Was a Jew? Rabbinic and Halakhic Perspectives on the Jewish-Christian Schism* [Hoboken, N.J.: KTAV, 1985] pp. ix–x). The three volumes published as a result of that project rank among the finest research produced in the twentieth century, but do not, so far as I can tell, deal with the critical question, what is Christianity? Under the series title *Jewish and Christian Self-Definition* (henceforth JCSD) the volumes are as follows: E. P. Sanders, ed., vol. 1: *The Shaping of Christianity in the Second and Third Centuries* (Philadelphia: Fortress, 1980); idem, ed., with A. I. Baumgarten and Alan Mendelson, vol. 2: *Aspects of Judaism in the Greco-Roman Period* (1981); and Ben F. Meyer and E. P Sanders, eds., vol. 3: *Self-Definition in the Greco-Roman World* (1982).

The juxtaposition of the term "self" with the concept of community is singularly modern, even probably post-Freudian. Nevertheless it has the advantage of relating to a sociological description of early Christian communities. It pursues this question, Did the early Christians have a view of themselves as a community of believers? Can the phenomenon of early Christian communities be approached fruitfully with the question, What were their normative self-definitions?[3]

One can see relatively little difficulty with the word "normative." Certainly the early church had norms, or at least one norm: the acceptance of Jesus of Nazareth as the one whom God had made the Christ and the Lord of the church. Central as the affirmation of the lordship of Christ was to the existence of the church, a reminder is in place that the Johannine letters and to some degree the Fourth Gospel as well do not use the term "Lord."[4] Whatever reason one may give for this, the fact needs to be recorded.

Nevertheless we ask: Would the earliest Christians have felt at home with the concept of "norm" as we moderns understand that term? Surely an early Christian would have said that to affirm the lordship of Christ or his messiahship as norm is not saying enough even though what it seeks to affirm is true and essential. If all we are saying with the term "normative" is that there was a standard or canon by which being a follower of the Way was tested, a quick reading of 1 John, for example, makes it clear that the author is indeed concerned about applying certain "norms," or "tests of life," as Robert Law called them.[5]

The term "self-definition" also creates some difficulties. When it is applied to a group, can one really say that groups, especially groups as young, dynamic, and plastic as the early Christian communities, have time for the kind of reflection assumed in the term "self-definition"? It has been argued that the early church was too busy being the church to step back and reflect on the nature of the church. Theological reflection on the topic of the boundary limits of the church surely did not come about until much later in the church's history. That agenda was then forced on them, however, by the course of events.[6] In part it was tied to the mission of the church.

Consequently even from earliest times in the church one can cite the inclusion of the Samaritans, the gentiles, and conversely the exclusion of Simon the Samaritan magician (Acts 8), Elymas, the sorcerer, "that utter impostor

---

3. R. A. Markus, "The Problem of Self-Definition: From Sect to Church," JCSD 1. 1–15, is a superb contribution to the discussion.

4. Except as "Sir" (see John 4:11, 15, 19, 49; 5:7; 6:34, 68; 9:36; 11:3, 12, 21, 27; et al.); but see 4:1; 6:23; 11:2; 20:2, 13, 28.

5. Law, *The Tests of Life* (Edinburgh: T. & T. Clark, 1909; 3d ed., 1914) — still one of the best books on 1 John.

6. Sanders notes that one of the options facing Judaism and the early church was "retaining a great deal of diversity" (JCSD 1. ix).

and charlatan, son of the devil and enemy of all goodness" (Acts 13:10–11). He is accused by the Paul of Acts as "falsifying the ways of God," as if the previous titles are not damning enough. In this category too are the disciples of John who have to submit to rebaptism (Acts 19). And then there are the Jewish exorcists, the seven sons of Sceva in Acts 19:13–20. The various groups of ascetics and protognostics to whom Colossians and 1 John, as well as the Apocalypse, make reference illustrate that early Christians were quite familiar with drawing boundary lines. It is inconceivable that the question "Who belongs to us?" did not come up among the disciples. Indeed, in the tradition it was "dealt with" in two ways: the one who is not against us is for us (Mark 9:38–41), and the one who is not with me is against me (Matt 12:30; cf. Luke 9:50).[7]

Implicit, nevertheless, in the writings of the early Christians is the awareness that it is important to write about what Jesus stood for in his life, what he did, what he taught and what was involved in forming communities that gathered around allegiance to him. Once that is granted, it surely is legitimate to use the category of "normative self-definition." In fact it is as free of intellectual bias as any one might suggest, and this paper will therefore attempt to draft an outline of the ingredients that must go into any discussion of the nature of the early church or the shape taken by Christianity in the first century.

My hypothesis is that the categories the early Christians used to describe themselves carry within them self-definitions and that these definitions, or better, descriptions, had a normative character. Before we proceed to analyze some of these, we may be reminded that while all such exercises have their limitations, they also have a distinct value, especially for teaching purposes. When the impact of Ludwig Feuerbach's essay *The Essence of Christianity*, delayed as it was, is recalled,[8] and the continuing influence of Adolf Harnack's lectures at the beginning of this century on the essence of Christianity is again noted,[9] it is clear that such exercises are worthwhile. This is the case

---

7. James D. G. Dunn has also pointed out that diversity had its limits and that the "centre (Jesus Christ) also defined the circumference" (*Unity and Diversity in the New Testament: An Inquiry into the Character of Earliest Christianity* [Philadelphia: Fortress, 1977] 379).

8. Feuerbach, *The Essence of Christianity*, was translated by George Eliot (=Mary Ann Evans, 1819–90) and first published in English in 1854 (German original, 1841); it was reprinted with a foreword by H. Richard Niebuhr and an introduction by Karl Barth (New York: Harper & Row, 1957). In the preface to the second edition, Feuerbach himself said: "[I] have shown that Christianity has in fact long vanished, not only from the reason but from the life of mankind, that it is nothing more than a *fixed idea*, in flagrant contradiction with our fire and life assurance companies, our railroads and steam-carriages, our picture and sculpture galleries, our military and industrial schools, our theatres and scientific museums" (p. xliv).

9. Harnack, *What Is Christianity?* (London: Williams and Norgate; New York: Putnam, 1901; repr. New York: Harper, 1957), originally published in German under the title *Das Wesen des Christentums* (Leipzig: Hinrichs, 1901), comprises lectures which Harnack delivered extempore and which a student took down in shorthand. Harnack justified their publication by saying in

even when one possesses neither the exact historical details that Harnack had at his fingertips nor the profound philosophical insights of Feuerbach.

It is a formidable task. Nevertheless every generation owes it to its younger students and to historical research to attempt it. The one who undertakes it must do so with fear and trembling, with modesty and yet a certain boldness prepared to articulate a position so that readers, including the scholarly community, can respond to it with the usual critical tools. I move, then, to some early Christian self-definitions.

Early Christians as Followers of the Way

In recent scholarship the NT usage of the term ὁδός has received considerable attention. It was noted as a self-designation some time ago and extensively discussed as such in a monograph published in 1964 by Eero Repo.[10] The fact that it has been seen by a number of scholars as a clue to the structure of the gospel of Mark[11] would seem to indicate that it is not a Lukan construct brought into the book of Acts but had its origins in the earliest Jewish Christian communities directly from the OT, or perhaps from Jesus himself. While scholars are generally reluctant to push an idea back from the evangelist to Jesus, no serious reasons have been advanced that would make this designation implausible as part of the teachings of Jesus. If we accept the designation of "prophet" which the early church applied to him, possibly following Jesus himself, then there is no reason to assume that he did not see himself as God's instrument in bringing to the peoples of divine choosing a way of repentance and renewal. Such a new understanding would proceed along the lines of the prophets, who themselves had looked forward to the time or times when God would prepare a way for the chosen peoples to rekindle their enthusiasm for the covenant and restore them to a life in obedience to the God who had called a people through Abraham, Moses, and now the prophets.[12]

Some sections of the church did not hesitate to call Jesus the way, but the term "way" did not emerge as a major christological title. Nevertheless,

---

the preface that "the theologians of every country only half discharge their duties if they think it enough to treat of the Gospel in the recondite language of learning and bury it in scholarly folios." The 1957 reprint includes a long preface by Rudolf Bultmann.

10. Repo, Der "Weg" als Selbstbezeichnung des Urchristentums: Eine traditionsgeschichtliche und semasiologische Untersuchung (Annales academiae scientiarum fennicae B-132/2; Helsinki: Suomalainen Tiedeakatemia, 1964).

11. Willard M. Swartley, "The Structural Function of the Term 'Way' in Mark's Gospel," in William Klassen, ed., The New Way of Jesus: Essays Presented to Howard Charles (Newton, Kans.: Faith and Life, 1980) 73–86.

12. One must assume that this is what the translators of the NEB had in mind when they translated ὁδός "new way" in Acts 18:26; 19:9 and as "Christian movement" in 19:23. In my opinion both translations are unfortunate.

"followers of the way" was used as a churchly self-designation and could easily be used as both a self-designation and as a designation for Jesus himself, since it was affirmed that what Jesus had done was to prepare the way, in fact, to lead on in the way to life. Jesus was in that sense called the pioneer both in the sermons in Acts (3:15; 5:31) and also in the epistle to the Hebrews (2:10; 12:2).

The term "way" has normative connotations. Even when it is granted that there can be many ways, the Christians gave a normative nuance to the term "way," to judge from the absolute manner in which it appears in Luke and Mark. And it is not likely that Mark or Luke had any impulses from the Greek world to use this designation. More likely it arose through Jewish convictions that the law had been given to God's people to serve as the way on which they should walk, and the use of the term "way" relates early Christians directly to the *halakah* of Judaism. After all, Christians saw Jesus as being the fulfillment of the law, that is, he had kept God's law by having learned obedience through suffering unto death. Through his faithfulness he had made it possible for his followers to walk on that way as well.

For Paul this same imagery means not that Christ is somewhere on the way ahead of his people but that he is on the way with the believer. Paul's favorite phrase to describe this relationship is that the believer is "in Christ."[13] Whether or not one calls this "Christ-mysticism" (Deissmann), it is clear that Paul sees the union between Christ and his church in very intimate terms, so that the church can in fact be called the body of Christ — the presence of Christ on earth.[14]

In this connection Paul can also speak of imitating Christ. This concept, much discussed a generation or more ago,[15] does not refer to any of the external aspects of the life of Jesus, such as his celibacy or even to his putative homelessness. Instead it is applied to his decision to become poor, and above all to what in Paul's world was called *humanitas*, or φιλανθρωπία: the willingness to suffer for the good of others and to take their hurt upon oneself. As he was just (Acts 3:14) and, according to the κήρυγμα ("proclamation"),

---

13. A carefully nuanced study of this theme is given in Eduard Schweizer, *Lordship and Discipleship* (SBT 28; London: SCM; Naperville, Ill.: Allenson, 1960).

14. Still basic to this discussion is J. A. T. Robinson, *The Body: A Study in Pauline Theology* (SBT 3; London: SCM; Naperville, Ill.: Allenson, 1952).

15. See, e.g., the work of Hans Dieter Betz, who as early as 1967 stressed the motif of imitation in Greek thought (*Nachfolge und Nachahmung Jesu Christi im Neuen Testament* [BHT 37; Tübingen: Mohr (Siebeck), 1967]); also Anselm Schulz, *Nachfolgen und Nachahmen: Studien über das Verhältnis der neutestamentlichen Jüngerschaft zur urchristlichen Vorbildethik* (SANT 6; Munich: Kösel, 1962); and Hans Kosmala, who traced this theme extensively in Jewish sources in *Essenismus und Christentum* (Leiden: Brill, 1959); idem, *Hebräer, Essener, Christen: Studien zur Vorgeschichte der frühchristlichen Verkündigung* (SPB 1; Leiden: Brill, 1959); idem, "Nachfolge und Nachahmung," *ASTI* 2 (1963) 38–85; 3 (1964) 65–110; P. J. Du Plessis, *ΤΕΛΕΙΟΣ: The Idea of Perfection in the New Testament* (Kampen: Kok, 1959).

suffered injustices joyfully for others, so too the Christian was prepared to suffer abuse knowing that in this way the kingly rule of Christ could be shared (1 Cor 5:8). Paul here enunciates a theme that is found in 1 Peter as well, in the Apocalypse, and in the Pastoral Epistles. Indeed, it likely goes back to the early years of the Jesus movement; certainly it had a very strong representation in Stoic and Cynic thought of the first century, and its roots go back to Isaiah[16] and to Plato.[17]

The Early Christians as κοινωνία of Brothers and Sisters

By using the category of κοινωνία (*communio*) of brothers and sisters, the early church availed itself of categories present in both Judaism and the surrounding Greco-Roman world. At the same time, perhaps through their experience with Jesus and the freedom he displayed in relating to women and (other?) outcasts, it may have been given a deeper meaning than it had for others.

In this connection it should not be overlooked that it was never debated whether women should belong to the church; that was simply taken for granted. One may perhaps judge that only the strong initiative of Jesus in this regard was able to keep that issue out of the discussion. Harnack's repeated stress on the brotherhood of humankind was not wrong. It was simply not developed along the inclusive lines that it had in the NT. For it would seem clear that at least in 1 John the concept of ἀδελφός was restricted to those who are within the κοινωνία; indeed, it has been argued that in 1 John love for the neighbor is already displaced by love for the fellow Christian. Whether this was actually true within the Johannine community would be hard to show. What does seem clear is that the first concern of the author of 1 John is that love within the fellowship be unfaltering, and it must seem a contradiction to speak of love for the outsider if the insider is being hated.[18] From everything we can gather about the nature of the Christian community, it is apparent that in a situation in which aberrations of many kinds existed in the communities the ideal of caring, loving, forgiving, and sharing

---

16. See now Bernd Janowski, "'Er trug unsere Sünden': Jes 53 und die Dramatik der Stellvertretung," in idem and Peter Stuhlmacher, eds., *Der leidende Gottesknecht: Jesaja 53 und seine Wirkungsgeschichte, mit einer Bibliographie von Jes 53* (FAT 14; Tübingen: Mohr [Siebeck], 1996) 27–48.

17. For the Cynics, Ragnar Höistad, *Cynic Hero and Cynic King: Studies in the Cynic Conception of Man* (Uppsala: Bloms, 1948), is an unsurpassed foundation. Ernst Benz (*Der gekreuzigte Gerechte bei Plato, im neuen Testament und in der alten Kirche* [Wiesbaden: Steiner, 1950]) first developed the similarity between early Christian views of the humiliation of Christ and the suffering of the just man in Plato's *Republic*. Arnold Ehrhardt ("Ein antikes Herrscherideal [Phil. 2.5–11]," *EvT* 58 [1948–49] 101–110, 569–72) contrasts early Christian views of ruling with those of Stoics and Cynics.

18. See William Klassen, "Love (NT)," *ABD* 5.207–12.

of financial resources flourished in the community to a degree virtually un-known in other Greco-Roman brotherhoods. Absent from the early church, it seems, was a concern with minute details of behavior as found, for exam-ple, in the Essene writings from the Dead Sea (though there is no reason to believe that the Essenes did not experience a similar warmth of fellowship and caring for each other). So Josephus tells us that the Essenes exceed all others in righteousness and have done so for a long time (*Ant.* 18.1.5), and that although Jews by birth, they "seem to have a greater affection for each other than the other sects have" (*J.W.* 2.8.2); in both places Josephus lauds them for their selfless sharing.

Can we speak of anything distinctive, then, in the κοινωνία concept of the early church? An analysis of early Christian texts yields the following ob-servations. For the early Christians, κοινωνία retains its secular base; that is, it designates the participation between business partners which is so close that when one succeeds, the other does, and when one fails, the other fails, too. Purposes and goals as well as destiny hang together. While one's individ-uality remains, it is far from autonomy, since in Pauline terms one reckons the other better than oneself (Phil 2:3; Rom 12:10, 16) and restricts one's own freedom if by the exercise of that freedom the fellow member is destroyed.

Beyond that secular foundation, however, lies the conviction that Chris-tian κοινωνία is ultimately partnership with the Father (1 John 1:3) and with God's Son (1 Cor 1:9), made possible through the fact that the latter shed his blood (1 Cor 10:16) — gave up his life for all. This vertical dimension of participation in God and God's Son has a corresponding social dimension: "We declare it to you, so that you and we together may share in a common life" (1 John 1:3); further, "If we claim to be sharing in his life, while we walk in darkness, our words and our life are a lie ... for to walk in the light is to share a common life" (1 John 1:6–7). For Paul this means that without hes-itation he can refer to the collection raised by the Christians of Macedonia and Achaia for the poor at Jerusalem as a κοινωνία (2 Cor 8:4; 9:13; Rom 15:26). This he saw as important enough to deliver in person, so he gave up his freedom and allowed himself to be taken into captivity when he arrived with it in Jerusalem.

The Gift of Oneness

In Luke's description of the early church in Acts this κοινωνία expresses itself not only in faithfulness to the apostolic teaching — the common meal, prayer, unaffected joy, the sharing of goods (κοινά, 2:45) — but also in an uncom-mon degree of unanimity among the early believers. No less than six times Luke describes them as being unanimous — ὁμοθυμαδόν (1:14; 2:46; 4:24; 5:12; 15:25; "one in heart and mind," 4:32). Paul repeatedly sets this out as the goal towards which the Christian community must work. His prayer is that the Romans "may agree with one another after the manner of Jesus Christ, so that with one mind and one voice you may praise the God and Father of our Lord Jesus Christ" (15:6). Moreover, the way in which "the God of peace," a peculiarly Pauline designation for God, will soon "crush Satan under their feet" is by their refusal to allow people to divide them and rob them of their solidarity (Rom 16:17–20).

It is clear from Luke's later account that achieving this goal was not always easy, and that in some cases it was impossible. Nevertheless, the fact that Paul in his later epistles holds it up as a distinct possibility makes it evident that this aspect of early Christianity's understanding of itself was not considered merely part of the first flush of enthusiasm so often characteristic of a new movement. Unanimity was a gift of Christ, and the role of the Spirit was to continue to seek its presence and expression. Paul wants to have the assurance that the Philippian Christians are "standing firm, one in spirit, one in mind, contending as one for the Gospel faith" (Phil 1:27–28). To share in the Spirit results in "thinking and feeling alike, with the same love for one another, the same turn of mind, and a common care for thinking alike" (τὸ ἓν φρονοῦντες, 2:2; there is a strong but inconsequential variant, αὐτό ["same"] for ἕν ["one"]). He rules out rivalry and personal vanity: "you must humbly reckon others better than yourselves" (2:3).

J. Paul Sampley has proposed that Paul's analogue for κοινωνία is *societas*, the Roman practice of partnership with legal sanction. Gaius, who in the second century CE codified the legal practice before his time, states it thus: "A partnership (*societas*) lasts as long as the parties remain of the same mind (*in eodem sensu*)"; likewise, "the society went forward with the unity of all partners or it did not proceed."[19] Sampley further concludes that τὸ αὐτὸ φρονεῖν has become for Paul "a shorthand phrase to refer to the *societas Christi*."[20] He investigates the various dimensions of relationships between Paul's understanding of the church and the Roman *societas* concept, such as Paul's account of the Jerusalem council, his use of the term κοινωνία, the dissembling of Cephas, and the discussions Paul had about his right to be supported. At the end of his essay Sampley lists five implications he sees in relating the Roman *societas* to our understanding of early Christian community:

1. As *societas*, the Christian community is distinguished and characterized by its common source and shared goal, not by mutual admiration, common

19. Sampley, "*Societas Christi*: Roman Law and Paul's Conception of the Christian Community," in Jacob Jervell and Wayne A. Meeks, eds., *God's Christ and His People: Studies in Honour of Nils Alstrup Dahl* (Oslo: Universitetsforlaget, 1977) 158–74; quotation from p. 160.
20. Ibid., 162.

social status, or such externals. Sampley cites the example of the letter to Philemon.

2. As *societas*, the Christian community depends on mutual trust and confidence among the partners.

3. As *societas*, the Christian community is voluntary, and is freely entered; similarly it is governed not by compulsion, but counts on the partners freely choosing to cooperate, to seek the good of others.

4. As *societas*, the Christian community is characterized by reciprocity, by give-and-take, by sharing the joys and tribulations of others. As a particular example Sampley cites Phlm 17: "So if you consider me your partner, receive him as you would receive me." The Greek evokes even more explicitly the terminology of *societas*: εἰ οὖν με ἔχεις κοινωνόν: "if you have fellowship (*societas*) with me," then "receive him as me."[21]

5. As *societas*, the Christian community may be torn apart by many factors, chief among which are fraud, deceit, exploitation of the partners, or renunciation by one or more partners. Fraud terminates *societas*, which may explain why Paul makes every effort by his conduct to occasion no suspicion of such action.

Clothed in Humility

Paul seems, however, to go beyond the Roman concept of *societas* in stating that Christians not only consider one another equal, but that in fact all rivalry and personal vanity are ruled out ("but you should humbly reckon others better than yourselves" [Phil 2:3]). The word-group "humble/humility" (ταπεινός/ταπεινοφροσύνη), used throughout the NT as a positive attitude, is also used throughout the OT to describe positively one's attitude towards God.[22] The gospel tradition uses it, for example, in the song of Elizabeth (Luke 1:52) and as an attribute of Jesus, who is "meek and lowly of heart" (Matt 11:29) and therefore can invite people to take his yoke of grace upon them. The humility that Paul saw in Jesus, "who humbled himself and became obedient" (Phil 2:8), he himself sought to emulate in his own ministry. Hence in Luke's account Paul tells the Ephesians that he has "served the Lord with all humility" (Acts 20:19). To the Corinthians he describes God along the lines of Elizabeth's song — as the one who lifts up the humble (2 Cor 7:6). His own refusal to take support is "lowering myself to help in raising you" (2 Cor 11:7); yet he fears that when he comes to them again, "my God may humiliate me in your presence," so that he must shed tears about those who have not repented of their deeds (2 Cor 12:21).

---

21. Ibid., 170–71.

22. Adolf Harnack, "'Sanftmut, Huld und Demut' in der alten Kirche," *Festgabe für Julius Kaftan zu seinem 70. Geburtstag, 30. September 1918* (Tübingen: Mohr, 1920) 113–29.

In close agreement with the words of Jesus he urges that the Romans "not pursue lofty things, but allow yourself to be swept away by humble things (or persons?)" (12:16). The Colossians are urged to put on the garments befitting God's people, among which he lists humility (3:12), and the Ephesians are admonished "always to be humble and gentle and patient" (4:2) and thus to live up to their calling. The Colossians are warned to avoid the false self-humiliation which does not have its origin in Christ (2:18, 23), for that has an air of wisdom but is a forced piety and has no effectiveness in combating sensuality.

The Petrine epistles urge that community to "wrap themselves in the garment of humility towards one another, because God sets his face against the arrogant, but favors the humble. Humble yourselves then under God's mighty hand, and he will lift you up in due time" (1 Pet 5:5–7). Like Paul, this author combines humility with oneness of mind: "Be one in thought and feeling, all of you, be full of brotherly affection, kindly and humble-minded" (3:8).

In the OT this attribute is used sparingly to depict one's attitude towards fellow humans. Here however it is applied to relations to one's fellow human being. Thus the ascetic dimension is absent, and it becomes a norm by which attitudes toward the neighbor are measured. Its roots could well lie in the teachings of Jesus, e.g., the parable told of the Pharisee and the tax collector in the temple (Luke 18:9–14), directed, Luke says, at those who were sure of their own goodness and looked down on everyone else. The punch line of that parable is: "For everyone who exalts the self will be humbled; and whoever humbles the self will be exalted."

Harnack has shown how widespread this idea was in early Christianity. He sees the three words ἐπιείκεια, πραΰς, and ταπεινοφροσύνη as specifically Christian and designates them as "central ethical concepts (ethische Hauptbegriffe) of the new religion" which have been foreshadowed in the OT. They are beloved words (Lieblingsworte) of the primitive Christians. He furthermore sees these three concepts as standing in a parallel relationship to three other Christian terms: faith, hope, and love. To be sure, all of these concepts have a strong eschatological drive behind them. But they direct themselves to a community here and now and deny the possibility that a person can find fulfillment in the self alone, or even in one's relation to God alone. Later in the church these attributes were given much use in the ascetic disciplines. But this was not the case in the early church, where they retained a theocentric perspective.[23]

The basic insight here is that the person as such has no rights even though the soul itself is valuable beyond limits. The whole origin of decisiveness with which nascent Christianity defied the world of individual rights in order

---

23. Harnack, " 'Sanftmut, Huld und Demut,' " 123.

to conquer it can be explained from this point of view. Nevertheless, Harnack says, "the early Christian Church was made of living stones and not of sponges. For the structure of Christianity which was built up in two generations could not have been built up by weak people who only absorbed things from their environment."[24]

Some Other Terms

In his larger work, *The Mission and Expansion of Christianity,* Harnack goes into some detail to describe the titles Christians used for themselves, among which he isolates "disciples" (which soon fell into disuse), "saints," "brethren," and "church of God."[25] Of these latter three, "saints" became soon to be restricted to a few, and the terms "brother" or "sister" also came eventually to be limited, so that priests and nuns might use it for each other. In the mid-third century, Cyprian would feel it necessary to say that on occasion the confessor may also use it for the one to whom confession is made.

The "church of God" is a designation that endures, perhaps because it stresses the grounding of the community in an act of God and points to its difference from other assemblies that meet for different purposes. The term "friends" lacks the depth of the terms "brother" or "sister" and therefore also never became widespread, even though the Greco-Roman world made much use of it. Likewise, the term "soldier of Christ" had a fairly high degree of popularity, especially in the West, but it did not displace others which had a more irenic ring and connoted more intimacy and a deeper level of sharing.

The term "Christian," which Luke suggests began as a term of derision in Antioch and appears as a title given to believers by others in one other passage in the NT, did not make much headway in the first centuries, though the term is used by Ignatius quite freely — understandably, since he was from Antioch.[26] Origen's modesty was most likely shared by many people: "I wish to be called by the name of Christ and to have the name which is blessed over the earth. I long to be and to be called a Christian, in spirit and in deed" (*Hom. in Luc.* 16). As this modesty disappeared and the importance of the distinction between being *called* a Christian and *being* one was lost, the term came into vogue and has been with us ever since. Far too seldom in the history of the church have Christians been as conscious of the honor of bearing the name of Christ as was Origen.

---

24. Ibid., 124.

25. Harnack, *The Mission and Expansion of Christianity in the First Three Centuries* (2d ed.; London: Williams and Norgate; New York, Putnam, 1908) 399–421.

26. Justin Taylor, "Why Were the Disciples First Called 'Christians' at Antioch? (Acts 11:26)," *RB* 101 (1994) 75–94.

In the book of Acts, Christians are described as "those who have made trouble all over the world" and as those who "flout the Emperor's laws, and assert there is a rival king, Jesus" (17:7–8). This description of Christianity has caused some trouble for specialists in Roman law like A. N. Sherwin-White, who despaired of the text — such "laws" were not intended for persons of Paul's rank, and they should not have been applied in an independent city or called "decrees" in any case.[27] E. A. Judge, however, discovered inscriptions showing that the oath of personal loyalty to Caesar stood outside any system of law, embraced Romans and non-Romans alike, that it was administered through the cities, and that it was expressed in more prescriptive terms than previously known. Thus it might easily have been spoken of as a "decree."[28]

The word translated "troublemaker" is used elsewhere for "revolutionary" (ἀναστατόω, Acts 21:38), and one would not expect Luke to present this report since it is part of his goal to show Theophilus that Christians do not threaten the security of the Roman Empire. But just as Jesus is quoted as saying that he came not to bring peace but a time of division, so too the early church is portrayed as forcing an assessment of all values — cultural and social but, first and foremost, religious and political. Justin Taylor observes that "in the non-Christian 1st century sources, the names Christ and Christian are invariably associated with public disorders and crimes," beginning with the first event recorded from the year 41 (Dio Cassius 60.6.6). Josephus, too, sets the name in the context of a series of disturbances (*Ant.* 18.64).[29] Taylor concludes that "the name was thenceforth (after 39–40) synonymous with sedition and crime."[30] The fact that "Christian" also appears as a self-designation in the *Didache* (12.4) perhaps indicates that the author wished to bring together the "two ways" imagery and the term "Christian."

What emerges from this brief survey is that the church exercised a high degree of liberty in adopting and adapting titles for itself. At the same time, a basic thrust towards oneness is evident precisely in the search for identity.

Diversity in Early Christianity

Any discussion of norms must also take into consideration the issue of deviation from those norms. The traditional approach to this question has been to assume that the orthodox faith came first and that heresy or deviation

27. Sherwin-White, *Roman Society and Roman Law in the New Testament* (Oxford: Clarendon, 1980), chaps. 3 and 4.

28. Judge, "Paul and Classical Society," JAC 15 (1972) 19–36, esp. 26.

29. This passage, the celebrated *testimonium Flavianum*, is much disputed. For a judicious review of the problems, see John P. Meier, *A Marginal Jew* (2 vols.; ABRL; New York: Doubleday, 1991–93) 1. 59–69.

30. Taylor, " 'Christians' at Antioch," 84, 94.

from that faith followed later. Ever since the monumental work by Walter Bauer it has been impossible to take this traditional point of view.[31] Rudolf Bultmann and his students have been especially persistent in calling attention to the diversity of the NT theological ideas, and in observing that a norm or an authoritative court of appeal for doctrine did not exist during the earliest period of the church's history. Bultmann holds that the term "faith" distinguished early Christian congregations from Jews and pagans but did not yet designate orthodoxy. Although several scholars have tried valiantly to disprove or at least soften Bauer's thesis,[32] the tendency has been to speak of "trajectories" along which the various movements in early Christianity proceeded.[33]

James D. G. Dunn, however, prefers to speak of "unity and diversity," and thus seeks both differences and similarities among early Christians. Dunn's investigation led him to conclude that there are five types of Christianity in the NT: Jewish Christianity; Hellenistic Christianity; Enthusiastic Christianity; Apocalyptic Christianity; and Early Catholicism. Each was just one part of the diversity that was first-century Christianity. Dunn's conclusion is that "there was no single normative form of Christianity in the first century." The unity of first-century Christianity focuses (often exclusively) on Jesus the man now exalted, Christ crucified but risen.[34]

Conclusion

I venture that too much of our thinking about the early church is still conditioned by the realm of ideas and a rational discourse of faith. What deserves more scrutiny is the ethos of the early church, the fundamental characteristics of its communal life.[35] What shape did the community take? How was deviance dealt with? What conditions for entrance applied? What role did discipline play? How were cultural distinctions between Jew and Greek, male and female, bond and free, both honored and transcended? How could "love for enemies" and vilification of opponents or competitors be reconciled?

---

31. Bauer, *Rechtgläubigkeit und Ketzerei im ältesten Christentum* (BHT 10; Tübingen: Mohr, 1934); in ET as *Orthodoxy and Heresy in Earliest Christianity* (Philadelphia: Fortress, 1971).

32. Notably H. E. W. Turner, in *The Pattern of Christian Truth: A Study in the Relations between Orthodoxy and Heresy in the Early Church* (London: Mowbray, 1954); also Thomas A. Robinson, *The Bauer Thesis Examined: The Geography of Heresy in the Early Christian Church* (Lewiston, N.Y.: Mellen, 1988).

33. The term "trajectories" became fashionable especially with the publication of James M. Robinson and Helmut Koester, *Trajectories through Early Christianity* (Philadelphia: Fortress, 1971).

34. Dunn, *Unity and Diversity*, 372–73.

35. An important beginning has been made in this direction by Jerome Murphy-O'Connor, in *What Is Religious Life? A Critical Appraisal* (Wilmington, Del.: Glazier, 1977) and *Becoming Human Together* (Wilmington, Del.: Glazier, 1977).

Was there another community in which women were fully treated as equal, with the exception of some of the mystery cults? The profound divisions between Jew and Greek were transcended in the church, but this is a topic that deserves and receives further exploration.[36]

From more than just Gal 3:28, however, it would seem to be clear from the NT that a new way of building community had come into being through Jesus and that, as far as we know, no other community, whether Therapeutae, Stoic, Cynic, Epicurean, or Essene, that approached the church in its inclusiveness, intimacy, and above all its power to transform people. None of the books, to my knowledge, which have dealt with normative self-definitions have explored this aspect. Nor has enough attention been paid to the threat that Christianity posed to the larger Roman society and its vaunted *Pax Romana* — a threat very real precisely because, far from the individual dissent represented by a Socrates or Stoics like Musonius or Epictetus, Christians were a corporate body, unified and recognizable as dissenters against the prevailing values.[37]

Although there have been many fine studies of the church since Harnack's important book, few have related the church concept of the NT to its surrounding culture. Attempts to draw lines of convergence between Jesus and the Cynics, or between Paul and the Stoics, must note the vast gulf that separates them on this point alone. Certainly the Cynics are more noted for their individualism. But where are the Stoic-Cynics who are prepared to curb personal liberties for the good of fellow Stoic-Cynics? The research of the future must pay attention to this dimension. Whatever we say about the way in which the church saw itself, we cannot avoid the fact that it was as a corporate entity that it visualized itself. Small wonder that early in the second century the designation emerged of the Christians as a "third race." For by then Christians were accused of hatred of the empire and of the emperor, and of uselessness from an economic point of view. Thus Celsus charged that the Christians were trying to cut off the branch on which they sat: "Were all to act as you do, the emperor would soon be left solitary and forlorn, and affairs would presently fall into the hands of the wildest and most lawless barbarians. Then it would be all over with the glory of your worship and the true wisdom among men" (Origen *C. Cels.* 8.68).

Clearly a critique such as Celsus undertakes already assumes that Christians existed in much larger numbers than they did in the first century.

---

36. Luise Schottroff, *Lydia's Impatient Sisters: A Feminist Social History of Early Christianity* (Louisville, Ky.: Westminster/John Knox, 1996), makes an excellent contribution to this discussion.

37. A point not noted by many who draw Jesus and the "Q community" into the Cynic orbit; see my review of Leif Vaage, *Galilean Upstarts: Jesus' First Followers according to Q* (Valley Forge, Pa.: Trinity Press International, 1994) in *RB* 102 (1995) 425–28, esp. 427–28.

Already in the early second century, Christians could refer to themselves as a "third religion."[38] And when Tertullian reports in 197 that Christians are *being called* a "third race" (*Ad nat.* 1.8: *tertium genus dicimur*), he is anticipating by only a half-century Pseudo-Cyprian's statement in 242–43 that "*We are* the third race."[39]

Surely soon after the destruction of the temple and Jerusalem in the year 70 some early Christians began to affirm that they were not really Jews any more. But for the most part the NT writers, with the probable exception of the writer to the Hebrews, are comfortable with being considered a "sect" within Judaism while others candidly claimed to be the true Israel. The emphasis laid on corporate images for the church and the stress laid on community life made a separation between Judaism and Christianity inevitable, quite apart from any differences in ideas about Jesus. The conclusion I am driven to is that early Christianity in all of its varieties was united in its common commitment to being a people striving for peace and unity among themselves and towards the outsider. Perhaps we need to pay more attention to the central place which the commandment "Seek peace and pursue it" (1 Pet 3:11; cf. Heb 12:14; Rom 14:19) had among the early Christians.[40]

For at least the past four centuries, since the days of Luther, it has been our constant temptation to ignore the corporate dimension of Christianity. In doing so we have lost its heart and transformed Christianity into a mystery cult or a program of self-renewal. R. A. Markus, following E. R. Dodds, suggests that the early church offered their members "a sense of belonging, fostered by direct fellowship within an intimate group, warmth, closeness and mutual support."[41] Perhaps the modern church, so eager to name itself after the christological title by calling itself "Christian," might learn from its ancient ancestor some basic elements of what it means to *be* the church.

---

38. This is probably how the epithet τρίτον γένος is to be understood in the *Preaching of Peter* (quoted in Clement of Alexandria *Strom.* 6.5.41); it is so translated in ANF 2. 489: "we, who worship Him in a new way, *in the third form*, are Christians." Further discussion in Harnack, *Mission and Expansion* (see the following note).

39. Documentation in Harnack, *Mission and Expansion* 1. 266–78. Markus ("Problem of Self-Definition") deals with this development. Typically the "third" referred to is in the sequence Romans, Jews, Christians.

40. See my article "'Pursue Peace': A Concrete Ethical Mandate," in Klaus Wengst et al., eds., *Ja und Nein: Festschrift für Wolfgang Schrage* (Neukirchen-Vluyn: Neukirchener Verlag, 1998) 195–207.

41. Markus, "Problem of Self-Definition," 2.

7

ONE LORD, ONE FAITH, ONE GOD, BUT MANY HOUSE CHURCHES

John Reumann

The house church in early Christianity has been rediscovered within our lifetime. Floyd V. Filson's brief article in 1939 is commonly regarded as the starting point for scholarly attention to "the church in the house of so-and-so," though William Sanday and Arthur C. Headlam, among others, had called attention to the phenomenon four decades earlier, and it is only in the last twenty years or so that investigation has mushroomed.[1] Yet for all the aspects we know reasonably well, there remain many more unclear areas and unresolved questions.

Graydon F. Snyder, a friend whom I join in honoring with this essay, has been one of the contributors to our knowledge of evidence, especially archaeological evidence, about early church buildings. He concluded that "the New Testament Church began as a small group house church (Col. 4:15) and it remained so until the middle or end of the third century"; and with reference to the same NT text he had earlier observed that "early Christians undoubtedly met in private homes..., though it should not be forgotten that Christians, like the Jews (Acts 16:13), also met in open places (Pliny, *Letters*, 117), mar-

---

1. Filson, "The Significance of the Early House Churches," *JBL* 58 (1939) 105–12; Sanday and Headlam, *The Epistle to the Romans* (1st ed.; ICC; Edinburgh: T. & T. Clark, 1895) 420–21 (on Rom 16:5): "There is no decisive evidence until the third century of the existence of special buildings used for churches. The references seem all to be to places in private houses, sometimes very probably houses of a large size.... There is no reason to suppose that this Church [at the house of Prisca and Aquila] was the meeting-place of all Roman Christians; similar bodies seem to be implied in vv. 14, 15." I shall cite the considerable secondary literature about house churches selectively, in a skeletal way.

kets, and hired halls (Acts 20:8)."[2] He has rightly dealt with house churches along with topics in christology, ecclesiology, worship, and the state.[3]

Of course, the place of the house church ought not to be overstated, even though it has implications, rightly, we may think, for Christian life today.[4] For there existed alternative models in antiquity which early Christians could employ: the synagogue (and not just "house synagogues"); voluntary associations in the Greco-Roman cities, such as guilds, clubs, and burial associations; and philosophical and rhetorical schools.[5]

There is also the danger of getting caught up in the "politically correct" trends of our own day. It may well be that in Philippi women like Euodia and Syntyche (Phil 4:2–3) were among the "heads of house-congregations" in "a relatively well-structured organization," with ἐπίσκοποι and διάκονοι (1:1).[6] But it is important to test such possibilities, which seem self-evident in a time of feminist studies, by evidence and, where possible, by presentations from investigators in a time and climate different from what is so common in North America in the 1990s.[7]

---

2. Snyder, *Ante Pacem: Archaeological Evidence of Church Life before Constantine* (Macon, Ga.: Mercer University Press, 1985) 166, 67. More recently, in *First Corinthians: A Faith Community Commentary* (Macon, Ga.: Mercer University Press, 1992), Snyder treats the "Christ party" of 1 Cor 1:12 as "a gnostic house church" (p. 246) comprised of πνευματικοί (36): they had eliminated sexual intercourse (94), yet did not mourn but were "puffed up" about the case recounted in 5:1–5 (59–60); they raised the question about eating meat offered to idols (120–21). Slogans from "the Christ house church" appear in 1 Cor 6:13; 8:8 (127); and 12:3 (the historical Jesus is anathema) (165).

3. Ibid., 165–69.

4. So, e.g., Del Birkey, *The House Church: A Model for Renewing the Church* (Scottdale, Pa.: Herald, 1988). See also an extensive German Roman Catholic literature, e.g., Hans-Josef Klauck, "Der Gottesdienst in der Gemeinde von Korinth," *Pastoralblatt für die Diözesen Aachen, Berlin, Essen, Köln, Osnabruck* 36 (1984) 11–20, repr. in idem, *Gemeinde – Amt – Sakrament: Neutestamentliche Perspektiven* (Würzburg: Echter, 1989) 46–58; Rudolf Pesch, *Paulus und seine Lieblingsgemeinde: Paulus – neu gesehen: Drei Briefe an die Heiligen von Philippi* (Freiburg: Herder, 1985), in connection with the "integrierte Gemeinde" in Munich. Are house meetings a way that U.S. "megachurches" use to achieve intimate groups?

5. Wayne A. Meeks, *The First Urban Christians: The Social World of the Apostle Paul* (New Haven, Conn.: Yale University Press, 1983) 74–82; for Meeks, "the household remains the basic context." While a house synagogue existed at Dura Europos, the first de novo Jewish synagogue construction in the diaspora has now been reported in Ostia; see L. Michael White, "Synagogue and Society in Imperial Ostia: Archaeological and Epigraphic Evidence," *HTR* 90 (1997) 23–58.

6. So D. Peterlin, *Paul's Letters to the Philippians in the Light of Disunity in the Church* (NovTSup 79; Leiden and New York: Brill, 1995) 228 (cf. 123–25); also John Reumann, "Contributions of the Philippian Community to Paul and to Earliest Christianity," *NTS* 39 (1993) 446–50.

7. Valerie A. Abrahamsen (*Women and Worship at Philippi: Diana/Artemis and Other Cults in the Early Christian Era* [Portland, Me.: Astarte Shell, 1995] 82–86) notes that NT commentators tend to "skip quickly over Euodia and Syntyche," but she herself says little about them. See W. D. Thomas, "The Place of Women in the Church at Philippi," *ExpTim* 82 (1972) 117–20; S. C. Agourides, "The Role of Women in the Church at Philippi," *Deltion Biblikon Meleton* [Athens] 1 (1980) 77–85; F. X. Malinowski, "The Brave Women of Philippi," *BTB* 15 (1985) 60–64; Lilian Portefaix, *Sisters Rejoice: Paul's Letter to the Philippians and Luke-Acts As Seen by First-Century Philippian Women* (ConBNT 20; Stockholm: Almqvist & Wiksell, 1988) 137–38, 141; but also J. A. Beet, "Did Euodia and Syntyche Quarrel?" *ExpTim* 5 (1893–94) 179–80; J. C. Watts, "The

A final caution has to do with the individuality of various local Christian churches in antiquity. Granted, they were mostly located in houses, in a common Greco-Roman Mediterranean world, sharing many common traits. But Rome and Philippi were different from Antioch, Corinth, or Alexandria. The size of the city, societal structures, economics, the makeup of the population, local religious influences, the presence or absence of a Jewish community, and the origin and variety of Christian contacts — in all of these variables the communities doubtlessly differed considerably.[8]

About Households and Churches

The words and concepts "house" and "household" have extensive background in the ancient Near East and Greco-Roman world. The senses of the Hebrew בַּיִת as dwelling, palace, temple, patriarchal family, clan, tribe, estate, and the relationships of husband and wife, father (parents) and children, master and dependents, have often been noted.[9] Similarly with the Greek "house(hold)," οἶκος often suggests dwelling (hence the areas of architecture and archaeology), οἰκία the extended family (and attendant sociological analysis).[10]

Not always noted is the way in which Jesus and early Christianity affirmed, but also placed a question mark over and posed a threat to, the household and family structures of the day. The positive strand involved the use made by Jesus of hospitality in houses at Capernaum (Mark 1:29; 2:15), Bethany (Luke 10:38–42; Mark 14:3–10), and even Tyre (Mark 7:24); the disciples, similarly (Mark 6:10; Matt 10:12–13//). The itinerant preachers of the Q community continued the practice. The house that keeps appearing in Mark (2:1; 3:20; 7:17; cf. 4:10–13; 10:1–12, for instruction) and the promise, to

---

Alleged Quarrel of Euodia and Syntyche," *ExpTim* 5 (1893–94) 286–87. The tendency in some treatments to make these two women leaders responsible for a massive disunity in the Philippian church is much overstated.

8. In "Contributions of the Philippian Community" (see above, n. 6) I have tried to show not merely that, if Paul's letters to Corinth had been sent, say, to Philippi, or 1 Thessalonians to Corinth, the letters would have been "off-target," but also that each community developed in its own way and made distinct contributions to Pauline Christianity. May we not also suppose that in any given city certain house churches exercised specific influence(s)?

9. Harry A. Hoffner, "בַּיִת," *TDOT* 2 (1975) 107–16; K.-H. Bieritz and Christoph Kähler, "Haus III. Altes Testament," *TRE* 14.479–80; E. Dassmann and G. Schöllgen, "Haus II (Hausgemeinschaft), b. Jüdisch," *RAC* 13 (1986) 843–54; John S. Holladay, "House, Israelite," *ABD* 3.308–18 (chiefly concerned with domestic architecture).

10. Otto Michel, "οἶκος, οἰκία, κτλ.," *TDNT* 5 (1967) 119–34; *TRE* 14.480–81 (Latin *domus* and *familia*); E. Dassmann, "Haus II, c. Christlich," *RAC* 13 (1986) 854–901; P. Weigandt, "οἰκία" and "οἶκος," *EDNT* (German ed. 1981) 495, 500–503; P. H. Towner, "Households and Household Codes," in Gerald F. Hawthorne and Ralph P. Martin, eds., *Dictionary of Paul and His Letters* (Downers Grove, Ill.: InterVarsity, 1993) 417–19. An overview of "household" in the ancient world, in Paul, and in three apostolic fathers is provided in Harry O. Maier, *The Social Setting of the Ministry As Reflected in the Writings of Hermas, Clement, and Ignatius* (Dissertations SR 1; Waterloo, Ont.: Wilfrid Laurier University Press, 1991).

one leaving "house, brothers, sisters, mother, father," of houses and such relationships "a hundredfold now in this age," not to mention "eternal life in
the age to come" (Mark 10:29–30//), reflect the new house communities of
the Jesus movement. But the negative strand has thereby been indicated:
rejection of existing household and family (Mark 3:31–35); indeed, hatred
of biological family (Matt 10:37; Luke 14:26).[11] A tension existed between
these two outlooks on households.

These dual aspects continued in the Pauline mission, as we meet house
churches in the apostle's own letters and the Acts accounts. On the one
hand, Paul and his missionary team move from place to place as itinerants,
supporting themselves with the work of their own hands (1 Thess 2:9; 1 Cor
4:12), dependent often on hospitality from others (Rom 16:23; Phil 4:10, 16),
giving up certain rights to food and drink or to be accompanied by one's wife
(1 Cor 9:4–6, 12b, 15–18). On the other hand, Paul and his coworkers made
the households of converts their base of operations and centers for cells of believers in the city regions where they worked. The household thus remained
for Christians the basic unit of familial relationships, economic enterprise
(1 Thess 5:14 indicates an early exception), and engagement with society.
But Paul put down no roots in a home of his own, and the house-critical
aspect of the Jesus movement translated for the Pauline churches into an eschatological tension: with the *parousia* the end was expected of all structures
of this age, though for the time being the household of believers was where
one experienced the promises fulfilled of new relationships. In such households, faith found space, a certain security, stability, and continuity for its
life, a discernible locus for activities.[12]

The NT references to "the church in/at the house of X" (ἡ κατ᾽ οἶκον
+ genitive + ἐκκλησία) occur at 1 Cor 16:19 and Rom 16:5 (of Prisca and
Aquila; see below on 16:10, 11, 14, 15); Phlm 2; and Col 4:15 (of Nymphia,
in Laodicea). To these must be added references in Acts about someone's being "baptized together with his/her whole household" (16:15, 35; cf. 16:31,
32, 34; 11:14; 18:8; κατ᾽ οἶκον at 5:42; 12:12, the house of Mary, mother
of John Mark), not to overlook house references at 2:1; cf. 4:23, 31; 8:3,
τὴν ἐκκλησίαν κατὰ τοὺς οἴκους; 20:20, cf. vv. 7–8; and 28:30–31. For
hospitality in private homes, see Acts 9:11, 17; 17:5; 21:8; 21:16. In the Pastoral Epistles the "household of Onesiphorus" (2 Tim 1:16; 4:19) provides
an example; cf. also 1 Tim 5:13; 2 Tim 3:6 and 2:20, and the developed
image of "the church of the living God" as "household" (1 Tim 3:15; cf. Heb

---

11. *TRE* 14.483–84; Gerd Theissen, *Sociology of Early Palestinian Christianity* (Philadelphia:
Fortress, 1978); Carolyn Osiek, "The Family in Early Christianity: 'Family Values' Revisited,"
CBQ 58 (1996) 1–24.

12. *TRE* 14.484–85; Meeks, *First Urban Christians*; Theissen, *The Social Setting of Pauline
Christianity: Essays on Corinth* (Philadelphia: Fortress, 1982).

10:21), with its leaders as good house managers (1 Tim 3:4–5, 12).[13] Further, there are 2 John 9–10 and 1 Peter (2:5, 9; 4:17), where the οἶκος becomes "the focus, locus and socioreligious nucleus of the ministry and mission of the Christian movement."[14] All this provides an extensive database, much of which has received considerable attention in the last twenty years. There are also pertinent Christian texts outside the NT.[15]

Some Questions and Answers

One ambiguity underlying discussion of "house churches" in light of such data is whether one means "the (extended) household — family and dependents — of a home owner and master" or "a group which meets at the home of a particular person," or both. The first understanding would involve the *patriapotestas* of a Roman father or grandfather (*paterfamilias*) and fits well with baptisms of whole households: what the Roman jailer in Philippi decides for applies to all in his household (Acts 16:31–34) — a sort of *cujus regio, ejus religio* principle. (Lydia's household in 16:15 is presented as a parallel, but we lack evidence that women held such *potestas*.) The second understanding suggests more a "benefactor" or "patron" (προστάτης; feminine προστάτις at Rom 16:2, of Phoebe), who provided a meeting place and a certain legal security for a group made up not of "family" or even just "clients" but, more broadly, believers from a geographical area of a city or with ties of trade or other background or language. Did the jailer's group at Philippi attract "those of Caesar's household," slave and freed persons, government employees, or military veterans, perhaps with some use of Latin? Did those *chez* Lydia involve others in the purple-cloth trade, non-Romans, people perhaps with some acquaintance with Judaism? Or did some gatherings involve both immediate family and others attracted by contacts of other sorts? Much is speculation here, but necessary if we are to ascertain what early Christian conventicles were like.

In all likelihood several house churches resulted in each city where Paul worked; likewise in places like Rome where he was not mission founder. The number of such house churches likely grew as years went by, some fading

---

13. *TRE* 14.485–86, reflecting considerable secondary literature; B. B. Blue, "House," in Ralph P. Martin and Peter H. Davids, eds., *Dictionary of the Later New Testament and Its Developments* (Downers Grove, Ill.: InterVarsity, 1997) 507–20 (including D. G. McCartney, "House, Spiritual House"; idem, "Household, Family"; P. H. Towner, "Household Codes"; see also "Architecture, Early Church"; Lorenz Oberlinner, *Die Pastoralbriefen*, vol. 3: *Kommentar zum Titusbrief* (HTKNT 11/2; Freiburg: Herder, 1996) 78–101.

14. John H. Elliott, *A Home for the Homeless: A Sociological Exegesis of 1 Peter, Its Situation and Strategy* (Philadelphia: Fortress, 1981) 222; cf. 197–98, 204, 220–23.

15. See Hans-Josef Klauck, "Die Hausgemeinde als Lebensform im Urchristentum," MTZ 32 (1981) 9 nn. 45–47 (repr. in idem, *Gemeinde*, 20 nn. 45–47); idem, *Hausgemeinde und Hauskirche im frühen Christentum* (SBS 103; Stuttgart: Katholisches Bibelwerk, 1981) 62–66, 69–77; E. Dassmann, *RAC* 13 (1990) 890–91.

from the picture, new ones arising. For Rome, Sanday and Headlam suggested three meeting places, a view accepted by C. E. B. Cranfield eighty years later.[16] But Peter Lampe's analysis has concluded that there were seven groups in Trastevere and other regions of the city, as well as Paul's rented house in Acts 28:30–31. For Philippi we may assume two on the basis of Acts 16 (Lydia and the jailer; not the girl exorcised of a Pythian spirit); certainly two from Phil 4:2–3 (Euodia, Syntyche, but note also Clement and Paul's "loyal companion," γνήσιος σύζυγος — Syzygus?), and Epaphroditus (2:25–31). Or are some of these to be equated with householders in Acts 16? In busy retirement, Graydon Snyder can contemplate further how many house churches existed in Corinth besides that of Aquila and Priscilla (16:19), the οἰκία of Stephanas (16:15), a synagogue group at the house of Titius Justus next door (Acts 18:7–8, and Crispus, 1 Cor 1:14), and that of the "Christ" group (1:12–13).[17] By the time of 2 Corinthians and "the revolt against the presbyters," concerning which *1 Clement* was written to Corinth, the house-church situation was even more complex and explosive.[18]

What functions did house churches have? What transpired at the house of Prisca and Aquila, in Corinth or Rome? Just about everything that one can list as purpose or activity in early Christianity — or perversion or problem. At assemblies of the sisters and brothers, prayer, preaching, teaching, and study took place; baptism, *agape*, and Lord's Supper; prophecy, speaking in tongues, hymn singing, lessons read aloud from the Septuagint, revelation, and interpretation — 1 Cor 14:26, the "service of the word";[19] healings and miracles (1 Cor 12:28–30); developing plans and programs to aid mission witness, members in need, prisoners, and of course Paul's collection for the saints in Jerusalem (Rom 12:6–8; 1 Cor 16:1–4; 2 Corinthians 8–9; Rom 15:25–29).

---

16. Sanday and Headlam, *Romans*, 421 (Rom 16:5, 14, 15); Cranfield, *The Epistle to the Romans* (2 vols.; ICC; Edinburgh: T. & T. Clark, 1975–79) 1. 22; 2. 786, 795; Lampe, *Die stadtrömischen Christen in den ersten beiden Jahrhunderten: Untersuchungen zur Sozialgeschichte* (2d ed.; WUNT 2/18; Tübingen: Mohr [Siebeck], 1989) 124–53, 301–2, 358; idem, "The Roman Christians of Romans 16," in Karl P. Donfried, ed., *The Romans Debate* (rev. ed.; Peabody, Mass.: Hendrickson, 1991) 229–30, listing "the house-church around Aquila and Prisca," "four other pockets of Christians" (Rom 16:10, 11, 14, 15) and two others from the remaining names in Romans 16, along with the Pauline center of Acts 28: all eight were "worshiping 'house-congregations,'" but "some [were] also held together by kinship or household ties," e.g., slaves (16:10), and "freed(women)" (16:11), possibly independent of the patron.

17. Snyder, *First Corinthians*, 21, 23, 216; Snyder judges house churches to be more likely than "amorphous networks which never met as congregations."

18. Maier (*Social Setting*, 93) sees divisions among patrons of house churches in Corinth as the setting for *1 Clement* (so also in *Hermas*).

19. Walter Bauer, "Der Wortgottesdienst des ältesten Christen" (1930), repr. in idem, *Aufsätze und kleine Schriften* (Tübingen: Mohr [Siebeck], 1967) 155–209, remains a basic analysis. Cf. Snyder, *First Corinthians*, 183–84; on the *agape* or Lord's Supper, 156–62. The meal of food and drink for bodily nourishment, with its abuses of economically poorer, lower-class Christians, was probably already being separated in Paul's day from the sharing of Christ's bread and cup; cf. John Reumann, *The Supper of the Lord* (Philadelphia: Fortress, 1985) 8–16, for stages of development.

What form hospitality was to take as new needs arose must have been a frequent concern, perhaps in the face of lack of money. Can we picture the Philippians discussing how to "exercise citizenship in a manner worthy of the gospel" (Phil 1:27), not only with regard to a πολίτευμα in heaven (3:20) but also in their present life in a Roman κολωνία (Acts 16:12), economically, socially, and politically? Consider how much postbaptismal catechesis must have been needed in the case of a house church where dependents (of a person like the Roman jailer or Lydia) were baptized along with the head of the house but without the conversion experience their earthly master had undergone! It is staggering to contemplate the range of contacts for evangelization that members of a household would have had with peers in city life.

To carry through these many tasks, house churches inevitably had to develop leadership structures. Each city seems to have created its own, and sometimes house churches in the same city might have had different organizational patterns. In Corinth the need for order attracted Paul's attention more than promoting ecstasy (1 Cor 14:33, 40), but in Thessalonica he urged believers not to "quench the Spirit" or "despise the words of prophets" (1 Thess 5:20–21). The apostle applied no uniform plan but let his congregations work out their own structures. For example, "those who toil (in mission) and care for" community members, in 1 Thess 5:12; "overseers and ministers," in Phil 1:1; "elders" never appear in Paul's acknowledged letters.[20] Varieties in leadership no doubt account for some of the differences and problems among house churches, perhaps including Euodia and Syntyche (Phil 4:2–3), the "parties" in 1 Corinthians 1–4, and "the strong" and "the weak" mentioned in Romans 14. As Filson remarks, "The existence of several house churches in one city goes far to explain the tendency to party strife in the apostolic age."[21]

Unity among House Churches

Given the pluralism in house churches, our question for early Christianity becomes not, "Why the differences?" but, "What held the communities of Jesus Christ together?" Sometimes this has been addressed as the question of unity between Jewish and gentile Christianity, or among Pauline, Petrine, and

---

20. On method — a topic Graydon Snyder appreciates (*Ante Pacem*, 5–11) — see my "Church Office in Paul, Especially Philippians," in Bradley H. McLean, ed., *Origins and Method: Towards a New Understanding of Judaism and Christianity: Essays in Honour of John C. Hurd* (JSNTSup 86; Sheffield: JSOT Press, 1993) 82–91. To respond to a question that I have been asked in light of that terse essay: Yes, ἐπίσκοποι first appeared in Christianity, as far we know, in Philippi, from local origins, involving in some cases women as heads of households. Later at Philippi the leaders seem to have been called πρεσβύτεροι. But there is no single NT or *jure divino* model of ministry for the ecumenical church today.

21. Filson, "Significance," 110; cf. *RAC* 13 (1986) 891–94.

Jacobean Christianities, or Palestinian versus diaspora, or apocalyptic versus gnostic Christianity. More basically one must also ask what united the several house churches in a given city region, even where the house churches all had the same missionary founder. Doubtless, interlopers were another problem.

There is no lack of passages where unity or oneness is urged. Paradigmatic is the confession of faith incorporated at 1 Cor 8:6. It is built around the εἷς θεός of the *Shema* (Deut 6:4) and the confession κύριος Ἰησοῦς Χριστός: one God and one Lord.[22] Philippians speaks of Christians having "the same attitude, one attitude" (τὸ αὐτὸ/τὸ ἓν φρονεῖν, 2:2). The Fourth Gospel's prayer that disciples "may be one" as the Father and the Son are one (17:11, 21, 22, in function, not ontologically) has become a favorite proof-text even for ecumenists who usually disdain proof-texts, a somewhat ironic outcome, given the history and independence of the Johannine community.[23] Eph 4:4–6, about the oneness given from the Spirit (4:3), has been dubbed "the Apostles' Creed in reverse": "one body and one Spirit,...one hope..., one Lord, one faith, one baptism, one God and Father...." Its triadic picture of God, its call to faith, and its eschatology actually begin with ecclesiology, but not house churches or "one church" (μία ἐκκλησία); rather, "one body." This ἓν σῶμα goes back to Paul's analogy about Christ and many members in a single body (1 Cor 12:12–27); whether its origin lies in the "one bread" of the Lord's Supper (1 Cor 10:16–17) or in Stoic political thought about the community (as in the fable of Menenius Agrippa, in Livy *Urb. cond.* 2.32) continues to be debated. But in Ephesians, instead of permeating the whole, Christ has become the Head (1:22–23, as in Col 1:18).

Imagery about unity grows more elaborate in the so-called apostolic fathers. There should be, not groups individually, but together "one prayer, one petition, one mind, one hope in love,...one temple of God,...one altar, one Jesus Christ, who came forth from one Father and returned (to him) and is one (with him)" (Ignatius *Magn.* 7.1–2); "one eucharist,...one flesh..., one cup for the oneness of his body, one altar, just as one bishop..." (Ignatius *Phld.* 4; cf. *Eph.* 20.2: "one faith..., breaking one bread").[24] This line of development was to seek unity through eucharist and episcopacy. Another way was to look for "one body, one attitude, one mind, one faith, one love" *after* the church of God is cleansed of evil hypocrites and other undesirables, at or before the eschaton (*Herm. Sim.* 9.18.4; cf. 9.13.5). One way or another, "one holy, catholic, and apostolic church" became an article of faith.

---

22. Analysis in John Reumann, *Creation and New Creation* (Minneapolis: Augsburg, 1973) 24–31.

23. See Raymond E. Brown, *The Community of the Beloved Disciple* (New York and Mahwah, N.J.: Paulist, 1979).

24. In Ignatius "unity" means "the solidarity of the Christian community," not "unity with God" (William R. Schoedel, *Ignatius of Antioch* [Hermeneia; Philadelphia: Fortress, 1985] 21).

But earlier, in Paul's day and in the NT period generally, how did diverse house churches find unity? The most obvious ways, as the passages already cited (1 Cor 8:6; 12; Philippians 2; John 17; Ephesians 4) suggest, centered on Jesus, christology, and faith. One could also speak of the Spirit, who is one, while the gifts of the Spirit were diverse (1 Cor 12:4). Whatever "the degree of unity that was achieved through all the differences and varieties, . . . the common factor holding all together is devotion to the person of Jesus Christ — the historical Jesus acknowledged as continuous with the one now acknowledged [after Easter] as the transcendent Lord."[25] House assemblies were an element of continuity from Jesus' own ministry, on into the Jesus movement, and then in the early church. One Jesus, many christologies about the crucified and risen Lord in whom the *kerygma* summoned people to believe, to trust, and to obey. One cannot say of Paul, or of the NT period in general, that the organization of the church — either in one particular form (episcopal, presbyteral, or congregational) or beyond the house churches of a city region (conciliar, Petrine/papal, or even a networking of friends) — was the hallmark of Christian unity. In the total picture, house churches prove to be a sort of "wild card," something that traditional (ecclesial) or past (historical-critical) or even more recent (literary) approaches have not sufficiently noticed in the first two centuries or so. But the role of the house churches is beginning to be perceived, e.g., in sketching Pauline thought or explaining the origins of Christian ministry and ecclesiology.[26]

The notion that the eucharist provided unity is a view long and widely held (cf. Ignatius *Phld.* 4, cited above). The claim amounted to this: "One Lord, one faith, one church, one eucharist." It carried the implication that only one eucharistic celebration should be held in a city such as Philippi or Rome.[27] This idea of a single eucharist, of all the people together in one place, has been defended particularly by Nicolas Afanassieff, though he does face up to the dawning recognition of the importance of "house churches."[28] Afanassieff takes ἡ κατ' οἶκον ἐκκλησία to mean not a house church ("église domestique") but the local church which assembled in a house, excluding multiple assemblies in the same city. Hence regarding Jerusalem the phrase κατ' οἶκον in Acts 2:46 means "from house to house" (see NRSV,

25. So C. F. D. Moule, *The Birth of the New Testament* (3d ed.; HNTC; San Francisco: Harper & Row, 1981) 17. Cf. my discussion of "The Oneness of the Many in New Testament Faith," in John Reumann, *Variety and Unity in New Testament Thought* (Oxford and New York: Oxford University Press, 1991) 277–92, also relevant for house churches.

26. See, e.g., James D. G. Dunn, *The Theology of Paul the Apostle* (Grand Rapids: Eerdmans, 1998) 541–42; more fully, Jürgen Becker, *Paul: Apostle to the Gentiles* (Louisville, Ky.: Westminster/John Knox, 1993) 241–55; cf. 420–30.

27. So, e.g., Carl Andresen, *Geschichte des Christentums*, vol. 1: *Von den Anfängen bis zur Hochscholastik* (Theologische Wissenschaft 6; Stuttgart: Kohlhammer, 1975) 3.

28. Afanassieff, "L'assemblée eucharistique unique dans l'église ancienne," *Kleronomia* [Thessaloniki] 6 (1974) 1–36.

note *q*), in the sense that disciples met in a different house each day because of "fear of the Jews." The three thousand persons baptized (Acts 2:41) and the five thousand at 4:4 are explained as Jewish pilgrims who immediately returned to their homes. The conversion of Cornelius in Acts 10 raises the question of where he participated in the eucharist. Not in a "domestic church" at his own house in Caesarea, Afanassieff argues, nor necessarily at Joppa (10:42–43), because believers in Caesarea and Joppa would at first have taken part in the service at Jerusalem(!).

Eventually, Afanassieff allows, it is possible that there were several eucharistic assemblies in Jerusalem, as also in Alexandria.[29] In Rome, the bishop became the symbol of unity, and for a time the idea of "one eucharist" was sustained by the device of the *fermentum:* the fragment of the bread from the papal mass sent to presbyters at *tituli* churches. But the original idea was one of the eucharist ἐπὶ τὸ αὐτό (Acts 1:15; 2:1, 47, et al.) — not just "with one mind" but "in the same place."

More likely, in spite of such liturgical-ecclesial ideology, each house church in early Christianity had its own *agape* and/or Lord's Supper. But did the several assemblies in, say, Philippi, ever meet together? Corinth provides a good test case, for 1 Cor 14:23 refers to ἡ ἐκκλησία ὅλη coming together ἐπὶ τὸ αὐτό. Opinions vary, but Dunn concludes that probably "church gatherings consisted of more regular small house groups interspersed with less frequent (weekly, monthly?) gatherings of 'the whole church.'"[30] One might then decide that the Lord's Supper was celebrated only when all the Corinthians assembled "as a church" (11:18 NRSV), all together. But "when you come together ἐν ἐκκλησίᾳ" might mean simply "in assembly at each house." Each house assembly would then be fully "church." Alternatively, since the reference in 14:23 is to "the service of the word" and not to "the Lord's Supper" (10:16–17; 11:17–34), one could conclude that the *agape*/eucharist occurred in each house church, for that intimate group, but that occasionally all the Christians in a city came together — out of doors, perhaps. But this would be a more public type of assembly, which unbelievers could observe and hear — and so perhaps be converted (14:16, 23–25).

Concluding Questions

This considerable, though not unlimited, evidence for house assemblies raises two further questions. First, did Paul and other early Christians capitulate to

---

29. Afanassieff, "L'assemblée eucharistique," 26–27, 29–33; for Alexandria, presbyteral organization is involved.

30. Dunn, *Theology of Paul*, 541, with reference to Robert J. Banks, *Paul's Idea of Community: The Early House Churches in Their Historical Setting* (Grand Rapids: Eerdmans, 1980; 2d ed. Peabody, Mass.: Hendrickson, 1994) 35–41.

the culture of the day in embracing the household, diminishing the "house-critical aspect" noted above? It was inevitable that all religious groups of the day had to deal with this basic unit of society, which went back to what Hesiod spoke of as a man together with his "οἶκος, wife, and an ox for the plow" on the family farm (*Op.* 405; cf. Aristotle *Pol.* 1.2.1258a), and with its developed forms in an increasingly urban, even technological, and empire-wide society. Jews, the Mithra cult, and other religious groups employed the house as cult center and communal meeting place until they grew strong enough and had legal permission to build a synagogue, temple, or shrine. House churches were inevitable. But Paul in the acknowledged letters did not make much use of the "household codes" of the day — rules that often accompanied the institution and governed relationships within the house-hold. That remained for Col 3:18–4:1; Eph 5:22–6:9; 1 Pet 2:13–3:7; and other NT writings to revise and employ (and Rom 13:1–7 may also reflect the theme).

While recent work on Paul and "friendship" suggests that the apostle em-braced many conventions of the day on φιλία, it is more likely, upon a further look, that he was selective and at points critical of certain conventions con-nected with this institution and its networking. The *do ut des* reciprocity of Greco-Roman patterns of friendship is something from which Paul removes himself in Phil 4:10–20, even in his relationship with his beloved Philippi-ans.[31] As a recent commentator says of Philippians with regard to "social convention" and "theological conviction," the theme of " 'friendship and fi-nances' can hardly be said to capture the essence of why or what Paul writes in this letter."[32] Where there existed a patron-client relationship, Paul sought an "emancipated clientele."[33]

Finally, given the many local household communities, whence the notion of a "universal church," as in Ephesians or Matt 16:18 (in contrast to the local assembly in 18:15–17)? Most likely, it came about via the develop-ment of christology. A universal Lord calls for a universal body of Christ the κοσμοκράτωρ — the "Lord of the universe." This would parallel an under-standing of God as universal ruler. But it must be remembered that, in Greek thought since Aristotle, the οἶκος was considered a building block for, and

---

31. See John Reumann, "Philippians, Especially Chapter 4, as a 'Letter of Friendship': Obser-vations on a Checkered History of Scholarship," in John T. Fitzgerald, ed., *Flattery and Frankness of Speech: Studies on Friendship in the New Testament World* (NovTSup 82: Leiden and New York: Brill, 1996) 83–106; idem, "Philippians and the Culture of Friendship," *Trinity Seminary Review* [Columbus, Ohio] 19 (1997) 69–83.

32. Markus Brockmuehl, *The Epistle to the Philippians* (Peabody, Mass.: Hendrickson, 1998) 40, with reference to Ben Witherington, *Friendship and Finances in Philippi: The Letter of Paul to the Philippians* (New Testament in Context; Valley Forge, Pa.: Trinity Press International, 1994).

33. The phrase is from Lukas Bormann, *Philippi: Stadt und Christengemeinde zur Zeit des Paulus* (NovTSup 78; Leiden and New York: Brill, 1995) 217.

part of, the πόλις and, in turn, of the κόσμος. There was thus in the concept of the household itself a dynamic to relate the local, basic unit of society to the πολιτεία (city-state and world empire) and eventually to the universe. To be part of a house church, in Philippi, Corinth, or Rome, pointed one beyond — to the full reign of God, already acknowledged in the fellowship of kith and kin and like-minded believers.

8

NEW TESTAMENT
MONASTERIES

J. C. O'NEILL

The community that first made Graydon Snyder and me friends was Westminster College, Cambridge, called Westminster after the Confession, not the
Parliament. Ernst Troeltsch once called the Calvinism that lay at the root of
the faith communities, to which Graydon and I in our different ways belong,
an attempt to create an "inner-worldly asceticism":

> Calvinism...creates an intramundane asceticism which logically and
> comprehensively recognizes all secular means, but which reduces them
> to means only, without any value in themselves, in order that by
> the use of all the means available the Holy Community may be
> created.[1]

Neither Graydon nor I likes the idea that the means were "means only, without any value in themselves," but we can't help recognizing some truth in
the suggestion that Calvinism built the Holy Community on the monastic
model, but within the world. As a historian, I offer Graydon these further
reflections on a question that has long troubled me: Did the monastery itself,
which Luther and Calvin rejected, actually exist as a Christian faith community from the beginning? Are there telltale traces of monastic communities
in the pages of the NT?[2]

---

1. Troeltsch, *The Social Teaching of the Christian Churches* (2 vols.; London: Allen and Unwin;
New York: Macmillan, 1931) 2. 607.
2. For an earlier attempt to canvass this question see J. C. O'Neill, "The Origins of Monasticism," in Rowan Williams, ed., *The Making of Orthodoxy: Essays in Honour of Henry Chadwick*
(Cambridge: Cambridge University Press, 1989) 270–87; also Adalbert G. Hamman, "Les orig-
ines du monachisme chrétien au cours des deux premiers siècles," in Cornelius Mayer with Karl

Once we concede two points, it is hard to deny the likelihood that there were monastic communities in existence from the beginning. First, the Dead Sea Scrolls were guarded by a monastic community, and there were other communities like it, as archaeology and the reports of Philo make plain. This first point shows that Christianity did not invent monasticism, if monastic communities were to be accommodated. Second, the two Egyptian monks Antony (ca. 251–356) and Pachomius (ca. 290–346) usually credited with the foundation of Christian monasticism never suggested that they were doing anything particularly novel, and no one accused them of novelty. Eusebius thought that Philo had met St. Peter in Rome, that he was familiar with the asceticism of many of the men and women who were converted by Mark in Egypt, and so was able to write *On the Contemplative Life* about Christian monasticism (*Hist. eccl.* 2.16–17). He said that Philo's treatise contained the rules that were still being observed by the church in his own day (*Hist. eccl.* 2.17.1). Eusebius knew more about the ins and outs of the social life of Christians than we do, and his explicit affirmation of continuity cannot be lightly dismissed.[3] This second point at least allows for the possibility that monastic communities existed from the start and forbids us to despair of finding traces of their existence in the NT.

I begin by asking how Jews in the centuries before the birth of Jesus Christ would have justified monasticism and what terms they would have used to mark off from their fellow faithful Jews the men and women who embraced monasticism. I then ask whether these justifications of monasticism and these terms turn up in the NT. I focus on two particular pieces of evidence: in the Synoptic gospels, the first beatitude taken with the story of the rich man who refused to sell all he had; and in the Johannine epistles, the information that we can gather about the communities to which they were addressed. Finally I

Heinz Chelius, *Homo Spiritalis: Festgabe für Luc Verheijen Osa zu seinem 70. Geburtstag* (Cassiciacum 38; Würzburg: Augustinus, 1987) 311–26. I found this essay only after mine was published.

3. James E. Goehring, "The Origins of Monasticism," in Harold W. Attridge and Gohei Hata, eds., *Eusebius, Christianity, and Judaism* (SPB 42; Leiden and New York: Brill, 1992) 235–55. Goehring (p. 326) is more cautious than I am: "The evidence should neither be used to support Eusebius' knowledge of 'organized monastic communities in Palestine' before 300 CE" (here citing Timothy D. Barnes, *Constantine and Eusebius* [Cambridge, Mass.: Harvard University Press, 1981] 195) "nor to argue, since he elsewhere mentions no known Christian communities, that such communities did not yet exist" (here citing Hermann Weingarten, "Der Ursprung des Mönchtums im nachconstantinischen Zeitalter," *ZKG* 1 [1877] 6–10). G. Peter Richardson argues that "Eusebius takes the Therapeutae over as an explanation, perhaps even a defence, of the fledgling monastic movement of his day" ("Philo and Eusebius on Monasteries and Monasticism: The Therapeutae and Kellia," in Bradley H. McLean, ed., *Origins and Method: Towards a New Understanding of Judaism and Christianity: Essays in Honour of John C. Hurd* [JSNTSup 86; Sheffield: JSOT Press, 1993] 356). He does not doubt that Christian monasticism *began* in Eusebius's day. Richardson rightly draws attention to the many striking physical parallels between the settlement of the Therapeutae and the Kellia, but the most he will allow is the possible influence of one on the other.

ask why the traces of monasticism that can be discovered were so difficult to discern that most biblical scholars, of all confessions and none, simply assume that monasticism is a late development in the history of the church.

The Dead Sea Scrolls

The discovery of the Dead Sea Scrolls has posed a hard question to biblical scholars. The scrolls were found stored in caves in pots made in a settlement at which there is, besides some secondary cemeteries, one carefully planned male burial ground containing about 1,100 tombs.[4] The *Manual of Discipline* was discipline for a male celibate community that gave up all private property: a community bound by poverty, chastity, and obedience.

Yet few scholars read the Hebrew Bible in a way that would lead them to see in it the origins of monasticism.[5] Likewise, few scholars read the NT in a way that would lead them to see in it the existence of monastic communities alongside married communities where individuals owned property. The idea that there were two ways of serving God, the active way and the contemplative way, was accepted as a matter of course by the Qumran community. The *Damascus Document* (CD) from the Cairo Geniza, published fifty years before the DSS came to light but copies of which have been found at Qumran, distinguished clearly between the Perfect and those who chose to marry (CD 7.4–6, 6a-8=19.1–4). The flourishing Egyptian monasticism of the third and fourth centuries made the same assumption: Leah active, Rachel contemplative; Martha active, Mary contemplative. The contemplative life was assumed

---

4. Roland de Vaux, *Archaeology and the Dead Sea Scrolls* (London: Oxford University Press, 1973) 45–47.

5. The two outstanding exceptions are Leonhard Rost ("Gruppenbildungen im Alten Testament," *TLZ* 80 [1955] 1–8) and Gerhard Wallis ("Die Gemeinde des Tritojesaia-Buches: Eine traditionsgeschichtliche Untersuchung" [unpublished Habilitationsschrift, Humboldt University, Berlin, 1958]). Erhard S. Gerstenberger has written a fine essay on how scholars have neglected to study the way the prophetic words were received and treasured by later congregations, but he does not seem to have noticed the possibility of monastic-type communities as the locus of transmission ("'Gemeindebildung' in Prophetenbüchern? Beobachtungen und Überlegungen zum Traditions- und Redaktionsprozess prophetischer Schriften," in Fritz Volkmar, Karl-Friedrich Pohlmann, and Hans-Christoph Schmitt, eds., *Prophet und Prophetenbuch: Festschrift für Otto Kaiser zum 65. Geburtstag* [BZAW 185; Berlin: De Gruyter, 1989] 44–58). Professor Wallis has drawn my attention to an essay by Hans Seidel that takes the discussion a stage further. Seidel isolates six criteria that would have to be fulfilled by the groups that could possibly have handed on the OT traditions: a chain of individuals, able to edit, wanting to preserve the tradition, with a library, economically viable from generation to generation, who venerated the founder. He does not think that Gerstenberger's congregations meet these criteria, but he identifies three relatively clear groups that do: the priesthood, the musicians, and the scribes ("Die Trägergruppen alttestamentlicher Überlieferung," in H. Michael Niemann, Matthias Augustin, and Werner H. Schmidt, eds., *Nachdenken über Israel, Bibel und Theologie: Festschrift für Klaus-Dietrich Schunck zu seinem 65. Geburtstag* [Beiträge zur Erforschung des Alten Testaments und des Antiken Judentums 37; Frankfurt am Main: Lang, 1994] 375–86).

by all Christians to be a higher and a better way, without denigrating the active way.

Traditionally this social phenomenon was traced back to Elijah, an unmarried prophet who established communities of the sons of the prophets at least in Bethel and Jericho (2 Kgs 2:3, 5, 7, 15), and to Elisha, his unmarried successor (2 Kgs 19:20). We read of a widow of one of the sons of the prophets and her two sons (2 Kgs 4:1). There may have been married communities, or married couples may have accepted monastic discipline late on in their marriage (as perhaps was the case with the unfortunate Ananias and Sapphira in Acts 5:1–11). Similar bands to Elijah's sons of the prophets existed earlier, in the time of Samuel (1 Sam 10:5, 10).

The challenge to biblical scholars is to entertain the possibility that monasticism is one more example of the phenomenon that basic beliefs and practices which shaped the regular pattern of life of countless believers are often not to be found in the documents of those communities, or are to be found only fleetingly or much later.[6] As far as the NT is concerned, we recall the paucity of traces of the observance of Sunday, of infant baptism, and of the ordination of ministers to preside at the Lord's Supper: all ancient customs universally observed and of central importance in community life.

There is one massive indication that Jesus and his earliest followers assumed that some who accepted his message would continue under monastic discipline or would seek to enter it. Prophets before him had done so, and he continued the practice. The massive indication is his habit of giving teaching to some that he did not give to all. The saying, "To you is given the mystery of the Kingdom; to others, not" (Matt 13:11; Mark 4:11; Luke 8:10), assumes that there is an arcane teaching only given to some. I do not need to defend its authenticity or the authenticity of other similar sayings, since, even if the saying does not go back to Jesus, it reflects the natural assumption of the community that later created and treasured it. In Matt 13:34//Mark 4:33–34 the disciples seek private teaching from Jesus about why they had failed to heal with a word where he had succeeded. At the beginning of the collection of eschatological teachings, the disciples are portrayed as asking privately when the end of the age would come (Matt 24:3; Mark 13:3–4; cf. Luke 21:7). In the saying, "What I say to you, I say to all," it is assumed that not all teaching is for all (Mark 13:37). In Luke 12:41, Peter asks whether certain teaching is "for us or for all." John's gospel contains a large private discourse directed specifically to the disciples (John 14–17).

The jar in which the first copy of the *Manual of Discipline* was found in a cave near the Wadi Qumran was in itself significant. The community that

---

6. Herein lies Hermann Gunkel's basic challenge to Julius Wellhausen; see J. C. O'Neill, "Gunkel versus Wellhausen: The Unfinished Task of the *Religionsgeschichtliche Schule*," *Journal of Higher Criticism* 2/2 (1995) 115–21.

made that pot was charged, as one of its main tasks, with the duty of preserving the secret commands of the Lord alongside the open commands of the Lord in the Torah, the Prophets, and the Writings. The double tradition was held to go back to Moses. There were secret things that belong to the Lord God — and, by implication, to his prophets — and the revealed things that belong to all the people from generation to generation (Deut 29:29). According to a later Jewish tradition, Moses on his deathbed commanded Joshua to anoint the secret books with the oil of cedar and put them away in earthen vessels in the place God had made from the beginning of creation that his name should be called on, until the day of repentance in the visitation with which God would visit them in the consummation of the end of the days (T. Mos. 1.16–18). Like Moses, Daniel sealed books up to the end (Dan 12:4, 9). The secret books "fragrant with myrrh" were said to be brought out by an archangel for Enoch (2 Enoch 22.11 [A]). When all the books on earth were burnt at the time of Ezra, Ezra was told to take five shorthand writers up a mountain, where God dictated to him the twenty-four books of the revealed canon and the seventy books of the secret canon (4 Ezra 14:1–9, 26, 44–47). The prophets were commanded to hand down "another law" to their sons so that these traditions might be transmitted from generation to generation (1 Enoch 81.6; 82.1; 2 Enoch 47.1; 48.6–7). The Temple Scroll found in Cave 11 at Qumran may well be a secret version of the Law of Moses meant for the community alone.[7] Jesus and his disciples simply followed an established pattern, and the secret teaching he gave was only written down and promulgated more widely because of the belief that the messianic age had already dawned with his coming.

The First Beatitude

The Sermon on the Mount, with its severe counsels, would seem an obvious example of secret teaching, at first for those who accepted the contemplative way, but later made more widely known. It would be beyond the scope of this essay to examine the whole Sermon, but the first beatitude may be taken as typical of the whole. The first beatitude, I shall argue, was a specific endorsement of the monastic life.

In pronouncing the blessedness of the poor, Jesus was not likely to be assuring the starving and the homeless of their eventual blessedness in the kingdom of God since blessings, in the Bible and in Jewish literature in

---

7. See Ben Zion Wacholder, The Dawn of Qumran: The Sectarian Torah and the Teacher of Righteousness (HUCM 8; Cincinnati: Hebrew Union College Press, 1983), esp. chap. 1, which "advances the hypothesis that the Qumranic Torah presented itself as a copy of a Torah which God had ordained to Moses on Mount Sinai. The text would be revealed to Israel only at the time of the eschaton, when the messianic epoch would be inaugurated" (33).

general, are always pronounced in a religious setting where behavior pleas-
ing to God is being recommended for its easiness, success, and happiness:[8]
"Blessed is the one who turns back from the changeable path and walks along
the straight path" (*2 Enoch* 42.10); "Blessed is the one to whom wisdom is
given.... Blessed is the one who does it" (4Q185 frg. 1, col. 2, ll. 8, 13).

But nor can the beatitude be recommending an intellectual insight into
the human condition as a condition of poverty, desolation, and misery.[9] This
reading is represented by the NEB translation of Matt 5:3: "How blest are
those who know that they are poor; the kingdom of Heaven is theirs" (1961
edition), changed in the second edition of 1970 to "How blest are those who
know their need of God...."

The phrase ענוי רוח has turned up in 1QM 14.7 (cf. 1QH 14.3), and
frgs. 8–10 of 4QM\ now enable us to decipher the previously unintelligible verb and read ובעניי רוח [לוא מר]חם מר[חם לבב קושי, "By the poor of spirit
[... not having pi]ty on the hard of heart."[10] Maurice Baillet conjectures that
the equivalent line 5 in 4QMᵃ frgs. 8–10 reads ובעניי רוח ר]שות לבב קושי[,
"[dans les pauvres d'esprit (est) l'au]torité sur le coeur (plein) de dureté."[11]
The *War Scroll* continues: "By the perfect of the way will all the peoples
of wickedness be destroyed" (1QM 14.7). The πτωχοὶ τῷ πνεύματι are not
those who know that the human condition is miserable. They are the warriors
fighting God's last battle against the massed forces of Belial. These warriors
are "perfect in spirit and flesh," not poor in spirit (1QM 7.5). The Greek represents a Hebrew construct. The רוח is almost certainly the Holy Spirit, and
there is a parallel in Hos 9:7, איש הרוח, "a man of the Spirit" or "a prophet,"
which gives us the true meaning. The Poor and the Perfect are communities
of men or women (or of men and women) who are a distinct yet separate part
of Israel. When the prophet Zechariah broke in two the staff called Beauty,
it was "the poor of the flock" that waited on him who knew that it was the
word of the Lord (Zech 11:7, 10–11). The first beatitude was a statement
that the poor of the Spirit would assuredly inherit the kingdom.

The story of the rich man who asks Jesus what he must do to inherit eternal life is an incident in the gospels that shows the same assumption that

---

8. Walther Zimmerli, "Zur Struktur der alttestamentlichen Weisheit," *ZAW* 51 (1933) 185–
86 n. 1.

9. Hans Dieter Betz, *The Sermon on the Mount* (Hermeneia; Minneapolis: Fortress, 1995)
114–18; idem, *Essays on the Sermon on the Mount* (Philadelphia: Fortress, 1985) 26–35.

10. The two letters after the lacuna are usually read סם[, but the ס is uncertain and meaningless; read ח (a reading suggested by a close inspection of the photographs on the computer
scanner at New College, Edinburgh).

11. Baillet, *Qumrân Grotte 4: III (4Q482–4Q520)* (DJD 7; Oxford: Clarendon, 1982) 21–
22; J. Duhaime in James H. Charlesworth, ed., *The Dead Sea Scrolls: Hebrew, Aramaic, and
Greek Texts with English Translations*, vol. 2: *Damascus Document, War Scroll, and Related Documents* (Princeton Theological Seminary Dead Sea Scrolls Project; Tübingen: Mohr [Siebeck];
Louisville: Westminster/John Knox, 1995) 124–25, 149.

there was a twofold expectation in the minds of Jesus and his earliest followers: a way of life for the contemplative distinct from the way of life of the
active (Matt 19:16–22; Mark 10:17–22; Luke 18:18–23). This man is told to
keep the commandments. He says that he has always kept them. The possibility that he lacks one thing is raised in different forms in Matthew, Mark,
and Luke. Mark says that Jesus looked on him and gave him a loving greeting (Mark 10:17). Matthew has Jesus say, "If you want to be perfect." Jesus
then asks him to sell all he has and to give it to the poor (the community of
the poor?) and follow him. Here is clear distinction between the commands
of the Law (the moral commandments of the Ten Words, to which Matthew
adds Lev 19:18) and the counsels of perfection, the former of which apply to
all believers and the latter only to the monks and nuns.

W. D. Davies and Dale C. Allison list six arguments against drawing this
conclusion.[12] The first is the most formidable — that there is nothing in Matt
5:48, the only other occasion in Matthew's gospel that the word "perfect"
is used, to suggest that only a few are to be perfect: "Are not all called to
imitate God in his love?"[13] This argument begs the question. If God lays the
Ten Words on all and perfection only on some, he is showing clear limits to
human behavior to all, and recommending a special characteristic of his own
to some volunteers. Only if Jesus could be shown to destroy this standard
distinction between two sorts of discipleship could his words about perfection
be taken as a command laid on all. If the distinction can be shown to apply in
the case of the young man, then it must also apply in the case of Matt 5:48.

Second, Davies and Allison argue, quite correctly, that one cannot deduce
from the command "Leave the dead" that Jesus issued a general order to ne-
glect the deceased. But that is just the point they think they are demolishing:
some are called to leave the dead as some are called to sell all they have and
give it to the poor.

Third, Davies and Allison think that Matthew's interest in money and his
"nuanced attitude towards wealth" counts for their position, not seeing that
the traditional distinction between the commands laid on all and the duties
required of the active, on the one hand, and the counsels of perfection, on
the other hand, are just this nuanced attitude to wealth they rightly find in
Matthew.[14]

Fourth, they say that Matt 6:2–4, the duty of giving alms secretly, implies
the continued possession of wealth that Matt 5:48 would say had ceased if
perfection implied poverty. Monastic communities, however, did hold prop-

---

12. Davies and Allison, *The Gospel according to Saint Matthew* (3 vols.; ICC; Edinburgh:
T. & T. Clark, 1988–97) 3. 47–48.
13. Ibid., 3. 47.
14. Ibid.

erty and wealth, and they did give alms; it is only that the individual members were deprived of individual possessions.

Fifth, Davies and Allison concede that Matt 19:12, the saying about eunuchs for the sake of the kingdom, refers to voluntarily chosen celibacy.[15] They argue from those parts of Matt 19:1–15 that show the disciples belittling marriage (v. 10) and children (v. 13) that Jesus is portrayed as opposing a negative view of family life: celibacy is not for everyone and children are to be welcomed.[16] They conclude from the fact that Jesus in Matthew does not rate the life of celibacy over family life that he does not envisage two sorts of believers.[17] Surely he does envisage two sorts of believers, but does not necessarily endorse the denigration of either form.

Finally, Davies and Allison argue that Matt 19:22–26 sees as the indispensable way of life what the rich man had refused to do. Not so. Jesus' teaching about the difficulty the rich will have in entering the kingdom of heaven does not imply that any particular rich person — say, the one who has just refused the invitation to sell all he has — will fail to enter the kingdom because of that refusal. Jesus specifically denies the conclusion that no rich people can be saved (vv. 25–26).

Davies and Allison concede that this rich man was challenged to give up his wealth, and they recognize that another rich man, Joseph of Arimathea, was a disciple (Matt 27:57–61). Only by condemning this rich man — without evidence — to the loss of eternal life do they manage to avoid the clear inference that Jesus recognized two sorts of the faithful: those who lived an active life in their own families, who married and had possessions, and those who lived the contemplative life in obedience in a community, renouncing marriage and private possessions and putting themselves under a military-like discipline.[18]

This incident provides a key to the Sermon on the Mount and the Sermon on the Plain. My reading of it chimes in with my reading of the first beatitude. The sayings collected in the two sermons are, on this argument, chiefly counsels of perfection. Mark's gospel, although it contains an account of the refusal of the rich man to sell everything, does not contain the special counsels of perfection laid on the poor of the Spirit.

---

15. Ibid., 22–25.
16. Ibid., esp. 36.
17. Ibid., 48.
18. This reading of Matt 19:16–22 is supported by Béda Rigaux, *Témoignage de l'évangile de Matthieu* (Brussels: Desclée de Brouwer, 1967) 231–33; ET *The Testimony of St. Matthew* (Chicago: Franciscan Herald, 1968) 167. George Wesley Buchanan argues that "it seems likely that Jesus was inviting that man to fulfill the qualifications for belonging to a perfect, celibate community for which giving all of one's possessions was only part of the requirement. . . . The commandment to be perfect may have been a commandment to become a monk" (*Jesus: The King and His Kingdom* [Macon, Ga.: Mercer University Press, 1984] 187).

The new evidence from Qumran must raise more sharply the question of whether Jesus did not assume that organized communities of men or women (or men and women together) might not continue to exist, in Israel and among the gentiles, as more and more people came to acknowledge him as messiah. Commentators can hardly deny that there were cases of voluntary celibacy and voluntary poverty. This evidence, given the practice of the Essenes, would strongly suggest that individuals who embraced poverty and chastity would also seek to place themselves in obedience under an abbot or abbess in a community. But is there, in fact, evidence in the NT that there were communities of members bound by poverty, chastity, and obedience?

The Johannine Letters

The clearest case is the community addressed in 1 John. As Pheme Perkins has reminded us, "the author clearly conceives his audience as men."[19] 1 John was compiled out of old traditions in a male community of the apostles' τεκνία or παιδία organized into two divisions of πατέρες and νεανίσκοι (2:12–14).

There is the same heightening of the commandments into counsels of perfection that we observed in the teaching of Jesus. The one who hates his brother is a murderer (1 John 2:15). It is possible not to sin (3:6, 9; 5:18; cf. 2:6). Nevertheless, all have sinned (1:10), but it is assumed that future sins will be avoided. Future sins are either sins unto death (for which no intercession is possible) or sins not unto death (for which intercession works; 1 John 5:16). This would seem to correspond to sins against the Ten Commandments, which are "unto death," and sins against the "counsels of perfection."

The "counsels of perfection" would seem to cut off the members of this community from the possibility of active life in the world:

> Do not love the world
> Nor the things in the world.
> If anyone loves the world
> There is not love for the Father in him.
> For everything in the world:
> The lust of the flesh
> And the lust of the eyes
> And the pride of life
> Is not from the Father
> But is from the world.

---

19. Perkins, *The Johannine Epistles* (New Testament Message 21; Wilmington, Del.: Glazier, 1979) xi.

> And the world is passing away,
> And its lust;
> But the man who [perfectly] does the will of God
> remains for ever. (1 John 2:15–17)

The two short epistles appended to 1 John share the vocabulary and ideas of the longer writing. But they are clearly epistles in a way that 1 John is not. Is there any evidence that these epistles could have belonged to a monastic milieu rather than to that of the active life of secular Christians?

2 John is written by the Presbyter to an Elect Lady. This Elect Lady has "children" (v. 4). She and they need to be warned to repel preachers who come denying Christ, so losing the Father along with losing the Son (v. 9). The Presbyter is also able to pass on to this Elect Lady greetings from her Elect Sister, who also has "children" (v. 13).

Heinrich Julius Holtzmann summed up the nineteenth-century view, which went back to Cassiodorus (ca. 485–ca. 580), that the frequent changes from the second person singular address to the Lady to a second person plural address show that the Lady is a church personified and that her "children," with whom she is identical, have to be understood as the members of that church.[20] Judith Lieu, in her careful study of 2 and 3 John, comes to the same conclusion, although she cautiously notes that "the use of this imagery [of κυρία as a church] in the address of a letter is without parallel."[21]

It is of course true that a Lady can personify a church (e.g., in *Herm. Vis.* 2.4.1), but there is no example in the one discourse of a Lady representing the church and, at the same time, of her children also representing the church. For example, Ignatius *Trallians* addresses the Elect Church, (*proem.*), but then speaks in the body of the epistle of "your bishop" (1.1; 3.2). He does not speak of the Elect Church and the children of the Elect Church, but, rather, he assumes that the Elect Church and the members of the Elect Church are conterminous.

The concluding greeting in 2 John is often taken as one of the strongest indications that the Lady represents the whole church, but in fact it counts against that assumption. The greeting comes from the children of the Elect Sister of the Lady addressed in our epistle. If the Elect Sister were a symbol for a church, the Elect Sister and her children would have most likely sent the greeting to the Elect Lady and her children. But the Elect Sister's children send greetings to the Elect Lady. The Elect Sister is distinguished from her

---

20. Holtzmann, *Evangelium, Briefe und Offenbarung des Johannes* (HKNT 4; 2d ed.; Freiburg-im-Breisgau: Mohr, 1893) 268.

21. Lieu, *The Second and Third Epistles of John* (Studies of the New Testament and Its World; Edinburgh: T. & T. Clark, 1986) 65–58, esp. 66. The only modern scholar I know who rejects the usual position is Ernst Gaugler, in his posthumously published commentary, *Die Johannesbriefe* (Auslegung neutestamentlicher Schriften 1; Zurich: EVZ, 1964) 282–83, 289.

children, just as the Elect Lady is distinguished from her children. The implication seems to be that, just as the children of the Elect Sister honor their head, so they honor the head of a sister-house, the Elect Lady of 2 John, and greet her as a sign of their unity.

It is far from the case that the change of those addressed (from the singular, referring to the Elect Lady, to the plural, referring to her children) is an indication that the Elect Lady stands for the church. On closer examination, the changes are deliberate and well marked.

In v. 4 the Presbyter reports that he has found a number of the children of the Elect Lady who were walking in the truth. In v. 5 he beseeches the Lady to join with him and others in loving one another. This loving seems to refer not to the general duty of loving one's neighbor but to the specific need to keep a close loving relationship both between houses and within houses. Love consists in walking according to "his commands." At this point the Presbyter turns to the Elect Lady's children and repeats his admonition: "that, as you have heard from the beginning, you should walk in [love]" (v. 6b).[22]

In v. 7 the Presbyter turns to the people who are threatening the loving unity of the houses:

> [It is the case] that many deceivers have gone out [from the houses] into the world, deceivers who do not confess that Jesus Christ is to come in flesh. If anyone does not confess Jesus Christ is to come in flesh,[23] this one is the deceiver and an antichrist.[24]

Verse 8 is still addressed to the children of the Elect Lady. The Elect Lady may well be included in the first person plural of the verb ἐργάζομαι (A B Ψ 0232^vid 81 323 614 et al.):

---

22. The text of 2 John 6b is in disarray:

ℵ*   ινα καθως αυτη εστιν η εντο [sic] αυτου ινα καθως ηκουσατε απ αρχης ινα εν
      αυτη περιπατησητε

B   αυτη η εντολη εστιν καθως ηκουσατε απ αρχης ινα εν αυτη περιπατητε

33   αυτη η εντολη εστιν ινα καθως ηκουσατε απ αρχης εν αυτη περιπατητε

The change from ἐντολάς (plural) in v. 6a to ἐντολή (singular) in v. 6b is difficult to explain. Then, the final pronoun in ἐν αὐτῇ refers most peculiarly to ἡ ἐντολή, whereas it must refer to the remote subject, ἡ ἀγάπη. What would most easily explain the disarray would be to suppose that αὕτη ἐστὶν ἡ ἐντολή ("this is the commandment") was originally a gloss to the sentence ἵνα καθὼς ἠκούσατε ἀπ᾽ ἀρχῆς ἐν αὐτῇ περιπατῆτε ("so that, as you have heard from the beginning, you may walk in it"). The gloss was taken from John 15:12 and 1 John 3:23. The glossator, of course, took the ἐν αὐτῇ to refer to ἡ ἀγάπη; only when the gloss was incorporated into the sentence (note, in an absurd place in ℵ*) did the ἐν αὐτῇ appear to refer, quite impossibly, to the command. The Presbyter has turned from addressing the Elect Lady to addressing her children.

23. The longer reading of 398 (396), which seems to have been omitted by homoioteleuton.

24. Omitting the article with ℵ 322 323 1241* 1846 2464.

[You children,] look to yourselves that you do not lose what we [the Presbyter and the Elect Lady] have achieved [in you], but receive a full reward. Everyone who steps out of line and does not remain in the teaching concerning Christ does not have God. As for the one who remains in the teaching, this one has both the Father and the Son. If anyone comes to you [children] and does not bring this teaching, do not [you children] receive him into the house and do not even speak a greeting to him. The one who speaks a greeting to him shares his wicked deeds.

The crucial transition from a direct exhortation to the Elect Lady to strict instructions to her children is clear. There is never any suggestion that the Elect Lady represents the corporate community. Her children are directly admonished, but she is besought, with an apology for mentioning what she has long known (v. 5).

The question remains. Is the Lady the owner of a house that is used by the local Christians as a place of worship, or is the Lady the head (because she is perhaps the owner) of a resident community of men and women? Against the first possibility and in favor of the second is the situation envisaged in vv. 10 and 11. The visitor is not a visiting preacher whose message is first heard and then, perhaps, rejected, as in *Did.* 11.1–2. The visitor is met at the gate of the compound of the house by the porter on duty. He is not a traveler seeking hospitality but a member of a similar house. He either gives the correct password ("Christ is to come in flesh"?) or he does not. If he does not, he is not even to be greeted in return, let alone admitted. The love that binds together other houses, including the house of the Elect Sister and her children, with the house of the Elect Lady and her children, all under the oversight of the Presbyter, excludes those who deny Christ is to come in flesh.

At every service of worship there were probably doorkeepers who decided whether men or women from other congregations, bearing letters of recommendation, were to be admitted to worship (*Const. apost.* 2.58.1). These doorkeepers — a recognized "order" in the church at least from the early third century — ensured that all the men and women and children who entered sat or stood in the appropriate parts of the congregation (see 1 Cor 14:16, τὸν τόπον τοῦ ἰδιώτου, "[one in] the place of an outsider"; *Const. apost.* 2.57.10), that catechumens and penitents left before the eucharist, and that unbelievers did not enter during the eucharist (*Const. apost.* 2.57, end). However, here in 2 John 10 the expression μὴ λαμβάνετε αὐτὸν εἰς οἰκίαν ("do not receive him into the house") suggests not so much entry into a congregation about to worship as entry into a house as a guest (cf. Luke 10:5).

The odds are that the word "house" in 2 John 10 refers to a residential community living according to a rule under the government of a mature woman. Her spiritual children are referred to by masculine pronouns and participles, and the masculine gender is likely to refer to both men and women. The only communities in which it would be possible to have women at the head were monastic communities of men and women. There is no doubt that mixed monastic communities existed later in the history of the church. Such a community is described by Gregory of Nyssa in his *Life of Macrina*, and Basil the Great gives rules for houses ruled by women in which male monks also lived.[25]

In 3 John, it is necessary to explain the relations between the Presbyter, Gaius (the beloved recipient of the epistle), Diotrephes, and Demetrius. We must start with the opening words of v. 9, for which there are five well-attested readings:

1. εγραψα τι τη εκκλησια $\aleph$* A 048^{vid} 1241 1739 bo^{mss}

2. εγραψας τι τη εκκλησια   B co

3. εγραψα αν τη εκκλησια   33 81

4. εγραψα αν τι τη εκκλησια   323

5. εγραψα αν τι τη αληθια $\aleph^2$

The original reading that explains all the others is (3).[26] No one would change the definite information that the Presbyter had written something to the church (1) into the indefinite statement that the Presbyter was deterred from writing by anyone like Demetrius. This would be far worse than supposing that the letter had been written and rejected. The reading of the Codex Vaticanus (2) is presumably another reverential alteration to save the face of the Presbyter: Gaius's epistle could be knocked back by Diotrephes because of Gaius's known alliance with the Presbyter, but not the epistle of the Presbyter himself.

Once we accept reading 3, we need no longer suppose that the church to which the Presbyter did not write was a church other than Gaius's, ruled over by Diotrephes. It is possible now to accept the natural assumption that

---

25. For Gregory, see Pierre Maraval, ed. and trans., *Grégoire de Nysse: Vie de sainte Macrine* (SC 178; Paris: Cerf, 1971); ET in V. W. Callahan, trans., *Gregory of Nyssa: Ascetical Works* (FC 58; Washington, D.C.: Catholic University of America Press, 1967); also Basil the Great *Regulae brevius tractatae* (PG 31. 1079–1306), e.g., Rule 154. See Susanna Elm, *"Virgins of God": The Making of Asceticism in Late Antiquity* (Oxford Classical Monographs; Oxford: Clarendon, 1994).

26. This was also the conclusion of Adolf von Harnack, *Zur Revision der Prinzipien der neutestamentlichen Textkritik: Die Bedeutung der Vulgata für den Text der Katholischen Briefe* (Beiträge zur Einleitung in das Neue Testament 7; Leipzig: Hinrich, 1916) 73.

Diotrephes belongs, with Gaius, in the one church.[27] Demetrius would also most naturally belong to the same church.

I suggest that the most economical reading of the circumstances of 3 John is as follows. The Presbyter is writing to Gaius to commend him for offering hospitality to missionaries who do not accept financial support from the gentiles among whom they work but rely on places like the church of Gaius. These missionaries have come back and reported favorably on Gaius's hospitality to the church that sent them out. The Presbyter would have written his letter to Gaius's church instead of to Gaius himself but for the fact that he knew that Diotrephes did not accept his position on missionary maintenance. And Diotrephes wanted to be Prior (i.e., head of the community). In the phrase φιλοπρωτεύων αὐτῶν I take it that αὐτῶν ("them," "of them") refers to the members of that church over which Gaius was for the time being Prior. The word φιλοπρωτεύω is, apart from a quotation of this verse in Palladius (ca. 365–425) *V. Chrys.* 131.19 (PG 47.5), found in Greek literature only once: in a discussion by Nilus of Ancyra about a vain monk who did not want to yield his office in the monastery to another. This does not prove that it is a private, monastic word, but it at least shows that it fits the monastic world.[28]

When the Presbyter comes, he will, in a gathering of the church in council, either *bring up* Diotrephes's works or, accepting the reading of Ψ (αὐτούς for αὐτοῦ), remind them of his works. The works (apart from the prating) are unlikely to be actual works in any case — and are not actual works, on the assumption that Diotrephes is a member of Gaius's church. The present tenses should be taken as conative.[29] His prating against the Presbyter (or against Gaius, on the noteworthy reading in v. 10 of 056 0142: ὑμᾶς for ἡμᾶς) has even taken the form of trying to refuse to play his part in entertaining the missionaries, of trying to forbid those who want to do so, and of planning to have them expelled from the community. The Presbyter ends by recommending Demetrius as a worthy successor as Prior. He sends greetings to Gaius from his friends and asks Gaius to greet by name the known friends of the Presbyter in the church.

Only the acceptance of the reading of v. 9 that connects this Third Epistle

---

27. A. E. Brooke, who rejects the reading (3) that I accept, still takes τῇ ἐκκλησίᾳ in its natural sense to refer to "the local Church of which Gaius and Diotrephes were members" (*The Johannine Epistles* [ICC; Edinburgh: T. & T. Clark, 1912] 187).

28. See *LPGL*, s.v. (p. 1480a); the text of Nilus is in *PG* 79. 496B.

29. Brooke Foss Westcott, *The Epistles of St. John* (4th ed.; London: Macmillan, 1902) 241: "The verbs do not necessarily express purpose and effort." Rudolf Schnackenburg earlier accepted this reading of the present tense (*Die Johannesbriefe* [HTKNT 13/3; Freiburg: Herder, 1953] 293), but retracted in the 5th edition of his commentary (1975); ET in *The Johannine Epistles* (based on 7th ed., 1984; Tunbridge Wells, Kent: Burns and Oats; New York: Crossroad, 1992) 298.

with either the Second or the First requires us to put Diotrephes in an actual position of authority in a church distinct from Gaius's. The ecclesiastical word φιλοπρωτεύω lets us see a situation where one member of the community is aspiring to be elected as head of that community. The Presbyter can only persuade. He will do that at a council when he comes, but meanwhile he recommends another member, Demetrius, as a far better candidate.

The relations as here set out fit far better a monastic community than a local congregation. The word ἐκκλησία looks more like the council of the community, with an elected head, than a church with a bishop. The Presbyter is not here concerned with doctrinal matters. His wish is to ensure that Gaius's house continues to support missionaries sent from afar for the work among the natives. He has the right to visit Gaius's house and address the council, but he cannot do more than defend Gaius to the brothers and try to ensure that a more acceptable man like Demetrius become the next Prior.

The network of houses belonging to the same order was always threatened with breakaway houses. Someone like the Presbyter of 3 John would seem to be writing to an ally, a Prior coming to the end of his term of office, to ensure that the missionary strategy of the order as a whole is duly supported by this house, and that such support will continue in the future.

1 and 2 John have already shown that doctrinal differences led members of the communities to go out into the world, but that was not the only threat to monastic life. There is no need to press 3 John into a procrustean bed made up out of bits of 1 John, 2 John, and the Fourth Gospel. If we can dare to entertain the hypothesis that the Fourth Gospel as well as the three epistles of John came from monastic communities, we have made room for all the peculiar features of the corpus: the preservation of secret teaching revealed to seers from heaven (a particularly strong feature of the Fourth Gospel); the contrast between the commandments designed for all and the counsels of perfection for the monks and nuns; the constant threat of both heresy and breakaway movements; and the institution of houses of men and women under women as head.

Why has the distinction between the two separate ways of following the Lord, the active and contemplative, been so hard to discern in the pages of the NT? Simply because both ways were possible for all who would follow, and there was no longer any need to keep the way of perfection shut in the houses of perfection, for the messiah had come.

PART THREE

COMMON LIFE
IN THE GOSPELS
AND ACTS

9

THE JESUS TRADITION IN THE COMMON LIFE OF EARLY CHRISTIAN COMMUNITIES

Daryl D. Schmidt

New Testament scholarship has devoted much attention these past two decades to historical reconstruction, first of the historical Jesus and now of early
Christianity. One of the issues most debated is the amount of continuity between the earliest traditions about Jesus and the shape of the religion that
became "Christianity." Most reconstructions reveal a significant amount of
discontinuity between the historical Jesus and the christologies in the canonical literature of the later institutional church. The arguments are usually
framed within the world of ideas found in the written documents of early
Christianity.

Graydon Snyder has taken a significantly different approach to the world
of early Christianity. His *Ante Pacem* presents a picture of early Christian
communities based on nonliterary remains from before the time Christianity
became a public religion in the fourth century.[1] As Snyder's subtitle indicates,
the nonliterary remains provide a glimpse of common church life during this
era. He has assembled the traditions preserved in popular forms of early
Christian community life without imposing on them the official interpretation
of canonical Christian literature.

Historical reconstructions of Jesus and early Christianity are typically
based primarily on literary evidence. The historical Jesus is reconstructed
from the surviving gospel materials, and the resulting profile is then compared
with the earliest Christian writings, the letters of Paul and other canoni-

---

1. Snyder, *Ante Pacem: Archaeological Evidence of Church Life before Constantine* (Macon, Ga.:
Mercer University Press, 1985).

cal writings. The trajectory from Paul to the establishment of Constantinian Christianity in the fourth century seems almost inevitable. By the end of the second century the debate over orthodoxy had already given "scriptural" status to the letters of Paul and the four gospels, the very writings that now provide the primary literary evidence for early Christianity. Any historical reconstruction based on that literature faces the critical challenge of recovering what otherwise might have been lost. Although Snyder's evidence does not begin until late in the second century, it nonetheless provides a valuable test of the survivability of the earliest layers of tradition identified in any historical reconstruction based on literary material.

The goal of this study is to assess the degree of convergence between these two pictures — the historical reconstruction of early Christianity based primarily on written documents and the world pictured in Snyder's *Ante Pacem*. I begin with a sketch of the common life of early Christian communities, as reflected in the evidence accumulated by Snyder, and then compare it with the results of current reconstructions of the historical Jesus. This comparison will in effect test the hypothesis: whether Snyder's evidence is more than a random sample or actually correlates in important ways with the historical reconstruction of the oldest layer of tradition preserved by the earliest communities of Jesus' followers.

Although the written traditions about Jesus derive from gospels usually dated to the last quarter of the first century, most scholars judge that these documents used sources from a generation or so earlier. Such sources would then belong to the first generation of Christians. In contrast, Snyder notes that there are no identifiable Christian artifacts that survive until a century later than the gospels. Any significant degree of continuity between these two sets of data thus would suggest that the earliest Jesus tradition was sustained in the common life of early Christian communities independently of its legacy in the development of canonical literature.

Nonliterary Evidence for the Common Life of Early Christianity

The nonliterary evidence assembled by Snyder presents a quite consistent picture of the common life of early Christian communities. Even though literate Christians developed mostly narrative gospels, the earliest nonliterary evidence Snyder finds is entirely nonnarrative. Indeed, Snyder maintains that "one would not expect to find, and indeed does not find, narrative art prior to the peace of Constantine" (p. 13). The earliest surviving visual images are not part of narrative sequences from gospel stories but rather function as symbols for aspects of Christian life, e.g., the anchor, fish, boat, dove, bread, and good shepherd. Only when the narrative gospels are presumed to be the necessary interpretive framework for understanding all early Christian imagery do these symbols become windows into larger narratives. Since Snyder eschews such an assumption, he is able to sustain a strong argument that there are no pre-Constantinian images that necessarily require a narrative interpretation.

Snyder's contention is further supported by the complete lack of any early pictorial representation of the dominant feature of the narrative gospels, the death and resurrection of Jesus. In fact, "there are no early Christian symbols that elevate paradigms of Christ suffering . . . or even motifs of death and resurrection" (p. 14). Instead, the gospel narrative scenes most frequently represented are taken from healing and miracles stories, such as the paralytic, the loaves and fish, and the raising of Lazarus. There are also scenes of Jesus as teacher, the woman at the well, and Jesus' baptism. Snyder lists thirty-one "pictorial representations" related in some way to Jesus: seven of healings, six of baptism, five of Lazarus, three of fishermen, two each of the loaves and fish, Jesus teaching, and the woman at the well, one each of the wisemen, walking on water, women at a tomb, and Christ Helios (p. 43). The lack of anything connected with suffering and death is quite noticeable.

Snyder interprets these scenes as indicative of popular Christian emphasis on Jesus as one "who could bring peace and opportunity to those in desperate circumstances," and the Christian community as the "effective agent of that deliverance" (p. 166). This interpretation is reinforced by the most frequent of all pictorial representations, that of Jonah. The more than one hundred scenes of Jonah do not narrate the biblical story but feature primarily Jonah tossed into the sea and Jonah at rest, again presumably representing "peace in an alien environment." Snyder finds here (and in the Noah and Daniel scenes) a common pattern in which "the biblical scene provides a scriptural backdrop for a symbol taken from the social matrix" (p. 47). In the context of these popular OT scenes, those of Jesus seem clearly related to the theme of deliverance, whether from hunger or illness or social setting — or death. The obvious implication for Snyder is that this overwhelmingly consistent pattern must be a reflection of the way popular Christian faith communities understood their life together. For them salvation was expressed as deliverance from alienation, not redemption from guilt achieved through suffering. Hence "Jesus does not suffer or die in pre-Constantinian art" (p. 56). This Jesus as deliverer is depicted in the image of a young wonder-worker or itinerant philosopher.

The contrast between these two views is exemplified in the frequent visual symbols of meals, usually both bread and fish and often five or seven baskets, making clear that the image is taken from the feeding stories (multiplication of the loaves and fish), not from the Last Supper. In scenes of meals, "there is no early representation of the meal without fish" (p. 25). For Snyder this combination clearly indicates that the common meal shared by the Christian faith community was without explicit sacramental overtones.

An important function of the common meal, as depicted in cemetery art, was the *refrigerium*, or "eating with the family dead and the special dead" (p. 65). The social matrix for the common meal tradition, including the "cult of the dead" meal, was small communities that did not yet need architectural forms for accommodating larger gatherings. Snyder locates the transition between the two social contexts in the private home remodeled into a house church, such as discovered at Dura-Europos (pp. 68–71). However, archaeological remains do not provide evidence to establish the antecedents for the meal tradition in the house church.

The architectural tradition in early Christianity appears to have followed a parallel development with the meal tradition, but the direction of influence is impossible to determine. Several recent studies provide a good overview of the issues involved. The architecture of early Christianity is usually divided into three pre-Constantinian phases: first, private homes where Christian groups met; second, homes remodeled for intentional use as "house churches" (*domus ecclesiae*); and third, larger meeting halls that were predecessors to the first fourth-century official "church buildings," the basilicas sponsored by Constantine. The most careful recent analysis of the stages of development in early church architecture is provided by L. Michael White. White emphasizes the contextual nature of the evidence, argues for different rates of development in different locations, and notes the transitional features between stages of development.[2] The general consensus still seems to hold that the *domus ecclesiae*, the private house remodeled into suitable space for a house church meeting, did not begin to appear before the second half of the second century, the period that provides the earliest evidence for Snyder.

A crucial corollary to the scholarly reconstruction of early Christian architecture has been the study of meals in Greco-Roman social history.[3]

---

2. White, "*Domus Ecclesiae-Domus Dei*: Adaptation and Development in the Setting for Early Christian Assembly" (Ph.D diss., Yale University, 1982), published as *The Social Origins of Early Christian Architecture* (2 vols.; HTS 42–43; Valley Forge, Pa.: Trinity Press International, 1996–97). White's survey of the evidence is presented in his *Building God's House in the Roman World: Architectural Adaptation among Pagans, Jews, and Christians* (ASOR Library of Biblical and Near Eastern Archaeology; Baltimore, Md.: Johns Hopkins University Press, 1990); for a more popular summary see idem and Eric M. Myers, "Jews and Christians in the Roman World," *Archaeology* 42 (1989) 26–33. There is a critical appraisal of White's approach in Paul Corby Finney, "Early Christian Architecture: The Beginning (A Review Article)," *HTR* 81 (1988) 319–39, esp. 333–36. The archaeological evidence is now succinctly presented in Carolyn Osiek and David L. Balch, *Families in the New Testament World: Households and House Churches* (Louisville, Ky.: Westminster/John Knox, 1997) 5–35. Osiek and Balch note contrasts downplayed by White.

3. See Dennis E. Smith, "Social Obligation in the Context of Communal Meals: A Study of the Christian Meal in 1 Corinthians in Comparison with Graeco-Roman Communal Meals" (Ph.D. diss., Harvard University, 1980), summarized in idem and Hal Taussig, *Many Tables: The Eucharist in the New Testament and Liturgy Today* (Philadelphia: Trinity Press International; Lon-

Archaeological evidence reinforces the centrality of common meals in the practice of most Greco-Roman social groups. The frequency of meal scenes and food symbols in early Christian iconography is predictable for any Greco-Roman social group. Snyder's caution against an overtly sacramental interpretation, based on the archaeological evidence, is that the earliest surviving Christian meal scenes completely conform to the expectations of Greco-Roman meal traditions. In the context of catacomb art, images of banquets and food do not suggest explicit eucharistic themes. The more natural interpretation, as Snyder suggests, would be a coalescing of a scene from the multiplication of the loaves with the practice of the *agape* meal in the social matrix of the meal for the dead. For Snyder the unavoidable conclusion is that the earliest locus for the common meal of the Christian community was in *martyria*, "places for the faithful to eat with the special dead," although the historical relationships between these factors are not clear (p. 65). Within Greco-Roman culture, "memorial meals for the dead" were one of the common types of group meals.[4] As with all Greco-Roman group meals, these commemorative banquets would have included basic religious features, such as invoking the gods.[5]

If indeed the *martyria* were the first distinctive sites for early Christian meals, they would not have been the only context in which early Christian faith communities shared meals. The comparisons already cited between the Greco-Roman dinner party and the Corinthian "potluck dinner" make clear that this meal tradition developed alongside that of the *refrigerium*. The Pauline house churches, already in their early stages, apparently had a common meal practice that greatly resembled the well-established Greco-Roman tradition of meals hosted in private homes.[6]

This study does not require us to review the scholarly debate over the Pauline understanding of the eucharist, but only to note that recent scholarship has called attention to the common meal context in which the eucharistic issues are set. Whatever problems are being addressed in 1 Corinthians 10–11, the common meal setting is clearly similar to the other common meal traditions we have already discussed. What cannot be estab-

---

don: SCM, 1990) chap. 2; and in Smith, "Greco-Roman Meal Customs," *ABD* 4.650–53. See also Kathleen E. Corley, *Private Women, Public Meals: Social Conflict in the Synoptic Tradition* (Peabody, Mass.: Hendrickson, 1993); Osiek and Balch, *Families,* 193–204.

4. Stanley K. Stowers, "Elusive Coherence: Ritual and Rhetoric in 1 Corinthians 10–11," in Elizabeth A. Castelli and Hal Taussig, *Reimagining Christian Origins: A Colloquium Honoring Burton L. Mack* (Valley Forge, Pa.: Trinity Press International, 1996) 68–83.

5. The basic features of the Greco-Roman dinner party easily compare with the "potluck dinner" tradition that provides the social setting for the issues Paul addresses in 1 Corinthians; see Peter Lampe, "The Eucharist: Identifying with Christ on the Cross," *Int* 48 (1994) 36–49, esp. the chart on p. 37.

6. Osiek and Balch present archaeological evidence that suggests that such meals could be considerably larger than has often been supposed (*Families,* 193–204).

lished, from either archaeological or literary evidence, is either the historical or social relationships between the various common meal traditions, especially that of the *refrigerium,* the commemorative meal for the dead held in burial settings, and the regular (weekly?) common meal held in the house churches. It is unlikely that there is any singular simple line of development between the two. For the purposes of this study we need only note the popularity of these common meals and that they are in fact variations of the same common meal tradition. The overall evidence clearly suggests that the Last Supper tradition, whatever its history of development, is not to be associated with every instance of a Christian faith community gathered for a meal.[7]

Antecedents of the Common Life of Early Christianity in the Jesus Tradition

The popular Christianity Snyder describes is based on archaeological evidence that begins about a century and a half after the death of Jesus. Two obvious questions follow: Does this tradition go back to Jesus, and if so, how was it transmitted in the face of a variant "official" tradition?

I begin simply by noting that much recent historical Jesus research has identified the meal tradition as part of the authentic core of Jesus material.[8] Virtually all reconstructions of the historical Jesus give great weight to the relationship between Jesus and John the Baptist. Whatever the continuities between the two, the most important contrast can be stated succinctly as "fasting versus feasting." In contrast to John's fasting, Jesus was known for "open commensality," to use John Dominic Crossan's term.[9] Even scholars more inclined to attribute controversy stories involving eating to early communities still readily acknowledge that "Jesus could be characterized as one who preferred banquets, in contrast to John," and further that "this was seen to be consistent with his overall message."[10]

Robert W. Funk presents a similar picture of Jesus by beginning with the tradition of Jesus as teller of parables. The plot structure of parables most likely to be authentic emphasizes the reversal of fortune between insiders and outsiders. The notable feature of the meal tradition associated with Jesus is likewise its variance from the social customs of the day, especially as regards

7. The eucharistic prayer in *Didache* 9, which includes thanks for the "life and knowledge" made known through Jesus (v. 3), has no Last Supper context.

8. Dennis E. Smith ("The Historical Jesus at Table," SBLSP 28 [1989] 466–86) gives this assessment: "a wide variety of scholars who disagree on virtually everything else include this motif in their respective pictures of the historical Jesus" (p. 466).

9. Crossan, *The Historical Jesus: The Life of a Mediterranean Jewish Peasant* (San Francisco: Harper, 1991) 261–64; idem, *Jesus: A Revolutionary Biography* (San Francisco: Harper, 1994) 66–70.

10. Smith and Taussig, *Many Tables,* 46, 47.

those with whom it is appropriate to share table.[11] It seems highly likely that the tradition of common meals practiced by early Christian faith communities is in direct continuity with traditions preserved by the Jesus movement as part of its legacy of the historical Jesus. This part of the Jesus tradition is captured in a series of statements that the members of the Jesus Seminar voted to be most likely historical: (1) Jesus consorted openly with social outcasts; (2) one label for social outcasts was "toll collectors and sinners"; (3) Jesus was criticized for eating with social outcasts; and (4) Jesus justified his practice of sharing an open table in aphorism and parable. These statements form the basis for judging that the story of Jesus' dining with sinners (Mark 2:15–17//) contains a historical core.[12]

Jesus' practice of an open table is treated as a central feature of the authentic Jesus tradition by a wide array of scholars, including those quite at odds over its significance. N. Thomas Wright, for example, concedes that "most writers now agree that eating with 'sinners' was one of the most characteristic and striking marks of Jesus' regular activity." However, this "symbolic praxis of feasting with his followers, and of weaving stories around this practice," is interpreted by Wright as the result of an "implicit messianic claim" on the part of Jesus, which would not be supported by most critical scholars.[13]

Jesus as healer is a second prominent feature in Snyder's archaeological evidence that also is well attested in recent historical Jesus research. Even though the Jesus Seminar was skeptical that individual healing stories in the gospels were actual reports of Jesus' healings, the Seminar affirmed the statements that "Jesus cured some sick people" and "Jesus drove out what were thought to be demons" as part of the authentic tradition of Jesus as "itinerant teacher" who "proclaimed the kingdom of God."[14] Crossan combines the two features of healing and eating, "magic and meal," into the twin pillars of the Jesus tradition.[15] Jesus as healer also figures prominently in other recent reconstructions of Jesus.[16]

One of the more popular healing scenes noted by Snyder is the healing of the paralytic. It can serve to illustrate my assessment of its role in the Jesus tradition. The paralytic is the only healing scene to appear more than once in

---

11. Funk, *Honest to Jesus: Jesus for a New Millennium* (San Francisco: Harper, 1996), part 2, "The Gospel of Jesus" (pp. 143–216), esp. p. 192.

12. Robert W. Funk and the Jesus Seminar, *The Acts of Jesus: The Search for the Authentic Deeds of Jesus* (San Francisco: Harper, 1998) 66–67, 567.

13. Wright, *Christian Origins and the Question of God*, vol. 2: *Jesus and the Victory of God* (Minneapolis: Fortress, 1996) 431, 532.

14. Funk, *Acts of Jesus*, 171, 566.

15. Crossan, *Historical Jesus*, 303–53.

16. See, e.g., Marcus J. Borg, *Jesus-A New Vision: Spirit, Culture and the Life of Discipleship* (San Francisco: Harper & Row, 1987) 57–75; John P. Meier, *A Marginal Jew: Rethinking the Historical Jesus*, vol. 2: *Mentor, Message, and Miracles* (ABRL; New York: Doubleday, 1994) 678–772; E. P. Sanders, *The Historical Figure of Jesus* (London: Penguin, 1993) 144–49.

Snyder's inventory of pre-Constantinian representations (three times total). In fact, of all miracles only Lazarus appears more (five times). Snyder calls these scenes nonnarrative because they are not retelling the story. The typical visual image of this scene is simply a man carrying a bed, in one instance in response to Jesus' gesturing toward him. The other healings and the raising of Lazarus are never portrayed more elaborately than this: Jesus pointing or touching (or being touched) and the person who is healed (pp. 59, 61). The tradition preserves the image of Jesus as deliverer without recalling the actual stories.

The historical analysis of the healing stories as told in the gospels involves factors similar to those applied to the visual tradition. The variations in the details of each story are regularly taken as evidence of the imagination of the storyteller, not as historical reminiscence of actual healings. In the Jesus Seminar's report, therefore, the high level of historical certainty that Jesus was indeed an exorcist and a healer is not reflected in any of the specific stories. The paralytic and several other healings (Peter's mother-in-law, the leper, the woman with a hemorrhage, and the two blind men) are judged to have some likely historical kernel to them, but in each instance contain narrative embellishments.[17] No exorcism story, in fact, is judged to be a report of an actual exorcism, even though Jesus most likely performed some exorcisms.

The visual images of Jesus in pre-Constantinian art thus dovetail in several important ways with the contemporary reconstruction of the historical Jesus derived from the gospels. In both instances we find snapshots of scenes that capture historical moments without necessarily giving reliable reports of specific events. The focus of attention in both cases is aspects of Jesus' life(style) that remain vital to the life(style) of Christian faith communities. Two of the most crucial elements of that way of life are shared meals and healed lives. Snyder is surely correct in looking to the social matrix of the community for a link between these two dimensions.

The Jesus Tradition in Transition

Snyder makes a strong case that the surviving pre-Constantinian archaeological evidence presents a different view of the common life of early Christian faith communities than the "official" view found in most canonical texts, especially the narrative gospels and the Pauline writings. Paul insisted on

---

17. Funk, *Acts of Jesus,* 64, reflecting the color-coding used for each story: basic features are colored pink (as probable), with embellishments gray (improbable) or black (highly unlikely), in contrast with the red (highly probable) used for general statements. It is also noted in most instances that Meier's analysis of the healing stories comes out about the same, e.g., that the story of the paralytic reflects considerable development in its transmission.

a "know-nothing" gospel — that he would choose to know nothing except Christ crucified (1 Cor 2:2). The creed authorized at Nicea vindicated Paul's choice, requiring assent to belief in Jesus' birth, death, burial, and resurrection, without a word about any aspect of his earthly life between birth and death. The complete lack of any images related to Jesus' death in pre-Constantinian art is thus all the more striking — and most likely not just accidental. Snyder's contention that this archaeological evidence represents popular Christianity must be taken seriously. If there is indeed continuity between the historical Jesus tradition and the common life of Christian faith communities in the second and third centuries, other traces of evidence must survive that indicate popular channels of transmission for traditions not contained in the creed and canon of official Christianity. Those other traces can be seen in the literary remains of the Jesus tradition outside the canonical gospels.

The next step is to assess these literary remains by identifying the degree of corroborating evidence they provide for Snyder's picture of popular pre-Constantinian Christianity. The noncanonical (or extracanonical) gospel evidence is especially pertinent in this case because of its circumstantial parallels to Snyder's archaeological evidence.

Snyder's surviving nonliterary evidence derives from the period beginning ca. 180 CE. This is the same general date customarily given for the emergence of the fourfold gospel tradition, as evidenced both by the appearance of Tatian's *Diatessaron* and in the use of the term fourfold gospel (τετράμορφον τὸ εὐαγγέλιον) in Irenaeus (*Adv. haer.* 3.11.8). The oldest surviving canonical list naming the four gospels, the Muratorian Canon, is usually dated only a decade later, ca. 190 CE.[18] Early in the next century we have the earliest surviving four-gospel codex, Chester Beatty I (designated 𝔓⁴⁵). By the beginning of the third century, therefore, the fourfold narrative gospel would seem to have been a well-established tradition.[19]

We need not review here the rest of the canonization process of NT literature, but only recall that the Pauline corpus had already attained the status of "scripture" (2 Pet 3:16), at least in some (official) circles. The ethos of Paul's insistence on "nothing but Christ crucified" (1 Cor 2:2) surely contributed to a collection of canonical gospels that contains only narrative gospels whose most obvious similarity is that they culminate in Jesus' passion narrative. It is thus all the more remarkable that it is precisely during this period that the popular Christianity described by Snyder leaves no trace of interest in

---

18. This dating has been challenged, of course, most notably in Albert C. Sundberg, "Canon Muratori: A Fourth-Century List," *HTR* 66 (1973) 1–41.

19. The evidence has been surveyed most recently in Graham Stanton, "The Fourfold Gospel," *NTS* 43 (1997) 317–46. Stanton accepts the arguments for regarding 𝔓⁴ as part of the same codex as 𝔓⁶⁴,⁶⁷, which would make this the earliest extant four-gospel codex (p. 327).

the death of Jesus. The fourfold narrative gospel tradition was clearly not the only "gospel" tradition thriving in pre-Constantinian Christianity.

Several kinds of evidence demonstrate the diversity of gospel traditions in the second and third centuries. It is in fact difficult to determine what "the gospel" refers to in many early references. Origen provides an example of a completely noncanonical saying, which he calls "the commandment of Jesus," namely, "Be skillful money changers." He then immediately cites 1 Thess 5:21–22 accurately as "the teaching of Paul." Evidently the saying "Be skillful money changers" was extremely popular in early Christianity, surviving in seventy versions. It is said to be in "the gospel," "the gospels," "the scripture," and is attributed to "the Savior," "the Apostle," "the blessed Paul," "the apostolic voice."[20] Origen also preserves a version of *Gos. Thom.* 82, "Whoever is near me is near the fire, and whoever is far from me is far from the kingdom." Even a scholar otherwise skeptical about noncanonical traditions, Otfried Hofius, regards this as a likely authentic saying of Jesus.[21]

The second century is replete with similar examples. *1 Clement* 13 presents a collection of eight sayings prefaced by the phrase "remembering the words of the Lord Jesus." The set of eight is not found in any other text. The series culminates with, "The measure you give will be the measure you get." A somewhat different version of this saying is found in each of the synoptic gospels. The other seven sayings reflect a wide range of similarities and differences with other existing texts, including one without other parallels: "As you are kind, so will kindness be shown to you." This set of sayings in *1 Clement* takes on a life of its own, with versions in Polycarp, Clement of Alexandria, the *Didascalia,* and the *Apostolic Constitutions.* The introduction is always "The Lord/our Savior said/taught us."[22] This becomes a common pattern: a familiar tradition is attributed to Jesus, without claiming to be quoting a source or reproducing verbatim an earlier version of the material.

Several important examples are found in *2 Clement.* For example, *2 Clem.* 8.5 introduces the following text with "The Lord says in the gospel": "If you can't guard a small amount, who will give you a large amount? For I say to you, the one who is trustworthy with the least thing is trustworthy with the most." There is no existing early Christian writing that has this text in it, although it echoes some of Luke 16:10–12. Helmut Koester concludes that *2 Clem.* 8.5 is the "oldest and most original form" of a saying that "must have been circulating in the free tradition of sayings" incorporated into the source

---

20. William D. Stroker, *Extracanonical Sayings of Jesus* (SBLRBS 18; Atlanta: Scholars Press, 1989) 125–28.

21. Hofius, "Unknown Sayings of Jesus," in Peter Stuhlmacher, ed., *The Gospel and the Gospels* (Grand Rapids: Eerdmans, 1991) 336–60.

22. Stroker, *Extracanonical Sayings,* 198–200.

used by *2 Clement*.[23] A wealth of material associated with Jesus in the second and third centuries preserves a mix of extracanonical material and "remembrances" that echo the canonical gospels, without citing them directly. At least for the early Christians who composed these texts, the preference was clearly for oral traditions over written ones, and not limited to material from the narrative gospels.

Another important indication of the amount of Jesus tradition circulating in pre-Constantinian Christianity is seen in the overall manuscript evidence that survives from second- and third-century gospels.[24] Few papyri fragments can confidently be dated before the beginning of the third century, when for the first time significant parts of entire codices survive: $\mathfrak{P}^{45}$ of the four gospels and Acts; $\mathfrak{P}^{66}$ of John; and $\mathfrak{P}^{75}$ of Luke and John. The remaining papyri fragments are typically pieces of single gospels:[25]

Matthew[26]	$\mathfrak{P}^1$ $\mathfrak{P}^{53}$ $\mathfrak{P}^{64,67}$ $\mathfrak{P}^{70}$ $\mathfrak{P}^{77}$
Luke	$\mathfrak{P}^4$ $\mathfrak{P}^{69}$
John	$\mathfrak{P}^5$ $\mathfrak{P}^{22}$ $\mathfrak{P}^{28}$ $\mathfrak{P}^{39}$ $\mathfrak{P}^{52}$ $\mathfrak{P}^{66}$ $\mathfrak{P}^{80}$ $\mathfrak{P}^{90}$ $\mathfrak{P}^{95}$

Of these, only $\mathfrak{P}^{52}$ and $\mathfrak{P}^{90}$ of John are dated earlier than "late second century." There are also multiple fragmentary copies of noncanonical gospel materials:

Egerton Gospel	PEgerton 2 + PKöln 255
Gospel of Mary	PRylands 463, POxy 3525
Gospel of Thomas	POxy 1, 644, 655
Gospel of Peter	POxy 2949, 4009
Infancy Gospel of James	PBodmer 5
POxy 1224[27]	

The one fragment here dated earlier than "late second century" is the *Egerton Gospel*. *Egerton* and the *Thomas* fragments use the same *nomina sacra* abbreviations for Jesus and God that are found in manuscripts of canonical gospels, perhaps suggesting these texts were "scripture" for the faith communities that preserved them.[28] Each of these noncanonical texts contains some narrative

---

23. Koester, *Ancient Christian Gospels: Their History and Development* (Philadelphia: Trinity Press International; London: SCM, 1990) 359–60.

24. See Funk, *Honest to Jesus*, 118.

25. Unless, as noted earlier, $\mathfrak{P}^4$ proves to belong to the same codex as $\mathfrak{P}^{64,67}$.

26. The latest volume of Oxyrhynchus papyri (vol. 64, 1997) includes six small fragments of codex pages of Matthew. POxy 4405 is part of $\mathfrak{P}^{77}$ and POxy 4403 may be from the same codex; POxy 4401 and 4402 are likely from the third century; POxy 4404 is assigned to the "late second century"; POxy 4406 is dated fifth/sixth century. These fragments increase the extant pre-Constantinian papyri of Matthew to about the same number as extant papyri of John.

27. All of these gospel fragments can be found in ET in Robert J. Miller, ed., *The Complete Gospels: Annotated Scholars Version* (rev. ed.; Sonoma, Calif.: Polebridge, 1994).

28. See A. H. R. E. Paap, *Nomina Sacra in the Greek Papyri of the First Five Centuries A.D.: The Sources and Some Deductions* (Papyrologica Lugduno-Batava 8; Leiden: Brill, 1959).

material, but none of them, in the form in which they survive, is a "narrative gospel" in the mode of the four canonical gospels. Apart from the *Gospel of Peter,* which survives only as a passion and resurrection narrative, the other noncanonical texts contain no mention of Jesus' death. This array of gospel manuscripts that survive from before the fourth century (about one-third from noncanonical gospels) presents a highly pluralistic picture of early Christianity. With the virtual fixing of the canon in the fourth century and the production of the first complete Bible codices, reinforced by a normative creed, this diversity of gospels soon disappeared. One vital segment of early Christianity also disappeared — except for the archaeological evidence so well documented by Graydon Snyder.

Conclusion

The common life of early Christian communities, for at least the first three centuries, preserved important elements of the historical Jesus tradition. Two of the most enduring memories of that tradition were Jesus' healings and Jesus' table fellowship. In neither case was the focus the retelling of stories from the narrative gospels, least of all merely for the sake of preserving those stories. Rather, these images sustained the continuing common life of successive faith communities, as they must have done for the communities that first preserved this Jesus tradition before it became a written text. In this way, archaeological evidence for the common life of early Christian communities confirms important continuities with the earliest Jesus tradition.

10

LEADERSHIP AND GOVERNANCE IN THE MATTHEAN COMMUNITY

William Richard Stegner

The presuppositions that I bring to this essay are shared by many who work with the gospel of Matthew today. The first presupposition concerns the *Sitz im Leben* — the social and religious situation — of the Matthean community for whom the gospel was written. Matthew was composed about AD 85 for a Jewish Christian community. This community was observant in that it kept the written law and much of the oral law. Further, this community was engaged in a struggle with the leaders of formative Judaism for the future and loyalty of the Jewish people.

Regarding source criticism, I accept the priority of Mark and the four-source hypothesis. Matthew knew Mark and carefully edited his Markan source to fit the needs of his second-generation community. Regarding redaction criticism, therefore, I have come to reject the presupposition that guided Ernst Käsemann in writing his famous article entitled "The Beginnings of Christian Theology." In that article he proposed that "apocalyptic" was the beginning or cradle of Christian theology and that prophecy, enthusiasm, and typology were all part of that apocalyptic worldview. The author of Matthew had preserved these remnants of the Jewish Christian past, though the author himself was "well on the way to a Christian rabbinate."[1]

Today many would affirm that the author redacted his sources and even wrote much of the gospel himself. However, the author did not focus so much

---

1. Käsemann, "The Beginnings of Christian Theology," in idem, *New Testament Questions of Today* (London: SCM, 1969) 82–107; the German original appeared in *ZTK* 57 (1960) 162–85. The seminal statements — that "it was apocalyptic which first made historical thinking possible within Christendom" and that "apocalyptic was the mother of all Christian theology" — are on pp. 96, 102. Käsemann's comment on "a Christian rabbinate" is on p. 85; cf. p. 84: "Matthew... [is] the representative of an incipient Christian rabbinate."

on preserving the past as on addressing the contemporary conflict with formative Judaism. Thus he causes Jesus to address the contemporary needs of the community and redacts his sources to that same end. So apocalypticism, prophecy, and typology are not so much echoes of the past as aspects of the author's horizon, or worldview.

Let me briefly summarize the purpose of the article and then give greater precision to that summary. While it is not particularly controversial, today, to posit some kind of scribal leadership for the Matthean community, I shall explore the kind of scribal leadership we find within that community. Further, I shall briefly explore the implications of this kind of scribal leadership for the governance of the community.

At this point a brief definition of "scribe" is called for. Scribes were a learned class. They could write when many others could not. They wrote legal documents like bills of divorce and court decisions. They copied Torah scrolls. Accordingly, many, if not most, scribes were experts in the interpretation of the law and, thereby, of the hermeneutical rules by which interpretation was governed.

I shall begin by examining several passages that point indirectly to scribal leadership and then move to two passages that speak directly of scribal leadership. This kind of scribal leadership might well be found within the larger Jewish community, as well as in Matthew's community. Other passages will suggest that the Matthean scribes were the recipients of revelation and visions. And this category of scribal leadership would not necessarily characterize the scribes in the larger Jewish community.

Passages Pointing to Scribal Activity

The first passage is taken from the famous scene at Caesarea-Philippi in which Jesus says to Peter, "whatever you bind on earth shall be bound in heaven, and whatever you loose on earth shall be loosed in heaven." (Matt 16:19b). What is binding and loosing? Binding and loosing is a scribal prerogative since it deals with the interpretation of the law. Indeed, there is a widespread consensus that the power of binding and loosing refers to the right to teach "authoritative *halacha*."[2]

Further, this power seems to be given to Peter alone. While some exegetes maintain that Peter is a representative of the disciples, and therefore that the power is given to the disciples and to the whole church, two facts point in

---

2. W. D. Davies and Dale C. Allison, *The Gospel according to Saint Matthew* (3 vols.; ICC; Edinburgh: T. & T. Clark, 1988–97) 2. 787; this is judged "the major opinion of modern exegetes" (p. 638). See also Graham Stanton, "Ministry in Matthean Christianity," in Douglas A. Campbell, ed., *The Call to Serve: Biblical and Theological Perspectives on Ministry in Honour of Bishop Penny Jamieson* (Sheffield: Sheffield Academic Press, 1996) 157.

the opposite direction. First is the singular pronoun "you": the statement is addressed to Peter. Second, v. 19b is preceded by v. 19a: "I will give you the keys of the kingdom of heaven." J. Andrew Overman observes that in the first century the term "keys . . . is a polemical term that provoked questions about true and faithful leadership."[3] Accordingly, this passage is saying that Peter is the true leader of the people of God and the leadership of formative Judaism is not.

In order to understand the full implications of the power of binding and loosing, we must place it within the contemporary context in which the Matthean community was situated. These terms were far from abstract: they carried "civic, judicial, and political freight." These were the powers that the leaders of formative Judaism claimed for themselves, and indeed used against the Jewish Christians. With these words the leaders of the Matthean community claim the same powers for themselves: "What [Matthew] does assert here . . . is that his community can fulfill these tasks internally and can try not to depend on the external offices and authorities outside his church."[4]

How can the leaders of the Matthean community claim the authority that was given to Peter? Again, the evangelist seems to have his eye on the contemporary situation as he describes the past: "the figure of Peter oscillates between representing the quintessential disciple and being a type of model of a community leader." Just as Matthean Christians identified with the disciples, so the leadership of the church wears the mantle of Peter: "In this instance [Caesarea Philippi], Peter emerges more as a transparent type for a community leader."[5]

Another indirect indication of scribal activity involves the changes the author of Matthew made to Markan conflict stories. Mark reports that Jesus engaged in running legal debates with the Pharisees in stories like Mark 2:23–28. In this story the disciples pluck ears of grain on the Sabbath and the Pharisees accuse them of breaking the Sabbath by reaping — a form of work. In Mark, Jesus justifies the conduct of the disciples by citing a precedent from scripture: David distributed the bread of the Presence (reserved for priests) to satisfy the hunger of his men. In Matthew's retelling, Jesus further justifies the conduct of the disciples by citing a precept from scripture: the priests work in the temple on the Sabbath and are guiltless. Since "something greater than the Temple is here" (12:6), the disciples are also guiltless.

---

3. Overman, *Church and Community in Crisis: The Gospel according to Matthew* (New Testament in Context; Valley Forge, Pa.: Trinity Press International, 1996) 242. See also Davies and Allison, *Matthew* 2. 639. For a contrary opinion, see Stanton, "Ministry," 158.

4. Overman, *Church and Community*, 244–45.

5. Ibid., 240. See also Ulrich Luz, *The Theology of the Gospel of Matthew* (New Testament Theology; Cambridge and New York: Cambridge University Press, 1995) 77: "Jesus' disciples are paradigmatic figures that allow his readers to be contemporary with Jesus."

We see, then, that the Matthean addition in 12:5–6 unfolds according to "the Jewish legal framework."[6] A *halachic* argument must be based on some "precept" found in scripture. Here the precept is that "temple service takes precedence over the sabbath." Further, the argument must be derived from the precept by a recognized hermeneutical rule. Here the rule is *qal wa-homer*, from the light to the heavy. The words "something greater than the temple is here" indicate that either Jesus or the kingdom of God is greater than the temple. So, if the priests who work in the temple on the Sabbath are guiltless, the disciples who work on the Sabbath for Jesus/the Kingdom of God are not at all guilty. The greater sophistication of the argument in Matthew shows familiarity with scribal thinking. Further, it renovates the argument for polemical purposes.

Similarly, the well-known citation formulas, which indicate the fulfillment of OT passages in the life and ministry of Jesus, point to scribal activity. The citation formulas introduce both a kind of typology and passages that (for Matthew) find their fulfillment in Jesus.[7] Scribes were truly people of one book, and the explication of scripture was their specialty.

Now, let us turn to two passages that directly mention scribal leadership. The first and most important is Matt 13:52: "Therefore every scribe who has been trained for the kingdom of heaven is like a householder who brings out of his treasure what is new and what is old." At the end of the discourse on the parables in Matthew 13 there is a brief scene in which Jesus asks the disciples whether they have understood the parables. They answer affirmatively. Then Jesus speaks the above saying. According to a literal reading of the text, the disciples are here declared to be "scribes discipled [trained] for the kingdom of heaven."

While this interpretation is possible, Matt 13:52 seems to address the contemporary situation of the Matthean community in a different way. An indication of this is the positive use of the term "scribe," whereas the majority of uses of the term carry strongly negative connotations. Further, numerous interpreters look upon this verse as the author's self-portrait, or signature. Hence Overman writes of this Jewish-Christian scribe that "the scribe of the Matthean community will be a leader in the community and will provide treasure for its life. These scribes parallel and rival the scribes of formative Judaism."[8]

---

6. Davies and Allison, *Matthew* 2. 313. I follow Davies and Allison closely in writing this paragraph.

7. The definitive work on the "formula quotations" in Matthew is Krister Stendahl, *The School of St. Matthew and Its Use of the Old Testament* (2d ed.; Philadelphia: Fortress, 1968).

8. Overman, *Matthew's Gospel and Formative Judaism: A Study of the Matthean Community* (Minneapolis: Fortress, 1990) 117; Davies and Allison likewise consider Matt 13:52a redactional (*Matthew* 2. 445).

Another positive reference to scribes is found in 23:34: "Therefore I send you prophets and wise men and scribes, some of whom you will kill and cru- cify, and some of whom you will scourge in your synagogues and persecute from town to town. . . . " This saying is located in a passage in which the scribes and Pharisees are denounced: "Woe to you, scribes and Pharisees, hypocrites!" (23:29a). While the combination "scribes and Pharisees" carries negative connotations, "prophets and wise men and scribes" are pictured pos- itively. Indeed, the prophets and wise men and scribes "seem to be Christian missionaries," and the saying emphasizes the reception these missionaries re- ceive.[9] The words "your synagogues" emphasize the distinction between the missionaries and their persecutors. The saying and the passage in which it is located seem to reflect the contemporary situation of the Matthean commu- nity. Whether the compound "prophets and wise men and scribes" describes three different kinds of leaders or represents "facets or modes" of scribal leadership will be explored below.[10]

However, another well-known passage seems to challenge the claim that there was scribal leadership within the Matthean community — indeed, to question whether there was any leadership class at all. Matt 23:8 reads, "But you are not to be called rabbi, for you have one teacher, and you [plural] are all brethren" (RSV). So what does 23:8 indicate? Indeed, generations of Christians have used Matt 23:8 as their virtual justification in creating egalitarian communities.

Was This an Egalitarian Community?

At the start I urged that the writer of Matthew addressed the story and words of Jesus to the contemporary struggles of his community. Today, a scholarly consensus holds that chapter 23, and particularly v. 8, was directed to those struggles.[11] For example, if the key terms in v. 8 — "rabbi," "one teacher," "all brothers [and sisters]" — refer to the contemporary situation, they are addressing an audience different from that of Jesus' day. By now the term "rabbi" is no longer a title of honor bestowed on a distinguished person. Rather, "rabbi" describes the increasingly technical training a teacher was receiving in formative Judaism.

Let us look again at the social significance of the words: "But you are not to be called rabbi, for you have one teacher, and you [plural] are all

---

9. Daniel J. Harrington, *The Gospel of Matthew* (Sacra Pagina 1; Collegeville, Minn.: Litur- gical, 1991) 322, 328. See also David E. Orton, *The Understanding Scribe: Matthew and the Apocalyptic Ideal* (JSNTSup 25; Sheffield: Sheffield Academic Press, 1989) 156. The saying in Matt 23:34 is Matthew's version of the Q saying found in Luke 11:49.

10. Orton, *Understanding Scribe*, 156.

11. Overman, *Matthew's Gospel*, 123; Harrington, *Matthew*, 322.

brothers [and sisters]." These words reject the title "rabbi," the hierarchy it exemplifies, and the privileges given to such teachers. In contrast, Jesus is the only teacher for the Matthean brethren. Further, Matthean Christians are to treat each other as brothers in a family, as participants in an egalitarian community. Clearly this is the message that Matthew, wishing to reflect the mind of Jesus, is teaching.

However, these words are addressed to Matthew's community. While they hold up a specific social ideal, they are doubtless addressing a different reality within that community. Recent interpreters have otherwise described the reality Matthew was striving to correct: "'Do not be called "Rabbi"'... implies striving for scribal honor in the church, possibly by converted scribes belonging to the Pharisees."[12] But "this passage alone virtually establishes the presence of certain institutional roles and a developing hierarchy within the Matthean community."[13] Matt 23:8, then, has a double edge: it is directed against both a tendency within the church and the Jewish leadership outside the church.

Revelation and Vision

Now that I have examined the more conventional kind of scribal leadership within the Matthean community, I turn to an esoteric kind of scribal leadership. A growing number of interpreters are pointing to the importance of revelation and vision in the pages of this gospel. Of course, a vision is one means by which revelation is transmitted. Further, there is evidence that the Matthean scribes, as well as some other scribes of the time, claimed to be recipients of revelation through the medium of visions.

Key passages emphasize the theme of revelation. The famous scene at Caesarea Philippi emphasizes revelation: after Peter identifies Jesus as "the Christ, the Son of the living God" (16:15), Jesus in turn replies that "flesh and blood has not revealed this to you, but my father who is in heaven" (16:17). Similarly, the Matthean version of the famous Q passage — the celebrated "Q thunderbolt" in Matt 11:25–27 — twice points to revelation. Jesus thanks God because "thou [God] hast hidden these things from the wise and understanding and revealed them to babes...." Then in v. 27 we read, "and no one knows the Son except the Father, and no one knows the Father except

---

12. Robert H. Gundry, *Matthew: A Commentary on His Handbook for a Mixed Church under Persecution* (2d ed.; Grand Rapids: Eerdmans, 1994) 457.

13. Overman, *Matthew's Gospel*, 123. To describe the contradiction between reality and ideal, Michael H. Crosby coins the phrase "normative dissonance" (*House of Disciples: Church, Economy, and Justice in Matthew* [Maryknoll, N.Y.: Orbis, 1988] 285); this phrase is an obvious play on the phrase "cognitive dissonance," popularized in the late 1960s.

the Son and any one to whom the Son chooses to reveal him." So even knowledge of God comes through revelation from the Son.

Much the same teaching is found near the beginning of the discourse on parables in Matthew 13. After Jesus tells the parable of the sower in Matt 13:3–9, the disciples ask him why he speaks to the crowds in parables. The reply is given in v. 11: "To you it has been given to know the secrets of the kingdom of heaven, but to them it has not been given." The word "it has been given" is of course a divine passive. It means that God has revealed the mysteries of the kingdom of heaven to the disciples and not to the crowds. Significantly, this discourse ends in v. 52 — in which the disciples are called scribes "trained for the kingdom of heaven." They are "trained" because God has revealed the secrets of the kingdom to them, and (or hence) they understand the parables!

Matthew's editorial work further emphasizes the importance of these three revelation words. It is instructive to document what Matthew adds to Mark's statement. Jesus speaks in parables to "those outside," "so that they may indeed see but not perceive..." (Mark 4:12). Matthew adds to that simple statement a citation formula and then quotes Isa 6:9–10 (already quoted or strongly alluded to in Mark 4:10–12). Matthew then adds the Q saying, "But blessed are your eyes, for they see...." Further, Matthew adds v. 12 at the beginning and changes Mark's "so that" to "because." He is really concerned to say that God has revealed "the secrets of the kingdom of heaven" to the contemporary members of the community — but not to those Jews outside.

Similarly, Matthew frames the Q passage in 11:25–27 with the woes pronounced on the Galilean cities and, in 11:28–30, with the statements concerning the easy yoke: "Come unto me..." (11:28). There is judgment for those outside, but an easy yoke for the recipients of revelation inside. Further, the reader will have noted the importance of the placement of Caesarea Philippi and the transfiguration: they are back-to-back. Both contain important christological statements, and emphasize important roles for the disciples. At Caesarea Philippi, Peter receives revelation, and through him the contemporary scribal leadership also receives its revelation — commission, orders, mission. Again, in the transfiguration story (Mark 9:2–9//), Peter, James, and John experience a vision.

In addition to the revelation described in these three passages, revelation through dreams is recorded in the birth narrative and in the scene before Pilate. Let us now turn to the transfiguration.

The Transfiguration

The story of the transfiguration emphasizes the importance of vision in Matthew. The following paragraphs will examine various aspects of this story. In both Matthew and Mark the *form* of the story is best described as an apocalyptic vision. For example, there are both verbal and formal correspondences between the transfiguration and the apocalyptic visions recorded in Daniel.[14]

However, Matthew emphasizes the visionary nature of the experience *to the disciples* by his redactional touches. As Peter, James, and John come down the mountain, Jesus' vague statement in Mark 9:9, "tell no one what they had seen...," is replaced with Matthew's precise "tell no one the vision..." (17:9). Matthew converts Mark's "what they had seen" into a technical term for vision, ὅραμα.[15] Indeed, Matthew's redacted statement in 17:9b, "Tell no one the vision, until the Son of Man is raised from the dead," seems to point specifically to the LXX of Dan 7:13. There ὅραμα and "son of man" appear in immediate juxtaposition. Matthew also adds 17:16 to the Markan account: "When the disciples heard this, they fell on their faces...." First, Matthew stresses what the disciples *heard* in the vision. In an apocalyptic vision hearing is a central concern because the hearer must report the future to the community. In visions to scribes hearing is equally important: there the concern is the correct interpretation of scripture or the correct *halachic* judgment. Then Matthew notes the response: prostration. Prostration is frequently a response to visions, particularly in apocalyptic texts.[16]

Having examined these formal elements, let us now turn to the content of the story. Certainly, the words of the heavenly voice are the climax of the story. Indeed, the story focuses on Jesus as Son and as an authoritative teacher of Torah. Since the voice quotes the very words "listen to him" that Moses spoke concerning the coming eschatological prophet, the role of that prophet-like-Moses is assumed by the Son (cf. Deut 18:15).[17] However, on a secondary level — and this is my concern — the story says something significant about Peter, James, and John. *They* experience the vision and *they* hear the voice from heaven. Having experienced the vision and heard the words, they now know something no one else knows.

Now recall Overman's comment, already quoted, about Peter at Caesarea Philippi: "in this instance Peter emerges more as a transparent type for a community leader." Do Peter, James, and John also emerge as community leaders

---

14. See Howard Clark Kee, "The Transfiguration in Mark," in John Reumann, ed., *Understanding the Sacred Text: Essays in Honor of Morton S. Enslin on the Hebrew Bible and Christian Beginnings* (Valley Forge, Pa.: Judson, 1972) 149; M. Sabbe, "La rédaction des récits de la transformation," in E. Massaux, ed., *La Venue du Messie: Messianisme et Eschatologie* (RechBib 6; Paris: Desclée de Brouwer, 1962) 67–70; William Richard Stegner, *Narrative Theology in Early Jewish Christianity* (Louisville, Ky.: Westminster/John Knox, 1989) 83–87; Celia Deutsch, "The Transfiguration: Vision and Social Setting in Matthew's Gospel (Matthew 17:1–9)," in Virginia Wiles, Alexandra Brown, and Graydon F. Snyder, eds., *Putting Body and Soul Together: Essays in Honor of Robin Scroggs* (Valley Forge, Pa.: Trinity Press International, 1997) 124–37.

15. Sabbe, "La rédaction," 67.

16. Deutsch, "The Transfiguration," 129.

17. Ibid., 133; the words "Listen to him" in Matt 17:5 are quoted from the LXX.

after this experience? Paul seems to give an answer in Gal 2:9, when he refers to them as "pillars." In Celia Deutsch's judgment, "Matthew 17:1–9 is a scribal visionary text, legitimating not only the teaching authority of Jesus, but also that of the scribes who exercise some of the leadership functions in the Matthean community."[18]

The rest of the NT also supports this assessment. Outside the gospels, the only other mention of the Transfiguration is 2 Pet 1:16–19. There the author claims that the vision confirms his message: "And we have the prophetic word made more sure" (1:19). Like Matthew, he stresses hearing: "we heard this voice borne from heaven...." Further, Paul cites a similar experience in 2 Cor 12:1–5 and boasts that his "visions and revelations" support his credentials against "these superlative apostles" (12:11c). Like Matthew and 2 Peter, Paul also tells us that he *heard* (same verb and tense) things that cannot be said.

Deutsch's interpretation also receives strong support from apocalyptic circles outside the NT. In the Dead Sea Scrolls knowledge of God's will was considered a gift from God, as the Hymns celebrate (1QH 12.11–12). In 4 Ezra, God commissions Ezra by means of a vision (14:1–8), and Ezra "sees" many visions. In *2 Apocalypse of Baruch*, Baruch "sees" visions and then teaches the people. In the *Apocalypse of Peter* from Nag Hammadi (NHC 7,3) Eduard Schweizer notes the first direct evidence of "an ascetic Judaeo-Christian group...still experiencing heavenly visions and prophetic auditions."[19] John J. Collins concludes his study "The Sage in the Apocalyptic and Pseudepigraphical Literature" with this statement: "There are...some consistent features of apocalyptic wisdom that distinguish it from traditional Hebrew wisdom. Most fundamental of these is the claim to have, and reliance upon, a supernatural revelation. Even a sage like Ezra, who disavows heavenly ascents, still relies on dreams and visions."[20] Thus the claim that vision and revelation legitimate the Matthean scribes in their leadership roles has support both within the NT and outside it in apocalyptic circles.

Having sketched the kind of scribal leadership portrayed in this gospel, let us return to 23:34 to tie up a loose end. David E. Orton raises the question whether the phrase "prophets and wise men and scribes" describes three different kinds of leaders or "facets or modes" of scribal leadership. The ghost or influence of Käsemann's approach still seems to hover as some ascribe a separate and distinct role for each category. For example, were the prophets

---

18. Ibid., 125.

19. Schweizer, "The 'Matthean' Church," *NTS* 20 (1974) 216. Further, Stanton ("Ministry," 156) finds that the Jewish-Christian 5 *Ezra* instructs Ezra "to go and convey to the Christian community his prophetic vision (2.48)."

20. Collins, "The Sage in the Apocalyptic and Pseudepigraphical Literature," in John G. Gammie and Leo G. Perdue, eds., *The Sage in Israel and the Ancient Near East* (Winona Lake, Ind.: Eisenbrauns, 1990) 353.

"Christian prophets" who proclaimed "the kerygma"? Did the wise men exhibit "other charismatic gifts in the church"? Were the scribes "the Christian
teachers"?[21] Orton is probably correct in refusing to drive a "wedge" between these three "designations." Indeed, if the above study is correct, the
scribes, who experienced revelation through visions, taught, prophesied, and,
in addition, probably exhibited other charismatic gifts.

This study has convinced me that the scribes exercised a primary leadership role within the community. They studied scripture; they taught; they
issued definitive *halacha,* etc. On the other hand, this is not an exhaustive
account of leadership within this community. I have made no attempt to deal
with the economic life of the community or with the leadership of house
churches, if, indeed, the church met in houses at all.

Governance

While the scribes were the primary leaders of the community, human leadership does not seem to explain all that is involved in the governance of the
community. For example, there are three crucial — and strategically placed —
passages that seem to complete the picture of governance. These passages are,
first, "lo, I am with you always" (28:20b); second, "his name shall be called
Emmanuel...God with us" (1:23b); and third, "For where two or more are
gathered in my name, there am I in the midst of them" (18:20). Governance
seems to be a blend of scribal leadership, on the one hand, and the presence
of Jesus with his church, on the other. The point of contact is revelation
and vision. What we seem to have here is not so much a theocracy as a
Christocracy. I am sure that this is how *they* understood governance.

While there are many discussions of the community's leadership, I have
not read one that would bring together human leadership and the role of
their Lord's continual presence. Most studies simply describe Jesus' continuing presence as an adaptation of the Jewish teaching about the *Shekinah,* and
that probably is true.[22]

I suggest that Matt 18:15–20 could be a case study in relating Jesus'
presence to the governance of the community. In most commentaries vv. 15–
17 are portrayed as showing a logical progression and describing a possible
continuous *process.* But then vv. 18–20 are treated as independent sayings,
somehow tacked on to v. 17. I am suggesting that vv. 15–20 as a whole made
sense to the author and his church even though they baffle some modern

---

21. Orton, *Understanding Scribe,* 156. I follow Orton closely in this paragraph.
22. See David D. Kupp, *Matthew's Emmanuel: Divine Presence and God's People in the First
Gospel* (SNTSMS 90; Cambridge and New York: Cambridge University Press, 1996). Kupp's work
is a very fine theological and exegetical study of Jesus' continuing presence with the church, but
it barely mentions any practical implications for governance.

commentators. These verses describe the case of a sinning member who could be expelled. Verse 18 gives the theological justification for the decision; v. 19 tells of an agreement in a church dispute whose resolution God ratifies; then v. 20 mentions Jesus' presence: "For where two or three are gathered in my name, there I am in the midst of them."

However, Matt 18:20 raises three critical questions when it is compared with 28:20b and 1:23b. First, there is the phrase "gathered in [*or:* into, εἰς] my name. . . ." The phrase "into my name" occurs only here in Matthew. W. D. Davies and Dale C. Allison suggest that the phrase may mean more than the mere act of coming together as Christians. Rather, it may correspond to 1 Cor 5:4: "When you are assembled, and my spirit is present, with the power of our Lord Jesus. . . ."[23] Second, the phrase "in the midst" (ἐν μέσῳ) differs from the preposition "with" (μετά) which precedes "you" (plural) in 28:20b and "us" in 1:23b. Finally, who are the "two or three"? Surely they are not the whole church, not even the "eleven disciples" (28:16), not the "people" whom Jesus would save from their sins (1:21b). Does this different language and smaller number point to a different kind of experience of presence?

I suggest that the "two or three" are scribes and that the more intense language of presence indicates revelation or vision. Through vision or revelation the two or three guide the church to the right decision. Here is a possible blend of scribal leadership and the presence of Jesus in governing his church.

---

23. Davies and Allison, *Matthew* 2. 789. I am indebted to their careful analysis showing the independent origins of vv. 18, 19, and 20; these verses were added to clarify v. 17. J. Duncan M. Derrett argues cogently (on the basis of vocabulary and content) that v. 19 has less to do with prayer than with the resolution of an internal church dispute ("Where Two or Three Are Convened in My Name," *ExpTim* 91 [1979] 83–86).

11

COMMUNAL DISCIPLINE IN THE SOCIAL WORLD OF THE MATTHEAN COMMUNITY

JOHN KAMPEN

The recent publication of fragments from the Cave 4 finds at Qumran have contained additional evidence concerning the sectarian interpretation and presumably use of the laws of reproof as stipulated in Lev 19:15–18. Already known from 1QS (the Rule of the Community) and CD (the Damascus Document), this material permits the development of a fuller picture of their use in these texts and suggests the central role of these laws in sectarian life. This paper will evaluate the interrelationship of the evidence from the Qumran documents, suggesting a development in their purpose and function within the sectarian history. Similarities in the sectarian interpretation of these laws to their formulation in Matt 18:15–20 are also apparent. These similarities will be evaluated and, where applicable, employed to help determine their purpose and function within the Matthean community. The significance of these observations for our understanding of the social world of the Matthean community will conclude the discussion.[1]

---

1. Portions of this paper were incorporated into presentations for the Canadian Society of Biblical Studies at Memorial University, St. John's, Newfoundland, June 13, 1997, and "An International Congress: The Dead Sea Scrolls — 50 Years after Their Discovery," Israel Museum, Jerusalem, June 20–25, 1997.

Reproof in the Qumran Texts

The preliminary publication of 4Q477 (Rebukes of the Overseer)[2] and 4Q286–290 (4QBerakhot)[3] have helped to highlight the significant role of the laws of reproof in the lives of those sectarian Jews who were related to the site of Qumran. This unexplored material, unknown to most researchers until recently, also brings into greater prominence those passages previously available in the Qumran corpus. An analysis of the citations concerning the laws of reproof within the context of the literary development of the Qumran corpus should begin with CD 6.11–7.6.

The importance of this passage in the development of the legislation of the sect can be clearly demonstrated. Jerome Murphy-O'Connor includes this passage of precepts in a section he referred to as a "Memorandum," reminding adherents of the new covenant in the land of Damascus of the basis of their identity and what distinguished them from other Jews,[4] and he details the further specification given to the Holiness Code in the legal section of CD. Building on Murphy-O'Connor's work, Philip R. Davies dubbed the statements of general practice or principle in this section "injunctions," thereby differentiating them from the laws in later texts.[5] He considered them to be an introduction of the basic tenets of the Qumran halakah. A literary analysis supports the contention that these texts appear at an early stage in the development of the legislation described in Qumran texts and do not represent the type of case law found in CD 9–16 to be discussed below.

The importance of Lev 19:15–18 for the author of this section of CD is apparent. That the legal principles and practices specified in CD 6.20–7.3 undergirding the way of life proposed for the adherents of the "new covenant in the land of Damascus" find their biblical warrant in this pas-

---

2. Esther Eshel, "4Q477: The Rebukes by the Overseer," *JJS* 45 (1994) 111–22.

3. Bilhah Nitzan, "4QBerakhot (4Q286–290): A Preliminary Report," in George J. Brooke, ed., *New Qumran Texts and Studies: Proceedings of the First Meeting of the International Organization for Qumran Studies, Paris 1992* (STDJ 15; Leiden: Brill, 1994) 53–72; idem, "4QBerahot^{a-e}(4Q286–290): A Covenantal Ceremony in the Light of Related Texts," *RevQ* 16 (1995) 487–506; idem, "The Laws of Reproof in 4QBerakhot (4Q286–290) in Light of Their Parallels in the Damascus Covenant and Other Texts from Qumran," in Moshe Bernstein, Florentino García Martínez and John Kampen, eds., *Legal Texts and Legal Issues: Proceedings of the Second Meeting of the International Organization for Qumran Studies, Cambridge 1995, Published in Honour of Joseph M. Baumgarten* (STDJ 23; Leiden: Brill, 1997) 149–65.

4. Murphy-O'Connor, "A Literary Analysis of Damascus Document VI, 2–VIII, 3," *RB* 78 (1971) 210–32, esp. 216–20. CD 6.11–7.4 is characterized as "le petite code des douze préceptes" by Albert-Marie Denis, *Les thèmes de connaissance dans le Document de Damas* (Studia Hellenistica 15; Louvain: Publications Universitaires de Louvain, 1967) 124.

5. Davies, *The Damascus Covenant: An Interpretation of the "Damascus Document"* (JSOTSup 25; Sheffield: JSOT Press, 1983) 125–42; idem, *Behind the Essenes: History and Ideology in the Dead Sea Scrolls* (BJS 94; Atlanta: Scholars Press, 1987) 47–48. Note also the discussion in Hartmut Stegemann, *Die Entstehung der Qumrangemeinde* (Bonn: Rheinische Friederich-Wilhelms-Universität, 1971) 150–65.

sage is quite demonstrable. Using Lev 19:18, the initial phrase in 6.20, לאהוב איש את אחיהו כמהו, states an authoritative general principle to under-gird the practices which follow.[6] Using the same grammatical structure whereby the infinitive is used to convey the imperative mood,[7] we find in CD 7.2 the mandate concerning reproof, להוכיח איש את אחיהו, based on Lev 19:17, and the injunction to not bear a grudge, ולא לנטור, from Lev 19:18. Once these obvious passages utilized by the sectarian author are identified, thereby establishing the link with Lev 19:15–18, other phrases also require further examination.

The presence of these verses from Leviticus is apparent in a number of other cases. In 6.21 we find the injunction ולהחזיק ביד עני ואביון וגר ("to strengthen the hand of the poor, the needy and the stranger"), a sectarian in-terpretation of Lev 19:15: לא תעשו עול במשפט לא תשא פני דל ולא תהדר פני גדול ("You shall not do an injustice in judgment, you shall not be partial to the poor or favor the rich").[8] While the biblical phrase speaks of impar-tiality in legal decisions, the sectarian text appears to emphasize support for all of the members of the "new covenant." Elsewhere in CD the verb חזק is used to speak of those who "hold fast to" the sectarian commandments and statutes.[9] The phrase of 6.21–7.1, ולדרוש איש את שלום אחיהו ("a man should seek the peace of his brother"), would then be the sectarian interpretation of Lev 19:16, לא תעמד על דם רעך ("you shall not stand upon [or 'against'] the blood of your neighbor"). The author is not only quoting but very actively in-terpreting this section of Leviticus from the standpoint of the "new covenant in the land of Damascus." There is, however, one phrase in CD 6.20–7.3 which is not as obviously linked to Leviticus 19.

CD 7.1–2 reads as follows: [10]ולא ימעל איש בשאר בשרו להזיר מן הזונות כמשפט ("a man shall not sin against the kin of his flesh; he shall refrain from fornication, according to the commandment"). I have elsewhere identified זנות ("fornication") as one of the central issues in sectarian self-identification addressed in the Damascus Document.[11] Commandments concerning incest,

---

6. The alteration in CD 6.20 to אהיהו from the biblical רעך of Lev 19:18 is noted in Louis Ginzberg, *An Unknown Jewish Sect* (New York: Jewish Theological Seminary, 1976) 202–3. He explains this as an obvious attempt to emphasize the sectarian theology of the author.

7. Jacob Licht, מגילת הסרכים ממגילות מדבר יהודה (Jerusalem: Bialik, 1965) 35–37; Elisha Qimron, *The Hebrew of the Dead Sea Scrolls* (HSS 29; Atlanta: Scholars Press, 1986) 71; Elisha Qimron and John Strugnell, *Miqsat Maase Ha-torah* (DJD 10; Oxford: Clarendon, 1994) 80–81.

8. In his commentary Solomon Schechter points to Ezek 16:49 (*Documents of Jewish Sectaries: Fragments of a Zadokite Work* [prolegomenon by J. A. Fitzmyer; vol. 1; New York: Ktav, 1970] xxxix [71]). The author of CD appears to be utilizing Ezekiel's interpretation of Lev 19:15.

9. CD 3.12, 20; 7.13; 8.2; 19.14; 20.27; cf. Chaim Rabin, *The Zadokite Documents* (2d ed.; Oxford: Clarendon, 1958) 25.

10. That the Hebrew word here is meant to be understood as הזונות is already recognized by Schechter (*Fragments*, xxxix [71]).

11. John Kampen, "The Matthean Divorce Texts Reexamined," in Brooke, *New Qumran Texts*, 149–67, esp. 152–59.

divorce, polygamy, and impurity with regard to menstruation, child birth, etc., all come under this category. Thus we can see that the author of this section of the Damascus Document has integrated a major issue of sectarian identification into a biblical exegesis of Lev 19:15–18. The author argues that adhering to the sectarian interpretation of the laws of זנות is included in the biblical injunction ואהבת לרעך כמוך ("to love your neighbor as yourself"). The same case is to be made for the final clause, ולהבדל מכל הטמאות כמשפטם ("to separate from all [manner of] uncleanness in accordance with their commandment"). Purity is the other issue for sectarian identity emphasized in the Damascus Document. Adherence to the sectarian commandments with regard to such central issues as fornication and purity is the way the member of the new covenant fulfills this biblical commandment. The author has integrated these issues into an exegesis of Lev 19:15–18, thereby providing a biblical justification for their importance in the lifestyle advocated within the document. Since this passage appears to offer an exegetical justification for a surprisingly large number of texts from Qumran with references to reproof, we can see its importance in the development of sectarian legislation.

Within the legal sections of the Damascus Document we find a second passage which is structured as an exegetical comment on the laws of reproof.[12] CD 9.2–8 begins with the citation formula ואשר אמר ("as to that which it says") and then quotes Lev 19:18 with regard to taking vengeance or bearing a grudge. A commentary on the biblical verse follows which concludes with a quotation of the reproof injunction in Lev 19:17, again introduced by the formula אשר אמר. Since the next phrase begins על השבועה ("concerning the oath"), the connection of the quotation from Lev 19:17 with the previous section is clear. That the interpretation of the law of reproof is the major theme is also evident from the content of the passage. The adherent of the covenant who in anger or in order to make the elders despise him presents against his fellow member a case which has not been the subject of reproof before witnesses is said to be violating Lev 19:18. This sectarian stipulation is reinforced by a quotation from Nah 1:2 concerning the same subject. Then CD 9.6 continues: "If he kept silent towards him from day to day[13] and then in anger he reported it and it was a capital offense,[14] he [i.e., the accuser] has testified against himself that he did not keep the commandments of God,

---

12. Lawrence H. Schiffman, *Sectarian Law in the Dead Sea Scrolls: Courts, Testimony and the Penal Code* (BJS 33; Chico, Calif.: Scholars Press, 1983) 89–90. If, when he states that "the requirement of reproof is exegetically derived" with regard to this passage, he means its historical priority over other Qumran texts which discuss the same subject, I would have to disagree and argue for CD 6.11–7.6.

13. See Schiffman, *Sectarian Law*, 91.

14. Schiffman (*Sectarian Law*, 92) asks whether the intent of the passage is to limit it to capital cases.

which tell him, 'You shall surely reprove your brother and not bear sin because of him'" (my translation). While a clear exegetical method is employed
to make the point in this passage, it is important to note that the subject
under consideration is much more specific and well defined than in CD 6–7.
This passage is not justifying the use of the laws of reproof, it is dealing with
one very specific issue in their implementation.[15] It would appear to be the
kind of issue which arises when they are, or at least an attempt is being made
to make them, operational.[16]

Further questions concerning the implementation of the laws of reproof
can be found later on the same folio, CD 9.16–10.3. This section deals with
the capital crime where the violation had only one witness. The issue of the
reproof procedure with regard to a capital crime had already been raised in
CD 9.6. The argument presented in this section is that conviction on a capital crime is possible if the offense has been repeated either two or three times
and one witness is present on each occasion.[17] It seems furthermore to indicate that two witnesses will suffice on issues of property or finance.[18] Also
spelled out in this passage is the role of the מבקר ("overseer") in the process
of reproof: his role is to be present and to record the occasion when a witness
comes forward to make a public reproof.[19] This officer was responsible for
keeping a record of the public rebukes, and it seems likely that he presided
over the procedures. The public nature of this event and the emphasis upon
the written record are both features of this legislation which appear here for
the first time in Jewish history. What about the text which is sandwiched
between the two sections on reproof in CD 9?

The section on oaths in CD 9.8–16 appears to be of consequence for the
development of our subject.[20] While the link between 1 Sam 25:26, a modified citation of which begins this section, לא תושיעך ידך לך ("you shall not

---

15. This approach recasts the argument of Schiffman, who suggests that this text is "the full
explanation of the Qumran law of reproof as a requisite for punishment" (*Sectarian Law*, 93).

16. On this section, see Schiffman, *Sectarian Law*, 89–109. I am less convinced of the implied
chronological relationship between the sections in his claim that CD 7.2–3 "is worded so as to
constitute a direct reference to the law of CDC 9:2–8" (p. 93).

17. While the extent to which this legislation differed from the rabbinic materials has been
noted, there is some disagreement about the particulars of this text, particularly on the number
and nature of the witnesses. See Baruch A. Levine, "Damascus Document IX, 17–22: A New
Translation and Comments," *RevQ* 8 (1972–75) 195–196; Jacob Neusner, "'By the Testimony
of Two Witness' in the Damascus Document IX, 17–22 and in Pharisaic-Rabbinic Law," *RevQ* 8
(1972–75) 197–217; Lawrence H. Schiffman, "The Qumran Law of Testimony," *RevQ* 8 (1972–
75) 603–12; idem, *Sectarian Law*, 73–88.

18. Schiffman, *Sectarian Law*, 96.

19. Charlotte Hempel, "Who Rebukes in 4Q477?" *RevQ* 16 (1995) 655–56; *contra* Eshel
("4Q477," 111–12), who seems to argue that the overseer is the one who carries out the public
rebuke.

20. While Schiffman is correct in pointing to the literary unity of CD 9.10–23, the section
should be viewed as one unit on the law of reproof rather than testimony (*Sectarian Law*, 95).
The literary divisions argued for in this paper also are somewhat broader than his.

seek vindication with your own hand"), and the injunction of reproof may not be apparent, there is good evidence to suggest such a connection.[21] In 1QS 6.27 this same biblical passage is linked with penal procedures, and in 4Q286 the phrase ואל יושע can be found in the column dealing with questions of reproof.[22] More importantly, however, the introductory phrase על השבועה ("concerning the oath") makes sense only if it is understood to be applying to the oath of the witnesses in the cases requiring reproof discussed in the previous, and presumably the following, sections. There is no reason to relate 1 Sam 25:26 to the question of oaths if this is not the case. It is because of the legal requirements for a public and recorded reproof that "whoever causes another to swear in the field instead of before judges or at their decree 'seeks vindication with his own hand.'" The author is linking 1 Sam 25:26 with the laws of reproof in Lev 19:17, presumably because of its sectarian connection with the injunction not to take vengeance. The remainder of the paragraph relates to the use of the oath in cases of missing property: anyone knowing about the missing property of an owner who has sworn a public oath attesting to its absence is himself guilty of theft if he does not come forward. Thus CD 9.2–10.3 is to be understood as one literary unit dealing with the topic of reproof.

The identification of this larger literary unit helps to clarify the breadth of the offenses covered by the laws of reproof in the Damascus Document. The term דבר מות ("capital case") appears in both CD 9.6 and 17 in clauses where the ambiguous syntax makes it difficult to determine whether the legislation is limited to capital cases.[23] CD 9.22–10.3, however, a continuation of the previous paragraph, applies these procedures to a broader range of cases. Issues of property similarly are discussed in ll. 10–16. Nitzan points to the words כל דבר אשר ימעל איש בתורה ("any matter in which a man sins against the law") in 9.16 to demonstrate the breadth of the violations covered by this procedure, "whether . . . ethical, criminal, religious, or those concerning the community's discipline."[24] Capital crimes, of course, as the "worst case scenario," would be the most difficult and hence would require the most clarity in legislative and judicial procedures.[25] Not incidental to the question of the development of this sectarian history is the attention paid to capital offenses. They presumably would not have commanded this amount of attention in an isolated monastic community with a maximum population at any one time of two hundred residents.

---

21. That it is to be understood as a biblical quotation is evidenced by the use of the characteristic opening phrase אשר אמר in CD 9.8–9.
22. Nitzan, "Laws of Reproof," 160.
23. Schiffman, *Sectarian Law,* 92.
24. Nitzan, "Laws of Reproof," 156.
25. Ginzberg, *Unknown Jewish Sect,* 41; Schiffman, *Sectarian Law,* 92.

While the term יכה is not mentioned in CD 8.4–13, the reliance on the earlier interpretation of Lev 19:15–18 is evident in the description of the traitors who rebelled and wallowed in the ways of whoredom and wicked wealth. In ll. 5–6 it is said that "[every] man took revenge and bore a grudge against his brother, [every] man hated his neighbor, [every] man sinned against the kin of his flesh." This passage is further evidence of the importance of this tradition for the adherents of the new covenant in the land of Damascus.

In the legislation spelling out stipulations for life within the *yahad* was included, according to 1QS 5.24–6.1, the obligation for members to reprove one another:

להוכיח איש את רעהו בא[מת] וענוה ואהבת חסד לאיש אל ידבר אלוהיהו
באף או בתלונה או בעורף [קשה או בקנאת] רוח רשע ואל ישנאהו
[בעורלת] לבבו כי ביום יוכיחנו ולוא ישא עליו עוון וגם אל יביא איש על
רעהו דבר לפני הרבים אשר לוא בתוכחת לפני עדים

> ...to reprove his neighbor in truth, humility, and loving charity for one another. No one is to speak to a companion with anger or ill-temper or stubbornly or with a mean spirit of wickedness. He shall not hate him with his uncircumcised heart but on that day he shall reprove him so as not to incur guilt because of him. A man also shall not bring before the association[26] an issue against his neighbor without a prior rebuke before witnesses.[27]

This apparently composite document of communal legislation provides evidence for the importance Lev 19:17–18 held in the life of the sect. These lines follow the section specifying the importance of ranking in communal life based on the annual examination of both inductees and all members. The laws of reproof are set within the context of a communal lifestyle with a high degree of accountability for individual actions. One of the distinguishing features of this text is the role of the law of reproof as an action preliminary to a more public, and what we would assume to be, judicial process, a perspective already identified in CD 9.2–10.3.[28] In 1QS it appears to have been adapted to meet the needs of the *yahad*, the type of social organization not yet fully developed in the Damascus Document.[29]

---

26. This is my attempt to provide an English equivalent for רבים, which is probably quite close to a synonym for יחד in this document, even though the latter is the more specific term, which I assume was used uniquely to designate the sectarian body. See the comment by Eshel, "4Q477," 121.

27. My translation; text in Eshel, "4Q477," 118.

28. James L. Kugel, "On Hidden Hatred and Open Reproach: Early Exegesis of Leviticus 19:17," *HTR* 80 (1987) 43–61; Nitzan, "Laws of Reproof," 150.

29. The term היחיד appears in CD 20.1, 14, 32.

The fundamental importance of the biblical laws of reproof for the development of sectarian legislation is much clearer from the evidence found in the 4QD materials.[30] I have just identified the manner in which the exegetical basis of the laws of reproof is evident in CD 6.20–7.3, how these principles are developed in CD 9.2–10.3 as the basis for the legislation which follows in the subsequent folios and then summarized very briefly in 1QS 5.24–6.2. Prior to the consideration of the 4QD materials the only evidence of the penal code in CD was the fragmentary text at 14.20. 4Q266 (D[a]) 10 i–ii; 4Q267 (D[b]) 9 vi; and 4Q270 (D[e]) 7 i all attest to the presence of a penal code in the D materials.[31] Since CD 14.20 is paralleled in the opening line of the penal code in 1QS 6.24, it seems reasonable to propose that this was the opening line for two or more versions of it.[32] The literary structure of both compositions undergirds the claim that the laws of reproof seem to have functioned as the first step in a process which leads to a more public judicial process for violations of sectarian legislation, for which the penalties were spelled out in its penal code.[33] Other compositions attest to the importance of this legislation for the life of the sect.

4Q286–290 (4QBerakhot), published in preliminary editions by Bilhah Nitzan already cited, appears to contain the fragmentary remains of a covenantal ceremony. Included in these fragments is a description of some laws of reproof that have many similarities to those already described. Nitzan rightly suggests that the literary structure of the extant portion of the laws of reproof can be divided into two sections. Lines 1–4a present the interpretation of Lev 19:17–18 understood by the sectarian author. If the proposed reconstruction is essentially correct, the remainder of the extant material develops the function of these laws within the community.[34] It is important to note that both 1QS 5.24–6.2 and CD 9.2–10.3, which develop the sectarian interpretation of Lev 19:17–18, are followed by a description of the sectarian leadership structure. In 4QBerakhot the subject of instruction and the role of the מבקר

---

30. I assume that 1QS follows CD in the literary tradition of the Qumran documents. For such an argument concerning related legislation, see Joseph M. Baumgarten, "The Cave 4 Versions of the Qumran Penal Code," *JJS* 43 (1992) 268–76. The possibility that some versions of D may have been revised by the community which lies behind 1QS is argued by Charlotte Hempel, "The Penal Code Reconsidered," in Bernstein, *Legal Texts and Legal Issues*, 337–48.

31. See Baumgarten, "The Cave 4 Versions of the Qumran Penal Code," 268–76; idem, *The Damascus Document (4Q266–273)* (DJD 18; Oxford: Clarendon, 1996) 72–75, 110–11, 162–66.

32. Ibid., 72–73.

33. Schiffman, *Sectarian Law*, 94–96; idem, "Reproof as a Requisite for Punishment in the Law of the Dead Sea Scrolls," *Jewish Law Association Studies II: The Jerusalem Conference Volume* (Atlanta: Scholars Press, 1986) 59–74; Nitzan, "Laws of Reproof," 157. *Contra* Moshe Weinfeld (*The Organizational Pattern and the Penal Code of the Qumran Sect: A Comparison with Guilds and Religious Associations of the Hellenistic-Roman Period* [NTOA 2; Freiburg: Universitätsverlag; Göttingen: Vandenhoeck & Ruprecht, 1986] 38–41, 74–76), who dubs the injunctions for reproof "moral sermonizing."

34. Nitzan, "Laws of Reproof," 158–60.

("overseer") in the process of reproof follows the opening exegetical explanation.[35] Thus the literary structure, at least at the level of content, resembles
1QS and CD on this point. The appearance of the word ענש ("punish") in
l. 8 also signals the beginning of a penal code. The remaining lines resemble
the code of 1QS 6.24–7.25, as well as the fragments of 4Q266 (D[a]) 10 i-ii;
4Q267 (D[b]) 9 vi; and 4Q270 (D[e]) 7 i, all of which emphasize the treatment
of fellow members of the sect. This is an extraordinary parallel, pointing both
to the importance and to the consistency of the laws of reproof within the
sectarian social structure.

Noteworthy throughout the Qumran literature discussed to this point is
the educational function of the injunctions related to reproof. It could be
argued that this role is central in the development of a sectarian way of
life. This purpose is specified in CD 15.13–15; 20.1–8; 1QS 8.16b–19; and
4QBer[a] 14.[36] CD 20.3 spells out this responsibility concerning the erring
member: "According to his offense shall men of knowledge reprove him until
the day when he will again stand in the formation of the men of holy perfection."[37] The sectarian membership is not to lose sight of the basic function
of reproof.

Conclusive evidence of the use of the laws of reproof within the sectarian
social structure is found in 4Q477, the Decrees of the Sect.[38] These fragments
contain the phrases [אנשי ה]יחד] ("men of the [commune]") and [מ]חני הרבים]
("[c]amps of the Many"), thereby indicating its usage within the sectarian social structure. In the first fragment, the line [ל]הזכיר את נעויתם] ("[to] make
their offenses be remembered") points to the purpose of this text. Offenses
recorded within the text include "doing evil" in some manner which concerns the רבים ("many"), since this is the word which begins the next line.
Attributed to Johanan ben Ar is the charge that he is קצר אפים ("short-
tempered"), likewise that he possessed a רוח פאארה ("haughty spirit").[39] When
we come to Hananiah Notos, we learn that he "disturbed the spirit of the yahad" and that he לערב, here probably from the root meaning "to mix"; but
the object of this "mixing" is missing from the fragment. The issue of "mixing"
is mentioned in both 11QT and 4QMMT.[40] Of either Hananiah or someone

---

35. This term is reconstructed by Nitzan at this point, though not present in the fragments.
While one cannot be certain about this reconstruction, the presence of the phrases [אנש]י יחד,
[בהו]כיחו לפני ע]דים] and [י]סרו בכול attests to the general subject discussed in these lines.

36. Nitzan, "Laws of Reproof," 157 (note the error in the citation of 1QS).

37. Schiffman, *Sectarian Law,* 170.

38. Eshel, "4Q477," 111–22; Hempel, "Who Rebukes in 4Q477?" 655–56.

39. Since there is a lacuna between the first and second charges it is difficult to say with
certainty that the latter offense should be attributed to Johanan, even though it seems most
likely.

40. The importance of this issue in Qumran literature is amply documented. In 11QT 35.12
and 37.11 the term is used to maintain the separation of the priests and their sacrifices from
the remainder of the Israelites. In 4QMMT C 8 those who "separated from the majority of

else missing from the fragments, it is then charged that וגם אוהב את שיר בשרו ("he also loves his near kin"), presumably because of some failure to reprove him.[41] There is good evidence to support the proposal that שיר in Qumran orthography refers to שאר, thereby referring to "near kin," also alluded to in CD 7.1; 8.6; and 19.19.[42] In CD 7.1 this injunction is found in the context of the discussion concerning reproof discussed above. Finally, Hananiah ben Sim[on] is charged: [וג]ם אוהב את טוב [הצואר] ("[al]so he loves the fair [neck]"), reconstructed on the basis of CD 1.18–19 and alluding to Hos 10:11.[43]

Reproof in the Gospel of Matthew

The interpretation and application of NT texts that concern communal discipline have been both a practical and theoretical problem since the time of their composition. Matt 18:15–20 has been a central text for the discussion of this issue throughout Christian history. While sometimes interpreted within the context of an intra-Christian debate, on the assumption that it reflected tensions over issues of legalism within the early Christian community, alternately interpreters have looked to the work's Jewish context for an explanation of its meaning. Hence it was rabbinic literature that provided the context for an explanation of this passage's meaning.[44] Similarities to passages from 1QS and CD were also recognized quite early in the process of the analysis of the Qumran materials.[45] Nevertheless, as by now I have made clear, it is only with the publication of the additional fragments from Cave 4 that the significance of the exegetical tradition of Lev 19:15–18 in the Qumran texts can be more fully appreciated. This recognition compels us to a more thorough examination of the similarities between this passage in Matthew and the material in the documents from Qumran.

It is clearly demonstrable from the above survey of the interpretive tradition of Lev 19:17–18 that Matt 18:15–17 is closely related to the texts from Qumran. The use of kinship language ("brother") is already rooted in the biblical text, and this is one explanation for the importance of this passage in

---

the people" also distinguished themselves from "being mixed in these matters," apparently with regard to defilement and impurity. It is used with regard to contact with expelled members in 1QS 7.24–25.

41. Eshel, "4Q477," 117–18.

42. Ibid., 112, 117–18.

43. Ibid., 118.

44. Relevant texts are cited in W. D. Davies and Dale C. Allison, *The Gospel according to Saint Matthew* (3 vols.; ICC; Edinburgh: T. & T. Clark, 1988–97) 2. 781–91; the importance of the Dead Sea Scrolls for vv. 16–17 is duly noted (p. 784).

45. See, e.g., Krister Stendahl, "Matthew," *PCB*, 789; Schiffman, *Sectarian Law*, 92; Kugel, "On Hidden Hatred," 55; Eshel, "4Q477," 121.

the sectarian legislation from Qumran. A similar usage can be demonstrated in Matthew, where extensive use is made of this kinship language.[46] The procedure spelled out in Matt 18:15, however, does start out at a different point than the steps recorded in CD 9 and 1QS 5–6. Here the member of the community who saw, or perhaps was victim of,[47] the offense is enjoined to approach the offender privately. This is a significant difference which will receive more discussion below.[48] After this step, however, the similarities are more apparent.

As in both CD 9.3 and 1QS 6.1 the next step, recorded in v. 16, concerns the necessity of witnesses. At this point both traditions have integrated Deut 19:15 into their interpretation of Lev 19:17–18. All three texts point to the necessity that the reproof be stated in the presence of witnesses. Not only do these texts agree concerning this step in the process, they also share the exegetical support required to justify it within their respective processes. Furthermore, both traditions interpret Deut 19:15 as supplying warrant for the necessity of having witnesses to the act of reproof, not to the action that necessitated a response.[49] This interpretation is not self-evident from the biblical text, but there is a remarkable convergence at this point, not only in the practice but also in the exegetical tradition supporting it.

The next step involves an appeal to the assembly, in CD 9.4 to the זקנים ("elders") of the "new covenant in the land of Damascus," in 1QS 6.1 to the רבים, and in Matt 18:17 to the ἐκκλησία. The only other place where the latter term is found in the gospel literature is Matt 16:19. "Church," the usual translation of this word in Matthew, distorts its meaning. It is used in LXX to translate the Hebrew קהל, with reference to an "assembly."[50] In other words, it is the equivalent of the יחד or the רבים in the Qumran texts. The assembly of the community is the final authority in all three cases. The similarity, however, also breaks down at this point. The focus of the legislation in 1QS and CD is to assure proper procedure prior to the hearing of the case before the assembly. The formality of this process is emphasized by the description of the role of the מבקר in CD 9.18 and the records of reproof in 4Q477. The connection of the penal code with this process also emphasizes the formal and

---

46. See, e.g., Anthony J. Saldarini, *Matthew's Christian-Jewish Community* (Chicago: University of Chicago Press, 1994) 91–93.

47. The phrase εἰς σέ ("against you") in Matt 18:15 is absent from a number of ancient MSS; see Bruce M. Metzger, *A Textual Commentary on the Greek New Testament* (2d ed.; London: United Bible Societies, 1994) 36.

48. Kugel, "On Hidden Hatred," 55.

49. Davies and Allison, *Matthew* 2. 784–85; Donald A. Hagner, *Matthew 14–28* (WBC 33B; Dallas: Word, 1995) 532.

50. John Kampen, *The Hasideans and the Origin of Pharisaism: A Study in 1 and 2 Maccabees* (SBLSCS 24; Atlanta: Scholars Press, 1988) 82–87; cf. Davies and Allison, *Matthew* 2. 785: "The local community is here meant, not the church universal."

final decisions of the assembly.[51] We do have to remember, however, that the sectarian membership did have literary reminders of the educational function of reproof with regard to its erring members, cited in passages such as CD 15.13–15; 20.1–8; 1QS 8.16b–19; and 4QBer[a] 14. The Matthean legislation, in contrast, emphasizes the earlier stages in the process, the personal appeal in the first instance and then the presence of two or three other members of the sect as witnesses. In Matthew the appeal to the assembly is described as significant only after the failure of these other steps. The significance of this difference in emphasis requires further examination.

Matthew 18 constitutes a redactional unity, with only a limited amount of material found in synoptic parallels.[52] As has been noted, Matt 18:15–20 is surrounded by material which emphasizes inclusion and forgiveness. Verses 6–7 concentrate on care for "the little ones," and vv. 10–14 reflect concern for the lost sheep who has gone astray. Significantly, the author of the first gospel describes this sheep with the verb πλανάω ("go astray") rather than ἀπόλλυμι ("lose"), as in Luke 17:14.[53] Erring members of the sect are the concern of this parable in Matthew. Following the section on communal discipline we find an explicit discussion of the meaning of forgiveness for the adherents of the Matthean group, including the question about the number of times forgiveness is required and the parable of the unforgiving servant.[54] The meaning of the communal legislation for the Matthean group can be determined only within this context. What, then, is the meaning of the second half of the passage, which begins at Matt 18:18: "Truly I tell you, whatever you bind on earth will be bound in heaven and whatever you loose on earth will be loosed in heaven"?

This phrase also appears in Matt 16:18–20, in this case in the singular and addressed to Peter. As already observed, this is the only other place in the gospel where we also find the term ἐκκλησία. In this passage Peter is given the keys to the kingdom of heaven. A full analysis of the role of Peter is a subject far beyond the scope of this paper. There seem to be two primary interpretations given for the meaning of the binding and loosing in these two passages: it is either a mandate to provide authoritative legislation regarding issues pertaining to the life of the early Christian community addressed in the book or gives the authority to exclude people from that community and

---

51. The obligatory and formal nature of the laws of reproof in CD 9.28 is also emphasized by Davies, *Damascus Covenant*, 132.

52. J. Andrew Overman, *Matthew's Gospel and Formative Judaism: The Social World of the Matthean Community* (Minneapolis: Fortress, 1990) 101; Margaret Davies, *Matthew* (Sheffield: JSOT Press, 1993) 129.

53. Overman, *Matthew's Gospel*, 101.

54. Ibid., 102–3; Saldarini, *Matthew's Christian-Jewish Community*, 92; M. Davies, *Matthew*, 129.

reinstate them.[55] To understand the phrase we need to examine the imagery which lies behind it.

We must begin with the keys of the kingdom. J. Andrew Overman has pointed to passages such as 2 Bar. 10.18 in post-70 Jewish literature in which the priests give up the keys of the temple because of their failure to exercise proper stewardship of their divinely appointed trust: "You, priests, take the keys of the sanctuary, and cast them to the highest heaven, and give them to the Lord and say, 'Guard your house yourself, because, behold, we have been found to be false stewards.' "[56] G. W. E. Nickelsburg has pointed to parallels between 1 Enoch 12–16; T. Levi 2–7; and this commissioning story in Peter.[57] This and other evidence suggests that Peter is sometimes modeled after the high priest; more importantly, that this sectarian community of the followers of Jesus was inspired by the model of a glorious and perfect future temple in which Jews would be able to live as God wanted.[58] The sectarian community incorporated aspects of this future temple into their communal life.

This viewpoint, of course, is also familiar to us from a number of Qumran texts, and the significance of this line of argumentation for the meaning of the binding and loosing texts in Matthew is then clear. Priests in the temple had the authority both to provide the authoritative interpretations of the purity laws which would safeguard that institution's sanctity and to enforce those laws by prohibiting entry to violators. In Matthew 16 and 18, Peter and the early Christian community are given the authority to legislate the way of life of the early followers of Jesus. Presumably this legislation also incorporated their hopes for the future life of the Jewish community. The conclusion of the work, in Matt 28:16–20 (often referred to as the "Great Commission"), suggests fairly grandiose expectations that the entire gentile world would also be interested in the perfect life desired by the Jewish God.

The role of reproof within the formal legal structures specified in the texts from Qumran has been outlined above. 1QS 5.25–6.1 situates the injunction to reprove within the context of the moral expectations of the sect and sets forth its importance in the communal procedures for addressing wrongs within the group. Regarding CD 9, I noted the manner in which the injunction to reprove is integrated into a discussion of the issue of the number of witnesses required for conviction. Here Lev 19:17–18 is dealt with as a literary unit so that reproof is related to the commandments not to take

---

55. G. W. E. Nickelsburg, "Enoch, Levi, and Peter: Recipients of Revelation in Upper Galilee," JBL 100 (1981) 575–600, esp. 594. A variety of interpretations are listed in Davies and Allison, Matthew 2. 635–41.

56. Overman, Matthew's Gospel, 20–21, with reference to 2 Bar. 10.18; 4 Bar. 4.4 (Jeremiah casts the keys toward the sun).

57. Nickelsburg, "Enoch, Levi, and Peter," 590–600.

58. John Kampen, "A Reexamination of the Relationship between Matthew 5:21–48 and the Dead Sea Scrolls," SBLSP 29 (1990) 34–59, esp. 48–50.

vengeance or bear a grudge. As noted, this text moves the discussion into the more serious infractions regarding crimes which involve capital punishment. The serious nature of this penal code means that the analysis of Moshe Weinfeld must be called into question when he proposes the following conclusions concerning this text: "As in other issues, this issue also deviates from legal, formalistic wording and passes into moral sermonizing."[59] While this might be true when compared with materials in the Iobacchi codes, the above analysis of the development of this interpretive tradition suggests otherwise. Given the manner in which this issue appears in a variety of sectarian compositions, its importance for the functioning of a religious group is not to be underestimated. Of the greatest significance is the fact that it is part of a penal code prior to Matthew.

An examination of the Matthean code within the context of the history which has been sketched above helps to clarify its intent and purpose. When we compare Matt 18:15–20 with the range of perspectives and roles regarding reproof in the Qumran documents, we find that it is closest to the legislation in 1QS, where the adherent is charged with the obligation "to reprove his neighbor in truth, humility, and loving charity for one another"; where, moreover, "no one is to speak to a companion with anger or ill-temper or stubbornly or with a mean spirit of wickedness." The motivation behind these prescriptions seems to be the maintenance of a satisfactory level of personal relationship among its members. The purpose of the legislation in CD 9 appears to be more legalistic, i.e., interested in the development of a strict legal code by which the Qumran group could regulate acts of perceived deviance among its membership. The educational function of reproof (noted in CD 15.13–15; 20.3–8; 1QS 8.16b–19; and 4QBer[a] 14) would have served an important purpose for both sectarian groups. Joseph Baumgarten has suggested that 1QS reflects a later period in the development of the Qumran legal code than CD and related fragments from Cave 4.[60] This means that from among the Qumran writings on this subject 1QS would be chronologically closest to the time of composition of Matthew.

It is quite clear from the context of Matthew 18 described above that there is a fundamental difference in the ideology undergirding the legislation between the Matthean group and the viewpoints reflected in the Qumran texts. Understanding the procedures for the appeal of grievances within the context of an emphasis on "brotherly" relationships is not peculiar to that study, and has been noted in recent studies of the social world of Matthew, including references to the repetition of brotherhood language throughout the work (especially in the Sermon on the Mount and chapter 18).[61] The explanation

---

59. Weinfeld, *Organizational Pattern*, 40.
60. Baumgarten, "The Cave 4 Versions of the Qumran Penal Code," 268–76.
61. Goran Forkman, *The Limits of Religious Community: Expulsion from the Religious Community*

for this emphasis in recent studies of the social history of Matthew "is that Matthew has shaped and constructed this traditional material in such a way as to provide instruction for his community about dealing with dissension and erring members.... The whole of chap. 18...aims at dealing with the problem of division within the community...."[62] This perception appears to be rooted in earlier redaction-critical work which argued that Matthew's use of the law had a twofold purpose: to describe the relationship of the Matthean community to Judaism and to counter antinomian tendencies within the Christian movement. A twofold emphasis appeared necessary to these redaction critics because they were unable to provide a comprehensive viewpoint that would account for the apparent variety of views concerning the Torah to be found in Matthew. If, however, there was more than one Torah in the Jewish community of Matthew, new possibilities for understanding open up.

Implications for Social History

In this paper I have made two assumptions that must be identified, but also clarified. The first is that I am willing to deal with the text of the first gospel as representing "the Matthean group and its spokesperson, the author of the Gospel of Matthew."[63] While recognizing the somewhat naive nature of the claim, I consider this assumption necessary to advance the study of social history related to this document. I do not find that we possess demonstrated methodologies that can permit us adequately to distinguish between the text and the social context it assumes. A surface reading, particularly of the didactic portions of the text — the Sermon on the Mount, for instance — suggests to me that in any case this assumption is warranted for the gospel of Matthew.

The second assumption is that the manuscript evidence from the caves near Wadi Qumran comprise some of the literary remains of a Jewish movement that was spread throughout Judea and Galilee in the latter centuries of the Second Temple era. While I accept the identification of the Essenes both with this literature and with the Qumran site, the evidence suggests a complex history and a diversity of viewpoints which are not to be simplistically harmonized.

Earlier I identified sectarianism with regard to our conception of Qumran. It is also an issue when we attempt to understand the social world of

---

within the Qumran Sect, within Rabbinic Judaism, and within Primitive Christianity (ConBNT 5; Lund: Gleerup, 1972) 123; Overman, Matthew's Gospel, 102–3; Saldarini, Matthew's Christian-Jewish Community, 92.

62. Overman, Matthew's Gospel, 101.

63. So Saldarini, Matthew's Christian-Jewish Community, 1. This explicit statement with regard to the assumption that there is a direct connection between the text, its author, and the community out of/for which it was written undergirds the present study as well.

Matthew, a topic I have discussed elsewhere.[64] I will not repeat the detailed argumentation that I presented before, but rather summarize some specific observations concerning the topic addressed in this paper.

In his study of the Matthean community Overman describes the sectarian context of first-century Judaism. Helpful for the purposes of this essay is Overman's discussion of the definition of the term "sect":

> While avoiding a comprehensive definition of the term sect, we follow J. Blenkinsopp in taking the term sectarian to mean a group which is, or perceives itself to be, a minority in relation to the group it understands to be the "parent body." The sect is a minority in that it is subject to, and usually persecuted by, the group in power. The dissenting group is in opposition to the parent body and tends to claim more or less to be what the dominant body claims to be.[65]

The evidence presented in this paper suggests that both groups saw themselves as a minority in opposition to a parent group. When we examine the history of interpretation of the laws of reproof, it appears that the Matthean version was subsequent to the evidence from Qumran and aware of the interpretive traditions represented in those texts. This evidence suggests that the author of this gospel was in dispute with a variety of movements. We cannot account for the evidence of a clear historical development through the Qumran literature which continues into Matthew without recognizing the importance of that observation. The scattered evidence for the presence of legislation from Qumran throughout the first gospel can best be explained by the hypothesis that there were persons within the same Jewish community who knew and presumably lived by that legislation. In the case of Matt 18:15–20 we see enough evidence of the Qumran process for dealing with reproof to argue that there is a connection. Similarly the initial personal appeal and a relative lack of emphasis on a formal process for the entire assembly suggests a disagreement with this rival sect. If this is true, then we need to reevaluate the social history of the Matthean community in the following manner.

---

64. John Kampen, "The Sectarian Form of the Antitheses within the Social World of the Matthean Community," *DSD* 1 (1994) 338–63, esp. 357–63.

65. Overman, *Matthew's Gospel*, 8–9; citation of Blenkinsopp from "Interpretation and the Tendency to Sectarianism: An Aspect of Second Temple History," in E. P. Sanders, A. I. Baumgarten, and Alan Mendelson, eds., *Jewish and Christian Self-Definition*, vol. 2: *Aspects of Judaism in the Graeco-Roman Period* (Philadelphia: Fortress, 1981) 1–26 (pp. 1–2 for this discussion). See also L. Michael White, "Crisis Management and Boundary Maintenance: The Social Location of the Matthean Community," in David L. Balch, ed., *Social History of the Matthean Community: Cross-Disciplinary Approaches* (Minneapolis: Fortress, 1991) 211–47, esp. 223–24. This article builds on his earlier discussion, "Shifting Sectarian Boundaries in Early Christianity," *BJRL* 70 (1988) 7–24.

The Pharisees and the scribes were the emerging leadership of the Jewish community in which the adherents of the way of life advocated in the first gospel were located. However, they were not the only Jewish rivals of the followers of Jesus in this community. Other sectarian groups were also present. Because we by accident came across their literature, we can find evidence of the group described in the Qumran sectarian compositions. The nature of this discovery should caution us against assuming that this was the only other sectarian group represented in that Jewish community. These sectarians probably agreed in their appraisal of the Pharisees and scribes. Such agreement, however, did not make these groups friends. I would argue that they were in vigorous competition with one another for the heart and soul of that community. Each group believed that the future of Judaism was at stake. This means that the debates about the nature and fulfillment of the law in Matthew were probably not representative of various groups within the first-century Christian movement. This study suggests rather that these followers of Jesus were in competition with a variety of perspectives found within the Jewish community of which they were a part.

This provides evidence of other sectarian Jewish groups which existed in the same Jewish community as Matthew. Issues such as the definition of group membership, the ideology around which group cohesiveness was constructed, and the appropriate methods for dealing with deviant members were of paramount importance. The community identified with Matthew was not merely in conflict with whatever historical reality was behind the portrayal of the Pharisees in that composition. The claim of authority, implicit in the statements concerning the keys of the kingdom, was also directed to other sectarian groups with whom the Matthean followers of Jesus were in conflict.

12

LUKE'S PORTRAIT OF SIMEON
(Luke 2:25–35)

Aged Saint or Hesitant Terrorist?

James LaGrand

The Simeon who held the baby Jesus in his arms in the temple has been old for a very long time.[1] Christmas church bulletin covers and Sunday school pictures take their places in a long tradition of iconography which represents the saint as an age-mate of the eighty-four-year-old Anna. Stained glass church windows, Renaissance paintings, medieval frescoes, and ancient mosaics of "the Presentation in the Temple" all agree about Simeon's place in Anna's age cohort — and the text stating Anna's age perhaps should be interpreted as 108 instead of eighty-four.[2]

If there is an ancient or modern picture anywhere representing Simeon as a young man, I have not seen it. Nevertheless, a fresh reading of Luke's text suggests a portrait of an eager, devout young man seeking divine direction in the temple, where he meets the newborn messiah and is transformed by a prophetic vision of the peaceable kingdom.

An examination of Luke's text in its historical setting supports this picture of an intensely religious youth deflected from terrorism. Before turning to the text, however, we should consider the weight of the long tradition of

---

1. As a gift to Graydon Snyder this essay can be compared to the tennis balls that the shepherds in the medieval mystery play bring to the baby Jesus. Like those shepherds, I can present only what I have. Professor Snyder's interest in early Christian art, his lifelong commitment to careful reading and rereading of biblical texts, and his imaginative persistence in relating scripture to personal and social experience give me confidence that he will accept my awkward questions graciously, even if he remains unconvinced by my answers.

2. Depending, that is, on whether the number refers to her actual age or the length of her widowhood.

written interpretation that supports the concept projected by the icons of
an aged saint. The idea seems to have been well established already in the
third century. Origen describes an old man eager to be released "from the
bonds of the body."[3] Although Origen himself warns against taking "refuge in
allegories,"[4] a picture emerged from his and like interpretations which makes
Simeon the representative of the OT prophets now stepping aside (to die) in
order that the infant messiah might usher in the new age.[5] The ideology of
this formulation is as clear as it is in the New Year's eve cartoons on modern
newspapers' editorial pages: the creaky figure of the Old Year hands over to
the baby wrapped in a ribbon, inscribed "New Year."

The liturgies of the church, allusions in European literature, and innumer-
able sermons have established the Simeon of the canticle Nunc Dimittis as
an important model of a believer ready and willing to cast aside the burdens
of life for salvation and a peaceful death.[6] Somewhat surprisingly, very early
Christian art does not include pictures of Simeon, although there are pictures
of the magi.[7] When Simeon is portrayed in a fifth-century mosaic in Rome,
he is already old.[8] The text of the eighth-century Latin *Gospel of the Nativity
of Mary* specifies his age as 113,[9] which gives him seniority over Anna even
if we understand Luke's text to mean that she had been "a widow for eighty-
four years." "Old Simeon" is portrayed frequently in early Italian Renaissance
painting and, memorably, by Rembrandt. Modern visual aids follow up on the
Christmas story with the picture of a very old man holding the baby Jesus.
This universal artistic agreement would therefore seem to pass Vincent of
Lérins's test of what is believed in all times and in all places by all the faithful.

Besides the conservative pressures to protect traditional icons and the
pious impulse to preserve humane values associated with accepted teachings
of the church, there are also new methods in the field of biblical studies
which discourage any attempt to determine Simeon's age cohort. Simeon and

---

3. Origen *Hom. in Luc.* 15; ET in Joseph T. Lienhard, *Origen: Homilies on Luke, Fragments
on Luke* (FC 94; Washington, D.C.: Catholic University Press of America, 1996) 62. Origen says
something similar in his *Dialogue with Heraclides*.

4. Origen *Hom. in Luc.* 6 (Lienhard, *Origen: Homilies*, 67).

5. Cf. Ephrem, writing in the fourth century: "The words of Simeon, 'You may dismiss your
servant in peace,' apply to the Law" (ET in Carmel McCarthy, trans., *Saint Ephrem's Commentary
on the Diatessaron: An English Translation of Chester Beatty Syriac* MS 709 [JSSSup 2; Oxford:
Oxford University Press, 1993] 67).

6. The *Shorter Oxford English Dictionary* defines "to sing (one's) Nunc dimittis" as "to declare
oneself contented to depart from life or from some occupation," a definition that preserves the
ambiguity of the biblical text, as do the liturgies of the church.

7. See Graydon F. Snyder, *Ante Pacem: Archaeological Evidence of Church Life before Constantine* (Macon, Ga.: Mercer University Press, 1985) 58.

8. See Beat Brenk, *Die frühchristlichen Mosaiken in S. Maria Maggiore zu Rom* (Wiesbaden:
Steiner, 1975).

9. Cited in F. W. Farrar, *The Gospel according to St. Luke* (Cambridge: Cambridge University
Press, 1889) 72.

Anna are seldom treated as historical figures by modern NT scholars. Even so, it is hard to deny that Luke's narrative is historical, or at least historicizing: either Luke thought Simeon and Anna actually saw the baby Jesus, or the author supposed that it would be instructive for his first readers to imagine two such persons in the time and place he describes. Accordingly, it makes sense to attempt a close reading of the text in its historical context for an understanding of the portrait of Simeon that Luke intended his readers to see.

At the risk of unsettling senior citizens whose pastors have offered them comfort with the picture of old Simeon going peacefully to his grave, and with the certainty of confusing Sunday school children and annoying their teachers, I propose a picture of Simeon as a young freedom fighter. In our new age of icons it is probably necessary to project the video before recording the arguments. Imagine, then, a man of military age, inclined to fight against God's enemies, but hesitating until arrested by a flash of insight that "It is not lawful for me to fight" — like the fourth-century Martin of Tours.

The Setting of Luke 2:25–35 in Prerevolutionary Palestine

Luke wrote his two-part treatise before AD 135, perhaps, as Adolf Harnack thought, before AD 67.[10] The setting of the narrative of Luke 2 is earlier, "in the days of Herod of Judea" (Luke 1:5). Herod himself was a catalyst for zealous opposition to Roman rule and a tyrant able to keep such opposition under control. The violence unleashed immediately after his death in 4 BCE shows that the Jewish freedom fighters were more than bandits (λῃσταί).[11] Following a protest by "teachers of the Law" (ἐξηγηταί, Josephus *Ant.* 17.216), Herod's designated successor Archelaus ordered his troops to attack the Passover crowd, scattering them and killing three thousand. Fifty days later, while Archelaus was in Rome, a vast number of Jewish pilgrims organized themselves into three camps to protect the Temple. Varus, the governor of Syria, led the Roman troops to disperse the rebellious crowd. Although the mob lacked the organization and discipline to fight the Roman

---

10. Harnack, *Neue Untersuchungen zur Apostelgeschichte und zur Abfassungszeit der synoptischen Evangelien* (Leipzig: Hinrich, 1911), cited in Ernst Haenchen, *The Acts of the Apostles: A Commentary* (Philadelphia: Westminster, 1971) 32. Note more recently the survey and argument in John A. T. Robinson, *Redating the New Testament* (London: SCM, 1976) 86–117.

11. See Martin Hengel, *The Zealots: Investigations into the Freedom Movement in the Period from Herod I until 70 A.D.* (Edinburgh: T. & T. Clark, 1989) 41, where Hengel reviews the various names given to the Jewish freedom movement and its protagonists. In our own time as well, established governments, such as the former apartheid regime in South Africa, typically refer to freedom fighters as terrorists. Both "assassins" (NRSV) and "terrorists" (NIV) are appropriate translations of σικάριοι in Acts 21:38.

troops, Varus saw enough coherence in the movement to track down and crucify two thousand of the "principal culprits" (Josephus *J.W.* 2.75).[12]

Judas of Galilee who is designated, famously, by Josephus as the founder of "the fourth school of philosophy among the Jews" was already active in the year of Herod's death, capturing for a time the royal armory at Sepphoris.[13] This Judas is also cited by Luke in Gamaliel's speech during the apostles' trial (Acts 5:37).[14] According to Josephus, Judas the Galilean (together with Saddok, a Pharisee) "established the roots of the evils that occurred at a later period by a doctrine of a kind that had never been heard before" (Josephus *Ant.* 18.9). The fundamental doctrine and defining characteristic of the philosophy was that "it recognized only God as ruler and Lord." Adherents would "call no man Lord (δεσπότης)."[15] Josephus's characterization of the movement as a "school of philosophy" can be explained variously, but it seems that Judas was a teacher as well as a warrior.[16] Building on traditions of pious zeal, Judas's teaching achieved the unique focus which Josephus deplored in the sect's response to the Roman census of AD 6.

In different ways, both Josephus and Luke stress the importance of the census of AD 6 and the resistance movement's totalitarian demand of loyalty to God. The literary function of Augustus, Quirinius, and the census in Luke 2 is clear.[17] As a source of historical information, however, Luke 2:2 (together with Luke 1:5) is notoriously problematical. This is not the place to attempt to settle that issue, except to refer to John T. Nolland's recent survey of the arguments and his own acceptance of Luke's account as documentary evidence for an enrollment in the days of Herod.[18] Nolland translates Luke 2:2 "This registration happened before Quirinius became governor of Syria." If this position can be sustained, the argument for accepting Luke's

---

12. Quoted in Hengel, *Zealots*, 327. Cf. William R. Farmer, "Judas, Simon and Anthronges," *NTS* 4 (1957–58) 147–55.

13. Josephus *J.W.* 2.117–19; *Ant.* 18.9. Hengel's reading of Josephus convincingly identifies Judas, son of the "robber captain" Hezekiah, with Judas the Galilean (*Zealots*, 327).

14. Note here, first, that the high priest and those with him were "filled with zeal" (ἐπλήσθησαν ζήλου, Acts 5:17), and second, that Luke's Gamaliel confuses the historical order of Theudas and Judas the Galilean if, as modern translators agree, μετὰ τοῦτον is taken to mean "after him."

15. Quoted in Hengel, *Zealots*, 77.

16. "Judas the Galilean, the son of Hezekiah, is spoken of . . . as one of the scholarly Hasidim," according to K. Kohler ("Zealots," *Jewish Encyclopedia* 12 [1906] 641); cf. Hengel, *Zealots*, 87, 332–34. Kohler's article remains a very useful summary of the development of what might be called the theology of zeal; cf. William R. Farmer, "Zeal," *IDB* 4 (1962) 936–38.

17. See Joel B. Green, *The Gospel of Luke* (NICNT; Grand Rapids: Eerdmans, 1997) 125; Joseph A. Fitzmyer, *The Gospel according to Luke I–IX* (AB 28; Garden City, N.Y.: Doubleday, 1981) 399–406; Raymond E. Brown, *The Birth of the Messiah: A Commentary on the Infancy Narratives in Matthew and Luke* (Garden City, N.Y.: Doubleday, 1977) 412–18.

18. Nolland, *Luke 1–9:20* (WBC 35A; Dallas: Word, 1989) 99–105; see also Nolland's extensive bibliography on the census (ibid., 94–96); cf. I. Howard Marshall, *The Gospel of Luke: A Commentary on the Greek Text* (NICNT; Grand Rapids: Eerdmans, 1978) 104.

representation of Simeon as historical (rather than as historicized) would be strengthened. At best it could mean that not only the oracle recorded by Luke but also other things Simeon said in his lifetime might have been re-membered and cited after Pentecost. In any case, an appreciation of Luke's portrait of Simeon requires an awareness of the claims made on pious Jews by zealous propaganda during the last years of Herod and the census of AD 6.

Many modern scholars prefer to limit the use of the label "Zealots" to the partisans in the final conflict of AD 132–35, and as a strict designation this is doubtless correct.[19] But already at the time of Jesus' birth and during his ministry, some pious young men were engaged in disciplinary violence against persons thought to be introducing the pollution of the nations into Israel. Luke was certainly aware of this zealous piety, as his description of the character and actions of the young Saul/Paul shows (Acts 9:1).

Luke's Simeon

Young men in many different times and cultures have felt called to serve in their country's armed forces or in underground resistance against foreign oc-cupying forces. Accordingly, some intense, devout teenagers and young adults in the time Luke describes would have struggled to decide if God were calling them to military engagement — perhaps even to suicide attacks against over-whelming force. In Luke's account, Simeon seems to be just such a young man, focused on the coming messianic age. He was watching and waiting for (προσδεχόμενος) "the consolation of Israel" (Luke 2:25; cf. Isaiah 40); in-deed, "it had been revealed to him by the Holy Spirit that he would not see death before he had seen the Lord's Messiah" (Luke 2:26, NRSV).

Luke says nothing about Simeon's age, but he specifies his gender, current residence, and reputation, as well as telling his name. The grammar of the first sentence Simeon speaks, often misrepresented in translation, is crucial to Luke's portrait. These first words testify to Simeon's self-understanding and, I propose, mark his conversion. Reference to "the nations" declares his new position and mark his lasting contribution to the messianic movement, in anticipation of Pentecost. Finally, the imagery of the sword concludes the oracle and completes Luke's portrait.

Simeon's name is itself significant. Simeon and Levi (Genesis 34; cf. Jdt 9:2–4), along with Phinehas (Num 25:1–8), Elijah (1 Kgs 18:40; 19:10–14), and the Maccabees, were models in the piety of zeal. Simon, the second son

---

19. See David M. Rhoads, *Israel in Revolution, 6–74 C.E.: A Political History Based on the Writings of Josephus* (Philadelphia: Fortress, 1976) 2; Richard A. Horsley, *Jesus and the Spiral of Vi-olence: Popular Jewish Resistance in Roman Palestine* (San Francisco: Harper & Row, 1987) 56–58, 77–89; Sean Freyne, *Galilee, Jesus and the Gospels: Literary Approaches and Historical Investigations* (Philadelphia: Fortress, 1988) 162–64, 195.

of Mattathias, was a leader in the Jews' fight against Seleucid rule. One of the sons of Judas the Galilean who was crucified in about AD 48 was also named Simon (Josephus *Ant.* 20.102). The only disciple of Jesus designated by Luke as a "Zealot" (Luke 6:15; Acts 1:13) was a Simon. Many other examples could be cited.[20] On the one hand, if Luke were creating a character to represent a zealot (a young recruit of the *sicarii*, perhaps) stopping at the Temple for divine confirmation of wavering convictions, he probably would have called him "Simeon," "Phinehas" or "Elijah." On the other hand, if Luke's character was a historical person who actually met the baby Jesus in the Temple, it is not hard to imagine that such a Simeon would have grown up feeling pressure to play the part of the famous ancestor after whom his parents had named him. In any case, in Luke's narrative Simeon has come to the Temple confident that he will receive divine direction. There, like Saul/ Paul on the road to Damascus (Acts 9:1–19), Simeon received a revelation and experienced a conversion.

Luke's description of Simeon as "righteous and devout" (δίκαιος καὶ εὐλαβής, 2:25) would not have shocked Theophilus, but these words together might represent the direction and focus that Paul indicated in his description of his early life (Gal 1:13–14; Phil 3:5–6). The coupling of "righteous" (δίκαιος=צדק) and "devout" could describe those engaged in disciplinary violence against other Jews: "Everyone who sheds the blood of godless men is like one who offers a sacrifice."[21] Unlike Paul, however, Simeon had not yet crossed the line between intense piety and fanatical violence. Luke's various references to the Spirit "resting on him" (v. 25), "revealing to him" (v. 26), and "directing him" (v. 27) assure the reader that Simeon will make the right move.

"Now" (νῦν) the moment has come (v. 29). The watchman has completed his assignment; he is free to go in peace. Indeed, the Spirit enables Simeon, with the baby Jesus in his arms, to see and understand that the arrival of "the Lord's Messiah" (v. 26) fulfills the promises of God. The Almighty (Δέσποτα, v. 29) is establishing a new order, worldwide, "in the presence of all peoples": "a light for revelation to the nations and for Israel's glory." Simeon is not simply released to resume his watch another day. The messianic age has begun. Simeon and all people everywhere can now truly begin to live in peace.

---

20. Simeon bar Kokhba, the most obvious example, came after Luke. The different forms of the name, represented in English by "Simeon" and "Simon," are used interchangeably by Josephus, e.g., *J.W.* 4.159; *Life* 190. Luke seems not to have used both forms for the same individual.

21. *Gen. Rab.* 21.3 (on Num 25:13), cited in Hengel, *Zealots,* 85; cf. John 16:2 and Paul's "clear conscience" in Acts 23:12. Supporting Bo Reicke's characterization of Simeon as an Essene prophet is "the strongly increasing attestation of חסיד/חסידים in the Qumranic writings," according to Rainer Riesner ("James's Speech, Simeon's Hymn, and Luke's Sources," in Joel B. Green and Max Turner, eds., *Jesus of Nazareth, Lord and Christ: Essays on the Historical Jesus and New Testament Christology* [Grand Rapids: Eerdmans; Carlisle: Paternoster, 1994] 277).

The figure of a watchman on the walls of Zion is an important biblical motif, especially in the prophets (see Isa 21:6; Jer 6:17; Ezek 3:17) and in the psalms (see Ps 127:1; 130:5–6). The military idiom of Simeon's opening lines has been noted by careful commentators. Already a century ago Alfred Plummer observed that "Symeon represents himself as a servant or watchman released from duty, because that for which he was commanded to watch has appeared. Comp. the opening lines of the Agamemnon of Aeschylus, where the sentinel rejoices at his release from the long watch for the fire-signal respecting the capture of Troy."[22] More recently, Joseph A. Fitzmyer also grasped the image projected by these first line: "Simeon casts himself in the role of servant-watchman posted to wait for the arrival of someone. He praises God as 'Lord.' ... He sings of his release from duty."[23] Unfortunately, both commentators return to the icon of "an old man about to die" for direction in their interpretations.

The master-slave idiom is also notable in these lines, with "release" (δεσπότης-δοῦλος) compared to manumission. This language seems to reflect the piety of that zeal which insisted on the absolute sovereignty of God. Understood in this way, the idiom does not suggest an alternative to the watchman image but simply clarifies the relationship of the watchman to the commander. As already noted, δεσπότης is the name for God which Josephus uses when representing "the fourth philosophy" (*Ant.* 18.23–25). Both Josephus and Philo use the term elsewhere as well, but it is an infrequent word in the NT.

The present active, second person singular form of the verb "you set free" or "release" (ἀπολύεις) gives no encouragement for a translation referring to the release of death. Nevertheless, mesmerized by the icon of "old Simeon," most commentators struggle to interpret the verb in context as a euphemism for "let me die in peace." Even though following this line with the majority, I. Howard Marshall admits that "the use of the present tense is difficult."[24] Nolland makes a clean break from the release-of-death tradition, citing P.Oxy 2760.2–3 for the use of this verb form in "a cavalryman's discharge."[25] Jacob's dying words in Gen 46:30, cited in the margin of the Nestle-Aland text, are a faint echo at best. Not even the traditional pictures represent Simeon on his deathbed.

If, as I suggest, Luke's Simeon is instead a religious youth determined to do what is right, even if it kills him, what he sees in his messianic vision gives him a new lease on life. It is not possible to say with certainty what "the

---

22. Plummer, *The Gospel according to S. Luke* (1st ed., 1896; 4th ed.; ICC; Edinburgh: T. & T. Clark, 1901) 67–68.
23. Fitzmyer, *Luke I-IX,* 422.
24. Marshall, *Gospel of Luke,* 119, listing the various standard attempts to avoid the obvious.
25. Nolland, *Luke 1–9:20,* 119.

consolation of Israel" (v. 25) might have meant to him before he was "guided
by the Spirit" (v. 27), but what is said about Israel and the nations in the
Hebrew Bible (and in extrabiblical literature in circulation at the beginning
of the first century AD) gives us some clues.[26] A sharp ambiguity in attitudes
towards foreigners appears. More remarkable, and immediately relevant to
Simeon's new vision (Luke 2:30), is the apparent contradiction within the
same scroll of the Bible and even within the same section. For example, Isa
49:13 speaks of Yahweh comforting his people, but this comfort is detailed
a few verses later in terms of foreign leaders licking the dust from the feet
of the faithful (49:23). Other texts, even in the scroll of Isaiah, can be interpreted as prescriptions for violence against foreigners and traitors.[27] Under
the guidance of the Holy Spirit, Luke has Simeon's eyes see the will of God
to be the opposite of the zealous vision.

Mary and Joseph are amazed. Simeon now shows that his newfound peace
is not an otherworldly escape from reality. Simeon's vision of the future includes "the falling and rising of many in Israel and a sign of contradiction"
(Luke 2:34) even in the messianic age. The baby Jesus, as "the Lord's Messiah," will face opposition in the establishment of peace. Simeon concludes
with the redirected military imagery — "a sword" (ῥομφαία) piercing Mary's
heart (v. 35).

Was Simeon Remembered?

Luke, who focuses on Paul's missionary journeys in his second volume, introduces Simeon as a prophet of the messianic mission to all peoples at the
beginning of Luke-Acts. NT scholars are divided about the value of Acts as
a source of information about Paul, but nobody doubts that Paul existed.[28]
Simeon, if he ever existed at all, vanishes from Luke's narrative and from
critical consciousness as soon as he sings his Nunc Dimittis. Nevertheless, in
ancient times at least one important theologian and preacher did remember
Simeon, as Rainer Riesner has demonstrated recently.[29]

John Chrysostom, in a series of sermons preached in Constantinople in AD
400 or 401, identified the Simeon cited by James in Acts 15:14 as the Simeon

26. For a survey of texts and scholarship on the theme "Israel and the nations," see James
LaGrand, *The Earliest Christian Mission to 'All Nations' in the Light of Matthew's Gospel* (Univer-
sity of Southern Florida International Studies in Formative Christianity and Judaism 1; Atlanta:
Scholars Press, 1995) 75–94.

27. When Luke reports Jesus' sermon on Isaiah 61 (Luke 4:18–19), he omits the reference in
our text to "the day of vengeance of our God" (Isa 61:2).

28. Even those scholars who are most skeptical about Luke's reliability nevertheless commonly
emphasize the fact that Paul was born in Tarsus, something they would not know except for
Acts 23:2 (as noted in W. C. van Unnik, *Tarsus or Jerusalem: The City of Paul's Youth* [London:
Epworth, 1962] 14).

29. Riesner, "James's Speech," 263–78.

quoted in Luke 2. In 1953, Edgar R. Smothers argued convincingly from textual criticism that Chrysostom had indeed made this identification.[30] Riesner
confirms Chrysostom's identification of the Simeon cited by James as Simeon
of the Luke 2:25–35, acknowledging that "modern interpretation of Acts
has hardly noticed this patristic testimony."[31] After calling into doubt the
usual explanations for Luke's use of the name "Simeon" for Simon Peter in
the council, Riesner scores three solid exegetical points against the common
modern assumption that James begins his contribution to the council's delib-
erations with a reference to Simon Peter's opening speech in Acts 15:7–11.
Riesner concludes with two additional arguments relating to Luke's possible
sources and the text-forms which Luke represents James as using.

First, if James had cited Simeon's revelation and his interpretation of Isaiah (as in Luke 2), the words "Simeon has interpreted" (Συμεὼν ἐξηγήσατο)
in Acts 15:14 would be exactly right. But the choice of words seems odd
and uncharacteristic of Luke for a simple reference to a preceding speech —
"As Simeon has just said" (or "recounted, reported, explained"). With reference to the other uses in Luke-Acts and also by Philo and Josephus, Riesner
observes that "in the Greek of NT times the verb [ἐξηγεῖσθαι] is predominantly used in religious contexts and usually has the sense 'to interpret' (e.g.,
Holy Scripture, dreams, oracles)."[32]

The second point supports the first. If James intended to cite Peter, he
seems to have forgotten why: "The brother of the Lord offers an independent argument and appeals exclusively to the prophetic testimony of both
the present and earlier period as the basis of his judgment."[33] As presented
in Acts 15:13–21, James's argument, and especially his citation of Amos, is
reminiscent of Luke 2:29–32 and can be seen to expand and build on it.

Riesner's third point fits tightly with the first two and drives the three
home together. Peter certainly claims seniority over the other apostles in the
mission to the nations, and over Barnabas and Paul as well. But Cornelius
was not the first convert from the nations known to Luke's readers. Besides
the Ethiopian baptized by Philip (Acts 8:26–39), the messianic mission to
the nations had been brilliantly predicted and explained with reference to
ancient prophecy by Simeon already at the very beginning of the messianic
age (καθὼς πρῶτον, Acts 15:14).[34]

Riesner's additional arguments regarding "the Jewish-religious background
of James and Simeon" and his suggestions about Luke's sources are relevant

---

30. Smothers, "Symeon Is Simon Peter," *HTR* 46 (1953) 212; less convincingly, he argued
that Chrysostom was wrong.
31. Riesner, "James's Speech," 263.
32. Ibid., 273.
33. Ibid., 274.
34. Ibid., 274–75. To be fair, Riesner's statement of the case is diffident in comparison with
mine.

to the question whether Simeon was remembered. Specifically, Riesner suggests that a pre-Lukan tradition linked Acts 15:14 and the birth narrative. It is Riesner's brief discussion of James's use of Amos 9:11–12, however, that is especially important for an evaluation of Luke as author of a tightly integrated narrative, perhaps even of his reliability as a reporter. The old argument, that Luke's account of James's speech is uncharacteristically dependent on an LXX reading of Amos 9:11–12, was seriously undermined by Nils A. Dahl's 1958 article relating the crucial phrase "a people for his name" to a congeries of texts in the old Palestinian Targum.[35] Riesner expands on Dahl's inventory with reference to Qumran material. He further suggests the possibility, which Hebrew texts found at Qumran seem to support, that "both the LXX and Acts 15:17 together rest on a Hebrew text of Amos 9:12 slightly different from that of the MT."[36]

Chrysostom's reading, if correct, proves that Luke recalled what his Simeon had said at the beginning of Luke-Acts. The reintroduction of Simeon at the council in Jerusalem implies an explanation of the development of the mission to all nations from the time of the messiah's birth. This explanation is interestingly different from most modern scholarly reconstructions, especially from the model proposed by the Tübingen School. Whether Luke created Simeon for this purpose or recorded, from reliable traditions, what was actually said to Mary and Joseph in the Temple is of course another question.

To speculate a little: If, indeed, a young man held the baby Jesus in his arms and thereafter avoided violent confrontation with the Romans, he might have continued prophesying in the messianic movement which Luke describes. James's reference might even be understood to mean that Simeon was in attendance at the council in about AD 48. In any case, the idea that Paul of Tarsus initiated the mission to the nations is no longer a safe assumption in NT studies. It now seems more likely that the mission to the nations itself attracted Paul to those in the Way — to kill them. The positive importance of Paul in the messianic mission after his conversion is not minimized by Luke, but he locates the beginnings with others: Simeon, Stephen, Philip, John, and Peter, to mention the few of whom we have record. Peter's speech at the council in Jerusalem emphasizes his own strong vocation in the mission. James reminds the assembly that Peter was not the first to speak in favor of a mission to all peoples, but that this direction — established at Pen-

35. Dahl, "'A People for His Name' (Acts xv.14)," NTS 4 (1957–58) 319–26; see esp. 323: "Acts xv.14 is modelled upon the general pattern [of Ezek 36:24, 28; Zech 2:15, et al.] rather than upon any individual passage." See also Richard Bauckham, "James and the Jerusalem Church," in idem, ed., The Book of Acts in Its Palestinian Setting (Grand Rapids: Eerdmans; Carlisle: Paternoster, 1995) 455–62.
36. Riesner, "James's Speech," 271; for Amos 9:11 Riesner cites CD 7.16; 4QFlor 1.12.

tecost — had been revealed from the very beginning (καθὼς πρῶτον) by the revelation to Simeon and his explanation of ancient prophecy.

In this essay, I have not attempted to define the piety of zeal except with reference to a few biblical texts. These texts, along with citations and allusions in other literature in circulation when Luke committed Simeon's canticle to writing, indicate a widespread, multifaceted ideology susceptible of very sharp focus in the emerging Zealot party's campaign against Rome. More immediately to the point, this zealous piety, from which the later rabbis and church leaders recoiled in horror, had the power in Luke's time to enlist pious young men such as Saul/Paul for individual acts of violence against fellow Jews — against those, that is, perceived as introducing the pollution of the nations into Israel and so threatening Israel's covenant with God.

In Acts, Luke shows how Paul turned from conspiring to murder those involved in the earliest Christian mission to become, himself, a Christian missionary to the nations (Acts 9:1–2; 13:2). So too, at the very beginning of the messianic era (καθὼς πρῶτον) a pious young man waiting in the temple for marching orders was released from the violent assignment he anticipated and allowed to go in peace. His prophetic words to Israel and the nations become the charter for the Christian church and likewise a signal instance of "the pattern Luke develops in Acts where Jews and Gentiles are seen as parallel beneficiaries of that salvation which is offered in the name of Jesus."[37]

---

37. Nolland, *Luke 1–9:20*, 120.

13

COMMON LIFE WITH JESUS

The Parable of the Banquet in Luke 14:16–24

KLYNE SNODGRASS

A parable dealing with table fellowship is a particularly fitting focus for an essay in a volume honoring Graydon Snyder and the tradition from which he comes, and I congratulate him for his contribution to scholarship and to the church. This parable is one of the longer and more important parables from Jesus, which is reason enough to focus attention on it. Further justification for revisiting this parable derives from recent suggestions that it is not so much an image of the eschatological banquet with God but a story about the conversion of the host to a different understanding of honor.[1]

The attention given in the gospels to meals is well known. As a primary context for understanding Jesus, his meals are an embodiment of his acceptance of outcasts and a demonstration of the grace and presence of the kingdom. Of all the material in the gospels, most NT scholars would view the emphasis on Jesus' table fellowship as among the most trustworthy and instructive.[2]

Luke gives more attention to eating and table fellowship than the other gospel writers; in fact, almost every chapter in Luke has some mention of eating. The parable of the banquet in 14:16–24 is a climactic treatment of this theme. At least in some explanations this parable lies at the center of Luke's chiastically shaped travel narrative, a narrative which serves as the

---

1. Most notable, Willi Braun, *Feasting and Social Rhetoric in Luke 14* (SNTSMS 85; Cambridge and New York: Cambridge University Press, 1995).

2. This has been challenged recently by Dennis Smith ("Table Fellowship and the Historical Jesus," in Lukas Bormann, Kelly del Tredici, and Angela Standhartinger, eds., *Religious Propaganda and Missionary Competition in the New Testament World: Essays Honoring Dieter Georgi* [NovTSup 74; Leiden: Brill, 1994] 135–62). However, Smith's writing off the meal traditions as a literary convention is based on questionable assumptions and is overly pessimistic.

framework for Jesus' teaching on his way to Jerusalem.[3] Luke's redactional shaping of chapter 14 around the banquet theme is obvious: a healing at a Sabbath meal in a Pharisee's home (14:1–6); Jesus' instructions on humility for those invited to banquets (14:7–11); instructions to his host as to who should be invited to such meals (14:12–14); a macarism from a guest about eating bread in the kingdom (14:15); to which the parable of the banquet (14:16–24) is a response.[4]

Less frequently recognized, however, is the way that other parts of the travel narrative prepare for the parable or deal with the same themes. Similar to the parable's exclusion of the persons originally invited (14:24), 13:24–27 describes some who will wish to enter through the narrow door but will not be able. The exclusion theme is even more specific in 13:28–29 where the endtime banquet is pictured with God's people, the patriarchs, and the prophets gathered to celebrate, but the hearers cast out. This is followed in 13:30 by an affirmation of reversal: the last will be first and the first will be last. In the parable itself the original guests were unwilling to come at the servant's invitation, which is anticipated in the lament over Jerusalem (13:34–35) by the rejection of God's messengers and the unwillingness of Jerusalem's children to be gathered. We may justly say that the material in 13:24–35 serves as an introduction to the banquet sayings of chapter 14.[5] Furthermore, the three excuses in the parable (14:18–20) parallel the three dialogues on discipleship in 9:57–62 and the three requirements of disciples in 14:26–33. In all three passages the case is made that preoccupation with possessions and family involvements is incompatible with discipleship.[6] These anticipations and parallels, along with the central place the parable has in the travel narrative, demonstrate just how important the parable of the banquet is for Luke.

For all its importance, this parable continues to be the focus of considerable debate. Several questions require attention. How is one to assess the parallels in Matt 22:1–14 and *Gos. Thom.* 64 and their relevance for determining the original form of the story? Against which of several suggested

---

3. See Craig L. Blomberg, who, like others, suggests that Luke adopted a chiastic parable source ("Midrash, Chiasmus, and the Outline of Luke's Central Section," in R. T. France and David Wenham, eds., *Gospel Perspectives*, vol. 3: *Studies in Midrash and Historiography* [Sheffield: JSOT Press, 1983] 242–43). On other chiastic arrangements of the travel narrative this parable is set opposite 13:1–9 or 13:18–30.

4. For a helpful treatment of issues pertaining to the social importance of meals, see Jerome H. Neyrey, "Ceremonies in Luke-Acts: The Case of Meals and Table Fellowship," in idem, ed., *The Social World of Luke-Acts: Models for Interpretation* (Peabody, Mass.: Hendrickson, 1991) 361–87.

5. Note too the parallels between the healing of the man with dropsy in 14:1–6 and the woman bound by Satan in 13:10–17.

6. See W. Gregory Carey, "Excuses, Excuses: The Parable of the Banquet (Luke 14:15–24) within the Larger Context of Luke," *IBS* 17 (1995) 177–87. Cf. also 12:14; 17:26–31.

backgrounds should the story be read? What is the intent of the parable, and what may be discerned about Jesus and his message from that intent? Do the elements of the story have allegorical significance so that, for example, the second invitation to substitute guests in 14:23 represents the missionary task to the gentiles?

Because of limitations of space, and because questions linger as to whether Matt 22:1–14 renders the same parable, attention will be confined here to the account in Luke.[7] The typical procedure in approaching parables is to strip them of introductions, conclusions, and all redactional or allegorical elements so as to return to a simpler, more "original" account. Adolf Jülicher's reconstruction of the banquet parable is perhaps the most blatant, in that he found the original parable to have been Luke 14:16, Matt 22:4 (without ἄλλους, "other") and 22:5, Luke 14:21ab, Matt 22:9–10, and possibly Luke 14:24.[8] How this original could have resulted in our two accounts, or could itself be discerned from these accounts, is hard to imagine. Today, although less radical reconstructions are offered, many express an uneasy awareness that such attempts are methodologically suspect.[9] The "original" version which results is often so simplistic and banal that one wonders why the story would be told.

---

7. Not only is Matthew's account much more political in tone; few actual correspondences exist between Matthew and Luke other than the basic framework. Of 223 words in Matt 22:1–14 only twelve appear in Luke 14:15–25 in the identical form, and only seven more in a related form. This is not evidence of the fluidity of the tradition, as a comparison with the triple tradition shows (contra Willard Swartley, "Unexpected Banquet People [Luke 14:16–24]," in V. George Shillington, ed., Jesus and His Parables: Interpreting the Parables of Jesus Today [Edinburgh: T. & T. Clark, 1997] 177). Nearly everyone grants that Jesus told a given parable on a number of occasions and with adaptations; see, e.g., Robert W. Funk, Language, Hermeneutic, and Word of God (New York: Harper & Row, 1966) 163 n. 1. Few, however, take this fact seriously when it comes to discussing individual texts. If Jesus' teaching was a warning to Israel, the theme of refusal to come to a banquet could have been used often in his teaching, and it is not surprising to find a basic structure developed in two different ways. This does not result in a caricature of an impoverished Jesus who imitates himself, as Adolf Jülicher argued (Die Gleichnisreden Jesu [2 vols.; Freiburg: Mohr (Siebeck), 1888–89] 2. 407).

I have argued elsewhere that the Gospel of Thomas is later than and dependent on the canonical gospel tradition and represents a secondary orality; see Klyne Snodgrass, "The Gospel of Thomas: A Secondary Gospel," SecCent 7 (1989–90) 19–38. Specifically with regard to this parable, Thomas shows contact particularly with Luke, has expanded the excuses to four, and — along with two other parables in Gos. Thom. 63, 65 — has directed this parable against businessmen and merchants. See Jean-Martin Sevrin, "Un groupement de trois paraboles contre les richesses dans l'Évangile selon Thomas (63, 64, 65)," in Jean Delorme, ed., Les Paraboles Évangéliques: Perspectives nouvelles (LD 135; Paris: Cerf, 1989) 425–39.

8. Jülicher, Gleichnisreden 2. 431.

9. See David Flusser, Die rabbinischen Gleichnisse und der Gleichniserzähler Jesus, vol. 1: Der Wesen der Gleichnisse (Judaica et Christiana 4; Bern: Lang, 1981) 63, 125–26; Richard Bauckham, "The Parable of the Royal Wedding Feast (Matthew 22:1–14) and the Parable of the Lame Man and the Blind Man (Apocryphon of Ezekiel)," JBL 115 (1996), esp. 472–73, 482–83, 488; Louise Schottroff, "Das Gleichnis vom großen Gastmahl in der Logienquelle," EvT 47 (1987), esp. 194–96 (still assumes a Q version). Michael D. Goulder (Luke: A New Paradigm [2 vols.; JSNTSup 20; Sheffield: JSOT Press, 1989] 2. 592) refers to "the featureless rump to which the Q hypothesis [and such procedures] tend," but he goes too far in the direction of assigning the parable almost entirely to Luke.

Often the allegory that is removed is more in the mind of the interpreter than in the gospel accounts.[10] And while Jülicher's complaints against allegory still influence us, the supposed distinctions between allegory and parable do not stand up to literary analysis. Redactional traces must be identified, but they may provide little that allows one to recreate an original structure. The more one accepts the possibility that stories were told more than one time and with variations, the less one can think of returning to *an* original. In my opinion such attempts are abortive, and parable research is better served by determining how the analogy in the parable functions, how the teaching of the parable may be correlated with Jesus' teaching elsewhere, and how the parable explicitly serves the redactional interests of the evangelist — without our reading into the text theological meanings that require a divining rod to discern.

The Background of the Parable

Possibly the most important question is that of the background against which the banquet parable is to be read. Several suggestions have been made, each of which affects one's understanding of the parable.

Joachim Jeremias, in an attempt to save the story from allegory — though ironically allegory that is retained in his interpretation — argued that Jesus' banquet parable was consciously drawn from a story in the Palestinian Talmud of a tax collector named Bar Maayan, who gave a banquet for the city councillors; when they refused to come, he gave orders that the poor should come and eat the food.[11] This suggestion has not found much acceptance, and rightly so. Even apart from the question of the late date of this account, nothing in Luke suggests we are dealing with a tax collector. Further, in the talmudic story the poor are brought in only so that the food is not wasted, not as actual participants in the banquet.

---

10. Joachim Jeremias sees a full salvation history in Matthew's account, even saying that entry into the banquet hall is a reference to baptism (*The Parables of Jesus* [3d ed.; New York: Scribner; London: SCM, 1972] 68–69). Detlev Dormeyer finds a reference to the apostolate in the word ἀπέστειλεν ("sent," Luke 14:17), to the eucharist and Christian believers in the meal itself, and suggests that the wrath of the "master" (κύριος) in v. 21 refers to the wrath of the resurrected one ("Literarische und theologische Analyse der Parabel Lukas 14,15–24," *BibLeb* 15 [1974] 206–19, esp. 217). Anton Vögtle argues that the three invitations in Luke refer respectively to the invitation to Israel, to gentiles who have accepted so far, and to the continuing mission to the gentiles (*Gott und seine Gäste: Das Schiksal des Gleichnisses Jesu vom großen Gastmahl* [Biblisch-theologische Studien 29; Neukirchen-Vluyn: Neukirchener, 1996] 37). Hans Weder does not find a contrast in the parable between two groups of people, but suggests that those who refuse the invitation and those who accept point to two sides within the hearers themselves (*Die Gleichnisse Jesu als Metaphoren: Traditions- und redaktionsgeschichtliche Analysen und Interpretationen* [FRLANT 120; Göttingen: Vandenhoeck & Ruprecht, 1978] 189).

11. Jeremias, *Parables*, 178–79, with reference to y. *Sanh.* 6.23c and y. *Ḥag.* 2.77d. Jeremias holds that the earthly setting of the story confirms that Jesus did not tell it as an allegory of the feast at the time of salvation, but also that he may have had this in mind (p. 69)!

Several scholars have suggested that the background of Luke 14 is to be found in Greek symposia, discussions of which are frequent enough that one may speak of a literary genre dealing with this theme.[12] Without question, banquets in the ancient world were contexts for philosophical and religious instruction. However, Luke's account is too brief and too specifically focused on Jesus to fit a symposiastic genre; it is more a monologue from Jesus than a dinner conversation. In fact, Luke's account parallels antisymposia traditions in some ways.[13] This literature does give us a deeper appreciation of the degree to which honor (and shame) were associated with attendance, seating arrangements, and the events happening at meals. At the same time, one does not have to go to a hellenistic context to find such ideas, for similar understandings of the association of honor and meals are evident in Jewish literature.[14] So, while much is to be learned from this background, it is not the key to interpretation.

The key determiner for the parable is the OT and Jewish expectation of an eschatological banquet marking the beginning of endtime salvation. Obviously the redactional shaping by Luke as evidenced in 13:28–29 and 14:14–15 indicates that this is the background against which he wants the parable read. The mere mention of a banquet is not, of course, sufficient ground to point to the endtime banquet, but evidence for an eschatological understanding of this image is strong. The more one accepts that Jesus preached an eschatological message, talked about reclining with Abraham, Isaac, and Jacob in the Kingdom (Matt 8:11–12//Luke 13:28–29) and intentionally ate with sinners (and disciples) as a demonstration of the presence of the Kingdom, the more one is compelled to view the banquet imagery as pointing to the eschatological banquet. Luke 22:29–30 is often overlooked in this regard, but these verses describe Jesus as giving the Kingdom to his disciples so that they may eat at his table in his kingdom and sit on thrones judging the twelve tribes of Israel.

The origin of the eschatological banquet imagery is apparently Isa 25:6 (NRSV): "On this mountain the LORD of hosts will make for all peoples a feast of rich food, a feast of well-aged wines . . . " (cf. Isa 65:13–14). Later, the promi-

---

12. See Plato *Symposium;* Plutarch *Moralia* (esp. "Dinner of the Seven Wise Men"; "Table Talk"). For discussion of Luke 14 against this background, see X. de Meeûs, "Composition de Lc. XIV et genre symposiaque," *ETL* 37 (1961) 847–70; E. Springs Steele, "Luke 11:37–54 – A Modified Hellenistic Symposium?" *JBL* 103 (1984) 379–94; Josef Ernst, "Gastmahlspräche: Lk 14,1–24," in idem, Rudolf Schnackenburg, and Joachim Wanke, eds., *Die Kirche des Anfangs: für Heinz Schürmann* (Freiburg: Herder, 1978) 57–58.

13. Willi Braun, "Symposium or Anti-Symposium? Reflections on Luke 14:1–24," *Toronto Journal of Theology* 8 (1992) 70–84.

14. The discussion of the Pharisaic *haburah* ("fellowship") often focused on meals, as in *m. Dem.* 2.2–3 and the parable in *Midr. Lam.* 4.2.3–4; see also the excursus, "Ein altjüdisches Gastmahl," Str-B 4. 611–39. Of course, typically no segregating of the influence of hellenistic meals and ideas from Judaism is permissible.

nence of the endtime banquet is evidenced in the Qumran scrolls, the pseud-epigrapha, and the rabbinic writings so strongly that it cannot be ignored.[15]

As a further elaboration of the end-time banquet imagery, the suggestion has been made that the excuses in the parable allude to Deut 20:5–7, which specifies exemptions from involvement in military campaigns for those having built a new house, having planted a vineyard, or having become engaged, and to Deut 24:5, which exempts those newly married.[16] This suggestion, which has been accepted by many, assumes that the real issue is allegiance to the messiah when troops are summoned to the final battle with which the end-time banquet is connected. That expectations included both a holy war and a banquet is verified by 1QSa 2.5–9 and Rev 19:9–16. The hypothesis of C. F. Evans that the central section of Luke was consciously modeled on Deuteronomy strengthened this argument.[17] Still further support is found in m. Soṭa 8.1–7, which offers a midrash on Deut 20:2–9 and begins "When the Anointed for Battle speaks unto the people...."[18] However, as the context indicates, "anointed for battle" seems to be a reference to the priest anointed for battle, not the messiah.

At first encounter these allusions to Deuteronomy seem attractive, but further reflection makes their acceptance extremely difficult. As Humphrey Palmer points out, the battle imagery is in Matthew's similar parable, but the excuses are in Luke.[19] Matthew gives as reasons for the guests not accept-ing the invitation only that they did not care and that one went to his field and one to his business (22:5). (Interpretation of the parable both in Mat-

---

15. 1QSa 2.5–9 (on which see below) describes those granted admission to the messianic banquet; 1 Enoch 62.15–16 says that the elect will eat, rest and rise with the Son of man forever, and shall wear garments of joy and life; 2 Enoch 42.5 describes the rest prepared for the righteous as a banquet of joy; 3 Enoch 48A.10 (whatever its date) speaks of the kingdom of Israel being gathered from the four quarters of the world and eating with the messiah and with the gentiles; 2 Bar. 29.3–8 says that those who are left when the messiah comes will feast on Behemoth and Leviathan (cf. 2 Esdr 6:49–52); m. 'Abot 4.16 teaches that "this world is like a vestibule before the world to come: prepare thyself in the vestibule that thou mayest enter into the banqueting hall"; Pesiq. R. 41.5 speaks of the banquet God prepares for the righteous in the time to come as the banquet of redemption; Midr. Qoh. 3.9.1 tells a parable of a banquet to which people bring their own seats, and interprets it of the hereafter; Midr. Qoh. 9.8 (cf. b. Sabb. 153a) relates a parable about guests who do not make preparations for a banquet, and applies it to the hereafter; b. Pesaḥ. 119b, concerning the Passover, describes God's great banquet on the day he manifests his love to the seed of Isaac. Of course, Rev 19:9 points to the same idea, and Mark 2:15–17 presupposes the eschatological banquet.

16. See esp. Paul H. Ballard, "Reasons for Refusing the Great Supper," JTS n.s. 23 (1972) 341–50; J. Duncan M. Derrett, "The Parable of the Great Supper," in idem, Law in the New Testament (London: Darton, Longman & Todd, 1970) 126–55 (Derrett finds allusions to Tg. Zeph 1.1–16).

17. Evans, "The Central Section of St. Luke's Gospel," in D. E. Nineham, ed., Studies in the Gospels: Essays in Memory of R. H. Lightfoot (Oxford: Blackwell, 1955) 37–54.

18. ET (and capitalization) from Herbert Danby, trans., The Mishnah (Oxford: Clarendon, 1933) 301.

19. Palmer, "Just Married, Cannot Come," NovT 18 (1976) 241–57.

thew and in Luke is hampered when elements from the one are read into the
other.) Palmer actually accepts the allusions to Deuteronomy in the Lukan
parable, but thinks they were intended to be a joke — excuses that would
exempt one from battle as a response to a dinner invitation add extra spice
for those who catch the allusion.[20] This is hardly convincing, but more importantly, as both Ballard and Humphrey admit, the parallels between the
excuses in Luke and the exemptions in Deuteronomy do not fit precisely. Actually, they do not correspond much at all. In Luke 14:18–20 the excuses
are that one guest has bought a field, one has bought five oxen, and one has
recently married. In Deut 20:5–7 one is exempt from battle if he has built
a house, planted a vineyard, or become engaged; Deut 24:5 adds that one
is exempt who has recently married. Only Luke's third excuse has a parallel,
and despite the popularity of this view I do not think that is sufficient to call
to mind the context of Deuteronomy.[21] In addition, the process of thought
assumed by the allusions is contorted. The excuses must be recognized as
legitimate exemptions from military service, although the parable has no military imagery, but then one must discern that such excuses are not legitimate
in a religious war,[22] all before the parable is half told.

By way of summary, unless some other compelling explanation were to
take precedence, the background against which the parable is to be read
should be confined to the expectation of an eschatological banquet marking
the beginning of endtime salvation. The suggestion of allusions to military
exemptions in Deuteronomy is neither convincing nor helpful in interpretation, even if one is otherwise convinced that the travel narrative is shaped
by material from Deuteronomy.

Does the Parable Tell of the Conversion of the Host?

A few recent studies have downplayed the eschatological background of the
banquet imagery and have found compelling reasons instead to focus on social factors. As a result these studies conclude that this fictional tale — there
is hesitation even to admit that we are dealing with a parable[23] — is about
the transformation/conversion of the host from one understanding of honor
to an entirely different schema of honor. On this understanding the host
gives a dinner in a quest for honor, but when he is snubbed, he rejects the
whole system of valuation and transfers his social life to a different group.
The parable is understood as addressing the wealthy in Luke's church, who

---

20. Ibid., 248–49.
21. Swartley ("Unexpected Banquet People," 184–85) for some reason says that the parallels
are remarkable and suggests that the oxen (in Luke) tilled the vineyard (in Deuteronomy)!
22. As m. Soṭa 8.7 shows.
23. Braun, Feasting and Social Rhetoric, 64.

in the desire to maintain status in the society are refusing associations with poorer Christians. Willi Braun provides the most detailed presentation of this thesis, but with variations it is advocated by Detlev Dormeyer, Richard L. Rohrbaugh, Bernard Brandon Scott, and Joel B. Green.[24]

Dormeyer's study is the first notice of this approach of which I am aware. He views the progression of invitations as a process of learning for the host. The refusal of the first guests leads the host to realize that he has overvalued their relation to him. The invitation to the poor leaves him still in danger of being isolated, for he is not a partner to these first substitute guests. Only with the second invitation to substitute guests does the relearning come to fruition, for now with the host's "open door policy" a new social ordering is in place that has no anxiety about contact with other groups.[25] One should note that this policy seems to have been derived from "everyone you find" in Matt 22:9, with which nothing in Luke's parable corresponds.

If Dormeyer's study is the first advocating this approach, Rohrbaugh's has most influenced those holding this position. Both Braun's and Rohrbaugh's studies provide valuable information on the structure of ancient cities, on understanding the relation of the wealthy and the poor, and on the system of honor that accompanied meals. In addition to sociological arguments supporting this theory, literary and theological motives also led to its development. Green accepts this interpretation because he, like others, feels the eschatological banquet approach gives an unflattering portrait of a God who extends invitations originally in a way consistent with the socially elite of Luke's world and only turns to the poor when rebuffed by the rich.[26] This "distortion of grace" had earlier caused Ernst Haenchen to reject the parable entirely as a work of the early church.[27] Further, Luke 14:24 is often viewed as inconsequential in the story, for it threatens exclusion to those who do not wish to come anyway.[28] Braun argues that v. 24 — although it may also include a threat of exclusion — is the host's announcement of his conversion,

---

24. Braun, *Feasting and Social Rhetoric*, esp. 98–131; Dormeyer, "Literarische und theologische Analyse"; Rohrbaugh, "The Pre-Industrial City in Luke-Acts: Urban Social Relations," in Neyrey, *Social World*, 137–47; Scott, *Hear Then the Parable: A Commentary on the Parables of Jesus* (Minneapolis: Fortress, 1989) 173–74; Green, *The Gospel of Luke* (NICNT; Grand Rapids, Mich.: Eerdmans, 1997) 554–63. Robert C. Tannehill also adopts Rohrbaugh's reading, but advocates a polyvalent approach that also accepts the eschatological meal interpretation and a third reading based on Luke 10:1–24, which sees the experience of early Christian missionaries reflected in the parable ("The Lukan Discourse on Invitations [Luke 14,7–24]," in F. Van Segbroeck, C. M. Tuckett et al., eds., *The Four Gospels, 1992: Festschrift Frans Neirynck* [3 vols.; BETL 100; Louvain: Leuven University Press, 1992] 2. 1603–16). But this is to confuse meditation on the parable with hearing it in its original context.

25. Dormeyer, "Literarische und theologische Analyse," esp. 213–14.

26. Green, *Gospel of Luke*, 556.

27. Haenchen, "Das Gleichnis vom großen Mahl," in idem, *Die Bibel und Wir: Gesammelte Aufsätze* (Tübingen: Mohr [Siebeck], 1968) 153–55.

28. So, e.g., Scott, *Hear Then the Parable*, 173.

his relinquishing the quest for belonging to the social elite and his redefining himself in relation to the socially marginal.[29]

While these studies have valuable aspects to them, in the end the parable is not about the conversion of the host, and this approach cannot succeed. Certainly the social values of the Kingdom are different, and this whole section seeks to promote a Kingdom view of self and others. Resonances of concern for the poor are obvious and have been emphasized redactionally by the conformity of v. 21 to v. 13. To focus on the conversion of the host, however, is a distortion for several reasons:

1. Nothing suggests the host gave his banquet as a quest for honor or that he needed instruction, and no conversion language is present either.[30]

2. This approach downplays both the Jewish and eschatological context too severely, including the Jewish literary background, the eschatological teaching of Jesus that sometimes focused on meals, and specific elements in the text such as the words "already it is ready" (14:17), to say nothing of 14:15.[31]

3. The parable gives too much prominence to the invitations spurned by one group and extended to others unexpectedly, and too little to a change in the host, to allow a reader to conclude what this theory demands.

4. This approach ignores the emphasis on the language of election.

5. Except for the treatment of Green, little or no attention is given to the *Sitz im Leben Jesu,* even though those advocating this view — if they express themselves at all on the matter — take the parable, or at least an earlier form of it, to be dominical. All the emphasis in this hypothesis assumes that the real discussion is the situation of Luke's community, but the result of such "mirror reading" has to be laid on the parable, not drawn from it.[32] For Green, the parable is an exemplar

29. Braun, *Feasting and Social Rhetoric,* 126.

30. Braun recognizes this (ibid., 128).

31. Braun will not even grant that the people in the story are Jews (ibid., 84–85). But if the story was told by Jesus in Palestine to Jews, on what grounds should we assume that some other ethnic group is in mind, especially given the presence of the language of election? Braun views v. 15 as entirely a Lukan creation (p. 64; also p. 54 for his downplaying of eschatology). I do not see any evidence that 14:15 alludes to the delay of the parousia, as Scott concludes (*Hear Then the Parable,* 164), following Erich Grässer (*Das Problem der Parusieverzögerung in den synoptischen Evangelien und in der Apostelgeschichte* [2d ed.; BZNW 22; Berlin: Töpelmann, 1960] 196–97).

32. Dormeyer grants the eschatological background, but emphasizes the change that has occurred in Luke's community. He then struggles to contrast the Jewish understanding of the parable on a human level with a Christian understanding that is more theological ("Literarische und theologische Analyse," esp. 216–18). The theology he finds is extreme; see above, n. 10.

of Jesus' teaching in 14:12–14.[33] But if this were the case, why were the first guests even invited, and why is so much attention given to their excuses?

The attractiveness of this view is that it latches on to themes present in Luke 14:7–14: the rejection of status seeking and concern for the marginalized. Nothing, however, equips a hearer or reader to know that the host in the parable needed to, or did, change his attitude. All the emphasis is placed on the failure of the first guests and their exclusion from the banquet. The parable is indeed about honor — not the host's quest for honor, but the guests' failure to find honor. The assumption of the story and of the exclusion statement is that attendance at the banquet is an honor which even the first guests desire — at least, if they understand it. Their failure is in being so preoccupied with possessions and relations that they do not recognize the importance of the invitation. Their preoccupation leads to exclusion from a banquet they would wish to attend. While the macarism about eating bread in the Kingdom (v. 15) is not essential to the parable, the parable at least addresses such thinking.

The complaint that the parable portrays an unflattering view of a God who turns to the poor only after being spurned by the wealthy betrays methodological assumptions that should be challenged. The assumption is that parables give complete theological pictures and that parable time is real time, neither of which is true. Parables are not to be stretched onto theological or chronological grids. They are arguments by analogy, and the degree to which a given analogy parallels reality will vary. Several correspondences may exist between a parable and the reality it portrays (despite Jülicher), but parable interpretation is not so much about listing correspondences as it is about determining how the analogies function.[34] This parable does not present an analogy concerning God's character, but one concerning the stance of the preoccupied guests and its result.

The Intent of the Parable

If the parable is not about the conversion of the host, then precisely what is its intent, and what may be discerned from the parable about Jesus and

---

33. Green, *Gospel of Luke*, 557–63.

34. In fact, apparent correspondences can sometimes mislead, as Nathan's parable to David in 2 Sam 12:1–7 shows: it is not the lamb (Bathsheba) that dies in reality, but the poor man (Uriah). Such misleading correspondences help parables to "deceive into the truth," in Kierkegaard's memorable phrase (Howard V. Hong and Edna H. Hong, eds. and trans., *Søren Kierkegaard's Journals and Papers* [7 vols.; Bloomington, Ind.: Indiana University Press, 1967] 1. 288). On parables as analogies, see esp. John W. Sider, *Interpreting the Parables: A Hermeneutical Guide to Their Meaning* (Grand Rapids: Zondervan, 1995); Peter Dschulnigg, "Positionen des Gleichnissverständnisses in 20. Jahrhundert," *TZ* 45 (1989) 348.

his teaching and about Luke's purposes? Although the parable has resonances that address issues of shame and honor and resonances concerning
attitudes to the marginalized, the question the parable addresses is neither
"What counts as shame and honor?" nor "What is the proper attitude toward the poor?" The question it addresses is instead "Who will be present at
the banquet?"[35]

The most helpful explanations are those that draw attention to the parable's
confrontation with Jewish assumptions about election. J. A. Sanders's article
has been most influential. He argues that Luke's central section presents Jesus
as giving a prophetic critique against abuses of Deuteronomy's theology of
election. While Deuteronomy stresses that obedience brings blessing and disobedience a curse, the conclusion was easy that suffering indicates one is not
elect, whereas prosperity indicates one is.[36] The relevance of Deuteronomy
once again becomes a question for interpreting the parable. Sanders accepts
the allusions to Deut 20:5–7 (which I have argued against) and C. F. Evans's
argument that Luke's central section is modeled after Deuteronomy 1–26. But
even if one rejects entirely theories that require the influence of Deuteronomy, the parable is still directed against presumptions about election. Sanders
draws attention to 1QSa 2.5–9, which describes those granted admission to
the Qumran community and the messianic banquet and assumes the latter is
already reflected in the daily life of the community:

> And no man smitten with any human uncleanness shall enter the as-
> sembly of God; no man smitten with any of them shall be confirmed in
> his office in the congregation. No man smitten in his flesh, or paralyzed
> in his feet or hands, or lame, or blind, or deaf, or dumb, or smitten in
> his flesh with a visible blemish; no old and tottery man unable to stay
> still in the midst of the congregation; none of these shall come to hold
> office among the congregation of the men of renown, for the Angels of
> Holiness are [with] their [congregation].

These exclusions are drawn partly from Lev 21:17–23, and a similar list of
those excluded from battle appears in 1QM 7.3–7. Sanders suggests that it
is as though the banquet parable was specifically constructed to contradict
the sort of membership or guest lists now known from Qumran.[37] Although
the community at Qumran was probably not the specific target, at least the
parable contradicts such thinking, which was doubtless present in various
sectors of Judaism.

---

35. This too, of course, is an issue of honor.
36. Sanders, "The Ethic of Election in Luke's Great Banquet Parable," in James L. Crenshaw
and John T. Willis, eds., *Essays in Old Testament Ethics: J. Philip Hyatt, in Memoriam* (New York:
KTAV, 1974) 245–71; see also Eugene E. Lemcio, "The Parable of the Great Supper and the
Wedding Feast: History, Redaction, and Canon," *HBT* 8 (1986) 1–26.
37. Sanders, "Ethic of Election," 262.

The NT, too, cautions against presumptions about election. The gospels report that John the Baptist warned his hearers not to presume they have Abraham as a father, for God is able to raise children for Abraham from the stones (Matt 3:9//Luke 3:8). The teaching of Jesus and Paul shows similar emphases.[38] The presumption of many ancient Jews, particularly of those who considered themselves pious, was that as God's elect they would be at the messianic banquet (or at least victorious and living with God) when evil was defeated.[39] The parable is directed against such presumption. The election motif, which is dampened when καλεῖν ("call") is translated "invited," is intrinsic to the parable and is also present in the Matthean parallel. Luke has given prominence to this motif by using the verb twelve times in 14:7–24.

The focus on election indicates that this parable and the related parable in Matthew are descriptions of the response of many in Israel, and especially the leaders, to the proclamation of the kingdom in Jesus' ministry. Other parables and sayings in this central section of Luke also point to the failure of Israel and the crisis the nation faces with Jesus' proclamation: most obviously, the parable of the fig tree (13:6–9), the lament over Jerusalem (13:34–35), the parable of the prodigal and elder sons (15:11–32), and the parable of the pounds (19:11–27). Rather than being some distance in the future, the kingdom banquet is "already ready" (v. 17) and awaits response from those invited. The intent of the parable is best summarized by a statement and a question. The statement: God is giving a party *now*, an outcast-embracing, forgiving party. The question: Are you going to come? The intent of the parable of the prodigal and elder sons is virtually the same.[40] These parables are strong evidence of Jesus' belief in the presence of the Kingdom in his ministry. His table fellowship with tax collectors and sinners and his dispensing forgiveness to them are indeed demonstrations of the presence of the kingdom.

The rejected invitations receive a prominence that should not be neglected. The excuses betray a preoccupation with everyday business and relations and presume people of some financial standing. The average farmer — to say nothing of the poor — does not buy five yoke of oxen, which would require that the man have at least one hundred acres.[41] Whether the excuses are legitimate or paper thin is debated, but for Luke this question is

---

38. See, e.g., Matt 8:11–12//Luke 13:28–29; Matt 11:20–24//Luke 10:13–15; Matt 12:33–37; Romans 2; 9:6; 2 Cor 13:5.

39. See, e.g., *1 Enoch* 1.1–9; 5.7–10; 58.1–4; 62.1–10; *2 Bar.* 13.8–12.

40. Cf. Eta Linnemann's comments on the parable of the prodigal son (*Parables of Jesus: Introduction and Exposition* [London: SPCK, 1966] 80).

41. Jeremias, *Parables,* 177. On the basis of *Ep. Arist.* 116 Goulder describes this man as belonging comfortably to the middle class (*Luke: A New Paradigm* 2. 594).

irrelevant.[42] His point is that no excuse is valid when one faces the kingdom. Possessions and relations are not to prohibit discipleship.

Nothing suggests, however, that the parable is a rejection of Israel or the Jewish people. Such a conclusion is a reading into the parable of Christian triumphalism. Nor are the strong words "None of those men invited will taste my meal" (v. 24) a rejection of Israel. Nothing suggests that either of the two groups of substitute guests (vv. 21, 23) refers to the gentiles. Despite the popularity of this suggestion from early in the church's history to present scholarship, I think such a conclusion is an allegorizing or, maybe better, a "christianizing" of the parable. If Luke thought this was the reference, he has done nothing to indicate it. Of primary importance is the description of the substitute guests in v. 21: the poor, the crippled, the blind, and the lame. As several people comment, no evidence exists to suggest that these groups or their location must refer to gentiles.[43] Further, no one suggests that the same list in 14:13 (the order is only slightly different) should be interpreted as referring to gentiles. How is a reader to know that the referent has changed in v. 21?

The significance of this grouping, however, is often overlooked. When John the Baptist sends emissaries to ask Jesus if he was the coming one, Jesus' response is that the messengers should tell John that "the blind are recovering sight, the lame are walking, the lepers are being cleansed, the dead are being raised, and the poor are receiving the good news" (Luke 7:22; cf. Matt 11:5). These words are taken from the description of God's salvation in Isa 29:18–19 and 35:5–6.[44] From this description John is to know that God's salvation has arrived. That three of the five groups in Luke 7:22 reappear in 14:21 surely is no coincidence. Rather than being a reference to the gentiles, these groups — the poor, crippled, blind, and lame — point to those people who responded to Jesus' ministry, that is, *Jews* benefitting from the presence of the Kingdom.

The parable is a challenge and a warning to those who assume election and their participation in the future Kingdom. The preoccupied guests who are excluded from the banquet are analogous to the preoccupied hearers of Jesus' message who do not discern the time and the importance of his ministry. Election does not derive from birth, and the intent of the parable is, as Sanders puts it, "that those who are confident they shall be at the eschato-

---

42. At least the first two excuses are not very impressive. No urgency exists with either excuse, and one is unlikely to have made the purchases without first examining the product. Linnemann's suggestion that the persons invited intended to come late is without basis and is only obtained by excluding v. 20 (*Parables*, 89, 159–62).

43. Schottroff, "Das Gleichnis vom großen Gastmahl," 204, 208; Braun, *Feasting and Social Rhetoric*, 89; Lemcio, "Parables," 9, 12–13.

44. The description obviously coincides with the themes of Isa 61:1–2 (and 42:7) quoted in Luke 4:18–19.

logical banquet in all likelihood will not be."[45] Attendance at the banquet is based on *response* to the invitation of God conveyed by Jesus, not on the title "invited one." The response called for cannot be put off to a future day while one goes about the routine of life, for the banquet has already begun with the ministry of Jesus.[46] A similar warning without the banquet motif is conveyed by the parable of the two sons (Matt 21:28–32) and sayings concerning those who presume entrance into the Kingdom because they have performed works in the Lord's name (Matt 7:21–23).

Luke 14:24 deserves further attention. At this point the narrative shifts from the singular to the plural "you" (ὑμῖν). Whereas the host had been addressing his servant, here the host or Jesus addresses all those present (or those who read). In all likelihood the voice of Jesus and the host merge at this point. The hearer or reader is to know that attendance at the banquet is determined by response to the message of Jesus.[47] An implicit christology is obvious, but it is left implicit.

Reflections

Of several matters still meriting comment, one is methodological. Jülicher's rejection of allegorizing was essential in his day, but his distortion of the parables as having only one point of correspondence between image and reality continues to haunt parable research, even though many have shown the inadequacies of this approach. A glance at the end of his treatment of the banquet parable reveals how much difficulty his views create.[48] He correctly interprets the parable as an analogy: as a man left in the lurch by his guests will not wait until they find it convenient to come, but will get other thankful guests, so will God since despite his work, his call to the Kingdom through Jesus has not been successful and others will take "your" place. But then, realizing that more than one correspondence exists, he confesses that this parable tempts one strongly towards a spiritual interpretation, and he grants the correspondences between the host and God, those invited and entrance into the Kingdom, the servants and God's messengers (especially Jesus). His comments become very brief at this point, but he still clings to

---

45. Sanders, "Luke's Great Banquet Parable," 259. As Sanders concludes, κεκλημένοι in Luke means "apparently elect" or "those who consider themselves elect" (ibid.).

46. In the words of Bruce Chilton, "Meals in Jesus' fellowship became practical parables whose meaning was as evocative as his verbal parables. . . . Each meal was a proleptic celebration of God's kingdom; the promise of the next was also an assurance of the kingdom" (*Pure Vision: Jesus' Vision of God* [Grand Rapids: Eerdmans, 1996] 86).

47. Derrett's suggestion that this verse alludes to the practice of sending portions of the meal to absent guests is without basis, so far as I can determine ("Parable of the Great Supper," 141, 155).

48. Jülicher, *Gleichnisreden* 2. 432.

the view that the allegorical elements were added later to a simple, fresh, and clear parable. But without the correspondences the analogy cannot work. This parable compels us to grant that various correspondences may exist in analogies, but those correspondences may be either clear or inexact. Parable interpretation is about discerning how analogies work, not merely about listing correspondences.

A second area for reflection has to do with the theological significance of meals in Luke. John R. Donahue argues for a three-level correspondence between the meals of the earthly Jesus, the eucharist, and the eschatological banquet.[49] Jesus' meals with sinners and the marginalized were, it seems to me, undoubtedly demonstrations of the presence of the kingdom, and several sayings use banquet imagery in describing the endtime. Luke does not explicitly connect the eucharist to the earthly meals, but, looking back, such a connection is hard to resist. The Qumran community, like the early church later, saw meals as an anticipation of the eschatological banquet. Luke does connect the eucharist and the endtime banquet. Possibly the most important text for this discussion is Luke 22:14–30, in which Luke's account of the initiation of the eucharist is framed with future kingdom references in vv. 16, 18, and 30. If the kingdom is given to the disciples in anticipation of that future eating and drinking in the kingdom (v. 30), and if the eucharist is a remembrance of Jesus (and his common life with them), then the connection of the earthly meals, the eucharist, the meal with the risen Christ on the road to Emmaus, and the eschatological banquet all partake of one reality: the celebration of God's reign and enjoyment of life in the presence of God. The parable assumes this celebration is taking place, but the point of the parable is a warning to those who may well exclude themselves by their attention to the wrong things.

The parable is also fertile ground for reflection about gospel and mission. To the degree that people have a sense of a celebration of life with God both in the present and the future, the invitation to participate still goes out, and the warning against preoccupation is still relevant. The parable is not about mission, but it can be a worthwhile tool for reflection on mission. In all such reflection, however, caution and balance are necessary, for the extremes justified by this passage, particularly the clause "Compel them to come in" (14:23), are a stain on the history of the church.[50]

Finally, what does this parable teach us concerning common life with Jesus? Possibly most important is the rejection of all triumphalism. Presumption is as much a danger for Christians as it was for first-century Jews, and

49. Donahue, The Gospel in Parable (Philadelphia: Fortress, 1988) 140, 143–45.
50. See Frederick A. Norwood, "'Compel Them to Come In': The History of Luke 14:23," Religious Life 23 (1954) 516–27.

we need to remind ourselves that those who presume they are elect and will be at the endtime banquet may not be. At the same time, the parable still invites people — including those who do not belong — to come and celebrate the presence of the reign of God. With this comes a focus on discerning the time, for the presence of the Kingdom brings with it a sense of urgency and a warning against preoccupation with the pedestrian aspects of life. By implication the parable also rejects boundaries that exclude people deemed deficient and encourages a concern for the poor. "Happy is the one who eats bread in the kingdom of God" (Luke 14:15).[51]

---

51. Appreciation is expressed to the Pew Foundation for partial funding of my research on parables.

14

THE BEGINNINGS OF
CHRISTIAN LIFE IN JERUSALEM
ACCORDING TO THE SUMMARIES
IN THE ACTS OF THE APOSTLES

(Acts 2:42–47; 4:32–37; 5:12–16)

ANDREAS LINDEMANN

The NT writings tell us relatively little of the ordinary daily life of people in the first century. The social, economic, and cultural circumstances that determined the life of the individual Christian are hardly alluded to either in the epistles or in the narrative texts, and so ordinary daily life is known to us only indirectly.[1] The authors of the first Christian narratives had apparently no intention of informing their readers of the social circumstances surrounding their tales, and the writers of the epistles were generally not at all interested in informing their addressees of the social situation they were in or in taking any position relative to it. A certain exception appears among the epistles in Paul's letters to the Corinthians[2] and in the narratives of Luke's two volumes.[3] The third evangelist takes up the question (which does not

---

1. There is no direct archaeological evidence of the communities mentioned in the NT, which is a distinct disadvantage for any "sociological" analysis of early Christian lifestyle. The problem is precisely described in Graydon F. Snyder, *Ante Pacem: Archaeological Evidence of Church Life before Constantine* (Macon, Ga.: Mercer University Press, 1985) 7–11, esp. 10.

2. 1 Corinthians and the two "collection letters" in 2 Corinthians 8 and 9 offer some information but little in detail. See the treatment in Reimund Bieringer, ed., *The Corinthian Correspondence* (BETL 125; Louvain: Leuven University Press, 1996), and esp. Hans Dieter Betz, *2 Corinthians 8 and 9: A Commentary on Two Administrative Letters of the Apostle Paul* (Hermeneia; Philadelphia: Fortress, 1985).

3. The name "Luke" will be used here to designate the otherwise unknown author of the third gospel and the Acts of the Apostles.

seem to be of any interest to the other authors of the story of Jesus) of how the Jesus movement financed itself (Luke 8:1–3), and thus informs us at least in summary fashion about the daily life of the "primitive community," that is, of the group of Jews in Jerusalem who believed in the resurrection of Jesus (Acts 2:42–47; 4:32–35, 36–37; cf. 5:12–16).

The question of whether and to what extent the reports in these "summaries" can be called historically trustworthy is disputed, but this will not concern us further here.[4] Also the question whether Luke had literary sources at his disposal or created freely can remain unanswered.[5] The question here is rather that of the literary function of these summaries and thus their theological meaning: Why is it that Luke offers not *one* but *three* general summaries of his beginning history of the post-Easter Jesus movement in Jerusalem, which partly overlap but also seem to be partly in tension with and partly complementary to one another? If one is unwilling to explain the existing text simply by saying that Luke found differing traditions and worked them into his text, then one must try to explain the present text from the totality of Luke's work.[6] Although the third summary's content is quite different from the first two, it performs much the same narrative function,[7] and thus is to be included in this discussion.[8]

Acts 2:42–47

In Acts 2, Luke narrates the "Pentecost experience" (vv. 1–13) and follows it with a sermon of Peter's explaining the events that have just occurred. The center of the sermon includes complete quotations of Joel 3:1–5 LXX (vv. 17–21) and of Ps 15:8–11 LXX (vv. 25–28). The purpose of the ser-

---

4. On this, see the summaries of research in Ernst Haenchen, *Die Apostelgeschichte* (KEK 3; 14th ed.; Göttingen: Vandenhoeck & Ruprecht, 1965) 155–58; Heinrich Zimmermann, "Die Sammelberichte der Apostelgeschichte," *BZ* n.F. 5 (1961) 71–82, esp. 71–73; Gerd Theissen, "Urchristlicher Liebeskommunismus: Zum 'Sitz im Leben' des Topos ἅπαντα κοινά," in Tord Fornberg and David Hellholm, eds., *Texts and Contexts: Biblical Texts in Their Textual and Situational Contexts: Essays in Honor of Lars Hartman* (Oslo and Boston: Skandinavian University Press, 1995) 689–712, esp. 689–91. Theissen develops the idea, against the current critical consensus, that it was the "Hellenists" in Jerusalem who attempted to bring about the ἅπαντα κοινά, and that after the expulsion of this group from Jerusalem the experiment ended quickly, but indirectly continued in the form of the Pauline collection for Jerusalem (706–10).

5. On this see Zimmermann, "Die Sammelberichte," and Rudolf Pesch, *Die Apostelgeschichte* (EKKNT 5; Zurich: Benziger; Neukirchen-Vluyn: Neukirchener Verlag, 1986) 129–30 (on Acts 2:42–47).

6. See the posing of the question in S. J. Noorda, "Scene and Summary: A Proposal for Reading Acts 4.32–5.16," in Jacob Kremer, ed., *Les Actes des Apôtres: Traditions, Rédaction, Théologie* (BETL 48; Gembloux: Duculot; Louvain: Leuven University Press, 1979) 475–83, esp. 479.

7. Noorda ("Scene and Summary," 480) sees 4:32–5:16 as a narrative unit, as also 2:1–47 and 3:1–4:31. He argues correctly that the "summary reports" are to be read as part of the composition of Acts, and not as "interruptions" of the individual stories.

8. On what follows compare the synopsis of the three summaries at the end of the article.

mon is the allusion to the exaltation of the crucified Jesus corresponding to the witness of David in Ps 109:1 LXX (vv. 34–35).[9] To their question "What should we do?" the audience is told to repent, to have themselves baptized in the name of Jesus, and to be rescued from "this perverse generation" (vv. 34–40).[10] Luke then narrates that "on that day" (v. 41, connecting directly to v. 1) there were three thousand people baptized. If the narrative of Acts 3:1–10 were to follow immediately, we would not notice anything missing. But Luke offers his readers at this juncture a summarizing overview of the way of life of the baptized in Jerusalem (2:42–47). Whether a new section then begins with v. 42 or with v. 43 is hard to decide.[11] On the one hand, no subject is expressly mentioned in v. 42,[12] so we are apparently to think that the 120 faithful of 1:12–15, and especially the newly baptized three thousand, are meant, so that the summary would begin with v. 43 (ἐγίνετο . . . φόβος). On the other hand, after v. 41 Luke abandons the description of specific individual experiences and goes into organizational data and the material basis on which such a large group came into being so quickly.[13] This points to a beginning of the summary at v. 42.

The first declaration in 2:42a refers to the steady holding fast (ἦσαν προσκαρτεροῦντες) to the "teaching of the apostles," by which Luke makes clear that the twelve apostles already referred to (1:26; cf. 2:37) are sufficiently without change to ensure the unity and continuity of the teaching of Jesus.[14] The second statement (τῇ κοινωνίᾳ) points to the community as it had been pictured (though without the term) in 1:13–14. And so Luke emphasizes that in spite of the increase in size of the group of the baptized, it was still possible to maintain the structure in every aspect. To this common

---

9. For an analysis of the speech and the context, see Marion L. Soards, *The Speeches in Acts: Their Content, Context, and Concerns* (Louisville, Ky.: Knox, 1994) 31–38.

10. Luke T. Johnson (*The Literary Function of Possessions in Luke-Acts* [SBLDS 39; Missoula, Mont.: Scholars Press, 1977] 184) notes the parallelism between Acts 2:37–41 and Luke 3:10, 11. Johnson adds, "What Luke has to say about possessions in the following verses [42–47] falls within the context of conversion." There is, however, a difference whether the Baptist *demands* a readiness to distribute alms as part of the penitence connected with baptism or whether Peter in answer to the question τί ποιήσωμεν; demands conversion and baptism and then the social reality of the baptized is *described*.

11. See the different treatment of the text in Nestle-Aland, 25th edition, where the new paragraph begins in 2:43, and the 26th and 27th editions, where it begins in 2:42.

12. One meets continually in the literature the formulation that Luke here depicts the life of the "Christian community," but we must note that Luke avoids using any name for the group (the word ἐκκλησία shows up for the first time in 5:11).

13. It is of no importance in this connection that the number three thousand is completely unrealistic; what is important is that Luke uses this to show that the way of life described in 2:42–47 involves not just a small group but a large unit.

14. The word διδαχή appears in Luke's two-volume work up to now only in Luke 4:32 (=Mark 1:22); in Acts 1:1 the activity of Jesus is described with the words ποιεῖν and διδάσκειν. Thus the διδαχή is actually the teaching of Jesus. In the rest of Acts διδαχή (5:28; 13:12, διδαχὴ τοῦ κυρίου; 17:19) and especially the verb διδάσκειν characterize concepts of the teaching of the apostles.

religious life belong also the "breaking of bread" and "prayer" (2:42b). The phrase κλάσις τοῦ ἄρτου refers right back to Luke 24:35: since the "breaking of bread" by Jesus is the sign of recognition for the disciples at Emmaus, the phrase points out that the larger group had come to hold fast to the religious practice of the pre-Easter Jesus tradition. The much-discussed question whether the "breaking of bread" here refers to the eucharist or to another common meal does not much matter here.[15] In any case it is a specific activity tied to the person of Jesus, which then continues unchanged after Pentecost.[16] The fourth mark of the group mentioned are the προσευχαί, where the notion of continuity is central, and indeed the continuity both with the already begun post-Easter practices (see Acts 1:14) and with the prayer practice of Jesus (cf. Luke 3:21; 5:16; 6:12; 9:18, 28; 11:2–4). So Luke shows in Acts 2:42 that everything that was valid for the small group of believers immediately after Easter continues to be binding on the completely differently sized group after "Pentecost." Thus it is no coincidence that the reference to the διδαχή of the apostles is emphasized, since for him everything else derives from this.

When we look at the parallel texts, 4:32–37 and 5:12–16, from the viewpoint of 2:42, it is no wonder that echoes are missing. Luke would weaken the statements formulated there by repeating them; yet in fact they are programmatic for the whole presentation that follows. It is only after the "departure" of Paul that open peril will arise to the unity and correct belief of the community (20:29–31).

After he has pictured the "internal view" of the community in 2:42, Luke changes the perspective in v. 43: What impression does the community of believers make on its surroundings? Everyone (πᾶσα ψυχή) in Jerusalem is filled with fear. According to the idiom of the gospel it is clear that φόβος does not mean "anxiety" here, but rather the "fear" or "awe" which corresponds to a revelatory event (Luke 1:12; 2:9; 7:16; and often).[17] The immediate cause of this fear is only mentioned afterwards, namely, the miracle working of the apostles. The allusion to the τέρατα καὶ σημεῖα is of course surprising, for there has been no report of miracles in Acts thus far.

---

15. For later pictorial representations of the bread or of the meal, see Snyder, *Ante Pacem,* 64–65.

16. One may question whether Luke even accepts a post-Easter repetition of the meal of Luke 22:15–20, and then whether he would pass this on with the abbreviated κλάσις τοῦ ἄρτου without any mention of the cup. Luke describes the last meal of Jesus with the two cups emphatically as a Passover meal. But then he gives a command to repeat this only with the bread (Luke 22:19; cf. 1 Cor 11:24) whereas with the one chalice there is neither the command to repeat (cf. 1 Cor 11:25b) nor any correspondence to the Markan ἔπιον ἐξ αὐτοῦ πάντες (Mark 14:23; cf. Matt 26:27, πίετε ἐξ αὐτοῦ πάντες). Does Luke mean possibly that the Last Supper should *not* be repeated in the way he has described it?

17. See Hans Conzelmann, *Die Apostelgeschichte* (HKNT 7; Tübingen: Mohr [Siebeck], 1972) 37: "Awe before the holy community."

But the word spoken by God in the text from Joel quoted in 2:19 had mentioned that God ("I") would perform τέρατα in the heavens and σημεῖα on earth, so that v. 43b seems to be the fulfillment of this announcement.[18] Accordingly the apostles are not thought of as the actual miracle workers, but rather those *through whom* the miracles occur. The first miracle story within Acts occurs immediately afterwards, in 3:1–10; thus through this general remark in 2:43 Luke has established that the miracle of the healing of the lame man appears as *one* miracle among many.

There is no parallel to the statement of 2:43 in the second summary (4:32–37). Luke appears to be satisfied to have referred wholesale to the miracle working of the apostles and then to have put in a concrete miracle story as an example. In the third summary (5:12–16) there is a drastic change, which concentrates essentially on the miracle working of the apostles and so even verbally alludes to 2:43.[19] Apparently Luke saw, after the story of 5:1–11, the need to have a fuller treatment of the healing, and helping miracles "at the hands of the apostles" follow the story of the two punishment miracles.

In 2:44a Luke states that πάντες οἱ πιστεύοντες[20] were ἐπὶ τὸ αὐτό[21] ("together"), so the situation of 1:15 and 2:1 has not basically changed. But — and here Luke introduces a whole new emphasis — "they held all things in common" (v. 44b). In the commentaries it is commonly pointed out that the phrase ἅπαντα κοινά expresses a classic ideal of friendship.[22] How

---

18. The term σημεῖα is used in 2:19, though not in Joel 3:3 LXX; thus the quotation is perhaps changed in anticipation of the statement of 2:43.

19. The formulation διὰ τῶν ἀποστόλων (2:42b) is varied in 5:12a to διὰ τῶν χειρῶν τῶν ἀποστόλων.

20. Luke here for the first time expressly mentions the ones whose life he is describing. A few manuscripts, including א and B, instead of the present participle πιστεύοντες read the aorist πιστεύσαντες; the broader, atemporal present participle denotes simply "the believers," so "the Christians."

21. Brian J. Capper ("Community of Goods in the Early Jerusalem Church," ANRW 2.26.2 [1995] 1738–40) opines that ἐπὶ τὸ αὐτό here and in 2:47 (προσετίθει…ἐπὶ τὸ αὐτό) is an indication of the use of a Semitic-language source: ἐπὶ τὸ αὐτό "is the Semitic equivalent of יחד," which is found very often in the Community Rule from Qumran (1QS); hence "an early Semitic source behind these two verses would have read: 'All the believers belonged to the יחד, and selling their property and possessions distributed them (i.e. the proceeds) to all....'" (1740). From this Capper judges in favor of the historicity of the community situation depicted in Acts 1–6: the first Christians in Jerusalem took over the property regulations from the Essenes at Qumran. According to Rainer Riesner ("Das Jerusalemer Essenerviertel und die Urgemeinde," ANRW 2.26.2 [1995] 1775–1922), this is connected with the proximity of the first community to the Essene Quarter in Jerusalem. But to be noted is that Luke has already used the phrase ἐπὶ τὸ αὐτό in Acts 1:15 and 2:1 certainly without the use of any source (cf. also 1 Cor 7:5 and esp. 11:20; 14:23). In the LXX ἐπὶ τὸ αὐτό is used for לבד (Exod 26:9); in Judg 6:33 the LXX has συνήχθησαν ἐπὶ τὸ αὐτό for ויאספו יחדו, where יחד is not a technical term (similarly Ps 2:2). ἐπὶ τὸ αὐτό of itself says nothing about the property relationships of those assembled.

22. Citations from classical Greek philosophy (Plato, Aristotle) and later hellenistic philosophy (including Philo) are frequently given; see, e.g., Conzelmann, *Die Apostelgeschichte*, 37;

Luke wants the phrase to be understood he says himself in 2:45:[23] the believers sold property[24] and possessions[25] and distributed the proceeds according to the need of each. Here the tenses used by Luke are of particular importance: the imperfects ἐπίπρασκον and διεμέριζον show that the "believers" did not at one stroke give up all their possessions, but that in any case of need sold off possessions in order to be able to help out the needy.[26] The idea is therefore obviously not that there was a common purse with common access, rather that those who held extra wealth beyond what was necessary for living sold that off in favor of those in need.[27] This is the part of the first summary that is made more fully precise in the second summary (4:32–35), in which decisive statements and concepts are repeated verbatim.[28]

With 2:46 Luke connects the report with the beginning of the summary (2:42) and also with the end of the gospel (Luke 24:53). We hear that the faithful collected harmoniously in the temple daily,[29] but that the "breaking of bread" was held in the houses of the believers. That the believers still visited the temple has not been mentioned before, but the information is immediately illustrated in the narrative of 3:1–10. The formulation at the start of v. 46a leads one to think that the believers had assembled as a group (ὁμοθυμαδόν) in the temple. Whether and to what extent that is realistic is for Luke of no import;[30] the decisive thing is that the believers on

Theissen, "Liebeskommunismus," 696–97. On the question whether Luke himself coined the phrase or found it already in earlier Christian tradition, see ibid., 696–700.

23. The καί that begins 2:45 is obviously epexegetical. Research often notes a contradiction or at least a tension between 2:44 and 2:45, since the latter presupposes no common possession of everything. Yet Luke clearly wants to show in 2:45 how this ἅπαντα κοινά really looked. Alan C. Mitchell ("The Social Function of Friendship in Acts 2:44–47 and 4:32–37," *JBL* 111 [1992] 255–72) notes emphatically that the principle expressed in κοινὰ τὰ φίλων was interpreted quite variously in antiquity: "Authors like Aristotle, Cicero, Seneca and Plutarch used the friendship maxim to uphold the social order of their day. They did not use it to advocate reform and social leveling. If anything their interpretations of the maxim support social distinctions" (264). Luke then is supposed instead to want to address the problem of the social order: "Luke had more in mind than alluding to a primitive Christian utopia when he incorporated elements of the Greco-Roman friendship ideal in his summary descriptions of the early Jerusalem community. The context of the maxims ἅπαντα κοινά and ψυχὴ μία directs their function toward the practical problem of how property will be held in his community and how those who have it will benefit those who do not by adopting a new view of friendship" (272). Admittedly the term φίλος appears in Acts only in 27:3; it seems there to be Luke's conscious reflecting the φιλανθρώπως treatment by the centurion Julius.

24. ὕπαρξις elsewhere in the NT only in Heb 10:34.

25. This must be the meaning of αὐτά.

26. καθότι in the sense of "each"; ἂν εἶχεν is past iterative.

27. Codex D reads expressly ὅσοι κτήματα εἶχον ἢ ὑπάρξεις, clearly to avoid the impression that all the Christians could have been wealthy.

28. This concerns the central statements ἅπαντα κοινά and καθότι ἄν τις χρείαν εἶχεν and the verb πιπράσκω.

29. The vocable προσκαρτερέω is repeated, although the meaning has changed since the verb now has a local sense.

30. After all, Luke is thinking here of more than "three thousand" people.

the one hand are obviously Jews, who would naturally visit the temple, and on the other hand are also a special, identifiable group. The second statement in v. 46a (κλῶντες... ἄρτον) pinpoints the reference to the κλάσις τοῦ ἄρτου in 2:42: by "the breaking of bread" is meant not a cultic action, which would be tied to a particular place, but the common mealtime held in houses, though we must remember that Luke has specified a very large number of participants. That there were noncultic meals we see from v. 46b (μετελάμβανον τροφῆς), while the emphatic reference to the (eschatological) ἀγαλλίασις (joy) and to the ἀφελότης (simplicity) of the heart[31] shows the religious dimension of the meetings "in the houses."

In 2:47a, with the reference to the praise of God the picture of 2:46a is strengthened: the believers praise God (not Christ), and thus again show themselves believing Jews (cf. again Luke 24:53, εὐλογοῦντες τὸν θεόν). This leads to the special respect they enjoy from the whole populace — that is, at least the Jewish public in Jerusalem noticed the pious and overall exemplary life of the "believers."[32]

The summary closes in 2:47b with the notation that Christ (ὁ κύριος) daily "added" further σῳζόμενοι to the ἐπὶ τὸ αὐτό. With this Luke on the one hand picks up 2:40 (σώθητε) and 2:41 (προσετέθησαν...); on the other, he underlines that the added ones will not change the structure of the existing group (ἐπὶ τὸ αὐτό, as in 2:44).[33] In the designation οἱ σῳζόμενοι (cf. 1 Cor 1:18) is contained of course the thought that the eschatological redemption will come only to those who stand in relation to Christ (cf. Acts 4.12); at the same time the formulation shows that those meant in no way represent any special group outside Judaism; hence also the temple scenes in Acts 3 and the description of the hearing before the Sanhedrin in Acts 4.[34]

There is a further hint of the growing number of believers in 4:4, where Luke, in connection with the temple sermon of Peter, similar to 2:41, mentions a large number ("five thousand men"). In the third summary, which is primarily concerned with miracles, Luke emphasizes the continual accretion of believers (5:14), while the second summary (4:32–35) offers no parallel to 2:46, 47; it seems that it has a clearly different function from the first summary.

Luke gives notice that in spite of the huge growth in the number of the baptized (2:41) there is an unbroken continuity from the time of the pre-Easter Jesus and beyond to the Easter situation: the guarding of the teaching,

---

31. There is no need for some suspicion or other about the character of these mealtimes lurking behind this statement.

32. Noteworthy is the correction in Codex D, which speaks not only of κόσμος instead of λαός, but beyond that in v. 47b introduces the catchword ἐκκλησία, thus introducing the "church" as the conceptually nameable special group.

33. See n. 21 above.

34. The large number of manuscripts (mostly later ones) which read τῇ ἐκκλησίᾳ at the end of 2:47 show that this idea, decisive for Luke, had been forgotten.

the community, the common meal according to the instruction of Jesus, the prayers, together with the miracle working activity through the apostles — all of these are outwardly visible and thoroughly recognized signs of those who have had themselves baptized and are therefore οἱ σωζόμενοι, without any change at all in their status as Jews who frequent the temple and praise God. Community ownership, that is, the readiness to give up possessions to help the needy, is one of the signs of the believers (2:44–47). But this is in no way *the* prominent mark, and especially is this not the practice that was particularly noticed from without. While in 2:42–43 and in 2:46–47 there is mention of the "outward effect" of the living and faith practice of the baptized, there is no corresponding parallel in 2:44–45. Does Luke perhaps precisely wish to avoid the impression that the effort for social equality was particularly attractive to outsiders?[35]

It is important that the summary in Acts 2:42–47 looks not to the past but forward, and offers an encompassing picture of the life of the community. Except for the mention of the "teaching of the apostles" and the "breaking of the bread," with which Luke takes up things already mentioned, all the other statements are only narratively illustrated in the following parts of Acts. The summary thus sets up for the reader an expectant tension with the question how one can concretely imagine what is described here only in hints.

Acts 4:32–37

The second summary, in Acts 4:32–37, is contextualized quite differently from the first summary. Luke does not place it after 4:4.[36] Instead, after 4:4 he notes the great missionary success which followed Peter's sermon and arrest in Solomon's portico and describes Peter's hearing before the council (4:5–22) and the subsequent gathering and prayer of the ἴδιοι (4:23–30).[37] He concludes by noting the public preaching which followed the outpouring of the Spirit on the group. The scenario depicted in 4:23–30 is unrealistic because according to 4:4 five thousand men (i.e., males) would have had to be involved, but this is of no importance to Luke.

Unlike 2:42, Luke's second summary in 4:32 is not formulated in relationship to what has already happened. Instead, interrupting the narrative account, it depicts the contemporary situation. The life of the community is not described in its entirety. Instead the focus is on a single point: how possessions are dealt with within the community. The practice is first briefly

---

35. According to the satirical depiction of the Christians by Lucian (*Peregr.* 13), it was characteristic of them that they supported financially those who had fallen into need, so that a sly con man could quickly get rich.

36. The statement of 4:4 matches 2:41.

37. On this, see Soards, *Speeches in Acts*, 47–50.

described in 4:32–35 (along the lines of the earlier summary in 2:44–45) and then illustrated, first by a positive example in 4:36–37 and then by a negative example in 5:1–11. A new element, not found in 2:44–45, is that the group being described is explicitly identified. The phrase πλῆθος τῶν πιστευσάντων is obviously meant to include all those whose adherence is recorded in the first four chapters of Acts.[38] The phrase καρδία καὶ ψυχὴ μία ("one heart and soul") emphasizes the inner unity of the whole group of "those who had come to believe." Of special importance is the assertion that "the company of those who believed were of one heart and soul."[39] This description summarizes in one succinct formulation everything said at greater length in 2:42–44a and 2:46–47a.[40]

The real theme is introduced in 4:32b: the believers did not refer to their possessions as "belonging" (ἴδιον εἶναι) to them.[41] The idea seems to be not that τὰ ὑπάρχοντα (possessions, belongings) were given up but, because individual possessions were placed at the disposal of all, that any private claim on possessions was renounced. (This is similar, of course, to the admonition in the "Teaching of the Two Ways" in *Did.* 4.8 and *Barn.* 19.8: οὐκ ἐρεῖς ἴδια εἶναι.) The phrase ἅπαντα κοινά is taken word-for-word from 2:44. All this corresponds to Luke's description of the practice of the women who accompanied Jesus (Luke 8:3, διηκόνουν αὐτοῖς ἐκ τῶν ὑπαρχόντων αὐτοῖς).

The surprising thing is that vv. 34–35 do not follow immediately after this introductory verse. Instead, in 4:33 Luke inserts a brief reference to the missionary preaching of the apostles for which there are no parallels in Luke's first summary. That first summary mentions the τέρατα καὶ σημεῖα performed by the apostles. In this second summary Luke speaks of apostles bearing witness with great δύναμις (power) to the resurrection. This confirms that 4:32–37, more much than 2:42–47, includes the description of a new state of affairs. Luke clearly wants to communicate to the reader that the reality depicted in 4:32, 34–35 stems from the proclamation of the resurrection.

---

38. As before, Luke avoids the term ἐκκλησία.

39. μία ψυχή is like κοινὰ τὰ φίλων (similar to ἰσότης φιλότης and γόνυ κνήμης ἔγγιον, "the knee is closer than the calf," a Greek proverbial statement; cf. Aristotle *E. N.* 9.8.1168b.6–8); the connection of καρδία and ψυχή is biblical language (Deut 6:5). David L. Mealand ("Community of Goods and Utopian Allusions in Acts II–IV," *JTS* n.s. 28 [1977] 96–99) sees behind the Greek tradition corresponding to 4:32 less an ideal of friendship than a utopian model.

40. Again it is noteworthy that the reading of codex D (and Cyprian) finds it necessary to emphasize that there is no διάκρισις (differentiation, quarrel) between them (codex E: no χωρισμός [separation]). Here is reflected ecclesial reality, which Luke surely already knows but at this point will not even marginally allude to.

41. See Friedrich Wilhelm Horn, *Glaube und Handeln in der Theologie des Lukas* (GTA 26; Göttingen: Vandenhoeck & Ruprecht, 1983) 40: "Private ownership remains, but the owners consider it not as private but as common possession"; Horn gives examples of the distinction between ἴδιος and κοινός.

Thus it is appropriate that, like 2:43a and especially 2:47, 4:33 ends with another reference to the external effects of this proclamation. The phrase χάρις μεγάλη refers not to "God's great grace" but to the "great state of favor, or good will," conferred upon all.[42] The reason for this — γάρ (for, because)[43] — is identified in v. 34a: not a single needy person was to be found among all the thousands of believers. In other words, though Luke does not say this explicitly, the injunction of Deut 15:4, read as a promise, has become a reality.[44]

Luke describes how this is achieved in 4:34b–35. Those who owned land or rental properties sold them and brought the proceeds to the apostles.[45] Verse 35b should be read as saying that the apostles then undertook the task of distributing this money to those in need. In 4:34b–35 Luke repeats from 2:45 the key verb πιπράσκω and the important expression καθότι ἄν τις χρείαν εἶχεν. But a precision he adds to 2:45 should also be noted. On the one hand, Luke avoids repeating from 2:45 the unqualified phrase τὰς ὑπάρξεις ἐπίπρασκον and says explicitly that properties, not possessions ab- solutely necessary for life, were involved.[46] On the other hand, in place of the equally unqualified expression διεμέριζον αὐτὰ πᾶσιν ("distributed them to all," 2:45) a rather exact description of how the money obtained by these transactions was handled is added. In the two narratives that follow Luke re- peats the expression ἐτίθουν παρὰ τοὺς πόδας τῶν ἀποστόλων ("laid [it] at the apostles' feet"), thus showing that the apostles were accorded the right to dispose of the money involved.[47] The money was not distributed arbi- trarily. Rather the highest authority, the circle of the apostles, undertook

---

42. According to Haenchen (*Apostelgeschichte*, 188 n. 5, on Luke 2:40), in Acts 4:33 Luke has in mind not the "advantage" of the people but the grace of God. But Luke 2:40 says expressly χάρις θεοῦ ("grace *of God*"); as parallel to Acts 4:33, Acts 2:47 is closer. On χάρις in Acts with no further designation, see 7:10.

43. Richard B. Hays (*The Moral Vision of the New Testament: A Contemporary Introduction to New Testament Ethics* [San Francisco: Harper, 1996] 123) emphasizes correctly the γάρ in v. 34; he likewise understands χάρις μεγάλη in the sense of the "grace" of God: "The absence of needy persons in the community is itself the warrant for the preceding theological claim that 'great grace was upon them all.'"

44. In Deut 15:4 it is stated that in connection with the year of remission no one among the people should be in need (cf. LXX: ὅτι οὐκ ἔσται ἐν σοὶ ἐνδεής, ὅτι εὐλογῶν εὐλόγησει σε κύριος ὁ θεός σου ἐν τῇ γῇ ᾗ κύριος ὁ θεός σου δίδωσίν σοι ἐν κλήρῳ κατακληρονομῆσαι αὐτήν).

45. On the supposition that the "houses" were according to Luke's treatment rented houses, the often-mentioned contradiction disappears when in Acts 12:12 there is mention of "the house of Maria."

46. The χωρία (pieces of land, fields) and οἰκίαι (houses) mentioned here are obviously not the homes of those doing the selling. It is (presumably) not the view of Luke that a farmer should sell his fields or that one should sell the house he or she lives in and thus become homeless.

47. See Jouette M. Bassler, *God and Mammon: Asking for Money in the New Testament* (Nash- ville: Abingdon, 1991) 124–25. Biblical examples of the phrase "to lay at someone's feet" are 2 Sam 22:39; Ps 8:7; 110:1. Theissen ("Urchristlicher Liebeskommunismus," 694 n. 23) notes a remarkable parallel in Cicero (*Flacc.* 68).

responsibility for its distribution. This corresponds to what is mentioned in 2:45 ("as any had need"), but guarantees that any abuse in the distribution of the money is excluded. It is true that the logical subject of the passive verb διεδίδετο ("distribution was made") is not identified. Nevertheless, the prior reference to the apostles makes their direct involvement very probable. The change from πᾶσιν ("to all," 2:45) to ἑκάστῳ ("to each," 4:35) should also be noted. Luke seems to want to convey that "each individual" had to present evidence of his or her need before receiving the required money from the apostles.

Thus the summary in Acts 4:32–35 offers as exact a description as possible of the "social" dimension of the "believers'" life together. It is striking that the focus is on those who give, not on those who receive. This shows that Luke is more concerned with those in his own time who have possessions than he is with the needy. To this topic I shall return below. The two narratives that follow fit into this framework. Barnabas sells an acre of land (not all his possessions) and dutifully hands over the money to the apostles (4:36–37). Ananias and Sapphira, on the other hand, secretly retain for themselves part of the money from a similar sale and are immediately punished because they have attempted to deceive the Holy Spirit of God (5:1–10).

Acts 5:12–16

The third summary, in Acts 5:12–16, is different from the first two in that here the theme of "property" plays no role whatsoever. Instead the theme of "miracle" stands strongly in the foreground, a theme only hinted at in the first summary and completely absent in the second.[48] Luke sees himself led, after the miracle of punishment in 5:1–11, to follow with a condensed reference to healing miracles. The comment that these miracles happen ἐν τῷ λαῷ ("among the people") emphasizes the characteristic that the apostles are consciously turning outward, beyond the circle of their own group, with their miraculous activity.[49] The reference to "Solomon's Portico" (5:12) indicates that Luke has special concern for the story of the healing of the lame man: the formulation in 2:46 (ὁμοθυμαδὸν ἐν τῷ ἱερῷ, "attending the temple together") is carefully connected with 3:11 in that "Solomon's Portico" is presented as a place where all can gather together.[50] The rest of the visitors to

---

48. See the synopsis on pp. 214–15 for the closeness of the language used.

49. The miracles have to a certain extent a missionary function, as Peter's statement in 3:6 and the commentary of the narrator in 3:8 show.

50. The question where this building was is of no importance here. In any case Luke gives his readers the impression it was somewhere in the temple area. Johnson (*Literary Function*, 195 nn. 1, 3) suggests that ἅπαντες means "all the *apostles*," and that in Acts 5:13 Luke is saying that no one dared to get close to them (in a physical sense): "All the uses of κολλάω in Acts (8:29; 9:26;

the temple do not dare to join (5:13a), while the reaction among the rest of the people is very positive.[51] With ἐμεγάλυνεν αὐτοὺς ὁ λαός ("the people held them in high honor," 5:13b) Luke again takes up in a substantially positive vein the pronouncements of 2:47 (ἔχοντες χάριν...) and 4:33 (χάρις τε μεγάλη ἦν ἐπὶ πάντας αὐτούς). Thereby the observation in 5:14, that the group of the "believers" has grown further, makes perfect sense (cf. 2:47; in the second summary such a reference was missing). Luke expressly notes in the process (5:14b) that it had to do with "men and women."[52] The formulation πιστεύοντες τῷ κυρίῳ is important: they trust in the Lord and this has the result (ὥστε, at the beginning of 5:15) that they bring the sick and the lame to the apostles to seek healing. Finally, a decidedly new emphasis appears in 5:16 as people also from the region around Jerusalem begin bringing sick people to find healing.[53]

The third summary says almost nothing about the life of those who believe in Jesus; it concentrates primarily on the external effects of the miraculous deeds of the apostles, which of course contribute considerably to the further growth in the number of believers. But like the two earlier summaries the third also stresses the unity of those who profess their belief in Jesus (ὁμοθυμαδόν in 5:12b, as in 2:46; cf. 4:32, καρδία καὶ ψυχὴ μία).

10:28; 17:34) make perfectly good sense when understood as indicating physical proximity. The element of 'spiritual allegiance' discerned in 17:34 is supplied by πιστεύω. Luke's use of κολλάω in the story of the Lost Son (Luke 15:15) indicates physical attachment but hardly an allegiance of mind and heart." Johnson adds that "the verse further emphasizes the majesty of the Apostles, lending them an aura of the numinous."

51. Daniel R. Schwartz ("Non-Joining Sympathizers [Acts 5.13–15]," *Bib* 64 [1983] 550–55) understands the statement of 5:13a from this perspective: because of the fate of Ananias and Sapphira, many feared "to cleave to the community as full members, namely by sharing their property"; in 5:13b and especially 5:14 Luke would then be saying that "many did associate themselves with the Christian community of Jerusalem, much as the well-known 'fearers of heaven' (or 'fearers of the Lord' or 'sympathizers') associated with contemporary ancient Judaism" (554). Here the short notice of Luke seems to be overinterpreted. Conzelmann (*Die Apostelgeschichte*, 47) thinks that "the apparent contradiction between v. 13 and v. 14 is a simple awkwardness of the narrator. Favor and fear produce the position of the community in the world," where οἱ λοιποί ("the rest") are the non-Christians. Against this Pesch (*Die Apostelgeschichte*, 206) prefers to see in the λοιποί the rest of the community members — those "who do not participate in the forbidden public sermon" — but this explanation is excluded by 4:31. Likeliest is the notion of Alfons Weiser (*Die Apostelgeschichte* [2 vols.; Ökumenischer Taschenbuchkommentar zum Neuen Testament 5; Gütersloh: Gütersloher Verlagshaus; Würzburg: Echter, 1981–85] 1. 150): the λοιποί are the outsiders who had not dared "as unauthorized to take part in the assemblies of the Christians." This, *contra* Johnson (see previous note), is the meaning of κολλᾶσθαι, at least in Acts 8:29; 9:26; 10:28 (otherwise only in 17:34, but even there it could mean that some joined Paul and followed him as he left the Areopagus).

52. Here the statement of Acts 4:4 recalling Luke 9:14 (five thousand *men*) gets a certain corrective.

53. Here the emphasis of 2:5–11 is strengthened: the apostles' activity was not limited to Jerusalem.

Acts 2:42–47

42 Ἦσαν δὲ προσκαρτεροῦντες
τῇ διδαχῇ τῶν ἀποστόλων
καὶ τῇ κοινωνίᾳ τῇ κλάσει τοῦ
ἄρτου καὶ ταῖς προσευχαῖς.
43 ἐγίνετο δὲ πάσῃ ψυχῇ φόβος,
πολλά τε τέρατα καὶ σημεῖα
διὰ τῶν ἀποστόλων ἐγίνετο.

44 πάντες δὲ οἱ πιστεύοντες
ἦσαν ἐπὶ τὸ αὐτὸ

καὶ εἶχον ἅπαντα κοινά

(ἔχοντες χάριν πρὸς ὅλον τὸν λαόν)

45 καὶ τὰ κτήματα καὶ τὰς ὑπάρξεις

ἐπίπρασκον
καὶ διεμέριζον αὐτὰ

πᾶσιν
καθότι ἄν τις χρείαν εἶχεν·

Acts 4:32–37

32 Τοῦ δὲ πλήθους τῶν πιστευσάντων
ἦν καρδία καὶ ψυχὴ μία
καὶ οὐδὲ εἷς τῶν ὑπαρχόντων αὐτῷ
ἔλεγεν ἴδιον εἶναι
ἀλλ᾽ ἦν αὐτοῖς ἅπαντα κοινά.
33 καὶ δυνάμει μεγάλῃ ἀπεδίδουν
τὸ μαρτύριον οἱ ἀπόστολοι
τῆς ἀναστάσεως τοῦ κυρίου Ἰησοῦ,
χάρις τε μεγάλη ἦν ἐπὶ πάντας αὐτούς.
34 οὐδὲ γὰρ ἐνδεής τις ἦν ἐν αὐτοῖς·
ὅσοι γὰρ κτήτορες χωρίων ἢ οἰκιῶν
ὑπῆρχον, πωλοῦντες ἔφερον τὰς τιμὰς
τῶν πιπρασκομένων
35 καὶ ἐτίθουν
παρὰ τοὺς πόδας τῶν ἀποστόλων·
διεδίδετο δὲ ἑκάστῳ
καθότι ἄν τις χρείαν εἶχεν.

Acts 5:12–16

12 Διὰ δὲ τῶν χειρῶν τῶν ἀποστόλων
ἐγίνετο σημεῖα καὶ τέρατα πολλὰ
ἐν τῷ λαῷ.
καὶ ἦσαν ὁμοθυμαδὸν ἅπαντες
ἐν τῇ στοᾷ Σολομῶντος,
13 τῶν δὲ λοιπῶν οὐδεὶς ἐτόλμα
κολλᾶσθαι αὐτοῖς,

ἀλλ᾽ ἐμεγάλυνεν αὐτοὺς ὁ λαός.

46 καθ' ἡμέραν τε προσκαρτεροῦντες ὁμοθυμαδὸν ἐν τῷ ἱερῷ, κλῶντές τε κατ' οἶκον ἄρτον, μετελάμβανον τροφῆς ἐν ἀγαλλιάσει καὶ ἀφελότητι καρδίας, 47 αἰνοῦντες τὸν θεὸν καὶ ἔχοντες χάριν πρὸς ὅλον τὸν λαόν. ὁ δὲ κύριος προσετίθει τοὺς σῳζομένους καθ' ἡμέραν ἐπὶ τὸ αὐτό.

(χάρις τε μεγάλη ἦν ἐπὶ πάντας αὐτούς)

36 Ἰωσὴφ δὲ ὁ ἐπικληθεὶς Βαρναβᾶς ἀπὸ τῶν ἀποστόλων, ὅ ἐστιν μεθερμηνευόμενον υἱὸς παρακλήσεως, Λευίτης, Κύπριος τῷ γένει 37 ὑπάρχοντος αὐτῷ ἀγροῦ πωλήσας ἤνεγκεν τὸ χρῆμα καὶ ἔθηκεν πρὸς τοὺς πόδας τῶν ἀποστόλων.

14 μᾶλλον δὲ προσετίθεντο πιστεύοντες τῷ κυρίῳ, πλήθη ἀνδρῶν τε καὶ γυναικῶν,

15 ὥστε καὶ εἰς τὰς πλατείας ἐκφέρειν τοὺς ἀσθενεῖς καὶ τιθέναι ἐπὶ κλιναρίων καὶ κραβάττων, ἵνα ἐρχομένου Πέτρου κἂν ἡ σκιὰ ἐπισκιάσῃ τινὶ αὐτῶν.
16 συνήρχετο δὲ καὶ τὸ πλῆθος τῶν πέριξ πόλεων Ἰερουσαλὴμ φέροντες ἀσθενεῖς καὶ ὀχλουμένους ὑπὸ πνευμάτων ἀκαθάρτων, οἵτινες ἐθεραπεύοντο ἅπαντες.

Conclusion

The first two summaries in Acts (2:42–47; 4:32–35) are substantially different from one another, but it is pointless to investigate them for tensions and contradictions and as a result to become entangled in hypotheses as to the history of the tradition or conjectures about the historicity of the events reported. In the context of the broad outline of Acts the summaries refer to different phases in the history of the "believers" in Jerusalem, and in so doing they describe different aspects of the life of the community. It is clear that Luke is not portraying a *community of possessions*, in either the first or the second summary, roughly corresponding to the purported community of possessions (and production) of the Essenes found in the Qumran writings or in the description in Josephus (*J.W.* 2.122–23).[54] Luke in no way states that the "believers" (πιστεύοντες) or, more exactly, "those who had become believers" (πιστεύσαντες) gave up all personal property and put the money into a common purse. The phrase ἄπαντα κοινά, appearing twice, is not meant to indicate an arrangement in which each individual might completely have given up his or her property or even the power to dispose of it. Theissen finds a contradiction between 4:32 and 4:34–35 because the first of these two texts deals with a "community of ownership without private ownership" whereas the second concerns "communal ownership that forms the basis for private usages."[55] Theissen supposes as a result that the "original Christian 'love communism'" became one of the accepted categories among the reform ideas of the Greeks within the community of Jerusalem, corresponding to the community of Qumran.[56] But the inner contradictions disappear if one reads already formulated in the summaries the concrete particulars of regular dealings with property as an explication of the basic expression ἄπαντα κοινά: Luke says that there was a readiness to forego property that was not necessary for life if thereby the basis for life could be established for others. Stress is laid on giving up possessions in favor of the needy, but this picture is connected with the viewpoint introduced in the second summary (and the attached stories), namely, that money made available in this manner would be administered properly by the apostles.

The question as to the actual, historical background of these summaries is of considerable interest, but it can hardly be answered. Of course, on the one

---

54. See Hans-Josef Klauck, "Gütergemeinschaft in der klassischen Antike, in Qumran und im Neuen Testament," in idem, *Gemeinde-Amt-Sakrament: Neutestamentliche Perspektiven* (Würzburg: Echter, 1989) 69–100, esp. 74–89.

55. Theissen, "Urchristlicher Liebeskommunismus," 704.

56. Ibid., 707: "The thought would be in this case not of the ever lagging reality at first pursued (the usual view), but rather it could have preceded it." On the problem of the idea of a "love communism," first broached by Ernst Troeltsch, see Gottfried Brakemeier, *Der "Sozialismus" der Urchristenheit: Experiment und neue Herausforderung* (KVR 1535; Göttingen: Vandenhoeck & Ruprecht 1988) 12–13.

hand it is entirely probable that the successors of Jesus coming from Galilee did not have an income that would guarantee them a life in Jerusalem, and that therefore they were forced to rely on "contributions" of the local inhabitants.[57] On the other hand, it is striking that the one definite report of a "contributor" refers to a Jew of the diaspora, so that at a minimum it cannot be excluded that it has to do with a very specific individual case.[58] But above all we should remember that we know absolutely nothing about the size and the social composition of the group of Christians in Jerusalem.

Did Luke reach back to tradition in composing the summaries? This question likewise cannot really be answered. Theissen concludes from the strikingly large number of *hapax legomena* that Luke did not formulate the summaries "freely."[59] But this argument is at least problematical. Both of the summaries that portray the life of the "believers" are entirely unique within the framework of the Lukan two-volume work, so it is easily imaginable that here Luke is also making efforts to deal with an especially nuanced language.

In contrast, it is probably easier to provide insight into the oft-discussed problem whether Luke wanted to describe a binding norm for the contemporary church with his two summaries or whether he simply wanted to show that the community of Jerusalem in the early days of the church conformed to a typical ideal (Greek as well as Jewish).[60] We must not overlook the fact that Luke does not describe structures of a small "original community," but rather the social constitution of a "large group" with several thousand members; his picture thereby raises the claim that it is valid not only for small communities but also for "large churches." Consequently the readiness to give up possessions in favor of the needy is, for Luke, presumably not the mark of a long buried "ideal" past; instead, Luke expects, or rather proposes, that this readiness exists everywhere and at all times.[61] In the process the further definition of the statements in 2:44–45 through the second summary in 4:34–35 shows that Luke by no means had a naive picture of an "ideal communism" which could function without more ado among such people as the "believers" or "those being saved."[62]

---

57. See Haenchen, *Die Apostelgeschichte*, 192.

58. Theissen ("Urchristlicher Liebeskommunismus," 703) thinks, with a nod to Martin Hengel, that Barnabas, coming from Cyprus, was perhaps mentioned only because "he was the best known case outside Jerusalem." Klauck mentions this too ("Gütergemeinschaft," 97).

59. Theissen, "Urchristlicher Liebeskommunismus," 702–3. Horn (*Glaube und Handeln*, 36–39) comes to a different conclusion: "The summary reports are marked with Lukan language; a pre-Lukan component is not in evidence linguistically."

60. This last is Conzelmann's thesis (*Die Apostelgeschichte*, 37): "this way of life is not pictured as a norm for the contemporary church. It is supposed to show the uniqueness of the ideal first years."

61. On the parenetic function of the summaries, see Horn, *Glaube und Handeln*, 43–47.

62. Klauck ("Gütergemeinschaft," 97) formulates it thus: there was in the original Jerusalem community, which we should not imagine very large, those who practiced a community of pos-

Instead, Luke lets it be known that the disposition of the available financial resources demanded meticulous supervision, in consequence of which the
apostles themselves took on the task. That this portrait indirectly contains a
binding instruction[63] for the whole subsequent history of the Jesus group, or
"church," becomes clear not least through the fact that in the further continuation of Acts Luke again speaks on this theme only in the Miletus speech of
Paul.[64] The readers therefore ought to understand that what is described in
both summaries is to be thought of as enduringly valid. Luke sketches a realistic picture, despite its "utopian" framework, and in doing so he demands, at
least in principle, its realization later on as well.

---

sessions with a charismatic-enthusiastic basis. "Charismatic" here means it was voluntary, not
forced, and was modeled on the renunciation of possessions exemplified by Jesus in his command
to love. The poor, who were to profit by this renunciation by the will of Jesus, were present in
plenty. "Enthusiastic" means that it was influenced by the imminent expectation of the end, a
consequence of the apocalyptic interpretation of the Easter experience. In this view any concern
for the future was virtually meaningless, and a complex organization was superfluous. No wonder,
then, that this would not go well in the long run, and so it came to the conflict described in 6:1.
Whether this thesis is *historically* accurate is not to be determined; *Luke* in any case does not at
all describe the reality of the community from this standpoint.

63. The action described in 6:1–6 has nothing to do with a dissolving of the organizational
control of 4:35 by the installation of the seven "deacons."

64. See Acts 20:35. In my opinion, Theissen's reflection ("Urchristlicher Liebeskommunismus," 695) is too modern — that Luke would have wanted to show in 20:32–35 that the
communities could exist "independent of wealthy donors." That Tabitha herself was in need
and could "exercise compassion only through her own handwork" (so Theissen, ibid., n. 25) is
not the natural meaning of Acts 9:36–39.

PART FOUR

COMMON LIFE
IN THE LETTERS
AND OTHER WRITINGS

15

PAUL AS ORGANIC INTELLECTUAL

The Shaper of Apocalyptic Myths

CALVIN J. ROETZEL

Books, sometimes multivolume books, offer critical descriptions of Paul's theology; detailed studies explore Paul's activity as a theologian. Given Paul's single-minded preoccupation with God's activity in the world, such treatments are natural, inevitable, and sometimes helpful. None to my knowledge, however, deals with Paul the intellectual even though Paul may be the foremost intellectual of the NT. In this essay I attend to Paul as an intellectual. I have been helped by Cornel West, who, following Antonio Gramsci, offers a broad and finely nuanced definition of intellectual activity as an *organic* exercise. An organic intellectual is a person bringing a high level of intellectual acuity to bear on the practical or social world, bringing parts of the whole into a meaningful connection.[1] Since Paul was passionately concerned with the community, and since his intellectual energies were devoted to persuading the community of the truth and power of his gospel, the expression *organic intellectual* may well describe the apostolic activity that gave his gospel a concrete, corporate significance. In the letters we see his fertile mind at work addressing his religiously uprooted converts, shaping their identity as the eschatologically elect, creating new forms of religiosity, and establishing an ethos for the "saints" in a new community. His skillful blending of activity and ideology was no disengaged, individualistic exercise, but a pas-

---

1. See Quintin Hoare and Geoffrey Noel Smith, trans., *Selections from the Prison Notebooks of Antonio Gramsci* (London: Lawrence & Wishart; New York: International, 1971) 10; West, *Prophesy Deliverance: An Afro-American Revolutionary Christianity* (Philadelphia: Westminster, 1982).

sionate, involved, and creative work for the world. Attention to this aspect of Paul's religious activity, I trust, is consistent with the lifelong work of Graydon Snyder, whom I am very pleased to honor with this essay.

While acute intellectual activity is evident at every level of Paul's discourse, for the sake of clarity and brevity I have chosen to focus on only one dimension of his intellectual activity, namely, the way he translated and transferred apocalyptic paradigms, myths, convictions, and topoi for and to the small circles of his converts. In light of the recent recognition that the substance of apocalyptic thinking is less a product of popular folklore than a result of scribal or learned activity, this choice would seem to be a valid one.[2] Moreover, such a consideration of Paul's appropriation and adaptation of the apocalyptic idiom may offer a way out of the scholarly debate about whether or not Paul was an apocalypticist. A brief recollection of this scholarly debate offers a useful context for our discussion.

The Scholarly Debate

In 1960 the late Ernst Käsemann concluded his epochal essay "The Beginnings of Christian Theology" by expressing the hope that his study had convincingly presented "apocalypticism as the mother of all Christian Theology."[3] Käsemann's proposal created an uproar. His *Doktorvater,* Rudolf Bultmann, replied that "Paul's theology and concept of history came not from apocalypticism but out of anthropology, namely, an understanding of human existence." He argued further that while a detemporalized and existential eschatology was the mother of Christian theology, a crude apocalypticism was

---

2. See John J. Collins, *The Apocalyptic Imagination: An Introduction to the Jewish Matrix of Christianity* (New York: Crossroad, 1984) 30, following Jonathan Z. Smith, "Wisdom and Apocalyptic," in Birger A. Pearson, ed., *Syncretism in Antiquity: Essays in Conversation with Geo Widengren* (Missoula, Mont.: Scholars Press, 1975) 131–56, repr. in Paul D. Hanson, ed., *Visionaries and Their Apocalypses* (Issues in Religion and Theology 4; Philadelphia: Fortress; London: SCM, 1983) 115–40.

3. Käsemann, "The Beginnings of Christian Theology," in idem, *New Testament Questions of Today* (Philadelphia: Fortress; London: SCM, 1969) 102 (German original in *ZTK* 57 [1960] 162–85); see further his "On the Subject of Primitive Christian Apocalyptic," in *New Testament Questions,* 108–37, esp. 137. (Käsemann's German noun *Apokalyptik* is almost universally mistranslated in English as the adjective, "apocalyptic," rather than the noun, "apocalypticism.") Käsemann had been greatly influenced by Albert Schweitzer's work on apocalypticism, and in at least one sense they were kindred spirits. On the Ogowe steamer on St. Stephen's Day, 1929, Schweitzer began the preface to his *Mysticism of Paul,* and before the steamer docked in Lambaréné he had rounded off the introduction with a final flourish: "Just because Paul's mystical doctrine of Christ has more to say to us when it speaks to us in the fire of its primitive-Christian, eschatological, manner of thought than when it is paraphrased into the language of modern orthodoxy or modern unorthodoxy, I believe I am serving in this work the cause not only of sound learning but also of religious needs" (*The Mysticism of Paul the Apostle* [London: Black, 1931; New York: Seabury/Crossroad, 1968] x).

not.[4] Philipp Vielhauer stated emphatically that Jesus' preaching had "noth-ing in common with Apocalyptic"[5] and Hans Conzelmann, a former student of Bultmann's, argued that Paul's theology was "based on nonapocalyptic credal formulations."[6] Willi Marxsen agreed and categorically stated that Paul "was not an apocalypticist."[7] More recently E. P. Sanders has disputed Käsemann's thesis, suggesting instead that the "conventions of apocalypticism had...little influence on [Paul]."[8] Sanders has been joined by Robin Scroggs, who argues that Paul inherited a structure with apocalyptic coloration but into that structure he poured something else "truly unique and original."[9] And Abraham J. Malherbe's work on 1 Thessalonians, while recognizing the apocalyptic aspects of Paul's letter, has rightly drawn attention to their pare-netic aspects.[10] But Malherbe's treatment of 1 Thessalonians as a parenetic letter in which Paul skillfully uses philosophical traditions to instruct those under their influence gives scant attention to the apocalyptic character of 1 Thessalonians.

While some scholars continued to hold that the apocalyptic myth had a central role in Paul's life, Johan Christiaan Beker gave a passionate defense of "apocalyptic" as the integrating center of Paul's theology. Beker vigorously argued that the deep structure of Paul's thought was "apocalyptic," that "the heart of Paul's gospel" was "apocalyptic," and that Paul's outlook was "an-chored in the apocalyptic world view," which served as "the fundamental carrier of Paul's thought."[11] Beker forcefully maintained that "the death and resurrection of Christ in their apocalyptic setting constitute the coherent core of Paul's thought."[12] For Beker, "apocalyptic" was the core, basis, structure, and conduit of Paul's gospel — a dramatic, sweeping claim indeed. Although Beker's work offered a comprehensive defense of the role of apocalypticism in Paul's thought, it hardly ended the dispute.

---

4. Bultmann, "Ist die Apokalyptik die Mutter der christlichen Theologie? Eine Auseinander-setzung mit Ernst Käsemann," in *Apophoreta: Festschrift für Ernst Haenchen zu seinem siebzigsten Geburtstag am 10. Dezember 1964* (BZNW 30; Berlin: Töpelmann, 1964) 64–69.

5. Vielhauer, "Apocalyptic in Early Christianity," in Edgar Hennecke and Wilhelm Schnee-melcher, eds., R. McL. Wilson, trans. ed., *New Testament Apocrypha*, vol. 2 (Philadelphia: Westminster, 1965) 609.

6. Conzelmann, "On the Analysis of the Confessional Formula in 1 Corinthians 15:3–5," *Int* 20 (1966) 15–25 (German original in *EvT* 25 [1965] 1–11).

7. Marxsen, *Introduction to the New Testament: An Approach to Its Problems* (Philadelphia: Fortress, 1968) 273.

8. Sanders, *Paul and Palestinian Judaism: A Comparison of Patterns of Religion* (Philadelphia: Fortress, 1977) 543.

9. Scroggs, "Ernst Käsemann: The Divine Agent Provocateur," *RelSRev* 11 (1985) 261.

10. Malherbe, *Social Aspects of Early Christianity* (Baton Rouge, La.: Louisiana State University Press, 1977).

11. Beker, *Paul the Apostle: The triumph of God in Life and Thought* (Philadelphia: Fortress, 1980) 16–17, 135.

12. Ibid., 207.

To this day scholarly opinion remains divided on the importance of the apocalyptic myth for Paul. For some it is the *Magna Mater* of Paul's theology, while for others it is a distant cousin or no relative at all. 1 Thessalonians, which some see as the most apocalyptic of Paul's epistles, is to others only a parenetic letter. And as for Paul's appeal in 1 Thess 4:16–17 to the *parousia* of Christ announced by the archangel and signaled with a blast of the trumpet, as well as the promised ascent of the dead and the living to meet the Lord in the air, these appear to some as the apocalyptic nerve center of Paul's gospel and to others as a trivial vestige of a Jewish apocalypticism lingering in the shadows of Paul's gospel.

This confusion as to the significance of the apocalyptic myth in Paul's thinking is caused in part by the radical alterations Paul made in the apocalyptic myth he inhabited. Such changes may give the impression that Paul repudiated apocalypticism when he merely reshaped it for his own community. Moreover, his resistance to and qualification of the apocalyptic enthusiasm of the Corinthians may cause some to wonder if he abandoned the apocalyptic myth altogether. While it is common these days to acknowledge apocalyptic elements in Paul's thinking, what is less common is an appreciation of the peculiar Pauline application or translation of the apocalyptic vision — the ways Paul challenged the logical, but in his mind mistaken, appropriation of the apocalyptic vision. That turn, I shall argue, was dictated by the context and sprang from the intellectual genius and complexity of the apostle himself. Here I shall note some of the adjustments Paul made in the apocalyptic myth he inherited and attend to some of the ways he redirected the apocalyptic vision of his addressees. In doing so we may see that Paul sought not to tame, or displace, or demythologize the myth, but to provide constraints within which its vital energy could be experienced within a community threatened by an apocalypticism run amuck.[13] We may also observe how Paul sought to revive an apocalyptic vision which to some seemed to have failed.

Everywhere Paul's letters reveal an author who took for granted a pervasive, powerful apocalyptic myth. While one must acknowledge that there

---

13. The nature of Paul's apocalypticism is debated. The dispute has been influenced by the Society of Biblical Literature Genres Project, on which Collins reports in his *Apocalyptic Imagination*. That study discredited many older, simplistic definitions of apocalypses and provided valuable help in describing the structure, context, and complexity of apocalypses. Collins in particular questions the value of essentialist definitions that describe apocalypses thematically, e.g., as dualistic, pseudepigraphic, forensic, or as dealing with reversal, angels, and the like. He prefers instead the definition hammered out by the members of the Genres Project, in which "apocalypse" is defined as "a genre of revelatory literature with a narrative framework, in which a revelation is mediated by an otherworldly being to a human recipient, disclosing a transcendent reality which is both temporal, insofar as it envisages eschatological salvation, and spatial, insofar as it involves another, supernatural world" (p. 4). Others, such as Sanders, have found this definition too general; see his "The Genre of Palestinian Jewish Apocalypses," in David Hellholm, ed., *Apocalypticism in the Mediterranean World and the Near East* (Tübingen: Mohr [Siebeck], 1983) 447–59.

was no canonical model of apocalypticism in the first century, and that those who appropriated apocalyptic symbolism enjoyed enormous freedom in its development and application, Paul's apocalyptic ideology and idiom do show a family resemblance to that of Qumran in particular. The conviction that the fateful, cosmic contest between the agents of light and the minions of darkness was nearing a conclusive, convulsive climax appears in both (1 Thess 4:15–17; Rom 13:11–12; Phil 4:5; 1QM). Paul's view that the final catastrophe would radically alter or even dismantle the social and political structures of the day resembles that of Qumran. The conviction that the form of this world was passing away (1 Cor 7:31) and that the struggle between the "children of light" and the "children of darkness" was part of a powerful drama, cosmic in scope and temporal in inception and resolution, was shared by both (1 Thess 5:5–11; 1QS 3.18–4.18). The anticipated vindication of the "saints" in the impending judgment, hope for a messianic deliverer, and a scriptural warrant for that hope were shared by Paul and Qumran. And although there were profound differences between the Pauline and the Qumran myth, e.g., in the eschatological timetable, in the priestly orientation or lack of it, and in the roles played by Jesus and the Teacher of Righteousness, nevertheless both shared a myth of crisis. While few scholars believe that Paul had firsthand acquaintance with the Dead Sea community, his debt to and skillful appropriation of apocalyptic symbols reveal a fertile mind at work in treating apocalyptic dualism, apocalyptic disassociation, and apocalyptic simplification.

Paul and Apocalyptic Dualism

In *Purity and Danger*, Mary Douglas speaks of the use of taboos or rules to establish community boundaries. From Douglas we learn that the more threatened the community, the greater the need to define its borders. The more fixed the borders, the sharper is the contrast between the insider and outsider; and the sharper the contrast, the greater the tensions created by transactions across those boundaries.[14]

Many apocalyptic writings and the Pauline letters reflect those tendencies. The dualism of apocalypticism knows three sets of boundaries: between the world above and the world below (cosmic), between this age and the age to come (temporal), and between the insider and outsider (social). Whether driven by persecution or by repression and exclusion, or by other causes of distress and trauma, the authors of apocalyptic writings reveal the alienation felt by the community, and that alienation is mirrored in its experience of

---

14. Douglas, *Purity and Danger: An Analysis of Concepts of Pollution and Taboo* (London: Routledge & Kegan Paul; New York: Praeger, 1966).

space and time. Thus the social differentiation between insiders and outsiders is profoundly reinforced by a mythology cosmic in scope and breathtakingly comprehensive in temporal reach.

That this dualism was replicated in a virulent hatred of the Jerusalem priesthood and the Roman oppressors is well documented at Qumran. These same polarities, however, also appear in the pseudepigrapha: the fallen angels of *1 Enoch* stand opposite the host of heaven (*1 Enoch* 6–20); heaven and Sheol define the polarities of mythic space where the "prison house of the [fallen] angels" contrasts with the realm of angels and, hence, the sinners with the righteous (21.10); the final, cataclysmic fire below separates the wicked from the redeemed above in the *Sibylline Oracles* (2.285–310). The fate of the righteous is set in 4 Ezra by the challenge to Roman tyranny declared by the coming messianic kingdom (7:36; 12:32–34), and the nations and their idols are separated from Israel and its God in *2 Baruch* (13.12; 5.1; 7.2; 67.2; 5.2; 48.27; 85.9; 72.5). The sense of having one's fate dictated by a final, climactic, fateful struggle so characteristic of these writings is also evident in Paul's letters. The difference is that Paul, and certainly much of the early church with him, believed that the resolution of that struggle was now beginning. God's righteous act was manifested in the victory over death made evident in the resurrection of Jesus. This triumph marked the beginning of God's move to reclaim a creation that manifestly was also being claimed by dark, sinister powers. The human landscape Paul knew was a dreadful place — tyrannized by principalities and powers (Rom 8:38), fought over by a hostile "god of this world" (2 Cor 4:4), subjected to death (1 Cor 15:26, 54–55), enslaved by sin (Rom 6:20–23), and threatened by Satan (1 Cor 7:5), demons (1 Cor 10:20–22), and the rulers of this age. According to Paul's gospel, this dark, demonic hegemony which for some seemed more real, its claims more insistent than the rule of God, was now being overthrown, and the resolution of that final desperate struggle was at hand.

But how did this cosmic mythology infiltrate the discourse of Paul with the community? We know of obvious cases in 1 Thessalonians where he distinguishes those who worship God from those who worship idols (1:6), where he juxtaposes his apostleship and ministry of encouragement (παράκλησις) against the ministry of deceit, uncleanness, guile, flattery, and crowd-pleasing gestures of others (2:3–10), where he positions the believer opposite the immoral, passionate, lustful gentiles (ἔθνη) (4:3–5), and where he compares the "children of the day" with the children of "the night," the wakefulness of believers with the sleep of the unbelievers (5:5–6).

The same differentiation also appears in 1 Corinthians. 1 Cor 1:9 contrasts those "called out of the world into the fellowship of God's son" with the children of this world; 1:18 opposes those "perishing" to "those being saved"; 2:14–15 contrasts the "unspiritual" and the "spiritual," 5:1 the pagans and the believers, 5:7 the old dough and the new, and 6:1–11 the "washed," the "consecrated," and the "justified" with the immoral, idolaters, the greedy, and the abusive. This differentiation is so pervasive in Paul's letters that it hardly needs further documentation.[15]

Paul's dualism is distinguished not by a separation between the insider and outsider or believer and unbeliever but by a tension between separation and inclusion, or between differentiation and diffusion. Paul's adjustment of the boundaries deviates from the usual pattern of apocalyptic writings of his time or apocalyptic communities such as Qumran. By withdrawal from the evil priests in Jerusalem, by physically retreating to the wilderness, and by imposing a strict daily rule, the "sons of light" separated themselves from the "sons of darkness" (1QS 4.7–14). Their rule forbade the pooling of their property with the "men of falsehood" (1QS 9.8–9); it banned any disputation with "men of the pit" (1QS 9.16); it commanded them not to spend a Sabbath near gentiles (1QS 11.14–15), and it prohibited the selling of clean birds or beasts to the gentiles (1QS 12.8–9). And this rigorous separation was invoked under the threat of eternal destruction:

> He [the member of the Community] should swear by the covenant to be segregated from all the men of sin who walk along paths of irreverence. For they are not included in his covenant since they have neither sought nor examined his decrees in order to learn the hidden matters in which they err by their own fault and because they treated revealed matters with disrespect; this is why wrath will rise up for judgment in order to effect revenge by the curses of the covenant, in order to administer fierce punishments for everlasting annihilation without there being any remnant. (1QS 5.10–13)[16]

Of course, however powerful the symbolic and metaphorical rhetoric, the separation from outsiders was not absolute. The presence of Greek manuscripts in the Qumran collection suggests some interchange with the dominant culture. The sectarians continued to remit the temple tax. And readmission after a period of discipline could follow expulsion from the sect. Consequently, absolute separation between the insider and outsider was simply impracticable. Ultimately the question was not if there would be social and cultural intercourse between the "poor" and the "other" but what kind and how much of the foreign to admit and appropriate. Certainly the amount of admission and

---

15. Wayne A. Meeks has drawn attention to this language of separation in *The First Urban Christians: The Social World of the Apostle Paul* (New Haven, Conn.: Yale University Press, 1983) 84–96.

16. Translation in Florentino García Martínez, *The Dead Sea Scrolls Translated: The Qumran Texts in English* (2d ed.; Leiden and New York: Brill; Grand Rapids: Eerdmans, 1996) 8.

appropriation that Paul was willing to tolerate differed in degree, if not in kind, from that of the Qumran community.

While the threat of an alien symbolic world appeared no less monstrous to Paul than to the Qumran sectarians, his apostleship and his instructions to the churches more freely embraced the separated. Even when varying circumstances dictated sharply differing emphases, his outreach was consistent. His apostolic mission was directed towards outsiders, i.e., "gentile sinners" (synonymous terms; Gal 2:15). He cautioned enthusiastic celebrants of new life in the spirit in Corinth that they were to seek the honor, respect, and "amen" of the outsiders (1 Cor 14:16).

In Rom 12:14–21 Paul urged Roman believers not to retaliate against their adversaries but to bless their persecutors, to eschew revenge, to offer food and drink to the hungry and thirsty, and thereby to conquer evil with good. Thematic and linguistic ties between this passage and 13:8–14 suggest a linkage between nonretaliation and love (13:8). Note, for example, Paul's ironic use of the combat motif in 12:21, where he urges upon his hearers an alternative to convention: "Do not be conquered (μὴ νικῶ) by evil, but conquer (νίκα) evil with good." The combat motif recurs in 13:12–24, where Paul again ironically prescribes an "armor of light" for his addressees (13:12) and thus functionally forges a link between the nonretaliation encouraged in 12:14–21 and the love of 13:8–14. Moreover, already in 13:8 Paul has defined the neighbor for whom love is commanded in Lev 19:18 (Rom 13:9), not as an insider, as in Leviticus, but as "the other" (τὸν ἕτερον), i.e., the outsider. And whoever loves "the other," Paul notes, already "has fulfilled the law." So once again we see that Paul was careful to make a connection between the commandment to love and obligation to the outsider. If what I am suggesting is correct, Paul is certainly closer to the Matthean command to love the enemy (Matt 5:44) than is sometimes acknowledged.[17]

But what informed this nonretaliation? Krister Stendahl has shown how the sectarians' certainty of God's imminent visitation and destruction of the foe formed the basis of their view of nonretaliation: "I will not return evil to anybody, with good will I pursue man, for with God rests the judgment of every living being and he is the one to repay man for his deeds....And the trial of a man of perdition I will not handle until the Day of Vengeance."

---

17. Krister Stendahl holds otherwise. He has argued that Paul's motivation for nonretaliation parallels that of Qumran, i.e., that given the impending wrath one can eschew retaliation knowing that God will soon vindicate that righteousness completely ("Hate, Non-retaliation, and Love: 1QS x.17–20 and Rom. 12:19–21," HTR 55 [1962] 343–55; repr. in idem, Meanings: The Bible as Document and as Guide [Philadelphia: Fortress, 1984] 137–49). While the apocalyptic motivation does inform Paul's exhortation (see 13:11, "The hour is nearer now than when we first believed"), the apocalyptic element reinforces and energizes love for the outsider, not vice versa. On other grounds but supporting the position here, see James D. G. Dunn, Romans 9–16 (WBC 38B; Dallas: Word, 1988) 749–52, 755–56.

However, at this point the sectarian diverged from Paul: "However, I shall not remove my anger from wicked men, nor shall I be appeased, until he carries out his judgment" (1QS 10.20). This nonretaliation was "grounded in the eschatological intensity of the 'eternal hatred towards the men of perdition.' "[18] God's vengeance thus made their vengeance redundant, and each member of the community felt commanded to "love all the sons of light, each one according to his lot in God's plan, *and to detest* all the sons of darkness, each one in accordance with his blame in God's vindication" (1QS 1.9–11, emphasis added). While Rom 12:19–20, with its emphasis on giving food and drink to the enemy and in so doing "heaping coals of fire on his head," shares the apocalyptic spirit of Qumran, the command to love the outsider in Rom 13:8–9 sets Paul off from the Dead Sea community. Evidently Paul realized the danger of the hate customarily inspired by apocalyptic separation and chose another way.[19]

Paul's urban ministry and his gentile mission may partly explain his modification of conventional apocalyptic emphases on exclusivity. In a radical tour de force Paul turned the arguments of the conservative faction in Galatia on their head to make way for "gentile sinners" (Gal 2:15). Where they would limit access to the community to the law-observant, Paul pushed in another direction by recalling an inclusive baptismal formula that embraced Jew and Greek, bond and free, male and female (Gal 3:28). Even while Paul recognized separation and exclusion from "the present evil age" (1:4) and the immoral from the community (1 Cor 5:1–13), his gentile gospel inevitably introduced a high level of ambiguity into the community which provoked resistance.

Romans itself was written at least in part to answer charges arising from Paul's ministry of inclusiveness directed towards "Greeks and barbarians" (1:14). While Paul was concerned with the problems of getting in and staying in, as Sanders argues, he was also intensely involved in developing a protocol for the crossing of boundaries. In a complex sense he was not interested just in getting in and staying in, but also in an active, positive engagement with the outsider. As Paul puts it, "To the Jews I became as a Jew; to those under the law I became as one under the law in order that I might win those under the law; to those without the law as one without the law, not of those outside the law of God but in the law of Christ, in order that I might win those outside the law. To the weak I became weak in order to win the weak. I have become all things to all people in order that I might save some" (1 Cor 9:20–22). This active and positive mission to include the outsider expanded

---

18. Stendahl, "Hate, Non-Retaliation, and Love," 341.
19. Paul apparently shares this understanding with Matt 24:12: "the love of many will grow cold."

the embrace of the apocalyptic myth Paul inhabited, and this mission was not driven, as John G. Gager has suggested, by a failed apocalypticism but, on the contrary, by a continuing feverish expectation of the end.[20]

In 1 Cor 5:1–5 these inclusive and exclusive tendencies interweave in a complex manner. The situation Paul addressed there concerned a man who was living with his stepmother in what Paul believed, perhaps incorrectly, was an incestuous relationship.[21] The easy tolerance of the religiously enthusiastic congregation appeared to Paul to sanction such boundless behavior. Infuriated, Paul prescribed the deliverance of the man into the hands of Satan "for the destruction of the flesh" — action aimed not only at separating the deviant but also at defining the community. "Cleanse out the old leaven," Paul commanded in 5:7, "that *you may be* fresh dough" (emphasis added).

This tension between boundlessness and boundedness, as Victor Witter Turner has noted, is characteristic of the liminal stage of ritual and myth as well. Following the mythic structure developed by Arnold van Gennep,[22] Turner shows how in the liminal stage tensions are created by competing tendencies: a straining toward universalization (or boundlessness) and a desire to impose structure or limit on the surge toward universalization.[23] Turner's observation aptly describes what we see in 1 Cor 5:1–5, where Paul acts to reimpose structure on a community whose spiritual elites sought to rise above all human structures and, therefore, to promote an order that was highly antistructural.[24] As a "ritual of separation," the curse Paul called for secured the identity of the community by locating its boundary. The expulsion of the deviant forced the community to engage itself in conversation and to identify itself by ordering its experience through its myths and symbols. This separation of the deviant, however, did not include disengagement from the outsiders (1 Cor 5:9–10) but from the immoral insiders, or the deviants.

In the incident here described Paul and the charismatic Corinthians were

---

20. Gager, *Kingdom and Community: The Social World of Early Christianity* (Englewood Cliffs, N.J.: Prentice-Hall, 1975).

21. Whether this was a spiritual marriage, as John Coolidge Hurd allows for (*The Origins of First Corinthians* [London: SPCK, 1965] 277–78), or not, as Gerhard Sellin holds ("Hauptprobleme des Ersten Korintherbriefes," *ANRW* 2.25.4 [1994] 2970–72) and as Gordon D. Fee asserts (*The First Epistle to the Corinthians* [NICNT; Grand Rapids: Eerdmans, 1987] 198–213), is not germane, although Sellin and Fee seem to make too little of the fact that the man is doing this "in the name of the Lord Jesus."

22. Van Gennep, *Rites of Passage* (Chicago: University of Chicago Press, 1960) (French original, 1909).

23. Turner, *The Ritual Process: Structure and Anti-Structure* (London: Routledge & Kegan Paul; Ithaca, N.Y.: Cornell University Press, 1969); see also Turner, "Myth and Symbol," in David L. Sills, ed., *The International Encyclopedia of the Social Sciences* (17 vols. in 8; New York: Macmillan, 1972) 10. 576–79.

24. Richard A. Horsley's description of the apocalyptic enthusiasm in Corinth as "spiritual elitism" is apt; see his " 'How Can Some of You Say There Is No Resurrection of the Dead?' Spiritual Elitism in Corinth," *NovT* 20 (1978) 203–31.

obviously moving in opposite directions. With its cry of liberty, its charismatic fervor, its claim to heavenly wisdom, and its reaching for a transsexual, angelic state, the community strained for an apocalyptic resolution that was antistructural, or indeed otherworldly. They were universalizing, one might even say cosmicizing, the myth. In asking the community to expel the offender, Paul was implicitly calling for a recognition of error by a people claiming to be above fault. By ritually handing the man over to Satan, Paul argued, the community would necessarily redefine itself by accepting its own limits as a community. While in his call for the exclusion of the "old leaven" Paul followed the exclusionary tendencies of most apocalyptic writings of the day, his hope for the ultimate salvation of the offender placed him in tension not only with his addressees but also with his own apocalyptic myth.

In 5:5 Paul anticipated the "destruction" by Satan of the man expelled while at the same time expressing hope for the salvation of his spirit (πνεῦμα) "on the day of the Lord Jesus." The phrase "day of the Lord Jesus" as used by Paul commonly refers to God's final act of righteousness to be completed at the *parousia* of Jesus (1 Cor 1:8; Phil 1:6, 10; 2:16; 1 Thess 5:2; et al.). Thus his hope for the salvation of the offender on that day argues against the view that Paul expected the shock of expulsion to precipitate his repentance and rehabilitation.[25] Instead, as in 1 Cor 3:14–15 Paul here expressed the hope that in the judgment God would preserve authentic expressions of life in the Spirit in spite of misguided but nonmalicious deeds. This inclusive gesture contrasts dramatically with the practice at Qumran, where final expulsion offered no possibility of reinstatement, and the theology of the Apocalypse of John, which anticipates the final destruction of the external enemy and the internal deviant — everyone whose name was "not written in the book of life was thrown into the lake of fire" (20:11–15) for eternal destruction. In the tension Paul displayed here between exclusion and inclusion, and his expressed concern for the health of the community and the ultimate salvation of the offender, we see a vigorous intellectual engagement with the complex and conflicted situation of an apocalyptic community in confusion. In so redrawing the boundaries of the community, Paul does appear to draw back from the harsh implications of an apocalyptic dualism that he seemed to share at other points. The tensions in this passage between exclusion and inclusion are enormous. Driven by contrary impulses in Paul — his strong communal interests and profound hopefulness in God's grace — tensions were created which remain unresolved, and these tensions so skillfully balanced by this profound intellect may account in part for the continuing vitality of Paul's thought.

---

25. As held by Fee; see above, n. 21.

232   CALVIN J. ROETZEL

Paul's Qualification of Apocalyptic Disassociation

Although, as we have seen, Collins favors the definition of apocalypse forged
by the Society of Biblical Literature Genres Project which eschews any essentialist definition, he nevertheless does agree with the essentialists that Jewish
and Christian apocalypses share tendencies toward disassociation: "Detachment from this world, in the hope of the glory that is above or is to come,
is *a common characteristic* of the Jewish apocalypses." In Revelation, he adds,
the "impulse to martyrdom, and to the rejection of this world, is intensified
by the example of Jesus, who achieved his victory by his crucifixion. The impact of Christ then is to intensify an element that was already present in the
Jewish genre."[26] While Collins's view that detachment is a shared feature of
apocalypses needs qualification, detachment is most often a feature of apocalypticism generally.[27] Certainly the Qumran writings share that tendency, and
some would see the same tendency in Paul's letters as well.

Paul's use of αἰών ("age, world") and κόσμος ("world") as separate realities gives support to the view that Paul shared the disassociation of his native
apocalyptic myth. The prescript to Galatians, loaded with heavy, symbolic
language about the Christ who "gave himself for our sins to take us out of
this present evil age (ἐκ τοῦ αἰῶνος τοῦ ἐνεστῶτος)" (1:4), supports the
view that Paul tended toward disassociation.[28] Through participation in the
cross of Christ, believers were to be crucified to (or separated from) the world
(κόσμος) and the world to (or from) them (Gal 6:14). Salvation was rescue
from the chaos and confusion of a world in its final decline: "the form of
this world (τὸ σχῆμα τοῦ κόσμου τούτου) is passing away" (1 Cor 7:31b).
In 1 Corinthians the negative vision of the world appears to endorse the
disassociation of the enthusiasts: since "the appointed time has grown very
short," Paul urges "those who deal with the world [to act] as though they
had no dealings with it" (7:29, 31a). He likewise urged the Roman church
not to be "conformed to this world (τῷ αἰῶνι τούτῳ)" (Rom 12:2), and
he reminded the Philippians of their heavenly πολίτευμα, a citizenship or
commonwealth antithetical to its earthly counterpart (3:20).

In this respect, Paul's apocalyptic myth faithfully represents that of other
Jewish and early Christian apocalypticism known to us. Yet it is going too

---

26. Collins, *Apocalyptic Imagination*, 214.
27. As the late John Gammie once pointed out to me, Daniel looks forward to the re-
institution of sacrifice in Jerusalem; one might also mention the *Animal Apocalypse* in *1 Enoch*
90.18–19, which endorses armed revolt against the oppressors of this world.
28. Rudolf Bultmann (*New Testament Theology* [2 vols.; London: SCM; New York: Scribner,
1951–55] 1. 256) viewed this passage as an anthropological description of the human condition
prior to faith, but he failed to do justice to the strong apocalyptic connotation of the act of
deliverance. J. Louis Martyn makes a compelling case for the apocalyptic intent of the letter
("Apocalyptic Antinomies in Paul's Letter to the Galatians," *NTS* 31 [1985] 410–24).

far to suggest that Paul's apocalypticism was either physically or psychologically escapist. There is tension in Paul's view sustained by the qualification or "eschatological reservation" (Käsemann) that Paul used to qualify apocalyptic enthusiasm. This qualification sharply contradicted the premature apocalyptic resolution claimed by members of the Thessalonian and Corinthian communities. Paul's dilemma was how to announce the inbreaking of God's final act of righteousness while insisting that the final resolution of the redemption of the world remained outstanding. This straining between the present and the future created explosive tensions that are often underestimated.

We gain some insight into Paul's strategy for sustaining that tension in 1 Thess 4:9–11. Here Paul exhorts the God-taught (θεοδίδακτοι) to love one another, "to strive to keep calm (ἡσυχάζειν), to take care of your own affairs, and to work with your hands (ἐργάζεσθαι ταῖς χερσὶν ὑμῶν)." In this passage Paul was hardly following the Epicurean injunction to withdraw from public life for a type of labor or handwork, divorced from politics in the pursuit of honor and freedom.[29] The traditions of Paul's diaspora synagogue put Paul closer to Philo's outlook than the highly elitist philosophy of Epicurus.

The key to understanding the passage is the decipherment of the term θεοδίδακτοι, which to my knowledge appears only here in ancient literature. Philo frequently used the term αὐτοδίδακτος to refer to the person who learns without a teacher. Unlike the Greek philosophers, who spoke of the αὐτοδίδακτος as the self-made philosopher, Philo used the term to refer to the person receiving wisdom, virtues, or knowledge directly from God and, therefore, needing no human teacher. Isaac, Adam, Noah, Moses, Melchizedek and others he named as αὐτοδίδακτοι. The αὐτοδίδακτοι, according to Philo, were exempted from physical labor and will in the future "enjoy peace that never ends, released from unabating toils" (*Fug.* 173). Moreover, the injunction "to live in quietness" (ἡσυχία and cognates), according to Philo, was no admonition to political quietism but rather an eloquent silence coming from a simple reliance on God (*Mos.* 1.66), a confident waiting on God by Abraham to provide an animal for the commanded sacrifice (*Fug.* 135–36), or even the eschatological rest hovering over the land in the final days (*Praem.* 157). On that day, Philo promises, those mistreating the land will suffer curses, but the land "when she looks around and sees none of the destroyers of her former pride and high name, sees her market place void of turmoil and war and wrongdoing, and full of ἡσυχία and εἰρήνη (peace), and δικαιοσύνη (righteousness), she will renew her youth

---

29. Here I am obviously at odds with Ronald F. Hock, *The Social Context of Paul's Ministry: Tentmaking and Apostleship* (Philadelphia: Fortress, 1988).

and bloom and take her rest calm and serene...." In no case does Philo use ἡσυχία (quiet living) to refer to withdrawal from the public life.

While no one would suggest that Paul directly appropriated Philo's language or vision, the type of Jewish expression we see in Philo surely represents the outlook of the diaspora synagogue elsewhere. The simple facts of Paul's biography — born and reared in a diaspora Jewish setting, a Greek-speaker, steeped in the language of the Septuagint — suggest that Paul was influenced by that social and cultural milieu. Whatever their background, as citizens of the new age waiting for the imminent arrival of the Son of man, the Thessalonians would have been in an unusually strong position to claim a wisdom direct from God that needed no human teacher (note, e.g., 1 Thess 5:12), and therefore they could already claim "release" from toil (4:11; 5:14). Certain philosophical traditions as well as Jewish diaspora traditions could have encouraged that response to Paul's gospel.

Faced with this development, Paul coined the word θεοδίδακτοι to make explicit what was already implicit in αὐτοδίδακτος: he subordinated the possession of divine wisdom to the love command, and he urged the θεοδίδακτοι to work with their hands. In this manner Paul radically recast the traditional meaning of the term αὐτοδίδακτος, and reestablished the connection between the apocalyptic vision and the sweaty arena of daily life. The associated admonition to "keep calm" (ἡσυχάζειν) was hardly an exhortation to political quietism, or a repudiation of unseemly for seemly work, but a form of listening or faithful watching appropriate to the arriving eschatological kingdom. The waiting, as in Philo, was active, and its sphere was social. So in this manner Paul moved to qualify the apocalyptic disassociation of some Thessalonians and to link the apocalyptic vision with the tasks of this world.

This qualification of the tendency toward apocalyptic disassociation is hardly confined to 1 Thessalonians. In Romans, too, Paul reflects on a version of apocalypticism that encouraged withdrawal from the world and repudiation of a dying order. The commands in Rom 13:1 to "be subject to the governing authorities" and to pay "taxes to whom taxes are due" make sense only if some believers had understood liberation from this world to mean that one should be diffident toward or contemptuous of civil authority.[30] Paul, however, turned the very myth which had been invoked to encourage withdrawal from the world into a mandate for participation in it. So while encouraging the disassociation characteristic of apocalypticism, he was also urging a positive, fruitful participation in this world.

---

30. See, e.g., Günther Bornkamm, *Paul* (New York: Harper & Row, 1971) 213; Ernst Käsemann, *Commentary on Romans* (Grand Rapids: Eerdmans, 1980) 361.

Paul's Complication of the Trend toward Simplification

The mortal illness of a child, the siege of a city, or an emergency at sea all focus human attention and energy on survival. Similarly, most apocalyptic writings are or pretend to be crisis materials which simplify by directing the attention, behavior, and organization of the community toward an emergency. With its insistence on the final triumph of God's righteousness, the restoration of a new world, and the elimination of all vestiges of diabolical forces, Paul's myth of crisis, though far from simple itself, followed this pattern. Paul's own sense of mission and his understanding of his apostleship were driven in a single-minded way by the conviction that his was the last generation of the world. And although his apocalyptic gospel simplified social structures, deciphered the mystery of historical terror, and solved the enigmas of scripture, Paul's letters themselves reflect serious disagreements with his addressees over the nature and extent of the simplifying function of his apocalyptic gospel. I shall address here three aspects of this simplification: gender, suffering, and the interpretation of scripture.

First, *the simplification of gender.* Turner has drawn our attention to important social changes that occur in the liminal stage. As Turner has it, these myths are seen as "deep mysteries which put the initiand [the one to be initiated] temporarily into close rapport with the primary or primordial generative powers of the cosmos."[31] Sexlessness which characterized that primordial stage characterizes the liminal stage as well.[32] In our equation, where the liminal stage equals the transition from the old to the new age, a restructuring of the social and natural world is taken for granted. Like apocalypticism, a liminal myth deals extensively with death and rebirth, with the destruction of the old order and the emergence of the new. 1 Corinthians is the best example of Paul's struggle with a community attempting to free itself from this transitional phase.

As Paul's letter tells us, the Corinthians so experienced Paul's myth, and so identified with the Lord of glory, that they claimed to speak the language of angels (13:1) and were able to claim a transsexual status reserved for heavenly beings. Paul's own celibate state may have unwittingly reinforced the Corinthian inclination to celibacy. Under the slogan "it is better for a man not to touch a woman" (7:1) — and implicitly for a woman not to touch a man — celibacy became the norm of the redeemed (7:4).[33] Married couples

31. Turner, "Myth and Symbol," 577.
32. Turner, *Ritual Process,* 102.
33. See Hurd, *Origins of First Corinthians,* 157; similarly Robin Scroggs, "Paul and the Eschatological Woman," *JAAR* 40 (1972) 283–303; Wayne A. Meeks, "The Image of the Androgyne: Some Uses of a Symbol in Earliest Christianity," *HR* 13 (1974) 165–208; S. Scott Bartchy, *Mallon Chresai: First-Century Slavery and the Interpretation of 1 Corinthians 7:21* (SBLDS 11; Missoula, Mont.: Scholars Press, 1973) 127–55.

abstained from sex. Those married to unbelievers inclined toward divorce to maintain their celibacy (7:12–16). The unmarried remained unmarried even while "aflame with passion" (7:8–11). Moreover, the cult reflected the vision the community had of itself as a gender-neutral society. Their modes of dress and the egalitarian expression of charismatic gifts (prophecy, speaking in tongues, etc., in 11:2–6) blurred the distinction between women and men. What Paul had promised the Galatians, that in Christ there is "neither male nor female" (3:28), became a reality in Corinth and ironically Paul did not find it to his liking.[34] Thus for the Corinthians the great human absolute, *eros*, had given way to another great absolute, transsexual or asexual salvation. And the Corinthian experience of the new age cut through a maze of restrictions and complex rules designed and maintained to keep *eros* within the bounds of a given social order. This new androgynous order simplified all human relationships by equalizing them and served as a radical alternative to complex, confusing cultural patterns.

Even though at one level Paul was a cohort in the development of this Corinthian spirituality, at another level he vigorously resisted and qualified that spirituality. By insisting on the partiality of the experience of the new age, and the proleptic nature of participation in that arriving endtime, Paul complicated the Corinthian "wisdom" enormously. Since the full experience of God's rule will be deferred until the *parousia* of Jesus, believers must, according to Paul, live in the overlap between the present age and the age to come. Consequently they must share in the tension generated by the warring worlds. Even while insisting on the value of celibacy as a charismatic gift (7:7, 32–34), Paul encouraged each married partner to attend to the sexual needs of the other (7:3–6); he advised those with unbelieving partners to remain married and to "consecrate" the marriage through sexual union (7:12–16);[35] he encouraged single members "aflame with passion" to marry (7:8–11); and he admonished them all to acknowledge the distinction between and interdependence of man and woman (11:2–16). By affirming their sexuality they would, in Paul's view, be acknowledging their continued tie to this world. In so qualifying the Corinthians slogan "it is better for a man not to touch a woman" (7:1), Paul emphasized the transitional character of this dawning new age, deferring full participation in it until the imminent *parousia* of Christ.[36] The tie thus secured to the world gave the Corinthian myth a measure of realism that the community was dangerously close to forfeiting.

34. Note Paul's significant omission of the phrase "male and female" in his recitation in 1 Cor 12:13 of the baptismal formula quoted in full in Gal 3:28.
35. See David Daube, "Pauline Contributions to a Pluralistic Culture: Re-Creation and Beyond," in Donald G. Miller and Dikran Y. Hadidian, eds., *Jesus and Man's Hope* (2 vols.; Pittsburgh: Pittsburgh Theological Seminary, 1971) 2. 223–45.
36. Turner, *Ritual Process*, 103–10.

The second aspect of Paul's "complicating simplification" is *the interpretation of suffering*. Beyond the simplification of gender and social relationships, Paul's apocalyptic myth offered a simplified understanding of historical terror. Of course, this understanding was hardly new. Since the Maccabean revolt, apocalyptic writings had presented suffering, persecution, and martyrdom as marks of God's people (*Jub.* 23.13–22; *2 Bar.* 70.2–10; *4 Ezra* 5:1–12). 1 Thessalonians and 1 Corinthians offer immediate confirmation of Paul's place in that tradition even while revealing a simultaneous shift of emphasis away from it.

The cross of Jesus became for Paul an important metaphor through which all suffering and terror received its significance. Paul's own abuse, rejection, and hardship shared mythically in that cross and simultaneously served as a model for the churches. Through that model the churches participated in the cross and shared in the community of the suffering redeemed. If authentically Pauline, 1 Thess 2:14–16 shows how rejection by their own people (συμφυλέται, "compatriots") brought the suffering churches in Thessalonica and Judea together into a shared community of suffering.[37] More importantly, in 1:7–10 Paul linked the physical and psychological terror of the Thessalonians with that of believers in Achaia, Macedonia, and beyond. Not only did believers find consolation and hope in this community of suffering; they also found independent confirmation of their membership in the community of the redeemed. As Paul put it, "You yourselves know we were destined for such things" (3:3).

But clearly the Thessalonians found other interpretations of their suffering too immediate and too insistent to be ignored. The death of baptized friends raised questions about the truth of Paul's gospel, since it had led some to expect that all believers would live to welcome the returning Lord. Their own persecution inevitably raised questions about the delay of the return, and about signs of the return (4:13–5:11). With hope flickering the temptation was great to return to old, familiar ways (4:5–8). Fearing for their steadfastness, Paul dispatched Timothy to remind them of his teaching given "beforehand" (3:2–4) and to reassure them so that "no one may be troubled, or disturbed in your sufferings" (3:3). By recalling his own suffering and insults in Philippi (2:1) and strong opposition in Thessalonica (2:2), Paul emphasized the bond between himself and his readers. And by recognizing that their reception of the word brought "much tribulation" (θλίψις, 1:5) and that this suffering was also shared by churches in Judea (2:14), their com-

---

37. Birger A. Pearson's arguments against the authenticity of 1 Thess 2:13–16 are to me compelling ("1 Thessalonians 2:13–16: A Deutero-Pauline Interpolation," *HTR* 64 [1971] 79–94); but see now Robert Jewett, *The Thessalonian Correspondence: Pauline Rhetoric and Millenarian Piety* (FFNT; Philadelphia: Fortress, 1986) 36–42.

munity of suffering was extended to embrace the mother church itself. In their misery they gained company. And finally by refracting this experience through the death of Christ, Paul gave the chaos and confusion, dislocation, and death experienced by the Thessalonians (4:13–18) a transcendent, incandescent holiness (see also 2 Cor 4:7–12). Cosmic arrhythmia and decay became a prolepsis of the new age. Cataclysm was suffused with divine presence because the woes, like birth pangs, heightened the expectancy of the arrival of the new age. The more intense the trauma, the more chaotic the confusion, the brighter the hope!

Similarly in 2 Corinthians Paul speaks of the simplifying function of suffering. Even the acrid stench of the martyr's corpse found its micromimesis in the daily afflictions of life "in Christ." Their suffering, like that of Christ, became a prolepsis of the salvation of the world and proof of their own salvation. As Paul says elsewhere, "we are the aroma of Christ to God among those who are being saved and among those who are perishing, to one a fragrance from death to death, to the other a fragrance from life to life" (2 Cor 2:15). Through this pact with death, established in the mythical experience of the death of Christ, Paul sought to link the alienation and distress of the community with the source of all meaning and life. Thus Paul's myth ordered a chaotic world, and in doing so reinforced the community. And through its own suffering — either at the hands of such cosmic powers as death or from such human agents as one's own tribal associates — community solidarity was secured. In this sense Paul's apocalyptic outlook certainly offered a simplified understanding of social alienation and is fully at one with the apocalypticism of the day.

Earlier in 1 Corinthians Paul dealt with a situation brought about more by internal forces than by external competitors. Perhaps through a misunderstanding of Paul, the Corinthians claimed a total experience of salvation that was profoundly escapist. Paul's insistence on the incompleteness of the salvific process and the link he forged between the Lord of glory and the cross challenged the Corinthian identification. Paul's call to participate in the brokenness of this world with its human pain and incompleteness (1:12–13) questioned the Corinthians' escapism.

The complexity and tension that Paul interjected into the Corinthian myth can easily be seen in chapter 4. In vv. 9–16 Paul offered a brutally sarcastic contrast of the hurt and abuse he and his coworkers endured with the religious puffery of the Corinthians. The apostles, he noted, were exhibited by God as "last of all" (4:9), like persons under a death sentence, as spectacles to the world and angels, as fools, weak, dishonored, vulnerable, hungry, naked, thirsty, knocked about, toiling, cursed, slandered, treated like garbage and everyone's offscouring. His own experience contrasted dramatically with the claims of the "pneumatic" Corinthians to be wise, free, sated, powerful, rich, wise, mature, free, invincible, glorified, resurrected participants in the superior order of heavenly beings.

By citing his own humiliation and calling on his "children" to "be imitators of me" (4:15–16), Paul used his authority as father and as suffering apostle to qualify the claims of the Corinthians, and he did so without explicitly denying their pneumatic existence. As Paul stated elsewhere, the primeval symbiosis between *Endzeit* and *Urzeit* was anticipated in Christ, but the full realization of that embrace remains outstanding (Rom 8:22–23). One's hope in that imminent resolution established one's place in the eschatological drama, but the deferral of that resolution left one firmly involved in the swirl of confusion and dislocation endemic to human suffering and incompleteness. Thus we see the same tension between apocalyptic simplicity and complexity that informed Paul's insistence on a simultaneous disassociation from and involvement in the world.

The third aspect of simplification I wish to examine is *the interpretation of scripture.* While the least ambiguous trend toward simplification may be seen in Paul's apocalyptic interpretation of scripture, here also tension is evident. All scriptures, according to Paul, found their fulfillment in the arriving rule of God manifested in the death, resurrection, and return of Jesus. And while the methods of interpretation were ingenious and complex, and sometimes circuitous and convoluted, their destination was rarely in question. Abraham's seed is Christ (Gal 3:16), Paul claimed. The archetypal Adam of Genesis has an antitype in Christ (Rom 5:12–21). David's line gains its culmination in Jesus (Rom 1:4). Sarah and Hagar find their counterparts in the children of the Spirit and the children of slavery (Gal 4:22–28). The prophets, likewise, already anticipated the new age inaugurated in Jesus' death and resurrection. Of Paul's approximately forty references to or quotations from the prophets, all in one way or another apply to the dawning eschaton.[38] The prophets, Paul believed, predicted the apocalyptic era now dawning (e.g., Rom 1:2; 16:26). They foresaw the turning to the gentiles in the last days (Rom 3:29; 9:25–26; 10:20; 15:12). Their murder foreshadowed the death of Jesus (1 Thess 2:15), and their pronouncements forecast his elevation and return.

As with the Prophets, so with Torah and the Writings, scripture was unfailingly experienced as a treasure of wisdom and knowledge of the future which only now was yielding up its secrets. So while the mechanics of scripture interpretation were complex, the outcome of the exegesis was predetermined. Light from the apocalyptic myth illumined the secret wisdom of the scriptures and then was refracted back onto the community sharing the myth. From the end of the world back to the text and then back to the world again the loop

---

38. See Calvin J. Roetzel, *Judgement in the Community: A Study of the Relationship between Eschatology and Ecclesiology in Paul* (Leiden: Brill, 1972).

ran. In this orbit, through the text the myth of crisis gained a richer texture, a deeper substance, and a sacred framework. In this circle the community shared in the life of the text, and the text shared in the fabric of the community. The hermeneutical circle was initiated, then, through the myth of crisis. Through the vantage point given by the apocalyptic myth, the community gained a perspective on the whole of scripture and its place in it. And thus the myth cracked the code, finding the key to the text's secrets. In turn, the text validated the myth. "Yes," Paul says, "to this day whenever Moses is read a veil lies over their minds; but when a person turns to the Lord the veil is removed" (2 Cor 3:15).

This is hardly to say that tension was absent from Paul's interpretation of scripture. Perhaps nowhere is this tension more apparent than in Romans 9–11 which, as I noted above, still practically pulses in a reader's hands. The tension was created by the dialectic of an apocalyptic myth based on the promises of God to Israel that in fact embraced "gentile sinners" (Gal 2:15). The question raised by the inclusion of the gentiles who had accepted the gospel was whether God had excluded the Jews who had rejected the gospel. If so, what would that imply about this God? Had he reneged on his promises to Israel? Had his word failed (Rom 9:6)? Perhaps nowhere in Paul's letters is such a profusion of scripture passages summoned to address a single issue. This dazzling array of scripture reinforces one's sense of the gravity and difficulty of Paul's argument.

The argument pulls in contrary directions — affirming first God's freedom to include gentiles *qua* gentiles, even if that means rejection for Israel, and second, somewhat paradoxically, God's firm commitment to Israel's salvation. Citing Gen 18:10, 14 and 25:23, Paul justifies the inclusion of gentiles by showing how God has always chosen to bless some and not others, preferring Isaac over Ishmael, Jacob over Esau, and even Joseph over his brothers. Citing Exod 33:39; 9:16 and Isa 29:16, and alluding to a number of other passages, Paul responds to the question, If God acts so arbitrarily, rejecting the chosen and choosing the rejected (9:14), hardening the heart of some and making others receptive (9:19), how can Israel be faulted for rejecting the gospel? In 9:25–29 Paul strings together citations from Hos 2:25; 2:1; Isa 10:22; Hos 2:1; 11:5; Isa 28:22; Deut 5:28; and Isa 1:9 to respond to the question about the justice of God. Is God just, Paul allows his objector to ask, if he includes gentiles who did not pursue righteousness and excludes Israel who did pursue righteousness? Citing Isa 28:16, Paul notes that in its contest for righteousness Israel stumbled over a stone placed on the track by God himself (Rom 9:33)![39] Just when it appears that Paul's sports metaphor

---

39. See the excellent treatment of this passage in John E. Toews, "The Law in Paul's Letter to the Romans: A Study of Rom. 9:30–10:13" (Ph.D. diss., Northwestern University, 1977).

disqualifies Israel from the race, he returns to the metaphor with a rhetorical question, "I say, therefore, has she stumbled so as to fall?" and answers emphatically, "Absolutely not!" Near the end of his discussion Paul concludes: "I would not have you ignorant, brothers and sisters, of this mystery, that you [gentiles] may not be wise in your own estimation, that a hardening has come upon a part of Israel until the full number of gentiles come in, and *so all Israel will be saved*" (Rom 11:25–26, emphasis added). At this point Paul tilts against the expectation in sports that winners require losers. Since the gentiles have won, one expects the Israelites to lose. But Paul's answer is surprising. Both the gentiles who did not race and Israel who stumbled but recovered are winners.

The tension between these two contradictory assertions reaches the breaking point when Paul acknowledges that the question as to how this can be accomplished finds no human resolution. The answer according to Paul is hidden in the mystery of God's own being. Paul can only wonder at it as he launches into a concluding, soaring benediction (11:33–36): "O the depth of the riches, and wisdom and knowledge of God. How inscrutable are his judgments and untraceable his ways. For who has known the mind of the Lord? Or who has been his counselor? Who has first given him anything so as to be repaid by him? For out of him and through him and in him are all things. To him be the glory forever. Amen." Once again the tension in Paul's own gospel extended his logic to the breaking point. God will include gentiles while remaining faithful to his promises to Israel. The tension between these bold affirmations finds a resolution only in the future, and even then only in the divine mystery. So while Paul's scriptural interpretation found a simplification when refracted through the lens of his apocalyptic myth, his hermeneutic was complicated by inclusive tendencies set loose by his gospel.

Conclusion

In this discussion of the tension in Paul's apocalyptic eschatology and of his mastery of the idiom I have observed the organic nature of Paul's intellectual activity. I have noted creative applications of the idiom in its transfer from both Jewish and messianist sources. I have pointed to the tension in Paul's thought both with the idiom that Paul appropriated and within the fresh constructions he created. His attempt to correct the eschatological enthusiasm at Corinth, his efforts to encourage, to reassure, and to exhort those in danger of disillusionment at Thessalonica, and his insistence on the inclusiveness of his apocalyptic gospel in Rome all involved him in applications fraught with tension and ambiguity.

But how was the tension in Paul's apocalypticism different from that endemic to all apocalypticism, since all apocalypticism creates tension between two worlds? There always exists a tension in apocalypticism between this world as known through suffering and incompleteness and another world as known only through apocalyptic metaphor and myth. And the greater the enchantment with the other world, the greater the disenchantment with this world. In a world in which oppressive inertia holds sway, apocalypticism envisions change — radical, dramatic, revolutionary, convulsive change. A heightened awareness of a common danger and the deficiencies of all human systems inspires the seer's vision of a brighter world. The greater the sense of deprivation and loss, the more painful is the conflict between the chaos of this world and the regeneration of the next, between helplessness and vindi-cation, between the aroma of death and the odor of the new creation. That vision challenges accommodations to cultural norms, to political ideology, to institutional intransigence, and to the idols of the day. That vision judges complacency at the plight of the vulnerable, the distress of the victims, and the agony of the brutalized. And that vision offers consolation and hope to the marginalized visionaries. Inevitably such a vision creates tension. So how is the tension in Paul's version of apocalypticism different?

While all of these tensions exist in Paul's apocalypticism, they are com-pounded and heightened by added tensions. First, there are tensions between himself and congregations who seek escape from this world through absorp-tion into the world to come. (All apocalypticism, including that of Paul, encourages disassociation, but Paul, while allowing for disassociation, will not tolerate disengagement from the world.) Then there are tensions be-tween himself and the exclusivistic tendencies inherent in apocalyptic myth. (All apocalypticism, including that of Paul, draws sharp boundaries between the insider and outsider, but Paul's emphasis on love for the outsider re-quires a protocol for crossing those boundaries to embrace the persecutor; this emphasis introduces a high level of ambiguity into the boundary ques-tion: absolutely secure boundaries mitigate against change; adjustable or open boundaries make change possible but foster ambiguity; obviously de-cisions about the location and symbolic significance of boundaries make a difference in the way a tradition will grow.) And finally there are tensions between God's gospel to the gentiles and the historic promises to Israel. (All apocalypticism divides the custodians of the mysteries from the ignorant or incredulous, and so does Paul, except that Paul refuses to agree that the in-clusion of gentile sinners implies the exclusion of Israel. The tension of this paradoxical vision finds its resolution only in the future and in the mystery of God.)

Inevitably, to highlight the importance of the continuing tension in Paul's appropriation of the myth he inhabits is to caution against making the im-plied resolution — the future — the modus operandi for understanding Paul's present. As critics, we do well to use restraint in supplying for Paul's myth a solution that he himself can only anticipate.[40] Stories as we tell them may require a resolution, as do symphonies. But the full resolution of God's story (*mythos*) Paul never knew. The resolution of God's story he only dimly apprehended, even though he fully inhabited it. And that tension was experienced and prescribed by Paul as a continuing condition. It was this complexity, outreach, and tie to this world that made it possible for transition, or liminality, to become a permanent condition. This combination avoided the eschatological disappointment of the enthusiasts and the easy conformity and surrender to the status quo of the traditionalists. So in the vitality of Paul's thought, in the skillful adaptation of his native apocalyptic idiom, and in his creative interpretation of his apocalyptic gospel for a variety of contexts, we see an organic intellectual at work.[41]

---

40. See my review of Norman R. Peterson, *Rediscovering Paul: Philemon and the Sociology of Paul's Narrative World* (Philadelphia: Fortress, 1985) in *TToday* 43 (1986) 139–42. There I argue that Paul's gospel may implicitly suggest that Onesimus, the slave, be given his freedom; but this hardly means that Paul required Philemon to manumit him. A rich humanitarian tradition seems to obscure Peterson's understanding of Paul at this point. No resolution is apparent to this reader concerning Onesimus's ambiguous status as a Christian slave.

41. I am grateful to Jouette M. Bassler for reading an earlier version of this essay and offering many valuable suggestions for its improvement.

16

THE RHETORIC OF LOVE
IN CORINTH

From Paul to Clement of Rome

BARBARA E. BOWE

Common, everyday experience should convince us that it is always difficult, if not impossible, to assess accurately what motivates (whether consciously or unconsciously) the words and actions of others. On the one hand, naivete often prevents us from recognizing a verbal power play for what it really is, namely, a subtle (or not so subtle) attempt to control and dominate the life of another. On the other hand, misunderstanding or cynicism often inclines us to impute to others perverse motives when they are not, in fact, present at all. If this difficulty is true in a world of face-to-face communication, how much more difficult is the challenge to "read" accurately the motivation and intention of ancient writers like the apostle Paul or Clement of Rome?

Such is the dilemma one faces when reading the similar passages "in praise of love" in 1 Corinthians 13 and *1 Clement* 49 as shown on the facing page. Are these two lyrical, even sublime, passages manipulative rhetorical tools designed to silence dissenters and to bolster the authority and power of their respective authors, Paul and "Clement"? Or are they genuine expressions of the highest Christian ideal of love designed to move their hearers to abandon their divisive and factious discord and to embrace this Christian ideal in what Clement called the "harmony of love" (*1 Clem.* 50.5)? Are the motives of these two authors the same, or are they different? It is no exaggeration to observe that, for the most part, the history of exegesis until very recently has tended to judge Paul's aim in a positive light and Clement's more often than not as the manipulative twisting of Paul. Our honoree, Graydon Snyder, has himself praised Paul's words in 1 Corinthians 13 when he describes 1 Cor

1 Cor 12:31b–13:7	*1 Clem.* 49.1–6
And I will show you a still more excellent way. [1]If I speak in the tongues of mortals and of angels, but do not have love, I am a noisy gong or a clanging cymbal. [2]And if I have prophetic powers, and understand all mysteries and all knowledge, and if I have all faith, so as to remove mountains, but do not have love, I am nothing. [3]If I give away all my possessions, and if I hand over my body so that I may boast, but do not have love, I gain nothing. [4]Love is patient; love is kind; love is not envious or boastful or arrogant [5]or rude. It does not insist on its own way; it is not irritable or resentful; [6]it does not rejoice in wrongdoing, but rejoices in the truth. [7]It bears all things, believes all things, hopes all things, endures all things. (NRSV)	Let the one who has love in Christ perform the commandments of Christ. [2]The bond of the love of God — who is able to explain it? [3]The greatness of its beauty — who is sufficient to tell of it? [4]The height into which love lifts us is indescribable. [5]Love joins us to God; "love covers a multitude of sins"; love bears all things; endures all things. There is nothing vulgar in love, nothing haughty; love admits no schism; love does not engage in faction; love does all things in concord; in love all the elect of God have been perfected; apart from love, nothing is pleasing to God. [6]In love the Master received us; for the sake of the love which he had toward us, Jesus Christ our Lord gave his blood, by the will of God, for us, and his flesh for our flesh, and his life for our lives. (my translation)

13:4–7 in this way: "These verses contain a blue ribbon list of adjectives which describe how and why love builds up the faith community."[1] Gordon D. Fee is also typical when he comments that "this is one of the greatly loved passages in the NT, and for good reason. It is one of Paul's finest moments; indeed, let the interpreter beware lest too much analysis detract from its sheer beauty and power."[2] More recently, however, Graham Shaw, Elizabeth Stuart, and Antoinette Clark Wire, among others, have challenged these favorable readings of Paul and, instead, have seen in Paul's words a thoroughly manipulative purpose.[3] Moreover, *1 Clement*, it has been argued, disguises the manipulative will and hegemonic power of the Roman community behind its lyrical language of love.[4]

These two letters from the ancient world, both addressed to the Christians in Corinth, depict communities torn by jealousy, dissension, and faction. Both present themselves as appeals to restore harmony. Both urge their respective recipients to recognize that, as Christians, they are one body. Both exhort the addressees to strengthen their common ground. And for both, issues of communal leadership and authority rest in the balance. Furthermore, both

---

1. Snyder, *First Corinthians: A Faith Community Commentary* (Macon, Ga.: Mercer University Press, 1992) 175.

2. Fee, *The First Epistle to the Corinthians* (NICNT; Grand Rapids: Eerdmans, 1987) 625–26.

3. Shaw, *The Cost of Authority: Manipulation and Freedom in the New Testament* (Philadelphia: Fortress, 1982) 92; Stuart ("Love Is . . . Paul," *ExpTim* 102 [1990–91] 265) claims that "1 Cor 13 is Paul at his most manipulative. Its message is that it is only through Paul that the Corinthians can experience the love of God in Christ because only Paul, no other Christian teacher, possesses that love." See also Wire, *The Corinthian Women Prophets: A Reconstruction through Paul's Rhetoric* (Minneapolis: Fortress, 1990), esp. 138–39.

4. See James S. Jeffers, *Conflict at Rome: Social Order and Hierarchy in Early Christianity* (Minneapolis: Fortress, 1991) 137.

letters, it has been argued, are fine examples of the deliberative rhetorical genre. And within this rhetorical framework, both employ an encomium on love to emphasize their exhortative strategy.

In the limited space of this study, I propose to revisit the difficult question of epistolary strategy and rhetorical motivation evident in these two Corinthian letters. My focus will be restricted to a comparative study of 1 Corinthians 13 and 1 Clement 49 in an effort to assess the function of this "rhetoric of love" in Corinth. Accordingly, the paper addresses three areas of concern: first, the rhetorical character of these Corinthian letters; second, the literary form and context of each passage, with a comparison of method and style in Paul and Clement; and third, an analysis of the function of this "rhetoric of love" in Corinth.

Rhetoric and Letters

In a now famous study, George A. Kennedy justified the application of rhetorical method to the NT by noting that the early Christian authors sought "to persuade their audiences to believe in the message about Jesus, or to believe it more strongly."[5] Persuasion is their primary aim, he argued, and for that reason they are rightly described as rhetorical in character. They lend themselves, moreover, to study by means of rhetorical methods. Accordingly, in the last twenty years a virtual explosion of rhetorical studies of various NT texts has engendered a whole subdiscipline of NT study.[6]

It is important, however, not to confuse genre and function. While both 1 Corinthians and 1 Clement are persuasive communications addressed to the Corinthian community, they are both, at the same time, real letters governed by the dominant constraints of epistolary and not principally rhetorical

5. George A. Kennedy, New Testament Interpretation through Rhetorical Criticism (Chapel Hill, N.C.: University of North Carolina Press, 1984) 3.

6. The relevant literature grows daily, but see esp. the following recent bibliographic summaries and collections of essays: C. C. Black, "Keeping Up with Recent Studies, XVI: Rhetorical Criticism and Biblical Interpretation," ExpTim 100 (1987) 256–57; Duane F. Watson, "The New Testament and Greco-Roman Rhetoric: A Bibliographic Update," JETS 31 (1988) 465–72; JETS 33 (1990) 513–24; idem and Alan J. Hauser, Rhetorical Criticism of the Bible: A Comprehensive Bibliography with Notes on History and Method (Biblical Interpretation 4; Leiden: Brill, 1994); Duane F. Watson, "Rhetorical Criticism of the Pauline Epistles since 1975," Currents in Research: Biblical Studies 3 (1995) 219–48; D. L. Stamps, "Rhetorical Criticism of the New Testament: Ancient and Modern Evaluations of Argumentation," in Stanley E. Porter and David Tombs, eds., Approaches to New Testament Study (JSNTSup 120; Sheffield: Sheffield Academic Press, 1995), esp. pp. 130–35; Stanley E. Porter and Thomas H. Olbricht, eds., Rhetoric and the New Testament: Essays from the 1992 Heidelberg Conference (JSNTSup 90; Sheffield: JSOT Press, 1993); idem, Rhetoric, Scripture and Theology: Essays from the 1994 Pretoria Conference (JSNTSup 131; Sheffield: Sheffield Academic Press, 1996); idem, The Rhetorical Analysis of Scripture: Essays from the 1995 London Conference (JSNTSup 146; Sheffield: Sheffield Academic Press, 1997); Stanley E. Porter, ed., Handbook of Classical Rhetoric in the Hellenistic Period, 330 B.C.–A.D. 400 (Leiden and New York: Brill, 1997).

convention.[7] That both letters are, moreover, *self-consciously* epistolary in character is demonstrated not only by their epistolary form but also by repeated internal references. Paul can remind the Corinthians: "I write (γράφω) these things not to shame you, but to admonish (νουθετέω) you as my beloved children" (1 Cor 4:14).[8] And the author of *1 Clement* is equally straightforward in making reference to the letter he is writing: "Beloved, we are writing (ἐπιστέλλομεν) these things not only for your admonition (νουθετεῖν), but also to remind ourselves" (7.1).[9] As letters, therefore, both texts function to establish a favorable relationship between their authors and addressees.[10]

At the same time, ancient rhetorical categories are useful and legitimate tools for ascertaining the nature of the persuasive arguments in these two letters if used with appropriate caution.[11] Such caution requires the following observations: (1) there is no certain proof that Paul had any formal rhetorical training that would have equipped him with rhetorical sophistication and given him an overriding rhetorical intention in all his letters; (2) as Abraham J. Malherbe has shown, letter writing as such was not a formal part of the system of ancient rhetoric;[12] and (3) Paul's certain use of a secretary or amanuensis in his letter-writing activity (Tertius in Rom 16:22; see also Gal 6:11; 2 Thess 3:17) at least raises the possibility that any rhetorical features evident in his letters may be attributed to his secretary and not to Paul's own intent and strategy. With these cautions in mind, therefore, we may examine the general rhetorical features of these two Corinthian letters without attempting to delineate a precise rhetorical arrangement for each of them.

In a number of important studies, 1 Corinthians has been profitably examined as influenced by the form and strategies of ancient deliberative rhetoric.[13] Judicial (or forensic) rhetoric, epideictic rhetoric, and delibera-

---

7. Both exhibit the requisite epistolary elements: Salutation and Greeting (1 Cor 1:1–3; *1 Clem. praescript*), Thanksgiving (1 Cor 1:4–9; *1 Clem.* 1.1–3.1 [=modified "thanksgiving"], Body (1 Cor 1:10–16:18; *1 Clem.* 3.2–63.4), and Closing conventions (1 Cor 16:19–24; *1 Clem.* 64.1–65.2).

8. See also 1 Cor 5:9, 11; 7:1; 16:21.

9. See also *1 Clem.* 53.1; 62.2, 3.

10. Note the frequent use of ἀγαπητός: 1 Cor 4:14, 17; 10:14; 15:58; *1 Clem.* 1.1; 7.1; 12.8; 16.17; 21.1; 24.1, 2; 33.1; 35.1, 5; 36.1; 43.6; 47.6; 50.1, 5; 53.1; 56.2, 16.

11. See esp. the recent pleas for caution and methodological prudence in the use of ancient rhetorical categories for analysis of the Pauline literature: Stanley E. Porter, "The Rhetorical Justification for Application of Rhetorical Categories to Pauline Epistolary Literature," in idem and Olbricht, *Rhetoric*, 100–122; Jeffrey T. Reed, "Using Ancient Rhetorical Categories to Interpret Paul's Letters: A Question of Genre," in ibid., 292–324; Porter, "Paul of Tarsus and His Letters," in idem, *Handbook of Classical Rhetoric*, 533–85.

12. Malherbe, *Ancient Epistolary Theorists* (SBLSBS 19; Missoula, Mont.: Scholars Press, 1988) 3.

13. Chiefly see Michael Bünker, *Briefformular und rhetorische Disposition im 1. Korintherbrief* (GTA 28; Göttingen: Vandenhoeck & Ruprecht, 1983) (Bünker argues that only 1:18–2:16 is deliberative); Margaret Mitchell, *Paul and the Rhetoric of Reconciliation: An Exegetical Investigation*

248 BARBARA E. BOWE

tive rhetoric constituted the three species of ancient rhetoric as defined by
Aristotle (*Rhet.* 1.3), each one addressing a different time frame. According
to Aristotle, forensic rhetoric concerns the past, epideictic rhetoric concerns
the present, and deliberative rhetoric concerns the future, "for the speaker
advises for or against things to be done in the future" (*Rhet.* 1.3.4). As
Margaret M. Mitchell has convincingly argued, 1 Corinthians demonstrates
the four principal characteristics of deliberative rhetoric: (1) a focus on future time as the subject of deliberation; (2) employment of a determined set
of appeals or ends, the most distinctive of which is the advantageous (τὸ
συμφέρον); (3) proof by example (παράδειγμα); and (4) appropriate subjects
for deliberation, of which factionalism and concord are especially common.[14]

In an earlier study which expanded on the work of Wilhelm C. van Unnik, I argued the same thesis for *1 Clement*.[15] There I showed that the author,
intentionally imitating Paul, employed the traditional vocabulary and rhetorical strategies of deliberative rhetoric, summarized above, in order to urge the
Corinthians of his day to abandon their factionalism and to embrace concord.

Modern studies of the rhetorical character of early Christian texts have
focused especially on the rhetorical situation evident in the texts. In a now
classic definition, Lloyd Bitzer has defined "rhetorical situation" as

> a complex of persons, events, objects, and relations presenting an ac-
> tual or potential exigence which can be completely or partially removed
> if discourse, introduced into the situation, can so constrain human de-
> cision or action as to bring about the significant modification of the
> exigence.[16]

This definition and that of Kennedy, who drew on Bitzer's work,[17] nearly
equate "rhetorical situation" with the real, historical, or epistolary situation,
also known to the form critics as the *Sitz im Leben* of the text. But any facile
equating of the rhetorical situation with the actual, historical situation has

of the Language and Composition of 1 Corinthians (HUT 28; Tübingen: Mohr [Siebeck], 1991);
Insawn Saw, *Paul's Rhetoric in 1 Corinthians 15: An Analysis Utilizing the Theories of Classical
Rhetoric* (Lewiston, N.Y.: Mellen, 1995); Elisabeth Schüssler Fiorenza, "Rhetorical Situation and
Historical Reconstruction in 1 Corinthians," *NTS* 33 (1987) 396–89; J. Smit, "Argument and
Genre of 1 Corinthians 12–14," in Porter and Olbricht, *Rhetoric,* 211–30; Duane F. Watson,
"Paul's Rhetorical Strategy in 1 Corinthians 15," in Porter and Olbricht, *Rhetoric,* 231–49; L. L.
Welborn, "On the Discord in Corinth: 1 Corinthians 1–4 and Ancient Politics," *JBL* 106 (1987)
83–113; idem, "A Conciliatory Principle in 1 Cor 4:6," *NovT* 29 (1987) 320–46; Ben Wither-
ington, *Conflict and Community in Corinth: A Socio-Rhetorical Commentary on 1 and 2 Corinthians*
(Grand Rapids: Eerdmans, 1995).

14. Mitchell, *Rhetoric of Reconciliation,* 23.
15. Barbara E. Bowe, *A Church in Crisis: Ecclesiology and Paraenesis in Clement of Rome* (HDR
23; Minneapolis: Fortress, 1988), esp. 58–74.
16. Bitzer, "The Rhetorical Situation," *Philosophy and Rhetoric* 1 (1968) 6.
17. Kennedy, *Rhetorical Criticism* (see above, n. 5).

led to radically diverse interpretations and differing reconstructions of early Christian history.

Recently, Dennis L. Stamps has made a case for rethinking the notion of rhetorical situation.[18] He rejects the equation of the rhetorical with the actual, historical situation and claims instead that the "rhetorical situation" is best understood as "the way in which the text presents a *selected, limited and crafted* entextualization of the situation."[19] As a general rule, he suggests, the more prevalent the rhetorical topoi employed, the less able are we to discern the actual historical situation that lies behind the text. At the same time, letters between two groups who share a common identity and purpose demand that the entextualized situation correspond to the perspective of most of the audience, if the letter is to be effective at all. As Stamps observes, "in terms of the rhetoric of the letter, it is the textual presentation of the inscribed situation which is crucial to the argument of the letter."[20]

Stamps's observations provide a fresh caution in this investigation of the function of Paul's and Clement's rhetoric of love. To the extent that both authors employ the language and strategies of deliberative rhetoric, they *construct a textual situation* that encompasses the logic and assumptions of this rhetorical genre.[21] Central to the political concerns of the deliberative genre was the assessment that factionalism and discord were evils to be avoided and that harmony, concord, and love were their positive antidotes.[22] If the "rhetoric of love" is central to the argument of both 1 Corinthians and *1 Clement,* then it gathers force by establishing an opposing "rhetoric of arrogance."

This final rhetorical feature of the Corinthian letters concerns the way in which both authors depict and ridicule their opponents as persons motivated by pride, arrogance, and self-seeking. Vilifying one's opponent in this way, especially by means of standard rhetorical techniques and topoi, is a strategy employed in both 1 Corinthians and *1 Clement,*[23] where both Paul

---

18. Stamps, "Rethinking the Rhetorical Situation: The Entextualization of the Situation in New Testament Epistles," in Porter and Olbricht, *Rhetoric,* 193–210.

19. Stamps, "Rethinking," 193 (emphasis added).

20. Ibid., 210.

21. Wire (*Corinthian Women Prophets,* 12–38) examines this entextualized situation in 1 Corinthians and then uses it to construct what she judges to be the actual historical situation, a move that may be judged to go beyond what the text can bear.

22. See the discussion and comprehensive assembling of ancient sources on these deliberative themes of factionalism and concord in Mitchell, *Rhetoric of Reconciliation,* esp. 60–64; on 1 Corinthians, see also Welborn, "Discord in Corinth," passim; and for these rhetorical themes in *1 Clement,* see Bowe, *Church in Crisis,* 58–74.

23. On the language of vilification, see esp. Sean Freyne, "Vilifying the Other and Defining the Self: Matthew's and John's Anti-Jewish Polemic in Focus," in Jacob Neusner and Ernest S. Frerichs, eds., *"To See Ourselves As Others See Us": Christians, Jews, "Others" in Late Antiquity* (Chico, Calif.: Scholars Press, 1985) 117–43; Luke Timothy Johnson, "The New Testament's Anti-Jewish Slander and the Conventions of Ancient Polemic," *JBL* 108 (1989) 419–41; Harry O. Maier, "*1 Clement* and the Rhetoric of *Hybris,*" *Studia Patristica,* forthcoming (cita-

and Clement draw extensively on the language for hybris employed in the Greek rhetorical and political tradition.[24] Those accused of hybris demonstrated the "self-indulgent arrogant behavior of the rich and powerful and privileged youth which disregards and oversteps the limits of human and divine authority."[25]

So it is that Paul depicts the troubles in Corinth (1:10) as stemming from dissensions (σχίσματα) and quarrelings (ἔριδες) that have, in his judgment, been motivated by hybris. Drawing on the common rhetorical topos of hybris, Paul accuses them of foolishness (μωρία: 1:18, 21, 23; 2:14; 3:19; cf. ἄφρων, in 15:36), boasting (καύχημα: 1:29, 31; 3:21; 4:7; 5:6; 9:15, 16; 13:3), being puffed up or arrogant (φυσιόω: 4:6, 18, 19; 5:2; 8:1; 13:4), exhibiting satiety (κορέννυμι, in 4:8), and sexual excess (5:1). These vices reflect well the standard denunciations against the arrogant and demand that the "praise of love" in 1 Corinthians 13 be heard as the powerful antithesis to such displays of hybris.

The author of 1 Clement also exhibits — and even expands — these hybristic topoi. He inscribes within his letter a rhetorical situation identical in many respects to the dissension and faction (3.2–4) assumed in 1 Corinthians. Like Paul, he attributes the cause of the discord to arrogance and jealousy (14.1). His rhetorical strategy seeks utterly to discredit both the motivation and the actions of the instigators by exposing their hybris. With typical accusations, he denounces their hypocrisy (ὑπόκρισις, 15.1), caricatures their insignificance by referring to them as "a few rash and self-willed persons (ὀλίγα πρόσωπα προπετῆ καὶ αὐθάδη)" (1.1) who, later in the letter, have shrunk in size to only "one or two persons (ἐν ἢ δύο πρόσωπα)" (47.6), described as "senseless, imprudent, foolish, and uninstructed" people (ἄφρονες, ἀσύνετοι, μωροί, ἀπαίδευτοι) who wish to "exalt themselves in their own conceits" (ἑαυτοὺς βουλόμενοι ἐπαίρεσθαι ταῖς διανοίαις, 39.1). He therefore excoriates them for their inflated arrogance and self-esteem (αὐθάδεια, 1.1; 30.5; ἀλαζονεία, 14.1; 16.2; 21.5; 35.5; ὑπερηφανία, 16.2; 30.1–2). The instigators, in his depiction, are boastful (ἐγκαυχάομαι, 21.5; καυχάομαι, 13.1; καύχημα, 34.5); they exalt themselves (ἐπαίρω, 14.5; 16.1; 21.5; 39.1; 45.8)

tions are from the unpublished MS, with gratitude to Prof. Maier for allowing me to cite it); Peter Marshall, "Hybrists Not Gnostics in Corinth," SBLSP 23 (1984) 275–87; idem, Enmity in Corinth: Social Conventions in Paul's Relations with the Corinthians (WUNT 2/23; Tübingen: Mohr [Siebeck], 1987); Andrie du Toit, "Vilification as a Pragmatic Device in Early Christian Epistolography," Bib 75 (1994) 403–12.

24. See esp. (for 1 Corinthians) Marshall, "Hybrists Not Gnostics," and (for 1 Clement) Maier, "Rhetoric of Hybris"; also N. R. E. Fisher, Hybris: A Study in the Values of Honour and Shame in Ancient Greece (Warminster: Aris & Phillips, 1992); idem, "Hybris and Dishonor: I," Greece and Rome 23 (1976) 177–93; Christopher Forbes, "Comparison, Self-Praise, and Irony: Paul's Boasting and the Conventions of Hellenistic Rhetoric," NTS 32 (1986) 1–30; Marshall, Enmity in Corinth, 182–216, 364–81.

25. Marshall, "Hybrists Not Gnostics," 276.

and lead the community into utter ruin (46.9).[26] Yet the relationship between these pictures of the "encoded adversaries" and their real-life counterparts in both letters still remains a vexed issue.

To summarize, both letters to Corinth adopt rhetorical strategies and language common in the deliberative rhetorical genre addressing strife and faction. These strategies control both the way in which the authors depict the rhetorical situation and the way they vilify as hybrists those they judge to be irresponsible. Over against such hybristic behavior, they present love as the antidote and remedy to communal discord. Both letters depend on the deliberative argument from advantage to urge all in the community to put an end to their strife and divisions and to embrace love, the greatest of Christian virtues.

1 Cor 12:31b–13:7 and *1 Clem.* 49.1–6 in Context

Recent studies of 1 Corinthians 13 have settled many questions about the form and function of this so-called digression in Paul's letter and by application have also shed light on its parallel text in *1 Clement*.[27] These studies establish the growing consensus that 1 Corinthians 13 (and parallels) correspond to the rhetorical form of the encomium (ἐγκώμιον) whose elements normally included prologue, birth and upbringing (when speaking of a person), acts (πράξεις), comparison (σύγκρισις), and epilogue.[28] Rhetoricians regularly used the encomium form to praise various virtues, and examples of such rhetorical exercises can be found among the basic level of Greco-Roman educational materials.[29] Paul, moreover, was not the first to commend (δείκνυμι, 12:31b) the virtue of love as an antidote to faction. One finds similar tactics in Polybius (στέργειν, 23.11.3), in Plato (ἔρως, *Symp.* 197C–D), in Maximus of Tyre (ἔρως, *Diss.* 20.2), and in Aristotle (φιλία, *E. N.* 8.1.4) but none of these often-cited examples offers an exact parallel to either Paul or Clement. Mitchell amasses more convincing evidence of the constant

---

26. See du Toit, "Vilification," 405–10; Stephen M. Pogoloff, *Logos and Sophia: The Rhetorical Situation of 1 Corinthians* (SBLDS 134; Atlanta: Scholars Press, 1992) 223–31.

27. For a history of the interpretation of 1 Corinthians 13 from 1918 to 1965, see Jack T. Sanders, "First Corinthians 13: Its Interpretation since the First World War," *Int* 20 (1966) 159–87. More recent studies stressing especially the rhetorical character of the text include (in order of appearance) Carl R. Holladay, "1 Corinthians 13: Paul as Apostolic Paradigm," in David L. Balch, Everett Ferguson, and Wayne A. Meeks, eds., *Greeks, Romans, and Christians: Essays in Honor of Abraham J. Malherbe* (Minneapolis: Fortress, 1990) 80–98; J. F. M. Smit, "The Genre of 1 Corinthians 13 in the Light of Classical Rhetoric," *NovT* 33 (1991) 193–216; idem, "Two Puzzles: 1 Corinthians 12.31 and 13.3 — A Rhetorical Solution," *NTS* 39 (1993) 246–64; Jan Lambrecht, "The Most Eminent Way: A Study of 1 Corinthians 13," in idem, *Pauline Studies: Collected Essays* (BETL 115; Louvain: Leuven University Press, 1994) 79–107; James G. Sigountos, "The Genre of 1 Corinthians 13," *NTS* 40 (1994) 246–60.

28. Smit, "Two Parables," 248.

29. Ibid.

Greco-Roman rhetorical tradition linking *love* (under its many names) and *concord,* and there can be little doubt that Paul and Clement drew on this commonplace.[30]

These two passages in praise of love present not "digressions" in their otherwise deliberative arguments but are integral to their respective exhortative strategies.[31] The *contexts* of both passages situate their encomia within a larger frame: for Paul, the encomium functions as the heart and center of Paul's teaching on spiritual gifts in 1 Cor 12:1–14:40. Within this context, the praise of love illustrates the means to the unity extolled especially in 1 Cor 12:12–13 and stands as the superior virtue in comparison to any other charisms, whether faith, hope, prophecy, tongues, or revelations (13:13; 14:4, 5, 30–31). Unlike the other charisms, love alone enhances and builds up the body (οἰκοδομεῖν, 14:4). Links with other parts of the letter (ἀγάπη, 4:21; 8:1; 16:14, 24), and especially the specific enumeration of what love *is not,* confirm that Paul's praise of love coheres with his overall purpose and intent throughout the letter. As he had in chapter 9, Paul uses himself as an example of behavior which he recommends to the Corinthians.[32]

Clement, like Paul, employs an encomium on love (49.1–6) to bolster his overall argumentative purpose, that is, to dissuade the Corinthians from continuing their strife and discord and to persuade them instead to embrace the "concord of love" (50.5). The encomium falls within a larger section of the letter which begins in 47.1, where Clement urges the Corinthians to "take up the epistle of the blessed Paul the apostle," and which concludes with a formal oath formula and doxology in 58.2. In this section, Clement first contrasts the Corinthian situation in Paul's day with his own time (47.4–7) and then calls for the swift cessation of strife and the restoration of φιλαδελφία (48.1). Specific allusions to 1 Cor 12:8–9 lie behind *1 Clem.* 48.5–6:

> Let a person be faithful (πιστός), let him or her have power to utter knowledge (γνῶσις), let him or her be wise (σοφός) in the discernment of arguments, let him or her be pure (ἁγνός) in deeds; for the more they seem to be great (μείζων), the more ought they to be humble-minded (ταπεινοφρονεῖν) and to seek the common good (κοινωφελές) of all and not their own benefit.

The praise of love follows immediately after these verses; it therefore demonstrates for Clement the way of ταπεινοφρονεῖν and care for what is

---

30. Mitchell, *Rhetoric of Reconciliation,* 165–71.

31. Cf. Witherington, *Conflict in Community,* 264; W. Wuellner, "Greek Rhetoric and Pauline Argumentation," in William R. Schoedel and Robert L. Wilken, eds., *Early Christian Literature and the Classical Intellectual Tradition: in honorem Robert M. Grant* (Theologie historique 53; Paris: Beauchesne, 1978) 187 for a different view.

32. Holladay, "Paul as Apostolic Paradigm," passim.

κοινωφελές. As it had in Paul, so for Clement the context makes obvious the comparison drawn between the spiritual gifts of faith, knowledge, wisdom, and purity and the corresponding superiority of love. References to the theme of love continue in the direct exhortation that resumes in 50.2: "Let us beg and pray of [divine] mercy, that we may be found in love, without human partisanship, blameless." The macarism of 50.5 praises those who act out of concord and love: "Blessed are we, beloved, if we perform the commandments of God in the concord of love, that through love our sins may be forgiven." Exempla of love continue in Clement's argument in 51.2 (those who willingly give their lives for others), in 53.5 (in Moses' address to God), and in 54.1 (those who are filled with love will freely choose voluntary exile if they are a cause of strife and division). References to love occur finally in the summary of the letter in 62.2 and mark this theme as central to the purpose of the entire letter.

Paul's Encomium on Love

If the *contexts* and function of these two encomia are similar in Paul and Clement, their specific form and *contents* are less so. Paul's encomium begins in 12:31 with a transitional verse marked by a pointed irony: "But earnestly seek the higher gifts. And I will show (δείκνυμι) you a still more excellent way."[33] In the following verses, however, Paul will go on to argue the exact opposite: against zealousness (with which love has no countenance, 13:4), against those gifts deemed in Corinth as the highest (13:1–3), against any "showy display" of virtue as a "still more excellent way" (13:4). These contradictions can be easily explained only by recognizing Paul's use of irony, whereby he "ridicules the Corinthians for aspiring, as their highest end, after the spectacular charismata."[34]

1 Cor 13:1–3 presents the prologue of the encomium, which normally includes the speaker's assessment of praise or blame and often displays comparison and hyperbole. Here, love is compared to and set over against the gifts of tongues (13:1), prophetic powers (13:2), knowledge of mysteries (13:2), faith itself (13:2), relinquishment of possessions (13:3), and self-glorification (reading καυχήσωμαι, "that I may glory"). In every instance, Paul claims, a gift without love is useless and produces nothing (οὐδέν, 13:2, 3).[35] Angelic tongues, knowledge of mysteries, faith that moves mountains, surrendering all things — the hyperbole of these phrases heightens both

---

33. I am in agreement with those who see this verse as a transition in which Paul ironically invites the Corinthians to be *zealous* (ζηλοῦτε as imperative) for the greatest thing of all, namely, love — of which Paul himself will be the prime example. See esp. Holladay, "Paul as Apostolic Paradigm," 82–88; Smit, "Genre," passim; idem, "Two Puzzles," 247–53.

34. Smit, "Two Puzzles," 251.

35. Holladay ("Paul as Apostolic Paradigm," 88–94) is surely correct to link each of these

the comparison and the force of Paul's devaluation of them in comparison with love.

1 Cor 13:4–7 comprises Paul's demonstration of the "acts" of love. As in other encomia (e.g., 1 Esdr 4:38–39) the virtue is personified. The arrangement of 13:4–7 alternates between seven positive and eight negative deeds of love in an A-B-A^1 sequence. Love enables one to be patient and kind, to rejoice in the truth, to bear all things, to believe all things, to hope all things, to endure all things. Paul's apostolic behavior, as Holladay demonstrates, provides the model for each of these deeds of love.[36] "Patience, kindness, love, endurance, rejoicing," mark Paul's apostolic self-description in 2 Cor 6:6–7. The specific term στέγειν ("to bear") describes Paul's apostolic life in 1 Cor 9:12, whereas other less-specific allusions all point to Paul's depiction of himself as an apostolic example which inspires this encomium on love.

As one might expect, the negative listing is pointedly aimed at Paul's opponents. The activities that Paul says "love does *not*" are the very same vices that have been attributed to Paul's opponents in Corinth. Jealousy heads the list and recalls the opening remarks in 1 Cor 1:10–17 against party strife as well as the explicit accusation in 1 Cor 3:3: "while there is jealousy and strife among you. . . ." For Paul, jealousy, acting like a braggart, being puffed up, and, we could add, boasting (ζηλοῦν, περπερεύεσθαι, φυσιοῦσθαι, καυχᾶσθαι) describe his opponents' activities perfectly. In short, they are hybrists who care only for themselves and their own advantage. Accordingly, the center point of the list in 13:4–7 comes at v. 5: "Love does not insist on its own way" (οὐ ζητεῖ τὰ ἑαυτῆς). A paraphrase might render this verse, "Love is not out for itself," or "Love does not seek its own advantage," as Mitchell has suggested, in keeping with the strategy of deliberative rhetoric.[37] Paul's point is clear: his opponents care only for themselves and not for what builds up the body in Corinth.

In vv. 8–12 Paul draws an explicit comparison between the finality of love and the transitory character of the spiritual gifts. The comparison highlights the relative insignificance of "prophecy, tongues, knowledge," in comparison with love, the supreme virtue. Paul's encomium concludes with an emphatic claim: "the greatest of these is love" (μείζων δὲ τούτων ἡ ἀγάπη). This verse prepares for a discussion of gifts and the plea to "make love your aim." It explains why Paul now will encourage prophecy over glossalalia — because the one builds up *itself* while the other builds up *the church* (1 Cor 14:4, ἑαυτὸν οἰκοδομεῖ/ἐκκλησίαν οἰκοδομεῖ).

---

gifts to Paul's own apostolic experience referred to elsewhere in his letters. Paul's own apostolic identity is therefore at issue and at risk in this text.

36. Ibid., 95.

37. Mitchell, *Rhetoric of Reconciliation*, 169.

1 Corinthians 13 cannot therefore be seen as a "digression," if by digression we mean a turning away from the main point of an argument. Paul has employed a different rhetorical tool, the encomium, but has used it entirely for his larger deliberative purpose. That purpose compelled Paul to argue for the most advantageous course of action for his audience. They must choose, as Paul constructs the argument, between self-interest and the interests of the body which is the church, between love and love's opposites.

Clement's Praise of Love

Clement no doubt saw the power and persuasive force of Paul's praise of love and imitated it well in *1 Clem.* 49.1–6:

Prol.	Let the one who has love in Christ perform the commandments of Christ.	
	[2]The bond of the love of God, who is able to explain it?	
	[3]The greatness of its beauty, who is sufficient to tell of it?	
	[4]The height into which love lifts us is indescribable.	
A	[5]Love joins us to God;	(ἀγάπη κολλᾷ)
	"love covers a multitude of sins";	
	love bears all things,	(ἀγάπη πάντα ἀνέχεται)
	endures all things.	(πάντα μακροθυμεῖ)
B	There is nothing vulgar in love,	(οὐδὲν βάναυσον)
	nothing haughty;	(οὐδὲν ὑπερήφανον)
	love admits no schism;	(σχίσμα)
	love does not engage in faction;	(οὐ στασιάζει)
A[1]	love does all things in concord;	(ἀγάπη πάντα ἐν ὁμονοίᾳ)
Concl.	*in* love all the elect of God have been perfected;	
	apart from love, nothing is pleasing to God.	
	[6]*In* love did the Master receive us;	
	for the sake of the love which he had toward us, Jesus Christ our Lord gave his blood, by the will of God, for us, and his flesh for our flesh, and his life for our lives.	

The pattern and arrangement follow that of Paul: a threefold structure A-B-A[1], alternating positive, then negative, then positive statements. In the prologue (49.1–4), hyperbole marks the opening two rhetorical questions and the declaration of love's "height" (τὸ ὕψος). Statements about the acts of love (49.5–6), both positive then negative, follow. The four concluding statements are climactic prepositional phrases: "*in* love [2x] . . . , *apart from* love . . . , *for the sake of* love. . . . " The passage concludes with the exemplum of Jesus as the decisive point in Clement's case (compare the opening line, addressed to "the one who has love in Christ").

While there is surely an agreement with the general sense of Paul's passage, Clement shares exactly only the verb "endure" (μακροθυμεῖ) and the repetition of ἀγάπη, πάντα, and οὐδέν.[38] Clement's encomium is more emphatic, more pointed than Paul's in many respects. Exhortation frames the passage entirely, and so is more obviously integral to the exhortative strategy of the whole letter. *1 Clem.* 49.1 opens the encomium with the command to those who "have love" to "perform the commandments," and 50.2 concludes with the resumptive hortatory subjunctive: "Let us then beg (δεώμεθα οὖν) and pray (αἰτώμεθα)... that we may be found in love, without human partisanship (προσκλίσεως), free from blame (ἄμωμοι)."

Clement's encomium is no more a general praise of love than is Paul's. Both authors select precise terms for love's positive and negative qualities, words which unmistakably reflect the issues in debate in their respective communities. Love's "opposites" are especially telling. Compare "nothing haughty" (οὐδὲν ὑπερήφανον, the adjective occurring 4x in *1 Clement*) with 16.2, which affirms that Christ came not with haughtiness but humble-mindedness (ταπεινοφροσύνη), and with the vice lists in 30.1 and 35.5 against "abominable pride" (ὑπερηφανία). When Clement addresses the opponents directly in 57.1–2, he singles out for condemnation their haughtiness and prays in 59.3 to a God who "humbles the pride of the haughty."

Throughout Clement's letter three terms especially have described the dissension in Corinth, or its opposite: schism (σχίσμα, 5x), faction (στάσις, στασιάζω, 16x), and concord (ὁμόνοια, 15x). Love, therefore, abhors the former and creates their opposite, concord. Of special importance for the argument in the letter is the claim that "in love the elect of God are made perfect." "God's elect" is a favorite designation for the church in *1 Clement* (1.1; 2.4; 49.5; 58.2; 59.2), and "safeguarding the number of the elect" for their salvation and fulfillment is a constant preoccupation (2.4; 46.8; 59.2). As Paul had claimed, so now Clement also affirms that love alone lasts forever, bringing God's faithful to their awaited perfect end.[39]

Conclusion: The Rhetoric of Love in Corinth

This brief survey of the form and content of these two encomia in Paul and Clement permits us now to return to the questions posed at the beginning. How do we assess the motive and strategy of these two authors? Do we see their letters as exercises in manipulative rhetorical ploy or as genuine Christian appeals for harmony and the common good? As in John Fowles's novel *The French Lieutenant's Woman*, there are two endings to our story, two answers that must be proffered for consideration.

---

38. See the comparison of these passages in Donald Alfred Hagner, *The Use of the Old and New Testaments in Clement of Rome* (NovTSup 34; Leiden: Brill, 1973) 185–213.

39. See Bowe, *Church in Crisis*, 76–85; W. C. van Unnik, "Le nombre des élus dans le première épître de Clément," *RHPR* 42 (1962) 237–46.

The "best" answer hangs in the balance, entirely dependent on the veracity or distortion, the accuracy or misrepresentation, of the opponents' character. If those labeled as hybrists in each of these letters were indeed arrogant self-seekers who cared little for the common good but only for their own self-importance, then the rhetoric of love, in Paul and Clement, is a powerful and well-intentioned tool to counter those claims. If, on the other hand, the depiction of the opponents is mere rhetorical vituperation with little or no correspondence to the true character or intention of those so described, then the rhetoric of love is itself a "noisy gong and a clanging cymbal" — vacuous and manipulative.[40] Different scenarios, moreover, have been argued for 1 Corinthians and *1 Clement,* but in both cases the data decisive for an accurate judgment continue to elude our grasp. We simply cannot, with certainty, retrieve the actual historical situation prevailing in Corinth at the time either of Paul or of Clement of Rome.[41]

A hermeneutic of suspicion warns us to approach these letters with great care and to recognize vilification for what it is. We do well to reject a facile equating of the "encoded adversaries" with their real-life counterparts. But the laws of rhetorical *ethos* also remind us that the speaker risks shame and rejection if the depiction of the situation and of the characters involved bear no resemblance to actual fact.[42] As Andrie du Toit has said: "A disturbing discrepancy between *verba* and *res* would put the *sinceritas* of the author in jeopardy."[43]

Neither Paul nor Clement, it appears, could wield absolute power over the Corinthian church when facing the difficult matters being debated there. Each chose instead to influence his community by the force of persuasion. In the game of rhetoric they excelled — they were masters. And in that game, the rhetoric of love was their greatest weapon.

---

40. For 1 Corinthians, these opposing assessments have been ably argued by Mitchell (*Rhetoric of Reconciliation,* passim) and Wire (*Corinthian Women Prophets,* esp. 138–46). Mitchell concludes (p. 303) that Paul's strategy fails, that he has satisfied neither faction, and that by appealing to his own example he has left himself open to the charge of "self-recommendation" (see 2 Cor 3:1; 4:2). Wire, on the other hand, sees a manipulative Paul, one who succeeded in "controlling" the freedom of the Spirit evident in the Corinthian women prophets.

41. See Walter Bauer, *Orthodoxy and Heresy in Earliest Christianity* (Philadelphia: Fortress, 1971) 100; cf. Bowe, *Church in Crisis,* 31–32.

42. See, e.g., Aristotle *Rhet.* 1.2.4; 1.8.6; 2.1.3–5; 2.13.16; 3.14.7; 3.16.8; Isocrates *Ant.* 278; Cicero *Inv. Rhet.* 1.14.20; *Rhet. Her.* 1.4.8.

43. Du Toit, "Vilification," 411.

17

FAITH IN ROMANS 12 IN THE LIGHT OF THE COMMON LIFE OF THE ROMAN CHURCH

Lloyd Gaston

The word πίστις occurs in two phrases in Romans 12 — μέτρον πίστεως (v. 3) and τὴν ἀναλογίαν τῆς πίστεως (v. 6) — and each is usually thought to help interpret the other. That πίστις means "faith" is seldom questioned since, as J. D. G. Dunn puts it, "throughout the letter Paul uses this key word of the human act and attitude of believing, as the means through which God effects his saving work."[1] I shall discuss the appropriateness of this common understanding below. Because of the later importance of the theological concept of *analogia fidei*, the faith of Rom 12:6 in particular has tended towards an objective *fides quae creditur* understanding. But perhaps the most important issue concerns the nature of the genitive ("of") in the phrase "measure of faith" (12:3).

Most interpreters understand it to be partitive,[2] so that the phrase is understood to mean "a portion of faith" (Otto Michel), "a gift...a limit" of faith (Ernst Käsemann), "the measure of faith that is individually appor-tioned by God to each believer" (Heinrich Schlier), "the measure (amount) of 'faith'" or "the degree of the divine gift of 'faith'" (Matthew Black), "'faith,' dispensed by God in various degrees" (Joseph A. Fitzmyer).[3] Dunn's thorough discussion concludes that "as God has measured to each a measure of faith"

---

1. Dunn, *Romans 9–16* (WBC 38B; Dallas: Word, 1988) 722.
2. See BDF §164 (pp. 90–91).
3. Michel, *Der Brief an die Römer* (11th ed.; MeyerK; Göttingen: Vandenhoeck & Ruprecht, 1957) 265: "The concept of measure encompasses the differences and varieties of the gifts of grace"; Käsemann, *Commentary on Romans* (Grand Rapids: Eerdmans, 1980) 335; Schlier, *Der Römerbrief* (HTKNT 6; Freiburg: Herder, 1977) 367; Black, *Romans* (NCB; Grand Rapids: Eerd-mans; London: Marshall, Morgan & Scott, 1981) 169; Fitzmyer, *Romans* (AB 33; New York: Doubleday, 1993) 646. Both Michel and Käsemann seem influenced by 1 Cor 12:9 and the opposition to charismatics, as if the phrase were μέτρον πνεύματος (or χάριτος).

means that "each has been given some measure of faith": "Paul clearly sees [this] as a variable in different believers."[4] Similarly, J. Paul Sampley says that "faith is a gift variable in strength," and J. C. O'Neill calls it "a virtue in man, the level of ability God has pledged and granted to each individual."[5] Yet C. E. B. Cranfield rejects this view as "improbable," and Ulrich Wilckens even calls it "simply impossible."[6] So how can the issue be resolved?

It may be that attention to the social situation of those addressed would help resolve the question. Recent years have seen a number of important studies of the social world of the early church in general and of Christians in Rome in particular.[7] It seems that two writings from the end of the first century in Rome, *1 Clement* and especially the *Shepherd of Hermas,* might be the best starting point.[8] While the Roman Christians did not have a high social status, since they were mostly freedmen (*libertini*) and resident foreigners (*peregrini*), there were nevertheless relative differences of wealth and status comparable to those identified in Corinth.[9] Although well aware of the careful analysis of Lampe, Robert Jewett probably goes too far when he speaks of Roman "tenement churches" as opposed to "house churches."[10] While it is doubtful that Christians ever met in detached houses or villas in pre-Constantinian Rome,[11] an *insula* ("tenement"?) usually contained "luxury apartments" as well as shops and small rooms for the poor.[12] It is perhaps

4. Dunn, *Romans 9–16,* 721, 722.

5. Sampley, *Walking Between the Times: Paul's Moral Reasoning* (Minneapolis: Fortress, 1991) 48; O'Neill, *Paul's Letter to the Romans* (Harmondsworth, Middlesex: Penguin, 1975) 198 (though for O'Neill, of course, this is no part of the original text of Romans).

6. Cranfield, "μέτρον πίστεως in Romans 12.3," *NTS* 8 (1961–62) 349; Wilckens, *Der Brief an die Römer* (3 vols.; EKKNT 6.1–3; Neukirchen-Vluyn; Neukirchener Verlag, 1978–82) 3. 11.

7. See, e.g., Carolyn Osiek, *Rich and Poor in the Shepherd of Hermas: An Exegetical-Social Investigation* (CBQMS 15; Washington, D.C.: Catholic Biblical Association of America, 1983); Harry O. Maier, *The Social Setting of the Ministry As Reflected in the Writings of Hermas, Clement and Ignatius* (Diss SR 1; Waterloo, Ont.: Wilfrid Laurier University Press, 1991); Peter Lampe, *Die stadtrömischen Christen in den ersten beiden Jahrhunderten: Untersuchungen zur Sozialgeschichte* (WUNT 2/28; Tübingen: Mohr [Siebeck], 1989). Archaeology does not help for the period in question; see the important study of Graydon F. Snyder, *Ante Pacem: Archaeological Evidence of Church Life before Constantine* (Macon, Ga.: Mercer University Press, 1985).

8. See Maier, *Social Setting,* 58, for a possibly early date for *Hermas.*

9. See Gerd Theissen, *The Social Setting of Pauline Christianity: Essays on Corinth* (Edinburgh: T. & T. Clark, 1982); Wayne A. Meeks, *The First Urban Christians: The Social World of the Apostle Paul* (New Haven, Conn.: Yale University Press, 1983).

10. Jewett, "Tenement Churches and Communal Meals in the Early Church: The Implications of a Form-Critical Analysis of 2 Thessalonians 3:10," *BR* 38 (1993) 32. Carolyn Osiek is uneasy about the term "tenement church," preferring to speak of "apartment church" ("The Family in Early Christianity: 'Family Values' Revisited," *CBQ* 58 [1996] 19–20, 21). Note that Lampe (*Stadtrömischen Christen*) speaks of "social stratification" among Roman Christians in all three sources: Romans (p. 63), *1 Clement* (p. 69), and *Hermas* (p. 71).

11. Lampe believes he can trace nine of the *tituli* churches to the first and second centuries (*Stadtrömischen Christen,* 11–13); Snyder is not so optimistic (*Ante Pacem,* 75–82). Christians could of course dream of meeting in the house of the senator Marcellus, as in the *Acts of Peter.*

12. James E. Parker, "Housing and Population in Imperial Ostia and Rome," *JRS* 57 (1967) 80–95.

too modern and too romantic to posit an "agapaic communalism" of poor but equal Christians.[13] In any case it tends to obscure the very real social tensions in the common life of the Roman church.

In her important study, Carolyn Osiek sees the relationship between the (relatively) wealthy and the (quite real) poor as a major theme in *Hermas*.[14] She notes that exhortation is clearly all addressed to the rich and that the poor are referred to as the objects of their concern. In particular the wealthy leaders are encouraged to receive other Christians into their houses (or apartments): "Bishops and hospitable men [or: hospitable bishops] who at all times received the servants of God into their houses gladly."[15] *1 Clement* is not as specific about the situation in Rome, but nevertheless presupposes a community of poor and relatively rich and speaks both to and for the latter. In particular he must oppose the arrogance, pride, and haughtiness of the wealthy and urge humble-mindedness (30.2–8; also 2.1; 13.1–3; 16.1, 17; 19.1; 38.2; 62.2). Characteristic is the following: "Let the strong (ὁ ἰσχυρός) care for the weak and let the weak (ὁ ἀσθενής) reverence the strong. Let the rich one (ὁ πλούσιος) bestow help on the poor and let the poor one (ὁ πτωχός) give thanks to God, that he give him one to supply his needs; let the wise (ὁ σοφός) manifest his wisdom not in words but in good deeds."[16]

The situation of the Roman Christians reflected in Paul's letter seems to be comparable. There are relative differences in wealth and social status. On the one hand, there are those who have needs, including hospitality (12:13), who are lowly or poor (12:16), who need merciful deeds and the distribution of goods (12:8), who are powerless and have infirmities (15:1). On the other, there are some who can act as hosts for other Christians in their homes (16:5), who can travel and pay taxes and customs (13:6–7), who can help finance a mission to Spain (15:24). Also comparable to the later Roman writings is the observation that the implied addressees of Paul's exhortation are those with relatively higher wealth and status.[17]

The parenesis proper begins with the injunction "not to be conformed to this age" (12:2),[18] a temptation especially for the wealthy in *Hermas*. The renewal of the mind implies the injunction "not to be super-minded above

---

13. Robert Jewett, "Tenement Churches and the Pauline Love Feasts," *Quarterly Review* 14 (1994) 51.

14. Osiek, *Rich and Poor.*

15. *Herm. Sim.* 9.27.2; for the textual issues, see Maier, *Social Setting,* 82 n. 42. There is almost identical wording in 8.10.3: "they gladly received into their homes the servants of God." On the importance of hospitality, see the list of good actions in *Herm. Mand.* 8.10; also Rom 12:13; *1 Clem.* 10.7; 11.1; 12.1; and as the duty of a bishop, 1 Tim 3:2; Titus 1:8.

16. *1 Clem.* 38.2; see also the prayer in 59.4, which asks God to "raise up the weak."

17. See Stanley K. Stowers, *A Rereading of Romans: Justice, Jews, and Gentiles* (New Haven, Conn.: Yale University Press, 1994) 75–76 and passim.

18. On this section, see William S. Campbell, "The Rule of Faith in Romans 12:1–15:13: The Obligation of Humble Obedience to Christ as the Only Adequate Response to the Mer-

what one ought to be minded, but to set your mind on being sober-minded" (12:3).[19] The temptation to feel superior is an all-pervasive theme in Romans: "With respect to honor, esteem one another higher [than oneself]" (12:10); "Have the same regard for one another. Do not think haughty thoughts but associate with the poor. Do not be wise in your own eyes" (12:16).[20] The language recalls an earlier injunction: "Do not boast triumphantly over the branches.... Do not think haughty thoughts but fear [God].... I do not want you to be ignorant, brothers and sisters, of this mystery, lest ye be wise for yourselves [=in your own eyes]" (11:17, 20, 25). It has recently been argued that Romans 12–13 reverses the sketch of the Roman Christian past in 1:18–2:3, so that rational worship (12:1) replaces idolatry (1:25), renewal of mind (12:3) replaces the unfit mind (1:28, 31), the injunction to sober-mindedness (12:3) reverses a false claim to be wise (1:22).[21] Similarly, the arrogant braggart of 1:30, who judges others (2:1, 3), cannot be separated from those Christians who judge and despise one another in Romans 14.[22]

It is not the intention of this little essay to solve the question of the identity of the weak and the strong.[23] I am among those who find it doubtful that the reference is to identifiable groups in Rome. It is also hard to imagine an individual who would call himself or herself "weak in faith."[24] The "strong" person is by implication anyone who might be tempted to call someone else weak. We have been reminded recently that the contrast between strong and weak was not unusual in antiquity and referred much more to perceived social status than to theological, religious, or dietary differences.[25] The parallel between wealthy and strong (and wise) in *1 Clem.* 38.2, cited above, is an indication of this. The admonition to accept (προσλαμβάνειν) one another, not to pass judgment on one another, to pursue peace and mutual edification, to please the neighbor for good, to agree among one another according to Jesus Christ — all of these can apply on many different levels

---

cies of God," in David M. Hay and Elizabeth Johnson, eds., *Pauline Theology*, vol. 3: *Romans* (Minneapolis: Fortress, 1995) 259–86.

19. This fine translation is by Robert Jewett, in his *Christian Tolerance: Paul's Message to the Modern Church* (Philadelphia: Westminster, 1982) 66. Words from the φρον- root constitute almost a leitmotif in the parenesis of Romans; see A. J. M. Wedderburn, *The Reasons for Romans* (Edinburgh: T. & T. Clark, 1988) 76–78.

20. Paraphrasing 12:16a with Fitzmyer, *Romans*, 656.

21. Stowers, *Rereading of Romans*, 317–20.

22. See Wayne A. Meeks, "Judgment and the Brother: Romans 14:1–15:13," in Gerald F. Hawthorne and Otto Betz, eds., *Tradition and Interpretation in the New Testament: Essays in Honor of E. Earle Ellis for His 60th Birthday* (Grand Rapids: Eerdmans, 1987) 290–300.

23. I am intrigued but not yet completely convinced by the arguments of Mark D. Nanos (*The Mystery of Romans: The Jewish Context of Paul's Letter* [Minneapolis: Fortress, 1996]) that the weak are non-Christian Jews, as the parallel with Rom 11:13–24 might indicate.

24. See Michel, *An die Römer*, 298.

25. Campbell, "Rule of Faith," 269–70.

and thus cohere well with the overall parenetic thrust of the letter. All are
being addressed as strong, and all are urged not to look down on anyone
considered weak.[26]

Within that overall framework, however, it seems that the faith of some
is being disparagingly called "weak" by others. Paul is quite disturbed by this
particular kind of arrogance, perhaps even more than by the arrogance with
respect to "knowledge" in Corinth. I find Rom 14:22 to be a key: "The
faith which thou hast, keep to thyself before God."[27] Faith is not something to be paraded and compared so that one can say to another, "I have
more faith than you," or speak disdainfully of someone else being "weak in
faith." Douglas A. Campbell has argued that Paul's quotation of Hab 2:4 in
Rom 1:17 "conditions every use of ἐκ πίστεως that follows" and that the
phrase consistently refers to the faithfulness of God or Christ.[28] This appears
to be true also for 14:23: "Everything that is not done in response to the
faithfulness [of God] is sin." While Käsemann would not agree, he certainly
captures the proper sense: "Sin arises... when one goes beyond the gift of
God, instead of attending to one's own μέτρον πίστεως, and thus falls into
ὑπερφρονεῖν.... Christ remains the only measure for all. No one must make
his faith a norm for others as they seek to serve Christ."[29] No one should
compare someone else's faith unfavorably with his or her own, and this is
quite properly related to Rom 12:3, to which we now turn.

In 1961–62 Cranfield published a thorough study of Rom 12:3 in which
he concluded that μέτρον πίστεως must be understood as a "means of mea-
surement" rather than a "measured quantity" and that the genitive must be
one of apposition and not a partitive genitive.[30] He is surely correct. Certainly
consideration of Paul's consistent rhetorical stance in the parenesis of Romans and probably the social reality that occasions it would strongly support
Cranfield's arguments. There is no social or literary (12:3a!) context in which
it would be less appropriate to give the strong, the mighty, the haughty, the
opportunity to boast about their faith. Certainly in Rome Christians should

---

26. See J. Paul Sampley, "The Weak and Strong: Paul's Careful and Crafty Rhetorical Strategy
in Romans 14:1–15:13," in L. Michael White and O. Larry Yarbrough, eds., *The Social World of
the First Christians: Essays in Honor of Wayne A. Meeks* (Minneapolis: Fortress, 1995) 40–52.

27. Cf. 1 Cor 5:13: "if we have been in ecstasy, it is for God [*alone, and therefore none of your
business*]; if we are reasonable, it is for you."

28. Campbell, "The Meaning of Πίστις and Νόμος in Paul: A Linguistic and Structural Perspective," *JBL* 111 (1992) 91–103, esp. 101; see his further clarifications in idem, "Romans
1:17–A Crux Interpretum for the Πίστις Χριστοῦ Debate," *JBL* 113 (1994) 265–85; "False
Presuppositions in the Πίστις Χριστοῦ Debate: A Response to Brian Dodd," *JBL* 116 (1997)
713–19. Dunn (*Romans*, 828) also sees the almost technical use of ἐκ πίστεως in Romans but
does not draw the same conclusions.

29. Käsemann, *Romans*, 379.

30. Cranfield, "μέτρον πίστεως"; also idem, *The Epistle to the Romans* (2 vols.; ICC;
Edinburgh: T. & T. Clark, 1975–79) 2. 613–16.

measure the strength of their faith not against one another but in relation to an objective standard.

Why then has Cranfield not been more widely followed?[31] One unstated reason is probably the general Christian instinct to think faith important and to strive ever to increase and deepen it. Another is likely the reading of Rom 12:4–8 under the influence of the metaphor of the body and the list of *charismata* in 1 Corinthians 12 (where, however, the catalog of gifts is quite different, and in Romans 12 "faith" is not an item on the list at all). Another is the different conception of the social and religious situation in Rome which Paul addresses.[32] Finally, there might be a weakness in Cranfield's argument itself.

The ἀναλογία τῆς πίστεως in Rom 12:6 is clearly parallel to the "measuring rod of faith" in 12:3. In this context ἀναλογία cannot mean (as it can otherwise) "in proportion to" (as if Paul thought that prophecy depended on the prophet's faith!) but must mean "in agreement with." The reference is to an objective standard by which prophecy can be judged, and this should have influenced the interpretation of 12:3. The standard is called "faith," which therefore must be *fides quae creditur*.[33] The problem is that πίστις probably never means that in Paul. We must after all turn to the word almost always translated "faith" in Romans 12.

Cranfield considers translating πίστις "faithfulness" but then rejects the idea,[34] understandably so, since he wrote long before the current discussion of πίστις Χριστοῦ as the faithfulness of Christ. There is also the prospect that πίστις all by itself can refer to the faithfulness of God or Christ. In 1973, John J. O'Rourke surveyed all occurrences of πίστις in Romans to investigate this possibility and found that Rom 12:3 could well refer to "the standard of God's fidelity," parallel to "God's mercies" in 12:1, but then rejected this because of the "proportion" in 12:6.[35] Cranfield himself comes close when he concludes his study thus: "Since the all-important thing in Christian faith is not the activity of the believer but the Object believed in, to say that the Christian is to measure himself and all things by his faith is really to say that

---

31. He has been followed by Wilckens, *An die Römer* 3. 11–12; John Ziesler, *Paul's Letter to the Romans* (TPI New Testament Commentaries; London: SCM; Philadelphia: Trinity Press International, 1989) 295–96.

32. "The danger [Paul] sees confronting the Roman congregations is not so much of charismatic abuse and overenthusiasm, but of not giving enough weight to the immediate dependency of faith, and of superseding it or devaluing it by placing higher value on Jewish (or non-Jewish) identity" (Dunn, *Romans 9–16*, 728).

33. Indeed, Augustine even translates the phrase *regula fidei* (Michel, *An die Römer*, 267).

34. Cranfield, "μέτρον πίστεως," 347.

35. O'Rourke, "Pistis in Romans," *CBQ* 35 (1973) 188–94, esp. 193. Karl Barth translates πίστις twelve times "Treue (Gottes)" or the like but "Glaube" in Romans 12, perhaps in anticipation of the concept *analogia fidei* that was to become so important for him (*Der Römerbrief* [Zellikon-Zurich: Evangelischer Verlag, 1940]).

he is to measure himself and all things by Jesus Christ. μέτρον πίστεως is really Jesus Christ Himself as standard and norm."[36]

In a recent remarkable book, Stanley K. Stowers observes that "Paul does not name Christ in Rom 12:3, but after 3:25–8:39, readers could hardly hear about faithfulness and not think of Christ's and their share in it."[37] I conclude then that Rom 12:3 must be paraphrased as follows: "not to be super-minded above what one ought to be minded, but to set your mind on being sober-minded, as God has allotted to each one a standard of faithfulness [=Christ]"; and 12:6: "if prophecy, [then] in agreement with the faithfulness [of Christ]." For the sake of the common life of the Roman church it is best not to speak of human faith in Romans 12.

---

36. Cranfield, "μέτρον πίστεως," 351.
37. Stowers, *Rereading of Romans*, 319.

18

ARE THERE ALLUSIONS TO THE LOVE FEAST IN ROMANS 13:8–10?

Robert Jewett

The centrality of the common meal in early Christian life was confirmed by Graydon F. Snyder's *Ante Pacem*, which examined the symbols of bread, fish, the vine, and the depiction of the multiplication of loaves and fishes.[1] He summarized the "characteristics of the house church noted in the period's art" as "a democratic, close-knit group" that shared "the meal as social *diakonia*."[2] In recent years I have been following up on these insights in my study of Paul's letter to the Romans, taking account of the concrete situation of the early Christian groups in the various districts where the earliest evidence has been found.[3] Unlike the public churches that comprise the tacit framework of most modern interpreters, it is clear that the early Christians met in their living spaces, mostly in secret, and that their common life was organized on very different principles than churches after the time of Constantine. When Romans is read in the light of such groups, new possibilities of translation and interpretation begin to emerge. For example, the concluding verse in the pericope of Rom 13:8–10 includes two references to ἡ ἀγάπη that raise the possibility I would like to consider. Is there so direct an allusion to the common meal in this pericope that a translation such as "the *agape*" would be justified? To pursue this question, we need to investigate whether the earliest literary evidence in the NT augments the picture that Graydon Snyder drew.

---

1. Snyder, *Ante Pacem: Archaeological Evidence of Church Life before Constantine* (Macon, Ga.: Mercer University Press, 1985) 21–26, 64–66.

2. Ibid., 166.

3. The groundbreaking study on the social location of groups in Rome is Peter Lampe, *Die stadtrömischen Christen in den ersten beiden Jahrhunderten: Untersuchungen zur Sozialgeschichte* (WUNT 2/18; Tübingen: Mohr [Siebeck], 1987, 1989).

House and Tenement Churches as the Context
of Early Christian Meals

There is indisputable evidence for the traditional picture of house churches in early Christianity, starting with references to the "church in the house" of particular patrons, explicitly mentioned in Rom 16:5.[4] Although the word οἶκος can refer to the various Roman or Greek styles of houses or even an apartment in a tenement building,[5] most studies of house churches assume a building owned or rented by a patron, somewhat analogous to the situation of middle- or upper-class housing in contemporary Europe or North America.[6] Jerome Murphy-O'Connor's calculation of the maximum size of thirty to forty for a house church congregation rested on the premise of a freestanding villa.[7] His more recent work considers the possibility that the shop space on the ground floor of a tenement building might be used for a "house church" such as Prisca and Aquila sponsored in Corinth, Ephesus, and Rome; it might accommodate a group of ten to twenty believers.[8]

The social model of a house church presupposes a patron or patroness who controls the space used by the Christian community. A number of such persons are mentioned in the Pauline letters, including Phoebe, Erastus, Crispus, Stephanas, Gaius, Philemon, Apphia, and Nympha. A house church is thus assimilated into the hierarchical social structure of the Greco-Roman world, in which heads of houses exercise legal and familial domination over their relatives and slaves. In the words of Wayne A. Meeks, "The head of the household, by normal expectations of the society, would exercise some authority over the group and would have some legal responsibility for it. The structure of the οἶκος was hierarchical, and contemporary political and moral thought regarding the structure of superior and inferior roles as basic to the well-being of the whole society."[9] This model of a house church has led to the widely accepted theory of Gerd Theissen that such churches were marked by "love-patriarchalism," in which the hierarchical social order is retained while

---

4. See also 1 Cor 16:19 and the similar formulation in 1 Cor 1:11 and 16:15.

5. Hans-Josef Klauck, *Hausgemeinde und Hauskirche im frühen Christentum* (SBS 103; Stuttgart: Katholisches Bibelwerk, 1981) 15–20. See also Robert J. Banks, *Paul's Idea of Community* (rev. ed.; Peabody, Mass.: Hendrickson, 1994) 31–36; Vincent P. Branick, *The House Church in the Writings of Paul* (Wilmington, Del.: Glazier, 1989) 13–28.

6. Floyd V. Filson, for example, uses the model of the freestanding house at Dura Europos as the basis for understanding house churches ("The Significance of Early House Churches," *JBL* 58 [1939] 107–9). See also Joan M. Petersen, "House Churches in Rome," *VC* 23 (1969) 264–72; Banks, *Paul's Idea of Community*, 14–15.

7. Murphy-O'Connor, *St. Paul's Corinth: Texts and Archaeology* (Wilmington, Del.: Glazier, 1983) 156.

8. Idem, "Prisca and Aquila," *BibRev* (December 1992) 49–50.

9. Meeks, *The First Urban Christians: The Social World of the Apostle Paul* (New Haven, Conn.: Yale University Press, 1982) 76.

mutual respect and love are being fostered by patrons serving as leaders of the congregations in their houses.[10]

Studies of the evidence in Thessalonians and Romans have raised questions in my mind as to whether the house church model is adequate to explain all of the evidence about church life in the Pauline letters. The impressive investigation of Roman Christianity by Peter Lampe identifies the slum districts where the earliest and most dense evidence of Christian settlement emerged.[11] This led me to consider the possibility of "tenement churches," in addition to the traditional concept of "house churches," as forms of early Christian communities that might more naturally occur in the poorest areas of the city.[12] On the basis of the evidence in Rom 16:14–15, I inferred that the class structure of the two tenement churches was mono-dimensional. In contrast to house churches that have an upper- or middle-class patron along with his or her slaves, family, friends, and others, the tenement churches referred to in Rom 16:14 and 15 consisted entirely of the urban underclass, primarily slaves and former slaves. Lacking a patron who would function as a leader, the pattern of leadership appears to be charismatic and egalitarian in tenement churches. The two groups greeted in Romans have five persons named, who are probably the charismatic leaders of the community. If the persons named are the renters of family living spaces in the tenement building rather than charismatic leaders of the group, the social pattern still appears to be egalitarian. No one of the five appears to have a position of prominence over the others. The leadership pattern appears to be collective rather than hierarchical. So who provides the economic support, the resources for the Lord's Supper, and the means for hospitality and charity characteristic of early Christianity in such a community?

The path toward understanding the social context in which communal mutuality could have alternated with love-patriarchalism in early Christian churches has been available since 1951. Bo Ivar Reicke's classic study of the early Christian systems of diaconal service and the love feast showed that the eucharist was celebrated in the context of a common meal by a broad stream

---

10. See Theissen, *The Social Setting of Pauline Christianity: Essays on Corinth* (Philadelphia: Fortress, 1982) 11, 107: "This love-patriarchalism takes social differences for granted but ameliorates them through an obligation of respect and love, an obligation imposed upon those who are socially stronger. From the weaker are required subordination, fidelity, and esteem."

11. Lampe, *Stadtrömischen Christen*, 36–52.

12. This research led to the publication of three closely related studies: "Tenement Churches and Communal Meals in the Early Church: The Implications of a Form-Critical Analysis of 2 Thess 3:10," *BR* 38 (1993) 23–43; "Tenement Churches and Pauline Love Feasts," chapter 6 in *Paul the Apostle to America: Cultural Trends and Pauline Scholarship* (Louisville: Westminster/ John Knox, 1994) 73–86; and an abbreviated form of this essay in "Tenement Churches and Pauline Love Feasts," in *Quarterly Review: A Journal of Theological Resources for Ministry* 14/1 (Spring 1994) 43–58.

of early Christianity through the fourth century.[13] The direct references to the *agape* in John 13:1; Jude 12; Ignatius *Smyrn.* 6.2; 7.1; and 8.2 as well as the discussions of common meals in Acts 2 and 1 Corinthians 11 show that the eucharistic liturgy was combined with diaconal service, understood as serving meals in celebration with the faith community. Whereas researchers have often attempted to separate the sacramental celebration from the common meal, Reicke showed that early Christian sources, beginning with the biblical evidence, points toward the "single Christian sacrament of table fellowship," whether supported by patrons or by the contributions of all the members.[14] The evidence justifies calling all such celebrations in the early church "love feasts." Such meals were marked by eschatological joy at the presence of a new age and of a Master who had triumphed over the principalities and powers, overcoming shameful status and opening up the possibility of sharing. This joy was treated with ambivalence by early Christian writers because it tended toward excesses of zealous impatience with the continuation of a fallen world and sometimes resulted in licentious behavior. At times an overly realized eschatology in some of the *agape* meals led to excessive enthusiasm and conflicts in Paul's churches.

The communal dimensions of the *agape* meal documented by Reicke led me to wonder whether the frequent admonitions "to love the brethren" in the Pauline letters may not have been intended to encourage congregational support and participation in such sacramental celebrations. In groups organized as house churches, the primary admonition would obviously be to the patrons, encouraging their involvement in love-patriarchalism. But in the context of groups organized as tenement churches, to whom would these admonitions of love be directed? Certainly not to patrons, because they are not present within the community itself. I therefore proposed a second interpretive category to be used alongside "love-patriarchalism," namely "agapaic communalism" as the ethical framework suitable for the early Pauline tenement churches. The provisions for the meal in tenement churches would have to come from sharing between members, since patrons were not available. In a form-critical study of 2 Thess 3:10, "If anyone will not work, let not eat," I showed that the creation of this regulation presupposed communities that were regularly eating meals together, for which the willingness or unwillingness to work was a factor of sufficient importance to require regulation, and in which the power to deprive members of food was in fact present.[15] I went on to show that the references to "brotherly love" (1 Thess 4:9) and "well doing" (2 Thess 3:13) in close proximity to the discussion of labor for

13. Reicke, *Diakonie, Festfreude und Zelos in Verbindung mit der altchristlichen Agapenfeier* (UUÅ 1951/5; Uppsala: Lundequistska Bokhandeln, 1951).
14. Ibid., 14.
15. Jewett, "Tenement Churches and Communal Meals," 23–43.

bread made it likely that the food for the love feasts in Thessalonica was being provided by community members rather than by patrons. This raises a question that is new for Romans research, whether a similar system of self-supporting love feasts is visible in Romans.

The Obligation of Mutual Love

The admonition to love one another in Rom 13:8–10 begins with the theme of obligation developed in 13:7, opening with a sweeping reference to avoiding indebtedness. The expression "be obligated to no one in anything" employs a conventional expression for monetary or social indebtedness, as the parallels indicate.[16] August Strobel pointed to a striking parallel in a grave inscription that celebrated a Roman woman of pagan background who "lived well and owed no one anything."[17] This widely shared value of being free of debts is also expressed in a letter from a young man to his mother: "Don't you know that I would rather become a cripple than to owe a man even an obulos?"[18] Paul's admonition extends this traditional reluctance to incur indebtedness into all areas of life with the word "anything," which includes the list of taxes, customs, respect, and honor owed in v. 7. These and all other obligations are to be met, taken care of, paid off, so that Christians are free to devote themselves to their new obligations.[19] This implies the avoidance of falling under the control of creditors or remaining entangled with patrons that might erode the capacity of the members of house and tenement churches to shape their common life in Christ. This counsel is consistent with Paul's preference to avoid dependency relations, except for radical dependency as a slave of Christ, visible in 1 Corinthians 9, 1 and 2 Thessalonians, and Philippians 4.[20] He wants Christians to be slaves of no human, if they can avoid it, indebted only to mutual love.[21] Their former social obligations are to be replaced by a single new obligation to meet the needs of fellow members in the church.

The puzzle about the admonition in Rom 13:8a is whether the exception

---

16. See Friedrich Hauck, "ὀφείλω, κτλ.," *TDNT* 5 (1967) 559–60; BAGD, s.v. (pp. 598–99).

17. Strobel, "Verständnis von Rm 13," *ZNW* 47 (1956) 92, cited from *IGRom.* 1.104 (R. Cagnat, G. Lafaye, et al., eds., *Inscriptiones graecae ad res romanas pertinentes* [4 vols. in 3; Paris: Leroux, 1906–27; repr. Chicago: Ares, 1975] 1. 104).

18. Ulrich Wilckens, *Der Brief an die Römer* (3 vols.; EKKNT 6; Zurich: Benziger; Neukirchen-Vluyn: Neukirchener Verlag, 1982) 3. 67, cited from BGU II 846 (*Ägyptische Urkunden aus den Königlichen Museen zu Berlin* [9 vols.; Berlin: Weidmann, 1895–1937] 2. 846).

19. Leon Morris (*The Epistle to the Romans* [Pillar New Testament Commentary; Grand Rapids: Eerdmans, 1988] 467) observes that the present imperative form of the verb "will have a continuous force: 'Don't continue owing. Pay your debts.'"

20. See Dale B. Martin, *Slavery as Salvation: The Metaphor of Slavery in Pauline Christianity* (New Haven, Conn.: Yale University Press, 1990) 126–35.

21. See Jewett, *Paul the Apostle to America*, chap. 6.

clause was meant to be understood antithetically ("but you ought to love one another")[22] or inclusively ("except to love one another"), which is the more natural and convincing option.[23] If Matthew Black is right in discerning an Aramaic word play between "to owe" and "to love" behind the wording of this sentence, the inclusive alternative would be further strengthened.[24] A new obligation is to replace the social dependency on patrons or families, namely "to love one another." The succinct formulation without an article signifies a well-known command,[25] which has numerous parallels in Jewish and apocalyptic literature.[26]

I think it is crucial for the interpretation of this pericope to clarify the social context of this formulaic obligation. That Paul has in mind the new obligation to love the members of one's house or tenement church as the new fictive family in which believers are embedded is strongly indicated by the wording of this verse. "One another" clearly refers to fellow believers, as Theodor Zahn, Hans Lietzmann, and others have shown.[27] Some commentators are inclined to improve Paul's ethic by including "all with whom the Roman Christians would come in contact," to use J. D. G. Dunn's expansive phrasing.[28] But how could Paul be encouraging love toward non-Christians

22. Anton Fridrichsen provides a penetrating analysis of the issue in "Exegetisches zu den Paulusbriefen," *TSK* 102 (1930) 294–97, concluding that Theodoret, C. F. A. Fritzsche, and Bernhard Weiß were correct in perceiving a subjective obligation in v. 8b as opposed to the objective indebtedness in 8a. The verse thus contains "a simple and natural wordplay" on the term "obligation" (297). He was followed by Willi Marxsen ("Der ἕτερος νόμος Röm 13,8," *TZ* 11 [1955] 235–36); C. K. Barrett (*A Commentary on the Epistle to the Romans* [London: Black; HNTC; New York: Harper, 1957; 2d ed., 1991] 250); Hauck ("ὀφείλω," 564); and Franz-Josef Ortkemper (*Leben aus dem Glauben: christliche Grundhaltungen nach Römer 12–13* [NTAbh n.F. 14; Münster: Aschendorff, 1980] 126–27). Heinrich Schlier also appears to favor this option in *Der Römerbrief* (HTKNT 6; Freiburg: Herder, 1977) 294.

23. Most commentators since Origen, Chrysostom, Pelagius, and Johann Albrecht Bengel have accepted this alternative that retains the ordinary translation of εἰ μή as "except" (BDF §§376; 428.3 [pp. 191, 221]. The most cogent argument for this is in C. E. B. Cranfield, *The Epistle to the Romans* (ICC; Edinburgh: T. & T. Clark, 1975–79) 2. 674; Cranfield shows that the antithetical option requires that the verb ὀφείλω be supplied in v. 8b in a different sense and mood, which is highly improbable: it would appear in 8a as "owe" and in 8b as "ought to be obligated." Also the articular infinitive clause "to love one another" impedes the supplying of a verb; see BDF §§398–99 (pp. 205–6).

24. Black, *Romans* (NCB; London: Oliphants; Grand Rapids: Eerdmans, 1973, 1989) 185: "Paul is probably reproducing in Greek an Aramaic *sententia*, possibly a Christian, conceivable even a dominical pun." Although we have no such pun, this has been accepted by Michael B. Thompson, *Clothed with Christ: The Example and Teaching of Jesus in Romans 12.1–15.13* (JSNTSup 59; Sheffield: JSOT Press, 1991) 122.

25. BDF §399.1 (p. 205); see also Thompson, *Clothed with Christ*, 123.

26. See Thompson, *Clothed with Christ*, 123–24.

27. Zahn, *Der Brief des Paulus an die Römer* (3d ed.; KNT 6; Leipzig: Deichert, 1925) 562; Lietzmann, *An die Römer* (5th ed.; HNT 8; Tübingen: Mohr [Siebeck], 1971) 112; Marie-Joseph Lagrange, *Saint Paul: Épître aux Romains* (EBib; Paris: Gabalda, 1916) 315; Wilckens, *Römer* 3. 68.

28. Dunn, *Romans 9–16* (WBC 38B; Dallas: Word, 1988) 776; he acknowledges, however, that "the exhortation elsewhere would normally refer to fellow Christians" and concludes that

at this point by qualifying such love as toward "one another"? When Paul wants to refer to the attitude of Christians toward outsiders, he mentions strangers (12:13), persecutors (12:14), "all" (12:18), or "enemies" (12:20). The appropriate social context of the love ethic in this section is the small Christian congregations in Rome and, more concretely, the love feasts and sacramental celebrations in which members shared resources. This context, which was natural and close at hand for the early church — but alien and unacknowledged in the orientation of scholars except those who stand in Snyder's Anabaptist tradition — renders it unnecessary to theorize about an "eternal debt"[29] that can never be paid since it is owed to all people everywhere.[30] There is no indication in any of Paul's references to love that it was a boundless and thus impossible burden. That misconception is due to the social decontextualization of Paul's ethic in the mainstream of our theological tradition, replacing it with elaborate intellectual constructs that have boundless implications and hence contain the convenient corollary of being incapable of actualization. There is not a shred of support for this expansive and finally evasive understanding of love in this pericope. The obligation to love fellow believers is advocated in a self-evident and unambiguous manner, on the presumption that its motivation was understood by the hearers. It had been reiterated by the earlier chapters of Romans; Paul refers in Dunn's words to "a responsive obligation . . . which arises from what those addressed have received" from God,[31] namely, love shown to the ungodly through the gospel that calls hearers into new communities based on love.[32]

There is a translation problem in v. 8b, which provides a rationale for the preceding clause as indicated by the presence of "for." It is possible to translate this in an adjectival sense referring to "the other law" of the Mosaic covenant,[33] compared either with the law of love to be mentioned in 13:10[34] or with Roman law alluded to in 13:1–7.[35] Some identify the "other law" as

---

"it would be best to say that Paul has fellow believers particularly in view but not in any exclusive way." Joseph A. Fitzmyer takes the same line, apparently in an attempt to make Paul appear less narrowly sectarian (*Romans* [AB 33; New York: Doubleday, 1993] 678).

29. The Latin expression is from Bengel, *Gnomon Novi Testamenti* (Tübingen: Schramm, 1759) 557.

30. See Marxsen, "Röm 13,8," 236, referring to Ernst Gaugler, *Der Römerbrief* (2 vols.; Zurich: Zwingli, 1952) 2. 295; Cranfield, *Romans* 2. 675; Morris, *Romans*, 467–68.

31. Dunn, *Romans 9–16*, 776. Fitzmyer (*Romans*, 677) argues that Paul's formulation is an "oxymoron, for love cannot be 'owed,'" but this overlooks the earlier argument of the letter.

32. See also Victor Paul Furnish's somewhat more individualistic statement of this point in *The Love Command in the New Testament* (Nashville: Abingdon; London: SCM, 1973) 100: "Rather, the obligation to 'love one another' inheres in what God has done, in the new life he has granted the believer in Christ."

33. For example, see Luke Timothy Johnson's *Reading Romans: A Literary and Theological Commentary* (Reading the New Testament Series; New York: Crossroad, 1997) 192.

34. Johann Christian Konrad von Hofman, *Brief an die Römer* (Nördlingen: Beck, 1868) 542–43; Zahn, *Römer*, 562–63.

35. The most extensive case has been developed by Willi Marxsen in "Röm 13,8," 230–37;

the law of love in 8a.[36] Because the term "law" does not appear in 13:1–7, some commentators assume the reference in 13:8 must be to the Jewish Torah, since the context does not clearly indicate otherwise.[37] The reference to the "other law in my members" (7:23), referring to the law of sin, would make a confusing counterpart to any reference to "another law" here in 13:8. Since Paul frequently refers to other people with the term "other,"[38] it is likely that Paul wished to refer to the person being loved, with the expression "the other" functioning as the object of the participial expression "the one who loves."[39] A further consideration was pointed out by Zahn, that the expected object of the verb "to love" is either "brother" or "neighbor," which raises the question about the nuance that Paul intends in the odd choice of the term "other."[40] That it refers to a fellow believer is strongly indicated by the expression "love one another" in 8a, for which 8b provides the justification.

Paul's choice of the term "other" rather than "neighbor" or "brother" opens the door to consider the obligation to love Christians beyond one's small circle of the house or tenement church.[41] It is Paul's way of opening up the issue of overcoming boundaries formed by shameful status. This fits perfectly into the context in Romans because mutual acceptance of members and leaders from other Christian groups was a significant problem in the church there. This subtle widening of the love command to include the "other" Christian in v. 8b thus opens the door to the topic directly addressed in 14:1–16:23, the welcome of persons identified as the "weak." Since the "weak" were predominantly Jewish Christian conservatives, in contrast to the gentile Christian majority of the Roman churches, there was a significant cross-cultural element in this pluralism that Paul includes within the obligation of Christian love.

Love between Christians is presented in v. 8b as law's fulfillment, which is usually assumed to be a typically Jewish expression for Torah observance.[42]

---

he argues that the word "other" is never used as the object of the verb "love" in the other Pauline letters and is more frequently used in the adjectival than the substantive sense. Franz J. Leenhardt modifies this by perceiving a contrast between the Mosaic law, summed up in love, and the Roman law of 13:1–7 (*The Epistle to the Romans: A Commentary* [London: Lutterworth; Cleveland: World, 1961] 337–38).

36. See Walter Gutbrod, "νόμος, κτλ.," *TDNT* 4 (1967) 1071.

37. See Cranfield, *Romans* 2. 675; Otto Michel, *Der Brief an die Römer* (14th ed.; MeyerK 4; Göttingen: Vandenhoeck & Ruprecht, 1978) 409; Wilckens, *Römer*, 68; Ortkemper, *Leben*, 128–29; Dunn, *Romans 9–16*, 776–77.

38. Ortkemper (*Leben*, 128) points to Rom 2:1, 21; 1 Cor 6:1; 10:24, 29; 14:17; Gal 6:4; Phil 2:4.

39. See Daniel García Hughes, "Nota breve. Rom. 13,8ᵇ," *EstBib* 2 (1943) 308.

40. Zahn, *Römer*, 562.

41. See Barrett, *Romans*, 250, followed by Thompson, *Clothed with Christ*, 125; Douglas J. Moo, *The Epistle to the Romans* (NICNT; Grand Rapids: Eerdmans, 1996) 813–14.

42. See Michel, *Römer*, 410. This is based on a quotation from Rabbi Jonathan (ca. 140 CE): "Whoever fulfills the law in poverty will finally fulfill it in riches." But Henrik Ljungman has

Paul had used a similar expression in Gal 5:14, "For the whole law is fulfilled in one word: 'you shall love your neighbor as yourself.'" The use of "fulfill" in this context appears to be distinctively early Christian, probably shaped by a polemical interaction with Jewish demands to "do" or "perform" the Torah.[43] The closest parallels to the use of "fulfill" both in Pauline rhetoric and in Matt 5:17 are in Greco-Roman rather than in Hebraic material.[44] Just as in the parallel usage by Matthew, to "fulfill" the law means to accomplish its original intent and purpose.[45]

The scope of the argument in Romans moves beyond the Torah, however, because "law" is used here without the article, if in fact the article belongs with "other," as suggested above. This requires that one treat "law" in the generic sense in this sentence.[46] When commentators attach the article to "law," they in effect change the thrust of this sentence into a legitimation of Torah, arguing for its continuing relevance for Christians.[47] With the more likely general construal, Paul's formulation would include both Jewish and Roman law, and indeed any other law that could be mentioned. Law in general is fulfilled, according to this context, not by performing every duty prescribed in Leviticus or Deuteronomy or some other code but by following the lead of the spirit[48] in loving one's fellow believers in a local house or tenement church. It is not love in general, or in the abstract, but rather

---

shown this is a mistranslation and that the Aramaic term should be rendered "hold" or "stand"; see *Das Gesetz erfüllen: Matth. 5,17ff. und 3,15 Untersucht* (LUÅ n.F. 1.50/6; Lund: Gleerup, 1954) 26–33. Nevertheless most commentators understand "fulfill" as an equivalent to Hebraic expressions for "doing," "performing," or "keeping" the Torah. See Barrett, *Romans*, 251; Wilckens, *Römer* 3. 68, 71; Eckhard J. Schnabel, *Law and Wisdom from Ben Sira to Paul: A Tradition Historical Enquiry into the Relation of Law, Wisdom, and Ethics* (WUNT 2/16; Tübingen: Mohr [Siebeck], 1985) 274.

43. See Hans Dieter Betz, *Galatians* (Hermeneia; Philadelphia: Fortress, 1979) 275; Dunn, *Romans 9–16,* 777.

44. See BAGD, s.v. πληρόω 4.b (pp. 671–72).

45. See Georg Strecker, *Die Bergpredigt: Ein exegetischer Kommentar* (Göttingen: Vandenhoeck & Ruprecht, 1984) 57; Jan Lambrecht, *The Sermon on the Mount: Proclamation and Exhortation* (Good News Studies 14; Wilmington: Glazier, 1985) 84. Schnabel (*Law and Wisdom,* 275) argues in contrast that fulfillment implies "concentrated reference of the various individual commandments to one point of reference," citing Stanislas Lyonnet, "La charité plénitude de la loi (Rom 13,8–10)," in Lorenzo de Lorenzi, ed., *Dimensions de la vie chrétienne (Rm 12–13)* (SMB 4; Rome: Abbaye de S. Paul, 1979) 156.

46. Commentaries and translations are almost uniformly careless at this point, translating νόμος in 13:8 "the law"; see, for example, Lagrange, *Romains,* 315; Schlier, *Römerbrief,* 394; Barrett, *Romans,* 250; Cranfield, *Romans* 2. 673, 676; Morris, *Romans,* 468; Dunn, *Romans 9–16,* 774, 777; Fitzmyer, *Romans,* 676; Moo, *Romans,* 810, 814.

47. See Moo, *Romans,* 814–16. In *Paul's Letter to the Romans: A Commentary* (Louisville: Westminster/John Knox, 1994) 211, Peter Stuhlmacher shifts the subject of this sentence into the arena of law to place it within Paul's defense against the charge of "antinomianism."

48. Cf. Betz, *Galatians,* 275: "the prescriptions and prohibitions of the Jewish Torah stand before the Jew as demands 'to be done' by him, while love is the result of liberation and the gift of the Spirit." The context in Romans does not have the polemical antithesis found in Galatians, which disturbs a commentator like Ernst Käsemann (*Commentary on Romans* [London: SCM; Grand Rapids: Eerdmans, 1980] 361). In the light of cultural expectations and their implications

love in the everyday experience of the love feast and other intense inter-actions of small groups of urban Christians that is in view here. The contrast in tenses between the present participle, "the one who loves," and the per-fect verb, "he has fulfilled,"[49] points in the direction of the steady, everyday work of love on the local level that is seen here as the fulfillment of divine law. Willi Marxsen refers in this context to the "continuous activity" of love that constitutes the fulfillment,[50] but he and other commentators overlook the social setting of this formulation. It is not some theology of love or law that fulfills the divine intent but love as practiced among members of small church groups, with particular reference in this verse to their extension of hospitality to "the other," to members of other groups whose orientation and background may differ substantially.

Love Feasts as Law's Fulfillment

A proper interpretation of Rom 13:10 should continue the focus on local church relations throughout this pericope. But the persistent deletion by commentators and translators of the article "the" in connection with love in this verse serves to generalize the admonition and drive it in a theoretical direction not intended by Paul. He refers explicitly to ἡ ἀγάπη ("the love") twice in this verse, making clear that it is the specific and distinctive form of love as experienced by early house and tenement churches that is in view.[51] This verse provides a formal recapitulation of the pericope in chiastic form, moving from ἡ ἀγάπη in the opening words to ἡ ἀγάπη in the final words.[52] The accurate translation is therefore as follows:

> The *agape* does no evil to the neighbor;
> law's fulfillment is therefore the *agape*.

The logical social corollary to "the love" in this verse is the *agape* meal other-wise known as the love feast, the common meal shared by most sectors of the early church in connection with the Lord's Supper. The repeated arthrous use of "love" in this verse justifies the translation "the *agape*."

---

for local groups of Christians, both passages are equally revolutionary. Hans Hübner offers a partially satisfactory analysis of the differences between the two in "πληρόω-πλήρωμα," *EWNT* 3 (1983) 260.

49. See Zahn, *Römer*, 563.

50. Marxsen, "Röm. 13,8," 236.

51. See BDF §252 (pp. 131–32), where ἡ ἀγάπη is rendered "Christian Love," with reference to John 1:21. For a discussion of the fact that the Greek article derived from the demonstrative pronoun and retains its deictic quality of pointing to a specific or previously named topic, see Robert W. Funk, "The Syntax of the Greek Article: Its Importance for Critical Pauline Problems" (Ph.D. diss., Vanderbilt University, 1953) 31–56. He discusses the arthrous use of ἀγάπη as "a good example of an abstract that has been thoroughly Christianized" (106–12).

52. See Ortkemper, *Leben*, 131; Dunn, *Romans 9–16*, 775; Anselm L. Bencze, "An Analysis of 'Romans 13.8–10,'" *NTS* 20 (1973–74) 91.

The proper social context must be kept in view if v. 10a is to rise above the level of a conventional truism, as the parallels make plain.[53] Ps 15:3 defines the blameless person as the one who "does no evil to his neighbor,"[54] while the typical expression for inquiring into a misdemeanor in Greek sources is "whether anyone has planned or committed evil."[55] Although the admonition to do no evil to the neighbor was frequently used, none of these references speaks of "the love" in such specific terms as Paul does here. By employing an early Christian rule that was sure to gain assent among believers in Rome, Paul is able to place "the *agape*" as practiced by the Roman congregations within the context of the discrimination between good and evil stated in 12:9 and thereby to make a subtle point concerning the "other" that still echoes from 13:8. Rom 13:10 contends that the love feast is inconsistent with doing any form of harm to a neighbor, defined here as a fellow Christian who may or may not be a member of one's small congregation.

The social context of the *agape* meal also fits the reiteration that such love is the "fulfillment therefore of law," a term that requires a similar contextualization. It is not just any love that is in view here, but "the love" within the Christian congregation. And the greatest barrier against such love in the Roman situation, according to Romans 14–15, was the insistence on conformity to various forms of law, which divided the weak from the strong and prevented the celebration of the love feast together. It is essential therefore to translate "law" without the article, in conformity with the Greek text and in opposition to the usual formulation in commentaries and modern versions.[56] It is law as a principle, in its various forms, that is fulfilled in the *agape* meal. The meaning of "fulfill" in this sentence is the entire completion of law, not the sum total of its individual demands.[57] In effect Paul is claiming that the

---

53. Furnish (*Love Command*, 111) accepts Ceslas Spicq's view that 13:10a serves as a rhetorical *litotes*, "an understatement for the sake of emphasis" (*Agape in the New Testament* [3 vols.; St. Louis: Herder, 1963] 2. 60).

54. See also Sir 10:6; *Ep. Arist.* 168, 207; Tob 4:15; and esp. Zech 8:17: "Let none of you devise evil in his heart against his neighbor."

55. Plutarch *Mor.* 523A. See also Peder Borgen's discussion of the reciprocal form of this command in "The Golden Rule: With Emphasis on Its Use in the Gospels," in idem, *Paul Preaches Circumcision and Pleases Men and Other Essays on Christian Origins* (Trondheim: Tapir, 1983) 100–104.

56. Most commentaries and translations translate νόμος in 13:10 "the law"; see Lagrange, *Romans*, 317; Schlier, *Römerbrief*, 395; Barrett, *Romans*, 251; Cranfield, *Romans* 2. 673; Morris, *Romans*, 469; Dunn, *Romans 9–16*, 780; Fitzmyer, *Romans*, 677; Moo, *Romans*, 817. The only exception I have found is Johnson, *Reading Romans*, 193.

57. See BAGD, s.v. (p. 672), and Ortkemper, *Leben*, 132; Ortkemper follows Gerhard Delling on this point ("πληρόω, κτλ.," *TDNT* 6 [1968] 305). Delling shows that the translation "complete fulfillment" is required here rather than "sum," which would be redundant with "sum up" in 13:9. André Feuillet rejects this active sense of "fulfillment" in "Loi ancienne et morale chrétienne d'après l'épître aux Romains," *NRT* 92 (1970) 797: "la seule vertu de charité se trouve renfermée la totalité des préceptes de la Loi." C. F. D. Moule is ambivalent on this point (" 'Fulness' and 'Fill' in the New Testament," *SJT* 4 [1951] 83).

final goal of law, in whatever culture it manifests itself, is achieved in the love feasts of early Christian communities.

An interpretation within the concrete social context in Rome helps to avoid "a sentimental but unrealistic idealism" that so frequently afflicts explanations of the NT doctrine of love.[58] In Rom 13:8–10, "the call to love the other is in fact *limited* to the neighbor."[59] But I would like to go beyond this insight to insist on the precise social context in which such love was expressing itself: in the *agape* meals of house and tenement churches of Rome. These groups had previously been separated by ideological and cultural conflicts; they were refusing to invite one another into their sacramental meals. In this way the boundaries erected by Mediterranean systems of honor and shame were being reerected within the sacramental community. The message of Romans challenges them to begin living up to the command of love, the central moral obligation of the Christian faith both for them and for us today — a matter which Anabaptist interpreters like Graydon Snyder have long understood.

Greetings and Mutual Welcome into the Love Feast

The final three chapters of Paul's letter to the Roman Christians carry out the theme of mutual love that we find in 13:8–10. Commentators have only gone part way to define what "welcome" means in this context. Joseph A. Fitzmyer's recent commentary comes the closest, showing that the Greek term used here means "take to oneself, take into one's household."[60] But he does not develop the obvious implication: to welcome people is to welcome them into something, into a social space that the welcomer controls. The normal usage is to welcome someone into one's "household," which in the context of a house church would imply the living space of the patron. In the context of early Christians meeting in tenement buildings, the reference must be to the space the group is using for the common meal. In either context, to welcome someone is to invite him or her into the sacramental meal, which was the center of fellowship for the community. The admonitions in 14:1 and 15:7 are thus a direct extension of 13:8, "to love one another," in which the primary arena of such activity was the love feast.

A significant corollary emerges from this exegesis. Scholars have long been conscious that one of the main impediments against the idea of Romans as a comprehensive doctrinal treatise is that it allegedly has no discussion of the sacrament. If we are right in discerning the love feast as explicitly mentioned in 13:10, then the entire discussion in the last three chapters deals with a

---

58. Dunn, *Romans 9–16*, 783.
59. Ibid.
60. Fitzmyer, *Romans*, 689.

crucial sacramental issue: who is welcome to take part in the breaking of the bread and drinking of the cup? Paul's answer is, "Every Christian, whether Jew or gentile, strong or weak." The sacramental love feast is to be retained as the arena in which the boundaries of shameful status are overcome.

This theme of inclusive welcome is continued in the greetings of chapter 16. The "basic meaning" of the Greek term ἀσπάζομαι ("to greet") that Paul employs repeatedly in this chapter was "to embrace."[61] As Hans Windisch observes, the Pauline command to greet one another "expresses and strengthens the bond of fellowship with those who are engaged in the same task, and who serve the same Lord, i.e., with saints and brothers."[62] This gesture of welcome was ordinarily extended when a guest entered the house or space of a host. So the implication of this repeated admonition is the same as that implied in 14:1 and 15:7, to welcome people into your social space, which in the case of either house or tenement churches was primarily the occasion of love feasts. Outside of such occasions, the spaces of houses, apartments, or tenement niches were in the control of patrons or family groups rather than of churches, and it is clearly the latter that are implied in the inclusive second person plural forms of these admonitions.

The obligation to extend an inclusive welcome was a unique feature of early Christianity. Nowhere else in ancient letter-writing do we find such a series of commands to greet one another as in Romans 16, commands that include the entire community being addressed by the letter. This is so peculiar that some commentators have accepted the suggestion by Harry Gamble that "the imperative form of the greeting verb functions here as a surrogate for the first person indicative form, and so represents a direct personal greeting of the writer himself to the addressees."[63] But there is not a shred of evidence that the second person plural imperative form was ever used in this first person sense, and Gamble provides no illustrations in support of his suggestion, which reflects a misconception of the congregational situation of Romans. It is not so much Paul who needs to greet these competing factions in Rome but the Roman Christians themselves. The entire argument of Romans is aimed at helping these factions to find common ground, to recognize their commonality in Christ, and to begin cooperating so they can advance the crucial mission west to Spain.

More nearly on target, it seems to me, is the suggestion of Francis Watson that these admonitions to greet one another imply that the gentile Christian

---

61. See Hans Windisch, "ἀσπάζομαι, κτλ.," *TDNT* 1 (1964) 497.
62. Ibid., 501; see also Martin Luther Stirewalt, "Paul's Evaluation of Letter-Writing," in J. M. Myers et al., eds., *Search the Scriptures: New Testament Studies in Honor of Raymond T. Stamm* (Gettysburg Theological Studies 3; Leiden: Brill, 1969) 189–90.
63. Gamble, *The Textual History of the Letter to the Romans* (Studies and Documents 42; Grand Rapids: Eerdmans, 1977) 93. This view is accepted by Dunn (*Romans 9–16,* 891).

and Jewish Christian factions in Rome should "introduce themselves to one another."[64] It has to do with mutual acquaintanceship, the necessary prelude to any form of cooperation. In each greeting, the appropriate venue for such mutual welcome has been established by 13:8–10, i.e., the love feasts which are law's fulfillment. The admonitions of the final chapter of Romans there-fore provide additional evidence that the question raised in the title of this article should be answered in the affirmative. The central role of what Gray-don Snyder has called "the meal as social *diakonia*" thus receives decisive confirmation.

---

64. Watson, *Paul, Judaism, and the Gentiles: A Sociological Approach* (SNTSMS 56; Cambridge and New York: Cambridge University Press, 1986) 101–2.

19

ORDER IN THE "HOUSE" OF GOD

The Haustafel *in 1 Peter 2:11–3:12*

EDGAR KRENTZ

Graydon Snyder has a keen interest in social issues, both in the NT and in the contemporary world. I am happy to present this small πάρεργον relating to the social world of the provinces of Pontos, Galatia, Cappadocia, Asia and Bithynia about 100 CE in honor of my faithful friend and neighbor down Ridgewood Court, the street where we live.

1 Pet 2:11–3:12 is a fascinating passage. It includes a section that looks like a domestic code, though not a typical one. But the passage seems not to fit that form-critical identification when considered in literary and social context. It is addressed to "resident aliens" (πάροικοι καὶ παρεπίδημοι), both terms indicating outsider status within the social structure. The precise demarcation of that social status has become a matter of interest in recent years.[1] The interpretation of 1 Pet 2:11–3:12 is fundamental to determining that status. Though the passage reads smoothly at first, a number of issues are raised. There is disagreement about the unity of the passage, based on differing form-critical analyses: Is it a "station code" (see below) or a "household code"? The basic motif running through the passage is debated: Is it subjection or honor? Is 2:11–12 the introduction to 2:13–4:11 or only to 2:13–3:12?

There is general agreement that the passage is a development of the household code that Aristotle presents in his *Politics*, which correlates the structure of the *polis* with that of the household.[2] But beyond that there is

---

1. See, e.g., the debate between John H. Elliott and David L. Balch in Charles H. Talbert, ed., *Perspectives on First Peter* (Macon, Ga.: Mercer University Press, 1986) 61–101.

2. Aristotle *Pol.* 1.1253b.1–14; cf. *E. N.* 8.1160a.23–1161a.10; 5.1134b.9–18. Aristotle's list becomes a topos used by many philosophers of other schools over a long period of time.

a wide diversity of opinion, as David L. Balch demonstrates.[3] Balch himself regards Arius Didymus, the first-century BCE Stoic philosopher, as the most useful near-contemporary resource for locating the code in 1 Peter socially, though he also finds a much broader basis in first-century thought.[4] Arius Didymus, like Aristotle, regards the household (οἰκία) as the πόλις (city state) writ small, the πόλις as the household writ large. Both *polis* and household are organized in a relationship whose axis is power: the lesser to the greater.

Leonhard Goppelt identified the unit 2:13–3:7 as a "station code," citing parallels in Col 3:18–4:1; Eph 5:22–6:9 (these passages in Colossians and Ephesians are often called "household codes"); and "station codes" in the so-called pastoral epistles (1 Tim 2:[1,] 8–15; 6:1–2; Titus 2:1–10) and apostolic fathers.[5] Goppelt identifies the sequence in 1 Peter as unusual, moving from the largest unit ("the civil order surrounding all society") to the smallest, marriage; Colossians and Ephesians begin from the middle of the household (marriage) and move outward to slaves.[6] Paul J. Achtemeier identifies 2:1–12 as the introduction to 2:13–4:11. Within 2:13–37 he identifies 2:13–3:7 as a "Call to Appropriate Subordination"; 3:18–4:11 as a "Call to Right conduct." He identifies three units in 2:13–3:7: "All readers to civil authorities" (2:13–17); "Household slaves to their masters" (2:18–25); "Believing wives to their unbelieving husbands" (3:1–6); and "Believing husbands to show respect for their believing wives" (3:7). The separation of 2:13–17 from 2:18–3:7 leads him to describe the latter as a "regular part of the household code."[7] This formal analysis, of course, denies the unity of the passage, and this has implications for its social analysis.

Troy W. Martin applies form-critical analysis and social description in discussing the "Household/Situation Codes" (his heading).[8] He employs David C. Verner's analysis of the four marks of units in the household code: (1) an address to a group representing a social class, usually in the plural; (2) an imperative (or infinitive or participle equivalent to the imperative),

---

3. Balch, "Household Codes," in David E. Aune, ed., *Greco-Roman Literature and the New Testament: Selected Forms and Genres* (SBLSBS 21; Atlanta: Scholars Press, 1988) 25–36.

4. ET in Balch, *Let Wives Be Submissive: The Domestic Code in 1 Peter* (SBLMS 26; Atlanta: Scholars Press, 1981) 40–44. The text survives as a long quotation in Stobaeus *Anthologium* 2.7.26 (full Greek text in Curt Wachsmuth and Otto Hense, eds., *Ioannis Stobaei: Anthologium*, vol. 2 [2d ed.; Berlin: Weidmann, 1958]). David E. Hamm ("The Ethical Doxography of Arius Didymus," *ANRW* 2.36.4 [1990] 2935–3242) provides a good introduction to the ethical thought of Arius Didymus.

5. Goppelt, *A Commentary on 1 Peter* (Grand Rapids: Eerdmans, 1993) 162–65.

6. Ibid., 164; 1 Pet 2:11–12 is designated the introduction to the parenetic section.

7. Achtemeier, *1 Peter: A Commentary on First Peter* (Hermeneia; Minneapolis: Fortress, 1996) 169, 190.

8. Martin, *Metaphor and Composition in 1 Peter* (SBLDS 131; Atlanta: Scholars Press, 1992) 124–30.

often with an object; (3) amplification, whereby the imperative is defined so as to provide motivation; and (4) a reason or cause, introduced with γάρ, ὅτι, or ὡς.[9] These units are then brought together in a series by connectives such as καί, ὁμοίως, and καὶ ὁμοίως. The series is often given development in several areas. Martin argues that these criteria show that 2:18–3:9 is a household code, whose elements are "slaves, wives, husbands, and everyone" — all but the last linked by ὁμοίως. Martin thus treats 2:13–17 as a discrete unit, separate from the household code. It concludes with a general exhortation in 3:8–9, as 5:5 does the station code in 5:1–5.

The structure of 1 Peter supports the assessment of 2:13–3:9 (or 2:13–3:12) as a literary unit. But perhaps Martin's analysis is so heavily dependent on formal analysis that it misses the creative modification brought about by "Peter" in these two disparate units in 1 Peter.[10] 1 Pet 3:8–9 does not use the connective standard in the household code; yet Martin includes it in the household code, certainly on the basis of content, not form. But then the major argument for excluding 2:13–17 falls away. Form gives way to function and content in 1 Peter — something that form criticism must always take account of. The emphasis on subordination (ὑποτάγητε, ὑποτασσόμενοι, 2:18; 3:1) at the beginning of each section suggests that 2:13–3:6 forms a unified sequence.[11] Subordination is a way of showing honor to the superior. Thus the sequence is authorities-slaves-wives. The ὁμοίως ("in a similar fashion") in 3:10 does join the verse on husbands to wives, but τὸ δὲ τέλος ("finally") clearly introduces a conclusion that includes a list of virtues, while 3:9 has language reminiscent of 2:23. Thus 2:13–3:9 is a clear unit dealing with authorities, slaves, wives, and husbands, concluding with general directives.

The citation of Ps 34:13–17 in 1 Pet 3:10–12 forms a fitting conclusion and supports the fact that a new section, in which the motif of subjection disappears, begins at 3:13. It urges the proper response to opposition and persecution. 1 Pet 2:11–12 introduces the large central section, called by Goppelt "the center and focus of the letter," and not 2:13–3:13 alone;[12] but the note of a "fair way of life among the gentiles" (τὴν ἀναστροφὴν ἐν τοῖς ἔθνεσιν ἔχοντες καλήν, 2:12) certainly is apposite to the context.

---

9. Ibid., 125–26, with reference to Verner, *The Household of God: The Social World of the Pastoral Epistles* (SBLDS 71; Chico, Calif.: Scholars Press, 1983) 87–89.

10. I shall use "Peter" for the author, though the apostle Peter cannot be the actual author. See the magisterial summary in John H. Elliott, "Peter, First Epistle of," *ABD* 5.276–78; and the discussion of authorship in Goppelt, *1 Peter*, 48–54; Achtemeier, *1 Peter*, 23–49 (both in favor of pseudonymity); also Raymond E. Brown, *Introduction to the New Testament* (ABRL; New York: Doubleday, 1997) 718–22 (cautious support of authenticity).

11. Martin argues here that the unifying motif is not subjection but the imperative τιμήσατε ("Honor," or "Show fitting respect for," 3:17); but this requires that 2:13–17 belongs in the same unit as the so-called household code.

12. Goppelt, *1 Peter*, 20. Achtemeier (*1 Peter*, 73) aptly entitles it "Thwarting False Accusations by Good Behavior."

It is precisely the unique features of this passage that make it so instructive about the social setting of the community addressed and therefore of the message urged by the author. The section is addressed primarily to those who are at the bottom of the social ladder, as the ὑποτάγητε (in 2:13) and ὑποτασσόμενοι (in 2:18; 3:1) suggest, both in public life and in the household. 1 Pet 3:7, addressed to husbands, breaks the unity and has the marks of an appendix to the list's primary focus. Those addressed feel excluded from the majority society, even though they, as converts, came out of it (1:14–15). Society was organized in a pyramid of power and functioned well when each member knew his or her place.[13] People sought status and honor; Peter addresses those who have neither, whether by social position or as a result of becoming Christian.

Peter writes to enable his readers to fit into the social structure positively. Peter does not simply urge conformity, however. He has prepared for this section by describing the Christians addressed as people of high status (2:9–10), applying to them terms of honor originally used of Israel in the OT. As a result they are now God's people. Then 2:11–12 provides a social reason that covers the entire station code. Christians should live in such a way that people recognize their good actions. And in each case he provides a theological rationale for subservience.

He begins with submission to the governing authorities "because of the Lord" (διὰ τὸν κύριον, 2:13–17). The term "Lord" suggests that God is at the top of the pyramid. Secular authorities are his agents to praise those who do good, and God's will is that good actions should stop the accusations. In that way those addressed will be free people, even though they are socially at the bottom.

Slaves are at the very bottom of the social hierarchy. As Keith R. Bradley puts it, "Their relationship was just one, as it happens, of a sequence of asymmetrical relationships that tied individuals together, comparable to the relationships between emperor and citizen-subject, father and son, teacher and pupil or officer and soldier."[14] Their masters want loyalty and obedience from slaves, in a sense the same responses owed in the other relationships above.[15] From the slaves' point of view powerlessness, isolation, loss of rights,

---

13. Paul Zanker (*The Power of Images in the Age of Augustus* [Ann Arbor, Mich.: University of Michigan Press, 1988] 152) reproduces the social pyramid model developed by Geza Alföldy. James Malcolm Arlandson (*Women, Class, and Society in Early Christianity: Models from Luke-Acts* [Peabody, Mass.: Hendrickson, 1997] 22) gives a modified graph of Gerhard Lenski's model of ancient society.

14. Bradley, *Slavery and Society at Rome* (Cambridge and New York: Cambridge University Press, 1994) 4.

15. Bradley, *Slaves and Masters in the Roman Empire: A Study in Social Control* (Brussels: Latomus, 1984) 21–45.

and degradation characterized slavery.[16] This often led to different modes of resisting slavery: suicide, murder or assault of masters, refusing aid when masters are attacked, wasting time, destruction of property, defrauding masters of money or goods, insolence, faked sickness, playing truant, running away, and the like.[17] It may be assumed that slaves could be corrupted by bribery. Underlying all this was the assumption that slavery automatically led to a loss of moral character, as the Roman law codes make clear.

Peter addresses a particular class of slaves, household slaves (οἰκέται).[18] Household slaves lived in their owners' homes and were in many respects much better off than slaves who worked on country estates or served as shepherds or neatherds (herdsmen). When Peter urges house slaves to subject themselves to their masters, both good and harsh, he affirms the social structure of his day. He gives no hint that slaves might or should seek manumission as a goal, even though some modern scholars argue that manumission was an authentic possibility for slaves.[19] But he couples this with doing good as a slave (2:20; cf. 2:12, 14). Peter assumes that slaves have a moral character! The admonition to do good is a specific application of submission to governing authorities. 1 Pet 2:18–20 thus follows 2:13–17 logically as an application of the principle of subjection to governing authority. But Peter adds a theological grounding: slaves should follow the example of the suffering Christ, who referred his case to the [supreme] judge who judges righteously (2:23). That implies vindication in the future. Thus the eschatological motif broached in 2:12 recurs here.

It is striking that Peter discusses slaves before wives (and without discussing the role of masters!). This runs contrary to the household code tradition, which usually has slaves in the last position — after relationships in marriage and fathers and children. Slaves clearly are very important to Peter. Did slaves perchance make up a high percentage of the Christian population, while few Christians were slave owners? No precise answer is possible, but the omission of masters supports that possibility.

Peter next turns to wives and urges them to subject themselves to their non-Christian husbands (3:1).[20] In a patriarchal society the subordination of

---

16. Bradley, *Slavery and Society*, 29.

17. Ibid., 108–22.

18. LSJ, s.v. (p. 1202), points out that they are to be distinguished from slaves (δοῦλοι), citing Chrysippus *apud* Athenaeus *Deipn.* 6.267b: διαφέρειν δέ φησι Χρύσιππος δοῦλον οἰκέτου, γράφων ἐν δευτέρῳ περὶ ὁμονοίας, διὰ τὸ τοὺς ἀπελευθέρους μὲν δούλους ἔτι εἶναι, οἰκέτας δὲ τοὺς μὴ τῆς κτήσεως ἀφειμένους. ὁ γὰρ οἰκέτης (φήσι) δοῦλος ἐν κτήσει κατατεταγμένος (Johannes von Arnim, ed., *Stoicorum Veterum Fragmenta* [4 vols.; Leipzig: Teubner, 1903–24] 3. 86); cf. Plato *Laws* 763. In the "Revised Supplement" to LSJ, P. G. W. Glare rejects this distinction with the words "delete 'hence opp. δοῦλοι'" (p. 224).

19. Bradley, *Slavery and Society*, 162–65.

20. I take ὑποτασσόμενοι (2:18) and ὑποτασσόμεναι (3:1) to be true middles. It is noteworthy that there is no discussion of a woman's subjection to a Christian husband.

women to their husbands was affirmed in principle by both Greeks and Romans.[21] The position of a married woman resembled that of a grown child in a family.[22] But here the Greeks were probably more severe in the first century than the Romans. Plutarch argues that women should subordinate themselves to their husbands (*Coniug. praec.* 33.142D), while Cicero implies that husbands "did not have the ability to order their wives — perhaps not even their children *in potestate*, though they had the legal right.[23] Peter would agree with Plutarch that a wife's adornment is not cosmetics, jewelry, fine clothing, or anything else that adorns (κοσμεῖ) a woman, but "those things that put forward gravity that commands respect, being in the correct social posture, and modesty" (σεμνότης εὐταξία αἴδως, *Coniug. praec.* 19.141E). Peter sounds similar when he urges, "Let your adornment (κόσμος) not be the external ornament of braided hair, the putting on of gold, or of clothing" (3:3–4). Rather it is the pure way of life (ἀγνὴ ἀναστροφή, 3:2; cf. καλὴ ἐν τοῖς ἔθνεσιν ἀναστροφή in 2:12). In the past holy women, who subjected themselves to their husbands, ornamented themselves (ἐκόσμουν, 3:5), as Sarah called her husband Lord (κύριος). The coincidence of terminology between Plutarch and Peter shows that they think along the same lines about marriage. But there is one major difference. Plutarch advises a wife that she should take her husband's friends as her own; and since the best friends a man has are his gods, it is fitting (προσήκει) for a woman to "worship and know only the gods her husband regards" (*Coniug. praec.* 19.140D). Peter urges Christian wives to use their way of life as a means to convert their husbands to Christianity (3:1), and here he breaks the social mold of the time.

Peter's advice to the husband is that he be the protector of his wife since she is weaker than he. This may reflect the social convention that a wife was often much younger than her husband, who as a result stood in the relation of husband, teacher, and protector to her. Thus Isomachus's wife was fifteen years old when he married her, young and untutored. He educated her, making clear that husband and wife have a division of labor. She, being the weaker, tends to things inside the house; the husband, being stronger, cares for things outside the house (Xenophon *Oec.* 7.5–8, 17–28). Each has honor (τιμή) when doing that for which he or she is fitted by nature. Peter urges the husband to distribute honor to the wife (to assign her the proper household tasks?) as a coinheritor of the life of grace (3:7).

---

21. See Susan Treggiari, *Roman Marriage: Iusti coniuges from the Time of Cicero to the Time of Ulpian* (Oxford: Clarendon; New York: Oxford University Press, 1991) 205–28 ("Graeco-Roman Theories of Marriage"), esp. 209–10 on submission in marriage.

22. See Paul Veyne, "The Roman Empire," in Philippe Aries and Georges Duby, eds., *A History of Private Life*, vol. 1: *From Pagan Rome to Byzantium* (Cambridge, Mass.: Harvard University Press, 1987) 39–40.

23. Treggiari, *Roman Marriage*, 210.

There is no discussion of the relationship of fathers and children, a surprising omission. Instead, 1 Pet 3:8–13 gives a general list of positive characteristics (a virtue catalog) as the way of carrying out the directive not to return insult for insult, but rather to bless.

This passage fits well into the discussion of οἰκονομία as a description both of household management and of political structure. As already observed, Aristotle, like Arius Didymus, correlates the structure of the household with that of the πόλις. The city consists of parts called οἶκοι (houses). The complete (τέλειος) house, which comprises both slave and free, has its own distinctive parts: master and slave in a despotic relationship; husband and wife in a marital relationship; father and children in a paternal relationship (Aristotle *Pol.* 1.1253b.1–14).[24] The same structure, Aristotle will proceed to argue, will be seen in the well-founded city (cf. *E. N.* 8.1160a.23–1161a.10; 5.1134b.9–18).

Arius Didymus's interpretation of Aristotle shows that the ethos promoted by Aristotle was still considered effective in the first half of the first century BCE. Seneca the Younger testifies to its power more than a century later.[25] 1 Pet 2:11–3:13, mutatis mutandis, fits well into this ancient political theory. Peter urges conduct that will make the nascent Christian community survive, even thrive, in the social structure of the time. The section is a unit, organized around the theme of the subjection of the weaker to the stronger, or higher, authorities as a mode of good conduct. Peter concentrates on the weaker members of society. There is, for example, no trace of a theory of kingship, or of how owners should treat their slaves. And as already observed, the omission of parents and children remains puzzling.

John H. Elliott and David L. Balch, cited at the beginning of this essay, debated the intention of the author of 1 Peter. Elliott argued that he urged the separation of the Christians from the surrounding society as an expression of their being "the household of God." Balch argued in favor of acculturation, not segregation. Though the present study has a limited textual basis in 1 Peter, it supports Balch's position. How could slaves of non-Christian masters and wives of non-Christian husbands separate themselves from the general society? They had rather come to terms with it.

Graydon Snyder has devoted much of his scholarship to the relationship of early Christianity to its social, artistic, and cultural contexts. This essay seeks to add yet one more positive footnote to his work.

---

24. Aristotle points out that there is no technical term to describe the relationship of husband and wife.

25. See Balch, *Let Wives Be Submissive,* 39–44; Balch also discusses Philodemus and Cicero, both of the first century BCE.

20

"SIN IS LAWLESSNESS"
(1 John 3:4)

Social Definition in the Johannine Community

JULIAN V. HILLS

A peculiar type of vision — this is what I owe especially to Graydon Snyder. As a beginning master's student in Chicago, a little over twenty years ago, I cross-registered through the Chicago "cluster" of theological schools for a course on the sociology of the NT. That class, team-taught by Snyder and Robin Scroggs, opened my formerly text-bound eyes to the living world of real people just beyond or behind or outside the text. Snyder and Scroggs showed me something of the art, the architecture, the visible communal organization, that made those early Christian writers much more than simply authors or scribes; I could see them now as participants in a movement or movements with a rich and varied social texture.[1] But Snyder and Scroggs also offered me some theoretical and analytical tools to excavate those precious literary remains as testimony to more than ideas, doctrines, and propaganda.[2] They convinced me, in short, of the great value of nonliterary materials and of social-scientific analysis for understanding the early church; and hence, for eyes to see it, that a vast pictorial, spatial, even three-dimensional universe is evoked by what I might have taken to be contextless theological words.

---

1. Most memorably in pictures and commentary that were to appear in Snyder's *Ante Pacem: Archaeological Evidence of Church Life before Constantine* (Macon, Ga.: Mercer University Press, 1985).

2. Again memorably, for example, in our reading and discussion of Scroggs's then-recent and pioneering essay, "The Earliest Christian Communities as Sectarian Movement," in Jacob Neusner, ed., *Christianity, Judaism, and Other Greco-Roman Cults: Studies for Morton Smith at Sixty* (4 vols.; SJLA 12; Leiden: Brill, 1975) 2. 1–23; repr. in Scroggs, *The Text and the Times* (Minneapolis: Fortress, 1993) 20–45.

It is not the debt of literal, physical vision — the sight of catacomb art, church design, trade routes, and the like — that I wish in small part to re-pay to Professor Snyder in this essay. It is instead my debt for that other vision, that glimpse of the societal or communal structure, identity, and self-consciousness: the flesh-and-blood reality of one group among many groups that confessed allegiance to Jesus Christ, and in so doing defined itself as other, as set apart, over against not only the wider Greco-Roman world but also rival, even neighboring, Christian enclaves. And my particular canvas for this conceptual, and I hope almost visual, experiment is the first letter of John.

In what follows, over against much modern criticism I hope to show that a puzzling phrase, quoted above as this essay's title, is principally neither a warning about sin in general, nor a reminder about the dangers of heretics or their heresies, nor the evocation of a motif connected with the endtime. To be sure, one or more of these themes may be present at some secondary level of reflection. But the chief point of it, I shall argue, is as a piece of communal self-definition, in which "sin," that familiar word for wrongdoing against God, is now given fresh and decisive redefinition: sin is *the destruction of community.*

Put more graphically, or spatially: the community is asked to consider that "sin," conventionally understood as offense against God on the *vertical* plane, is also "lawlessness," to be understood as offense against the community on the *horizontal* plane. And if this reading can commend itself, several notori-ously difficult passages in 1 John come into clearer focus as part of the same framework, not of theological or ethical speculation only but of a life-and-death battle for the survival of a communion whose existence has so recently been threatened.

In the first part I shall describe some of the problems detected in 1 John 3:4 and their solution as proposed in representative examples of modern scholarship. In the second I shall elaborate on the hypothesis outlined above. Then, in the third part, I shall sketch some of the ways in which this specifi-cally communal reading can be of value in the interpretation of other passages in 1 John 3–5. Finally, my conclusions will suggest further, broader insights newly recoverable from the literary remains of the Johannine group.

The Problem

Scholarly opinion is more or less uniform that at the time 1 John was written — some time at the turn of the first to the second century CE — the Johannine community had recently suffered the loss of a portion of its membership: "they went out from us" (2:19). "They," of course, are the "secessionists," in Raymond E. Brown's apt epithet: those who (among other things) deny that Jesus is the Christ (2:22).[3]

One might reasonably conjecture an atmosphere of unease, doubt, suspicion, among those who remain. Who will be next to leave? Clearly the crisis is not over, since a warning has been issued: "I write this to you about those who would deceive you" (2:26, RSV). However, to complement the warning there is a word of reassurance: "but the anointing which you received from him abides in you, and you have no need that any one should teach you" (2:27) — not even the author, or so he writes. For a moment, then, calm prevails: "See what love the Father has given us..." (3:1). All is well, it seems: "we are called children of God, and so we are.... Every one who thus hopes in him purifies himself" (3:2–3).

But in 3:4 the epistle's audience is called once more to face the raw fact that "sin" is still around; that it has consequences; and that it will have to be dealt with. "Every one who commits sin (τὴν ἁμαρτίαν) is guilty of lawlessness (τὴν ἀνομίαν)," the author writes, and, as if to drive the point home, "sin is lawlessness (καὶ ἡ ἁμαρτία ἐστὶν ἡ ἀνομία)" (3:4). So what is going on that causes the author to pen this fresh definition, if such it is, of a word ("sin") that he has freely used six times (1:7, 8, 9 [twice]; 2:2, 12)? May we hazard a glimpse of what the writer (perhaps "the Elder" of 2 John 1; 3 John 1) saw, and what his first hearers heard — or rather, were being summoned to recognize?

There is, as a preliminary matter, the grammatical question: what to do with a clause in which both the subject and the predicate (once one has decided which is which) have the definite article.[4] Since both "sin" and "lawlessness" are abstracts (though each, of course, able to attract to itself concrete particulars), there is no evading this dilemma by an appeal to the status of one or the other noun. So we are left with a finely balanced proposition, that "sin" (however understood) is also "lawlessness."[5]

It is not at once clear, therefore, just what kind of wrongdoing ἀνομία stands for.[6] As is often reported, in the LXX the word is found in poetic parallelism with ἁμαρτία, which would suggest only a minimal difference

---

3. Brown, *The Epistles of John* (AB 30; Garden City, N.Y.: Doubleday, 1981); the choice of the term is explained on p. 70 n. 156.

4. A. E. Brooke notes that there is some late MS evidence for the omission of the definite article before ἀνομία (*The Johannine Epistles* [ICC; Edinburgh: T. & T. Clark, 1912] 85); but this is clearly secondary.

5. Though not common, sentences in which arthrous nouns (nouns with the definite article) stand on both sides of the copula are found expressing a variety of ideas. Six types are classified in F.-M. Abel, *Grammaire du Grec biblique* (Ebib; Paris: Gabalda, 1927) §29g (pp. 123–24); similarly BDF §§273 (p. 143). Abel speaks of "an equivalence between predicate and subject" in 1 John 3:4.

6. The lexicons offer a predictable array of definitions: LSJ, s.v. (p. 146b) "[1.] *lawlessness, lawless conduct*, opp. δικαιοσύνη [with refs.]; 2. *the negation of law*, opp. νόμος"; BAGD, s.v.

in meaning between the two terms.[7] Likewise, though a range of hellenistic Greek texts can be cited in which ἀνομία may conceivably bear a sense
relevant to the interpretation of 1 John, even from these it is not possible
to distill some technical meaning deriving from, say, political or legal theory
that might secure for us the nuance in the present passage.[8] And so we are
driven to the immediate and broader contexts of 1 John 3:4 to deduce the
force of ἀνομία here.[9]

The first and presumably the easiest solution is that the verse serves notice
that "sin" is to be taken seriously.[10] It is no merely personal wrong, to be
excused or absolved by some privately or communally executed cultic means,
but a transgression against God. Hence, "[the author's] intention is to insist
that in the whole discussion the terms 'sin' and 'righteousness' shall be taken
in their most uncomplicated, crude sense: sin is doing wrong; righteousness is
doing right."[11] Most plainly, then, "[the author] uses *anomia* here to mark sin

---

(pp. 71b–72a) *"lawlessness,* 1. as a frame of mind, opp. δικαιοσύνη...; 2. *a lawless deed";* LPGL,
s.v. (p. 147b) "1. *lawless act, transgression;* of heresy; 2. as a f.l. [*falsa lectio*] for ἀνομοίος."

7. Ps 31(32):1–2 (cf. Rom 4:7–8); 50:4, 7, 9 [51:2, 5, 11] (quoted in *1 Clem.* 18.3, 5,
9); Jer 31(38):34 (cf. Heb 10:17); synonymity is probable in Ps 58(59):4. Cf. *1 Clem.* 8.3
("Repent...from your *iniquity* [τῆς ἀνομίας];...If your *sins* [αἱ ἁμαρτίαι] reach from the
earth to heaven..."). A glance at the Hatch-Redpath concordance to the LXX (s.v. ἀνομία
[pp. 106b–107c]) shows numerous cases where ἀνομία competes with the variant readings
ἁμαρτία, ἀδικία, ἀσέβεια, and ἀνόνημα.

8. See, e.g., the authors quoted or cited in Georg Strecker, *Die Johannesbriefe* (MeyerK 14;
Göttingen: Vandenhoeck & Ruprecht, 1989) 160–62 and nn. 8, 11, 12; now in ET as *The
Johannine Letters: A Commentary on 1, 2 and 3 John* (Hermeneia; Minneapolis: Fortress, 1996)
93–96. It counts, I suppose, as only anecdotal (not to mention anachronistic) evidence that
the first Greek word associated with "anarchy" in S. C. Woodhouse, *English-Greek Dictionary:
A Vocabulary of the Attic Language* (London: Routledge & Kegan Paul, 1910) s.v. (p. 29), is
ἀνομία; the second (!) is ἀναρχία. But good examples of the meaning I have in mind — virtually
equivalent to the French *anomie* — are not limited to the Attic period. See, e.g., Sextus Empiricus
(second century CE) *Adv. math.* 2.33, quoted in Strecker, *Letters,* 95 n. 11.

9. So this is an instance where the two cardinal principles of lexicography both apply equally.
On the one hand, *words have meanings;* i.e., it is essential to scour all available materials for comparable uses of a word and foolish to argue for a meaning of word X that is nowhere attested in
extant contemporary evidence. On the other hand, where word X is found only rarely elsewhere,
or where the evidence leads us in several directions at once, we must resort to the maxim that
a word's meaning is established by its context. The present case is the more interesting because
ἀνομία, found 14x in the NT, occurs nowhere else in the Johannine literature.

Johannes P. Louw and Eugene A. Nida place ἀνομία alongside ἄνομος ("lawless"), ἄθεσμος
("lawless, unruly"), παρανομία ("lawless act, evil doing"), and ἀθέμιτος ("disgusting, bad") within
semantic domain 88, "Moral and Ethical Qualities and Related Behavior," sub-domain R, "Act
Lawlessly" (*Greek-English Lexicon of the New Testament Based on Semantic Domains* [2d ed.; 2 vols.;
New York: United Bible Societies, 1988–89] 1. 758).

10. Indeed, Ruth B. Edwards suggests of the whole of the second part of 1 John (3:4–5:12)
that "the main purpose seems to be to stress the seriousness of sin" (*The Johannine Epistles* [New
Testament Guides; Sheffield: Sheffield Academic Press, 1996] 98).

11. C. H. Dodd, *The Johannine Epistles* (Moffatt NT; New York: Harper, 1946) 73; so already
Brooke Foss Westcott, *The Epistles of St. John* (3d ed., 1892; repr. Grand Rapids: Eerdmans, 1966)
102: "Sin and lawlessness are convertible terms. Sin...is the assertion of the selfish will against a
paramount authority"; similarly John R. W. Stott: "the statement 'sin is lawlessness'...so identifies them as to render them interchangeable.... Lawlessness is the essence, not the result, of sin"

as a wrong act, wilfully done," as Kenneth Grayston puts it; "it is doing what is prohibited and omitting what is commanded."[12] This position is, of course, capable of various refinements. One of these shades the meaning towards the contravention of God's law as expressed in the OT.[13] Another is to identify the law that is broken as "the command to love the brothers,"[14] or again, with a little more specificity, to claim that sin here is "a matter of rule-breaking, a matter of regulation by the discipline of the community."[15]

The second standard solution is to connect 1 John 3:4 with those who have left the community, so as to make the verse a summary statement of how they have behaved. This view has been given perhaps its fullest expression by John Bogart: "[The author] is saying to his congregation, in effect, 'if you live like these gnostic libertines, you sin, and your sinning makes you lawless, as they are.'" Indeed, for Bogart "the term ἀνομία here reflects the antinomian stance of the libertines; as pneumatics they were above the law."[16]

A third solution takes its cue from this identification of the purveyors of ἀνομία as former members of the author's community, but pushes it a step further. "Lawlessness" now has an eschatological referent: those who sin participate in the regime of the false christ(s), of the once singular but now plural antichrist(s) (ἀντίχριστος-ἀντίχριστοι) mentioned already in 2:18, who is (or are, or will be) the visible agent(s) of evil in the endtime. Seen in this way 1 John 3:4 becomes a witness to an established tradition of the antichrist defined as "lawless" or connected with an era of lawlessness.[17] Thus Brown renders the verse, "Everyone who acts sinfully is really doing iniquity, for sin is the Iniquity," and maintains that the definite article in ἡ ἀνομία ("*the* Iniquity") "indicates a definite and well-known predicate."[18] Like Bogart

---

(The Epistles of John [Tyndale NT 19; Leicester: Inter-Varsity; Grand Rapids: Eerdmans, 1960] 122); F. F. Bruce: "John insists that sin, in the common sense of the term, is rebellion against God" (The Epistles of John [Grand Rapids: Eerdmans, 1979] 89).

12. Grayston, The Johannine Epistles (NCB; London: Marshall, Morgan & Scott; Grand Rapids: Eerdmans, 1984) 104.

13. This is presumably the idea behind the AV's translation of καὶ τὴν ἀνομίαν ποιεῖ as "transgresseth also the law"; the tradition continues in the NEB and REB: "to break God's law."

14. Brooke therefore suggests of 3:4a that "the sins of which the writer is thinking are failures to fulfil the law of love, rather than the grosser sins of the flesh" (Epistles, 85).

15. J. L. Houlden, A Commentary on the Johannine Epistles (Black NT; London: Black, 1973; repr. as 2d ed., 1994) 92.

16. Bogart, Orthodox and Heretical Perfectionism in the Johannine Community as Evident in the First Epistle of John (SBLDS 33; Missoula, Mont.: Scholars Press, 1977) 130; contrast Brooke, Epistles, 84: "ἀνομία here is, of course, not the antinomianism of the 'Gnostic.'"

17. This position has received classical exposition in Ignace de la Potterie, "'Le péché, c'est l'iniquité' (I Joh III,4)," NRT 78 (1956) 785–97; repr. in ET, with slight revisions, as "'Sin Is Iniquity' (I Jn 3,4)," in de la Potterie and Stanislaus Lyonnet, The Christian Lives by the Spirit (Staten Island, N.Y.: Alba, 1971) 37–55.

18. Cf. the similar claim of George Milligan with regard to ἡ ἀποστασία ("the rebellion") in 2 Thess 2:3 that it was for the epistle's readers a familiar term, "as the use of the def. art. proves" (St. Paul's Epistles to the Thessalonians [1908; repr. Minneapolis: Klock, 1980] 98).

before him, Brown attaches this announcement exclusively to the secessionists: "now their sins (toward which they are indifferent) are identified as manifestations of the expected Iniquity" — a judgment supported by an impressive catalogue of biblical and extrabiblical references,[19] not to mention the concurrence of other scholars.[20]

Not all the evidence falls so easily into place, however. That each of these proposals involves some difficulty is suggested in the more recent observations of Judith M. Lieu. Duly noting that ἀνομία, in addition to being "a general OT word for sin," can "designate the ultimate iniquity in opposition to God's rule which would be characteristic of the End-time" and that, in her judgment, in 1 John 3 "this meaning fits better than simply contravention of the Law or of the rules of the community," still Lieu is constrained to observe that this explanation "does not help define sin elsewhere in the letter."[21] It is of course true that those secessionists have concerned the author earlier in the epistle, and that soon the readers will be charged to "test the spirits" (4:1) — to check the credentials, creedal and moral, of roving prophets and/or missionaries.[22] But all of this still leaves us far short of a satisfactory resolution to the problem: why here, at approximately the midpoint of the epistle, "sin" should have earned this new designation "lawlessness."

---

19. Brown, *Epistles*, 399–400, citing 2 Cor 6:14–15; *T. Dan* 6.1–6 ("the time of the iniquity of Israel"); Mark 16:14 in the Freer MS W ("this is the age of *lawlessness* [τῆς ἀνομίας] and unbelief under Satan") — a reading apparently known to Jerome (*saeculum istud iniquitatis et incredulitatis substantia* [*sub Satan?*] *est*); *Barn.* 4.1–4 ("works of ἀνομία"="the error of the present time"); 18.1 ("the ruler of the present time of ἀνομία"); Matt 13:41; 24:11–12 ("ἀνομία will be multiplied"); Mark 7:22–23 ("Depart from me, you who work ἀνομία"); *Did.* 16.3–4 ("for in the last days . . . as ἀνομία increases . . . then shall appear the deceiver of the world"); and, most importantly (and most often quoted), 2 Thess 2:3–8 ("the man of ἀνομία, the son of perdition," also called ὁ ἄνομος: "the Iniquitous One" [Brown]). See also *Herm. Vis.* 3.6.1, where those who are "cast far from the tower [=the Church]" are "the sons of wickedness (οἱ υἱοὶ τῆς ἀνομίας)."
It is a good question, however, whether the strong variant reading in 2 Thess 2:3, where for "man *of lawlessness* (τῆς ἀνομίας)" there is substantial support for "man *of sin* (τῆς ἁμαρτίας)" (as printed in von Soden's *Handausgabe* of 1913), is evidence for or against the near synonymity of the terms: what, if such is the case, will have prompted the change? It is also worthy of note that while the UBS committee upgraded the reading "of lawlessness" from "C" to "B" from the 3d to the 4th editions of *The Greek New Testament*, the commentary on their decision remains unchanged (see TCGNT [1971] 635; [2d ed., 1994] 567).
20. See esp. Rudolf Bultmann, *The Johannine Epistles* (Hermeneia; Philadelphia: Fortress, 1973) 50; Stephen S. Smalley, *1, 2, 3 John* (WBC 51; Waco, Tex.: Word, 1984) 155. Observing that ἁμαρτία is in the predicate position, which "perhaps indicates a reference to something well-known," Smalley concludes that this reading satisfies three criteria: (1) it looks back to 2:18, "John's mention of the eschatological figure of antichrist"; (2) "it connects with 2:28–29" by showing that hope for the parousia and right Christian conduct are "impossible for one who rebels against God"; and (3) "it provides an apt preface to the warnings against sin" in 3:5–9.
21. Lieu, *The Theology of the Johannine Epistles* (New Testament Theology; Cambridge: Cambridge University Press, 1991) 52–53.
22. The same problem was to be grappled with only a few years later; cf. *Did.* 11.7–8: "Do not test or examine (οὐ πειράσετε οὐδὲ διακρινεῖτε) any prophet who is speaking in a spirit. . . . But not everyone who speaks in a spirit is a prophet, *except he have the behavior of the Lord.*"

1 John 3:4–10 as Communal Self-Definition

I have already suggested that a fresh route beyond the customary triad of interpretations may be opened up by a more communal — spatial, three-dimensional — reading of what on the surface appears to be a doctrinal (or at least an ethical) proposition. And while none of the three customary approaches to the question is without something to commend it, I suspect that in none of them do we yet hear the nuance that satisfies not only the immediate and wider literary contexts of the verse but also some plausible reconstruction of the situation the author was attempting to address. Here, then, in rather greater detail, is the interpretation I have already hinted at. I shall break it down into its three component parts: the situation, the crisis, and the solution.

(a) *The situation:* There is a fairly strong consensus that 2:18–19 reflects the "defining moment" that has occasioned the writing of 1 John.[23] The community has suffered the loss of some of its members, though whether they were the majority or the minority we cannot tell. These two verses are remarkable in several ways. They reveal a Christian leader struggling to explain how it is that a portion of his membership has chosen to go elsewhere; I know of no NT precedent for this.[24] They reveal him, moreover, quite uncompromising in the frame of reference he adopts by which to justify what has happened. It is not a matter of regret: "If only they had stayed and discovered the fullness of our gospel." It is not a matter of petition or intercession, as one might have hoped: "May God have mercy on them, teach them the error of their ways, and one day restore them to the fold." No such poignancy here. Rather: "Now that they are gone they have proved who and what they were, and are; and it was for the best that they left."

(b) *The crisis:* This rigorist message is, of course, clothed in suitable theological dress. The impulse to rationalization — to tell how in God's will this disaster can have come about — finds its explication in what is evidently a well-established antichrist myth ("as you have heard," 2:18). So it is that in a daring move this antichrist — Beelzebul, Belial, perhaps also "the Lawless One" of 2 Thessalonians — is now *demythologized,* in Rudolf Bultmann's justly famous term, or, more clearly in this present context, *historicized.*[25] He (*or:* they) is (*or:* are) no longer a mythical figure (singular or collective), to be

23. I have previously speculated that 1 John as a whole might be read differently were it not for exegetes' singular focus on 2:18–27 (see Hills, "A Genre for 1 John," in Birger A. Pearson, ed., *The Future of Early Christianity: Essays in Honor of Helmut Koester* [Minneapolis: Fortress, 1991] 375 n. 36).

24. There is a possible parallel in Gal 2:11–13, where Paul recounts his abandonment in Antioch.

25. Bultmann, *Epistles,* 50. In our own time, during the so-called Gulf War the leader of Iraq dubbed the final (and, for his own forces, fatal) confrontation "the Mother of all Battles" — a transparent appeal to identify the coming events as somehow supernatural in character.

expected at some divinely appointed future date. They are a part of the here and now: they are, that is, the members (perhaps better, the never-members) of the community who have left.

With 1 John 3 the scene has changed. It is no longer "they" who are the subject matter but "us," or "we" (see 3:1–2). And so "every one" in 3:3 is a part of this group — those who remain: "every one who thus hopes in him." In what follows (vv. 4–10) there is, as might have been expected, a corresponding demythologizing, or historicizing, except that this time it is of the faithful. On the positive side this is communicated easily enough: "He who does right is righteous, as he is righteous" (3:7).[26] But it is the negative side that requires fuller explanation, and it is here that the smooth axioms that had formerly served so well are now found wanting: "He who commits sin is of the devil" (3:8); "No one born of God commits sin" (3:9). These formulas, needless to say, were drawn up with that vertical dimension in mind, in that they are grounded in the above/below polarity and satellite concepts inherited from the Fourth Gospel.[27] To explain who is "in" and who is "out" — for the Johannine gospel most often the author's group and the Judeans, respectively — is not so difficult, especially in hindsight: the vertical and the horizontal can be portrayed as one and the same. But what rhetoric will sustain the force of both dimensions when those creedal and social boundaries have been crossed? This is the crisis that faced our author, this group — once, for sure, but perhaps many times.[28] It is a crisis of categories, but one that cannot simply be reduced to a competition between theologies or, more specifically, between an orthodox and a heretical "perfectionism." Such a distinction would imply that it was a matter of intellectual judgment — of what later generations would term "orthodoxy" over against "heresy" — when what our actual author has in mind is something far more down-to-earth. How has your belief affected your way of life? How close have you come to doing what might exclude you, or your fellow Christian, from this elect, chosen group?

(c) *The solution:* In 3:10b the vertical and the horizontal again collide. In the first part, the author writes that "whoever does not do right is not of God" — and this assertion of course simply rephrases those axioms recently

---

26. Though if "as" (καθώς) means "to the degree that" (BAGD, s.v. 2 [p. 391]), this is in itself exceptional in the NT writings.

27. See, e.g., John 1:13; 3:3, 5, 18, 20–21; 6:37, 39, 44, 64; 8:31–32, 47; 9:31; 10:14, 27–29; 12:37–40; 13:35; 14:21; 15:6, 16, 19; 17:6, 9, 16.

28. By "group" I allude specifically to the group/grid frame of analysis articulated by Mary Douglas (see esp. *Natural Symbols: Explorations in Cosmology* [New York: Random House/ Pantheon, 1970] 54–64), as commended to me those twenty and more years ago by Snyder and Scroggs and by then already used effectively, e.g., in Sheldon R. Isenberg, "Millenarism in Greco-Roman Palestine," *JR* 4 (1974) 26–46; more recently, see Bruce J. Malina, *Christian Origins and Cultural Anthropology: Practical Models for Biblical Interpretation* (Atlanta: Knox, 1986).

quoted. But then, in translating the second part, the RSV, otherwise so magnificent an achievement of accuracy and clarity, lets us down in completing
the verse "*nor* (καί) he who does not love his brother."[29] This καί in fact
bears an unusually heavy weight. It does not distinguish between one group
and another, as "nor" or any of its surrogates would seem to imply.[30] What it
does is to *define* "whoever does not do right" (on the vertical plane: whoever
sins) as "he who does not love his brother" (on the horizontal plane: whoever does not build up this community).[31] And this, a quite unexceptionable
reading, may turn out to have some important consequences.

1 John 3–5 in Communal Perspective

I have urged that the real force of 1 John 3:4 resides in its combination
of *vertical* (=traditional, theological) and *horizontal* (=relational, communal)
language. Part of the evidence for this position has emerged already in 3:10,
that "he who does not do right [and hence] is not of God" is *also* "he who
does not love his brother." But it will take several other strong test cases
to secure this insight, or at least to provide it with a hearing in mainstream
scholarship. Here, then, are three such cases.

(a) *1 John 3:12:* The equivalence just argued for might very soon appear
unfounded were it not for 3:12 and that very difficult reference to Cain (Gen
4:8; cf. Heb 1:4; Jude 11). It would surely have been enough to write off
this character as evil, as unworthy of the readers' or hearers' attention, were
it not for his ambiguous status. As a member of the original and elect "first
family," i.e., as the offspring — even the firstborn! — of Adam and Eve, Cain
naturally belongs *within* the circle of the chosen. Yet what he did (according
to Genesis 4) places him *outside* that group. Hence in 3:12 there is some
evident equivocation.[32] Cain killed his brother: and why did he kill him?

The answer we might have expected is this: "because he was born of the
evil one" (see 1 John 3:6, 8, 9; also John 8:44: the devil "was a murderer from
the beginning"). But this is not the answer that the author of 1 John supplies.
Cain killed Abel "because his own deeds were evil and his brother's [were]
righteous." It is not Cain's *origin* (his vertical heritage) that explains what he

---

29. The NRSV characteristically renders these singulars as plurals ("nor are those who do not
love their brothers and sisters"), hence gutting the line of its existential specificity; and "nor"
remains, as in NAB (cf. TEV "or"; Moffatt "neither").

30. I.e., that there is both a group A and a group B who fit this description.

31. Grammatically, then, καί here is epexegetical (*explaining* what has just been said); see
BDF §442.9 (p. 228); §471.3 (p. 248).

32. The Greek of this verse is difficult — perhaps deliberately elusive and ambiguous. Even
if there were a relative pronoun, "Cain, *who* (ὅς)" (as supplied by the RSV, JB, NRSV, NAB,
REB), the problem would not disappear because of the καί that precedes the verb ἔσφαξεν ("he
killed"): "*and so* he killed"? "*even so*, he killed"?

did, but his *actions* (the way he worked out his heritage on the communal, horizontal plane). The social reality that underlies such a claim is clear: your parentage, your particular family history, matters little or nothing in light of your Christian calling and the way you live it or fail to do so. The latter has canceled — or rather, it has redefined — your identity, both individually and communally. It is not, after all, *where you come from* that will matter, but how you treat your fellow Christian. This will tell us all that we need to know.[33]

(b) *1 John 3:15:* In years past, commentators regularly connected the key phrase of this verse ("any one who hates his brother is a murderer") with several other NT passages. The most obvious candidate has been Matt 5:21–22, where what was said of old, that "You shall not kill, and whoever kills shall be liable to judgment" (Exod 20:13; Deut 5:17; 16:18), is now revised so that "Every one who is angry with his brother" must now accept that liability.[34]

But there is more to this verse than the repetition of the principle articulated in Lev 19:17 and, as Grayston notes, reiterated in rabbinic tradition.[35] The previous verse, so redolent of the theology of the Johannine gospel (John 5:24, μεταβέβηκεν ἐκ τοῦ θανάτου εἰς τὴν ζωήν), announces no mere metaphor but a communal, social, reality: "We know that we have passed out of death into life (ἡμεῖς οἴδαμεν ὅτι μεταβεβήκαμεν ἐκ τοῦ θανάτου εἰς τὴν ζωήν)" (1 John 3:14). And if the boundary between those who are *in* and those who are *out* is as clear as this verse suggests, then it is plain that whoever "hates" his or her brother — here not only a clever allusion to the Cain and Abel episode but a technical term for a fellow Christian[36] — cannot now be considered a member of the author's community, either because his or her disposition is antithetical to the Christian gospel or because his or her actions have forced another member to leave. In this case, he or she has compelled a "brother" or "sister" from the realm of life to the realm of death. And this, of course, is an act of murder, because whoever is outside is as good as dead.[37]

---

33. The narrative of the man born blind (John 9) provides substantial commentary on this theological *and* social situation.

34. So, e.g., William Barclay, *The Letters of John and Jude* (rev. ed.; Philadelphia: Westminster, 1976 [1st ed., 1958]) 83: "There can be no doubt that John is thinking of the words of Jesus in the Sermon on the Mount."

35. Grayston, *Epistles,* 113, quoting Rabbi Joshua in *'Abot* 2.11: "The evil eye and the evil nature and hatred of mankind put a man out of the world" (Herbert Danby, trans., *The Mishnah* [Oxford: Clarendon, 1933] 449; Grayston's cited reference, "12.11," is an innocent error). Some context for this quotation is provided by *'Abot* 3.11: "R. Dosa b. Harkinas [a contemporary of R. Joshua, ca. 90 CE] said: Morning sleep and midday wine and children's talk [cf. 1 Cor 13:11] and sitting in the meeting-houses of the ignorant people put a man out of the world" (Danby, *Mishnah,* 451).

36. See BAGD, s.v. ἀδελφός 2 (p. 16).

37. For late-twentieth-century Christians in the Western world it may be almost impossible to sense the literalness of what we so easily take to be metaphorical language. But even now our Third-World brothers and sisters can teach us a timely lesson: that to be a Christian — to hold

(c) 1 John 5:16: There has been endless speculation as to what constitutes the "mortal sin" (or "sin *unto death*") that the author means to identify in the famous phrase ἁμαρτία πρὸς θάνατον.[38] It has been tempting, of course, to find here echoes of the pronouncement that "whoever blasphemes against the Holy Spirit never has forgiveness, but is guilty of an eternal sin" (Mark 3:29//),[39] or of the equally forbidding statement that "whoever is ashamed of me...of him will the Son of man also be ashamed" (Mark 8:38//).[40] But in both of these cases the relationship principally at stake is not that which obtains within the community but how those on the outside receive, or do not receive, these new prophets of the kingdom.

A second approach, also of considerable vintage, is to appeal — approvingly or otherwise — to the distinction between "mortal" and "venial" sin, or to some antecedent to this distinction (typically, as voiced by Tertullian). On this basis Bultmann judges that "the problem of the sin of Christians is thus formulated as the question of which sins can be forgiven and which not," a question that leads to an investigation of other texts in Judaism and early Christianity in which some supposedly unforgivable sin is identified.[41]

A third reading has been explored by David M. Scholer: that "the 'sin unto death' is one which a believer does not and cannot commit," or, stated positively (so to speak), that "the 'sin unto death' refers to the sins of nonbelievers."[42] This is an important suggestion since it greatly relieves the pressure otherwise placed on the exegete to explain how on earth a "brother" (and presumably "sister," too — in any case, a fellow believer) can be imagined committing so calamitous an act. But Scholer must pay a price for this relief. First, he must assert that the reference to a "sin unto death" is an "aside," i.e., that it is no essential part of the author's argument.[43] This is difficult

---

any religious conviction — involves a cost, not only financial but also social, familial, physical. In the NT, the Gospel of Mark already acknowledges as much (see, e.g., Mark 4:11–12, 17; 8:34–9:1; 10:29–31).

38. Probably every nuance documented in the history of exegesis through 1982 is catalogued in Brown, *Epistles*, 612–19.

39. On this saying, see, e.g., Gerd Theissen, *Sociology of Early Palestinian Christianity* (Philadelphia: Fortress, 1978) 28: "The Holy Spirit represents the wandering preachers and the prophetic spirit to which they give expression."

40. Again see Theissen, *Sociology*, 27: "The conflict between 'man' and 'Son of man' which appears in [these sayings] does in fact have a social foundation in the conflict between vagabond outsiders and 'human' society."

41. Bultmann, *Epistles*, 86. Bultmann, of course, judges that 1 John 5:14–21 is an appendix to the work, secondarily added by an "ecclesiastical redactor."

42. Scholer, "Sins Within and Sins Without: An Interpretation of 1 John 5:16–17," in Gerald F. Hawthorne, ed., *Current Issues in Biblical and Patristic Interpretation: Studies in Honor of Merrill C. Tenney Presented by His Former Students* (Grand Rapids: Eerdmans, 1975) 232, 238.

43. And he does so insist (ibid., 242, 244); so already Robert Law, *The Tests of Life* (3d ed.; Edinburgh: T. & T. Clark, 1914) 135: "the introduction of this [topic] is merely incidental." Nonetheless, Law judged that "it is a sin which may be committed by Christians, and *it is only as committed by Christians* that it is here contemplated" (137, emphasis added).

because there has been nothing to distract the reader of 1 John 5:16 from seeing the final part of the verse as a continuation of the thought of its open-ing: "If anyone sees *his brother committing....*" Second, Scholer must concede that, from this perspective, "actually, it is somewhat of a tautology for 1 John to suggest that believers do not 'sin unto death.'"[44] Third, while in his own translation of the verse Scholer adopts the language of the KJV and ASB ("sin *unto death*"), he speculates little as to the range of meaning that πρός in πρὸς θάνατον might have here.[45] It is as if πρὸς θάνατον must mean some-thing like ἐν θανάτῳ — "*in* death," or "*in the realm of* death," i.e., outside the community.[46]

But what if the "sin unto death" means instead some act that drives *either* its perpetrator *or* its victim outside the community — *from* life *to* (πρός) death? Now at last the physical (=communal) and the metaphorical (=spir-itual, theological) — the horizontal and the vertical — combine in one and the same meaning and the same result. This "sin unto death" now fulfills the definition already proposed, and for which I have tried to make a case in 1 John 3:4. In direct discourse: "If you do what sends you, or your fel-low Christian(s), outside the boundaries of this community of ours, you have committed murder: you have committed a sin to which I [the author] know of no antidote. I do not even request that you pray for such a person.[47] How could I, when, like Cain, it was not that he or she had the wrong pedigree — God alone knows about this — but that, *by the measure of what has been done*, he (or she) has now revealed that in the long run he would have no part of this community of God?"

Conclusions

Imagine yourself the leader of a community that believes that it alone — or it and a few others, some known, some unknown, considered now as a unity

---

44. Still, Scholer is willing to acknowledge that "1 John 2:2 may be the guarantee that one who commits the 'sin unto death' may still have hope" (ibid., 243 n. 64).

45. Scholer excuses John 11:4 from the picture, but perhaps prematurely: "the context of John 11:4 is so different that it offers no genuine solution" (ibid., 235 n. 25; on the translation, 230 n. 2).

46. Cf. "you will die *in your sins*" (John 8:21, 24 [twice]). Precisely this extension of Scholer's argument has now been worked out in Dietrich Rusam, *Die Gemeinschaft der Kinder Gottes: Das Motiv der Gotteskindschaft und die Gemeinden der johanneischen Briefe* (BWANT 133 [=7/13]; Stuttgart: Kohlhammer, 1993) 142–46. Rusam intends to show that this πρός (KJV "unto"; otherwise "leading to," or some equivalent) is intimately associated with the concept of *place*, with reference, e.g., to πρὸς τὸν πατέρα in John 1:2 ("*with* the Father"); 1 John 2:1 ("we have an advocate *with* the Father"); 3:21; 5:14.

47. In the phrase οὐ περὶ ἐκείνης λέγω ἐρωτήσῃ ("I do not say that one is to pray for that," RSV), οὐ λέγω may best be rendered "I do not *mean*," i.e., "this is not my purpose here" (cf. Mark 14:71; John 6:71; 1 Cor 10:21; Gal 3:17). Ironically, there may therefore be both promise and threat in 1 John 3:2: "we are God's children now; it does not yet appear what we shall be."

("other sheep, that are not of this fold," John 10:16) — has received knowledge of "that which was from the beginning" (1 John 1:1), of what alone
can provide "fellowship with us" and hence "with the Father and with his
Son Jesus Christ" (1:3). Perhaps within this group you are the only educated
member — the only one thoroughly schooled in the scriptures and trained in
debate, as well as endowed with the charism of leadership. You can *prescribe*,
in almost absolute terms, who ought to belong and who ought not to; and it
is surely part of the purpose of the Gospel of John to demonstrate that those
who "believe" belong and those do not (or will not) believe do not. But you
cannot, ahead of time, *describe* what those within, or without, will eventually
do. Some will stay and some will leave; and there is no telling what are the
decisive incentives or motivations in either case.

At some point, theology will yield to communal reality — will be reformulated in light of it, will have provisos and qualifications added to take account
of it. In short, the community of faith will find some language with which to
tell itself (and, putatively, the outside world) who and what it is, and why
things have turned out this way. Hence even in the almost dualistic narrative of John's gospel there is a gray area: "disciples" who "drew back" (6:66);
"Jews" (or "Judeans") who believe (8:31; 11:45; 12:11, 42); Judas, the disciple who betrays (6:70–71; 17:12). The narrator actually has Jesus informed
of this ambiguity when, in 2:23, after "many believed" in him as a result of
his Passover miracles, still Jesus "did not trust himself to them" (2:24): *later*
they would show who they really were.

The author of 1 John probably did believe that he was living in this latter era (2:18): when the secrets of all hearts would be revealed, when truth
would triumph over falsehood, right over wrong, knowledge over ignorance
("you know," 2:20–21). But like all of us he was also living in the meantime,
when some people do not do or say what they promised to; when things are in
flux, boundaries unclear; and when the future of the gospel appears — though
incongruously — in doubt. In this setting, "sin is lawlessness" doubtless appeals to the conventions of the day, and with varying degrees of interpretive
usefulness fits the three standard readings of it: it speaks to the seriousness
of sin; it reminds the community of the severe penalty already suffered by
those who have left; and, for those with the education to spot it, it describes
the metaphysical (or eschatological) dimensions of human wrongdoing. But
each of these readings has also a social location — a place where it must have
"made sense" — in the present life and conduct of the community, and it is
this that I have tried in part to recover.[48]

---

48. See in general Peter Brown, *The Making of Late Antiquity* (Cambridge, Mass.: Harvard
University Press, 1978) 11: "In this period [=between the second and fifth centuries], 'divine
power' came to be defined with increasing clarity as the opposite of all other forms of power.
The '*locus* of the supernatural,' where this unique power was operative, came to stand for a

Theological propositions can never lightly be reduced to raw social data, or even to human perception of social situations. Conversely, social situations cannot simply be mirror-read out of theological propositions. But unless they are part of a dead tradition the latter will inevitably have *social meaning,* just as the former can always be made intelligible within a theological framework. The Sons and Daughters of Light *today* may be the Sons and Daughters of Darkness *tomorrow:* this is a simple fact of life, though it may take considerable theological energy to accommodate it. And so it is that in this short phrase in 1 John 3:4 the author sought to avoid the necessity of expending such energy again. "Sin is lawlessness," he wrote: your sin will destroy both you and this anointed community.

---

zone in human life where decisions, obligations, experiences, and information were deemed to come from outside the human community. A highly privileged area of human behavior and of human relations was demarcated." This seems to me an uncannily accurate picture of the mindset of the author of 1 John, and of that "zone" wherein "sin" could be the most devastating "lawlessness."

21

WOMEN IN HOUSE CHURCHES

Carolyn Osiek

Some years ago I told a male cousin that I was teaching a course on Women in the Early Church. His response was, "It must be a short course." Today it would be a very long course. The topic for this essay is better delimited, but the subject of the house church, as we have become aware, raises most of the questions about early Christian life, and the bibliography on women in the early church multiplies exponentially. What I propose to do is to discuss some of the major questions and issues that have surfaced in recent study and offer some judgments.

Good things come in threes. First, I want to talk about three polarities that have pervaded the study of women in the early church — patriarchy vs. the discipleship of equals, public vs. private, and ascetic vs. domestic lifestyle — and to render some judgment about each. After that discussion I will lay out three working assumptions that I believe must inform our investigation: about masculine language, about the honor/shame system, and about how house churches functioned. But in order to engage effectively that final assumption on the workings of a house church, three questions must be asked, questions to which we all wish we knew the answers.

The first polarity is *patriarchy vs. the discipleship of equals*. Scholarship on the position of women in Greco-Roman antiquity and early Christianity has tended to fall into two camps. On one hand, legal and social historians and social-science interpreters have stressed the patriarchal social structures of the culture, in which the Roman *paterfamilias* had legal authority of life and death over everyone in his household, in which women could not administer their property and could not act as legal persons without a male *tutor*. Social-scientific analysis has shown the prevalence of the sexual double standard, the emphasis on female purity and exclusiveness, and the obligation of males to defend their women's honor.[1]

On the other hand, feminist and liberation writers, with a different reading of the sources, have argued for a new spark of insight in earliest Christianity, especially in the teaching of Jesus — a vision of a new way of relating as female and male in the church. According to this reading, the model of discipleship offered by Jesus broke through the barriers of social discrimination to a vision of true equality. But according to the model, this liberative tendency was not maintained by later disciples. The "fall from primal grace" occurred at different moments, depending on one's point of view: with Paul, or deutero-Paul, or just after the NT. Thus this model becomes a new version of the "early catholicism" argument, whereby the pristine origins degenerated at some point into accommodation with "the world."

A variation on this model is the suggestion that there were indeed moderate liberative tendencies at work in the period, but that they did not originate with Christianity. Rather, we can see the movement toward greater social freedom for women already happening in the Roman Empire independently of the influence of Christianity, which simply rode the wave of social development and followed these tendencies to a certain extent.[2] In this scenario, not much of the credit goes to the early church. As someone put it, Christianity was not the only game in town contributing to a transformation of patriarchy, but it was *one* of the games.

Jewish feminist scholars have made us quite aware of the implicit anti-Judaism that can lie behind the argument that Christianity created a discipleship of equals: Jesus liberated women from the oppression of Judaism.[3] So there are problems all around: if Jesus liberated women, he was unfair to his own Judaism; if he did and the church couldn't keep up with him, it has failed him in a major way; if patriarchy really held sway all along, then from the perspective of modern sympathies, Jesus may have been a failure.

I find myself most convinced by the position that holds a movement toward greater social freedom for women (not toward "liberation" in the

---

1. Especially David D. Gilmore, ed., *Honor and Shame and the Unity of the Mediterranean* (American Anthropological Association Special Publication 22; Washington, D.C.: American Anthropological Association, 1987); John G. Peristiany, ed., *Honour and Shame: The Values of Mediterranean Society* (Chicago: University of Chicago Press, 1966); idem and Julian Pitt-Rivers, eds., *Honor and Grace in Anthropology* (Cambridge: Cambridge University Press, 1992); Halvor Moxnes, "Honor and Shame," in Richard L. Rohrbaugh, ed., *The Social Sciences and New Testament Interpretation* (Peabody, Mass.: Hendrickson, 1996) 19–40.

2. See Kathleen E. Corley, "Feminist Myths of Christian Origins," in Elizabeth A. Castelli and Hal Taussig, eds., *Reimagining Christian Origins: A Colloquium Honoring Burton L. Mack* (Valley Forge, Pa.: Trinity Press International, 1996) 51–67.

3. Bernadette J. Brooten, "Jewish Women's History in the Roman Period: A Task for Christian Theology," *HTR* 79 (1986) 22–30; Judith Plaskow, "Christian Feminism and Anti-Judaism," *Cross Currents* 28 (1978) 306–9.

modern sense) that was happening already in Roman society, and in which Christianity partially participated. Indeed, we can trace in Roman society of the first century such a movement for women in a number of ways: the virtual disappearance of marriage by *manus* (transfer of the bride from the family and authority of her father to that of her husband); Augustus's incentive of freedom from *tutela* to women who bore a certain number of children; the evidence mentioned by several authors that respectable women were beginning to recline at public banquets alongside their husbands; evidence of women administering their own property, conducting business, and owning businesses.[4] Some strains of Christianity seem to have picked up on this movement and given it a religious motivation. Others represented a continuity of more traditional patterns. Both tendencies were probably at work.

The second polarity is *public vs. private*. Much work has been done on the analysis — one might almost say the creation — of these social structures in Greco-Roman antiquity. According to ancient texts and modern anthropological theories alike, the public domain of temples, theater, forum, assemblies, and law courts (or in the countryside among peasants, the town square and the fields) is the world of men in which women do not mix, while the domain of house and garden, domestic production, and child care is the private domain of women. In some earlier thinking, the two categories remained as rigidly fixed and separated as if the way they functioned today in the most conservative Islamic society were the way they functioned everywhere.

The model is not all wrong, of course. The *social* invisibility of women in public life in Greco-Roman antiquity is striking in comparison with many other cultures. But social invisibility is conceptual: it exists in the minds of those who articulate the ideal and may bear no resemblance to what is really going on. The fact that women may not be addressed in public settings does not mean that they were not there. The evidence for women in business and professions demonstrates that social invisibility is not actual invisibility.[5]

Moreover, the categories are overdrawn and often too rigidly applied. The Roman *paterfamilias* conducted much, if not most, of his business and politics — the two intrinsically interwoven through the patronage system — at home, in the front part of the house, to which Roman women, in contrast to Greek women, were not denied access. Here the stated differences between the Greek and Roman use of domestic space must be taken seriously into account. The elite Greek house, according to Vitruvius, did segregate

---

4. For references, see Carolyn Osiek and David Balch, *Families in the New Testament World: Households and House Churches* (Louisville, Ky.: Westminster/John Knox, 1997) 57–60.

5. See Susan Treggiari, "Jobs for Women," *American Journal of Ancient History* 1/2 (1976) 76–104; Deborah Hobson, "The Role of Women in the Economic Life of Roman Egypt," *Echos du monde classique/Classical Views* 28 n.s. 3 (1984) 373–90.

women in the back of the house, while the Roman house did not (*De arch.* 6.10.1–5).[6] To the extent that Roman customs penetrated the Greek East, romanizing changes can be presumed eventually in the East as well, at least for the relatively elite. Of course, an author like Vitruvius, and indeed most of the non-Christian ancient sources, do not envision dwellings of the lower classes and the poor, where lack of space would have made any kind of sexual segregation virtually impossible.

There has sometimes been an assumption that the house church, because it most often met in a domestic structure, also met under the rules of the private sphere, in which women are thought to have had greater freedom within the circle of the immediate family. But most often a house church meeting was not that of the immediate family, and this notion of "private rules" for it has been ably challenged by an analysis of Paul's expectations in 1 Corinthians.[7] Rather than thinking of the house church as a private haven, we should probably think of it as the crossroads between public and private, and the old Roman idea that "as goes the household, so goes the state" was equally applicable in the Christian community (see 1 Tim 3:4–5).

Again, we are warned that an implicit bias can lurk beneath the assumption that the synagogue was a public meeting, therefore more restrictive of women than the private Christian meeting in the house. The use and even the renovation of private houses for public meetings was common to Jews, Christians, and others, and nothing can be construed about social behavior by the use of domestic space; much less can comparisons be made between the relative freedom of Jewish and Christian women on this basis.[8]

The third polarity is *ascesis vs. normal domesticity*. How early did the ascetic lifestyle begin in Christianity, including the permanent embrace of prayer, fasting, and especially celibacy? Are we to assume that most of the women we hear about are ascetics or living normal family lives?

Already in 1 Corinthians 7, Paul seems to advocate a certain asceticism for eschatological motives, especially the discouraging of marriage and re-marriage. Given the symbolic weight already borne in the culture by women's

---

6. Discussion in Osiek and Balch, *Families*, 6–10. It has been argued by others that in fact the architectural evidence of Greek houses from the classical period does not support this gendered division of space in the Greek house; see Michael H. Jameson, "Domestic Space in the Greek City State," in Susan Kent, ed., *Domestic Architecture and the Use of Space: An Interdisciplinary Cross-Cultural Study* (Cambridge and New York: Cambridge University Press, 1990) 92–113, esp. 104, 109; idem, "Private Space and the Greek City," in Oswyn Murray and Simon Price, eds., *The Greek City from Homer to Alexander* (Oxford: Clarendon, 1990) 171–95, esp. 172, 186–92.

7. Stephen C. Barton, "Paul's Sense of Place: An Anthropological Approach to Community Formation in Corinth," *NTS* 32 (1986) 225–46.

8. Sharon Lee Mattila, "Where Women Sat in Ancient Synagogues: The Archaeological Evidence in Context," in John S. Kloppenborg and Stephen G. Wilson, eds., *Voluntary Associations in the Greco-Roman World* (London and New York: Routledge, 1996) 266–86, esp. 269.

chastity, it is reasonable to expect that celibacy as an ideal would be applied especially to women and eventually would appeal strongly to them as an alternative to marriage.[9] 1 Cor 7:36–38 speaks of a decision to be made by a man about a woman's marital status, and it is frequently interpreted as an indication that "celibate marriages" have already begun, at least in Corinth, where several kinds of unusual behavior seem to have been indigenous. Officially enrolled widows are not allowed to remarry in the church of Timothy, but younger widows are in fact encouraged to remarry (1 Tim 5:9, 14). They would have been a highly volatile group when they got together, just the kind of group that aroused unconscious fears of anarchy. They were young and not directly under male control; hence the advice to Timothy to get them remarried as soon as possible. Ignatius (Smyrn. 13.1) suggests the existence of an identifiable group of "virgins called widows" in at least one community of Asia Minor in the early second century. Bonnie B. Thurston has made the plausible suggestion that the term παρθένος be taken here in its broader sense of women of marriageable age, and that the reference refers to these "non-enrolled" widows young enough to remarry (see 1 Tim 5:11–14).[10] Acceptable "safe" older widows as an identifiable group who did not remarry, however, flourished in the church for several centuries, not only as objects of charity but as a recognized service organization.[11]

Celibacy for the kingdom did not appeal only to women. Hermas is told that his wife will "from now on be to you as a sister," presumably meaning that his new identity as a seer requires sexual continence (Herm. Vis. 2.2.3). Justin boasts in the middle of the second century that both men and women have been celibate from their youth into old age (1 Apol. 15, 29). Yet there can be no doubt that as time advanced the ethos of consecrated female virgins formed a strong characteristic in early Christianity, for a variety of reasons that cannot be examined here but that have everything to do with the female body as symbol of political, social, and theological integrity.

The idealization of virginity and female celibacy has so overshadowed the rest of the evidence that there has been a tendency to assume that women singled out as engaged in ministry were members of this ascetic group. It is only in recent years that we have begun to look at the accumulation of evidence on the other side, e.g., the married evangelists Prisca and Junia (Rom 16:3, 7), Mary mother of John Mark (Acts 12:12), the mother of Rufus (Rom 16:13), the wife of Epitropos (Ignatius Pol. 8.2), the married martyr

---

9. Kerstin Bjerre-Aspegren, The Male Woman: A Feminine Ideal in the Early Church (Uppsala Women's Studies: Women in Religion 4; Uppsala: Almqvist & Wiksell, 1990).

10. Thurston, The Widows: A Women's Ministry in the Early Church (Minneapolis: Fortress, 1989) 64–65.

11. Stephan Davies, Revolt of the Widows: The Social World of the Apocryphal Acts (Carbondale, Ill.: Southern Illinois University Press, 1980); Carolyn Osiek, "The Widow as Altar: The Rise and Fall of a Symbol," SecCent 3 (1983) 159–69; Thurston, Widows.

Perpetua, and her pregnant companion Felicitas (as a slave, not legally married), to name only a few. In spite of the obsession of that culture to classify women by sexual status, it is very interesting that so many women are named in the Pauline and Ignatian letters and elsewhere without such designation: Phoebe, Mary, Tryphaena, Tryphosa, Persis, Julia, and the unnamed sister of Nereus (Rom 16:1, 6, 12, 15); Euodia and Syntyche (Phil 4:2); Grapte (*Herm. Vis.* 2.4.3), Tavia (Ignatius *Smyrn.* 13.2), Alce (Ignatius *Pol.* 8.3; *Smyrn.* 13.2; *Mart. Pol.* 17.2), and Blandina (*Martyrs of Lyons and Vienne*), again to name only a few.

It is highly unlikely that all or most of them were ascetics. Margaret Y. MacDonald leads in the right direction with her suggestion that women in ministerial roles in the first centuries were more likely married or widowed than celibate ascetics, in spite of some evidence of a growing custom of consecrated celibacy.[12]

I turn now to three assumptions that must be discussed. The first is that masculine plural titles should not always presume men to the exclusion of women. The second is that the cultural values of honor and shame were at work, but differently in different situations. The third is that the principal activities of the house church were worship, hospitality, education, social services, and evangelization, and that women participated in all of these activities.

The first assumption, *that masculine plural titles should not always presume men to the exclusion of women,* should be obvious according to grammatical and social custom. In both domains, women were considered to be included with and embedded in men, as we still are in many languages and cultures. Yet discussions of the literature have not completely abandoned the assumption that masculine references refer exclusively to men when it comes to positions of leadership, in spite of the διάκονος Phoebe (Rom 16:1), the ἀπόστολος Junia (Rom 16:7), teachers of women like Grapte and the public gnostic teacher Marcellina in the mid-second century in Rome — the latter so effective, according to Irenaeus, that she "exterminated many" (*Adv. haer.* 1.25.6; cf. Epiphanius *Pan.* 27.6) — and a number of known women prophets, including "Jezebel" (Rev 2:20). Rationally, we assent to the principle and perhaps do not see a problem. However, when passages roll off our lips such as 1 Cor 12:28 ("God has established in the church first apostles, second prophets, third teachers") or Phil 1:1 ("to all the holy ones in Philippi with ἐπίσκοποι and διάκονοι") or Eph 4:11 (God provided "some to be apostles, some prophets, some evangelists, some pastors and teachers") or Eph 2:20

---

12. MacDonald, *Early Christian Women and Pagan Opinion: The Power of the Hysterical Woman* (Cambridge and New York: Cambridge University Press, 1996). It is therefore puzzling that she makes Tavia into the leader of a group of ascetics (p. 214–15), a judgment for which there is no evidence.

(the church is "built upon the foundation of the apostles and prophets with Christ Jesus as cornerstone") — even if we have acknowledged in that last one that the prophets referred to are Christian rather than ancient Israelite prophets — I do not think that most of us imagine groups composed of both men and women, and I am quite certain that the general Bible-reading population does not. We need continually to remind others and especially ourselves to readjust the mental picture.

The second assumption concerns *the function of the cultural values of honor and shame,* often considered the "pivotal values" of ancient Mediterranean culture. There has been a tendency in scholarship to introduce general formulations uncritically into any ancient situation and assume that the dynamic works in the same way from ancient Israel to Augustine, and from Spain to Babylonia, in spite of anthropologists' careful documentation and adaptation of cultural generalities to given situations.[13] Indeed, some anthropologists have questioned the existence of a single system of honor and shame across Mediterranean civilization, preferring instead to link the culture patterns in a north/south direction, taking in southern and northern Europe, rather than in an east/west direction, from Spain to the Middle East.[14]

There is no agreement on the exact way that honor and shame function within a given cultural context. Some would claim that in traditional Mediterranean cultures for a woman there is no real honor except that of her family and its dominant males, while for her there is only appropriate sensitivity to shame, expressed in shyness and sexual exclusivity. For others, women bear the responsibility for guarding not only family but national honor, and the honor of women is that of the family. In this case, the entire weight of corporate honor is projected onto the bodies of women.

In a society clearly divided along gender lines in its structures of work, leisure, and friendship, male anthropologists have access only to the male world of meaning and therefore derive their interpretations from it. Women anthropologists with access to the private world of women usually suggest that women in honor/shame cultures adapt to the more public male honor system, in which women are something like commodities to be guarded, raided, and traded, but privately such women operate on a different kind of honor system, one based not on competition for honor but on mutual confidence.[15] Still others argue that the honor/shame system has more to do with

---

13. A good introduction to this topic is Moxnes, "Honor and Shame." To the bibliography given there add Sally Cole, *Women of the Praia: Work and Lives in a Portuguese Coastal Community* (Princeton, N.J.: Princeton University Press, 1991); Jill Dubisch, ed., *Gender and Power in Rural Greece* (Princeton, N.J.: Princeton University Press, 1986).

14. See, e.g., Frank Henderson Stewart, *Honor* (Chicago: University of Chicago Press, 1994).

15. Lila Abu-Lughod, *Veiled Sentiments: Honor and Poetry in a Bedouin Society* (Berkeley: University of California Press, 1986); Dubisch, *Gender and Power,* passim but esp. Robinette Kennedy,

political ideologies or the presuppositions of the interpreter than it does with what is really happening in the culture.[16]

My growing conviction is that in the ancient Mediterranean, as today, there were significant variations according to time and place as to how the honor/shame code was actualized and that much of the difference in the first century depended on the degree of Roman influence. If Vitruvius (first century BCE) is correct that the Greek house was built to segregate the family's women from the business and entertaining conducted by the adult male members of the family, that is one system. If the Roman house was designed not to segregate but to display social status in which women participated, that is another. Both are honor/shame systems. It would seem that the strict segregation of women as described by Philo, in which married women were not to venture beyond the front door and unmarried women not even to get that far (*Spec. leg.* 3.31.169), was based on the most conservative upper-class male ideal of classical Athens, and that by the time of Philo it was pretty much a male fantasy. The veiling of women in public — still a requirement in some Islamic countries and an enduring custom in others — is meant to symbolize shame or sensitivity to honorable chastity by concealing beauty and sexuality, though the veil can certainly be worn in such a way that it augments those very qualities. Considerable evidence indicates that covering a woman's head with a veil was once customary throughout both Greek and Roman spheres of influence, but that it was much less prevalent in western Roman areas by the middle of the first century. Many official portraits of women continued to feature the suggestion of a veil, but it was more symbolic than concealing.[17]

One of the practices of a strictly segregated honor/shame society is that respectable women's names should never be spoken in public because such women should draw the attention of no one beyond the immediate family. If it is necessary to mention them in public, they should be referred to only by their relationship with a relevant male: the wife of A, the mother of B, the daughter of C, and so on. On the contrary, Roman aristocratic women were patrons of public associations, their names inscribed and their dedicatory statues on display.[18] Paul's direct naming of women friends, collaborators, and benefactors, in most cases without mention of their marital or familial status, contradicts this rule as well. It may not be coincidental, however, that the largest number of women whom Paul greets appear in his letter to the church

---

"Women's Friendships in Crete: A Psychological Perspective" (pp. 121–38); Uni Wikan, "Shame and Honor: A Contestable Pair," *Man* 19 (1984) 635–52.

16. Cole, *Women of the Praia*, 77–107.

17. Ramsay MacMullen, "Women in Public in the Roman Empire," *Historia* 29 (1980) 208–18; see Plutarch *Mor.* 267A on the veiling of women as the usual custom in the Roman East.

18. Partial lists in Osiek and Balch, *Families*, 50–52; L. Michael White, *The Social Origins of Christian Architecture* (2 vols.; HTS 42–43; Valley Forge, Pa.: Trinity Press International, 1996–97) 1. 45–46, 81–82, 106.

at Rome, which was probably the place where social change was happening most rapidly.

All of this is not to say that there was no operative honor/shame code or that it did not affect women in a different way than men. Roman society remained highly patriarchal and passed on this characteristic to Judaism and Christianity. Early Christianity created its own adaptations of the honor/shame code by proposing an alternate standard for honorable conduct based on its moral system and the inversion of values that accompanied a theology of the cross. Similarly, a different standard of shameful behavior consisted of failure to live according to those standards. But even apart from a different set of religious expectations, expectations of female chastity and passive virtue were undoubtedly higher than those of male sexual virtue.

The third assumption proposes that *the house church in the first generations of the Christian era was a center for worship, hospitality, education, social services, and mission.* Three further questions will help shape the reconstruction of church life in these communities. These are the questions to which we all wish we knew the answers. First, what kinds of houses are we envisioning when we talk about the "house church"? Second, where were women and how did they function at the common meals of the gathered community? Third, since some of the best evidence for women heads of households in the ancient Mediterranean world comes from the NT, how were women both patrons and heads of house churches in a culture in which male headship of the house was the norm?

We need first to talk about what kinds of houses are envisioned. In early January of 1998, at a meeting of the New Testament group of the Association of Chicago Theological Schools, I showed a collection of slides about Roman domestic arrangements that illustrate everyday life and the structures of various kinds of houses. Grady, our honoree, was asked to respond, and in his inimitable way he spoke to the effect that he, too, had stood in the House of the Vettii at Pompeii and imagined the gathering of a house church going on there. "But Lyn," he said, "it's all a delusion. Christians never met in houses like these." I must say I remain unconvinced. Some Christian groups must certainly have met in much more modest accommodations, even in some of the grimier *insulae* or "tenement churches," as Robert Jewett calls them.[19] But I see no reason, given the ample evidence for the ownership of some rather spacious houses at Pompeii by persons of modest social status but less modest wealth, why groups of worshiping Christians, like their Jewish or Mithraist neighbors, could not have met in peristyled (colonnaded) *domus*.[20]

19. Jewett, "Tenement Churches and Communal Meals in the Early Church: The Implications of a Form-Critical Analysis of 2 Thessalonians 3:10," *BR* 38 (1993) 23–43.
20. The large, luxurious House of the Vettii at Pompeii was probably owned by two freedmen

The best thing seems to be to leave open the possibility of a variety of different configurations for house church meetings in the earliest years at least. The households of Stephanas and of Prisca and Aquila in Corinth (1 Cor 16:15, 19) are likely to have been *domus,* even if ever so modest. "Those from Chloe" (1 Cor 1:11) may be messengers to Paul, but they may also be members of a gathering in more modest circumstances.

But the relevant question here is this: Would the position of women in the assembly have been any different whether it took place in a spacious and luxurious house, a more modest peristyled house, or a rented room in the corner of an *insula?* It is sometimes assumed that the larger and more imposing the *domus,* the more hierarchical and patriarchal the social structure, so that in less formal meeting situations more flexibility of leadership structures could be presumed. Perhaps, but most of the evidence of various voluntary associations and private cults suggests rather highly organized leadership structures, with less evidence of women as actual leaders than as patrons. We do not yet know enough about how patronage functioned in private associations, much less how women patrons functioned.

As has already been discussed, there seems to have been more of a tendency to segregate women from male company in Eastern houses than Western, with variations allowed for degrees of romanization or adherence to older traditions. The earliest traditions would allow for women to be present at meals with men only in intimate family circles, and even then, if men reclined, women sat next to their couch. More formal occasions would necessitate either the complete absence of women or their accommodation in separate dining rooms. The more official and public an event, the more likely that traditional customs would hold sway. Thus Valerius Maximus early in the first century CE tells us that the traditional Roman way of dining is for women to be seated next to their husbands' couches, but that Roman women were now reclining at banquets alongside their husbands. At approximately the same time, however, Livia, who is reported to have reclined next to Augustus at their wedding in the new way, still gave separate banquets for women when Augustus gave his banquets to celebrate important occasions and military victories (Dio Cassius *Hist. Rom.* 48.44.3; 55.2.4, 8.2; 57.12.5). In spite of the assumption that, by the first century, Romans in Italy would have fully integrated the newer customs of integrated couches, there are some house layouts in Pompeii that feature two rooms side by side, both of which would seem, by everything we know, to be intended as dining rooms.

There is also the question whether all who attended such meals reclined. In a gathering in a *domus,* there can be little doubt that the arrangement

---

brothers; the ample house of Caecilius Jucundus by the son of a freedman; and Julia Felix, owner of a large rental property in the southeast section of the city, was surely a freedwoman.

of the room designated the dining room could have been anything other than *triclinium* (dining room, supper room) or *stibadium* (semicircular seating arrangement), the latter a slightly more flexible arrangement that was already appearing in the first century but became common only much later, with hosts and most important guests reclining.[21] The question is, what about everyone else? We are simply lacking the information, but my educated guess is that the more solemn the occasion, the more likely that temporary couches would be set up to include at least all males in the formal position, and that the dining room of most houses would not have been large enough to contain the whole membership.[22]

The possible options for women at the common meal of a house church, then, are as follows: first, the absence of women and children, leaving the ritual meal to be eaten by men alone; second, separate dining rooms for men and women, children either excluded or brought in with the women; third, women and children seated next to their reclining male relatives; fourth, women and children seated in a place apart from the reclining men; and fifth, women and men reclining together, children either seated near them or together in a separate place. The first option, the complete absence of women from the ritual meal, is unlikely given the large number of women who were active in various kinds of ministry. The second, separate dining rooms, is also unlikely if all were supposed to share from the same table and hear the word read and preached. The third through the fifth options, however, are all plausible, depending on time and place, namely, women and children seated next to men's couches; women and children seated separately but in the same area; and men and women reclining together. The persistent accusation of suspicious outsiders and authorities against private associations, including Christian ones, that they indiscriminately mixed both sexes and all social ranks, probably had a basis in just such things as seating or reclining arrangements at official gatherings.

Given what we know about Roman colonies like Philippi and Corinth, it is more likely that reclining together was the style there than perhaps in some other Pauline churches. Eventually, of course, the couches and chairs disappeared, and everyone stood, probably men on one side of the room and women on the other. But that was to take at least another century. Hippolytus's prescriptions for such meals in the early third century still seem to presuppose some kind of seating arrangement.

---

21. Katherine M. D. Dunbabin, "Triclinium and Stibadium," in William J. Slater, ed., *Dining in a Classical Context* (Ann Arbor, Mich.: University of Michigan Press, 121–48).

22. See Kathleen E. Corley, *Private Women, Public Meals: Social Conflict and Women in the Synoptic Tradition* (Peabody, Mass.: Hendrickson, 1993) 24–34, 66–75. Already Jesus son of Sirach (ca. 180 BCE) issued this caution: "Never dine with another man's wife, nor revel with her at wine; lest your heart turn aside to her, and in blood you be plunged into destruction" (Sir 9:9).

A wider question is the role of women in the patronage system, specifically as patrons in Christian communities. Patronage was the backbone of the informal social system of cohesion among men, providing means for political and social advancement as well as economic benefits.[23] Women, too, exercised patronage; there is ample evidence of this, though it must have been in a somewhat different way. Elite women were actively though indirectly involved in politics.[24] There is no reason to assume that something analogous did not operate at other social levels. Women were public patronesses of guilds, clubs, synagogues, and other types of private associations. By the third century, we know of the tendency of Christian benefaction to be centered on giving at the ritual assembly so that all resources would be channeled through the hands of the bishop and his deacons.[25] But it was not always so. We must read in the light of patronage the stories of and references to Phoebe, Lydia, the mother of John Mark in Jerusalem, and others, bearing in mind that in the traditional Roman patronage system a patron was owed *obsequium* and *operae* by a client. Did Paul give suitable tribute to his patrons Phoebe and Lydia, and perhaps give them private instruction or repair leatherwork around the house, in exchange for the hospitality and financial assistance he received from them?

Patronage is one thing; managing a household is another. The literature on household management never raises the question of a female manager without the presence of a *paterfamilias*, and the idea was so contrary to the conservative theorists that they never discuss it. Yet we know that it happened. Some historians will assume that a reference to a house church meeting "in the house of" a woman refers merely to the name of the *owner* of the house — and women did hold property independently — but that it says nothing about who presided at social activities of the household. That is the question. Two examples from Roman social sources illustrate in part that, in certain circumstances, women did make the decisions and preside at social gatherings. Ummidia Quadratilla chose the dinner entertainment in her house until the age of 79, and her taste earned the disapproval of Pliny the Younger (*Ep.* 7.24). Matidia, great-aunt of Marcus Aurelius, housed the future emperor's daughters in her house, and she seems to have been fully responsible for them (Cornelius Fronto 1.30; 2.94–97). Can we envision something similar in the case of the mother of John Mark, Nympha, etc.?

---

23. John H. Elliott, "Patronage and Clientage," in Rohrbaugh, *Social Sciences,* 144–56.

24. Richard A. Bauman, *Women and Politics in Ancient Rome* (London and New York: Routledge, 1992).

25. L. William Countryman, *The Rich Christian in the Church of the Early Empire: Contradictions and Accommodations* (Texts and Studies in Religion 7; New York: Mellen, 1980); Charles A. Bobertz, "The Role of Patron in the *Cena Dominica* of Hippolytus' *Apostolic Tradition*," *JTS* n.s. 44 (1993) 170–84; idem, "Almsgiving as Patronage: The Role of Patroness in Early Christianity" (unpublished paper presented at the AAR Annual Meeting, San Francisco, November 1992).

Having discussed some of these free-floating questions, let us turn now to the functions of the house church: worship, hospitality, education, social services, and mission or evangelization. As discussed above, women were present for the principal act of worship, the ritual meal of the assembly, perhaps in background locations in some circumstances but in the foreground in others. They were, after all, half or more of the membership.

The best examples of houses led by women, probably in most cases widows, are from the NT: Mary mother of John Mark in Jerusalem (Acts 12:12), Lydia (Acts 16:14, 40), Nympha (Col 4:15), and perhaps Chloe (1 Cor 1:11). I do not think this means that the first generation of Christians was different in this regard, but that here we have unbiased social information from non-elite sources. I further think it correct to surmise that in such cases these women hosted formal dinners and presided at them, including the assembly of the ἐκκλησία. The sources would understandably be silent about this, not wanting to encourage more of it. In the absence of definite evidence we shall probably never know, but in the context of the slender evidence that we do have it makes sense.

Women have traditionally had chief responsibility for hospitality. This would include reception of Christian visitors, especially itinerant missionaries like the wandering apostle/prophets of the *Didache* or the founder of a church. A general pattern was probably to host such dignitaries in the house in which a house church assembled. Soon, however, this was a ministry entrusted particularly to those widows who would have the capacity to receive guests (1 Tim 5:10). Of course, in some cases the widow's house might also be the meeting place of the assembly, and she would be its patron. One wonders, for instance, about Ignatius's fondness for Tavia and Alce. The prisoner Ignatius may not have been allowed out overnight, but perhaps he was. These women must have performed some special service for Ignatius, and the most likely scenario is that they were widows who provided hospitality. It is highly unlikely that Ignatius would have referred to them alone, by name, if they had husbands.

These women's houses thus became important centers of communication and education. The Greco-Roman world is full of evidence of households that take in family members or friends of family members who require a place to live commensurate with their status, or even those in immediate need of safe housing. In similar situations in the Christian community the same kind of hospitality was undoubtedly practiced, and as always, women would have to have been in the forefront of making the practice effective.

The house church was also center of education, not only initial instruction but also continuing education in faith. Those who qualified for advanced instruction — for a "graduate degree," so to speak, such as that provided by professional teachers like Justin in mid-second-century Rome — must first have been through the regular instruction based in houses, at meetings other than that of the weekly assembly. Whatever instruction could be given through preaching at the weekly assembly could not have borne the entire weight of a program of religious formation. One is reminded of Pliny's account of Christians who meet very early in the morning to bind themselves by oath not to commit crimes, then hold a prayer service with singing (Pliny Ep. 10.96.7).

Given the culture, it is unlikely that all such religious instruction took place in mixed groups. Some, perhaps much of it, was gender-specific, with instruction oriented to the particular roles of women and men in the family. It is here that we have ample evidence of the special role of women teachers, a role often neglected even today because scholarly interest remains at the public, predominantly male, level. Every cultural and religious tradition that practices any kind of gender separation develops distinctive teaching traditions for men and women. The three religions of the book — Judaism, Christianity, and Islam — still do so, though not universally.

Allusions to the teaching of women by women tell us of a continuing custom of whose content we know very little: older women are to form character in younger women while male teachers do the same for young men (Titus 2:3–8). While Hermas delivers his revelatory message with the presbyters in the assembly, an otherwise unknown Grapte receives her own copy of the text to give special instruction to widows and their children, which implies some kind of regular assembly of persons in that category (*Herm. Vis.* 2.4.3).[26] Widows form a more or less distinctive group as the church grows, sometimes objects of charity but also a group of women on whom church leaders come to depend for a variety of services, one of them being instruction of other women. Later, in the Eastern churches, deaconesses will take over much of that work. It has been suggested that, since much teaching in oral cultures is done by storytelling, instructional stories told in these circles eventually emerged into the "malestream" as the apocryphal gospels and acts.[27]

Another function of the house church was as a center of social services for those members of the church who were in need. Again, young widows and their children come immediately to mind, from families which cannot support them. Apparently there were some attempts by families to sidestep their own responsibility in this regard and have their widow freeload on the church (see, e.g., 1 Tim 5:4, 5, 8, 16), just as some slaves began to expect from the church not only moral encouragement but funding for their manumis-

---

26. Full references in Osiek and Balch, *Families,* 167–73.
27. Dennis Ronald MacDonald, *The Legend and the Apostle: The Battle for Paul in Story and Canon* (Philadelphia: Westminster, 1983); Davies, *Revolt of the Widows.*

sion (Ignatius *Pol.* 4.3). Justin speaks of a common collection for orphans and
widows, the sick, the imprisoned, and visiting strangers (*1 Apol.* 67). Tertullian speaks of the monthly contribution for works of charity: food and burial
for the poor, support of orphans, old slaves and sailors, and those imprisoned
(*Apol.* 39.5–6). Already by the middle of the second century, therefore, a
common collection for relief of the needy was in place. This custom, eventually to be centralized in church leadership, did not, however, immediately
replace private deeds of patronage and benefaction, in which Greco-Roman
women in general were known to be active participants. Just as women were
patrons of clubs and synagogues, so they were of house churches as well. But
the private patronage of Christian women for the poor and needy will never
be adequately documented. We catch fleeting glimpses, for instance, of the
"enrolled" widow of 1 Tim 5:10 who is expected not only to have shown hospitality and washed the feet of visitors but to have relieved the afflicted and
done other kinds of good works, too.

Visiting the sick and the imprisoned was also included in the kinds of
charitable activity expected of Christians (Matt 25:36, 39). Much of this fell
to the deacons, once their position was in place. Deacons visit Perpetua and
her companions in prison (*Pass. Perp. et Fel.* 3.7), yet in Lucian's account
of the imprisonment of the then-Christian Peregrinus, widows and orphans
come in droves to visit him (*De mort. Per.* 12). Tertullian expects that among
the duties of a Christian woman, even one married to a non-Christian, are
visitation of both the sick and those in prison, duties that an unbelieving
husband will be reluctant to let her do (*Ad spon.* 2.4). Finally, the house
church was a center for mission and evangelization. Each family unit was a
locus for evangelization, including — perhaps especially — the mixed marriage. Paul considers the presence of the believer in the family to render it
holy (1 Cor 7:14), and 1 Peter sees the submission of Christian wives to their
non-Christian husbands as a means of converting them (3:1–2). Later, Tertullian would take a much dimmer view and try to discourage mixed marriages
(*Ad spon.* 2.4–7). There was as yet no "missionary school." Those who would
be sent as missionaries by local churches got their training and encouragement in local assemblies that would then commission them for their mission.
Paul claims the right, which he did not use, to bring a wife with him as the
other apostles do (1 Cor 9:5). Missionary couples like Prisca and Aquila and
Andronicus and Junia were able to put not only their houses but their assets
and their lives at the service of the gospel. Countless others did the same,
either singly or in pairs. For all we know, traveling missionary couples may
have been more the norm than the exception.

One final question to be asked here is this: How would early Christian
women have heard and received the household codes and related expressions
of their role as that of submission? Here M. Y. MacDonald makes an in-

teresting proposal.[28] Already accustomed to the rhetoric of submission, such women might have seen in Eph 5:21–33, which likens wife and husband to the church and Christ, a bestowal of new identity. Already used to bearing the symbolic weight of house, family, chastity, and the honor of family and city state, they may have been filled with an appropriate sense of their own importance as representatives of the church itself, that is to say, the whole gathered community, before Christ.

In the societies in which Christianity developed, social freedom for women was increasing to some limited extent. This new faith system was still working out its identity vis-à-vis its parent religion and the cultural origins of its members. Women were active contributors to the new Christian movement that would ultimately change the Mediterranean world and bring profound changes to male-female relationships, changes whose effects are still with us today, even if we have not yet completely lived up to the vision.

28. M. Y. MacDonald, *Early Christian Women*, 240–43, 247.

22

ART IMITATING LIFE

Suffering and Redemption in
an Early Christian Apocalypse

ROBERT C. HELMER

In the early fifth century CE, the Palestinian lawyer Sozomen sought to continue the legacy of Eusebius through the writing of his *Historia ecclesiastica*,
which he dedicated to the Emperor Theodosius II.[1] In this work, Sozomen
makes reference to the practices of several local communities in Palestine
regarding the use of an early Christian apocalypse, the *Apocalypse of Peter*.[2]
He reports that "as for the so-called *Apocalypse of Peter*, having been proven
completely spurious from the time of the fathers, we know that it is being
read in certain churches of Palestine still now once each year on the day of
Preparation, on which the people very devoutly fast at the recollection of the
suffering of the Savior" (*Hist. eccl.* 6.19).[3]

It is evident from Sozomen's account that he does not approve of this use
of the *Apocalypse of Peter*, and he indicates that the reason for its demise as
a text appropriate for use in the liturgy lies in its Petrine authorship having
been proven false.[4] So who was it that made this judgment regarding the use

1. Glenn F. Chesnut, *The First Christian Histories: Eusebius, Socrates, Sozomen, Theodoret, and
Evagrius* (2d ed.; Macon, Ga.: Mercer University Press/Peeters; 1986) 199–207; Johannes Quas-
ten, *Patrology*, vol. 3: *The Golden Age of Greek Patristic Literature* (Westminster, Md.: Christian
Classics, repr. 1983) 534–36.

2. The *Apocalypse of Peter* referred to here is that surviving in three Greek fragments and two
Ethiopic manuscripts. This *Apocalypse* is to be distinguished from the Nag Hammadi text (NHC
7,3) of the same name and, unfortunately, the same standard abbreviation. Unless otherwise
noted, the ET quoted in this essay is that of C. Detlef G. Müller, "Apocalypse of Peter," in
Wilhelm Schneemelcher, ed., R. McL. Wilson, trans. ed., *New Testament Apocrypha* (rev. ed.;
2 vols.; Cambridge: Clarke; Louisville, Ky.: Westminster/John Knox, 1991–92) 2. 620–38.

3. ET my own; Greek text in *PG* 67.1477.

4. Sozomen, as does Eusebius (*Hist. eccl.* 3.3.2), refers to this apocalypse as "the so-called

or nonuse of the *Apocalypse?* Certainly not the Palestinian communities that continued to employ this text in their worship. Sozomen's comment that it had been "proven completely spurious from the time of the fathers" points rather to an official judgment or decision of some sort, made by someone in the past.[5]

Regardless of the determination of the ecclesiastical scholars or authorities on the authenticity of this early Christian text, fifth-century Palestinian communities still found merit in hearing the words written centuries earlier. Here, then, is an example of what Graydon F. Snyder has described as a conflict between adherence to the great tradition and the practices of the local tradition.[6] In his groundbreaking work on the archaeological evidence for pre-Constantinian Christianity, Snyder proposes four processes that "are always at work as a revealed body of truth affects a social situation"; namely, (1) some elements of the great tradition are being accepted in the social matrix; (2) some elements of the great tradition are being accepted in the social matrix in a nonnormative manner; (3) some elements of the social matrix are being adapted by the great tradition; and (4) some elements of the social matrix are being accepted by the great tradition in a nonnormative manner.[7]

It is the second of these four that I propose is at work in the continued use of *Apocalypse of Peter* into the fifth century. The great tradition has handed down this early Christian text, once used by some of the very "fathers" from whose time it had been proven "completely spurious," according to Sozomen. By the fifth century, however, it has clearly fallen out of favor. A normative acceptance of the great tradition, therefore, would preclude the reading of this *Apocalypse* in a liturgical setting. Sozomen's observation of just that occurrence, then, is witness to the great tradition "being accepted in the social matrix in a non-normative manner."

Apocalypse of Peter (τὴν καλουμένην Ἀποκάλυψιν Πέτρου)." Certainly for Eusebius this Petrine apocalypse was noncanonical. He writes in *Hist. eccl.* 3.3.2 that "of the so-called *Revelation [of Peter]*, we have no knowledge at all in Catholic tradition, for no orthodox writer of the ancient time or of our own has used" it (ET in Kirsopp Lake, trans., *Eusebius Ecclesiastical History I* [LCL 153; Cambridge, Mass.: Harvard University Press, 1926, repr. 1992] 192–93).

5. It is surprising that Sozomen would make reference to "the fathers" as a legitimation for his own disdain for the *Apocalypse of Peter* since he was, in general, not well disposed toward ecclesiastical authority. See, for example, his remark concerning bishops who "convened councils and issued what decrees they pleased, often condemning unheard those whose creed was dissimilar to their own, and striving to their utmost to induce the reigning prince and nobles of the time to side with them" (*Hist. eccl.* 1.1.15).

6. Snyder, *Ante Pacem: Archaeological Evidence of Church Life before Constantine* (Macon, Ga.: Mercer University Press, 1985). Snyder built on the earlier work of Robert Thouless (*Conventionalization and Assimilation in Religious Movements as Problems in Social Psychology* [Oxford: Oxford University Press, 1940]); Robert Redfield (*Peasant Society and Culture* [Chicago: University of Chicago Press, 1956]); and McKim Marriott ("Little Communities in an Indigenous Civilization," in idem, ed., *Village India* [Chicago: University of Chicago Press, 1955] 197–200).

7. *Ante Pacem*, 10.

In what follows I will briefly look at the narrative of the *Apocalypse of Peter* and its place in early Christianity. This will lead to an examination of the place of suffering and the redemption that is promised to the righteous disciples of Jesus, to the successors of those original apostles, and to all who believe through them. Finally, I will conclude by noting the change in the function of this Petrine *Apocalypse*: from a moral treatise exhorting an acceptance of suffering on the part of the community to an affirmation of the redemptive suffering of Jesus rather than the community.

Content and Influence of the *Apocalypse of Peter*

Dating probably from the first third of the second century, the *Apocalypse of Peter* relates a postresurrection dialogue between Jesus, Peter, and other unnamed disciples while together on a mountain.[8] In the course of seventeen chapters Jesus reveals to his disciples the signs both of the end of the age and of his own return. He also discloses the fate of all, both sinners and righteous, in the afterlife. After Moses and Elijah appear glorified on the mountain, the narrative concludes with the ascension of Moses, Elijah, and Jesus. Throughout the discourse the greatest attention is paid to the lot of sinners. The tone of the narrative is established from the outset, as the prologue to the *Apocalypse* introduces the work as "The narrative of Peter (concerning) the second coming of Christ and the resurrection of the dead who died on account of their sins because they did not observe the commands of God their creator."[9] In all, ten full chapters are devoted to a "tour of hell," describing graphically the punishments awaiting those who fail to live a life of righteousness.[10] This emphasis serves as an exhortation to the community out of which this text was written: the message of Jesus revealed in the *Apocalypse of Peter* has been entrusted to the successors of those first disciples, and that message is to be heeded.

The *Apocalypse of Peter* quickly became a part of the great tradition. Patristic authors such as Clement of Alexandria, Methodius of Olympus, and Macarius Magnes quote from the work.[11] Indeed, for all three it is at or al-

---

8. For recent studies, see the following: Richard Bauckham, "The Apocalypse of Peter: An Account of Research," *ANRW* 2.25.6 (1988) 4712–49; Dennis D. Buchholz, *Your Eyes Will Be Opened: A Study of the Greek (Ethiopic) Apocalypse of Peter* (SBLDS 97; Atlanta: Scholars Press, 1988); Julian V. Hills, "Parables, Pretenders, and Prophecies: Translation and Interpretation in the Apocalypse of Peter 2," *RB* 98 (1991) 560–73; Bauckham, "The Apocalypse of Peter: A Jewish Christian Apocalypse from the Time of Bar Kokhba," *Apocrypha* 5 (1994) 7–111; Robert C. Helmer, " 'That We May Know and Understand': Gospel Tradition in the Apocalypse of Peter" (Ph.D. diss., Marquette University, 1998).

9. ET my own; the prologue does not appear in Müller's translation.

10. The term "tour of hell" comes from the work of Martha Himmelfarb, *Tours of Hell: An Apocalyptic Form in Jewish and Christian Literature* (Philadelphia: Fortress, 1983).

11. Clement *Ecl. proph.* 41; 48; Methodius *Symp.* 6; Macarius *Apocr.* 4.6.16; 4.7.

most on a par with scripture.[12] As regards liturgical practices, both the *Canon Muratori* and the *Codex Claromontanus* list this apocalypse among the NT writings considered canonical and acceptable.[13] And as late as the ninth century the *Stichometry of Nicephorus*, while maintaining that the *Apocalypse of Peter* (along with Revelation, *Barnabas*, and the *Gospel of the Hebrews*) is not recognized, does not go so far as to place it among the "apocrypha."[14]

Whence came the authority of this apocalypse? Within the narrative, the authority of Jesus and the authority of his disciples are intertwined. Jesus' authority is clear from the start. As the narrative opens, the resurrected Jesus is seated as teacher and the disciples worship him.[15] Jesus describes the signs of the close of the age and of his return, a discourse that serves as a preface to his climactic declaration that all this will take place so that "I might judge the living and the dead. And I will pay everyone back according to his deeds" (1.7c–8). Finally, in the concluding scenes of *Apoc. Pet.* 15–17, Moses and Elijah appear (both in glorified form) with Jesus on a mountain.[16] A voice from heaven affirms that "this is my beloved son, with whom I am pleased," and issues the command, "Obey him!" (17.1; ET my own). Thus the revelation of Jesus is validated and decreed normative.

The authority of Jesus is then passed on to the disciples who are with him, and to Peter in particular.[17] In *Apoc. Pet.* 1.2–3 the disciples ask for the signs of Jesus' coming and the close of the age. They seek this information both for themselves and for future believers. They explain further that they have made this request so that they "may perceive and mark the time of thy Parousia" (1.2), so that they may "instruct those who come after us, to whom

---

12. For example, Clement refers to the writing as "scripture" (ἡ γραφή); Methodius considers it as "among the inspired writings" (ἐν θεοπνεύστοις ἀγγέλοις). On Clement's concept of canon and use of the term γραφή, see James A. Brooks, "Clement of Alexandria as a Witness to the Development of the New Testament Canon," *SecCent* 9 (1992) 41–55.

13. Wilhelm Schneemelcher, "The Canon Muratori" and "The Catalogue in the Codex Claromontanus," in idem, *New Testament Apocrypha* 1. 34–36, 37. The former states that "of the revelations we accept only those of John and Peter"; the latter numbers the *Apocalypse of Peter* with Acts and Revelation as canonical.

14. Wilhelm Schneemelcher, "The Stichometry of Nicephorus," in idem, *New Testament Apocrypha* 1. 41–42.

15. In early Christian art, the figure of Jesus as teacher is found relatively infrequently. Snyder points to two sarcophagus sculptures possibly of a seated Jesus with an open scroll. According to Snyder, "the teaching Jesus had a function in the early faith community. While it implies the authority of Jesus, it stresses more the function of Jesus as mediator of revelation or authoritative teaching" (*Ante Pacem*, 61).

16. Presumably Jesus has already been glorified through the resurrection.

17. On the importance of Peter in early Christian writings, see David Henry Schmidt, "The Peter Writings: Their Redactors and Their Relationships" (Ph.D. diss., Northwestern University, 1972); Terence V. Smith, *Petrine Controversies in Early Christianity: Attitudes towards Peter in Christian Writings of the First Two Centuries* (WUNT 2/15; Tübingen: Mohr [Siebeck], 1985). Snyder notes that the graffiti under San Sebastiano include prayers written to "call upon the efforts of Peter and Paul. The importance of these graffiti cannot be overestimated, for they furnish us with a spontaneous picture of the life of the early Church" (*Ante Pacem*, 141).

we preach the word of thy Gospel and whom we install in thy Church, in order that they, when they hear it, may take heed to themselves that they mark the time of thy coming." It is the disciples (and their successors) that will carry forward the message of Jesus.

The second part of this rationale is reminiscent of Jesus' prayer in John 17:20–21: "I do not pray for these only, but also for those who believe in me through their word, that they may all be one; even as thou, Father, art in me, and I in thee, that they also may be in us, so that the world may believe that thou hast sent me." Here it is future Christians, perhaps the current community out of which John was written, that are envisioned.[18] Raymond E. Brown has commented regarding this Johannine passage that "the disciples are symbols of what believers should be."[19] In the context of *Apoc. Pet.* 1, the same is true. The signs and warnings are given to those first disciples of Jesus, and their proper response will ensure them the reward reserved for the righteous rather than the doom awaiting the sinful. But ultimately this *Apocalypse* is not about those disciples, whether in history or in tradition. Instead it is the response of future disciples, and in particular the response of the community out of which the *Apocalypse* was written, that concerns the author. As in John 17:20–21, Peter and the other disciples function as "symbols of what believers should be."

Suffering and the Reward of the Righteous

The disciples are repeatedly summoned to a life of righteousness, a righteousness that will lead to eternal reward. The rest that they are promised will be enjoyed with those righteous who preceded them in death, among whom are Moses, Elijah, Abraham, Isaac, and Jacob. The goal of all believers is to have their name included among "the names of the righteous in heaven" that are written in "the book of life" (*Apoc. Pet.* 17.7). The revelation of the *Apocalypse of Peter* is that to pursue righteousness is properly to discern the signs of the times and to accept willingly the suffering of the present age. To pursue righteousness does not entail a flight from this world. Rather, the suffering of this world is to be endured in the hope that God will provide reward and rest in the afterlife.

For example, in *Apoc. Pet.* 1.4–5 Jesus predicts the arrival of many false christs at the end of the age. He cautions his disciples, "Take heed that men

---

18. George R. Beasley-Murray notes that this is "the only explicit petition within the prayer [in John 17] on behalf of the Church in its historical existence" (*John* [WBC 36; Dallas: Word, 1987] 301).

19. Brown, *The Gospel according to John XIII–XXI* (AB 29A; Garden City, N.Y.: Doubleday, 1970) 773–74. See also Rudolf Schnackenburg, *The Gospel according to St. John* (3 vols.; HTKNT; 1975; New York: Crossroad, 1982) 3. 190.

deceive you not and that ye do not become doubters and serve other gods."
A little later Jesus continues the discussion about these false christs. He prepares the disciples for the suffering to come, warning them that a rejected
false christ will "kill with the sword, and there shall be many martyrs" (2.10).
Suffering is to be the lot of the disciples in this world. However, Jesus promises that "they that are slain by his hand...shall be reckoned among the good
and righteous martyrs who have pleased God in their life" (2.13).

At the close of the narrative the disciples behold the appearance of Moses
and Elijah in glorified form. It is not possible for the disciples to look at them
because light "which shone more than the sun" comes from their faces and
garments (*Apoc. Pet.* 15.2). This tradition of physical appearance manifesting
righteousness is found, among other places, in Dan 12:3 "And those who are
wise shall shine like the brightness of the firmament; and those who turn
many to righteousness, like the stars for ever and ever."[20] Upon witnessing
Moses and Elijah, Peter inquires of Jesus in *Apoc. Pet.* 16.1, "(Where then
are) Abraham, Isaac, Jacob and the other righteous fathers?" In response,
Jesus shows the disciples a "great open garden...full of fair trees and blessed
fruits, full of the fragrance of perfume" (16.2–3). Jesus declares that "this is
the honour and glory of those who will be persecuted for my righteousness'
sake" (16.5). The narrative concludes with Jesus, Moses, and Elijah ascending
into heaven and the disciples descending the mountain, praising God "who
hath written the names of the righteous in heaven in the book of life" (17.7).

The tradition of suffering in this world being followed by the restful reward of the righteous in the world to come has been documented by Snyder
in the pictorial evidence, particularly in sepulchral scenes, of early Christianity. Among these scenes the figure of the *orante* is prominent.[21] Snyder
concludes that the female figure of the *orante* occurs more frequently than
any other in Christianity ca. 180 and that "she must be the most important
symbol in early Christian art."[22] He notes the presence of the *orante* in such
OT narratives as the Jonah cycle, Daniel in the lion's den, the three young
men in the fiery furnace, and Susannah and the elders. In each instance, the
she represents "peace, which can come from God through the faith commu-

---

20. See also 4 Ezra 7:125: "the faces of those who practiced self-control shall shine more
than the stars"; *2 Baruch* 51.3: "those who proved to be righteous on account of my law...their
splendor will then be glorified by transformation, and the shape of their face will be changed
into the light of their beauty"; *2 Enoch* 66.7: "How happy are the righteous who shall escape the
Lord's great judgment; for they will be made to shine seven times brighter than the sun."

21. The *orante* is a "standing female figure with arms stretched above her head." This symbol,
inserted into biblical scenes, has "come from the local tradition but has adapted a translocal
scenario." Its Roman usage was to represent filial piety and security. This symbolism is then
taken over in Christian art, differing in its application primarily in that "the faith community
family was a religious association, not an extended blood relationship" (*Ante Pacem,* 19–20).

22. Ibid., 19.

nity whenever one faces individualized threat from external sources."[23] For example, the scene of the three young men "must surely represent survival and peace in a very hostile environment"; likewise, Susannah's appearance as an *orante* indicates her *pax* despite the harassment, which could end in capital punishment."[24] The presence of these scenes on sarcophagi indicates that, while the believer suffered in this life, the Christian community firmly believed that the suffering individual or group now enjoyed the restful reward symbolized by the *orante*.

This pictorial evidence mirrors the literary evidence of the *Apocalypse of Peter*. The world of the disciples is about to become hostile to them, full of deceivers, temptations, and suffering. The believer is challenged to produce the fruit of righteousness, unlike the unfruitful fig tree of *Apoc. Pet.* 2.5–6. The promise is made, however, that should a disciple prove worthy of his or her calling, then that one will enjoy the reward of the righteous along with these OT figures.[25]

From Moral Treatise to Statement of Faith

In tracing the figure of the *orante* in sepulchral art, Snyder makes the following observation: "When the environment was no longer hostile to the Christian, when the Christian community was no longer harassed qua Christian, then the pictorial symbol of a peaceful Orante amidst critical (biblical) situations no longer served a useful purpose. It lost its value in the social matrix."[26] The *orante*, then, once the "most popular element of early Christian symbolism," ceased to be used in the post-Constantinian world.

In similar fashion, the function of the *Apocalypse of Peter* evolved between the time of its origin in the second century and its use by Palestinian communities in the fifth century. In its original setting, the narrative of the *Apocalypse* centered on the conduct of the community out of which it was

---

23. Ibid., 49–50.

24. Ibid., 54, 50.

25. As the year 2000 draws ever nearer, there will be much discussion and much writing about the "signs of the times." No doubt a great deal of effort will be spent by various Christian communities trying to adapt the great tradition to their local practices and way of life. This will be particularly so of groups who perceive the world as unfriendly, even hostile, to the Christian way of life. One is hard pressed to wait in the checkout line at the local supermarket without encountering a variety of tabloid publications that proclaim the imminent fulfillment of some biblical prophecy (or better yet, a Dead Sea Scroll prophecy). For example, recall David Koresh or the Heaven's Gate movement of recent memory. These relatively small groups of believers interpreted the signs of the times (David Koresh specialized in biblical texts; the Heaven's Gate movement in the celestial course of the Hale-Bopp comet) and acted accordingly. When communities arrange their common life around nonnormative interpretations of the great tradition, how can the larger faith community intercede without appearing to be yet another example of the unfriendly and hostile world?

26. Snyder, *Ante Pacem*, 49.

written. It was a moral treatise, summoning the members of that community to lives of righteousness, perhaps in the face of persecution, suffering, even martyrdom. In this way, the punishments that await the sinful will be avoided, and the restful reward of the righteous will be attained.

By the time of the fifth century account of Sozomen, however, a change has seemingly taken place. It is not the righteousness and suffering of the community that is the focus, but rather the righteousness and suffering of Jesus. The moral exhortation of the *Apocalypse of Peter* has become a statement of faith in the saving grace of Jesus' death on the cross. As Sozomen writes, it is the "recollection of the suffering of the Savior" that is at the heart of the Good Friday observances, and it is in the course of these observances that the *Apocalypse* is read.

Early Christian art provides a striking parallel to this change. Through the time of Constantine, Jesus is represented in art as a wonder-worker. As Snyder notes, "from 180 to 400 artistic analogies of self-giving, suffering, sacrifice . . . are totally missing." Rather, in the pre-Constantinian era Jesus was understood "in an alienation-deliverance structure."[27] The world was a hostile place for Christians, and they were therefore in need of rescue. Granted, the fulfillment of the rescue would be achieved after death, but the deliverance was evidently real to the Christian believer nonetheless. And that deliverance came about through the young heroic redeemer, Jesus.

It is after Constantine that the figure of Jesus slowly assumes the role of suffering savior. Snyder observes that "the suffering Christ on a cross first appeared in the fifth century, and then not very convincingly."[28] The use of the *Apocalypse of Peter* in liturgical services in the fifth century provides literary support for Snyder's remarks on the beginnings of this new tradition. Gone is the call to righteousness, and in its place is the celebration that, rather than the individual's being summoned to judgment for his or her own sins, Jesus has already done the suffering for that person. The local practice of the fifth-century Palestinian Christians had adapted the great tradition to the common life of their communities.

---

27. Ibid., 165.
28. Ibid. Snyder documents that "the cross, as an artistic reference to the passion event, cannot be found prior to the time of Constantine" (ibid., 27).

PART FIVE

COMMON LIFE IN ART, ARCHITECTURE, AND MUSIC

23

PRESENCE AND ABSENCE IN EARLY CHRISTIAN ART

ROBERT E. WAGONER

When I traveled to Rome several years ago, my curiosity about early Christian art had been greatly stimulated by Graydon Snyder's *Ante Pacem,* so I made a point of visiting the Vatican museums, the catacombs, and as many of the oldest churches I could find in order to see for myself what could be learned. I was surprised both by what I saw and what I did not see. What I encountered did not seem to me to be recognizably "Christian," nor did it seem to be "art" by conventional standards. No images of Christ, the passion, crucifixion, or the resurrection. No pictures of judgment, heaven or hell. A few images seemed to correspond to the gospel narratives, but most appeared to be illustrations of oddly marginal OT scenes. Moreover, the quality of most of these images was rather crude and distinctly lacking in aesthetic appeal. What I found was puzzling, often enigmatic, and at variance with my naive expectations. The experience not only led me to reconsider my notions about art and how it functions but also to rethink what I thought I knew about Christian origins.

My first efforts to understand what I saw in Rome proceeded on the assumption that the absence of certain images was due to the hostility of the early church to anything suggesting idolatry. This understanding was stated most definitively by Ernst Kitzinger in 1954.[1] The emergence of artistic imagery in the fourth century, according to this argument, was due to pressures from the laity against the clergy's iconophobic adherence to the second commandment, another instance of the more general way in which hellenistic

---

1. Kitzinger, "The Cult of images before Iconoclasm," *Dumbarton Oaks Papers* 8 (1954) 83–150, esp. 89.

influence supposedly compromised the integrity of the early church.[2] Sister Charles Murray, however, has undertaken a careful review of the whole
matter and has shown rather conclusively that this argument depended on
reading the issues of the later iconoclastic controversy (726–843) back into
the early centuries. Her analysis of the documents found "very little indication indeed that the Fathers of the early Church were in any way opposed
to art,"[3] and therefore iconoclastic motives cannot be used to account for
the images that appeared, or did not appear, in the catacombs as early as the
second century.

Another supposition on my part was that fear of persecution may have
kept the early church from making images expressing the content of their
faith. But recent scholarship discounts this as a general and pervasive influence. Paul Corby Finney describes the environment of the early Christians as
"unfriendly in some places, hostile in others, and probably indifferent or even
friendly in still other places" — but not one of systematic persecution.[4] There
were martyrs, to be sure, but the fact that early Christian apologists — Tertullian being the most notorious — spoke out quite openly and aggressively
also makes it clear that early Christianity was quite capable of explicit verbal
expression, so why not artistic? Finney's thesis that they had simply not yet
achieved the appropriate material means to shape a sense of group identity
reduces the significance of early Christian art to being nothing more than an
early phase of economic development.[5] This set me to wondering: why not
look at these images as deliberate choices? Why not see them for what they
are instead of what they are not?

My intent here will be to show why I think most modern and traditional concepts of art are inappropriate to deal with the images devised by
the early Christian communities and to try to come away with a glimmer
of appreciation both for what is present in early Christian art and for what
is not present. To do this, we have to reconsider systematically some of our
cultivated preconceptions about art.

First, we have to recognize that the typically modernist preoccupation with
art in terms of "aesthetics" — values accessible only to a distinctive kind of
awareness — does not serve us very well with respect to the earliest examples of Christian art. To view something aesthetically, I must try to see it as

---

2. The history of this interpretation is summarized in Paul Corby Finney, *The Invisible God:
The Earliest Christians on Art* (New York: Oxford University Press, 1994) 3–14.

3. Murray, *Rebirth and Afterlife: A Study of the Transmutation of Some Pagan Imagery in Early
Christian Funerary Art* (Oxford: B. A. R., 1981); see chap. 1, "Art and the Early Church" (pp. 13–
36), esp. 34–36.

4. Finney, *Invisible God*, 19.

5. "The truth is simple and mundane: Christians lacked land and capital. Art required both.
As soon as they acquired land and capital, Christians began to experiment with their own
distinctive forms of art" (ibid., 108).

unique — as it is in itself — not comparable with other things, nor as something explainable by concepts or theories. The special function of art has to be understood on its own terms, not as a means to any end other than the *expression* of feeling or the representation of certain *forms* of feeling that engage our interest independently of practical value or moral approval. The notion of an "aesthetic object," in other words, requires an "aesthetic subject."[6] Highest priority is of course given to original and refined works of art capable of engaging sophisticated sensibilities. This is what "aesthetics" is all about. Whether in its elitist or populist form, however, the modern attitude holds that control of the value and meaning of an aesthetic object resides in an autonomous mentality — "Beauty is in the eye of the beholder."

But it would be difficult to see the fading images on the walls and ceilings of third-century Christian catacombs in Rome as aesthetic objects. To be sure, the dampness and stale air have not been kind to the images over the centuries. Even so, they appear rather amateurish — flat, sketchy, more like graffiti than works of art. There is little about them that grabs the eye in terms of expressive power and even less to admire with respect to technical skill or formal elegance. To contemplate these images for their aesthetic interest would be rather disappointing. There seems to be no attempt to draw the viewer's admiring gaze to the Christian message by means of aesthetic appeal, as later Byzantine art would do so successfully. Moreover, without foreknowledge of the biblical stories and Orphic scenes to which they refer, they would be unintelligible as well as unappealing. Perhaps the reason these images were not more artful was economic — that is, perhaps the Christian occupants could not afford the kind of artisans who could make aesthetically appealing images.[7] Or perhaps, as I shall argue, the makers or authorizers of these images did not consider them to be forms of art in the first place.

Interestingly enough, however, there are works of art belonging to Christians from the fourth century that have outstanding aesthetic appeal, such as the beautiful mosaic ceiling in the ambulatory of Santa Costanza (the mausoleum of Constantine's daughter)[8] and the elegant silver casket belonging to a Christian lady, Projecta (now in the British Museum).[9] The subject matter in Santa Costanza is entirely Dionysian — extraordinary mosaics depicting vintage scenes and vine tendrils with grapes, and a profusion of erotes, exotic

---

6. Immanuel Kant: "The judgment of taste is not a judgment of cognition, and is consequently not logical but aesthetical, by which we understand that whose determining ground can be no other but speculative" (*Critique of Judgment* [New York: Hafner, 1951] 37).

7. See Finney, *Invisible God*, 153.

8. André Grabar, *Early Christian Art* (New York: Odyssey, 1968) 187–91 (figs. 202–6).

9. Jas Elsner, *Art and the Roman Viewer* (Cambridge: Cambridge University Press, 1995) pl. 3, figs. 58, 59.

birds, as well as busts of Constantia and other persons — although apparently
the central dome originally included some OT scenes.[10] The designs on the
luxurious silver casket suggestively juxtapose the toilet of Venus with that of
Projecta herself. We know she is a Christian lady only by the inscription on
the edge of the lid — "SECUNDE ET PROJECTA VIVATIS IN CHRISTO."
Obviously neither the first Christian princess, Constantia, nor the Christian
lady, Projecta, disdained fine art, nor did either one see any problem in using artistic forms representing pagan deities. Art seemed to have nothing to
do with being Christian. And in the case of the catacomb painters, being
Christian had nothing to do with art. In these early centuries there seems to
be a definite disconnection between Christianity and fine art — not that the
latter was proscribed or prohibited but that there was no necessary relation
between them. Two quite different realms.

One important exception to this is the tomb of the Julii found in the third-
century necropolis excavated underneath St. Peter's basilica.[11] The walls and
ceiling of the tomb are decorated by an overall visual scheme in which three
wall images (fisherman, good shepherd, and Jonah) and a striking ceiling mosaic of a solar charioteer are linked together by a naturalistic depiction of
a vine with a profusion of tooth-edged leaves rendered in three different
shades of bright green. Obviously aesthetic considerations do play a role in
this tomb, and the overall effect is quite compelling. The vine-scroll is a familiar Dionysian motif in the hellenistic art of the day, carrying the ancient
meaning of wine as a life-giving divinity but also evoking the idea of Dionysus as a dying and rising god. Vine-scrolls were used to decorate and frame
compositions all over the Roman world,[12] sometimes for the specific celebration of the cult of Bacchus, sometimes for funerary purposes, but also for
more general representations of nature as peaceful and bountiful, as in the
ambulatory of Santa Costanza, which the decoration in the Julii tomb somewhat resembles. The curious thing about the vine in the tomb of the Julii is
the absence of grapes, which is explained by Murray as a deliberate omission
by its Christian owners in order to avoid any association with drunkenness.[13]
Possibly so, but the absence of grapes might also have been a matter of simplicity of design in order to focus attention on the vitality of the vine, rather
than its fruitfulness. Or perhaps the angler, the good shepherd and Jonah *are*
the fruits.

---

10. Susannah and the elders, Cain and Abel, Elijah on Mt. Carmel, among others, were
recorded in some Renaissance drawings; see Henri Stern, "Les mosaïques de l'église de
Sainte-Constance à Rome," *Dumbarton Oaks Papers* 12 (1958) 157–218, esp. 166–80.

11. Grabar, *Early Christian Art*, 80 (fig. 74); also Murray, *Rebirth and Afterlife*, figs. 17–19.

12. See "The Dionysos Mosaic" in R. M. Nagy et al., eds., *Sepphoris in Galilee* (Raleigh, N.C.:
North Carolina Museum of Art, 1996), for a recently excavated splendid example of Dionysian
art in the early third century CE, only four miles from Nazareth.

13. Murray, *Rebirth and Afterlife*, 89.

That it was a Christian tomb seems to be well established, even though the meaning of the Helios-Sungod figure is open to some question. Murray builds up a painstaking argument based on a careful analysis of writings of Tertullian and especially Clement of Alexandria to show that the images symbolize a soteriological sequence culminating in the "triumphant entry of the Christian believer into heaven, harnessed to the chariot of Christ, after he has died with him." Hence its appropriateness in the mausoleum of a believer, she concludes.[14] She may be right. The archeological and textual evidence assembled by Murray is in any case impressive, and her argument is cogent.

What strikes me, however, is that the images themselves are ambiguous, especially the Helios figure, widely disseminated at the time, which we should note also appears in slightly different form in a nearby *non-Christian* tomb. Does it refer to Christ or to the sun that dies and rises each day? Interpretation of the Helios becomes especially problematic if we consider reports that the Emperor Constantine raised a statue of himself in the guise of the sun atop a fifty-meter column and had another image of himself placed in a Sun-chariot to be driven among torches around the hippodrome.[15] The fact is that the doctrine of salvation that Murray attributes to the images is nowhere evident in the images themselves. I saw no believer hitched to the chariot, nor did I see anything to assure me that the Helios figure was indeed Christ. My point is that the coherent meaning provided by Murray's argument is the coherence of *theological doctrine*. Text and idea rule image. She is explicit about this in her introduction: "I believe a text is needed to control meaning in a picture. . . ."[16] Her approach, in other words, is a variation of the modern view that aesthetic significance is conferred and controlled by consciousness — in this case, a doctrinally informed consciousness.

Alternately, however, if one gives primacy to *visual* experience rather than to argument,[17] the coherence of images in the tomb of the Julii actually depends entirely on the exuberant vine and its very green leaves spreading up and around the chariot of Helios and down to the angler, good shepherd, and Jonah. What holds these disparate images together and energizes them is the vital physicality of the vine and its leaves. This is what fills the eye most immediately. Instead of a logical program of salvation, the vision presented in the tomb of the Julii is of irrepressible and superabundant *life* touching first one figure and then another as one's eyes move over the scene. The specific meanings of the charioteer, the angler, the shepherd, even Jonah, are elusive

---

14. Ibid., 95–96.
15. Ramsay MacMullen, "The Meaning of A.D. 312: The Difficulty of Converting the Empire," *17th International Congress of Byzantine Studies, Dumbarton Oaks, Washington, D.C.* (New Rochelle, N.Y.: Aristide Caratzas, 1986) 4.
16. Murray, *Rebirth and Afterlife*, 11.
17. See Maurice Merleau-Ponty, *The Primacy of Perception* (Evanston, Ill.: Northwestern University Press, 1964).

and open — who *are* these people? — but there is no mistaking the dynamic flow of life that connects them.

My general point here is that from a modernist standpoint these early Christian images are either trivialized as (not very satisfying) "aesthetic objects" or their genuine visual impact is overruled by subordinating them to canons of textual authority. Ambiguity is hard to live with — even when we recognize, as Murray certainly does, that "the very 'openness' of some of the symbols of early Christian art may be deliberate."[18] But actually confronting these uncertainties may yield more actual new insights than reiterating doctrines already known.

In major contrast to the subjectivity of modernist views of art is the great classical tradition that is forcibly impressed upon one simply by walking around the city of Rome. Everywhere one looks there are splendid examples of classical architecture and sculpture — the Ara Pacis, the Arch of Constantine, the jumble of temples in the Forum, the Pantheon. The museums on Capitoline Hill and the Museo Nazionale Romano in the Baths of Diocletian, as well as the Pio-Clementine at the Vatican, are full of superb examples of classical sculpture. But it is important to note that such works as the newly restored equestrian statue of Marcus Aurelius and the colossal heads of Constantine and Alexander the Great are more than mere representations of Roman and Greek emperors. The canons of symmetry and proportion that shaped them are just as essential as their resemblance to historical personalities. They and the sculptures of Greek gods by Pheidias and Praxiteles are the embodiment of transcendent ideals as much as they are imitations of human form. Art may be the imitation of nature, but nature itself must be seen as the replication of a reality still more perfect.

But when one descends to the third-century catacombs of Callistus and of Domitilla and Priscilla, the aesthetic ideal everywhere apparent above ground seems nowhere apparent below.[19] To be sure, the artifacts are fragile wall paintings rather than sculptures of stone, and the narrow corridors do not offer much scope for the development of architectural space. But it is obvious that the dim, shadowy figures are not attempts at naturalistic representation, still less attempts at idealization, even of heroes of the faith. Instead, one finds sketchy, impressionistic renditions of Daniel in the lions' den, the three Hebrew children in the fiery furnace, Susannah and the elders, Jonah and the whale, Noah and the ark, Abraham and Isaac, along with such symbols

---

18. Murray, *Rebirth and Afterlife*, 10–11.

19. "No distinctively Christian art predates the year 200," says Finney (*Invisible God*, 99); he finds the art of the Callistus tomb to represent "the first Christians committed to the use of pictures in religious places" (146–228). Grabar also finds no Christian art prior to 200 and takes the catacombs of Domitilla and Priscilla, particularly the so-called Greek chapel, as the best examples of the earliest Christian art (*Early Christian Art*, 81–121).

as fish, anchor, peacock, and dove. Of the few NT images, the raising of Lazarus is the most understandable, given the context.

Most perplexing is the near total lack of images of Jesus, or of Christ as suffering, crucified, and risen, or as moral teacher, lawgiver, or judge. "The absence of portraits, for example, of Jesus and Mary and the apostles, is indeed a striking feature of pre-Constantinian Christian art," observes Finney.[20] Erwin R. Goodenough makes a similar observation about the paintings found in the fourth-century Via Latina catacombs.[21] Since the catacombs by their very nature were relatively private places, and not very pleasant to visit, fear of scrutiny by imperial authorities or a hostile public seems unlikely. In an age known for its skills at portraiture, therefore, all the more puzzling is the deliberate avoidance of any attempt to make images based on physical resemblance or images that would register something distinct about Jesus' personality. Even Murray concedes that "in third- and fourth-century art Christ appears either as a symbolic figure: good shepherd, fisherman, or in the painted and sculpted scenes where he is shown in the teacher/philosopher type not really differentiated from the surrounding figures. He never appears isolated as a cult image, and there is no attempt to depict him as a real and distinctive personality."[22] That is, to push the point a bit further, what "appears" in these symbols is a notable absence: nothing in the earliest visual evidence is a sure indicator of the Christ-event, and this at a time almost exactly coincident with the formation of the NT canon. The quest of the *iconic* Jesus turns out to be even more frustrating and inconclusive than the nineteenth-century quest of the *historical* Jesus!

Even the paintings on the walls of the earliest known Christian church building found in Dura-Europos, Syria, also dating from the early third century, do not significantly alter this judgment. Specifically NT subject matters were depicted in this building — the three Marys at the tomb, the healing of the paralytic, Christ and Peter walking on the water, the Samaritan woman at the well, but again, very sketchy and unskilled artwork — and no representational images.[23] The making of these images paid no more attention to the imitation of natural forms than was necessary to suggest the story that they illustrated. Considerations of proportion or symmetry or ideal forms were ignored, as well as any individuating characteristics. By the standards of classical art one would have to say that these images were a failure. If art is

---

20. Finney, *Invisible God*, 86.

21. "No cross, let alone Crucifixion scene has appeared and this same absence is one of the most surprising features of catacomb art in general." There is no "Last Judgment," and "Christ himself never is presented directly as the 'firstfruits of those that sleep'" (Goodenough, "Catacomb Art," *JBL* 81 [1962] 136).

22. Murray, "Art and the Early Church," *JTS* n.s. 28 (1977) 329.

23. Grabar, *Early Christian Art*, 68–71, figs. 59–63.

defined as *mimesis* — the imitation of a natural reality or an ideal pattern — then early Christian images are not art.

This may have been part of a much larger change in Roman viewing practices in late antiquity. Jas Elsner has shown that there was a general turn away from simple naturalism toward a more symbolic mode of seeing in all forms of art — from architecture and rhetoric to wall painting and mosaics. Art became more abstract and exegetic, not because of lack of skill, but out of a desire to go "beyond" the illusions of ordinary sight. Typological images and allegorical interpretations were preferred because it was the vision of *meaning* that counted, not accurate visual representation.[24] The gain in intellectual depth, however, was at the price of stable understanding. The same image might be seen in profoundly different ways by Christians and non-Christians, even by the same person.

The irony is that the notion of art as mimesis, originally used by Plato (*Rep.* 10.596–98) to deprecate the use of visible images to represent invisible truth, was inverted by later Christian apologists and employed in successive steps to justify the use of icons — first as educational tools, then as intermediate anagogical reflections of divine reality, and finally, at the Trullan Synod of 692 (also known as the Quinisext or Fifth-Sixth Council), as visual declarations of the doctrine of the incarnation. "In Christ God had become man and therefore capable of visual representation," Kitzinger recounts, and this led to the conviction that images were not only permissible but "even a re-enactment" of the incarnation — virtually equivalent to the sacrament of the mass in their spiritual efficacy. This growing insistence on the naturalistic depiction of Christ as real man in real flesh-and-blood representations led to actual condemnation of the early church's use of abstract symbols. "The determination to eliminate even the last remnants of Early Christian symbolism is remarkable," notes Kitzinger.[25] This polarizing reversal soon erupted in the bitter and divisive iconoclastic controversy.

If neither modern nor classical theories of art seem to be the appropriate lenses through which to see the artifacts of pre-Constantinian Christians, then perhaps we have to give up looking at them as works of art. Hans Belting does just this in his "history of the image before the era of art,"[26] which argues that the significance of early medieval images is in their effectiveness as instruments of power rather than as aesthetic objects. To regard them as the latter is to miss the point. They were not so much *admired* for their beauty as they were *venerated* for their success in mediating divine power (miracles, for example). The "likeness" of these images to the divine did not consist

24. Elsner, *Art and the Roman Viewer*, 18–19.
25. Kitzinger, "Cult of Images," 142–43.
26. This subtitle of Belting's *Likeness and Presence* (Chicago: University of Chicago Press, 1994).

in their physical attractiveness or in their imitation of appearances but in their *effects*, what they made happen in the lives of their worshipers. They were kissed, clothed, paraded, knelt before — in other words, treated like personages who could *act*, not just be looked at.[27]

Holy images have always stood in tension with the theologians, argues Belting, because they acted directly on the lives of the faithful, quite independent of texts, canons, and ecclesiastical authority. Far from setting up images and instituting their worship, the theologians were usually in the position of trying to limit their influence: "Only after the faithful had resisted all such efforts against their favorite images did theologians settle for issuing conditions and limitations governing access to them. Theologians were satisfied only when they could 'explain' the images."[28] The struggle between the power of images and the power of the word climaxed in the iconoclastic controversy, which was resolved by near-total victory for images in the (Orthodox) East but only a qualified victory in the (Roman Catholic) West; the latter eventually led to complete subordination of images to the Word in the Reformation.[29]

Belting's richly documented history does not begin until after the Constantinian period — when funerary portraits for memorial purposes begin to acquire power as cult images — but his point stands: *images have power.* To regard them merely as static aesthetic objects or to read them as "reflections" or "expressions" of historical forces originating elsewhere fails to take seriously their own capacity to shape the world of which they are a part. Therefore, even though Belting does not deal with pre-Constantinian Christian artifacts, let us take his point as established that it would be a mistake to regard them as works of art that are to be accounted for by the usual kinds of iconographic or historical analysis. But there is no evidence to show that the earliest Christian images brought about miracles, cures, visions, or the like. Nor do they seem to have served as objects of worship and veneration through which access to the divine might be gained. So what kind of "power" did they have? How did these images "work" on their world?

"Don't think," said Ludwig Wittgenstein, "but look!"[30]

These frescoes and wall paintings are usually rough sketches, grouped sometimes one way, sometimes another, with no apparent central focus. Be-

---

27. Ibid., 6, 531–32.

28. Ibid., 1.

29. John Calvin: "The Holy Spirit is so bound to its truth that it can only express its power... when its word is perceived" (quoted in Belting, *Likeness and Presence*, 550).

30. Wittgenstein, *Philosophical Investigations*, vol. 1 (New York: Macmillan, 1953) 66 (31e). What Wittgenstein meant, of course, is not that simple perception resolves all difficulties, but that understanding of languages and images requires putting aside all extrinsic explanations about what they ought to mean and looking instead to see their implicit rules within context, intentions, etc., and accepting the way they are used as a "given." See also vol. 2, xi (193e–226e).

cause they are artistically unrefined, somewhat like crude caricatures, and therefore unappealing in themselves, the viewer's attention necessarily shifts to what they signify — the good shepherd, Jonah, Noah, Daniel in the lions' den, the three Hebrew children, Susannah and the elders. The images do not actually narrate the stories but point away from themselves like signs to remind viewers of stories they already know. In a general way, interpreters point out, the theme of most of the images is soteriological — referring to stories of salvation. They are "tokens of God's works and deeds," argues Finney. Instead of direct representations of the divine in a picture, "what they represented was God's *erga* personified in certain key figures who had been beneficiaries and recipients of God's deeds." They are "signs or tokens of divine intervention," Finney suggests, that may have served as visual "petitionary paradigms" or the focus for funerary prayers on behalf of the deceased.[31] But there is no evidence that such prayers preceded the images chronologically, nor is a connection between prayers and images anything more than supposition. In fact many of the same images do occur in other contexts, such as the Podgoritza plate that seems unlikely to have served such functions.[32] And the later insertion of three Jonah motifs in a (fourth-century) floor mosaic at Aquileia (in Venetia) alongside non-Christian images would suggest that their significance was not limited to funerary purposes and also that Christians saw no problem in putting Christian and non-Christian motifs together.[33]

The story of Jonah's sulky disobedience, moreover, doesn't exactly qualify him as a hero of faith, an appropriate focus for prayers. Perhaps the images of Jonah, Daniel, and Susannah are better understood not so much as soteriological but as *peripeteia* — "reversals" in which adverse expectations suddenly turn into their polar opposite. They are symbols of life lived contrary to ordinary expectations.

What about the good shepherd — is it an image of Christ? We know that Christians adopted it as their own, but we also know that it was a very popular image that originated long before Christianity and was, for Romans, a symbol of philanthropy.[34] While hiking in the mountains of Turkey, I once came upon a shepherd who was carrying a lamb across his shoulders in the "good shepherd" manner — but I could not tell whether he had rescued the lamb or was taking it home for slaughter. One of the oldest examples of this image, the similarly posed archaic "Calf Bearer" found on the Acropolis in

31. Finney, *Invisible God*, 281–83.
32. Ibid., 284–85.
33. Josef Engemann, "Christianization of Late Antique Art," *17th International Congress of Byzantine Studies*, 84–89.
34. "The sheep-carrier has a long pre-Christian history," notes Finney, "not just in Greece and Rome but also in the Near East," and it "acquired new (and often conflicting) levels of meaning" (*Invisible God*, 188–89).

Athens, was almost certainly carrying the animal to sacrifice.[35] The use of this image in the Christian baptistery at Dura-Europos, however, would not likely carry this implication — or would it?

One of the most enigmatic figures painted in six different Christian cata-combs as well as on early Christian sarcophagi is that of Orpheus charming the animals with his lyre.[36] One could readily imagine that the story of Or-pheus's rescue of Eurydice from the underworld might have been a helpful thought in the catacombs, but this episode is never pictured. Ancient tra-dition going all the way back to Plato (*Prot.* 316) and Pythagoras regarded Orpheus not as legendary but as a historical person and associated the mag-ical power of his music to tame wild beasts with the power of learning and philosophy to gain immortality through certain intellectual disciplines. This is strongly implied in the *Phaedo*, where Socrates, getting ready to face exe-cution, speaks of philosophy as "the highest music" and seeks, Orpheus-like, to "charm" his companions from their fear of death (61, 78). Orpheus, in other words, was a symbol of high culture, implying that personal immortality depended not on a "savior" but on taking proper care of one's soul. Murray explains how Christian apologists such as Clement of Alexandria worked hard to assimilate this Orphic intellectual eschatology to Christian purposes.[37] But the fact remains that there is nothing identifiably Christian about the image, and it could have been read in a way to make the message of the gospel quite superfluous.

Orphism seems to have been a sixth-century modification of Dionysian religion in Greece that introduced the idea of metempsychosis, the sepa-ration of the soul from the body at death and its reincarnation in succes-sive bodies.[38] A bone tablet found with the inscription, "life, death, life, truth, . . . Dio(nysoi), Orphikoi," could refer either to the transmigration of souls or to the continuation and rebirth of life itself (ζωή), not just of a sep-arable soul (ψυχή).[39] The ambiguity of the inscription may deliberately imply both meanings.[40]

"Dionysus," says Walter F. Otto, "is both life and death." In him life and

---

35. John Boardman, *Greek Art* (new rev. ed.; London: Thames and Hudson, 1985) pl. 65 (see also illustr. 54).

36. Murray, *Rebirth and Afterlife*, 37–63 ("The Christian Orpheus").

37. Ibid., 46–52.

38. In the *Meno*, Plato refers to "divinely inspired" poets who speak of the soul as immortal: "at one time it comes to an end — that which is called death — and at another is born again, but is never finally exterminated" (81B; also *Phaedr.* 249; *Rep.* 10.614).

39. Susan Guettel Cole, "Dionysus and the Dead," in T. H. Carpenter and C. A. Faraone, eds., *Masks of Dionysus* (Ithaca, N.Y.: Cornell University Press, 1993) 277.

40. The first line of two fourth-century BCE gold grave tablets found in Thessaly, cut in the shape of ivy leaves, reads: "Now you have died and now you have come into being, O thrice happy one, on this same day" (quoted in Fritz Graf, "Dionysian and Orphic Eschatology," *Masks of Dionysus,* 241). But why "thrice"?

death are not mutually exclusive, but are intertwined and even generated from each other.[41] As the god of wine he may be a personification of the process by which the crushed grape lives again in the joy-giving power of wine. But he is also known as the god of theater. Intoxication, dance, masquerade, trance, and illusion are his effects. Whenever he is present boundaries are blurred: human and divine, male and female, madness and sanity, ecstasy and brutality. Dionysus wears many masks, but they all "reveal their names to be Life and Death," says Otto.[42]

In Euripides Bacchae (406 BCE), Dionysus announces in his opening line, "I am the son of God (Zeus)," and then suffers rejection and abuse, but through the allure of sensual pleasure and his appeal to women, manages to subvert the establishment and bring about death and destruction. Some aspects of this play appear to anticipate certain Christian themes — its anti-establishment plot, the rejection and suffering of the "son of God," the benign and pacific appearance of the deity, and especially the affirmation of the "two powers supreme in human affairs," i.e., bread [Demeter] and wine [Dionysus] — as prototypical for the Christian eucharist.[43] Whether the Bacchae influenced early Christians is problematic,[44] although almost certainly the play would have been known by the Roman literati of the first few centuries, since it is mentioned already in Vergil Aeneid (4.469–90).[45]

What is basic to Dionysus is that, while he is a "son of Zeus," he is a chthonic deity, not one of the Olympian sky-gods. His transcendence is in pure immanence. His wildness is as much involved with birth and generation as it is with destruction. His contradictory forms make a mockery of mimesis, and as such he is the antithesis of form and clarity. "Dionysus represents obliteration of the western eye," notes Camille Paglia about his effects on art: "Apollo's solar torch is put out; the heart of creation is blind. In nature's female womb-world, there are no objects and no art."[46] The aniconism of the early Christian era might possibly have been as much due to Dionysian formlessness as to biblical hostility to representations of the divine.

In classical Greece, Dionysus was frequently portrayed in vase paintings grasping a grapevine, crowned with an ivy wreath, and dancing ecstatically with thyrsus-bearing women, although the violent tearing apart of his body

---

41. Cf. Plato Phaedo 72: "a generation from the dead to the living."

42. Otto, Dionysus: Myth and Cult (Bloomington, Ind.: Indiana University Press, 1965) 121, 190.

43. Philip Vellacott, trans., Euripides: The Bacchae and Other Plays (Harmondsworth, Middlesex: Penguin, 1954) 254–317, 200–201.

44. This case has been made by Arthur Evans in The God of Ecstasy: Sex-Roles and the Madness of Dionysos (New York: St. Martin's, 1988) 145–73 (=chap. 7, "Dionysos and Christ").

45. For this reference I am indebted to Steven Rutledge, of the department of classics at the University of Maryland.

46. Paglia, Sexual Personae (New York: Random House/Vintage: 1991) 88, 93.

and the ritual eating of his flesh to internalize the god and renew life is never pictured. In late antiquity the wild energy of Dionysus tends more towards pleasure-seeking and orgiastic excess, and the widespread use of Dionysian motifs is often no more than a decorative convention to express the joy of life: perhaps sometimes to draw the ironic contrast between the pleasures of life and the "wretched oblivion" of death.[47]

In my peregrinations around Rome I came across many Dionysian motifs, especially on sarcophagi: Bacchus and erotes with abundant grape clusters, dancing maenads, vine tendrils and leaves, and ivy leaves. Erwin Panofsky notes that "'Bacchic' sarcophagi surpass all other Roman funerary monuments not only in beauty of form and richness of content but also in numbers."[48] Initially, Christian sarcophagi almost randomly combined Dionysian motifs with Jonah and the good shepherd. But by the mid-fourth century they were sculpted in highly programmatic compositions.[49] In the well-known sarcophagus of Junius Bassus, an enthroned Christ centered between biblical scenes is balanced by grape harvest scenes, on one end, and by wheat harvest scenes, on the other.[50] Especially notable in the Basilica of Saint Agnes and the Vatican museums were the many grave markers and inscriptions from the catacombs with ivy leaf decorations, some also with Chi-Rho symbols and doves. But the distinction between Christian and non-Christian seemed very slight, and was often next to impossible to discern.[51] Leibnitz's "identity of indiscernibles" began to nag at me: if the differences were not very discernible, perhaps there wasn't much of a difference?

We know only very generally what meanings these images symbolized. It is in the nature of symbols to be equivocal. The multiple, sometimes contradictory, meanings they carry may be quite deliberate, since the reality they are identified with is itself equivocal. Symbolism reveals by its structure of double meaning the equivocalness of being, observes Paul Ricoeur: "Symbolism's *raison d'être* is to open the multiplicity of meaning to the equivocalness of being."[52]

The "work" of these early Christian images, in other words, is their am-

---

47. In some texts, "Dionysus is considered the source of something that has been lost in death, not something that has been gained" (Cole, "Dionysos and the Dead," 282).

48. Panofsky, *Tomb Sculpture* (New York: Abrams, 1992) 34.

49. See esp. the riot of vintaging erotes on the "Sarcophagus of the Good Shepherd" (Grabar, *Early Christian Art*, pl. 286–89).

50. See Elizabeth Struthers Malbon, *The Iconography of the Sarcophagus of Junius Bassus* (Princeton, N.J.: Princeton University Press, 1990).

51. "It is not always possible to determine whether or not the occupant of a given sarcophagus was a Christian" (Panofsky, *Tomb Sculpture*, 40).

52. Ricoeur, *The Conflict of Interpretations* (Evanston, Ill.: Northwestern University Press, 1974) 62–78.

biguity. Most of these images are very problematic in one way or another. Is Noah a figure of repentance or of baptism, for example? Why does his ark look more like a box than a boat?[53] Is Jonah going into or out of the whale? And why does he look like Endymion?[54]

The OT origin of most of these images implies Jewish interpretations, except that the texts that they refer to seem somewhat marginal over against the great themes of the Hebrew Bible — the Law and the Prophets. Charming as they are, Jonah is only an extended parable, and the stories from Daniel are edifying tales for the faithful. And one must look in the apocryphal additions to Daniel (chapter 13) to find the story of Susannah and the elders. The image of Noah, oddly enough, may actually have come into catacomb paintings by way of pagan Roman rather than Jewish sources in order to convey the notion of "death as a prelude to life."[55]

But beyond these iconographic puzzles lurks a more general and serious question. One cannot help but wonder that if God performed these saving acts in days of old, maybe a new "savior" is redundant. In fact, where is he?

Even the images with NT associations, other than the raising of Lazarus and the healing of the paralytic, seem oddly chosen. Why the woman with the issue of blood (Luke 8:43–48) or the woman of Samaria at the well (John 4:1–42)? Because of Dionysian openness to women? Because the role of women was more prominent in the first centuries than Paul's letters and the church fathers would lead us to think? The good shepherd, as we have seen, may or may not be a Christian image — and is ambiguous even if it is. Orpheus's charming the beasts may be no more than an evocation of a paradisaical notion of the afterlife, a common decorative motif in Roman times. Or it may be read in terms of certain eschatological expectations — but which ones? Other images, such as the Orans figure, had broad spiritual connotations for Romans before being used by Christians, but suggest nothing specific. Taken singly or together all of these images suggest a serene spirituality that is basically life-affirming and hopeful about the future, especially in the face of death. But not much more can be said with certainty. They are richly suggestive but impossible to fix with determinate meanings. They are polysemic and fundamentally aporetic.

Are these not signals of transcendence? Where God is present all meanings come loose. God is present when the last becomes first, when the stone that was rejected becomes the cornerstone of the building — that is, as open-

---

53. Murray, *Rebirth and Afterlife*, 99.

54. Endymion's lover was the moon-goddess, Selene, who bore him forty children. Portraying Jonah as Endymion in blissful repose may have been a reference to the *refrigerium interim* between death and heavenly revival (see Josef Engemann, *Deutung und Bedeutung frühchristliche Bildwerke* (Darmstadt: Primus, 1997) 112–13.

55. Murray, *Rebirth and Afterlife*, 98–111 ("The Christian Ark of Noah").

ness and equivocalness of being. The power of the early Christian images consists in the impossibility of making them reveal a univocal and authoritative meaning. Their "likeness to the divine" is precisely their equivocal presence. The fact that we cannot take any satisfaction in them as aesthetic objects or as representations of the divine or as images with univocal meanings actually demonstrates a strange kind of effectiveness. These early artifacts may not "say" what we want them to say because quite possibly they were intended to be open and aporetic. The strange disjunction between the absence of Christ in the catacomb images and the Christ-centered texts of the NT opens new possibilities of understanding. Instead of ruling images with the word, maybe the word should be ruled — or at least opened up — by the images.

In this light, then, perhaps we should undertake the "experiment in reading" that Henry Staten invites us to take in his critical revision of Rudolf Bultmann's interpretation of the Gospel of John.[56] The central issue is death. "If the dead rise not," says the apostle Paul in 1 Cor 15:32, "let us eat and drink, for tomorrow we die." Freedom from death is the key to the success of the gospel, Bultmann concurs, because otherwise human life is "sheerly unintelligible."[57] However, Bultmann's project is to "demythologize" the otherworldly implications of Jesus' promise of eternal life (3:16) so that we confront an eschatological reality that is already present here and now rather than a future otherworldly reward for present belief. In Bultmann's argument, says Staten, Jesus' words call for "authentic life" that results from "the resoluteness of the believer with respect to the future death that he/she now overcomes."[58] Staten accepts Bultmann's "this-worldly" focus on this crisis of decision — either to live a *real* life in the face of death or to live an inauthentic, trivialized, and *unreal* life — as the substance of Jesus' message. But, Staten asks, why not take Jesus' words about "life" literally — not allegorically, as orthodox Christians do, or philosophically, as Bultmann does? Staten's startling proposal is to read the Gospel of John naturalistically rather than transcendentally. By advancing a Dionysian reading of key Johannine texts over against Bultmann's existentialist interpretation, Staten suggests that "the Word became flesh" (1:14) may mean just what it says: that the divine is disclosed in the "truly radical descent to the flesh," in the natural corruptibility and continuity of life.[59]

What if Jesus really meant "I am the living bread . . . if you do not eat the flesh of the Son of Man and drink his blood you will not have life in you"

---

56. Staten, *Eros in Mourning — Homer to Lacan* (Baltimore: Johns Hopkins University Press, 1995), chap. 1, "How the Spirit (Almost) Became Flesh: The Gospel of John" (pp. 47–70).
57. Bultmann, *The Gospel of John: A Commentary* (Philadelphia: Westminster, 1971) 43.
58. Staten, *Eros in Mourning,* 57.
59. Ibid., 49.

(6:51–53)? That is, maybe it is the very fleshiness of human life — its inexorable vitality — rather than its spirituality, that has to be grasped. "He
who hears my word...has passed from death to life" (5:24). Perhaps Jesus'
mission — "the Father has sent me" — is to remind us dramatically that
death never has the last word: "Why should not the eternal *zoe* be conceived
as life itself, universal life that all living things share in common?...When
the food is bread, rather than meat, it is easy to forget that life subsists
on death, that ingestion and digestion are the exchange point at which life
dissolves back into life at the cost of life."[60] The decision Jesus confronts
believers with is the decision to accept the natural processes of life — that
all life feeds on other life. The agony of death is the dissolution of individuality that must be gone through in order to live anew: "Unless a grain of
wheat falls into the earth and dies, it remains alone; but if it dies, it bears
much fruit" (John 12:24). Death restores us to community with all living
things.

This does not do justice to the full development of Staten's argument,
but if we take seriously the absence of Christ and the cross in early Christian art, his otherwise bizarre "hyperliteral" reading of the Gospel of John
begins to seem plausible. After all, the Roman Catholic Church has for
centuries insisted on what may be called a literal reading of the words
of the eucharist, although reserving to itself the power to transform the
substances of bread and wine into the divine body and blood. In a naturalistic reading, however, transubstantiation occurs simply by eating and
drinking. The celebration of the eucharist in this view would be the ritual
(and actual) embrace of death as the means to new life, not a magical act
whereby one surpasses mortality. The "real presence" would be physical, not
metaphysical.

If early Christians understood the gospel in terms of *life-death-new life,* the
depiction of a "savior" would have been unnecessary. The crucifixion would
not have been a once-and-for-all act of atonement (to be artistically glorified)
but rather an enactment of the passage from life to life that all humanity
must pass through. The "alpha" and the "omega" is *life,* not the passage of
death. And neither would there be any moralistic distinction between those
who qualified for new life and those who did not. Death comes to all. No
judge. No law. The only question is whether death is affirmed as essential
to life or whether it must be "redeemed" by a deathless spirituality that is
beyond life.

We cannot know if this Dionysian meaning was in the minds of Christians
in the first few centuries. Undoubtedly the allegorical understandings offered
by the church fathers would have appealed to those who felt that the limits

---

60. Ibid., 60, 66.

of natural life could only be understood in terms of a transcendent spiritual life. Dionysian Christians, on the other hand, may have seen the power of the divine in the power of life itself rather than in a spiritual realm that was "other" than life. For them, representational images of Christ may have been absent because he was present, not as a divine personality, nor as one crucified, but as life — resurrected life.

24

GIVING TEXTS VISION AND IMAGES VOICE

The Promise and Problems
of Interdisciplinary Scholarship

ROBIN M. JENSEN

In the early fifth century, Paulinus, the aristocratic bishop of Nola, built a basilica dedicated to the martyr saint Felix, whose relics he had installed in his church. For this building, he commissioned a program of painted (and perhaps mosaic) images portraying Christ, the saints, and certain biblical stories. In many of his letters and poems, Paulinus describes these decorations and goes on to defend such artistic adornment of churches. Visual art in Christian buildings not only counters the popularity of pagan idols but also inspires and delights his flock, enticing them to come to church instead of seeking other, less-sanctioned religious entertainments — including the popular but dubious feasts at martyrs graves. Paulinus was the sort of church leader who knew how to use elements of popular culture, incorporating and transforming them for his own purposes of edification and conversion. While taking a critic on a tour of his new construction, he says this:

> Now I want you to look at the paintings along the portico, with which it is adorned in extended line. Crane your neck a little till you take in everything with face tilted back. The man who looks at these and ac-knowledges the truth within these empty figures nurtures his believing mind with representations by no means empty. The paintings in fact depict in the order prescribed by faith all that aged Moses wrote in his five books.... You may perhaps ask what motive implanted in us this decision to adorn the holy houses with representations of living per-

sons, an unusual custom. If you listen, I shall try to explain the reasons in a few words. Everyone is aware of the crowds which Saint Felix's fame brings here. Now the greater number among the crowds here are countryfolk not without belief but unskilled in reading. For years they have been used to following profane cults in which their god was their belly, and at last they have turned as converts to Christ out of admiration for the undisputed achievements of the saints performed in Christ's name. Notice in what numbers they assemble from all the country districts, and how they roam around, their unsophisticated minds beguiled in devotion.... This was why we thought it useful to enliven all the houses of Felix with paintings on sacred themes, in the hope that they would excite the interest of the rustics by their attractive appearance, for the sketches are painted in various colours. Over them are explanatory inscriptions, the written word revealing the theme outlined by the painter's hand.[1]

Like Paulinus, modern historians of Christianity may learn that their readers and students likewise can be beguiled, edified, and inspired when images of all kinds are brought to enrich and enliven textbooks and lectures. Material remains add a crucial visual dimension to prosaic summaries of events or to a scholarly examination of the great thoughts of ancient writers, and they offer another avenue for understanding the religious experience of the distant past. The combination of textual and material evidence moreover provides a far richer and undoubtedly more complete view of any era. Certain kinds of questions become central for historians who would make use of visual evidence. For instance, what was it that these early Christians actually saw when they went to church in the basilica in Nola? On what basis did the patrons or artists make their choices of theme, context, composition, and materials? How did those images shape or reflect the content of their faith, the practice of their religion, or their hopes or expectations for their lives as members of a Christian community?[2]

The incorporation of visual materials to the study, writing, or teaching of early Christianity hardly needs defense. Scholars have long recognized the limitations of exclusively text-based views of religion, whether it be Christianity or any other faith tradition. Archaeologists have already shown Bible scholars how much they can gain from juxtaposing texts with material remains. Modern historians of religion are regularly introduced to (if not trained in) the methods of sociologists and cultural anthropologists. Study

---

1. Paulinus *Poem* 27.511–83; ET in P. G. Walsh, *The Poems of St. Paulinus of Nola* (ACW 40; New York: Newman, 1975) 289–92. See Paulinus's description of the basilicas at Nola and Fundi (in *Ep.* 32, to Severus).

2. André Grabar offers a similar set of questions in the introduction to his *Christian Iconography: A Study of Its Origins* (Princeton, N.J.: Princeton University Press, 1968) xli–l.

of painting, sculpture, and mosaic, long closely managed by art historians, has begun to cross over into the databases of historians of Christianity, and is being put to far more profound use than simply illustrating or ornamenting textbooks. Historians are alert to the possibilities of a whole new field of data — the physical evidence supplied by art historians and archaeologists — and are venturing to speculate about aspects of early Christianity that were not readily apparent in the written documents alone. Sometimes these efforts challenge well-entrenched theories and offer fresh visions of the past.[3]

This kind of cross-disciplinary study has raised several challenging problems, however. Sculpture, painting, and remains of buildings rarely appear with explanatory inscriptions of the type that Paulinus provided of his (no longer extant) wall decorations.[4] We cannot know precisely how viewers experienced these art objects nor how they functioned in formation either of mainstream theology or popular piety. Scholars may work hard to match distinct bodies of evidence that are (at best) either chronologically contemporaneous or geographically proximate, while yet wondering if this is even the right approach. Scholarly methodologies and training also come into conflict. Traditionally trained historians often operate from the assumption that texts are fairly clear and their meanings mostly self-evident. For these scholars, art objects can be dauntingly enigmatic and uncommunicative. Since their usual approaches to critical interpretation of literature are inapplicable and unhelpful for the analysis of a visual image, they wish for a set of directions for constructing some preliminary theories about what certain images might have meant to ancient viewers. For this, training in the methods of art historians might seem required, but few have the time or the inclination to undertake an extended program of formal study.

These kinds of issues must be addressed as we embark on any interdisciplinary work — work that often brings together two disparate fields and subjects the data of one for consideration according to the methods of another. Such a process can lead to misunderstanding, accusations of mishandling of data, and conflict over appropriate scholarly methods as often as it leads to mutual enlightenment. Text historians, worrying about the degree of subjectivity seemingly inherent in an examination of artistic evidence,

---

3. See, for example, the work of W. H. C. Frend and J. G. Davies, both historians of Christianity who have relied extensively on the evidence of art history and archaeology. More recently, see the following exemplary works: Graydon F. Snyder, *Ante Pacem: Archaeological Evidence of Church Life before Constantine* (Macon, Ga.: Mercer University Press, 1985); Elizabeth Struthers Malbon, *The Iconography of the Sarcophagus of Junius Bassus* (Princeton, N.J.: Princeton University Press, 1990); Paul Corby Finney, *The Invisible God: The Earliest Christians on Art* (Oxford and New York: Oxford University Press, 1994); and L. Michael White, *The Social Origins of Christian Architecture* (2 vols.; HTS 42–43;Valley Forge, Pa.: Trinity Press International, 1996–97).

4. Also famous are Eusebius's descriptions of the Church of the Holy Sepulchre in Jerusalem, the Church of the Holy Apostles in Constantinople, and others whose decorations are no longer extant; see Eusebius *Vita Const.* 2.25–39; 3.50; 4.58–60; *Hist. eccl.* 10.4.44–46.

have been known to characterize art history as a kind of "soft field" compared to the world of written words and ideas. For surprisingly parallel reasons, art historians worry about letting textual historians make what they fear might be a ham-handed effort to interpret data that is essentially nontextual.

Disciplinary subspecialization and a growing emphasis on professional focus have fostered an unfortunate but understandable estrangement between these two broad scholarly worlds, that of art history and archaeology on the one hand and the history of Christianity on the other. Unfortunately, separate analyses of text and material object miss an opportunity to consider the broader context of both. Viewing either type of primary source as a discrete form of expression, without the benefit of the added interpretive data supplied by the other, deprives both fields of possible new insights. Yet the problem is eminently understandable. Good scholarship is understood to require mastery of a specialization, and few individuals can master more than one discipline. In a modern information-rich world, merely having a minimal idea of the literature in another field requires a high level of commitment.

Thus while many intellectual historians find visual art beautiful and interesting, even provocative, they may be unsure how to evaluate it as primary research data and intimidated by the scholarly apparatus of the practitioners of art history. If they resort to subjecting the art to a supporting role as illustration of text, they will certainly be charged with lacking appropriate appreciation for the significance or power of the art itself. But the problem also stems from the nature of the data itself. Most historians are trained in a verbal universe. They take their bearings from original, written, sources. Paulinus-like, they want their churches (or texts) to be supplied with pictures, but also quite naturally they want to provide captions for those images, giving the viewer some textual guidance to ensure their correct understanding of what the images were for in contrast to the idolatrous uses of art in contemporary Roman polytheistic society. They want to make their meanings clear.

The captioning of images was also a solution practiced by sixteenth-century Protestant reformers, who allowed paintings only insofar as they were labeled with appropriate scriptural quotations as primary reference. Without those captions, these reformers felt, images seemed perilously subjective and undisciplined, likely to lead viewers into heresy, superstition, and idol worship.

Like the sixteenth-century reformers, some text historians have presumed that Christian art was irrevocably tainted by its association with paganism, and as such needed to be seen as the work of popular, unenlightened, or perhaps consciously nonconforming believers.[5] Others, however, have gone

---

5. See Finney, *The Invisible God*, 3–38, on the subject of early Christian (and later academic) attitudes toward iconography as tainted by paganism; also Mary Charles Murray, "Art and the Early Church," *JTS* n.s. 28 (1977) 304–45.

beyond simply supplying texts as explanations of or controls on the visual art, viewing the art as corroborating their (sometimes confessionally biased) analysis of the Christian past. This kind of interdisciplinary scholarship is flawed by a kind of hunt-and-plunder data collection that subjects the material evidence to a kind of selective testing for its usefulness in making a particular argument, solving a problem, or proving a point — usually that the evidence of art shows the widespread harmony of the "orthodox" position, and as such served an apologetic function, almost like the rhetoric of the "defense of the faith."[6]

This kind of scholarly malpractice led in the 1930s to a challenge from the so-called Roman school, which developed new strategies and methods that arguably subjected material evidence to less subjective and more scientific analysis. That work was conducted in such a way that freed art objects from assumed dogmatic or liturgical conformity with written texts, merely reinforcing the "orthodox tradition." Exemplified by the work of Paul Styger, Erich Dinkler, and Theodore Klauser, this new scholarship tended to emphasize the continuity of Christian art with its pagan prototypes rather than with the writings of the Fathers. Its proponents saw themselves as giving objects of artistic output a kind of dignity, beauty, and cultural autonomy they had previously been denied in being made either subject to, or in conflict with, the prevailing mainstream (orthodox) faith.

For their part, art historians and archaeologists mostly study the objects as sufficient ends in themselves. They have been trained to consider material evidence as essential and primary historical data, often entirely apart from textual sources. Moreover, because of restrictions on their time or the emphasis of their education, many (if not most) of these scholars find themselves too limited by their specialization to invest in understanding the methods or data of the text historians. They often lack broad knowledge of the writings or the history of religious practices and symbols that might correspond in time and place with the artworks they were studying. Preoccupied with classifying and analyzing the formal aspects of art objects, or with tracing the origins of a motif, these scholars only indirectly address many questions that intrigue their colleagues in other fields — questions about the meaning or function of art as expressive of the religious faith or hope of a community. The questions of meaning, interpretation, or connection to the life of the faith from which the work springs may appear to the formal art historian as an intrusion of a very subjective or even suspect set of categories. Historians of religion who wish to raise these questions may seem naive at best; at worst, manipulative of the evidence for their own ends.

---

6. A summary of the history of scholarship, covering many of these same issues and providing bibliography, may be found in Thomas F. Mathews, *The Clash of Gods: A Reinterpretation of Early Christian Art* (Princeton, N.J.: Princeton University Press, 1993) 3–22.

Somewhere in the middle of the divide is a group of scholars who risk the venture into another scholarly domain for the sake of bridging disciplines and broadening their view of the culture or period they are studying. In order to protect themselves from the worst mistakes of bumbling amateurs, they may undertake collegial interdisciplinary research and dialogue, working with scholars from the other discipline and exchanging information. Given the realities of modern scholarly specialization, most will continue to reside in separate disciplines even while sharing allied concerns and exploring the same bodies of data. Questions that arise in one field of study must sometimes be directed to another. This is particularly true for scholars interested in the *interpretation* of art, interested in what it communicated to its audience — something broadly labeled the "study of iconography." Those scholars who have worked at the intersection between text and art history have essentially carved out a distinct field. In most cases these scholars began with the mastery of a "home discipline" and then acquired a broad working knowledge of another.[7] The future may depend on scholars working as teams, informing and critiquing one another.

Recently, in the midst of a lecture to an audience which included some art historians, I was asked to comment on the famous statement of Gregory the Great in response to an episode of iconoclasm in Marseilles. Gregory rebuked the bishop (Serenus) for destroying images of the saints by asserting that "what writing presents to readers, a picture presents to the unlearned who view it, since in the image even the ignorant see what they ought to follow; in the picture the illiterate read."[8]

This statement has sometimes been taken as the classic Western position on religious art — that religious pictures are the "Bible of the Unlettered." The questioner wished to construct an appropriate response to Gregory's argument. Without doubt, Gregory's viewpoint (widely shared, even today) presumes that visual art is inferior or subservient to verbal expression and suggests that images are the "food" for childlike minds, while theological texts contain the meat of adult formation. Such a stance would reduce frescoes, carved reliefs, sculptured portals, mosaic panels, or stained glass windows to being merely decorative or didactic — designed to teach children and the less educated the stories of the Bible or to present models of virtue in the images of saints. Rather than recognizing that visual expression can be as deeply theological or intellectually sophisticated as what is written in large tomes, the viewpoint presumes that the serious work of theology is carried on in the pulpit, lecterns, and the libraries of churches, universities, and theological

---

7. To name just a few of these pioneers: Erwin Panofsky, André Grabar, Ernst Kitzinger, and Kurt Weitzmann. The most interesting and productive contemporary interdisciplinary scholars include Hans Belting, Henry Maguire, and Mary Charles Murray.

8. Gregory I *Ep.* 13 (*PL* 77. 1027–28; 1128–30; ET in NPNF 2/13. 53–54).

schools. Gregory, like Paulinus, considered art an effective way to combat the pagan polytheism of his time, but almost unwittingly he endorsed an elitist stance against images. Like Clement of Alexandria's gnostic Christians, these latter groups seem to have risen above the masses and lived in a kind of spiritual or intellectual world quite superior to the supposedly simpler world of pictures and stories.

Serious students of early Christian visual art are profoundly convinced that art rather functions as a highly sophisticated, thoughtful, and often eloquent mode of theological expression. Even ordinary museum-goers realize that art can belong to the high culture just as well as the low. Certainly viewers require at least a basic familiarity with the biblical narratives and with the common traditions of scriptural interpretation to appreciate the subtlety of most of the surviving early Christian art objects. The need for study, indeed, exemplifies the mutual dependence of verbal and visual modes of religious expression. Visual images are neither necessarily distinct nor divergent from images found in written texts. Art cannot be presented as disconnected from literature or theological writing. In fact, early Christian visual images usually have direct parallels in early Christian literature. Visual symbols have their counterparts in textual metaphors. Viewers, like readers, are allowed, even expected, to be familiar with the many layers of the faith tradition as passed down in different forms, whether homilies, liturgies, dogmatic writings, or pictures.

However, since almost nothing was recorded in the documents (Paulinus and Gregory are rare exceptions), we have little evidence that theoretical reflection on the use of art exists from the early Christian period (unlike the later period encompassing the debate about icons). Such a conclusion can only be reached by analogy and comparison. For instance, scholars have studied the *theologoumenon* of "creation in the image of God" as a basis for a Christian philosophical view of the image's participation in the archetype. Others have undertaken a careful analysis of the theories of vision in the early church.[9] A more directly interpretive objective may be achieved by simultaneously considering specific texts and art objects (noting their points of similarity or parallel symbolism) as equally powerful tools of communication, directed at similar audiences. By collecting and comparing particular textual or artistic metaphors and typologies, one could then go on to build a theory that would argue that visual and verbal theologies are equally to be valued

---

9. See an excellent recent article by Mary Charles Murray, "The Image, the Ear, and the Eye in Early Christianity," in *Art, Religion, and Theological Studies* 9/1 (1997) 17–24; also Margaret R. Miles, *Image as Insight: Visual Understanding in Western Christianity and Secular Culture* (Boston: Beacon, 1985) 41–48; Jas Elsner, *Art and the Roman Viewer: The Transformation of Art from the Pagan World to Christianity* (Cambridge and New York: Cambridge University Press, 1995).

and necessarily related to one another.[10] Each of these efforts requires an interdisciplinary approach, using the methods of art historians in conjunction with the study of early Christian texts.

However, another problem inherent in finding a workable interdisciplinary methodology emerges in the question of how one approaches data in the first place: the matter of biases that govern the analytical tools or interpretive stance. Text historians, like art historians, will transfer particular skills and points of view to the analysis of new material, and their basic philosophical, theological, or political agendas may emerge as essentially governing the way they will undertake the work. Some interpreters are more literalistic in their approach, e.g., seeing most visual images as illustrations of specific textual narratives, while others will adapt aspects of modern rhetorical or genre analysis, socio-cultural criticism, or various kinds of structuralist or deconstructionist approaches.

For those who follow the more literalist approach, the task appears relatively simple. Visual images are understood to be harmonious with the mainstream tradition, and most of them are seen as illustrations of narratives or presentations of widely held dogmatic positions. Texts and images are assumed to be mutually reinforcing. Interpretation then becomes a matter primarily of keying images to texts and then turning to the textual tradition for answers to questions about the selection, composition, or significance of the image. Controversies are sparked, however, when the scholars' theological, sociopolitical, or religious backgrounds appear to direct their conclusions to particular ends.[11]

The other approaches, associated with modern and postmodern criticism, assume a less direct or obvious function for the art and look for the symbolic, covert, or even culturally subversive aspects of particular images and texts. Starting from the premise that art and text need not have the same religious or cultural purpose, the task is then one of looking for the obscure meanings found in codes, symbols, or signs that might or might not reinforce the messages sent by texts (and vice versa). Of particular significance to this kind of analysis are the social and cultural settings of the data and the contrasting categories of "elite" and "popular" art or religion. Since the production or use of texts presumes a certain degree of literacy (whereas art is often *supposed* to be more democratic), some historians have proposed an essential social distinction or even conflict between the users of texts and the viewers of art, sometimes in the face of examples of art objects that could only

---

10. See my *Understanding Early Christian Art* (London: Routledge, forthcoming 1999); also Jas Elsner, ed., *Art and Text in Roman Culture* (Cambridge and New York: Cambridge University Press, 1996).

11. See, for example, Mathews's evaluation of the work of Ernst Kantorowicz and Andreas Alföldi in *The Clash of Gods*, 16–20.

have been afforded by the most wealthy or "elite" members of a community. These scholars strenuously object to interpretations of art objects that rely on texts as primary mediators of their significance or meaning, and for them the discovery of discontinuities becomes a central part of the interpretative process.[12]

Meanwhile, the new field of "reader-response" criticism raises the parallel problem of getting into the mind of the ancient viewer. While text historians used to believe that they actually knew what words meant, even to ancient readers, now they are less certain and have begun to distinguish among writer, receiver, and the message sent. At the same time we must similarly note the clearly separated viewpoints of artisan and viewer and wonder which is the more important, or more accessible, for our purposes as historians — the artist's intention or the audience's perception. Finally, as with written documents, we really have no way to know that what we see bears any resemblance to what an artisan or patron more than a thousand years ago intended to express, or what an original viewer actually interpreted it to mean.

Texts and art are also different in another significant way. While texts come to us through generations of copying and being multiplied, art objects are normally unique or singular. We have a pretty good idea what they looked like when they were first created. Although art objects were sometimes copies of earlier works, each is a kind of original, in contrast to the extant documents of which we have almost no autographs. This situation removes us even further from the mind and intentions of the author in the case of texts and opens up the question of the long tradition and the gradual shaping or transforming of meaning over time.

Nevertheless, looking at art, like reading a text, is a process conditioned first by the particular situation and the character of the viewer, which is of course affected by the object in view. In other words, the viewer interprets the image for herself, but the object has its own reality by virtue of being seen, over time, by different people with different reactions. Thus the image can be said to have a presence and power that is transformed or experienced by different viewers, and perhaps itself changes the viewer's perception (perhaps even the viewer) in a large or a small way. Thus both image and viewer are transformed in their interaction and may be each time a single viewer returns to the same object. That this was as true a thousand years ago as it is still today is a pretty reliable assumption, an assumption that only makes the endeavor to arrive at some conclusive theories that much harder.

---

12. Miles, for example, focuses on the discontinuity between theological language and religious imagery (*Image as Insight*, 38 and passim); see also Snyder's distinction between the "great tradition" and the faith of "common folk" (*Ante Pacem*, 7–11).

The category "artist" in the ancient world was not like its counterpart today. Artists did not sign their work, nor did they give interviews to reporters.
In fact, quite other than the way we ordinarily treat most early Christian
theological writing, ancient art objects may have no single, individual pro-
ducers, but rather were the products of workshops. Likewise, few viewers
recorded or reviewed what they saw, claiming one object to be beautiful or
good, another ugly and useless. We can never know what they actually saw,
experienced, or thought about it all. Historians must gather enough material
to get a sample and then follow their intuition, guided mostly by intelli-
gence and imagination. But that, in all fairness, is a fairly adequate working
definition of writing history on any subject.

Out of all this one can only conclude that interdisciplinary scholarship is
filled with promise and fraught with problems. It is a pilgrimage through an
uncharted and dangerous wilderness that only adventurous and sturdy scholars should undertake. Almost no one will be safe from attack from one camp
or another. Scholars are not known for their show of hospitality and em-
pathy to strangers from other fields. If we could map a relatively safe route
through the territory, we might try a conservative and at least fairly familiar one, relying on known and available resources, which for text historians
means surveying documents from the same *general* context and era as selected
art objects or archaeological remains. If their relative proximity is established,
both kinds of data may be treated as sources of information to aid in mutual
interpretation. Whether they have roots in the very same social or cultural
milieu or not, at least they have come from the same world. That simple
overlap at least gives the analyst a historical foothold.

In attempting to establish geographical or chronological synchronicity,
however, interpreters must not overlook the basic character of the images
or the texts in themselves. Here we need to consider formal and stylistic aspects of the art: Is it expressionistic? Naturalistic? Of high or low quality?
What did the work cost, and who could have afforded it? Does it look like
other works of its kind, or is it unique? Is the object absolutely crowded with
images, or does it present a single figure, spaciously arranged on an open field?
Should we assume that the selection of images was made by the patron, by
the workshop of artists, or by a combination of both? And was the combination deliberate or more haphazard? Establishing the original context also is
crucial. Was the object made for a tomb or a dining room? Is this building a
martyrium or a baptistery? Is this the bishop's palace or the parish hall?

Texts also have their formal, contextual, rhetorical, and stylistic aspects.
Historians should not read all texts in the same way, though they sometimes do. Genre — whether a document is a theological treatise, liturgical
handbook, legal argument, homily, letter, or poem — will greatly affect the
way we must analyze it. Sometimes these documents are meant to instruct,

sometimes to inspire or move the emotions. Theoretical or doctrinal arguments are crafted so as to be as precise as possible. Homilies or prayers are far
more subtle and evocative. The content, composition, and context of these
written remains also feed us information crucial to the interpretive process.
However, scholars must be admonished not to treat texts like (the proverbial) haystacks, tossing aside most of the content while on a hunt for a few
nuggets of helpful information. Texts, like art, need to be examined as whole
compositions instead of as boxes of miscellaneous bits of information to be
mined and resorted as needed.

Like painting or sculptural programs, written documents may be abbreviated and simple or more detailed and complex. Their meanings may be plain
or obscure, single or multiple. Allegories, typologies, and metaphors provide
an indirect route to the heart of meaning, in this case a meaning which will
almost always be elusive and subjective. The frequency of a particular theme
or grouping of metaphors in a series of homilies may be reflected in the motifs
or entire compositions of decorative programs. When certain images appear
frequently and in proximity to one another, historians may begin to theorize
about parallels, patterns, and their meaning.

Liturgical documents might easily correspond to the physical remains of
worship spaces, or they might not. When they do, scholars may rejoice. When
they do not, those same scholars might make an important discovery. Homilies employ symbols and metaphors that may be repeated in visual form in
painting and sculpture — or not. Either way, the information is important in
establishing the effectiveness or the popularity of a particular verbal or visual
image. Yet all the while we must remember that preservation is often accidental and all hypotheses based on extant materials are merely provisional. Much
of what we have is left to us only because of the power, security, climate, or
propensity of communities to preserve what they wanted posterity to find and
to destroy what they disapproved of.

But more basic than trying to understand what individual art works or
written documents meant in late antiquity is the question of how art and
texts themselves functioned as both constructive and expressive factors in religious belief. We may discover that some images preceded texts and that the
texts then provided commentary on the visual symbols. Similarly, architectural spaces may have preceded liturgy and helped to shape it, rather than
vice versa. At the very least we can be certain that visual imagery never
merely retold or condensed a text into visual language. Rather it made meaning in its own right, using symbols and allegories often already present in
written expression (narratives, commentaries, etc.) in such a way as to become a communication mode in itself — one that paralleled, commented
upon, expanded, or even subverted the text (and its readers), rather then
merely amplifying or serving the text. Learning to "read" art works, therefore,

means learning to read a visual language, to become familiar with a visual idiom, not unlike a foreign tongue.

Moreover, this visual idiom is not necessarily less "rational" than verbal expression. Any such assumption reinforces unfortunate stereotypes about art and texts that in turn affect the ways that we study them — stereotypes that view art as an aid for the unlearned or for the popular manifestations of religion, and texts as the provenance of the social elite, the intelligentsia, or the official members of the religious organization, in other words as belonging particularly to the "high culture." Images and words together constitute sacred symbols, and neither has inherent primacy over the other. Neither is inherently more likely to have been made for, or enjoyed by, the upper classes. Homilies were heard by the unlettered, and paintings were commissioned by the wealthy. Understanding this might require that we transcend modern culture's tendency to disengage symbols and words and to value words as better or clearer communicative devices.

So how do we begin? By taking into consideration what we can — by looking simultaneously at these two modes of communication of meaning, texts and images. We cannot presume that these are inevitably or even often in conflict, and we cannot privilege either word or picture as being prior or more authentic. As I have already said, assuming that the image merely serves the word underestimates the importance of image as a powerful and basic element of communication. But to assume that the word is one or more steps distant from visual expression is to cut off a valuable resource for interpretation. Both word and image must be viewed as evidence of meaning making in a culture or in a religious faith, and must be seen as partners in the process.

Visual art has many different functions in the expression and development of the religious tradition. Among these are the decorative, the illustrative, and the didactic, but added to these are functions that might be characterized as exegetical, symbolic, liturgical, and iconic. The former are not to be denigrated. Beauty offers glory, and education brings illumination. However, the latter four functions assume that visual art is capable of mediating or even manifesting more complex theological ideas, including the incarnation and the presence of the divine in creation. These functions are subjective and often complex in a way that direct discourse might not be, and restricting such a supple and versatile medium would be nearly idolatrous. Still, art has meaning only insofar as it refers to something the viewers already *know* from some other level of their experience, and our main means of access to those other levels is usually through the study of surviving literature. Carefully and respectfully compared, texts and images can be mutually illuminating.

As exegesis, art interprets scriptures on many different levels, from the literal to the allegorical. As symbol, art acts as a bridge between a familiar reality and one that transcends ordinary expression. As liturgy, art may have a performative function that belongs to a particular space, time, and set of ritual actions. Finally, as icon art brings the viewer into direct contact with the holy, providing the mechanism for epiphany.

Another distinction exists between the content of religious images. Although we may draw too strict a distinction between narrative and iconic images, the purposes may not be exactly the same. The former may be more directly dependent on memory and familiarity with the tradition while the latter may be less culturally conditioned. But the eye and mind must be trained to read certain motifs, and this reading will always be culturally determined — a cultural determinism we may not be able to recover across time and space. What we may see only once may well have been as familiar to viewers of the past as the conventional images of the present are to us. Narrative images depend particularly on memory and use a kind of sign language to remind us of what we already know. They are not meant to be taken literally; rather they are intended to serve as openings to a far more complex set of layered meanings and significations.

Iconic images are not so related to memory or to textual referents. The image functions as a kind of stepping-stone, or mediator, between the invisible realm of the divine and the more direct world of the senses. In a way the image both presents and protects the divine, in the same way that apophatic theology does. Icons proclaim that the divine cannot be known in its essence, but only in its affect — the way we know without being told. Direct engagement with the divine is difficult to withstand. The icon therefore both reveals and protects both the viewer and the holy mystery.

My challenge, then, is the plea that text historians move beyond a view of the past that is mediated primarily through written documents and take scholarly risks to understand the power, the subtlety, and the beauty of sacred images; that they respect and attend to art as primary source data rather than as a mere visual aid for their prose. Parallel to this is the wish that those who attend primarily to the artistic materials become more familiar with the richness of early Christian texts in order to illuminate their understanding and deepen their appreciation for the art objects they cherish.

25

WHICH PATH
AT THE CROSSROADS?

*Early Christian Art as a Hermeneutical
and Theological Challenge*

David R. Cartlidge

To define art is akin to E. B. White's reported comment that to analyze humor
is like dissecting a frog: the subject dies, and the results are discouraging to all
but the most hardened scientist. As this paper involves what art is and does,
we will get the surgery out of the way quickly.[1] Susanne K. Langer insists
that there is in the world of art the whole range of human experience, from
the noetic to the emotive.[2] For Langer art is functional: "the function of art
is ... to acquaint [the audience] with something he [or she] has not known
before...." Art acts; it creates an illusion (with all the sense of play in the
Latin *illudere*).[3] It is the playful creation of art that draws the audience into
an illusory world which would otherwise be unavailable to it. The resultant
confrontation or dialogue of worlds, taking place between the audience and
the art form, creates an art event. To employ a term from the 1960s counter-
culture (which Langer does not), art is "a happening."

Paul Tillich, who was strongly drawn to the visual arts, extends into the
theological dimension the thrust of Langer's philosophical analysis:

---

1. Were superscriptions in order, I would have chosen two: "Ceci n'est pas une pipe" (inscription on a painting by Magritte); and "I did not suppose that the things from the books
would aid me much as the things from the living and continuous voice" (Papias of Hierapolis, in
Eusebius *Hist. eccl.* 3.39.1–7).

2. Langer, *Feeling and Form: A Theory of Art* (New York: Scribner, 1953).

3. Ibid., 19, 45–68.

The third expression of human freedom is from bondage to the given. Man is not only able to sketch something new in terms of means; he is also able to create something new in terms of ends. He is able to create the world of artistic forms which express and transform the given. Of this creative freedom we speak when we speak of the arts.[4]

For Tillich, as well as for Langer, art functions as a symbol; that is, it points to and participates in a reality which is beyond itself and which is available only through art.[5] When an art object interacts with an audience to create an event which draws the audience into a world different from its own, it challenges the audience's world (e.g., its narrative world; its world of space and time; its world of movement and body language).

Texts as well as the pictorial arts may and usually do function as arts. That judgment includes such texts as academic papers; the function of these papers is to draw the audience into the problem-solving world of the author. The particular problem-world addressed in this essay is that of the relationship between early Christian art and the early church's texts.

A central problem for those working with early Christian art is that the historiography of early Christianity has tended to plot the church's journeys with texts as the central cartographic topoi. This tendency relegated early Christian art to an important but ancillary role in the discipline's central purpose.[6] Art history, on the other hand, was inclined to see especially the earliest (ante-pacem) Christian art as a siding (if not a derailment) in the journey of normative art style; the aesthetic norm was always classical (Greek and Roman) naturalism. Christian and other late antique art was "disturbingly different."[7] It was only with the neoclassic revival in the post-Constantinian age that Christian art became part of the Western mainstream.[8] Ironically, rhetoricians treated early Christian literature in a similar fashion.[9]

4. Tillich, On Art and Architecture (New York: Crossroad, 1987) 18.
5. Ibid., 36–39.
6. On the history of this relationship, see Graydon F. Snyder, Ante Pacem: Archaeological Evidence of Church Life before Constantine (Macon, Ga.: Mercer University Press, 1985) 1–11; Walter Lowrie, Art in the Early Church (New York: Pantheon, 1–38); Brendan Cassiday, "Introduction: Iconography, Texts and Audiences," in idem, ed., Iconography at the Crossroads (Index of Christian Art 2; Princeton, N.J.: Princeton University Press, 1993) 1–15.
7. Peter R. L. Brown, "Art and Society in Late Antiquity," in Kurt Weitzmann, ed., The Age of Spirituality: A Symposium (New York: Metropolitan Museum of Art; Princeton, N.J.: Princeton University Press, 1980) 17.
8. Arnaldo Momigliano, "After Gibbon's Decline and Fall," in Weitzmann, Symposium, 7–16; George M. A. Hanfmann, "The Continuity of Classical Art: Culture, Myth, Faith," in ibid., 75–99. Overall evaluations of this condition are in Ernst Kitzinger, Byzantine Art in the Making: Main Lines of Stylistic Development in Mediterranean Art, 3rd–7th Century (Cambridge, Mass.: Harvard University Press, 1977); Weitzmann, ed., The Age of Spirituality: Late Antique and Early Christian Art (Catalogue of the Exhibition; New York: Metropolitan Museum of Art, 1979).
9. Ihor Sevcenko, "A Shadow Outline of Virtue: The Classical Heritage of Greek Christian

The partnership of art history and general historiography is currently undergoing a reevaluation in both academic camps. Rhetorical studies in early church historiography have begun to treat the early church's literature as an art form, and certain elements in art history are demanding that early Christian art must be allowed artistic and historiographical autonomy.[10]

Leo Steinberg charges that his own discipline is infected with "textism, [which] as I define it is an interdictory stance, hostile to any interpretation that seems to come out of nowhere *because it comes out of pictures,* as if pictures alone did not constitute a respectable provenance."[11] Thomas Mathews, in his discussion of images of Jesus in the early church treats pictorial art as a valid and powerful medium through which the church and its faithful expressed their faith. The pictorial expression is as meaningful and helpful to historiography and theology as are theological texts:

> To [the converts of the early church, Christ] was still utterly mysterious, undefinable, changeable, polymorphous. In the disparate images they have left behind they record their struggle to get a grasp on him; the images were their way of thinking out loud on the problem of Christ. *Indeed, the images are the thinking process itself.*[12]

In a volume intended to explore the emerging new methods and purposes of art history and iconography, Brendan Cassiday illustrates the significance of the book's title: it is "meant to suggest that iconography stands at the crossroads of several disciplines, all of which draw upon images as a source of information for their particular areas of inquiry." A crossroads demands decisions:

> [W]hat can iconography tell us about the past and what should we not expect it to tell us, or, put another way, where should we locate the limits of interpretation? . . . What is the epistemological status of the interpretation we elicit from the mute image and how are we to choose among conflicting interpretations of the same work? And finally, what kinds of relationship exist between texts and images?[13]

Contemplation of Cassiday's last question and of the history of both early Christian arts, the chirographic and the pictorial, suggests the following two propositions which are the issue in this essay:

Literature (Second to Seventh Century)," in Weitzmann, *Symposium,* 53–73, esp. 54–58 (on the "classicizing" of Christian rhetoric in the second century).

10. Amos N. Wilder, *The Language of the Gospel: Early Christian Rhetoric* (London: SCM, 1964) 18–20; Charles H. Talbert, *What Is a Gospel? The Genre of the Canonical Gospels* (Philadelphia: Fortress, 1977) 1–23.

11. Steinberg, *The Sexuality of Christ in Renaissance Art and in Modern Oblivion* (2d ed.; Chicago: University of Chicago Press, 1996) 220.

12. Mathews, *The Clash of Gods: A Reinterpretation of Early Christian Art* (Princeton, N.J.: Princeton University Press, 1993) 141 (emphasis added).

13. Cassiday, *Iconography at the Crossroads,* 3.

1. When we deal with both of these art forms, the rhetorical and the pictorial, as art forms, we are forced to consider that we are study-ing the traditions of the church's faith experience expressed in two parallel media.

2. Early church historiography is incomplete if it does not deal with the problems raised by the consideration of the first proposition, namely, that early Christian pictorial art is a theological tradition parallel with that expressed in chirographs. This consideration must overcome cer-tain inherent and problematic biases in both disciplines, namely, that both have traditionally given preference to texts.

Art history is a relatively new discipline, and it has from the beginning been a handmaiden to textual studies and other disciplines.[14] As Erwin Panofsky pointed out, the new field of art history had to fight its way free of "an entan-glement with practical art instruction, art appreciation, and that amorphous monster 'general education.'"[15] Panofsky found that when he came to the United States

> the early American art historians such as Charles Rufus Morey . . . were not the products of an established tradition but had come to the history of art from classical philology, theology and philosophy, literature, ar-chitecture, or just collecting. They established a profession by following an avocation.[16]

Thus the first struggle of the art historiography of the early church to be-come a discipline unto itself was to free itself from its being treated as a subset of "New Testament Archaeology." For this reason, Walter Lowrie, who was an archaeologist, felt impelled to state emphatically this liberation in the introduction to his book on early Christian art.[17]

Panofsky, with his colleague and mentor Aby Warburg, defined a pro-gram of art interpretation which consisted of the methods of iconography and iconology.[18] Panofsky considered art to be a "cultural symptom" or "sym-

---

14. Snyder (*Ante Pacem*, 1–11) has presented an excellent bibliography and summary of our subject. This study intends only to build upon Snyder's pioneering effort.

15. Panofsky, "Three Decades of Art History in the United States," in idem, *Meaning in the Visual Arts* (Garden City, N.Y.: Doubleday, 1955) 324.

16. Ibid.

17. Lowrie, *Art in the Early Church*, 19: "we are *not* dealing here with archaeology."

18. Iconography is the method of classifying an artwork by its subject, form, composition, and compositional elements. It is, in Panofsky's words, determining "the intrinsic meaning or content" of a work of art ("Iconography and Iconology: An Introduction to the Study of Renaissance Art," in idem, *Meaning in the Visual Arts: Papers in and on Art History* [Garden City, N.Y.: Doubleday, 1955] 40–41). The latter term is no longer much employed; its function has been assumed under iconography; see Cassiday, *Iconography at the Crossroads*, 6.

bol."[19] Art reveals the heart and soul of a culture. It is therefore essential that the meaning of an artwork join with other such symbols in culture, e.g., literary works, social structures, and political patterns, as well as with other arts, as clues to the substance of that culture. Art is as significant an indicator of a culture's nature as are other cultural symptoms. Panofsky developed the methods of iconography and iconology as programs to search for cultural "themes and concepts" by which to interpret pictorial art and to allow the art to enter into dialogue with other cultural symbols.[20] This methodology was interpreted by many of his followers to be a search for texts which would deliver the meaning of a work of art or verify the meaning which the art historian intuited from the art. The result was that

> [Panofsky] swept up in his wake scores of eager young historians in thrall to sheer intellectual excitement of his approach. . . . Many abandoned themselves to an orgy of text hunting in the indices of the *Patrologia Latina*, in search of that textual nugget that would reveal the secret of a Netherlandish triptych or an Italian fresco.[21]

Iconography, of course, as Cassiday points out, "would scarcely be possible without texts. It is rather the tendency to reduce art to illustration of particular kinds of texts and the inclination to account for . . . images as if they were verbal statements made by nonverbal means [that is problematic]."[22]

The text hunting in early church art history augmented a historically grounded tendency in Western culture to regard the pictorial images of the church as both subsidiary to and dependent upon the early church's texts. The Western academic tradition, driven both by its ecclesiastical and its hellenistic origins, has a deeply invested epistemological stake in the primacy of the text as the bearer of truth. Moreover, the tradition has a greater investment in a special collection of texts among others — the biblical canon.

The Western church officially included pictorial art in the church by its definition that church art was scriptures for the unlettered and the ignorant. Pope Gregory the Great's pronouncement in this vein is generally agreed to be the deciding factor against iconoclasm in the Western church:

> To adore images is one thing; to teach with their help what should be adored is another. What scripture is to the educated, images are to the ignorant, who see through them what they must accept; they read in them what they cannot read in books.[23]

---

19. Panofsky followed Ernst Cassirer in his use of these terms (Cassiday, *Iconography at the Crossroads*, 5–7).

20. Panofsky, "Iconography and Iconology," 40–41.

21. Cassiday, *Iconography at the Crossroads*, 6.

22. Ibid., 7.

23. Latin text of the *Epistula ad Serenum* (600 CE) in Conrad Kirsch, *Enchiridion Fontium Historiae Ecclesiasticae Antiquae* (7th ed.; Freiburg: Herder, 1956) 580. See Herbert L. Kessler,

Indeed, Gregory insisted upon the use of pictures as scripture for a significant
and specific enterprise, his missionary campaign in Gaul.[24] Nevertheless, his
relative ranking of the relationship of pictorial image and rhetorical image
became a general principle. Thus, the concept that pictorial art is precisely
verbal statements made by nonverbal means became an official ecclesiastical
decision.

The Eastern church, after a bloody struggle, finally subscribed to the theological views of John of Damascus (ca. 675–ca. 749), who argued that church
use of images is theologically validated in incarnational theology.[25] This made
it possible for figurative art to be cherished in Byzantium: "of all the cultural
families of Christianity — the Latin, the Syrian, the Egyptian, or the Arme-
nian — the Byzantine was the only one in which art became inseparable from
theology."[26]

Much of the early church's art did, in fact, begin with texts. Kurt
Weitzmann was certainly one of the first to discuss in a systematic and
comprehensive manner "the problem of how miniature and text are related
to each other in principle."[27] Weitzmann, building on the work of Johan
Jakob Tikkanen,[28] developed the hypothesis that book illustration was a well-
established industry in the hellenistic period. Hellenistic Jews and Christians
as well as pagans profusely illustrated rolls and then codices for their sacred
and classical texts.[29] The frescoes at the synagogue in Dura Europos, for example, exhibit the signs that they descended from either LXX rolls or "model
books" based on illustrated Septuagints.[30] The house church at Dura con-

"Pictorial Narrative and Church Mission in Sixth-Century Gaul," in idem and Marianne Shreve
Simpson, eds., *Pictorial Narrative in Antiquity and the Middle Ages* (Studies in the History of Art;
Washington, D.C.: National Gallery of Art; Hanover, N.H.: University Press of New England,
1985) 75–76; idem, "Pictures as Scripture in Fifth-Century Churches," *Studia Artium Orientalis
et Occidentalibus* 2 (1985) 22–31.

24. Kessler, "Pictorial Narrative," 75–91.

25. ET of John's argument in Cyril A. Mango, ed., *The Art of the Byzantine Empire, 312–1453*
(Sources and Documents in the History of Art; Englewood Cliffs, N.J.: Prentice-Hall, 1972)
169–72.

26. John Meyendorff, quoted in Thomas F. Mathews, "Religious Organization and Church
Architecture," in Helen C. Evans and William D. Wixom, eds., *The Glory of Byzantium: Art
and Culture of the Middle Byzantine Era, A.D. 843–1261* (Exhibition catalogue; New York:
Metropolitan Museum of Art/Abrams, 1997) 23.

27. Adolph Katzenellenbogen, review of Weitzmann, *Illustrations in Roll and Codex*, *Speculum*
23 (1948) 513.

28. Tikkanen, "Le Rappresentazioni della Genesi in S. Marco a Venezia e loro Relazione
con la Bibbia Cottoniana," *Archivo storico dell'arte* 1 (1888) 121–22; 257–58; 348–49; idem,
"Die Genesismosaiken von S. Marco in Venedig und ihr Verhältnis zu den Miniaturen der
Cottenbibel," *Acta Societas Scientiarum Fennicae* 17 (1889; repr. Soest, 1972) 72–98.

29. Weitzmann, *Illustrations in Roll and Codex: A Study of the Origin and Method of Text Illustration* (Studies in Manuscript Illustration 2; Princeton, N.J.: Princeton University Press, 1947; repr.
1970).

30. Weitzmann and Herbert L. Kessler, *The Frescoes of the Dura Synagogue and Christian Art*
(Dumbarton Oaks Studies 28; Washington, D.C.: Dumbarton Oaks, 1990).

tains a scene of David's decapitating Goliath which shows some indications that it descended from a LXX roll illustration; Weitzmann thus includes the house church fresco in his catalog and iconographic descriptions of the Dura synagogue's paintings.[31] William Tronzo and Kessler have used as illustrations of this hypothesis the frescoes in Cubiculum C of the "new cemetery" under the Via Latina in Rome, which contains "The Parting of the Red Sea," "The Sacrifice of Isaac," "Moses (or Peter) Striking the Rock," "A Man Holding a Scroll (Moses?)," all these on the walls, and a portrait of Christ, beardless, on the ceiling, as the focal point of the other illustrations.[32] Thus, the models of much early Christian art, especially that which employs portraits of characters or narrative scenes from the Septuagint rolls, are descended from text illustrations.

The church not only inherited this scriptural art tradition but early in its life began to produce its own illustrated gospels and acts. These served as exemplars for the decoration of churches in the late Constantinian and Justinian periods as well as for the explosion of religious art in the Middle Ages.[33]

Iconography has therefore had cause to assume that the source of pictorial images in the early church was chirographic. However, when someone from a background in literary studies examines iconographical analyses, he or she is likely to notice that the growing understanding of the complexity of early church and Jewish traditions, especially oral traditions, does not usually play a role. That is, the texts with which iconographers are accustomed to work are the received texts.[34] This is not to fault iconography or iconographers; *ars longa, vita brevis.*

The complexity of rhetorical traditions, however, might well come into play in the analysis of early Christian pictorial art. An example among many possible is one current analysis of the house church at Dura Europos. In the baptistery, the good shepherd, the Samaritan woman and the scene of Jesus and Peter's walking on water come together, with the good shepherd as the focal point, and indicate that

[a]ppropriate for the theme of baptism, the representation shows Adam and Eve on either side of the tree of knowledge, framed by trees of paradise. Above it, a broader presentation of a sheep carrier with his flock

---

31. Weitzmann and Kessler, *Frescoes*, 84–86.

32. Tronzo, *The Via Latina Catacomb: Imitation and Discontinuity in Fourth-Century Roman Painting* (University Park, Pa.: Pennsylvania State University Press, 1986) 51–66; Weitzmann and Kessler, *Frescoes*, 174–77; Antonia Ferrua, *Le Pittura della nuova Catacomba di Via Latina* (Vatican City: Pontifical Institute of Christian Archaeology, 1960) illus. xcviii; xcic; xxxv; xxxvii; xxxi, 1.

33. Kessler, "Narrative Representations," in Weitzmann, *Late Antique and Early Christian Art*, 449.

34. Cassiday, *Iconography at the Crossroads*, 6–8.

introduces a bucolic theme, which, in this context, *is to be understood as a symbolic reference to John 10:11.*[35]

To one steeped in the complexity of formation of ancient texts, especially of the oral and/or written sources underlying John's gospel, the attribution of the iconographic program to a particular text may appear facile. Dinkler's conclusion could be amended to read, "[the Good Shepherd] is to be understood as a symbolic reference to the same understanding of theological significance which also underlies John 10:11."

There are figurative images from the early church which necessarily raise the question of oral tradition and Christian art. Kessler examines the popular images which depict the meeting of Peter and Paul in Rome, an image which goes back at least to the end of the fourth century.[36] The date forces the author to consider that "legend" and "theological discussion" underlie the image, rather than a text. The earliest textual witness to this scene, which does not appear in the Acts of the Apostles, is the *Acts of Peter and Paul,* usually dated to the fifth or sixth century. As Kessler observes,

> the composition was, in fact, built up from the emblematic core motif and, with ad hoc additions, made to conform to the preceding [narrative pictorial images] in the cycle. Though stimulated, perhaps, by oral tradition or by written apocrypha describing Paul's meeting with Peter, the image is essentially a pictorial invention to express the idea of *concordia apostolorum.*[37]

In the case of the images of the meeting of Peter and Paul, we have a series of them which, on their own, express a theological motif which was incorporated into texts subsequent to the creation of the image. There are many other such images, for example, that of Peter's striking the rock[38] and that of John the Evangelist boiled in oil in Rome.[39]

The earliest extant Christian images, especially the funerary art, may also be interpreted as iconographic programs. I have already pointed to the program at the house church at Dura Europos and that in Cubiculum C of

---

35. Erich Dinkler, "Abbreviated Representations," in Wietzmann, *Symposium,* 390 (emphasis added); Snyder, *Ante Pacem,* 68–71.

36. Kessler, "The Meeting of Peter and Paul in Rome: An Emblematic Narrative of Spiritual Brotherhood," *Dumbarton Oaks Papers* 41 (1987) 265–75.

37. Ibid., 273.

38. Elizabeth Struthers Malbon, *The Iconography of the Sarcophagus of Junius Bassus* (Princeton, N.J.: Princeton University Press, 1990) 81; Erich Dinkler, "Die ersten Petrusdarstellungen: ein archäologischer Beitrag zur Geschichte des Petrusprimates," *Marburger Jahrbuch für Kunstwissenschaft* 11 (1939) 8–11; Ulrich Fabricius, *Die Legende im Bild des 1 Jahrtausend der Kirche* (Kassel: Oncken, 1956) 97.

39. This story is mentioned by Tertullian (*De praescr.* 36) but does not appear in a text before the *Acts of John in Rome.*

the Via Latina cemetery. Ernst Kitzinger applies such an interpretation to an early sarcophagus in the Museo Pio Cristiano (inv. 181). He "reads" the sarcophagus as if it were a script and interprets the sarcophagus as pictorial scripture:

> [The *kriophoros*, "ram-carrier"] gained enormous popularity among Christians because it called to mind the Gospel parables of the lost sheep (Luke 15) and of the shepherd who gives his life for his sheep (John 10). That is to say, it epitomized central tenets of faith — remission of sins and redemption through Christ's self-sacrifice. It did not, however, depict the historical Jesus. It evoked a verbal simile. *To be sure, Christ had used this simile in reference to himself....*[40]

The shepherd is the subject of the teaching discourse on the left; thus, "[w]e are meant to 'read' it in the manner of indirect speech. It is the embodiment of the true philosophy that has governed the couple's life and will assure their afterlife."[41]

There is another possibility of influence in respect to the *kriophoros* image and the rhetorical image of Jesus as "Good Shepherd." The sheep-bearer, as Kitzinger points out, is "age-old."[42] It precedes the rhetorical image in John 10 by centuries, both in pictorial and in rhetorical form (e.g., Psalm 23). One does not adopt an image from previous art without a price, that price being that the intent and meaning of the earlier image are never completely erased in the new. The composition and style of the *kriophoros* in Christian art is extremely close to that in pagan art. A cogent argument could be made that the Good Shepherd in John 10 is the result of influence from the pictorial images of the *bonus pastor*, which abounded in the Greco-Roman world. One may well suspect that third-century Christians, worshiping in the Dura baptistery, would find in the good shepherd a great deal more than a reference to certain Christian stories. Although the analysis of iconographic programs deals with art as art, Steinberg's accusation of "textism" in the discipline looms over many of these interpretations.

The earliest extant Christian art cannot be dated before the end of the second and the beginning of the third century; this lends weight to the concept that the pictures always refer to texts. Because we have extant examples of chirographs which are earlier than the extant figurative art, it is assumed that the latter must be derived from the former. These early texts are, of course, fragments. We are willing to assume (and, I believe, correctly), on the basis of the later, complete texts, that the preceding fragments are the

---

40. Kitzinger, "Christian Imagery: Growth and Impact," in Weitzmann, *Symposium*, 142 fig. 1.
41. Ibid.
42. Ibid.

remains of complete manuscripts. Yet we are unwilling to take that step with the church's pictorial art.

The usual explanation for the relatively late appearance of pictorial art in the early church is that the church interpreted the second commandment in the Decalogue to forbid the making of any images for any purpose; this was fortified by the early church's abhorrence of pagan cult practices. These factors make up what has been called the "classical" statement about the appearance of church art. But the classical consensus has been under cogent attack.

Sister Charles Murray, for example, has charged that the early church writers, generally considered enemies of Christian art, have been misrepresented.[43] Likewise, Kurt Schubert builds on the discovery of the synagogues at Dura Europos and Hammath Tiberias and of the house church at Dura. They raise strong doubts as to whether Judaism and Christianity interpreted Exod 20:3–4 as absolutely forbidding the production of figurative images. Schubert has assembled a formidable array of texts, archaeological data and a catalog of both Jewish and Christian images to demonstrate that the Jewish attitude toward the production of images was very different from what was previously supposed.[44] As Schubert persuasively argues, when the temple was destroyed in the war of 66–73 CE, Judaism's rather short-lived rigidity toward the prohibition of all images lost its focus, namely, the statue of the emperor which had been erected in the Holy of Holies. The general attitude expressed in the Midrashim and the Targumim is that images are acceptable so long as they were not worshiped as idols.[45]

Schubert also points out that the power of Hellenism was strong, beginning with the first century CE and especially in the diaspora. There are numerous reports of images in homes and places of worship supported by the ruling and the monied classes within hellenistic Judaism. In short, "a positive attitude towards images developed only in environs where images were appreciated."[46] These environs were precisely where Christianity began to expand after 70 CE.

Sociometric analyses of the growth of early Christianity show that increase would not have been on an arithmetic scale. Rodney Stark demonstrates that up until about the year 150, Christians would have made up only about 0.07 percent of the total population. Between 150 and 250, Christians would have

---

43. Murray, "Art and the Early Church," *JTS* n.s. 28 (1977) 303–45, with reference to Tertullian *De pud.* 10; Irenaeus *Adv. haer.* 1.23.4; 1.25.6; Clement of Alexandria *Paed.* 3.11. *Contra* Murray, see Kitzinger, "Christian Imagery," 141 n. 1.

44. Schubert, "Jewish Pictorial Traditions in Early Christian Art," in idem and Heinz Schreckenberg, *Jewish Historiography and Iconography in Early and Medieval Christianity* (CRINT 3/2; Assen: Van Gorcum; Minneapolis: Fortress, 1992) 143–59.

45. Ibid., 153.

46. Ibid., 150.

grown to 1.9 percent; from 250 to 350 they increased to 10.5 percent in 300, and to 56.5 percent by 350.[47]

The paucity of Christian artifacts before the year 250 is certainly as plausibly assigned to the very small numbers of Christians who would have been patrons of the arts as to an aniconism inherent in the religion itself. Further, the increase in art objects between 275 and 350 is exponential, just as is the increase of Christians themselves. Given the best estimates of the population of the Roman Empire (60 million), Stark suggests that, in 100 CE, there would have been all of 7,500 Christians (by 250 the number is 1,171,000). Just how much art would 7,500 people produce that would endure and be identifiable as Christian (and not as pagan or Jewish)?

It is difficult to know what would have been distinctively Christian in the earliest forms of Christian art. There is not one example of early Christian symbolism or figurative art that does not have antecedents in paganism or Judaism.[48] The religious association of such art must be determined by context. The sarcophagus which Kitzinger discusses as typically Christian pictorial scripture (see above, on Museo Pio Cristiano, inv. 181), upon which appear an *orante*, a teaching scene, and a good shepherd, is a case in point. It is usually dated at about 275 CE. Formerly, such a sarcophagus would have been considered Christian because of the combination of the three main figures. That hypothesis is now in doubt.[49]

Given the urbanization of Christianity in the hellenistic cities during the second half of the first century, the prolific use of cultic art in those cities, the growth scales presented by Stark, and the fact that the earliest Christian art pieces indicate that they are the product of already-developed traditions, it is difficult to believe that the first Christian art did not appear much earlier than did the earliest Christian art now extant. We do not have this art, or we may not have identified it. But we do have discussion of the use of art by Clement of Alexandria, Tertullian and Irenaeus. One ought to be able to assume that, by the time such discussion began, the use of pictorial art was widespread enough to attract the attention of these writers.

I now come to a preliminary conclusion. When one combines the textual scholars' understanding of the complexities of tradition that underlie texts with the iconographers' understanding of the complexities of image tradition that lies behind pictorial art, it is more and more likely that historical accuracy would demand that the pictorial images and the textual images be

47. Stark, *The Rise of Christianity: A Sociologist Reconsiders History* (Princeton, N.J.: Princeton University Press, 1996) 7.

48. Snyder, *Ante Pacem*, 13–29.

49. Giuseppe Bovini and Hugo Brandenburg, eds., *Repertorium der christlich-antiken Sarkophage*, vol. 1: *Rom und Ostia* (Wiesbaden: Steiner, 1967) no. 66, pl. 21, 66.2; James Nelson Carder, in Weitzmann, *Late Antique and Early Christian Art*, 518 (no. 462).

seen as parallel witnesses to the tradition, rather than to assume that the chirograph is the prior source.

The principal argument, however, for the treatment of the pictorial arts and the rhetorical arts as parallel and interdependent expressions of the early Christian experience is an aesthetic-theological one. If one were to demonstrate that every image in early Christian art was inspired by a patron's or artist's reading of a text, the resultant image would remain a new creation in its own art medium. The image might point to the text and bring the patron's and/or the artist's reading of the text's meanings to the viewer. But as Kitzinger has pointed out, once the orders from a patron are issued, the artist takes over.[50]

A pictorial artist of any period brings to his or her creation the accumulation of all the art forms in which he or she has previously worked. The pictorial image itself has become an experience in spatial aesthetics; it is no longer an art event in rhetorical aesthetics. To paraphrase Langer, the painter or sculptor has "destroyed" the text and has created a pictorial image. The result is not a combination of forms; it is a new art form and a new experience.[51]

The exegetical enterprise employs a multitude of methods to determine what, for example, Paul of Tarsus intended to say to the Corinthians and what the Corinthians will have read. The art historiographer, like the theologian, must work to determine what the early Christian who sat in the baptistery of the church at Dura Europos saw and experienced in that seeing. This experience was not free from narrative allusions. But it also brought with it the Greco-Roman aesthetic.[52]

Paul J. Achtemeier ends his SBL presidential address on orality in the early church's rhetorical practices with a challenge: "one suspects ... [that] scholarly suppositions have prevailed that are simply anachronistic when applied to the actual environment within which documents were written and read ... much work remains to be done — and redone!"[53] A like challenge is now put to early church historiography, if historians and exegetes will give to early Christian art and the aesthetics of late antiquity the attention they are due.

First we must deal with our commitment to texts, with the fact that we are "trained to interpret texts, impressed by the ubiquity of texts, and work-

---

50. Kitzinger, "On the Interpretation of Stylistic Changes in Late Antique Art," in idem, *The Art of Byzantium and the Medieval West: Selected Studies* (Bloomington, Ind.: Indiana University Press, 1976) 32–48.

51. Langer, *Feeling and Form*, 153.

52. See esp. Kitzinger, *Byzantine Art*, passim; Brown, "Art and Society," 17–27.

53. Achtemeier, "*Omne verbum sonat:* The New Testament and the Oral Environment of Late Western Antiquity," *JBL* 109 (1990) 27.

ing single-mindedly with texts...."[54] In such a situation, will pictorial art be allowed to speak for itself? We face a common situation in the challenge that oral tradition makes to historians and theologians who are dedicated to the superiority of chirographs: the original faith expression was in one art form (oral rhetoric); it was transformed into a second art form (written rhetoric) and, simultaneously, to a third (figurative arts).

The study of the chirographic remains of the first centuries of Christianity is turning to metahistorical methods to analyze and to interpret texts and to reconstruct the oral and written traditions that underlie those texts. Narratology, audience criticism, the various semiotic approaches to literature, and the anthropological study of folk tales and of epic singers are but a part of this revolution. History and theology no longer remain the reduction of faith experience to propositional statements; they are rather ways by which to engage the arts of the early church's faith experiences. Art history is in the same search.[55]

All of this activity results in a strong reminder to both historiography and theology that the *dabar YHWH* (in the NT the λόγος τοῦ θεοῦ) did not appear in the human community in chirographic form. On the contrary, the Word began as art event, as stories told by the singers of tales and as poetry chanted by the prophets. The love of new technologies — writing, the papyrus and vellum scroll, the codex, the printing press — caused the transformation of these art forms to the chirographic form and led to the coronation of the text as the designated bearer of the Word. But humans, as aesthetic creatures, are not inclined to limit themselves to one art medium for the expression of their faith.

Recognition of the great diversity of media that historically have transformed the Word opens up the pictorial arts' challenge both to historiography and to theology. It demands that theology go beyond the use of early Christian art as cover illustrations for NT introductions and for collections of documents for the study of early church texts.[56]

Once we recognize that the pictorial arts of the early church are not a subsidiary but a parallel tradition to that of the textual arts, we must take seriously the attempts of art historians to "see" as did the early Christians. Iconographers are profiting from strategies of interpretation akin to those who now analyze literature.[57] This analysis allows the historiographer

---

54. Werner Kelber, "Narrative as Interpretation and Interpretation as Narrative: Hermeneutical Reflections on the Gospels," *Semeia* 39 (1987) 120.

55. Mieke Bal and Norman Bryson, "Semiotics and Art History," *The Art Bulletin* 73/2 (June 1991) 174–208; Cassiday, *Iconography at the Crossroads*, 15.

56. As in the case of David R. Cartlidge and David L. Dungan, eds., *Documents for the Study of the Gospels* (Philadelphia: Fortress, 1980; 2d ed., 1994); the cover is an excerpt from the Sarcophagus of Junius Bassus.

57. Bal and Bryson, "Semiotics and Art History," 174–208.

to engage in a true humanistic exploration of other humans' experiences, without the reduction of these experiences to post-Enlightenment positivistic propositions.

A study of the early church's pictorial arts as arts reinforces new developments in the historical picture of the church as contemporary historiography reconstructs it. This suggestion derives from a puckish question: If we were to accept the parallel nature of early Christian pictorial art with the early church's texts as expressions of the theology of the church, would images of biblical scenes hold a value more sacred than do images that are not biblical? The question is not frivolous. The problem of canon haunts both chirographic and pictorial historiography. One need only observe the large number of publications of "the Bible in art"; and at the same time there are but two extant monographs on the art paralleled in Christian apocrypha, and they deal with the "influence" of "legends" in chirographic form upon canonical art.[58]

Early Christian artists — figurative or rhetorical — did not consider themselves bound by a canon. Images of extracanonical subjects exist alongside canonical subjects on artwork after artwork. In my own collection of images of Christian art paralleled in Christian apocrypha and other extracanonical literature there are some 48 works of art from the third century and over 180 from the fourth century that contain parallels to extracanonical traditions; most are on art that also displays "canonical" images.

Arguably the first nativity scene is a sarcophagus fragment that is now in the pulpit of the Church of St. Ambrose in Milan. It depicts an infant, wrapped in cloth and lying in a crib. The crib is flanked by an ox and an ass. The beasts are paralleled only in the *Gospel of Pseudo-Matthew* 14 (and derivative representations). As that gospel links the beasts with Isa 1:3 ("the ox knows its owner, and the ass its master's crib"), it seems likely that the carving is not "influenced" by *Pseudo-Matthew* but that a common tradition of Christian typology engendered both the literary and the pictorial versions of this typological link. The influence of this extracanonical tradition is such that one is hard-pressed to find a nativity scene in Christian art that does not include the ox and the ass.[59]

The NT accounts of the nativity do not speak of midwives. Several Christian apocrypha do, most notoriously the *Protevangelium of James*. There Salome, the doubting midwife, performs a gynecological examination to determine if the virgin Mary is still "intact" after she has given birth to the Holy Infant. Salome receives a withered hand for her audacity, and immediately

---

58. J. E. Weis, *Christus- und Apostelbilder: Einfluss der Apokryphen auf die ältesten Kunsttypen* (Freiburg: Herder, 1902); Fabricius, *Legende*.

59. David R. Cartlidge, "The Christian Apocrypha: Preserved in Art," *BibRev* 13/2 (June 1997) 24–26, fig. p. 26. The tradition is continued, e.g., in a cartoon in *The New Yorker*, December 15 (1997) 107.

turns to the Virgin and child for help. The scene was very popular in early art. It occurs in the Cemetery of Valentinus, on the wall of an arcosolium.[60] Of interest is that the scene with Salome's hand is accompanied by one of the visitation and of the bathing of the infant Jesus (with two midwives), a scene not associated with any Christian rhetorical tradition; it is common, however, in nativity scenes of pagan gods and heroes. This is a transitional stage from the "withered hand" scene to later standard iconography in which Salome actually becomes a saint. Few cycles of the "Life of the Virgin" in art exclude the midwives.

The mosaic image of Christ as Helios, in the Necropolis under St. Peter's, the Vatican,[61] is paralleled in an interesting combination of both canonical and extra-canonical legends. The fragment of an early Christian baptismal hymn in Eph 5:14 is probably completed in Clement of Alexandria *Prot.* 9.84:

> Awake, Sleeper
> Rise from the dead,
> And Christ will shine on you.
>
> The Sun of the Resurrection,
> He who was born before the dawn,
> Whose beams give life.[62]

There are literally dozens of examples of this canonical/extra-canonical mixing in art which is either *ante-pacem* or demonstrates that it likely had an *ante-pacem* precedent.

The influence of early Christian pictorial art and its combination of what we now would call canonical and extra-canonical traditions continues in the church and its theological discussions to the present.[63] There is no Eastern Orthodox church without an Anastasis (in the English version, "The Harrowing of Hell"), a scene which occurs very early in the church's art.[64] These scenes occur in relatively late rhetorical form in the *Gospel of Nicodemus* (*Acta Pilati*) 10.1. There is likely no one who would not recognize a portrait of Paul either on a third-century drinking glass or in a painting in a modern church. His pointed dark beard, receding hairline, and sharp features appear in the earliest art of the church. Behind these portraits is the same tradition about Paul that gave birth to *Acts of Paul* 3.

---

60. Fabricius, *Die Legende,* 58; Weitzmann, *The Fresco Cycle of S. Maria di Castelseprio* (Princeton Monographs in Art and Archaeology 26; Princeton, N.J.: Princetown University Press, 1951) fig. 54.

61. Snyder, *Ante Pacem,* pl. 31.

62. Wilder, *Language of the Gospel,* 116–18.

63. Cartlidge, "Christian Apocrypha," 24–31, 56.

64. At least as early as the fourth or fifth century. The scene is on the right forward column, niche 3, zone 7, of the Ciborium in San Marco, Venice (Gertrud Schiller, *Ikonographie der christlichen Kunst* [5 vols. in 8; Gütersloh: Mohn, 1966–91] vol. 3, fig. 145).

It is only an a priori ranking of canonical over extra-canonical literature that allows early Christian art to be considered the product of a *Volkreligion*, as Snyder rightly indicates.[65] One can maintain this assessment only if one assumes the theological purity of early church theology as defined by the canonical or "orthodox" chirograph.[66]

Such a priority has not ruled throughout the history of the church. One cannot imagine the faithful gaining from a typical crucifixion scene an impression which would recognize that, while most of the scene is faithful to the gospels, the loincloth shows the influence of the *Gospel of Nicodemus* 10.1, and Sol and Luna above the cross are either pagan or gnostic. Nor can one imagine a series of the "Life of the Virgin," in which the church carefully points out that the first images show the influence of the *Protevangelium of James*; the rest are canonical — except for the Dormition.

The elements are therefore in place for productive explorations in our reconstruction of the history of the early church, an odyssey which must face the challenges of "textism," of canon, and of early Christian aesthetics. This journey can take place only with a true cooperation between those whose focus of study is the pictorial arts and those who labor among the traditions which at some point became textual. This cooperation has begun. At the crossroads of iconography and rhetorical studies there is a great opportunity to "see rare beasts, and have unique adventures."[67]

---

65. Snyder, *Ante Pacem*, 6–7.

66. Snyder (ibid., 9–11) refers in this context to the significance of Walter Bauer, *Orthodoxy and Heresy in Earliest Christianity* (Philadelphia: Fortress, 1971).

67. W. H. Auden, *For the Time Being: A Christmas Oratorio.*

26

ARCHITECTURAL TRANSITIONS FROM SYNAGOGUES AND HOUSE CHURCHES TO PURPOSE-BUILT CHURCHES

Peter Richardson

Christianity stresses the formation of "kinship" community either where it had not existed before (1 Peter 2:10) or where it had been disrupted by the Jesus revolution (Mark 10:23–31). Early Christians undoubtedly met in private homes (Colossians 4:15), though it should not be forgotten that Christians, like the Jews (Acts 16:13), also met in open places (Pliny, *Letters*, 117), markets, and hired halls (Acts 20:8). There is no literary evidence nor archaeological indication that any such home was converted into an extant church building. Nor is there any extant church that certainly was built prior to Constantine. Consequently, we have *no evidence regarding the intentional structure of a Christian meeting place prior to the "peace."* But there are homes that were restructured to accommodate the Christian assembly.[1]

The emphasized words in Snyder's description are almost a commonplace: there is no evidence of purpose-built churches before 313 CE (the Edict of Milan). It is likewise a commonplace that Constantine inaugurated Christian basilicas in the period after 324 CE when he was sole emperor, to assume tacitly that later basilical churches derived from Constantine's initiative, and to imagine that this is a sufficient explanation.[2] I will emphasize that there

---

1. Graydon F. Snyder, *Ante Pacem: Archaeological Evidence of Church Life before Constantine* (Macon, Ga.: Mercer University Press, 1985) 67 (emphasis added).

2. J. B. Ward-Perkins, "Constantine and the Origins of the Christian Basilica," *Papers of the*

was a transitional period in the third century during which the example of Jewish synagogues was a critical factor.

Snyder and White on House Churches and House Synagogues

In *Ante Pacem*, Snyder gathered archaeological evidence for the character of early Christianity;[3] he emphasized the breadth of the evidence and the importance of the social-historical framework. Though now somewhat old, his book remains a skillfully devised compendium, useful for its drawings, bibliographies, analyses, and evaluations. One concern was to identify the earliest stages of the architecture of Christian meeting places, and he rightly put first the church at Dura-Europos, alongside the more complicated evidence of Capernaum, Aquileia, and the *Titulus* churches in Rome.[4] He argued that "Christians of the third century were not building new churches, but taking over existing architectural structures," as Dura-Europos (a house converted to Christian use sometime between 232 and 256 CE) shows unmistakably. He was more reticent about Capernaum, holding that it had little to tell us about house churches.

Some evidence, he said, was "borderline." He thought that the north church at Aquileia "may be the first Christian edifice created *de novo*," for he doubted that there was an earlier *domus ecclesiae* below it, emphasizing that these are "simply halls with mosaic floors." He considered a rival for this honor, Titulus Crisogoni: "If this hall was built in 310...then this, or possibly the north church at Aquileia, must be the earliest-known structure built specifically for the Christian assembly. We can note that this building...was a meeting hall...."[5]

Snyder also considered evidence for *insulae* or tenement churches, suggesting that in addition to remodeling middle- or upper-class houses, a similar practice obtained lower down the scale, where a church member turned over a modest apartment (in which much of the population lived) to the church.[6] The best example is SS. Giovanni e Paolo, where renovations carried out in the mid-third century CE created a two-story meeting hall.[7] Sny-

---

British School in Rome 22 (1954) 80, 121–22; Richard Krautheimer, *Early Christian and Byzantine Architecture* (3d ed.; Harmondsworth, Middlesex, and Baltimore, Md.: Penguin, 1979).

3. Recently he has emphasized the acculturation of Jewish and Christian communities in Rome; see Graydon F. Snyder, "The Interaction of Jews with Non-Jews in Rome," in Karl P. Donfried and Peter Richardson, eds., *Judaism and Christianity in First-Century Rome* (Grand Rapids: Eerdmans, 1998) 64–86.

4. Snyder, *Ante Pacem*, 67–117.

5. Ibid., 34–35, 74–75, 81–82.

6. Robert Jewett, "Tenement Churches and Communal Meals in the Early Church: The Implications of a Form-Critical Analysis of 2 Thess 3:10," *BR* 38 (1993) 23–43.

7. Snyder, *Ante Pacem*, 77–80.

der thought it likely that the third-century alterations were for Christian purposes, since early fourth-century changes were certainly Christian. This general picture fits well the complex social-historical developments of the third century. While Snyder allowed the possibility that there were purpose-built pre-Constantinian churches, he was skeptical because the evidence was slender. He cited several relevant inscriptions. For example, *P.Oxy* I.43 (ca. 295 CE) refers to two streets named after churches and *P.Oxy* XXXIII.2673 (February 5, 304 CE) refers to church possessions, both of which might presume publicly visible meeting places.[8] Basically, however, "Christian culture began to appear at approximately the end of the second century" when several features coalesced, "when [Christians] became involved with legal title to land and property; when they used organized labor, . . . when their church had public functions such as buying and selling; when the Church had visible, known leadership; and, above all, when Christians were willing to make their presence known to the larger public."[9]

Snyder's work has been partly upstaged by L. Michael White's study, which is fuller in its documentation of the relevant archaeological and literary evidence but narrower because limited to architecture.[10] He emphasizes the social context of early Christian architecture. Volume 1 analyzes early archaeological evidence for church buildings alongside evidence for Mithraea, synagogues, and other religious structures. Volume 2 provides a collection of primary data bearing on those analyses.[11]

White accepts a widely recognized commonplace, that churches had their earliest origins in the house church, and then examines "pre-basilical" churches in volume 1 archaeologically, emphasizing the successive adaptations to fit houses for use as churches. When patrons turned over their houses to a group, they provided for renovations to make the house more useful. The most informative archaeological materials come from Dura-Europos, where almost contemporaneous structures for Jews, Christians, Mithraists, and others can be compared. These structures were generally located against the city walls, in contrast to traditional religious structures in the urban center. The same situation obtains in Priene, where a synagogue, a cult dedicated to Alexander, and a Mithraeum were beside each other in a residential dis-

---

8. Ibid., 159.
9. Ibid., 163.
10. L. Michael White, *The Social Origins of Christian Architecture* (2 vols.; HTS 42–43; Valley Forge, Pa.: Trinity Press International, 1996–97). Volume 1 was originally published as L. Michael White, *Building God's House in the Roman World: Architectural Adaptation among Pagans, Jews and Christians* (Baltimore, Md.: Johns Hopkins University Press, 1990).
11. Volume 2 (*Texts and Monuments for the Christian Domus Ecclesiae in Its Environment*) is the most complete collection of data presently available on early Christian architecture; the texts in the original languages, with new translations and commentary, are most convenient.

trict near the western city wall. In both cities, substantial temples in the center contrasted with new house-based cults on the periphery.

Early Christianity was rooted in a specific set of social conditions involving patrons wealthy enough to have houses that could be renovated and given away. The status of Christians, the roles of patrons, and the honor system that lay behind such munificent gifts allow a better understanding of the church as it moved from being a reform movement within Judaism to the religion of the empire.

White includes discussion of synagogues but limits the evidence to the diaspora. Though understandable, the decision is regrettable: it eliminates instances of early purpose-built synagogues and overlooks important adapted synagogues; it exaggerates the closeness of the comparisons; and it overlooks other useful comparisons.

The data in volume 2, however, imply that not all pre-Constantinian churches were adaptive structures. Sometime in the third century, I suggest, Christians tentatively began to build more self-confident, more publicly visible meeting places that were purpose-built. The evidence suggests a transitional phase between the early informal adaptations of houses and the "true" basilicas of Constantine, though this period can be neither precisely dated nor fully studied. Such a transition period is potentially important and needs concentrated study, along the lines of the questions suggested at the end of this essay.

Chronological and Geographical Considerations

Chronologically, evidence from house synagogues is relevant.[12] At Dura-Europos a house was converted to a synagogue (second half of the second century CE) earlier than the church. The same pattern was present in Stobi (second or third century CE), Priene (probably second century CE), Ostia (second century CE), and Delos, the earliest such adaptation (second or first century CE).[13] While the social processes are the same, adaptations of synagogues were usually earlier than those of churches. Geographically, the Jewish

---

12. There is an immense amount of literature on synagogues. See recent lengthy bibliographies in Dan Urman and Paul V. M. Flesher, *Ancient Synagogues: Historical Analysis and Archaeological Discovery* (2 vols.; SPB 47; Leiden: Brill, 1995); Donald D. Binder, "Into the Temple Courts: The Place of the Synagogue in the Second Temple Period" (Ph.D. diss., Southern Methodist University, 1997). See also Peter Richardson, "Early Synagogues as Collegia in the Diaspora and Palestine," in John S. Kloppenborg and Stephen G. Wilson, eds., *Voluntary Associations in the Graeco-Roman World* (London and New York: Routledge, 1996) 90–109: synagogues existed in the pre-70 period, they originated in Egypt, and to non-Jews in the diaspora they looked and functioned like *collegia*, which had architectural forms similar to those that Jews and Christians adopted.

13. White, *Social Origins*, vol. 1, chap. 4; also L. Michael White, "Synagogue and Society in Imperial Ostia: Archaeological and Epigraphic Evidence," in Donfried and Richardson, *Judaism and Christianity*, 30–63. On Delos, see B. Hudson McLean, "The Place of Cult in Voluntary As-

diaspora provides excellent physical evidence for patron-inspired adaptations of houses as synagogues extending from the second century BCE through the third century CE. There is also good inscriptional evidence for the generous roles of patrons.

On the Christian side, the evidence is both better and worse. Early Christian literature coheres with archaeological evidence from a slightly later period, as many have demonstrated: churches met in houses of patrons, who either continued to share it or donated it outright.[14] A *domus ecclesiae* probably did multiple duty as meeting place, house, workshop, and social center, though as time passed the religious uses probably became more important, the earliest unassailable evidence for which is Dura. Generally, the literary and physical evidence pertains to areas outside Palestine. Since the links between first- and early-third-century literary and archaeological evidence is strong, we will not be far wrong to think that by the mid- or late second century CE Christians used adapted houses as churches.

In Judea the evidence for both house synagogues and house churches is weaker. Excavations at Caesarea Maritima, not well published, suggest a (probably) second-century house-synagogue; the house may have been late hellenistic.[15] At Herodium, the *triclinium* in Herod's Upper Palace was adapted for synagogue use by revolutionaries (66–74 CE), following the pattern elsewhere of adapting *triclinia*. A similar alteration occurred at Masada (same dates), though the room in the casemate wall was not originally residential.[16] Both renovations emerged from the exigencies of war in the late first century CE, not from patronage. The existence of pre-70 CE purpose-built synagogues such as Gamla does not compromise the importance of adaptation as a synagogue strategy, especially among less socially significant groups. Inclusion of Judean evidence leads to a more nuanced view of these Jewish developments. Christian architectural adaptation is less clear: in Galilee Capernaum is usually cited, though there are serious difficulties;[17] several examples nearby in Syria are better, especially Qirqbize, Umm al-Jimal, and

---

sociations and Christian Churches on Delos," in Kloppenborg and Wilson, *Voluntary Associations*, 186–225.

14. See Bradley B. Blue, "Acts and the House Church," in David W. J. Gill and Conrad Gempf, eds., *The Book of Acts in Its Graeco-Roman Setting* (=vol. 2 of *The Book of Acts in Its First Century Setting*) (Grand Rapids: Eerdmans; Carlisle: Paternoster, 1994) 119–222.

15. Caesarea Maritima was always a hellenized city; see Peter Richardson, *Herod: King of the Jews and Friend of the Romans* (Columbia, S.C.: University of South Carolina Press, 1996) 91–94. On the synagogue, see Michael Avi-Yonah, "Synagogues," in Ephraim Stern, ed., *The New Encyclopedia of Archaeological Excavations in the Holy Land* (hereafter *NEAEHL*) (4 vols.; Jerusalem: Carta; New York: Simon & Schuster, 1993) 1. 278–80.

16. Richardson, *Herod,* 183–86, on Netzer's views.

17. The fourth-century walled structure is discontinuous with the first-century house, and probably irrelevant for this question.

Dura.[18] Thus the evidence of diaspora and Holy Land, though not identical, coheres, and any history of general architectural developments should avoid too sharp a contrast. What follows will focus on relevant data from the eastern provinces, especially Palestine, in order to focus on the transitional period.[19]

Purpose-Built Synagogues

This description might imply that Christian communities learned how to adapt houses for their needs from Jewish and other communities, a likely but not yet demonstrable view. Certainly they developed similar strategies and thought about their buildings in similar ways, though the evidence is not well balanced.[20] One aspect of this emerges from an unlikely source.[21] When Eusebius quotes Philo's description of the Therapeutae's buildings and practices, he claims to be describing early *Christian* practices in Alexandria. Apparently monastic Jews were inconceivable, yet the description was attractively parallel to Christian monastics in his own day. Though Eusebius does not know it, Judaism had both eremitic and cenobitic monasticism, as did the church of Eusebius's day; both communities had developed the same types of monastic communities two centuries apart. When Eusebius borrowed from Philo, did he know what he was doing or was he deliberately obfuscating? The two Jewish monasteries known to us, Qumran and the Therapeutae, had long since been destroyed, and probably no trace of them remained in Eusebius's day. Since there was apparently no tradition of monastic Judaism, Eusebius was able (whether knowingly and tendentiously or ignorantly and innocently matters little) to apply Philo's description to Christian monasteries, which he did effectively. Were the two developments totally independent, or was there some residual borrowing by Christians from earlier Jewish practices? We cannot say; the literary evidence is insufficient to settle the historical and architectural questions, though most would assume the complete independence of the two architectural developments.

This exemplifies our problem. Basilical churches parallel basilical syna-

---

18. White, *Social Origins* 2. 135–52.

19. William L. MacDonald, *Early Christian and Byzantine Architecture* (New York: Braziller, 1962) 23, argues that there was more innovation in the hellenized East.

20. We lack Jewish texts on these matters, though note *m. Ned.* 9.2, on the dispute between R. Eliezer and the Sages whether a vow to turn a house into a synagogue was binding; see also *m. Meg.* 3.1–3, on selling a synagogue.

21. Peter Richardson, "Philo and Eusebius on Monasteries and Monasticism: The Therapeutae and Kellia," in Bradley H. McLean, ed., *Origins and Method: Towards a New Understanding of Judaism and Early Christianity: Essays in Honour of John C. Hurd* (JSNTSup 86; Sheffield: JSOT Press, 1993) 334–59.

gogues, though later.[22] Should we imagine influence, or are they independent developments?[23] Lee I. Levine holds that "many buildings, especially those in the Galilee and Golan, were patterned after some form of Roman civic building, others were patterned on the Christian basilica and featured a central nave, two aisles, an apse (or bema), a narthex (forehall), and an atrium."[24] This formulation obscures the situation for two reasons: Jewish synagogues *preceded* churches and *Roman* civic buildings were the model for the borrowing.

The word "basilica" is regularly used of churches and synagogues. The Roman basilica was a civic building, used for a variety of purposes: market, bank, stock exchange, tribunal, law court, meeting place.[25] Basilicas emerged in the Roman world by the second century BCE;[26] though the word is Greek ("royal building"), there is no known example of a Greek precursor to the Roman type. While the word indicates primarily function, not architectural form, the basilica was a rectangular building of varying proportions, with entrances in either the short or long sides, and with a higher central portion divided from two lower side aisles by rows of columns. Usually there were clerestory windows above the columns to light the central space; often there was a second floor over the side aisles. Sometimes there was an apse or a projection, used as a "tribunal," on one end or one side (later, sometimes

---

22. Some want to reserve "basilica" for the very large architectural creations of Constantine and later, but I will use the term for those and for smaller churches that share the same form.

23. Robert Milburn, *Early Christian Art and Architecture* (Berkeley and Los Angeles: University of California Press, 1988) 83, emphasizes that "the pagan basilica was, by the second or third century AD, being readily adapted to the religious uses of the Hebrews," and claims that "the synagogue may be said to have cleansed the basilica of its pagan associations and helped to prepare for the free use of the basilican style in Christian churches, but the influences run both ways...." Contrariwise, G. Foerster, "Dating Synagogues with a 'Basilical' Plan and an Apse," in Urman and Flesher, *Ancient Synagogues* 1. 87–94, argues that this class of synagogues was influenced by churches.

24. Levine, "Synagogues," in *NEAEHL* 4. 1421–24; here 1423.

25. Vitruvius (first century BCE), *On Architecture* 5.1.4–9, says: "Basilicas should be constructed on a site adjoining the forum and in the warmest possible quarter, so that in winter business men may gather in them.... It is thought that the columns of basilicas ought to be as high as the side-aisles are broad; an aisle should be limited to one third of the breadth which the open space in the middle is to have. Let the columns of the upper tier be smaller than those of the lower.... But basilicas of the greatest dignity and beauty may also be constructed in the style of that one which I erected, and the building of which I superintended, at Fano.... The two middle columns on [one] side are omitted, in order not to obstruct the view of the *pronaos* of the temple of Augustus... and also the tribunal which is... shaped as a hemicycle whose curvature is less than a semicircle.... Its curvature inwards is fifteen feet so that those who are standing before the magistrates may not be in the way of the business men in the basilica...." This description (eliminating most of Vitruvius's details about proportions) stresses the multiuse character of basilicas (Morris Hicky Morgan, trans., *Vitruvius: The Ten Books on Architecture* [New York: Dover, 1960] 132–36).

26. Basilica of Porcia in Rome, 189 BCE; Aemilian Basilica, 179 BCE; Basilica of Sempronius, 180 BCE; Basilica of Pompeii, 130 BCE or a little later. For comparative plans, see *Atlas d'architecture mondiale* (Paris: Stock, 1978) 230–34.

at both ends).[27] This basic shape was adopted by Christians and Jews for many of their purpose-built religious structures.[28] The word, however, is frequently used loosely of any room with columns. In the rest of this essay I shall use the term when a number of basilical elements are present.[29] Large halls without basilical elements are here called "meeting halls," following Snyder and White.

Roman basilicas appeared in the Roman East from the first century BCE onwards. The most important and probably the earliest (late first century BCE) was Herod's Royal Basilica, embellishing the southern side of Jerusalem's temple precinct; the basilica in Sebaste may also have been one of Herod's constructions. In the second century CE a basilica with apse was built in Tiberias alongside the Cardo Maximus leading south to Hammat Tiberias; another late-second-century CE basilica appears, surprisingly, in Beth Shearim. Beth Shean, Bostra, Qanawat (Canatha), Shaqqa (Maximinianopolis), and no doubt other important eastern cities, both hellenized and Jewish, had basilicas.

Jewish communities began building basilical synagogues relatively early. This basic architectural form was soon fashionable, though the significance of the basilical form itself is often ignored. But not all synagogues were basilical; alongside this form were a number of meeting halls. In Table 1 I have excluded house-synagogues but included meeting halls and basilicas; the line between them is not clear, and a more adequate typology still needs to be attempted. Though the division pre- and post-Constantine was not significant for synagogue architecture, that convention helps clarify their relation to church architecture.[30]

The table permits the following observations: (1) there is a more even chronological distribution from pre-70 CE synagogues through the fourth century than is usually thought; (2) the practices of Jewish communities in the eastern diaspora and Palestine were parallel; (3) architectural form within both diaspora and Palestinian communities shifted from more or less evenly balanced numbers of meeting halls and basilical synagogues to a substantial preponderance of basilical style; (4) while numerous synagogues were built on models other than basilicas, from the third century onwards (when Roman

27. Examples: near-identical Basilica A and Basilica B at Corinth, Augustica Raurica, Aspendos, Cosa; Trajan's Basilica Ulpia is the best-known example of double apses.
28. There are very few "true" basilicas in Judaism. Sardis's monumental synagogue might deserve the term, though it was not explicitly modeled on the basilica but was developed from an earlier renovation that had already combined several rooms of a gymnasium.
29. White (*Social Origins*) seems attracted to an idealized version of a Christian basilica and hesitates to apply the word to smaller churches. It seems preferable to retain the word for buildings whose components were derived from basilicas, regardless of their deviations from either Roman basilicas or later Christian applications.
30. The list, by no means complete, includes synagogues whose essential plan and features can be known reasonably well.

Table 1: Synagogues in the Roman East

SYNAGOGUES[31]	EASTERN DIASPORA	PALESTINE
I. Pre-Constantinian		
Meeting halls	Aegina	Jericho, Hasmonean Palace (70–50 BCE)[32]
		Gamla (1 c. BCE or CE)
		Shuafat (pre-70 CE)[33]
		Kiryat Sefer (pre-70 CE?)
		Nabratein 1 (2 c. CE)
		En Gedi phase 1 (late 2/early 3 c. CE)
		Khirbet Shema (3 c. CE)
		Caesarea stratum 4 (3 c. CE)
		Capernaum phase 1? (1/early 2 c. CE)
		Qasrin, phase 1 (3 c. CE)
		Hammat Tiberias phase I (3 c. CE?)
Basilicas	Gerasa (3 c. CE)[34]	Arbel phase 1 (2 c. CE)
	Sardis stage 3 (3 c. CE)[35]	Qazyon? (197 CE)[36]
		Nabratein synagogue 2a (3 c. CE)
		Chorazin phase 1 (3 c. CE)
		Baram, large (5 c. CE?) and small (3 c. CE)
		synagogues
		Gush Halav (3 c. CE)
		Ma'oz Hayyim (3 c. CE)
		Meiron (3 c. CE)
		Horvat Sumaqa phase 1 (3 c. CE?)
		Hammat Gader phases 1–2 (3 c. CE?)
		Horvat 'Ammudim (end 3/early 4 c. CE)
II. Post-Constantinian		
Meeting halls		Hammat Tiberias phase 2 (4 c. CE)
Basilicas	Sardis stage 4 (4 c. CE)	Qasrin Bldg A (4 c. CE)
	Miletus ? (3 c. CE?)	Chorazin phase 2 (early 4 c. CE)
	Apamea (ca. 391 CE?)	Beth Shearim (late 3/4 c. CE)
		Rehov (4 c. CE)
		Meroth (4 c. CE)
		Capernaum, phase 2 (late 4 c. CE)
		Samaritan synagogues (all 4 c. CE):
		Khirbet Samara, narthex, atrium
		Zur Natan (Khirbet Majdal), atrium
		el-Khirbe (Mt. Gerizim)
		Hazzan Ya'aqov Synagogue (Shechem)

31. For details of most, see *NEAEHL.* See also Dennis Groh, "The Stratigraphic Chronology of the Galilean Synagogue from the Early Roman Period through the Byzantine Period (ca. 420 CE)," in Urman and Flesher, *Ancient Synagogues* 1. 51–69.

32. See Abraham Rabinovich, *Jerusalem Post* (March 30, 1998) 1: Ehud Netzer reported a synagogue at the Hasmonean Winter Palace complex in Jericho (dated 70–50 BCE), with mikveh, benches, a small niche, courtyard, outbuildings, and columns on all four sides of the hall.

33. Abraham Rabinovich, *Jerusalem Post* (April 8, 1991) 1.

34. Gerasa is important for the way a Christian church was built from an earlier synagogue, while reversing its orientation.

35. Perhaps *m.* '*Abod. Zar.* 3.7 is relevant to Sardis: "if a house was built from the first for idolatry it is forbidden; if it was plastered and bedecked for idolatry...one need only remove what was done to it anew; but if a gentile did but bring in an idol and take it out again, such a house is permitted." See also 1.7 (on basilicas) and *m. Tohar.* 6.8.

36. Rachel Hachlili and Ann Killebrew, "Qazyon," paper read at the ASOR 1997 Annual Meeting, allow the possibility that Qazyon was a synagogue, but think it likelier that it was a pagan temple. The inscription, however, has more in common with synagogue inscriptions from Egypt and Rome: "For the salvation of the Roman Caesars / Lucius Septimus Severus Pius / Pertinax Augustus and Marcus / Aurelius Antonius and Lucius / Septimius Geta, their sons, by a / vow of the Jews," and within a wreath, "and Julia Domna Augusta." It can be dated to 197.

basilicas had become common in the area) basilical synagogues gradually became dominant, especially in the Holy Land.[37] These synagogues may not have aped in size or detail true Roman basilicas, but there was sufficient similarity to basilicas that their formal origins are not much in doubt. Thus the fundamental observation is that (5) basilical synagogues predate basilical churches.

Purpose-built "houses of prayer" in Egyptian Judaism originated in the second century BCE; inscriptional evidence refers to *exedrae* (CIJ 1444), gateways (CIJ 1441), *periboloi* (CIJ 1433), appurtenances (CIJ 1422, 1433), gardens (CPJ 1134).[38] The allusions are not as clear as we might wish, but some prayer-houses may have had basilical features. These earliest Jewish community structures, no doubt more like meeting halls than basilicas, may have been important antecedents of later basilical synagogues. This architectural development, traceable first in the diaspora, developed a little later in the homeland, as the pre-70 synagogues now show. Postdestruction Judaism had a strong tradition of purpose-built synagogues; these developed in several types,[39] but by the third century the strongest and most widespread tradition was that modeled on Roman basilicas. Like basilicas, they were for multifunctional communal purposes, had large crowds in view, with higher "nave" and lower side aisles, a double row of columns, perhaps clerestory windows, occasionally apses, doors typically (though by no means always) in the shorter end. Most of the decorative effects were concentrated in the interior; both were frequently embellished with mosaic floors; in Jewish towns they were often located in a central public area; both had a wide range of functions. In short, their functional, chronological, and design features suggest that synagogues drew much of the inspiration for their form and decoration from Roman basilicas. Just at the time synagogues followed the basilical model, however, they also began to mimic features of the temple in Jerusalem.[40] Decorative elements reminiscent of the temple began to appear only when Judaism had the self-confidence to construct once again purpose-built structures in the Holy Land. Thus there were two important attitudes: a deep sense of loss of the central shrine and, ironically, an accommodation to Roman standards of taste.

These later synagogues were not exactly like basilicas, of course. In several respects, especially interior features, they differed: seating was on benches around the walls;[41] they were oriented towards Jerusalem; they provided for

---

37. In the table specific instances of this shift can be seen.

38. Texts in Richardson, "Early Synagogues."

39. With both regional and chronological variations; e.g., in southern Judea there are uncolumned meeting rooms turned broadside and preceded by an atrium.

40. Binder, "Temple Courts," argues that synagogues were extensions of the temple from the beginning, but this seems very unlikely.

41. Three churches (two at Herodium) also had perimeter seating on benches; see Ehud Net-

the Torah scroll; they might be located away from the city square, even in the Holy Land.[42] While initially the structures were relatively simple meeting halls, when purpose-built synagogues became grander, the Roman basilica was the model of choice, both in homeland and diaspora.

Purpose-Built Churches

From 324 CE onwards imperial basilicas were built, the finest being those ordered by Constantine himself.[43] He built in Jerusalem (the Holy Sepulchre, and the Eleona on the Mount of Olives), in Bethlehem (the Church of the Holy Nativity), at Mamre (within Herod's enclosure of the oak tree associated with Abraham), and perhaps at Baalbek.[44] Yet, significant as Constantine's architectural program was, purpose-built churches may have preceded him. During some reigns and in some places, where Christianity was especially self-confident, purpose-built churches were erected. House churches no doubt became gradually more visible and public, as White has noted in connection with the Ostia synagogue, but when a Christian community acquired a site and erected its own structure, churches became significantly more public. This may have happened by the late third century, before the Constantinian settlement, to judge from the evidence White and Snyder have accumulated. The possibility that there were earlier examples in out-of-the-way places should not be excluded altogether. In the following I have used White, limiting the evidence to sites and sources from the East; I have included only those that may presuppose purpose-built churches prior to the flowering of "true" basilical churches after 324 CE.

Documentary Evidence

- P.Oxy I.43 (Egypt, ca. 295 CE): the papyrus alludes to North Church Street and South Church Street, not impossible if the allusion were to house churches but more likely to purpose-built churches. (White, no. 45)

---

zer, "The Churches of Herodium," in Yoram Tsafrir, ed., *Ancient Churches Revealed* (Jerusalem: Israel Exploration Society; Washington: Biblical Archeology Society, 1993) 219–32.

42. A second story over the aisles may have been used in the second or third century as a "women's gallery." Since there is no evidence of separation in earlier synagogues, the exclusion may have come only after adopting a building form that permitted it.

43. White would refer to these as "true" basilical churches, though I see no need to insist on such splendor as essential. He tends to avoid the term "basilical" in other cases; see *Social Origins*, 124, 192, 242 n. 189, among others. By contrast, Milburn (*Early Christian Art and Architecture* 86) argues that the term need not be used technically.

44. The first three were dedicated by Constantine's mother, Helena (ca. 329). Constantine also built in Rome (S. John Lateran, S. Costanza, S. Peter's), Constantinople, and Trier.

- Lebaba, Syria (318/319 CE): an inscription referring to a Marcionite "synagogue" built under the direction of the presbyter Paul. (White, no. 39)

- Laodicea Combusta, epitaph of M. Julius Eugenius (307–340 CE): the inscription mentions, while outlining his life, that he "rebuilt the entire church from its foundations and all embellishments around it, which contain *stoai* and *tetrastoa*, paintings, mosaics, a fountain and an outer gateway...." (White, no. 48)

Archaeological Evidence (see also table 2)

- Qirqbize in northern Syria (early fourth century): a small basilical church was found adjacent to a villa. (White, no. 38)

Non-Christian Literary Sources

- *Edessene Chronicle* 1 (8).1–2 (November 201 CE): the juxtaposition of church and king's palace implies a large visible structure; "...in the reign of Severus...the spring of water that rose in the great palace of Abgar the Great flowed more strongly than ever...so that the royal halls, the *stoai* and apartments began to stand in water.... They destroyed the great and magnificent palace of our Lord the King and tearing away everything that lay in their path and all the beautiful and splendid buildings.... They even destroyed the temple of the church of the Christians." (White, no. 26)

- Porphyry *Adversus Christianos* frg. 76 (268–70 CE): the Syrian Neoplatonist (234–305 CE) contrasted temples (*naoi*) and houses (*oikiai*): "But the Christians, imitating the construction of temples, erect great buildings in which they meet to pray, though there is nothing to prevent them from doing this in their own homes...." (White, no. 29)

- Maximinus, Rescript (after Eusebius *Hist. eccl.* 9.10.10) concerning Christians (313 CE): the language could refer to house churches or to basilicas; "And they are given concessions so that they might construct their dominical houses (*ta kyriaka ta oikeia*)." (White, no. 34)

- *Edessene Chronicle* 12.2 (313 CE): "bishop Kune laid the foundations for the church of 'Orhai [Edessa]; bishop Sa'ad built and completed it after him." (White, no. 26)

- Licinius and Constantine, *The Edict of Milan* 7 (June 13, 313 CE): "...if any appear to have bought them...let them restore the same to the Christians without charge and with no price on demand.... And since the said Christians are known to have possessed not only those places in which they were accustomed to meet, but others as well . . . you will order them . . . to return the same to the Christians, that is to their corporations and conventicles." (White, no. 33)

Christian Literary Sources

- Eusebius *Hist eccl.* 8.1.5 (ca. 303 CE),[45] looking back before the turn of the century: "with what favor one may observe the rulers in every church being honored by all procurators and governors. Or how could anyone describe those assemblies with numberless crowds and the great throngs gathered together in every city as well as the remarkable concourses in the houses of prayer? On account of these things, no longer being satisfied with their old buildings, they erected from the foundations churches of spacious dimensions . . . in every city. . . . " (White, no. 23)

- Eusebius *Hist. eccl.* 10.4.37–45 (324 CE), describing the new church, dedicated in 317 or 318 CE, built by Bishop Paulinus in Tyre: " . . . the whole area that he enclosed was much larger. The outer enclosure he fortified with a wall surrounding the whole, so that it might be a secure courtyard for the whole. He spread out a gateway, great and raised on high to ward off the very rays of the rising sun. . . . Marking off a great expanse between the temple and the first gates he adorned all around it with four transverse *stoai*, which enclosed the area in a kind of quadrangular figure with columns raised on all sides. He enclosed their intermittent spaces with wooden lattice-work partitions which reached an appropriate height, and he left an atrium in the middle for beholding the sky. . . . He erected opposite the front of the temple fountains . . . he made the entry passages to the temple wide openings by means of still more innermost gateways . . . he arranged the number of gateways for the *stoai* on either flank of the whole temple, and in addition to these he designed up above different openings to the building for still more light. . . . Now the Royal House [*basileion oikon*] he fortified with richer and even more lavish materials. . . . Nor did the pavement escape his care. Indeed this, too, he made brilliant with all kinds of ornate marble . . . he constructed ornate *exedrai* and large buildings on either side. . . . " (White, no. 23)

- Eusebius *Hist. eccl.* 10.2.1–3.1 (ca. 324), again looking back: "we beheld every place which, a short time before, had been torn down by

---

45. From the earlier edition of Eusebius. White suggests in several places that the phrase "erected from the foundations" means major renovations, not necessarily new structures.

the impious deeds of the tyrants. Reviving as from long and deadly mistreatment the temples were raised once again from the foundation to
a lofty height and received in far greater measure the magnificence of
those that had formerly been destroyed.... There came to pass many
festivals of dedication in every city and consecration of the newly built
houses of prayer...." (White, no. 23)

Alongside evidence for Eastern churches in a transitional period should be
placed sites up to the end of the fourth century (thus paralleling table 1).
Table 2 distinguishes in a preliminary way between halls, small churches or
chapels, and major basilicas.

While there was a good bit of architectural variation, after a bridge period during which large meeting halls were created, the dominant form for
purpose-built churches came to be the basilica.[46] Even within the one architectural form there were variations in size, proportions, embellishment,
apsidal arrangements, and so on; but most examples in the East resembled
the form well-known from Roman architecture. The situation is this: (1) the
pre-Constantinian period provided some evidence of purpose-built churches,
some of which may have been basilical; (2) Constantine adapted the basilica
for most of the noble structures he sponsored; (3) after Constantine, basilical churches that were not merely scaled-down versions of Constantine's
creations proliferated; but (4) basilical synagogues had already emerged as
an architectural type a couple of centuries earlier; and (5) these structures
are the nearest analogy for the modestly scaled fourth-century churches.
Synagogue and church developed in parallel fashions, but were they architecturally independent? Early on, both used houses donated by patrons; both
shifted to purpose-built structures; in a transitional phase both used meeting halls and basilicas; both eventually adopted the Roman basilica.[47] These
circumstances militate against the prevailing view that early Christianity and
postdestruction Judaism were bent on differentiating themselves from one another, for Jewish and Christian communities behaved rather similarly over a
long period of time. The key periods were the two transitional periods. Now
that the early adaptive strategies of the two communities have been eluci-
dated, the transition to purpose-built strategies — especially in the case of
Christianity — needs examination, as do the formal similarities (especially

---

46. In the Constantinian and post-Constantinian periods other architectural forms appeared,
the most important of which were centrally focused spaces; e.g., memorials were octagonal or
round, and other churches utilized square or cruciform plans, topped by concrete domes.

47. The case of Mithraism shows that there was nothing inevitable about these developments,
for it began with a similar architectural solution as Judaism and Christianity but did not continue to basilica-inspired communal buildings. A couple of instances of basilical Mithraea do not
undercut this general evaluation, as Roger Beck has privately confirmed.

Table 2: Early Churches in the Roman East

Meeting halls

Nazareth?, phase 1 (below Byzantine monastery) (3–4 c. CE)[48]
Capernaum, phase 2 (*domus ecclesiae?*) (4 c. CE)

Chapels (usually basilical)

Tabgha, Church of the Loaves and Fishes, phase 1 (4 c. CE)
Tabgha, Church of the Sermon on the Mount (4 c. CE)
Tabgha, Church of the Primacy of Peter (4 c. CE)
Nablus, Jacob's Well, cruciform church (ca. 380 CE)
'Agur (late 4 c. CE)
Mamre, church within Herodian enclosure (ca. 330 CE; apse earlier?)
Shavei Tzion (late 4 c. CE)
Magen, Building C (flanking Building B, below) (4 c. CE)
Burj Haidar (mid-4 c. CE)
Kharrab Shams (4 c. CE; Butler: before 370 CE)
Serjillah, small church (perhaps before inscription of 372 CE)
Fafertin, apse with semidome, bema (inscription 372 CE)
Antioch, St. Peter's (4 c. CE)
Barad, Syria, Julianos's Church (399–402)

Basilicas

Aqaba, mud-brick basilica (290 CE)[49]
Jerusalem, Church of the Holy Sepulchre (326–35 CE)
Bethlehem, Church of the Nativity (320s–330s CE)
Jerusalem, Eleona Church (330s CE)
Gerasa, Cathedral Church (reconstruction of Temple of Dionysus?) (ca. 365 CE)
Jerusalem, Gethsemane, Egeria's Church (379–84 CE)
Damascus, Church of St. John the Baptist (379 CE)
Bostra, third-century Roman basilica converted to church (4 c. CE)
Qanawat (Canatha), Roman basilica converted to church (4 c. CE)
Pella, Civic Complex Church (ca. 400)
Elusa, East Church (4 c. CE)
Mamshit, East Church (4 c. CE)
Sobata, South Church (late 4 c. CE)
Dor (late 4 c. CE)
Magen, Building B (4 c. CE)[50]
Ephesus, Church of the Councils, conversion of Roman basilica (4 c. CE)

---

48. B. Bagatti, "Nazareth," in *NEAEHL* 3. 1103–5, argues for third century, but this is too early.
49. On August 11, 1998, Mary Louise Mussell reported in the *Ottawa Citizen* and on CBC radio the discovery of a rectangular transitional basilical church, built of mud-bricks, with nave and side aisles but without apses (the sacristies on each side of the chancel), 28 by 16 meters. It was dated by pottery in the foundations to the late third century (290 CE), and was destroyed in the earthquake of 363 CE. The interior walls were painted in the first stage, with the indication of a cross. A cross has also been found in one of the mud-brick tombs in the associated cemetery. This structure appears to offer confirmation of the argument of this essay.
50. Vassilios Tzaferis, "Early Christian Churches at Magen," in Tsafrir, *Ancient Churches*, 283–85.

between some early Galilean synagogues and some early Syrian churches). Further research might consider the following:

1. Can specific comparisons of formally similar churches and synagogues clarify the architectural relationships between Jewish and Christian basilicas?[51]

2. How similar were Jewish basilical synagogues to the Roman basilica, and do eastern Roman examples influence specific Jewish structures?

3. How similar were small Christian churches to Roman basilicas, on the one hand, and to Jewish basilical synagogues, on the other?

4. Did Judaism influence Christian architectural developments in the transitional period (late third and early fourth centuries), or was Christian practice a parallel and unrelated acculturation?

5. Would architectural influence imply that "sibling" relationships between "related strangers" — Christians and Jews, both "Rebecca's children" — were relatively close for a long period?[52]

6. At a later period (fifth century, say) did Judaism borrow from Christianity?

7. Can efforts at self-definition and differentiation by both communities be architecturally discerned?

8. Were similar social changes occurring in both Christian and Jewish communities, and can they be traced in the shift to purpose-built structures (e.g., in reduced roles for patrons and increased community resources)? If so, would this require major revisions in understanding Jewish history?

9. Would an architectural inventory of both corpora of buildings from the same period establish reliably the relative wealth and resources of the two communities?

10. Would different architectural solutions to such matters as entry rites, seating, roles of leaders and participants, attitudes toward patrons, place of martyrs and relics, and the like provide a guide to differences in the character of each community?

---

51. There is unmistakable borrowing of both formal and decorative elements between a Temple of Apollo at Kedesh and the nearby Baram synagogue, first pointed out to me by Mordechai Aviam. Such cross-cultural borrowing is the issue here.

52. The titles of three books on the topic of the relationship in this period: Hayim Goren Perelmuter, *Siblings: Rabbinic Judaism and Early Christianity at Their Beginnings* (New York: Paulist, 1989); Stephen G. Wilson, *Related Strangers: Jews and Christians, 70–170 C.E.* (Minneapolis: Fortress, 1996); Alan F. Segal, *Rebecca's Children: Judaism and Christianity in the Roman World* (Cambridge, Mass.: Harvard University Press, 1986).

Ultimately, perhaps, there may be no assured answers, for the evidence is still thin for the transitional periods. But to raise these questions in an essay in Snyder's honor may show the need to follow in his footsteps, and that there is still room for deeper and better understandings of the relationships between Judaism and Christianity during this crucial *ante-pacem* period.

27

EARLY CHRISTIAN MUSIC

Stephen G. Wilson

The theme of this volume — the common life of the early church — provides
an opportunity not to be missed: to write on something where my interests
and ignorance coincide. The interest comes from many years of choral singing
in an Anglican setting and a curiosity about the life of early Christians; the
ignorance, from the realization that, apart from brief allusions to songs and
singing in Paul and the book of Revelation, I could not recall ever seeing
any sustained discussion of early Christian music. That, as I soon discovered,
was partly because I had never looked. But it was also partly because for the
first two centuries the evidence is extremely thin and that which does exist
is discussed in books and journals more likely to be read by musicologists or
liturgiologists than by historians of early Christianity.

From the third century on, Christian writers comment with increasing frequency on musical practices in church, synagogue, pagan cult, and everyday
life, and what they say has some bearing on the earlier period. I shall, however, concentrate on the first two centuries in this brief discussion. This has
the advantage of leaving aside more technical matters for which there is only
later evidence — musical notation, scale and pitch, or the origins of Grego-
rian chant — and permitting attention to be focused on two questions: Did
early Christians sing, and if so, what was the social context of this practice?[1]

A good way to begin is to recall two quotations and a picture. The first
quotation is from Pliny's much-quoted letter to Trajan:

> Moreover they maintained that this had been the sum of their guilt or
> error, that they had been in the habit of gathering together before dawn

---

1. The question is worded in this way because we know almost nothing about Christian use
of instrumental music in this period. The sources for the first few centuries are conveniently
collected in James W. McKinnon, ed., *Music in Early Christian Literature* (Cambridge Readings in
the Literature of Music; Cambridge and New York: Cambridge University Press, 1987).

on a fixed day and of singing antiphonally a hymn to Christ as if to a god (*carmenque Christo quasi deo dicere secum inuicem*), and of binding themselves by oath, not to some wickedness, but not to commit acts of theft or robbery or adultery, not to break faith, not to refuse to return money placed in their keeping when called upon to do so. (*Ep.* 10.96.7)[2]

The use of the phrase *carmen dicere* elsewhere to refer to singing and the apparent reference to antiphony — or perhaps more literally to singing "in turn" or "in orderly fashion" — suggest that Pliny alludes to the custom of Bithynian Christians of singing at their regular (Sunday?) gatherings. Pliny's report is based on the testimony of Christian apostates, but there is no reason for us to doubt their word any more than he did.[3]

My second quotation comes from Philo's account of the Therapeutae:

After supper they hold the sacred vigil which is conducted in the following way: They rise up all together and standing in the middle of the refectory form themselves into two choirs, one of men and one of women, the leader and precentor chosen for each being the most honored amongst them and the most musical. Then they sing hymns to God composed of many measures and set to many melodies, sometimes chanting together, sometimes taking up the harmony antiphonally, hands and feet keeping time in accompaniment.... Then when each choir has separately done its part... they mix and both together become a single choir. (*Vita* 83–85)

Philo is describing one of the great feasts of the Therapeutae and is deliberately contrasting them to the gluttonous, frivolous, and licentious banquets of the Greeks. He notes that even before the supper solos were sung, and that they occasionally inspired a communal refrain. But when, after supper, they divide into two choirs — deliberately mimicking the singing led by Moses and Miriam at the Exodus (Exodus 15) — and later join together in one, they become so carried away that they can continue their singing all night long. Philo's extended description of the musical life of the Therapeutae is unique

---

2. ET in Wynne Williams, trans., *Pliny: Correspondence with Trajan from Bithynia (Epistles X)* (Warminster, England: Aris and Phillips, 1990) 123.

3. Ralph P. Martin, "The Bithynian Christians' *Carmen Christo*," *StPatr* 8 (1966) 259–65; A. N. Sherwin-White, *The Letters of Pliny: A Historical and Social Commentary* (Oxford: Clarendon, 1966) 704–6. Jorg Christian Salzmann ("Pliny [*ep.* 10,96] and Christian Liturgy — A Reconsideration," *StPatr* 20 [1989] 389–95) surveys attempts to surmise the context of this "singing" — baptismal? eucharistic? or as part of a regular gathering for worship? *Carmen* can refer to an invocation, a prayer, or a magical incantation; the base reference is to a fixed form of words. For *carmen dicere* as "song," see Horace *Carm. saec.* 5–8; *Odes* 4.12.9–10; Seneca *Ep.* 108.1. Tertullian *Apol.* 2.6, in the first Christian reference to Pliny's letter, also sees a reference to singing (*canendum Christo:* "singing hymns to Christ" [ANF 3. 18b]). Johannes Quasten judges that the Christians may have been responding to the charge that they used magic ("Carmen," *RAC* 2. 901–10).

in Jewish sources of this period. Many issues would be resolved if we had an equivalent description of synagogue practice — but we do not. So how far we can extrapolate from the Therapeutae, an ascetic and monkish group, to other Jewish groups is a moot point. Nevertheless, Philo does not express any special surprise at the singing of the Therapeutae nor suggest that it was in any way odd. What he notes is that their songs were either newly minted or adaptations of ancient songs in Greek style (*Vita* 80).

We have, as my pictorial example, a mural from Herculaneum depicting a ritual in an Isaic temple; it is, in fact, a scene outside an Isis temple (see facing page).[4] At the top, descending the steps that have a base relief of a sphinx on each side, is a white-robed priest carefully carrying a vase in both hands. On one side is another priest and on the other a priestess. In the forefront another priest attends a small altar with a fire; around him are other figures, some holding *sistra*[5] and one playing a flute. The striking element in the middle is a group of devotees, divided into two sides, men and women, each three or four rows deep, and in the middle a sort of chorus master gesturing with one hand like a conductor. Precisely what kind of ritual this is remains unclear: an evening service closing the temple, a morning service opening it, an initiation rite, or a piece of religious theater in front of the temple have all been suggested. It is worth noting that the attention of the two main groups, evidently singing or chanting, is turned towards their leader in the middle, rather than towards the priest at the top of the steps or the person fanning the flames on the altar. In addition, the two choruses appear to be made up of men and women. The similarity to Philo's description of the Therapeutae is striking.

These three snippets of evidence, then, encourage us to ask what the musical practices of Christians, Jews, and pagans were, and how, if at all, they were associated.

Early Christian Music

Music is, in almost all the societies known to us, ancient and modern, all-pervasive. Rocking the baby, working the fields, celebrating the newlywed, and mourning the dead are just a few of the myriad occasions when human beings seem instinctively to turn to music. At this stage, however, we can re-

---

4. Thanks are due to the Ministero per i Beni Culturali e Ambientali, Naples, for permission to reproduce this photograph. On the meaning of the painting, see V. Tam Tinh Tran, *Le culte des divinités orientales à Herculanum* (EPRO 17; Leiden: Brill, 1971) 29–50. The connection with Philo is noted also in Peter Richardson and Valerie Heuchan, "Jewish Voluntary Associations in Egypt and the Roles of Women," in John S. Kloppenborg and Stephen G. Wilson, eds., *Voluntary Associations in the Graeco-Roman World* (London and New York: Routledge, 1996) 226–51, esp. 249 n. 44. Clement of Alexandria (*Strom.* 6.4.35) refers to hymns of the Egyptians cults.
5. Plural of *sistrum*, the metallic rattle used in celebrating the rites of Isis.

strict our inquiries to whether early Christians used music when they gathered
for worship. The evidence is slight and scattered, but it is not insignificant.

Paul mentions his own singing (ψαλῶ, 1 Cor 14:15 [twice]) and lists a
psalm or perhaps a hymn (ψαλμόν) as one item that Christians may contribute to common worship (1 Cor 14:26). Both could imply solo or small
group singing. Two later Pauline texts exhort the readers to sing and make
music to the Lord with "psalms and hymns and spiritual songs" (Eph 5:19;
Col 3:16) — contrasted in Ephesians with "drunkenness and dissipation,"
which Christian and Jewish writers elsewhere frequently associate with secular music making.[6] To be sure, Jas 5:13 recommends that the distressed pray

6. The three terms in Ephesians and Colossians — ψαλμοί, ὕμνοι, ᾠδαί — are roughly
synonymous; see esp. J. A. Smith, "First-Century Christian Singing and Its Relationship to Contemporary Jewish Religious Song," *Music and Letters* 75 (1994) 1–15; already idem, "The Ancient
Synagogue, the Early Church and Singing," *Music and Letters* 65 (1984) 1–16; A. A. Bastaiensen,
"*Psalmi, hymni,* and *cantica* in Early Jewish-Christian Tradition," *StPatr* 21 (1989) 15–26; William
Sheppard Smith, *Musical Aspects of the New Testament* (Amsterdam: Uitgeverij W. ten Have,
1962) 61–62. The attempt to make some fine distinction between the three words — as refer-

and that the cheerful sing (ψαλλέτω), but this does not in itself suggest a context for these activities.[7]

In a curious passage in the *Acts of John* 94–96 Jesus speaks to his disciples just before his arrest by the "lawless Jews":

> "Before I am given over to them, let us sing a hymn to the Father, and thus go to meet what lies ahead." So he bade us form a circle, as it were, holding each other's hands, and taking his place in the middle he said: "Answer 'Amen' to me." Then he began to hymn and to say. . . .[8]

The hymn that Jesus then sings mentions piping (on the αὐλός), and this may have accompanied their singing, as apparently did the dancing that is alluded to as well. *Acts of Paul* 9 describes Christians breaking their fast with a communal meal to the accompaniment of psalms and songs. Justin refers briefly to the use of prayers and hymns of thanksgiving as an alternative to sacrifice (*1 Apol.* 13) and apparently wrote a work entitled *Psaltes* that is no longer extant (Eusebius *Hist. eccl.* 4.18.5), but in his account of the Roman eucharist there is no mention of singing (*1 Apol.* 67). Gnostics and Marcionites, according to their opponents, made free use of psalms and songs — which led to suspicion of music on the part of some but, as at a later date, to the development of musical alternatives by others.[9] On the references to singing in the *Odes of Solomon* (7.22–23; 16.1–3; 41:1–2, 16) — themselves thought by many to be examples of hymns used at Jewish-Christian gatherings — Smith has recently made the following observations: that they should

---

ring, e.g., to biblical psalms, to syllabic songs of praise, and to melismatic (=relating to or having *melisma*, i.e., a song, or tune) charts respectively — is belied by known Jewish and Christian usage.

7. Of uncertain significance is the singing of Jesus and his followers at the Last Supper ("when they had sung a hymn," Mark 14:26; Matt 26:30 — a *hallel* psalm [="psalm of praise," but perhaps esp. of psalms sung at Passover]?): this may or may not reflect early Christian eucharistic practice. Likewise, the visions in Revelation referring to heavenly singing/songs (Rev 5:8–10; 15:3–4) may have nothing to do with mundane practice. Paul and Silas, while in prison, bolster their spirits with prayer and song before their miraculous release (Acts 26:25), but the context is not one of communal worship. And there is no reason to accept E. Werner's view that in 1 Corinthians 13 Paul denigrates instrumental music, as Jewish and Christian writers later do ("'If I speak in the tongues of men': St. Paul's Attitude to Music," *Journal of the American Musicological Society* 13 [1960] 20). It is merely a matter of rhetorical contrast; rightly, W. S. Smith, *Musical Aspects*, 115.

8. Wilhelm Schneemelcher, ed., R. McL. Wilson, trans. ed., *New Testament Apocrypha* (2d ed.; London: Clarke; Louisville, Ky.: Westminster/John Knox, 1991–92) 2. 181.

9. Tertullian *De carn.* 17.20; *Adv. Val.* 12.2; Hippolytus *Ref.* 5.6.5, 10.1; 6.36.6. On the dual reaction to "heretical" use of music, see Johannes Quasten, "The Liturgical Singing of Women in Christian Antiquity," *CHR* 27 (1941) 149–65, esp. 150–52; Josef Kroll, *Die christliche Hymnodik bis zu Klemens von Alexandreia* (Libelli 240; 2d ed.; Darmstadt: Wissenschaftliche Buchgesellschaft, 1968) 37–39.

be taken at face value; that they associate singing with worship; and that in two cases they refer to communal participation.[10] Finally, in *Orac. Sib.* 8.487–500 Christians' spiritual worship, which includes sacred song, is contrasted with the sacrificial cults of pagan worship.

What may we conclude? First, we should note that the allusions are all entirely positive. The overall impression we gain is that singing was a routine part of worship, accepted and encouraged by all Christians, "orthodox" and "heretic" alike. Sometimes it may have involved solo or small group singing, at other times the whole group. Certainly, the allusions are not extensive, but this is not so different from our knowledge of other, more central Christian rituals in the same period — baptism and the eucharist, for example. This suggests only that our evidence is haphazard and is not necessarily an indication of music's significance for early Christians. Moreover, the evidence is uniform in tone and scattered among the sources, producing a consistent picture. Second, there is no restriction on who participates: all Christians, men and women alike, apparently join in the sacred songs. Third, while occasionally a contrast is drawn with pagan practices (once directly, once perhaps by implication), no allusion is made to Jewish song, in the synagogue or elsewhere.

In many respects this contrasts dramatically with Christian evidence from the third century on, where with some exceptions attitudes to music range from guarded acceptance through suspicion to outright hostility: the singing of women, the playing of instruments, the use of nonbiblical songs, dancing and hand clapping, and the excessive use of music at funerals or martyr shrines were all criticized by many of the more eminent Christian leaders.[11] But that is another story, and the point of mentioning it here is merely to reinforce the conclusions drawn above. For what the leaders opposed the ordinary folk presumably did, and it may well be that it was precisely because certain musical habits had become so ingrained that they provoked such energetic opposition.

---

10. J. A. Smith, "First-Century Christian Singing," 13–14. Further on the dating (probably first or second century CE) and provenance of the *Odes*, see James H. Charlesworth, "Odes of Solomon," *OTP* 2. 726–27. Charlesworth dates them around 100 CE.

11. The fullest treatment is Johannes Quasten, *Music and Worship in Pagan and Christian Antiquity* (Washington, D.C.: National Association of Pastoral Musicians, 1983 [German original, 1929]). See also Everett Ferguson, "Toward a Patristic Theology of Music," *StPatr* 24 (1991) 266–83; H. F. Stander, "The Clapping of Hands in the Early Church," *StPatr* 22 (1989) 75–80; Carl Andresen, "Altchristliche Kritik am Tanz: Ein Ausschnitt aus dem Kampf der alten Kirche gegen heidnische Sitte," *ZKG* 72 (1961) 217–62. The most common reasons for suspicion of vocal and instrumental music were their association with the idolatry and immorality of pagan cults ("the devil's rubbish," as John Chrysostom called them) and a certain asceticism and extreme spirituality that suspected anything that might give undue pleasure.

Early Jewish Music

The story of early Christian music has for a long time been tied to that of the Jews. In the classic works from an earlier era it seemed natural enough to suppose that Christians, who began as a Jewish sect, depended on the Jews for their musical traditions as they did for much else (including other liturgical elements). The logic was roughly as follows: if Christians included singing in their worship, especially the psalms, they must have borrowed the custom from the Jews; and if they borrowed it from the Jews, it was most likely from the synagogues which, in turn, must have adapted the temple liturgy to their own needs — that is, until 70 CE when, following the destruction of the temple, music was banned as a sign of mourning for their tragic loss.[12]

Recent work has almost entirely undermined the logic of such arguments.[13] One stark fact has to be recognized from the outset: we know very little about worship in the synagogues of the prerabbinic period and nothing about their use of music. In particular, there is no evidence for the musical performance of biblical psalms, their use being restricted to scriptural reading and exposition. The evidence we do have suggests that, insofar as synagogues were used for common worship, this contained two elements: reading and exposition of the scriptures and prayer. In the absence of any hard evidence, the attempt to reconstruct synagogue musical practice used to follow two main lines: to read back from later, mostly rabbinic, evidence to the earlier period and to assume that whatever Christians did, they must have borrowed from the synagogues and, therefore, the synagogues must have done it before

---

12. For example, W. O. E. Oesterley, *The Jewish Background of the Christian Liturgy* (Oxford: Clarendon, 1925; repr. Gloucester, Mass.: Smith, 1965); Gregory Dix, *The Shape of the Liturgy* (1945; repr. New York: Seabury, 1983); C. W. Dugmore, *The Influence of the Synagogue upon the Divine Office* (1944; repr. Westminster, England: Faith, 1945); A. Z. Idelsohn, *Jewish Music and Its Historical Development* (New York: Holt, 1929); Eric Werner, *The Sacred Bridge: The Interdependence of Liturgy and Music in Synagogue and Church in the First Millennium* (2 vols.; New York: Columbia University Press, 1959–84); I. Adler and R. Flender, "Frühchristliche Musik," in *TRE* 23.446–52; Carl H. Kraeling and Lucetta Mowry, "Music in the Bible," in Egon Wellesz, ed., *The New Oxford History of Music* (London: Oxford University Press, 1957) 283–312; Bruno Stäblein, "Frühchristliche Musik," in Friedrich Blume, ed., *Musik in Geschichte und Gegenwart: Allgemeine Enzyklopädie der Musik* (4 vols.; Kassel and Basel: Barenreiter, 1949–86) 4. 1036–64. While their arguments vary and they do not agree on all points, these authors all take the same general approach.

13. Here I am merely summarizing the arguments of J. A. Smith ("First-Century Christian Singing"; "Ancient Synagogue" [see above, n. 6]) and of James W. McKinnon ("The Exclusion of Musical Instruments from the Ancient Synagogue," *Proceedings of the Royal Music Association* 106 [1979–80] 77–87; "On the Question of Psalmody in the Ancient Synagogues," *Early Music History* 6 [1986] 159–91). See also L. I. Rabbinowitz, "The Psalms in Jewish Liturgy," *Historica Judaica* 6 (1944) 109–22; Johann Maier, "Zur Verwendung des Psalmen in der synagogalen Liturgie (Wochentag and Sabbat)," in H. Becker and R. Kaczynski, eds., *Liturgie und Dichtung: Ein interdisziplinäres Kompendium* (2 vols.; Pietas liturgica 1–2; St. Ottilien: Eos, 1983) 1. 55–90. It should be noted that while their general line of argument is persuasive, J. A. Smith and McKinnon have a tendency to be inconsistent in the use of rabbinic sources, being sometimes alert to the historical problems, sometimes not.

them. The one argument fails, among other things, for chronological reasons; the other is entirely circular.[14] Added to this was a tendency to confuse what we know about the temple rituals — which contained a fairly elaborate musical element, vocal and instrumental — with what went on in the synagogues. But this was to assume that the synagogues were organized as substitutes for the temple, something which we can gradually trace from the second century CE on but not before. The silence in our sources about synagogue musical practices was further explained by assuming that music was banned after 70 CE, as a sign of national mourning for the temple but also perhaps because of a preference for spiritual worship and an antipathy to the sensuous musical ceremonials of pagan cults. Yet there is no evidence for any such move. The rabbinic sources usually quoted do, to be sure, express suspicion about the use of music at banquets and legislate about the playing of certain instruments on the Sabbath, but they do not anywhere suggest a ban on instrumental (or vocal) music in the synagogues.[15]

Perhaps the reason for this is that there was nothing to ban. For while it may be that the first century was for Jews and Christians a "heightened auditory environment" or "sonic landscape," and while they may instinctively have lapsed into "lyrical speech," we cannot leap from these to the existence of recitation, cantillation, or even full-scale song.[16] Or could we lean on the argument that the dearth of sources for everything in this period allows us to assume that things went on for which we have no specific evidence? After all, there is record of Jews singing to express experiences of communal grief or joy, to mark weddings and funerals, or to celebrate Passover, and Philo expresses no surprise that the Therapeutae used songs and had enough of them to sing the night away.[17] Some of these songs appear to have been common property, unless the singing was always extempory or responsorial, and they must have learned them somewhere. What more natural place than the synagogue?

This is not an unreasonable line of argument, but it runs up against an obstinate silence in the sources. For, unlike the case of the early Christians, we

---

14. J. A. Smith ("First-Century Christian Singing," 2 n. 10) notes a recent example of this circular argument in E. P. Sanders, *Judaism: Practice and Belief 63 BCE–66 CE* (London: SCM; Philadelphia: Trinity Press International, 1992) 202. On the basis of 1 Cor 14:26 ("When you come together, each one has a hymn, a lesson, … ") and the fact that Paul and his readers were christianized Jews, Sanders infers that singing took place in the synagogue, too.

15. See esp. McKinnon, "Exclusion," which in fact deals with more than the issue of musical instruments.

16. Edward Foley, though generally recognizing how little we can say, uses these vague categories to justify his conclusions (*Foundations of Christian Music: The Music of Pre-Constantinian Christianity* [American Essays in Liturgy; Collegeville, Minn.: Liturgical, 1996]).

17. Grief and joy: Philo *Flacc.* 14.121–22; 3 Macc 1:18; 4:2–4; 6:32, 35; 7:16; Esth 4:3. Weddings: 3 Macc 4:6–8; *m. Soṭa* 9.11; *m. B. Meṣ.* 6.1. Funerals: Mark 5:38; Luke 8:52; *m. Ketub.* 2.10; *m. Mo'ed Qaṭ.* 1.5; 3.8–9.

have not even a hint of musical activity in the synagogue, and this does not encourage us to surmise what might have been, except to suppose that the silence of the sources was matched by the musical silence of the synagogue.

Pagan Music

Against the general run of things G. Wille, in his massive study of Roman music, presents a sustained argument for the influence of Roman musical habits on the early Christians. From general observations — such as the growing separation of church and synagogue and the demonstrable musicality of the Romans, to which Christians were constantly exposed — as well as from the specific statements and claims of later Christian writers, he concludes that Christian practice is to be explained by Roman rather than Jewish influence.[18] The sweep of his brush is broad, covering all kinds of music making and stretching through five or six centuries. This reduces his value for our purposes, since many of his sources are late, but he points us perhaps to a way of refocusing the question.

What, in the social world of early Christianity, were the groups and meetings most like their own? They surely were those of the voluntary associations (the *collegia* or θίασοι), founded on common devotional, economic, or social interests, that were a prominent part of the social map of the Greco-Roman world.[19] Religious rituals were well nigh universal in these associations — sometimes their central concern (the mysteries), sometimes more peripheral (trade guilds) — and most of them involved music. This is clear not only in the patristic polemic against music because of its connection with pagan worship and other suspect social activities (sporting contests, the theater, etc.) but also in the inscriptional and artistic evidence from antiquity.

In my opening example from the cult of Isis we found depicted a double choir, made up of men and women occupied in some sort of communal ritual. They may represent the total membership of that temple or a select group within it. There is ample evidence to reinforce some of the features of this particular example.[20] The central role of music in associations is likewise

---

18. Wille, *Musica Romana: Die Bedeutung der Musik im Leben der Römer* (Amsterdam: Schippers, 1967) 367–405. Quasten (*Music and Worship*) had of course already pointed out the importance of pagan associations as a reason for patristic opposition to music. But while he sometimes indicates examples of influence (rather than analogy), as in funeral and martyr cults (pp. 149–75), his book is long on quotation of the sources but short on the interpretation of them. Stäblein ("Frühchristliche Musik," 1058–59) refers to the influence of pagan music as probable but largely unknown, and Kraeling and Mowry ("Music in the Bible," 310) suggest the influence of the mystery cults on some early Christian hymns, e.g., Phil 2:6–11; 1 Tim 3:16; Ignatius *Eph.* 7.2.

19. See Kloppenborg and Wilson, *Voluntary Associations*, passim.

20. Philip Harland, a graduate student at the University of Toronto, responded generously to my inquiry about this with a host of references and interpretative notes. I am most grateful and

strongly implied in two reliefs, one from Kyzikos (Asia) and the other from Apamea (Bithynia), each divided into three panels: the first, showing the dedication of a relief to Zeus Hypsistos, has the gods above, the association members reclining below, and dancers and musicians in the bottom panel; the second, honoring a priestess of Cybele and Apollo, is much the same except that in the top panel the gods are worshiped by a priestess, a flute-playing girl, and a sheep-tending boy.[21] Both of these indicate that music was a routine part of the associations' gatherings, though whether all members participated is not clear. An inscription containing the statutes of the Iobacchoi, which exhorts members not to sing on certain occasions or in a disruptive way, may imply that singing was normal on other occasions.[22]

Beyond this we know of guilds dedicated to music and dance, of which the best known are the peripatetic Dionysiac artists, who performed in their own cult but could be hired for other cults and festivals, too.[23] Singers (ὑμνῳδοί) appear in different guises in the inscriptions. Some were members of a singers' *collegium* with their own rituals, dedicated to gods or emperors.[24] Others appear to have been a group within a larger association (for example, of elders) or one group of functionaries among others (θεολόγοι, θέμιδοι).[25] Many inscriptions refer to individual singers (a ὑμνῳδός), but this usually does not imply that they were solo performers, since the evidence points in general to groups of singers rather than individual virtuosi.[26] Even so there were

depend on him in what follows. See further Erich Ziebarth, *Die griechische Vereinswesen* (1896; repr. Wiesbaden: Sändig, 1969) 90–92; Franz Poland, *Geschichte des griechischen Vereinswesens* (1909; repr. Leipzig: Zentral-Antiquariat der Deutschen Demokratischen Republik, 1967) 46–49, updated and expanded in "Griechische Sängervereinigungen im Altertum," *700-Jahr-Feier der Kreuzschule zu Dresden 1926* (Dresden, 1926) 46–56.

21. The Kyzikos inscription is GIBM IV.2 1007; the Apamea inscription I ApamBith 35 (119 BCE or CE) (epigraphical abbreviations follow G. H. R. Horsley and J. A. Lee, "A Preliminary Checklist of Abbreviations of Greek Epigraphy Volumes," *Epigraphica* 56 [1994] 126–69).

22. IGII2 1368 (ca. 177 CE). It does not say if or when they could sing, but the importance of music in Dionysiac groups is generally well established.

23. See Arthur Pickard-Cambridge, *The Dramatic Festivals of Athens* (2d ed.; Oxford: Clarendon, 1968) 279–305; also 246–62 on the more technical aspects of dance and music in drama.

24. IPergamon II 374 contains statutes for the mysteries and celebrations of the ὑμνῳδοί, an elitist guild dedicated to the emperors and gods of Rome, entrance to which required a hefty fee and the composition of a new hymn. See H. W. Pleket, "An Aspect of the Emperor Cult: Imperial Mysteries," *HTR* 58 (1965) 331–47, esp. 341–43; R. Mellor, *ΘΕΑ ΡΩΜΗ: The Worship of the Goddess Roma in the Greek World* (Hypomnemata 42; Göttingen: Vandenhoeck & Ruprecht, 1975) 192–93. See also IGBulg II 667, 668, which speak of φιλοσέβαστοι ὑμνῳδοί dedicating altars to Zeus/Hera/Apollo.

25. ISmyrna 644 (second century CE) and perhaps IGBulg II 666 (Nicopolis) appear to define ὑμνῳδοί as part of the γερουσία or πρεσβύτεροι. IEph 645 (Ephesus) speaks of ὑμνῳδοί, θεολόγοι, and θέμιδοι, and ISmyrna 697 of the first two of the three. The μολποί (singers) of Ephesus (IEph 900–901, 906) and Miletus (LSAM 50) who honor Apollo may have been a *collegium* in their own right or a subgroup within one.

26. Poland, "Sängervereinigungen," 48–49. IEph 742, 1004, 1600, 2446, 3247 (Ephesus) and ISmyrna 595 all refer to a singular ὑμνῳδός.

special roles for some individuals, such as the hymn teachers mentioned in
IPergamon II 485 (first century CE) and the choir leader in IGBulg II 666
(Nicopolis). Singers could be men or women, children or adults.[27] Some
groups were strongly associated with civic ceremonies, but since this could
include versions of the emperor cult and other religious rituals, a distinction
between civic and cultic roles is difficult to make.[28]

This kind of evidence — and it is only a selection — indicates that music
was a regular feature of the communal life of *collegia* and θίασοι. It was
typically performed by choirs and trained instrumentalists, a natural enough
arrangement then as now (note Philo's allusion to the "most musical" taking the lead). Presumably, as with the Therapeutae, this does not mean that
singing was confined to the trained or the more musical, since the more
skilled could have led the others in song (instrumental playing would have
been a different matter). If we are looking for musical practices analogous
to those of the early Christians, then they are surely to be found in the *collegia* and θίασοι of the Greco-Roman world. Among gentile Christians, at
least, the idea of singing in communal celebrations of all sorts — including
the more specifically devotional — would have been entirely natural, and it
should hardly be surprising if similar practices developed widely among the
early churches. It is interesting to note, too, that almost all investigations of
the background of early Christian music have tended to focus on Judaism,
where evidence is virtually nonexistent. Discussions have thus been marred
by anachronism and circular reasoning, while they might have focused on
those groups within pagan society for which there is a rich and pertinent
body of evidence.[29]

Does this mean, then, that we are now to discard Jewish analogies altogether? J. A. Smith would argue not, since for him the proper analogy is not
with the synagogues but with private Jewish associations — in particular the
Therapeutae, the Qumran community, and Jewish households. As to the musical practices of the last two we know very little, although the Therapeutae

27. Female singers (ὑμνήτριαι) appear in MDAI(A) 35 (1910) 457–59 (no. 40) and
MDAI(A) 37 (1912) 287 (no. 16) — both Pergamum. When named, most hymn singers are
men. On youth singers, see Martin P. Nilsson, "Pagan Divine Service in Late Antiquity," *HTR*
38 (1945) 63–69, esp. 66; Poland, "Sängervereinigungen," 49–50.

28. Ziebarth (*Die griechische Vereinswesen*, 91–92) emphasizes their civic role, but recognizes
that it spills over into cultic activity. See further Philip Harland, "Honours and Worship: Emperors, Imperial Cults and Associations at Ephesus (First to Third Centuries CE)," *SR* 25 (1996)
319–34.

29. I use the language of analogy rather than of influence to avoid the suggestion that the
practices of voluntary associations were the genealogical source of those of early Christians.
Jonathan Z. Smith, *Drudgery Divine: On the Comparison of Early Christianity and the Religions
of Late Antiquity* (Chicago: University of Chicago Press, 1990), warns against such false comparisons, and notes that in the past scholars have consistently dismissed pagan evidence on
ideological grounds.

are a somewhat different matter.[30] The problem with this argument is that it casts things in an unnecessarily narrow way. Why only *Jewish* private associations? Why not *pagan* associations, too? If we define voluntary associations to include an array of groups — Christian, Jewish, and pagan — as it has been argued we should, then the net can be cast far wider.[31] The result is that we gain a broader, more accurate, and more interesting picture of the social context of early Christian music.

30. J. A. Smith, "Ancient Synagogue," 9–15. He recognizes that there are only vague allusions to music in the DSS and that most of the evidence for household singing has to do with the singing of *hallel* psalms at Passover. Though admitting, therefore, the tentative nature of his conclusions, like many others Smith never looks beyond Judaism for the answer to his puzzle.

31. So Kloppenborg and Wilson, *Voluntary Associations,* esp. 1–15. This would in principle include synagogues as well, but the only musical aspect of this evidence is its silence.

GRAYDON F. SNYDER

CURRICULUM VITAE AND
COMPREHENSIVE BIBLIOGRAPHY

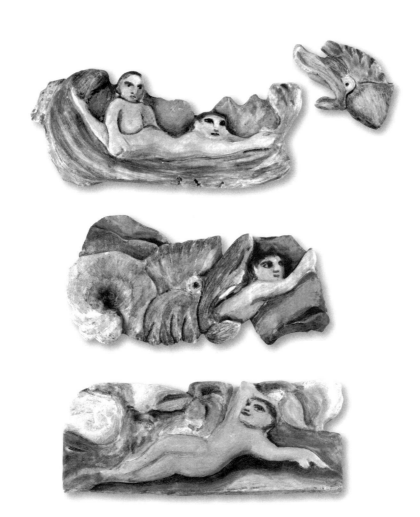

Curriculum Vitae of
Graydon F. Snyder

Graydon Fisher Snyder, younger son of Clayton and Irene (Fisher) Snyder, was born in Peru, Indiana, on April 30, 1930, and raised in Huntington, West Virginia. Graduating from Huntington East High School in 1947, he entered Manchester College, North Manchester, Indiana, from which he graduated with a B.A. in 1951, majoring in chemistry and with a minor in peace studies. (Thirty-nine years later, in 1990, his college alma mater would honor him with the Distinguished Alumnus award.) From Manchester, Snyder moved to Bethany Theological Seminary, Chicago, Illinois, where he received his B.D. in 1954. He was ordained in the fall of 1959, in Peru, Indiana, as a minister in the Church of the Brethren. While still in seminary he and Lois Horning were married, on June 13, 1953, and they have shared in his life of ministry and scholarship as well as in the nurture of their three children, Jonathan Edvard (born in Oslo, Norway, in 1958), Anna Christine (1960), and Stephen Daniel (1962).

Recognizing a call as both pastor and scholar, Snyder accepted a place as a doctoral student at Princeton Theological Seminary and began his studies there in 1955. But even before arriving at Princeton he was off for further study at Göttingen University in Germany (1954–55), and in 1958–59 he was awarded a Fulbright scholarship for research at Oslo University, Norway. Indeed, his graduate student days were characterized by extensive travel: to Egypt and the Near East in 1955; in Europe, especially Germany and Scandinavia, in 1955 and again in 1959; and in various countries behind the former Iron Curtain in 1959. He received his Th.D. from Princeton Theological Seminary *cum laude* in 1961; his dissertation, directed by Otto A. Piper, was entitled "The Continuity of Early Christianity."

Already in 1959 — two years before completion of the doctorate — Snyder was appointed to the faculty of Bethany Theological Seminary. In 1965 he was promoted to the rank of full professor, and ten years later he became dean; he was to serve in this office until 1986. In 1979 he earned the further distinction of being named to the Wieand Chair in New Testament studies. During these twenty-seven years at Bethany, Graydon and Lois's travels by no means ceased. Europe again beckoned in 1966–67 and in the mid- and late 1980s, especially Czechoslovakia and the former East Germany; Cuba in 1980; other parts of Central America in 1979 and 1983; the Pontifical Institute of Christian Archaeology, Rome, 1966–67; Cambridge University, 1973–74; and once more Rome, at the American Academy, on a grant from the Association of Theological Schools, in 1981.

Then in 1986, prior to the relocation of Bethany Theological Seminary to Richmond, Indiana, Snyder made what would be his final career move as a full-time teacher, scholar, and administrator. He accepted the position as professor of New Testament at Chicago Theological Seminary, where he would remain until his official retirement in 1996; from 1986 to 1990 he was also academic dean. Since 1996 he has continued at Chicago Theological Seminary as adjunct professor of New Testament.

Those travels mentioned earlier have included several stops nearer home, as visiting professor at Garrett Evangelical Theological Seminary, Evanston, Illinois, at the Lutheran School of Theology at Chicago, at the Evangelical Theological Seminary in Naperville, Illinois, and his appointment as theologian in residence at the Community Presbyterian Church of Clarendon Hills, Illinois. But his travels have also embraced an emerging new world of religious and theological endeavor: in China (1988) and in southern Africa (1990) — more specifically, at the University of Zimbabwe (1992).

In addition to the publication of his articles in such leading journals as the *Journal of Biblical Literature, Catholic Biblical Quarterly, New Testament Studies,* and *Vigiliae Christianae,* Snyder's professional academic credentials include his election as president of the Chicago Society of Biblical Research (1969, 1970) and the solicitation of numerous articles in what will continue to be standard reference works, including *The Interpreter's Dictionary of the Bible,* the *Anchor Bible Dictionary,* the *Mercer Dictionary of the Bible,* the *Encyclopedia of Early Christianity,* the *Dictionary of Biblical Interpretation,* and the *Encyclopedia of Catholicism.* He has also been a regular participant in the Society of New Testament Studies. For six years — from 1986 to 1992 — he served on the Accreditation Commission of Theological Schools.

Snyder has undertaken numerous ecclesiastical and community responsibilities alongside his academic work. Within his own denomination he has held several leading posts, for example, as moderator, First Church of the Brethren, Chicago (1968–present); as member of the Board of Education in District 88 (1970–73); as president of the *Brethren Journal Association* (1971–73; 1974–75); as member (and chairman, 1979–81) of the Board of Trustees and of the Governing Council of the Board of Trustees, Bethany Brethren Garfield Park Community Hospital (1981–present; as president, 1991–92). He has also been a board member of the Evangelical Health Foundation (1986–present), of the Brethren Health Foundation (1985–90); and a member of the Governing Board of the National Council of Churches (1986–91).

It remains to put on record the admiration his colleagues have developed for his courageous defense of academic freedom and freedom of inquiry. He has earned wide respect for his loyalty to scientific scholarship as well as to his denomination and theological tradition. His close relations with colleagues in the Chicago area, including regular and active participation in the New Testament Colleague group in the Association of Chicago Theological Schools and in the Chicago Society of Biblical Research, are especially noteworthy. Indeed, the fact that he has now retired from full-time teaching has clearly done nothing to lessen his intellectual vigor or his commitment to a very wide circle of friends, colleagues, and former students.

Bibliography of
Graydon F. Snyder

COMPILED BY
JULIAN V. HILLS, ROBERT JEWETT,
AND KENNETH M. SHAFFER, JR.

1954

"And Yours? An Open Letter to Brethren Parents" (with Lois Snyder), *GMess* 103/47 (November 27, 1954) 6–7, 11.

1955

"'Brethren' German Students on University Campuses," *GMess* 104/24 (June 11, 1955) 21.

1957

"Hidden Treasure" (with Lois Snyder), *Horizons,* October 6, 1957, 8–12.

1961

"The Continuity of Early Christianity: A Study of Ignatius in Relation to Paul," Th.D. dissertation, Princeton Theological Seminary, 1961.

"Exploring the Bible" (series), *BLead,* April 1961, 41–61: "Christ, Our Living Lord"; "The Source of True Wisdom"; "When the Righteous Suffer"; "When Human Wisdom Fails"; "When God's Wisdom Prevails."

"Exploring the Bible" (series), *BLead,* May 1961, 33–49: "Out of the Heart"; "Discipline in the Home"; "The Importance of Diligence"; "Self-Discipline: Why?"

"Exploring the Bible" (series), *BLead,* June 1961, 25–41: "A Search for Life's Meaning"; "Two Views of Life"; "Guarding the Tongue"; "The Fruits of Faith."

"Hark to the Ark! A Fantasy on Genesis 6–9," *GMess* 110/45 (November 25, 1961) 12–14.

1962

William Klassen and Graydon F. Snyder, eds., *Current Issues in New Testament Interpretation: Essays in Honor of Otto A. Piper* (New York: Harper, 1962).

"Exploring the Bible" (series), *BLead*, July–August 1962, 30–71: "Too Little, Too Late"; "Headed for Disaster?"; "Why Does God Let It Happen?"; "Patriotism – True and False"; "Hope beyond Tragedy"; "Conquered and Exiled"; "A Call to Repentance"; "God's Love Proclaimed"; "Tidings of Comfort and Joy."

"Exploring the Bible" (series), *BLead*, September 1962, 29–50: "Laying the Foundations"; "Faith to Rebuild"; "A Mind to Work"; "Draw Near to God"; "John Heralds the Christ."

"A Servant (Church) and the Sixties," *BLT* 7/3 (Summer 1962) 14–21.

"The Form of a Servant," *GMess* 111/35 (September 15, 1962) 20–21.

1963

"The Historical Jesus in the Letters of Ignatius of Antioch," *BR* 8 (1963) 3–12.

"Old Testament Studies: A Survey," *BLT* 8/3 (Summer 1963) 59–61.

"Christ and History," *GMess* 112/50 (December 28, 1963) 9–12.

Review of Paul S. Minear, *Images of the Church in the New Testament* (Philadelphia: Westminster, 1960), in *BLT* 8/1 (Winter 1963) 62–64.

Review of Paul Winter, *On the Trial of Jesus* (SJ 1; Berlin: De Gruyter, 1961), in *JBR* 31 (1963) 338.

1964

In His Hand (Elgin, Ill.: Brethren Press, 1964).

"The Assassination from a Christological Perspective" (with Donald E. Miller), *The Pulpit* 35/4 (April 1964) 20–22.

"Why I Wrote What I Wrote in the New Youth Curriculum," *BLead*, September 1964, 22–23.

"Biblical Images of the Church and Church Membership," *BLT* 9/4 (Autumn 1964) 3–16.

Review of Edgar Hennecke and Wilhelm Schneemelcher, eds., R. McL. Wilson, trans. ed., *New Testament Apocrypha*, vol. 1 (London: Lutterworth; Philadelphia: Westminster, 1963), in *JBR* 32 (1964) 156–58.

Review of Gerhard Kittel, ed., *Theological Dictionary of the New Testament*, vol. 1 (Grand Rapids: Eerdmans, 1964), in *JBR* 32 (1964) 364–65.

1965

"The Incarnation and Giving: A Response," *BLead*, December 1965, 4.

1966

"The Soul in Solid State," *Messenger* 115/15 (July 21, 1966) 5–6.

Review of Joachim Jeremias, *The Central Message of the New Testament* (New York: Scribner, 1965), Rudolf Schnackenburg, *The Moral Teaching of the New Testament* (New York: Herder, 1964), and Martin K. Hopkins, *God's Kingdom in the New Testament* (Chicago: Regnery, 1964), in *JBR* 34 (1966) 262–64.

1967

The Shepherd of Hermas=vol. 6 of Robert M. Grant, ed., *The Apostolic Fathers: A New Translation and Commentary* (New York: Nelson, 1964–68).

"Basic Tensions in the Church of the Brethren," *BLT* 12/1 (Winter 1967) 31–36.
"All This and Rachel, Too," *Seminarian*, Fall 1967, 1–3.
"A Day with Fortvnatvs," *Messenger* 116/24 (November 23, 1967) 3–6.

Review of Lage Pernveden, *The Concept of the Church in the Shepherd of Hermas* (Studia theologica Lundensia 27; Lund: Gleerup, 1966), in *JBL* 86 (1967) 357.

1968

"Chalmer Faw: Man on the Move," *Messenger* 117/11 (May 23, 1968) 2–4.
"The Text and Syntax of Ignatius *Pros Ephesious* 20.2c," *VC* 22 (1968) 8–13.

1969

"Servanthood Is Not Enough," *BLT* 14/1 (Winter 1969) 28–31.
"Survey and 'New' Thesis on the Bones of St. Peter," *BA* 32/1 (February 1969) 2–24.
"The Literalization of the Apocalyptic Form in the New Testament Church," *BR* 14 (1969) 5–18.
"Support Means Solidarity and Sanctuary," *ChrCent* 86/4 (January 22, 1969) 120–21.
"Reflections on Ezekiel 18," *Messenger* 118/20 (September 25, 1969) 4–7.

Review of Otto Betz, *What Do We Know about Jesus?* (Philadelphia: Westminster, 1968), in *Foundations* 12/1 (1969) 94–95.

1970

"The Ministry in the Early Church," *BLT* 15/1 (Winter 1970) 4–7.
"Survey and 'New' Thesis on the Bones of St. Peter" (see 1969), repr. in Edward F. Campbell and David Noel Freedman, eds., *The Biblical Archaeologist Reader*, vol. 3 (Garden City, N.Y.: Anchor, 1970) 405–24.
"Christian Ethics," *ChrMin* 1/5 (July 1970) 33–35.
"Obedience or Disobedience? An Understanding of Romans 13," *Messenger* 119/3 (January 29, 1970) 8–10.
"Early Christian Symbols," *Messenger* 119/7 (March 26, 1970) 10–13.
"He Lives...I Live [poem]," *Messenger* 119/26 (December 17, 1970) 4.

Review of Walter Schmithals, *The Office of Apostle in the Early Church* (Nashville: Abingdon, 1970), in *JBL* 89 (1970) 253–55.
Review ("Those Bones Again") of Daniel William O'Connor, *Peter in Rome: The Literary, Liturgical and Archaeological Evidence* (New York: Columbia University Press, 1969), in *ChrCent* 87/18 (May 6, 1970) 569–70.
Review ("Dovish Approach") of Robert F. Drinan, *Vietnam and Armageddon: Peace, War and the Christian Conscience* (New York: Sheed and Ward, 1970), in *ChrCent* 87/42 (October 21, 1970) 1264.
Review ("Valuable Collection") of Eberhart Arnold, ed., *The Early Christians after the Death of the Apostles: Selected and Edited from All the Sources of the First Centuries* (Rifton, N.Y.: Plough, 1970), in *ChrCent* 87/43 (October 28, 1970) 1289.

1971

"Power and Violence: A Biblical Study," printed in fascicle form with Rosemary R. Ruether, "Radical Social Movement and the Radical Church Tradition," as *Colloquium* 1 (Oak Brook, Ill.: Bethany Theological Seminary, 1971).

"John 13:16 and the Anti-Petrinism of the Johannine Tradition," *BR* 16 (1971) 5–15.

"Chitterling Communion: Breaking Cracklin' Cornbread Together," *Messenger* 120/7 (April 1, 1971) 14–15.

"Jesus Power: A Confrontation with Women's Lib at Corinth," *BLT* 16/3 (Summer 1971) 161–67.

Review ("Perspectives on the Early Church") of Arnold, *The Early Christians* (see above, 1970), and Henry Chadwick, *The Early Church* (Pelican History of the Church 1; Grand Rapids: Eerdmans, 1971), in *Messenger* 120/1 (January 1, 1971) 30.

Review of Arnold, *The Early Christians* (see above, 1970), in *BLT* 16/1 (Winter 1971) 62–64.

Review ("Off with the Mask!") of John M. Swomley, *American Empire: The Political Ethics of Twentieth-Century Conquest* (New York: Macmillan, 1970), in *ChrCent* 88/8 (February 24, 1971) 259.

Review ("On the Eco-Catastrophe") of Richard Neuhaus, *In Defense of People: Ecology and the Seduction of Radicalism* (New York: Macmillan, 1971), in *ChrCent* 88/50 (December 15, 1971) 1478.

Review ("The Jesus Story: Four Perspectives") of William E. Phipps, *Was Jesus Married? The Distortion of Sexuality in the Christian Tradition* (New York: Harper & Row, 1970), Hans J. Schultz, *Jesus in His Time* (Philadelphia: Fortress, 1971), Haim Cohn, *The Trial and Death of Jesus* (New York: Harper & Row, 1971), and William A. Emerson, *The Jesus Story* (New York: Harper & Row, 1971), in *Messenger* 120/23 (December 1971) 31.

1972

"Apocalyptic and Didactic Elements in 1 Thessalonians," SBLSP 1 (1972) 233–44.

"A Summary of Faith in an Epistolary Context: 1 Thess. 1:9, 10," SBLSP 2 (1972) 355–65.

"Dunkerness IV: Will Grandfather Snyder Wear a Red Tie?" *BLT* 17/1 (Winter 1972) 25–29.

"The Post-Apostolic Church: A Tunnel Time," *Guide* 87/2 (March–May 1972) 2–4.

"A History of Christian Symbols," *Sunday Digest*, May 7, 1972, 1–4.

Review of Leon Morris, *The Gospel of John* (NICNT; London: Marshall, Morgan & Scott; Grand Rapids: Eerdmans, 1972), in *Encounter* 33 (1972) 414–15.

Review ("God Above, God Ahead") of Walter H. Capps, *Time Invades the Cathedral: Tensions in the School of Hope* (Philadelphia: Fortress, 1972), in *ChrCent* 89/26 (July 5, 1972) 757.

Review ("Paul: Envoy, Exile, Brother") of Malcolm Muggeridge and Alec Vidler, *Paul: Envoy Extraordinary* (London: Collins; New York: Harper & Row, 1972), John J. Gunther, *Paul, Messenger and Exile: A Study of the Chronology of His Life and Letters* (Valley Forge, Pa.: Judson, 1972), and Richard L. Rubenstein, *My Brother*

Paul (New York: Harper & Row, 1972), in *Messenger* 121/19 (November 1, 1972) 22–23.

1973

Using Biblical Simulations, vol. 1 (with Donald E. Miller and Robert W. Neff) (Valley Forge, Pa.: Judson, 1973).

"The Authority of the New Testament," *BLT* 18/3 (Summer 1973) 117–30.
"Power and Violence," *Crux* 10 (1973) 9–18.
"'I Am': A Meditation on the Life of Jesus at the Time of His Death," *Messenger* 122/4 (April 1973) 18–20.
"The First Christian," *Guide* 88/4 (September–November 1973) 2–4.
"Interpreting the Bible" (series), *Guide* 88/4 (September–November 1973): "Victory in Suffering," 58–59; "Life in the Christian Community," 64–65; "Living Victoriously in Society," 70–71; "The Strong and the Weak," 76–77; "Always of Good Courage," 82–83.
"Galilee and Jerusalem," *Guide* 89/1 (December 1973–February 1974) 2–4.
"Interpreting the Bible" (series, with Kenneth M. Shaffer, Jr.), *Guide* 89/1 (December 1973–February 1974): "Why the Gospel of John?" 10–11; "Who Is This Jesus?" 16–17; "Belief or Unbelief?" 22–23; "The Word Dwelt among Us," 28–29; "Water for the Thirsty," 34–35; "Bread for the Hungry," 40–41; "Light for the Blind," 46–47; "Love among Believers," 52–53; "Life in Christ," 58–59; "Promise of the Counselor," 64–65; "Victorious in Defeat," 70–71; "Victorious in Death," 76–77; "The Resurrection Victory," 82–83.

Review of Wolfgang Trilling, *Untersuchungen zum zweiten Thessalonicherbrief* (ETS 27; Leipzig: St. Benno, 1972), in *JBL* 92 (1973) 613–14.
Review of Vernard Eller, *In Place of Sacraments: A Study of Baptism and the Lord's Supper* (Grand Rapids: Eerdmans, 1972), in *Foundations* 16 (1973) 188–89.
Review ("Demythologizing JFK") of Henry Fairlie, *The Kennedy Promise: The Politics of Expectation* (Garden City, N.Y.: Doubleday, 1972), in *ChrCent* 90/19 (May 9, 1973) 547–48.

1974

"Jesus Christ the Yes-Man," *Messenger* 123/2 (February 1974) 14–15.
"Exploring the Bible" (series), *Guide* 89/3 (June–August 1974): "The Thessalonian Witness," 9–11; "Pastor and People," 15–17; "Christ's Coming, Our Hope," 21–23; "The Christian's Hope and the Daily Task," 27–29; "God's Redeeming Grace," 33–35; "God's Eternal Purpose," 39–41; "Renewed in Mind and Spirit," 45–47; "Partnership in the Gospel," 51–53; "Pressing On toward the Goal," 57–59; "A Threatened Church," 63–65; "Christ above All," 69–71; "Freedom in Christ," 75–77; "Personal Relationships in Christ," 81–83.
"Exploring the Bible" and "Interpreting the Bible" (series), *Guide* 90/1 (December 1974–February 1975): "The Master Teacher," 35–39; "The Suffering Savior," 41–45; "The Lord of Life," 47–51; "All Empowered People," 53–57; "A Worshiping People," 59–63; "A Serving People," 65–69; "A Reconciling People," 71–75; "Living in Hope," 77–81.

Review of Ernest Best, *A Commentary on the First and Second Epistles to the Thessaloni-
ans* (HNTC; New York: Harper & Row, 1973), in *JBL* 93 (1974) 312–14.
Review of J. Reiling, *Hermas and Christian Prophecy: A Study of the Eleventh Mandate*
(NovTSup 37; Leiden: Brill, 1973), in *JBL* 93 (1974) 628–29.
Review ("View from the Left") of Sandy Vogelgesang, *The Long Dark Night of the Soul:
The American Intellectual Left and the Vietnam War* (New York: Harper & Row,
1974), in *ChrCent* 91/40 (November 20, 1974) 1107–8.

1975

Using Biblical Simulations, vol. 2 (with Donald E. Miller and Robert W. Neff) (Valley
Forge, Pa.: Judson, 1975).

"Sayings on the Delay of the End," *BR* 20 (1975) 19–35.
"Genesis: An Introduction," *Guide* 90/4 (September–November 1975) 5–9.

1976

Towards a Christian Lifestyle (with Kenneth M. Shaffer, Jr.) (Stewards Commission of
the Northern District of Indiana Church of the Brethren, 1976).
Texts in Transit: A Study of New Testament Passages That Shaped the Brethren (with
Kenneth M. Shaffer) (Elgin, Ill.: Brethren Press, 1976).

"The *Tobspruch* in the New Testament," *NTS* 23 (1976–77) 117–20.
"Repentance in the New Testament," in Keith Crum, ed., *The Interpreter's Dictionary
of the Bible: Supplementary Volume* (Nashville: Abingdon, 1976) 738–39.
"Church of the Brethren Stewardship 1976–2000," *Messenger* 125/11 (November
1976) 28–29.
"A Message of Reconciliation," *Guide* 91/4 (September–November 1976) 5–9.

Review of D. George Vanderlip, *Christianity according to John* (Philadelphia: Westmin-
ster, 1976), in *Foundations* 19 (1976) 187–89.
Review of J. L. Houlden, *A Commentary on the Johannine Epistles* (HNTC; London:
Black; New York: Harper & Row, 1973), in *Foundations* 19 (1976) 191–92.

1978

"The Shepherd of Hermas," in Jack N. Sparks, ed., *The Apostolic Fathers* (New York:
Nelson, 1978) 155–259.
"Homosexuality and the Covenant Community," *Messenger* 127/6 (June 1978) 22–24.
"Present Trends in Theological Education," *BLT* 23/3 (Summer 1978) 165–68.

Review of Robert McAfee Brown, *Theology in a New Key: Responding to Liberation
Themes* (Philadelphia: Westminster, 1978), in *ChrCent* 95/43 (December 27,
1978) 1268–69.

1979

"The Impact of Camping on the Life-Style of the Faith Community," *BLT* 24/1
(Winter 1979) 18–23.
"Take It or Leave It," *Guide* 94/3 (June–August 1979) 2–5.

"Exploring the Bible" and "Interpreting the Bible" (series), *Guide* 94/4 (September–November 1979): "God's Created Power," 9–13; "God's Saving Acts," 15–19; "God's Authority and Rule," 21–25; "Teaching the Faith," 27–31; "Vision of the Heavenly Kingdom," 33–37.

1980

"Sexuality: Its Social Reality and Theological Understanding in 1 Corinthians 7" (with Lauree Hersch Meyer), SBLSP 19 (1980) 359–70.

"The Social Ministry of Jesus," *BLT* 25/1 (Winter 1980) 14–19.

1981

"Theological Education from a Free Church Perspective," *Theological Education* 17 (1981) 175–81.

"*Texts in Transit* Reconsidered: Great Passages of the Bible for Brethren," *Guide* 96/4 (September–November 1981) 5–9.

Review of Arnold, *The Early Christians* (see above, 1970), in *Sojourners* 10/4 (1981) 30–31.

1982

"Coach [poem]," *Messenger* 131/2 (February 1982) 22–23.

"Resources for New Testament Study," *Guide* 98/1 (December 1982–February 1983) 2–9.

Review of Howard Clark Kee, *Christian Origins in Sociological Perspective: Methods and Resources* (London: SCM; Philadelphia: Westminster, 1980), in *JBL* 101 (1982) 448–49.

Review of Hans Freiherr von Campenhausen, *Urchristliches und altkirchliches: Vorträge und Aufsätze* (Tübingen: Mohr [Siebeck], 1979), in *SecCent* 2 (1982) 42–44.

Review of Matthew L. Lamb, *Solidarity with Victims: Toward a Theory of Social Transformation* (New York: Crossroad, 1982), in *ChrCent* 99/37 (November 24, 1982) 1207.

1983

Articles in *The Brethren Encyclopedia* (3 vols.; Philadelphia: Brethren Encyclopedia, Inc., 1983–84): "Bethany Brethren Hospital"; "Covenant Theology"; "Human Sexuality"; "Love Feast"; "Misíon Mutua."

Review of Walter H. Capps, *The Unfinished War: Vietnam and the American Conscience* (Boston: Beacon, 1982), in *ChrCent* 100/1 (January 5, 1983) 22.

Review of Myron Augsburger, *Matthew* (Communicator's Commentary 1; Waco, Tex.: Word, 1982) and Maxie D. Dunnam, *Galatians, Ephesians, Colossians, Philemon* (Communicator's Commentary 8; Waco, Tex.: Word, 1982), in *ChrCent* 100/16 (May 18, 1983) 505–6.

1984

"A West Side Story," *Messenger* 133/6 (June 1984) 12–13.

"Understanding Paul and His Letters: An Interview with Graydon F. Snyder," *Guide* 99/4 (September–November 1984) 5–9.

1985

Ante Pacem: Archaeological Evidence of Church Life before Constantine (Macon, Ga.: Mercer University Press, 1985).

1986

"Theological Reflections on Genetic Engineering," *BLT* 31/4 (Autumn 1986) 209–14.

1987

Review of Kenan T. Erim, *Aphrodisias: City of Venus Aphrodite* (London: Muller, Blond & White, 1986), in *BARev* 13/3 (1987) 11.

Review of James Stevenson, *The Catacombs: Life and Death in Early Christianity* (Nashville: Nelson, 1985), in *SecCent* 6 (1987) 43.

Reviews in *CTSReg* 77/3 (1987) 46–47: Elizabeth Struthers Malbon, *Narrative Space and Mythic Meaning in Mark* (New Voices in Biblical Studies; San Francisco: Harper & Row, 1986); Charles H. Talbert, *Reading Corinthians: A Literary and Theological Commentary on 1 and 2 Corinthians* (New York: Crossroad, 1987); Stanley K. Stowers, *Letter Writing in Greco-Roman Antiquity* (Library of Early Christianity 5; Philadelphia: Westminster, 1986); Jane Dillenberger, *Style and Content in Christian Art* (2d ed.; New York: Crossroad, 1986).

1988

Tough Choices: Health Care Decisions and the Faith Community (Elgin, Ill.: Brethren Press, 1988).

"Covenant Theology and Medical Decision Making," *BLT* 33/1 (Winter 1988) 27–35.

"Anabaptist Health Care and the Ten Commandments," *Mennonite Medical Messenger* 39/1 (July–September 1988) 12–21.

Reviews in *CTSReg* 78/1 (1988) 53–54: Doug Adams and Diana Apostolos-Cappadona, *Art as Religious Studies* (New York: Crossroad, 1987); Abraham Malherbe, ed., *Moral Exhortation: A Greco-Roman Sourcebook* (Library of Early Christianity 4; Philadelphia: Westminster, 1986).

Reviews in *CTSReg* 78/2 (1988) 43–45: Xavier Léon-Dufour, *Life and Death in the New Testament: The Teachings of Jesus and Paul* (San Francisco: Harper & Row, 1986); Gary Habermas and Anthony G. N. Flew, *Did Jesus Rise from the Dead? The Resurrection Debate* (San Francisco: Harper & Row, 1987); Ernest Gordon, ed., *The Gospel in Dostoyevsky: Selections from His Works* (Rifton, N.Y.: Plough, 1988); Robert J. Schreiter, ed., *The Schillebeeckx Reader* (Edinburgh: T. & T. Clark, 1984; New York: Crossroad, 1986).

Reviews in *CTSReg* 78/3 (1988) 48–49: Robin Scroggs, *Christology in Paul and John: The Reality and Revelation of God* (Proclamation Commentaries; Philadelphia: Fortress, 1988); Jane Schaberg, *The Illegitimacy of Jesus: A Feminist Theological Interpretation of the Infancy Narratives* (San Francisco: Harper & Row, 1987); John Shelby Spong, *This Hebrew Lord* (San Francisco: Harper & Row, 1988); Wolfgang

Trilling, *A Conversation with Paul* (London: SCM, 1986; New York: Crossroad, 1987); James D. G. Dunn and James P. Mackey, *New Testament Theology in Dialogue: Christology and Ministry* (Philadelphia: Westminster, 1987).

1989

Reviews in *CTSReg* 79/4 (1989) 64–68: David Rensberger, *Johannine Faith and Liberating Community* (Philadelphia: Westminster, 1988); Stevan L. Davies, *The New Testament: A Contemporary Introduction* (San Francisco: Harper & Row, 1989); James L. Kugel and Rowan A. Greer, *Early Biblical Interpretation* (Library of Early Christianity 3; Philadelphia: Westminster, 1986); Wayne A. Meeks, *The Moral World of the First Christians* (Library of Early Christianity 6; Philadelphia: Westminster, 1986); David E. Aune, *The New Testament in Its Literary Environment* (Library of Early Christianity 8; Philadelphia: Westminster, 1987); James M. Robinson, ed., *The Nag Hammadi Library in English* (3d ed.; San Francisco: Harper & Row, 1988); C. K. Barrett, *The New Testament Background: Selected Documents* (rev. ed.; San Francisco: Harper & Row, 1989); James L. Mays, ed., *Harper's Bible Commentary* (San Francisco: Harper & Row, 1989); Gerald P. Fogarty, *American Catholic Biblical Scholarship: A History from the Early Republic to Vatican II* (San Francisco: Harper & Row); Mary Hayter, *The New Eve in Christ: The Use and Abuse of the Bible in the Debate About Women in the Church* (London: SPCK; Grand Rapids: Eerdmans, 1987).

Review of S. Loren Bowman, *Power and Polity Among the Brethren: A Study of Church Governance* (Elgin, Ill.: Brethren Press, 1988), in *BLT* 34/1 (Winter 1989) 53–55.

1990

"Early Christian Symbols," *Biblical Literacy Today* 4 (1990) 12–14.

Articles in Watson E. Mills, ed., *Mercer Dictionary of the Bible* (Macon, Ga.: Mercer University Press, 1990): "Apostolic Fathers"; "Epistle of the Apostles"; "Epistle of Barnabas"; "Papias"; "Polycarp, to the Philippians"; "Second Clement"; "Shepherd of Hermas."

Articles in Everett Ferguson, ed., *Encyclopedia of Early Christianity* (New York: Garland, 1990): "Clement of Rome"; "Ignatius of Antioch"; "Polycarp."

"Pre-Embryos: A *Touch Choices* Update," *Health Missions Update*, Winter 1990, 1–2.

Reviews in *CTSReg* 80/1 (1990) 59–60: Calvin R. Mercer, *Norman Perrin's Interpretation of the New Testament: From Exegetical Method to Hermeneutical Process* (Studies in American Biblical Hermeneutics 2; Macon, Ga.: Mercer University Press, 1986); Jaroslav Pelikan, *The Excellent Empire: The Fall of Rome and the Triumph of the Church* (San Francisco: Harper & Row, 1988); William O. Walker, *Harper's Bible Pronunciation Guide* (San Francisco: Harper & Row, 1989); John Dart, *The Jesus of Heresy and History: The Discovery and Meaning of the Nag Hammadi Gnostic Library* (San Francisco: Harper & Row, 1988).

Reviews in *CTSReg* 80/2 (1990) 39–43: Richard A. Horsley, *The Liberation of Christmas: The Infancy Narratives in Social Context* (New York: Crossroad, 1989); Hendrikus Boers, *Who Was Jesus? The Historical Jesus and the Synoptic Gospels* (San Francisco: Harper & Row, 1989); Martin Kähler, *The So-Called Historical Jesus and the Historic, Biblical Christ* (1964; repr. Philadelphia: Fortress, 1988);

Robin Lane Fox, *Pagans and Christians* (New York: Knopf, 1987; San Francisco: Harper & Row, 1988); Marinus de Jonge, *Christology in Context: The Earliest Christian Response to Jesus* (Philadelphia: Westminster, 1988); Mary Condren, *The Serpent and the Goddess: Women, Religion, and Power in Celtic Ireland* (San Francisco: Harper & Row, 1989); William Richard Stegner, *Narrative Theology in Early Jewish Christianity* (Louisville, Ky.: Westminster/John Knox, 1989); Henri Crouzel, *Origen: The Life and Thought of the First Great Theologian* (San Francisco: Harper & Row, 1989).

Reviews in *CTSReg* 80/3 (1990) 40–42: Paul M. van Buren, *A Theology of the Jewish-Christian Reality: Christ in Context* (San Francisco: Harper & Row, 1988); Christopher Rowland and Mark Corner, *Liberating Exegesis: The Challenge of Liberation Theology to Biblical Studies* (Louisville, Ky.: Westminster/John Knox, 1990); Itumeleng J. Mosala, *Biblical Hermeneutics and Black Theology in South Africa* (Grand Rapids: Eerdmans, 1989); Thomas C. Oden, *First and Second Timothy and Titus* (Interpretation; Louisville, Ky.: Westminster/John Knox, 1990).

1991

Ante Pacem: Archaeological Evidence of Church Life before Constantine (repr. of 1985 ed.; Macon, Ga.: Mercer University Press/Seedsowers, 1991).

Texts in Transit II (with Kenneth M. Shaffer, Jr.) (Elgin, Ill.: Brethren Press, 1991).

Review of Del Birkey, *The House Church: A Model for Renewing the Church* (Scottdale, Pa.: Herald, 1988), in *BLT* 36/4 (Fall 1991) 294.

Reviews in *CTSReg* 81/1 (1991) 53–54: Marcus Borg, *Jesus – A New Vision: Spirit, Culture, and the Life of Discipleship* (San Francisco: Harper & Row, 1988); John Dominic Crossan, *The Cross That Spoke: The Origins of the Passion Narrative* (San Francisco: Harper & Row, 1988); David Tracy, *Plurality and Ambiguity: Hermeneutics, Religion, and Hope* (San Francisco: Harper & Row, 1987); Richard A. Horsley, *Jesus and the Spiral of Violence: Popular Jewish Resistance in Roman Palestine* (San Francisco: Harper & Row, 1987).

Reviews in *CTSReg* 81/2 (1991) 63–64: Paul Tillich, *On Art and Architecture* (New York: Crossroad, 1989); Walter Brueggemann, *Power, Providence, and Personality: Biblical Insight into Life and Ministry* (Louisville, Ky.: Westminster/John Knox, 1990); Naomi Shepherd, *The Zealous Intruders: The Western Rediscovery of Palestine* (London: Collins; San Francisco: Harper & Row, 1987); Barbara Krieger, *Living Waters: Myth, History, and Politics of the Dead Sea* (New York: Continuum, 1988); Ahmed Osman, *Stranger in the Valley of the Kings: Solving the Mystery of an Ancient Egyptian Mummy* (San Francisco: Harper & Row, 1988).

1992

First Corinthians: A Faith Community Commentary (Macon, Ga.: Mercer University Press, 1992).

Articles in David Noel Freedman, ed., *The Anchor Bible Dictionary* (6 vols.; New York: Doubleday, 1992): "The Christian Movements at Rome"; "Christianity at Rome"; "Early Christian Art"; "Hermas the Shepherd."

Review of Stanley Hauerwas, *Naming the Silences: God, Medicine, and the Problem of Suffering* (Grand Rapids: Eerdmans, 1989), in *BLT* 37/1 (Winter 1992) 67–68.

Reviews in *CTSReg* 82/1 (1992) 38–40: Elsa Tamez, *The Scandalous Message of James: Faith without Works Is Dead* (New York: Crossroad, 1990); Robert M. Grant, *The Greek Apologists of the Second Century* (Philadelphia: Westminster, 1988); Horst Balz and Gerhard Schneider, eds., *Exegetical Dictionary of the New Testament*, vol. 1 (Grand Rapids: Eerdmans, 1990); Richard Bauckham, *The Bible in Politics: How to Read the Bible Politically* (London: SPCK; Louisville, Ky.: Westminster/John Knox, 1990); R. David Kaylor, *Paul's Covenant Community: Jew and Gentile in Romans* (Atlanta: Knox, 1988); Macrina Scott, *Picking the Right Bible Study Programs* (Chicago: ACTA Publications, 1992); Herman Hendrickx, *The Miracle Stories of the Synoptic Gospels* (London: Chapman; San Francisco: Harper & Row, 1988).

Review of C. S. Song, *Jesus: The Crucified People* (New York: Crossroad, 1990), in *CTSReg* 82/3 (1992) 40.

1993

"Before the Canon: The Pre-Cultural Jesus Tradition," in Isabel Mukonyora, James L. Cox, and Frans J. Verstraelen, eds., *"Rewriting" the Bible — The Real Issues: Perspectives from within Biblical and Religious Studies in Zimbabwe* (Gweru/Harare, Zimbabwe: Mambo, 1993) 81–87.

Reviews in *CTSReg* 83/3 (1993) 14–20: Robin Scroggs, *The Text and the Times: New Testament Essays for Today* (Minneapolis: Fortress, 1993); Barbara Thiering, *Jesus and the Riddle of the Dead Sea Scrolls: Unlocking the Secrets of His Life Story* (San Francisco: Harper, 1992); Burton L. Mack, *The Lost Gospel: The Book of Q and Christian Origins* (San Francisco: Harper, 1993); Jerome H. Neyrey, *Paul, In Other Words: A Cultural Reading of His Letters* (Louisville, Ky.: Westminster/John Knox, 1990); J. Christiaan Beker, *Heirs of Paul: Paul's Legacy in the New Testament and in the Church Today* (Minneapolis: Fortress, 1991); Calvin J. Roetzel, *The Letters of Paul: Conversations in Context* (3d ed.; Louisville, Ky.: Westminster/John Knox, 1991); P. R. S. Mooney, *A Century of Biblical Archaeology* (Cambridge: Lutterworth; Louisville, Ky.: Westminster/John Knox, 1991); David E. Garland, *Reading Matthew: A Literary and Theological Commentary* (New York: Crossroad, 1993); William S. Kurz, *Reading Luke-Acts: Dynamics of Biblical Narrative* (Louisville, Ky.: Westminster/John Knox, 1993); Charles H. Talbert, *Reading John: A Literary and Theological Commentary on the Fourth Gospel and the Johannine Epistles* (New York: Crossroad, 1992); Gerd Theissen, *The Open Door: Variations on Biblical Themes* (Minneapolis: Fortress, 1991); James L. Bailey and Lyle D. Vander Broek, *Literary Forms in the New Testament: A Handbook* (Louisville, Ky.: Westminster/John Knox, 1992).

1994

"The Perfidy of Corban," in Theodore W. Jennings and Susan Brooks Thistlethwaite, eds., *Theology and the Human Spirit: Essays in Honor of Perry D. LeFevre* (Chicago: Exploration, 1994) 83–88.

Review of Massimo Grilli, *Communità e Missione: le direttive di Matteo: Indagine esegetica su Mt 9,35–11,1* (Europäische Hochschulschriften 23, Theologie 458; Frankfurt am Main and New York: Lang, 1992), in *CR* (1994) 191–92.

Review of Dale C. Allison, *The New Moses: A Matthean Typology* (Minneapolis: Fortress, 1993), in *ChrCent* 111 (1994) 829–30.

Reviews in *CTSReg* 84/3 (1994) 30–32: Otto Betz and Rainer Riesner, *Jesus, Qumran, and the Vatican: Clarifications* (London: SCM; New York: Crossroad, 1994); Abraham J. Malherbe, *Paul and the Popular Philosophers* (Minneapolis: Fortress, 1989); Thomas W. Overholt, *Channels of Prophecy: The Social Dynamics of Prophetic Activity* (Minneapolis: Fortress, 1989); Robert Jewett, *Paul, the Apostle to America: Cultural Trends and Pauline Scholarship* (Louisville, Ky.: Westminster/John Knox, 1994); Robert M. Grant, *Jesus after the Gospels: The Christ of the Second Century* (Louisville, Ky.: Westminster/John Knox, 1990); Arthur J. Droge and James D. Tabor, *A Noble Death: Suicide and Martyrdom among Christians and Jews in Antiquity* (San Francisco: HarperCollins, 1992).

Reviews in *CTSReg* 84/4 (1994) 36–40: Bruce J. Malina, *The New Testament World: Insights from Cultural Anthropology* (rev. ed.; Louisville, Ky.: Westminster/John Knox, 1993); idem, *Windows on the World of Jesus: Time Travel to Ancient Judea* (Louisville, Ky.: Westminster/John Knox, 1993); Richard A. Horsley, *The Liberation of Christmas: The Infancy Narratives in Social Context* (2d ed.; New York: Crossroad, 1993); Edward Schillebeeckx and Catharina Halkes, *Mary: Yesterday, Today, Tomorrow* (London: SCM; New York: Crossroad, 1993); Adalbert G. Hamman, *How to Read the Church Fathers* (New York: Crossroad); Jean-Pierre Prévost, *How to Read the Apocalypse* (New York: Crossroad, 1993); Robert Kysar, *John: The Maverick Gospel* (rev. ed.; Louisville, Ky.: Westminster/John Knox, 1993); Carl D. Schneider, *Shame, Exposure, and Privacy* (New York: Norton, 1992).

1995

Health and Medicine in the Anabaptist Tradition: Care in Community (Health/Medicine and the Faith Traditions; Valley Forge, Pa.: Trinity Press International, 1995).

"Archaeology, Christian," in Richard P. McBrien et al., eds., *The HarperCollins Encyclopedia of Catholicism* (New York: HarperCollins, 1995) 90–91.

Review of Walter H. Wagner, *After the Apostles: Christianity in the Second Century* (Minneapolis: Fortress, 1994), in *CR* 8 (1995) 422–24.

Review of Ernest D. Martin, *Colossians, Philemon* (Believers Church Bible Commentary; Scottdale, Pa.: Herald, 1993), in *BLT* 40/2 (Spring 1995) 130–31.

Review of Willard M. Swartley, *Israel's Scripture Traditions Behind the Synoptic Gospels: Story Shaping Story* (Peabody, Mass.: Hendrickson, 1994), in *BLT* 40/2 (Spring 1995) 123–24.

Reviews in *CTSReg* 85/2 (1995) 24–26: Dale Aukerman, *Reckoning with Apocalypse: Terminal Apocalypse and Christian Hope* (New York: Crossroad, 1993); Perry B. Yoder and Willard M. Swartley, eds., *The Meaning of Peace: Biblical Studies* (Louisville, Ky.: Westminster/John Knox, 1992); Willard M. Swartley, ed., *Love of Enemy and Nonretaliation in the New Testament* (Louisville, Ky.: Westminster/John Knox, 1992); Robert G. Hamerton-Kelly, *Sacred Violence: Paul's Hermeneutic of the Cross* (Minneapolis: Fortress, 1992); idem, *The Gospel and the Sacred: Poet-*

ics of Violence in Mark (Minneapolis: Fortress, 1994); James G. Williams, *The Bible, Violence and the Sacred: Liberation from the Myth of Sanctioned Violence* (San Francisco: Harper, 1991); Robert L. Brawley, *Centering on God: Method and Message in Luke-Acts* (Louisville, Ky.: Westminster/John Knox, 1990); Fred B. Craddock, *Luke* (Interpretation; Louisville, Ky.: Westminster/John Knox, 1990); Eduard Lohse, *Theological Ethics of the New Testament* (Minneapolis: Fortress, 1991).

Reviews in *CTSReg* 85/3 (1995) 46–47: Albert Nolan, *Jesus before Christianity* (rev. ed.; Maryknoll, N.Y.: Orbis, 1992); Priscilla Pope-Levinson and John R. Levinson, *Jesus in Global Contexts* (Louisville, Ky.: Westminster/John Knox, 1992); David B. Batstone, *From Conquest to Struggle: Jesus of Nazareth in Latin America* (Albany, N.Y.: State University of New York Press, 1991).

1996

"Jesus for Tomorrow," *BLT* 41/1 (Winter 1996) 29–33.

Review of Paul Corby Finney, *The Invisible God: The Earliest Christians on Art* (New York: Oxford University Press, 1994), in *Journal of Early Christian Studies* 4 (1996) 263–65.

Review of Bruce W. Winter, *Seek the Welfare of the City: Christians as Benefactors and Citizens* (Grand Rapids: Eerdmans, 1994), in *BLT* 41/1 (1996) 50–51.

Review of Brad Stetson, *Pluralism and Particularity in Religious Belief* (Westport, Conn.: Praeger, 1994), in *BLT* 41/1 (Winter 1996) 54–56.

Reviews in *CTSReg* 86/1 (1996) 24–26: Marion L. Soards, *The Speeches in Acts: Their Content, Context, and Concerns* (Louisville, Ky.: Westminster/John Knox, 1994); Bruce W. Winter and Andrew D. Clarke, *The Book of Acts in Its First-Century Setting*, vol. 1: *The Book of Acts in Its Ancient Literary Setting* (Grand Rapids: Eerdmans, 1993); Chalmer E. Faw, *Acts* (Believers Church Bible Commentary 5; Scottdale, Pa.: Herald, 1993); John A. Darr, *On Character Building: The Reader and the Rhetoric of Characterization in Luke-Acts* (Louisville, Ky.: Westminster/John Knox, 1992); Werner Stenger, *Introduction to New Testament Exegesis* (Grand Rapids: Eerdmans, 1993).

Reviews in *CTSReg* 86/2 (1996) 18–19: Stevan L. Davies, *Jesus the Healer: Possession, Trance, and the Origins of Christianity* (New York: Continuum; London: SCM, 1995); Bonnie Thurston, *Reading Colossians, Ephesians, and 2 Thessalonians: A Literary and Theological Commentary* (New York: Crossroad, 1995).

1997

Virginia Wiles, Alexandra Brown, and Graydon F. Snyder, eds., *Putting Body and Soul Together: Essays in Honor of Robin Scroggs* (Valley Forge, Pa.: Trinity Press International, 1997).

"The Social Context of the Ironic Dialogues in the Gospel of John," in Wiles et al., *Putting Body and Soul Together,* 3–23.

Articles in Everett Ferguson, ed., *Encyclopedia of Early Christianity* (2d ed.; 2 vols.; New York: Garland, 1997): "Clement of Rome"; "Ignatius of Antioch"; Polycarp."

Review of W. H. C. Frend, *The Archaeology of Early Christianity: A History* (Minneapolis: Fortress, 1996), in *BARev* 23 (1997) 75–77.
Review of Valerie A. Abrahamsen, *Women and Worship at Philippi: Diana/Artemis and Other Cults in the Early Christian Era* (Portland, Me.: Astarte Shell, 1995), in *JBL* 116 (1997) 557–58.
Reviews in *CTSReg* 87/1 (1997) 19–24: Burton L. Mack, *Who Wrote the New Testament? The Making of the Christian Myth* (San Francisco: HarperCollins, 1995); R. David Kaylor, *Jesus the Prophet: His Vision of the Kingdom on Earth* (Louisville, Ky.: Westminster/John Knox, 1994); Stevan L. Davies, *Jesus the Healer: Possession, Trance, and the Origins of Christianity* (New York: Continuum; London: SCM, 1995); Luke Timothy Johnson, *The Real Jesus: The Misguided Quest for the Historical Jesus and the Historical Truth of the Traditional Gospels* (San Francisco: HarperCollins, 1996); M. Eugene Boring, *The Continuing Voice of Jesus: Christian Prophecy and the Gospel Tradition* (Louisville, Ky.: Westminster/John Knox, 1991); Scott McCormick, *Behold the Man: Re-Reading the Gospels, Re-Humanizing Jesus* (New York: Continuum, 1994); Robert W. Funk, *Honest to Jesus: Jesus for a New Millennium* (San Francisco: Harper, 1996); Marcus Borg, ed., *The Lost Gospel Q: The Original Sayings of Jesus* (Berkeley: Ulysses, 1996); William Hamilton, *A Quest for the Post-Historical Jesus* (London: SCM, 1993; New York: Continuum, 1994); Lance DeHaven-Smith, *The Hidden Teachings of Jesus: The Political Meaning of the Kingdom of God* (Grand Rapids: Phanes, 1994).

1998 and Forthcoming

"Jesus before Culture," in *Recruitment, Conquest, and Conflict: Strategies in Judaism, Early Christianity and the Greco-Roman World* (Emory Studies in Early Christianity 6; Atlanta: Scholars Press, 1998) (forthcoming).
"Early Christian Meeting Places, Constantinian Basilicas, and Anabaptist Restorationism," *Mennonite Quarterly Review* (forthcoming).
"The God-Fearers in Paul's Speech at Pisidian Antioch," in Christine Thomas et al, eds., *Proceedings of the First International Symposium on Pisidian Antioch, July 2–4, 1997 at Yalvaç, Turkey* (forthcoming).
"The Interaction of Jews with Non-Jews in Rome," *Symposium on Romans* (SNTS) (Grand Rapids: Eerdmans, 1998) (forthcoming).
Articles in *The Dictionary of Biblical Interpretation* (rev. ed.; Nashville: Abingdon, forthcoming): "Otto Alfred Piper"; "Johannes Munck."
"The Retirement Home as Counter-Culture," *BLT* 63 (1998) (forthcoming).
Articles in *The Brethren Encyclopedia* (rev. ed.; Philadelphia: Brethren Encyclopedia, Inc., forthcoming): "Bethany Hospital"; "Wellness."

Review of Paul N. Anderson, *The Christology of the Fourth Gospel: Its Unity and Disunity in the Light of John 6* (WUNT 2/78; Tübingen: Mohr [Siebeck], 1996), in *JR* (forthcoming).
Reviews in *CTSReg* 88 (1998) (forthcoming): Gerd Luedemann, *Opposition to Paul in Jewish Christianity* (Minneapolis: Fortress, 1989); James D. G. Dunn, *Jesus, Paul and the Law: Studies in Mark and Galatians* (Louisville, Ky.: Westminster/John Knox, 1990); Judith M. Gundry Volf, *Paul and Perseverance: Staying In and Falling Away* (WUNT 2/37; Tübingen: Mohr [Siebeck], 1990); James W. Aage-

son, *Written Also for Our Sake: Paul and the Art of Biblical Interpretation* (Louisville, Ky.: Westminster/John Knox, 1993); Bruce J. Malina and Jerome H. Neyrey, *Portraits of Paul: An Archaeology of Ancient Personality* (Louisville, Ky.: Westminster/John Knox, 1996); Peter Stuhlmacher, *Paul's Letter to the Romans: A Commentary* (Louisville, Ky.: Westminster/John Knox, 1994); Ben Witherington, *Paul's Narrative Thought World: The Tapestry of Tragedy and Triumph* (Louisville, Ky.: Westminster/John Knox, 1994); Stephen Westerholm, *Preface to the Study of Paul* (Grand Rapids: Eerdmans, 1997); Wiles et al., *Putting Body and Soul Together.*

Index of Ancient Sources

The indexes were compiled by Robert C. Helmer

16:17	*152*
16:18–20	*169*
16:18	*116*
16:19	*148–49, 168*
17:1–9	*155*
17:5	*154*
17:9	*154*
17:16	*154*
18	*169–71*
18:6–7	*169*
18:10–14	*169*
18:15–20	*156–58, 167, 169–71*
18:15–17	*116*
18:15	*168*
18:17	*168*
18:18	*169*
18:20	*156*
19:12	*125*
19:16–22	*124*
19:22–26	*125*
21:28–32	*199*
22:1–14	*187–88*
22:4	*188*
22:5	*188, 191*
22:9–10	*188*
22:9	*193*
23:8	*151–52*
23:29	*151*
23:34	*151*
24:3	*121*
24:11–12	*291*
24:12	*229*
25:36	*314*
25:39	*314*
26:27	*205*
26:30	*394*
27:57–61	*125*
28:16–20	*170*
28:16	*157*
28:20	*156–57*

Mark

1:22	*204*
1:29	*108*
2:1	*108*
2:15–17	*191*
2:15	*108*
2:23–28	*149*
3:20	*108*
3:29	*296*
3:31–35	*109*
4:10–13	*108*
4:10–12	*153*
4:11–12	*296*
4:11	*121*

4:12	*153*
4:17	*296*
4:33–34	*121*
5:38	*397*
6:10	*108*
7:17	*108*
7:22–23	*291*
7:24	*108*
8:34–9:1	*296*
8:38	*296*
9:2–9	*153*
9:9	*154*
9:38–41	*93*
10:1–12	*108*
10:17–22	*124*
10:17	*124*
10:23–31	*373*
10:29–31	*296*
10:29–30	*109*
12:18–27	*15*
13:3–4	*121*
13:37	*121*
14:3–10	*108*
14:23	*205*
14:26	*394*
14:71	*297*
16:14	*291*

Luke

1:5	*177–78*
1:52	*99*
2	*178, 183*
2:2	*178*
2:25–35	*183*
2:25	*179–82*
2:26	*179–80*
2:27	*180, 182*
2:29–32	*183*
2:29	*180*
2:30	*182*
2:34	*182*
2:35	*182*
3:8	*197*
3:10–11	*204*
3:21	*205*
4:18–19	*182, 198*
4:32	*204*
5:16	*205*
6:12	*205*
6:15	*180*
7:22	*198*
8:1–3	*203*
8:3	*210*
8:10	*121*
8:43–48	*340*

Clement of Alexandria _____
  Ecl. proph.
    41   318
    48   318
  Paed. 3.11   366
  Prot. 9.84   371
  Strom. 6.4.35   392

1 Clement _____
  1.1   247, 250, 256
  2.1   260
  2.4   256
  3.2–4   250
  7.1   247
  8.3   289
  10.7   260
  11.1   260
  12.1   260
  12.8   247
  13.1–3   260
  13.1   250
  14.1   250
  14.5   250
  15.1   250
  16.1   250, 260
  16.2   250, 256
  16.17   247, 260
  18.3   289
  18.5   289
  18.9   289
  19.1   260
  21.1   247
  21.5   250
  24.1   247
  24.2   247
  30.1–2   250
  30.1   256
  30.2–8   260
  30.5   250
  33.1   247
  34.5   250
  35.1   247
  35.5   250, 247, 256
  36.1   247
  38.2   260–61
  39.1   250
  43.6   247
  45.8   250
  46.8   256
  46.9   251
  47.1   252
  47.4–7   252
  47.6   247, 250
  48.1   252
  48.5–6   252

49   244, 246
49.1   256
49.1–6   245, 251–52, 55
49.5   256
50.1   247
50.2   253, 255
50.5   244, 247, 252–53
51.2   253
53.1   247
53.5   253
54.1   253
56.2   247
56.16   247
57.1–2   256
58.2   252, 256
59.2   256
59.3   256
59.4   260
62.2   247, 253, 260
62.3   247

2 Clement 8.5 _____ 144

Codex Claromontanus _____ 319

Epiphanius _____
  Pan. 27.6   305

Eusebius _____
  Hist. eccl.
    2.16–17   119
    2.17.1   119
    3.3.2   316
    4.18.5   394
    8.1.5   385
    10.2.1–3.1   385
    10.4.37–45   385
    10.4.44–46   346
  Vita Const.
    2.25–39   346
    3.50   346
    4.58–60   346

Gregory the Great _____
  Ep. 13   349
  Ep. ad Serenum   361

Herm. Mand. 8.10 _____ 260

Herm. Sim. _____
  8.10.3   260
  9.13.5   113
  9.18.4   113
  9.27.2   260

Index of Modern Authors